INDIA'S COLONIAL ENCOUNTER
ESSAYS IN MEMORY OF ERIC STOKES

India's Colonial Encounter

ESSAYS IN MEMORY OF ERIC STOKES

Second Revised and Enlarged Edition

Edited by
MUSHIRUL HASAN
NARAYANI GUPTA

MANOHAR
2004

ISBN 81-7304-536-4

First published 1993
Second edition 2004

Published by
Ajay Kumar Jain for
Manohar Publishers & Distributors
4753/23 Ansari Road, Daryaganj
New Delhi-110002

Typeset by
AJ Software Publishing Co. Pvt. Ltd.
New Delhi-110005

Printed at
Lordson Publishers Pvt. Ltd.
Delhi-110007

Contents

IV

Preface to the Second Edition

The first edition of this book has been out of print for a number of years. We are pleased to introduce this revised and enlarged edition. The revision is, however, limited to my paper that was substantially modified and updated recently in my book *Islam in the Subcontinent: Muslims in a Plural Society* (2002). The additions are significant. I am extremely grateful to the British Academy and Chris Bayly for letting us reprint his paper that was published in *Proceedings of the British Academy—1997 lectures and memoirs*, 1998. My senior friend Walter Hauser has been gracious enough to let us include his unpublished paper. Like many of us, he has been a long-standing admirer of Eric Stokes and his scholarship.

We are grateful to a number of reviewers, Mahesh Rangarajan, Thomas R. Metcalf and Sumit Sarkar included, for their generous comments on *India's Colonial Encounter*. We hope that the two papers included in this addition would enhance the value of this commemoration volume.

August 2003 MUSHIRUL HASAN

Contributors

DAVID BAKER taught at St. Stephen's College, University of Delhi.

C.A. BAYLY is Vere Harmsworth Professor of Imperial and Naval History at the University of Cambridge.

BINAY BHUSHAN CHAUDHURI was Professor of Modern Indian History at the University of Calcutta.

RAVINDRAN GOPINATH is Reader in History, Jamia Millia Islamia.

J.S. GREWAL was Director, Indian Institute of Advanced Study, Shimla.

SUMIT GUHA is Professor of History at the University of Rutgers.

NARAYANI GUPTA is Professor of History, Jamia Millia Islamia.

MUSHIRUL HASAN is Professor of History and Director, Academy of Third World Studies, Jamia Millia Islamia, New Delhi.

WALTER HAUSER was Professor of History, University of Virginia, Charlottesville.

GORDON JOHNSON is President, Wolfson College, Cambridge.

ATIYA HABEEB KIDWAI is Professor at the Centre for Regional Development, Jawaharlal Nehru University, New Delhi.

MEERA KOSAMBI was Professor at the S.N.D.T. University, Bombay, and the University of Pune.

D.A. LOW was Vice-Chancellor of the Australian National University and Smuts Professor of the History of the British Commonwealth, University of Cambridge.

RUDRANKSHU MUKHERJEE, a historian, currently works with *The Telegraph*.

RAJAT KANTA RAY is Professor of History, Presidency College, Calcutta.

FRANCIS ROBINSON is Vice-Principal, Royal Holloway, University of London.

GYAN PRAKASH SHARMA is Professor of History, Jamia Millia Islamia.

Eric Stokes
(10 July 1924 - 5 February 1981)

NARAYANI GUPTA

As I walked past St. Catharine's College on that bleak February afternoon in 1981, I noticed something unusual about the College flag. It was flying at half-mast. It took me a little time to realize what it meant. Eric Stokes was no more.

One of the most enduring aspects of Indo-British relationship has been the bond between teachers and students. London, Cambridge, Oxford, Sussex and other universities have been meeting-grounds where British tutors have supervised Indian students, and the libraries of these universities, together with the India Office Library and Records in London, have provided the material from which so many theses have been spun. Some teachers have been remembered longer and with deeper affection than others. Of Eric Stokes it would be true to say that his premature death was as much a blow to those who had studied with him or had known him as a friend, as to his own family. Eric had undergone surgery in the summer of 1980. It was a great shock when at Christmas, he was seriously ill again. Even while painfully—and terminally—ill, he made it a point to travel to Oxford to conduct the *viva voce* examination for Rudrangshu Mukherjee because, as he said, it was important that the results of overseas students should not be delayed, since they were living in Britain on limited funds. Days before he passed away, he telephoned the College to ensure that the fellowship of Sugata Bose was extended.

Sugata recalls his first encounter with Eric Stokes. Instead of a homily in a sombre book-lined study, Sugata's first tutorial was a bracing walk through the lovely town of Cambridge, its history and its beauty unfolded for him by someone whose wit matched his knowledge. The late Ratnalekha Ray, who produced a brilliant thesis on Bengal agrarian society under the supervision of Eric Stokes, used to love relating the story of the day she invited her supervisor to join them in celebrating Holi. Later, the professor walked into the South Asian Studies Seminar quite oblivious of the streaks of colour across his forehead, and the startled glances of his colleagues!

Never complacent, never satisfied, Eric could mock gently and spur students on to doing better and better. The tutorial supervision system of Oxford and Cambridge often brings out the best in students and fosters a rewarding relationship between them and their tutors. Eric did a little more. As Chris Bayly put it, 'he concealed an ideal of service beneath the jocular and the circumstantial...At the personal level, the Commonwealth idea had substance'. This was strengthened by the fact that he was backed by a very happy family; lonely students were always made to feel welcome at their home, something Indian students were always grateful for. Perhaps this had something to do with the fact that Eric himself had spent many years away from Britain.

It was while Eric was studying at Cambridge that the War had broken out. Called up for military service, he was a subaltern in the Indian Mounted Artillery in Burma. Later, a teaching assignment took him to the University of Malaya in Singapore, in 1950. There he completed his doctorate, under the supervision of Percival Spear, who had returned to Cambridge after many years of service at Delhi University. *The English Utilitarians and India*, published by the Clarendon Press in 1959, arose from Eric's interest in classical political theories and in Indian history. A stint as Professor at the University College of Rhodesia and Nyasaland, Salisbury, widened his horizons and gave him an abiding interest in comparative Commonwealth history. In 1963 he returned to Cambridge to teach in the History Faculty, and became the Smuts Professor of the History of the British Commonwealth in 1970. Later, he was honoured by being elected a Fellow of the British Academy. In these years he worked on Indian history, and published *The Peasant and the Raj: Studies in Agrarian Society and Peasant Rebellion in Colonial India* (Cambridge, 1978). His unfinished work on the Revolt of 1857 was to be later edited and published by Chris Bayly as *The Peasant Armed: The Indian Revolt of 1857* (Oxford, 1986). Other essays and reviews gave expression to his wide range of interests.

Indian history was the poorer for his untimely death. It is fitting that those who knew Eric Stokes should pay tribute to his memory. This thought prompted us, in 1988, to write to various scholars inviting them to contribute to a commemoration volume. Such collections, as all editors know, sometimes take a long time to get together. If we had waited for some of the contributions which had been promised, it would have been delayed still further.

What we do have is a collection of articles which relate to some of Eric Stokes' many research interests—British Indian ideologies, agrarian history and the Revolt of 1857. Some of the articles stray beyond these, secure in the conviction that Eric would have listened to them with the humourous twinkle and the half-smile which many of us remember from encounters at the India Office Library, the Cambridge South Asia seminars and the National Archives in Delhi. 'There is room for everyone', he once said to a student expressing diffidence about a research subject.

I

Eric Thomas Stokes
1924 - 1981

C.A. BAYLY

Eric Stokes was born on 10 July 1924 in Hampstead, London into a Cockney working-class environment. His father, Walter John Stokes, had fought in the Rifle Brigade in the First World War and had been severely traumatized. After the War he was only able to take casual jobs. Eric Stokes's mother, Winifred came from a Welsh Baptist family. Her religious beliefs and love of poetry, strongly influenced the young Stokes. He won a scholarship to Holloway School and received an uneventful education until the outbreak of war, when his school was evacuated from London and he was sent to Towcester, Northamptonshire. Boarded in village houses, Stokes was thrown together with Frank King (MA Christ's College, Cambridge; Headmaster, Highbury Grove School, 1955), the history master of Holloway School, who was a formative influence on his intellectual life and later took him to visit Cambridge. T.E. Lawrence's *Seven Pillars of Wisdom*, which King recommended to Stokes, seems to have awakened an early interest in travel. As a boy, Stokes had spent much time wandering around London streets and churches which also gave him a strong sense of the lived past. During the War he sometimes hitch-hiked to the capital with friends to observe the bomb damage at first hand. He always retained his affection for London and, in later years, he sometimes took his graduate students on long rambles from one Wren church to the next on the way from King's Cross Station to the India Office Library on the South Bank.

In December 1941 Stokes won an Exhibition to Christ's College, Cambridge to read History.[1] The life of the University was severely disrupted by War but Stokes developed a life-long interest in the History of Political Thought, which was already a major subject in the Historical Tripos. Michael Oakeshott, the philosopher and political theorist, had been a Fellow and College Lecturer at Gonville and Gaius College and was a member of the History Faculty until 1940. He was to take up this position again in 1947, by which time Stokes had himself returned to Cambridge. Herbert Butterfield was also lecturing in the Faculty and had begun his campaign to return political philosophy and religion to a central place in the analysis of historical change.

In the meantime, however, Stokes was 'tossed casually by war half-way across the globe and brigaded willy-nilly with men of diverse Commonwealth nations and races'.[2] In 1943 he was called up as an officer cadet and sent by a long and circuitous sea route to India. Avoiding U-boats, his troopship zig-zagged across the Atlantic before passing through the Mediterranean and Arabian seas. Two-thirds of the soldiers on board were suffering from dysentery and sunburn by the time their boat finally docked in Bombay in the spring of 1944.

Eric Stokes's years in India from 1944-6 were the formative influence on his view of the world. He found his later periods in Malaya and Africa challenging, but it was India to which he was most attached and where he felt most at home. His experience there taught him the 'conviction, or if you will, illusion . . . that part of the total meaning of things was to be discovered in this encounter with the world outside the European continent',[3] especially as this experience lay 'beyond the confines of urban, industrial civilisation'.[4] In the spring of 1944, he reported as an officer cadet trainee to the Cadet Wing, School of Artillery, India Command at Deolali near Bombay.[5] Later in the year he moved for further training to Ambala in the Punjab. Stokes was commissioned as a Lieutenant in the Royal Artillery and finally, in early 1945, allotted to the 30th Indian Mountain Artillery Regiment. He spent the first half of 1945 in a Reinforcement Camp for South-East Asia Command at an unidentified location 'east of the Brahmaputra'.[6] He never set foot in Burma during wartime because the dramatic Japanese surrender intervened.

Mountain Artillery units were still an essential fighting arm in the difficult terrain of southern Asia. Yet the spirit of Stokes's new unit seemed to hearken back to the days of Kipling's 'Barrack-room Ballads' and the struggles of martial races on the mountainous rim of India. The Colonel under whom he was to serve was reputed to be 'very horsey', disliking 'stinking mechanical vehicles'.[7] Stokes used to remark ironically that in the 1940s, when the rest of the world was engaged in a death-struggle which was resolved by mass air-bombardment and nuclear warfare, the Indian authorities were still apparently more concerned with uprisings on the North-West Frontier. Pathan millenarian leaders seemed to bulk as large in their strategy as Adolf Hitler or Marshal Tojo.

Stokes was trained by his martinet unit commander as a connoisseur of the pack mules and small horses which pulled the Mountain Artillery over the Indian ranges. He learned that white mules were always to be purchased in preference to brown ones and that the bruising inflicted by falling off them was mild by comparison with the abuse that he received from his superior officers when he did so. He was wary of the mules, which frequently bit or kicked him. But he wrote to his sister, Jessie Muirhead, that he preferred working with the animals alongside Indian troops to the brittle and formal life of the officers' mess.

Eric Stokes's early contacts with Indians made him much more open with his Indian colleagues and graduate students of later days than many of his peers. In 1944 he wrote from India of his pleasure of meeting Indians on equal terms as compared with 'the mercenary servility which is the normal rule here'.[8] He was always prepared to chide and joke with them in a manner which initially startled, but ultimately charmed even the most prickly members of the Indian intelligentsia whom he later encountered. Here the Subaltern of Mountain Artillery was perhaps of some service to the later historian of India. In one respect, though, Stokes did not put his Indian experiences to the service of his academic scholarship. He learned a considerable amount of Urdu in the Army. His notes for artillery manoeuvres are written in romanized Urdu, and he received friendly letters from his Indian NCOs in the language.[9] When he began to work on Indian social history in the 1970s, he never built on this proficiency in spoken Urdu. Perhaps the hiatus had been too long, or the Arabic script was too daunting.

Relatively few of Stokes's letters to his family during these years contain general comments about the situation in South Asia. He records his life as a rigid and often tedious routine, enlivened by games of chess and second-rate American films. To ease the boredom, which was not broken until the unit was ready for action in the very month that the atomic bomb was dropped, he made observations of the tropical night-sky and distantly admired the grace of Indian women during early morning rides around the military stations. His sister sent him *The New Statesman* and *Penguin New Writing* which sustained his strong political and literary interests.

Occasionally Stokes's broader reflections broke through the circumstantial detail of these letters. Visiting Bombay, he was struck by the wealth of Malabar Hill, home of the local elite, and compared it with the poverty of the 'depressed classes or untouchables, the biggest blot on Indian life and a crying condemnation of the caste system which perpetuates it'.[10] He felt the hostility of the residents of the major towns to the British, now clinging to their great South Asian Empire by their finger tips. Walking through the Indian neighbourhoods of Calcutta in his uniform, he realized with 'what cold hatred the politically conscious people (clerks, etc.) regarded me' and felt 'rather like a Nazi officer must have felt, walking along a Paris Boulevard'.[11] Visiting Calcutta University's History Department he fell into strenuous debate with its lecturers, trying to persuade them that 'we English weren't such blackguards as they tended to think'.[12] Stokes remained ambivalent about the British Empire, being born into it and yet criticizing it from the inside. He remarked that his Calcutta opponents were rational men who could see both sides of the argument. They could hardly be expected to view the British dispassionately. In an abject failure of colonial rule, 'two million peasants had died a mere two years ago'[13] during the great Bengal famine of 1943.

Stokes was in Delhi, on leave from Ambala, during the visit of the Cabinet Mission in April 1946. This was the British delegation which failed to bring about a final compromise between the Indian National Congress and the Muslim League, and so paved the way for the Partition of August 1947. At this time he recorded his sympathy for the Hindus in a striking manner. Deploring the preponderance of Muslim buildings in Delhi, he wrote 'From the beginning out here I have been more attracted towards Hinduism than Islam, which I instinctively regard as something alien to India.'[14] He recognized that Hindus and Muslims had lived together in reasonable harmony for a thousand years, and that a considerable exchange of values and practices had taken place. Contemporary communal hatreds were, he thought, not so much a consequence of British policies of divide-and-rule, but resulted instead from 'a growing knowledge of and realisation of the past. . . . The Hindu is become growingly aware of the devastation of his culture which the Muslims carried out. There is hardly a Hindu temple of any age or note in the whole of the north Indian plain.' These thoughts about Indian religion mirrored quite directly the ideology of the emergent Hindu right wing.

Eric Stokes's early views on Indian religion are also intriguing on a personal level. He recorded his preference for friendship with Muslims. His own strong, but rather abstract Christian convictions might have been expected to find a sympathetic echo in Islam, as with many Britons who disliked what they took to be the 'idolatry' of Hinduism. But here we begin to glimpse the attraction to paradox and ambiguity which was an important component of his attitudes. Having read some of the Hindu scriptures in translation, Hinduism itself appeared to him to be congenial religion of paradox and diversity. Complex to the end, he finished the letter to his sister about Delhi's architecture by wondering if he had been too harsh about Muslim culture.

Caste divisions also seemed to be a critical feature of Indian life to Stokes at this time. On an earlier visit to Bombay, Stokes had speculated that here was a good chance that 'when the British bayonets left India' the wealthy Parsi Zoroastrian community of Bombay might be subject to 'a scourge greater than the pogroms of the Middle Ages' from a revolution of the untouchables.[15] His attitudes mirrored the conventional British view that Indian society was irrevocably split on the lines of caste and religion and that the Raj was the only thing that lay between Indian and anarchy. That view was at least plausible in the last two years of British rule.

The young British officer's casual observation of the strong communal divisions which permeated the Indian Army confirmed these judgements of racial essence. Stokes noted that the Mountain Artillery regiments took the pick of Indian troops, especially 'Sikhs and [Muslim] Punjabis. The former are definitely more clever, but the Punjabi are easily the most lovable.'[16] He also wrote that he had intervened in a dispute between a Muslim Sanitary Havildar and a Hindu Gurkha soldier who complained that his food had been polluted by the Muslim.[17] In Malaya in the following year, he complained that his Ahir troops were to be replaced with Dogras (Kashmiri Hindus). The Ahirs (pastoralists and peasants from north India) 'are not soldiers by instinct, and hence need a lot of supervision' but 'they were very likeable individually'.[18]

When, in the early 1960s, Stokes first began to write on Indian social as opposed to intellectual history, he still thought of castes and religions as concrete and sharply defined social units. His later experience of the African 'tribe' had already raised many questions for him about the ultimate value of these colonial social categories. But the early analyses of the Rebellion of 1857 tend to describe the castes as the major actors.[19] In the 1970s, however, he was to be influenced at Cambridge by the social anthropology of Edmund Leach and Stanley Tambiah, which held that castes were not the hard-edged entities that Stokes had once thought. Close reading of British Indian revenue and rent-rate reports of the nineteenth century was to convince him that factions and interests within broad caste groups were the most important units of analysis.[20] In this respect, he was to quietly move from the colonial to the post-colonial in his own thinking.

Meanwhile, in India Command, Stokes noted what he regarded as the ominous failure of the Army to recognize Victory in Asia Day (15 August 1945). He speculated that units such as his, which had recently finished their training, would be used to reoccupy the former South-East Asian territories of the British Empire. In the event, his unit left Bangalore on 21 September 1945 and carried out occupation duties near Rangoon and Bangkok. It was finally stationed in Malaya for a brief period in early 1946. Here its main duty was to disband the Indian National Army, the force which had been raised by the nationalist leader, Subhas Chandra Bose, to fight alongside the Japanese against the British.

Stokes's first introduction to Malaya, where he and his wife were later to spend five years, was not suspicious. The country had been wrecked by warfare; rations and commodities were hard to come by. Stokes also felt the people of the Far East were 'inscrutable' and never imagined forming the links with them which he believed he had developed with Indians.[21] Yet he thought that he had had a 'very easy war' and had missed 'very sticky' fighting on the Burma Front by the 'skin of his teeth'.[22] Writing from the Royal Artillery Mess in Peshawar on 22 July 1946, he remarked that, despite the heat of the North-West Frontier, he would have preferred India to the grim England of 1946, but Cambridge would probably not keep open his place unless he returned for the Michaelmas Term 1946.

Another consideration dampened Stokes's interest in going home. A confirmed democrat of twenty-one years of age in the days of Attlee's popular government, he nevertheless wrote that he would find it a great wrench to break with 'a society where relations are still unmarred by twisted views of equality' which prevailed in the West.[23] Dealing with Indian troops, who looked to the British officer for their welfare and happiness created 'a very happy, idyllic relationship' so different from the 'national and class struggles' of Europe. Such romantic and paternalist attitudes had been essential to the British Empire, and explain why so many of its servants found it difficult to live in post-war Britain, preferring Africa or Australasia in Eric Stokes's case, they also chimed with his continuing interests in Michael Oakeshott's ideas, the role of Victorian idealist philosophy in the British Empire and the poetry of Tennyson or Kipling.

Demobilized under an early release scheme, Stokes returned to Christ's for the Michaelmas Term 1946 along with so many other members of the wartime generation. History teaching at Christ's had been galvanized by the arrival there as Fellow of J.H. Plumb, who had worked in intelligence during the War. Stokes was to take Plumb's special subject in Part II of the Tripos and was also supervised by Anthony Steel, the medieval historian. The moral and intellectual life of the University had been transformed more broadly by the return of hundreds of mature and experienced men and women. Acutely aware of the loss of life and promise they had witnessed, they were determined to make every moment count.

Stokes pursued his academic interests in British history and the History of Political Theory. He was inspired by Plumb's lectures on the eighteenth century and Pevsner's on English architecture, besides following the lectures of David Knowles, Michael Postan, Helen Cam, John Saltmarsh, and Edward Miller. His growing interest in the peasantry, in sharp contrast to his concerns in intellectual history, was also galvanized by reading Marc Bloch's studies of France.

The returning 1946 year included Charles Parkin, whom Stokes had met in India (Fellow and College Lecturer, Clare College, 1948-83) and Frank Spooner (Fellow, 1951-7, later Professor of Economic History at Durham, 1966-85) who became close friends of his. Parkin was another enthusiast for the History of Political Thought and later wrote on Edmund Burke. Other contemporaries and later correspondents were 'Bill' E.T. Williams (later Warden of Rhodes House, Oxford), James Mossman (later Foreign Office Intelligence and foreign affairs journalist) and Kenneth Ballhatchet (later Professor of History at SOAS, London University), Christie Eliezer, a Tamil mathematician from Sri Lanka was also a close friend with whom Stokes was to serve in Malaya. All these men helped develop his historical interests. The letters written between them over the next two decades ranged over politics, religion, and current affairs. Almost Victorian in tone, they are testimony to high-minded ideals of scholarship and service and to a day-to-day literary stylishness, which are now difficult to reproduce.

Two other important developments occurred at this period. In 1947 Eric Stokes, who had always been of a questioning but spiritual frame of mind, was confirmed as an Anglican Christian in Christ's College Chapel. The officiating priest was Canon I.T. Ramsey, an important influence on Stokes's religious life. About this time, he met Florence Mary Lee, then a student teacher at Homerton College, whom he married in 1949. They were to bring up their four daughters in Malaya and Rhodesia.

After graduation in 1949, Stokes's experience of India and interest in the history of political thought drew him, by a stroke of cleverness, to combine two fields that were to become very significant in post-War Cambridge: extra-European history and the history of political thought. He began to work on the influence of James Mill and the British utilitarians on the government of the East India Company. This work was finally presented as a Ph.D. thesis in 1952 and was published as *The English Utilitarians and India* in 1959. His supervisor in this work was Dr. T.G.P. Spear (graduate of St Catharine's College and Bursar of Selwyn), formerly of the Government of India Information Service in Delhi, who had returned to Selwyn College as Fellow and Bursar after Independence. Spear proved an enthusiastic but somewhat distant supervisor (apparently he did not finally read the thesis in full until after it had been examined in late 1952).[24] Spear's own interests in eighteenth- and early nineteenth-century Delhi fitted well with those of Stokes. One of Stokes's examiners was to be C.H. Philips (later Director of SOAS and Vice-Chancellor of London University), an expert on the history of the East India Company. Philips also proved to be a strong supporter of Stokes throughout his career.

The opportunities for university teaching in straitened post-War Britain were limited. By 1950 Stokes had decided he was unlikely to secure a position in Britain. Now married, he began to look for academic posts overseas. This attracted him because he was acutely aware of the importance of training a generation of local people to occupy positions of responsibility, now that British rule in Asia was ending. At this period, lecturers' posts in the Empire were still dispensed by the Inter-University Board for Higher Education which worked closely with the Colonial Office. Stokes went to London for an interview in answer to an advertisement for a history post in the Caribbean. Instead, on arrival, he was sent down the corridor to the door marked 'Malaya', where he secured a lectureship in the new University of Malaya in Singapore.

The federation of Malaya (present-day Malaysia and Singapore) to which Eric and Florence Stokes embarked in the middle of 1950 was a different place from the devastated society which he had briefly visited four years before. The region was now beginning to embark upon the long economic boom which was to make it the world's most dynamic economic region. The old colonial society patterned on the Indian model with its huge bungalows, lush gardens, and innumerable servants had been destroyed by Japanese occupation and the horrors of internment in Changi Gaol. It had given way to a more modest, and less racially segregated expatriate community of middle-class people with restricted incomes of whom the Stokes were typical. In the University, European, Malay, and Chinese staff and students lived together. The Chinese element was dominant among the undergraduates, accounting for 564 out of the 859 students in 1951-2. Malay men were better represented on the Arts side, though Malay women were notable by their absence throughout the University.[25]

Government policy, too, had changed quite rapidly immediately before the Stokeses' arrival, reflecting Britain's need to cling on in an area of great strategic and economic importance. It was only recently that the authorities had decided to transform the venerable Raffles College, an undergraduate teaching institution, and an associated medical college into the University of Malaya, which was to have advanced English-medium teaching and research facilities.[26] The developmental aspects of colonial rule were to be stressed in what John Lonsdale has called 'the imperialism of the welfare state'. The new History Department taught British, European, and Commonwealth history (all of which Stokes tried his hand at). But Malcolm MacDonald, who was both High Commissioner and Chancellor of the University, along with some of his officials, believed that a sense of common Malayan identity should also be fostered.[27] Malayan and Chinese literature and some South and South-East Asian history made its appearance in the advanced classes at the University.

Although in retrospective comparison with Central Africa, South-East Asia was a relatively open and progressive colonial society, the British authorities faced serious unrest. One local correspondent informed Stokes before he set sail in late 1950 that there were now a dozen murders a day in the Federation.[28] He added that it was unsafe to travel beyond Johore Baru a few miles away from Singapore, and that the population 'though not pro-Bandit . . . was certainly not pro-British' and that the authorities were totally incompetent. Soon after the Stokeses arrived in Singapore, they found the city paralysed and in flames following the so-called Maria Hertogh riots (11-13 December 1950).[29]

Further riots and disturbances followed in the next two years as the Malayan Communist Party mobilized for war against the British. Their insurgency was only brought to an end by the vigorous and authoritarian rule of General Sir Gerald Templer, who instituted the scheme of protected villages to seal off the Chinese squatter farmers from Communist infiltration.

In the rich Chinese commercial city of Singapore, these problems seemed relatively distant, the disturbances concentrated up-country in the rubber estates. Living in the protected environment of the University of Malaya, the Stokeses encountered a few radical activists such as James Puthucheary, who was later imprisoned by the authorities. Letters from students and colleagues in other parts of the colony, however, spoke of the tense situation. On the occasion of one riot, the students came to the campus armed with hockey sticks to protect their white teachers from molestation. As a former officer, Stokes joined the local Volunteer Corps. He appears to have believed that the best way to defeat Communist insurgency was to continue the 'Asia for the Asians policy' which had been announced by Malcolm MacDonald.[30] Stokes's natural contacts among indigenous intellectuals included people such as Eunice Thio, a lecturer in History, who believed in nationalist political activity, but was hostile to Communist radicalism.[31] More, rapidly than most expatriates, including academics, Stokes had begun to believe in managed, but quite brisk decolonization.

Stokes's attitudes to Malayan political issues had formed rapidly, and, as in India, he was well ahead of official and expatriate thinking. Yet his ideas were still tinged with idealistic paternalism. In a talk for University Staff he delivered in November 1952 he discussed the 'Basis of a Malayan Nation'. A nation, he wrote anticipating Benedict Anderson's main thesis, was a 'modern community' acutely aware of its own special identity which was created by economic structure and the 'intercommunication of ideas'. Malayan society was a 'frontier society' whose 'main cluster of roots went back less than three generations'.[32]

In Malaya, Stokes argued, the sense of Malayaness' was initially developed amongst a new class, the upwardly mobile Chinese and Indian immigrants. The problem for Malaya, he thought, was that this middle class mobilization against the British had opened up a divide not only between the commercial elites, the Malayan peasants and Chinese squatters, but even between the Chinese bourgeoisie and the old Malayan official class.[33] In these conditions 'ancient race prejudice' could flourish as it had done in India where the modern hatred of the Hindu moneylender 'rallied the ancient hostility of religion' to fight on its side and bring about Partition.

In India, though, there was a central administration and a core of nationhood which was strong enough for the British to devolve power to and ready to fight militant Communism. That was not so in Malaya or South-East Asia as a whole.[34] The British still had one final task in presiding over the emergence of a new, democratic Malaya. A successful outcome had become more likely, he told an Adult Education Class in 1953, as new Chinese immigration had ceased during the War and the new Malay-born Chinese elite was disenchanted with the Communist government in China. Yet racial antagonisms were still so strong that an independent Singapore might have to be created.[35] Here Stokes anticipated events nearly a decade ahead, when Singapore finally split from the newly independent Malaysia.

Nevertheless, in 1953 Stokes thought that there was still the basis for a democratic Malay nation which included Singapore. The prospects were brighter than in other Asian societies whose 'hopeless poverty makes freedom meaningless'. It depended largely on how the predominantly Chinese middle class conducted itself. The middle class would need to compromise internally between different races. More important, he thought, it would need to turn its back on its 'gross materialism', which had been intensified by Western secularism, and improve its 'moral conduct' through social provision and community development. The British government also had a role here, he thought. It had a duty to do nothing to promote communalism politically. It should not, for instance, institute separate communal electorates as it had done in India. Instead, working with the trade unions it should promote social welfare. It must 'prepare the administration for the transfer of power by ensuring that now Asians of high quality are given training'.[36]

In a small way Stokes attempted to put these ideals into action in his own sphere of authority. Soon after he arrived, he had noticed that the staff's indigenous servants were housed in cramped and unventilated quarters. He intervened with the University authorities to improve their conditions, though embarrassingly it transpired that they preferred their old quarters to the new, custom-built accommodation created for them. Still the officer of sepoys, he also wanted to provide entertainments and Christmas boxes for members of the subordinate staff to 'improve the general spirit of relationships among us'.[37]

Biography is easier when the subject retains a straightforward and predictable moral or political position throughout his life. Fundamentally, Stokes probably did remain the Christian idealist revealed by many of his letters. But his intellect was always attracted to paradox and humour and he was constantly on the lookout for an occasion to tease, amuse, or shock his audience. While believing strongly in the historical influence of ideas, he would still sometimes take up a surprisingly materialist, even cynical position. Less than two years after his lecture on the need for a moral basis of Malay nationhood, we find him addressing a pious British Council 'Conference on Commonwealth Studies' and arguing that the Commonwealth bond was ultimately based on commercial interest, and nothing more. There was a message here. Britain's 'shrewd commercial instinct' had 'preserved her from those dangerous delusions of power and prestige which have misled other colonial powers'. He presumably had the imminent French defeat at Dien Bien Phu in mind.[38]

Stokes's desire to shock people from current orthodoxies or pieties mirrored his historian's opinion about the complexity of historical causation. He felt that neither ideological not economic interpretations of historical events could possibly be sufficient on their own. As he wrote in a Singapore student magazine, monocausal arguments necessarily moved out of the realm of historical explanation into that of political ideology.[39]

In general, though, it was the problems of building up a young history department, writing lectures to cover much of modern history and taking up once again the history of the English utilitarians in India that occupied Stokes in Malaya. On campus at least, relations between the races were quite good, with Muslims, Chinese, Eurasians and Europeans, working and living side by side. Stokes was distantly impressed by the energy and bravura of its head, C.N. Parkinson, a historian of Asian trade, best known, of course, for Parkinson's Law. Stokes also encouraged students and younger members of the Department to move away from European Political History to studies of the local Chinese and Malay communities. Wang Gungwu, one of his students and later friends in the Malayan and Singapore university system, was later to make major contributions to the historical sociology of pre-colonial and colonial South-East Asia which took up in detail some of the issues to which Stokes had briefly alluded in his talks and unpublished papers.[40]

Yet while Stokes himself wrote history about Britain, India, and Central Africa, he published nothing significant about South-East Asia. His only historical exploration of the region was contained in lectures on the Malay princes and indirect rule, a form of government which he wrote about more fully in the case of Africa. Why was this? The main reason was certainly that he had not finished revising his doctoral thesis for publication. He also seems to have accepted the common Raj attitude that South-East Asia was really a poor man's India. In an unusually savage review of John Bastin, *The Native Policies of Sir Stamford Raffles in Java and Sumatra* (Oxford, 1957) in the journal *History*, he asserted that Sir Stamford Raffles was 'not a man of settled principle but . . . a mecurial opportunist', who derived anything that was important in his programmes from Indian precedents, which Bastin had supposedly ignored. Bastin responded negatively to this attack, and with some justice.[41] Ironically, the historiography of South-East Asia began to develop quite quickly about the time of Stokes's departure and he unwittingly made some contribution to its development.

By 1954, Stokes was, according to his letters to Charles Parkin, beginning to feel a sense of drift in his life in the University of Malaya. The Ph.D. thesis was passed but not yet published. Cambridge University Press committed an error of judgement by stating that it did not publish dissertations when Percival Spear showed the final draft to them in 1953.[42] In the meantime, Stokes had neither the leisure nor the inclination to continue the modifications to the thesis which Spear had proposed.

The situation in Malaya was also changing. The Communists had been defeated, but the Malays had emerged in a very strong position. What Stokes had called 'the Gamble on Independence'[43] was in train and he may have felt that the future for expatriate academics was less rosy than it had been. Most important, the education of the Stokeses' two children was a looming problem. While educational standards were good in the Federation, many of the British residents, still scarred by memories of Japanese occupation and Communist violence, sent their children home.

Moving out of the colonial into the domestic university world, Stokes was appointed to a lectureship in History at the University of Bristol where he spent the years 1955-6. Stokes found his new colleagues pleasant, but he never really adjusted to the large civic university after the intimacy and novelty of Malaya or the traditions of Cambridge. By comparison with anthropology departments, British university history departments were still disinclined to teach overseas history, even of the constitutional and ideological sort which Stokes then practised.

Distant temporarily from the colonial frontier, Stokes had time in Bristol to consider the relationship between his recent experiences and the political thought which still preoccupied him. He was naturally attracted to the organic understanding of state and society of which Burke was the leading British proponent. He rejected abstract rights theories of the European and socialist tradition. But in view of his experience of colonial war and repression, he worried about where the state and individual rights fitted into Burke's scheme. Was the expansion of Europe with its injustices, slaughter, and expropriation of native peoples 'natural' in the Burkean sense? 'Do you, like Burke, throw a decent veil over the beginning of states?'[44] How was the day-to-day repression of the colonial state in Cyprus, Malaya, Kenya (and very shortly Suez) to be reconciled with the idea that power was a gift from God to the rulers?

The contemporary study of political ideas in Britain seemed to have little to say on such matters. 'What in your view', he asked Parkin, 'is the relationship of the academic study of historical ideas to our own political situation?'[45] Ultimately, Stokes must have answered himself. Direct action in their appropriate spheres by educated men, inspired by the best of both the liberal and the organic traditions, was the most that could be hoped for. Besides, Stokes was suffering 'regret and nostalgia over leaving Malaya'. Among other things, return to England had checked his fuller acceptance of Christianity and revived some long-standing problems he had about belief in the Divinity of Christ. He sometimes depicted himself as more of a deist or unitarian than an orthodox Christian.[46] He also began to 'feel deeply that I am not fitted for the life of an academic recluse. . . . I would like to make some contribution to the awful African problem.[47] It was this thought that went back with him to the colonial frontier in Salisbury, Southern Rhodesia.

Despite his staleness with the work and the place, it was during his period in Bristol that Stokes completed most of the revisions to his Ph.D. thesis which was to be published in 1959 as *The English Utilitarians and India.* The work has been called 'a minor classic in the History of Political Thought' (F. Rosen),[48] and it was received with extremely favourable reviews. One reason for this was its literary quality. It won Stokes a 'Silver Pen Award, 1955-9' from the 'Journal Fund' of New Jersey in the same group as Henry Kissinger. Samuel Huntington, George Kennan, and Ralf Dahrendorf. It also appeared at the right time. Twelve years after Indian Independence, the British were beginning to consider their former South Asian Empire with greater objectivity. Spurred by the centenary of the Mutiny Rebellion of 1857, Indians were also beginning to reassess the so-called Age of Reform of the 1830s which was thought to have been a prelude to the Rebellion. Most important, the book appeared to show political ideas inaction and analyse the first major Western attempt to modernize the 'Third World'. It attracted American interest at a time when Americans were in the grip of modernization theory and beginning self-consciously to take up the 'White Man's burden'.

Inevitably, for a classic nearly forty years old. *The English Utilitarians* has suffered as much emulation as refutation over the years. The metaphor Stokes applied to Robinson and Gallagher's *Africa and the Victorians* applies as well to his own book. Like some ancient and scarred African bull elephant, tusks splintered, one-eyed, carcass bristling with embedded spears, it still crashes on through the bush. Of the main contentions it contained, the great importance of evangelical thought on the government of Britain and its empire in the first half of the nineteenth century has been continuously vindicated. If anything, Boyd Hilton's *The age of Atonement* (Cambridge, 1989) and continuing work by Andrew Porter show this theme being extended and developed.

By contrast, the role of utilitarianism in Indian government and Indian revenue systems has appeared to dwindle over time. The earliest line of attack on this idea was from historians of the Indian localities. These scholars showed either that Indian social structures reproduced themselves underneath the turmoil of land-revenue settlements, blunting or rendering insignificant British policy initiatives, or that the British themselves were prevented by their lack of money and knowledge of the country form effecting much change. Yet here some of Stokes's argument can be preserved. The detailed work of Peter Penner[49] has shown that men of the R.M. Bird and James Thomason school of revenue administration did actually but the 'levelling' doctrines of net-produce rent theory into practice in some districts of northern India. Later work on the history of agrarian Punjab also suggested that broadly utilitarian and evangelical ideas were important, and were acted upon by officials such as Robert Cust and Robert Montgomery.

Another, and more recent line of critique has been directed at Stokes's reading of the domestic context of utilitarian ideas. Lynn Zastoupil has argued that Stokes associated John Stuart Mill too easily with James Mill's position on Indian government. Zastoupil argues that the Younger Mill moved much closer in his views to Burke and the organic tradition which valued the customs and language of subject peoples.[50] F. Rosen has likewise argued that Stokes relied overmuch on Elie Halevy's view of the utilitarian tradition.[51] This led him to over-emphasize its authoritarian implications and ignore the extent to which both James Mill and Jeremy Bentham drew rigid limits to the exercise of state power by their repeated insistence on the need for representative government.

This still leaves us with the problem of locating the ideological basis of the clear authoritarian and interventionist tone of Indian government after 1818. The answer may lie in the inheritance of the era of Lord Wellesley, whose aggressive aristocratic paternalism, inspired individuals such as Charles Metcalfe without benefit of utilitarianism. Yet Stokes's arguments may still have some force. For instance, C.E. Trevelyan, a key figure in Lord William Bentinck's 'Age of Reform', was nearer to the model of a utilitarian evangelical and in both India and Ireland, his commitment to representative government was very weak. Controversies such as this demonstrate that it is the capacity of *The English Utilitarians and India* to continue to raise historical questions which marks it out as a seminal work on the history of British government and India.

Before the book's long and somewhat painful gestation was completed, Stokes himself had been translated to another field of imperial crisis. In 1956 the British Government decided to extend its policy of developing higher education to Central Africa and founded the University College of Rhodesia and Nyasaland at Salisbury. Roland Oliver having rejected the Chair of History, the authorities offered it to Stokes, who accepted. But the posting was a difficult one. Florence Stokes remembers that arriving in Rhodesia in 1957 was like 'landing on the moon', a far cry from the cosmopolitanism of Singapore. The journey on the Union Castle Line to South Africa was followed by a three days' train journey up into the High Veld, a reminder of the continuing social and political dependence of Central Africa on the huge white bastion to the south. Though the new Principal, Walter Adams (later Director of LSE), met the Stokeses off the train, the University house they occupied was at that time 4 miles outside Salisbury in deep elephant grass with no telephone or public transport.

These practical problems were dwarfed by political and social ones. This was the period shortly before the acrimonious breakup of the Central African Federation into black and white dominated national units. In Southern Rhodesia the power of the new generation of white settlers who had fled post-War Britain or who were seeking a new beginning outside South Africa was visibly growing.[52] Racial attitudes were much harsher than they had been in Malaya and black people were treated with barely concealed contempt. Initially, there were no black members of staff at the College. Black students had to pay fees for education beyond the age of eleven unless they were in mission schools while white students had their education free. Blacks were subject to rigorous pass laws which meant, for instance, that the Stokeses' African servants were unable to bring their wives or husbands to stay in the white township, although the law allowed this in the University enclave to which the Stokeses later moved.

Not the least distasteful feature of Rhodesia was that white neighbours in their first housing colony snooped on each other and informed the police of fraternization with the blacks. African nationalism was rigidly controlled in the colony, but white political activity in sympathy with African aspirations was already growing and was strongly represented among the young British and South African teachers on the Campus. Lecturers from the University who carried out extra-mural classes in the black suburb of Harare, including Stokes, were regularly tailed by police agents. Shortly before Stokes left the Campus in 1963, one of his politically active colleagues in the History Department, Terence Ranger, was deported from the colony by the government of Sir Roy Welensky as white Southern Rhodesia slipped towards the inglorious interlude of UDI and white domination.

As Professor responsible for the future of a major department of a new university, Stokes's attitude was more cautious than that of his activist colleagues. His position was that 'the true British political tradition was the spirit and practice of representative government'. Democracy was still a distant ideal in Central Africa because of the great gap in education between rich and poor. But representative government was not, and educated Africans should be rapidly 'admitted to a share of political power' as representatives of all Africans.[53] Elsewhere he justified this position by arguing that the genius of the British political tradition was not that of the abstract European Rights of Man, but of 'representative rather than democratic government'.[54] It was uniquely suited to the type of political gradualism which was needed in Central Africa: 'the European is required to enter into close relations with the African, to wrench him from his tribal society, to congregate him in factories and towns, to look to him as a market, to instruct him in western tastes and values. . . . For in such attunement lies the preordained harmony where interest and morality coincide.' While Stokes saw this modernization process as inevitable, he was not sanguine about its results and regretted the rapid destruction of old beliefs and communities.

Stokes's attitudes were not informed only by his reading of political thought. As in Malaya, he was fearful that either a too fast or a too slow advance towards the goal of full representative government would pitch the country into the hands of Communist radicals. He disliked doctrinaire socialism both because it was godless and because it overrode individual rights. On this—and on this alone—he was sat one with the Salisbury white oligarchy. He gave several talks to the African Broadcasting Studios. One of these (15 September 1960) was a subtle intervention in the official campaign to counter Communist influence among the black population. He argued that Communist rule in Russia did not mean equality, as some black nationalists were arguing. Instead, the Soviet Government 'deliberately kept wages low and the shops half empty of foodstuffs and household goods in order that Russia might have the world's largest standing army and such expensive toys as rockets to the moon'. The Communist danger was quite real because Africa was 'ripe for the totalitarian messianism of the Right (e.g., Egypt) or the Left'.[55]

On the other hand, the University College of Rhodesia and Nyasaland was a place of considerable intellectual buoyancy, expanding its numbers of history lecturers. As Professor. Eric Stokes had to lecture across an even wider range of medieval and modern history than had been the case in Singapore. His witty, irreverent side relished the 'delightful, music-hall comedy feel to life' as panjandrum in a new but very remote college.[56] More interesting, it had been in the previous fifteen years that African history had come of age as an academic discipline in African, British, and American universities. Basil Davison's *Old Africa Rediscovered* (1960) and *Black Mother* had given the subject visibility, though Stokes thought that they were somewhat sentimental.[57]

The 'scientific' historical work, however, had been done by Roland Oliver (London) G.P. Murdock (Yale) and many historians in South African universities. In Salisbury itself. Terence Ranger was taking the lead in charting the history of black experience under colonialism. A British historian from Christ's, Richard Brown set himself to study the pre-colonial societies of Central Africa. Clyde Mitchell, head of anthropology (later Professor in Manchester and Oxford) was also a powerful force in departmental politics and, as a friend of Stokes and successor to Gluckman, a firm supporter of cooperation between anthropology and history.[58] In this he was aided by Jaap van Velsen (author of *The Politics of Kinship: A Study in Social Manipulation among the Lakeside Tonga of Nyasaland* (Manchester, 1964). The ancient historian, C.R. Whittaker, was another who nudged the department towards the study of a broad social history.

With the *English Utilitarians* a recently published critical success, it was not to be expected that Stokes would give up his interest in the influence of ideas on historical change or his Indian concerns. But he devoted some of his time to the history of Zambezian Africa and the government of South Africa. The focus on smaller administrative units, tribal structures and even popular resistance was slowly to move his Indian work, too, in a different direction. He and his colleagues recognized that 'the prevalent trend in historical writing is unquestionably affected by the rise of African nationalism and the belief in the need for examining the African past with renewed sympathy and insight'.[59]

A powerful influence here was the Rhodes-Livingstone Institute which, through the work of the anthropologist, Max Gluckman, and others had brought Central Africa into the forefront of anthropological theory. During Stokes's time, two seminal conferences were held. The first, the Leverhulme History Conference (Salisbury, September 1960) brought together historians and anthropologists, including African intellectuals. Another at Lusaka in September 1963 was devoted to the new African social and political history. Some of the papers at this meeting drew on oral history techniques which were being pioneered at this time by Jan Vansina. Others considered novel topics such as the role of spirit medium cults. The historical role of these cults in the formation of African kingdoms and their resistance to European invasion was highlighted by their contemporary importance in African nationalist movements.

Terence Ranger and Richard Brown were in the forefront of this work, but a new generation of indigenous male and female history graduates of Stokes's department, such as Mutumba Mainga and Lishoma Muuka (later of the Zambian Ministry of Foreign Affairs) also made one of their first appearances before white academic audiences at this meeting.[60] To Terence Ranger's delight, Stokes had put him in charge of the first History Honours Group of students out of which Mutumba Mainga and several other future Ph.Ds were drawn.[61] In addition to the new African history, a major influence on all the participants in these meetings was the school of British social anthropology. The references in the papers to 'segmentary states' and 'acephalous societies' distantly echo the seminal work of Edward Evans Pritchard. A more direct influence in Salisbury were the South African based anthropologists. Max Gluckman, Meyer Fortes (later Stokes's colleague at Cambridge), and Audrey Richards.

As in politics, so in academic matters, Stokes was a liberal rather than a radical. He approved of the new Central African 'school of sociological [i.e. anthropological] history', but seemed to echo Ronald Robinson in arguing that it was 'deficient in analysis' and was condemned to mere antiquarianism unless it elucidated broad, comparative issues.[62] This was to be a theme in Stokes's later Indian historical writing. On the one hand, he always insisted on full primary documentation. For instance, writing some years before to Parkin who felt that appropriate 'historical explanation' had no necessary connection with primary documentary evidence, Stokes asserted that 'without original sources, there is no feel of history'.[63] On the other hand, he believed that all history was essentially comparative history. The comparative element for Stokes was generally supplied by the structures and policies of colonial administrators, even at the level of local administration. In his Cambridge years, he seemed to accept some of Geoffrey Elton's critique of 'soft', social history topics.

Though he took up anthropological taxonomies of kingdoms and states, Stokes was critical of the concept of culture, which he thought meaningless as an analytical term. In later years he viewed with puzzlement the headlong rush in American studies of India towards what he regarded as essentializing 'ethno-history'. He had little time for gender studies, believed there were iron limits to the worth of the history of mentalities and paid strangely little attention to religion in his own work. Stokes, however, was in no sense an academic conservative. He always received novel intellectual positions with the fascination of the student of thought. His critique of them was pointed, but rarely dismissive.

In these circumstances, it is not surprising that Stokes's contribution to African historiography was to be largely in examining the micro-structures of Central African colonial administration and the taxonomy of the more solidly founded African kingdoms. The book he edited with Richard Brown, *The Zambezian Past* (1966), which issued from the Lusaka Conference, contained a part introduction and two articles by Stokes. This work, like much of what was done in the University College, had arisen out of the need to teach undergraduate special subjects to whites and Africans in Central African History[64] and to assign archivally-based projects to advanced students.

Stokes believed that he was the only member of the department who did not really 'come off' as an African historian as such. He felt he had spent too much time finishing off his Indian work and running up the successive 'impasses', as he thought, of Milnerism and Indirect Rule. Neither of these produced much published work for him. Milnerism came to nothing because Milner himself seemed *sui generis* in British imperial history, an authoritarian failure who was of little significance compared with the idealist school of Lionel Curtis. Despite copious note-taking, Indirect Rule also seemed a dead fruit, with lord Lugard himself already having said all that needed to be said.

It was Roland Oliver who pointed Stokes to the issue of the British pacification of Central Africa. Stokes, therefore, began to research and write on the fall of Yao power on Lake Malawi and the attenuated survival under British paramountcy of King Lewanika's Barotse kingdom in the far west of the Zambezian Valley. In a retrospective comment of 1974 he argued that these essays were 'period pieces'. Because of their emphasis on the paramount importance of British motives and policies, he felt they defied the trend of Africanization. This was then running strongly and reached its apogee as far as Barotseland was concerned in Gwyn Prins's, *The Hidden Hippopotomus* (1982).

Even in 1960, however, Stokes believed that it was 'important to preserve the truth that there had actually been a historical phenomenon called imperialism and the European motives and actions still deserved continued study'.[65] That view has been amply endorsed more recently. For African historians were to come to realize in the following twenty years that to account for African resistance and African social forms, from spirit cults to 'tribes', still required a steady concentration on the nature of European power which moulded them and provided the conditions in which they could reproduce themselves.

Stokes's two essays in *The Zambezian Past* and his contribution to the volume's introduction marks the transition between his early work on the political theory of empire and his later articles on Indian social history. Indeed, until Stokes and T.R. Metcalf began to work on social change in the north Indian regions in the 1960s, there was nothing remotely resembling this style of work in modern Indian historiography. In *The Zambezian Past*, Stokes is happy to concede the importance of African agency. The centralized states of pre-colonial Africa had the capacity and sometimes the will to resist European invasion. Similarly, decentralized or 'acephalous' polities also often threw up long standing resistance movements, he argued. By contrast, it was semi-centralized but segmentary kingdoms which, with their internal divisions, were easy prey to the white conquerors. He later applied some of these arguments to nineteenth-century India.

But such historical sociology could only go so far, Stokes asserted. Purposive European imperialism had also to be taken into account. Analysing Sir Harry Johnston's destruction of the Malawi kingdoms between 1893 and 1903, Stokes noted the practical constraints within which British conquest operated. Given considerable military and political resources, Lord Lugard could afford to crush indigenous resistance quickly in northern Nigeria but then totally recast native authority in the form of 'indirect rule'. The model, Stokes believed, was the Indian experience of Lord Dalhousie's period which Lugard quoted. And the key was not so much the Indian native states, but the operation of British authority in the so-called non-regulation provinces.[66] In Malawi, Johnston had no such resources. Paradoxically, he therefore set himself to systematically subvert African authority and effect a piecemeal, but complete conquest.[67] Yet even these practical constraints were not the whole story. Johnston himself was a protégé of the 'aggressive' modernizing imperialism of Joseph Chamberlain and the British politicians of the 1890s.

In these essays and other papers, Stokes tried to reach behind the formal distinction between direct and indirect rule. He also sought to distance himself somewhat both from the 'Africanist' theories of his Salisbury colleagues and from the view that 'local crises' explained British policy in its entirety. This view had been powerfully reinforced by Robinson and Gallagher two years earlier in their *Africa and the Victorians.*

Sometime before completing his Zambezian work, Stokes had already made one final general statement on the role of ideas in the British Empire of the later nineteenth century. His inaugural lecture given in the University College of Rhodesia and Nyasaland in 1960 was published as *The Political Ideas of English Imperialism.* Thirty-eight pages in length, it stands as sketch for a volume on the intellectual history of the British Empire of the later nineteenth century which he never published. He did, however, do a considerable amount of work on state papers in the UK and Africa and published several preliminary articles which were facilitated by a Rockefeller grant which he received in the late 1950s.

Stokes's inaugural in Rhodesia is particularly illuminating because it is much more self-reflective that *The English Utilitarians* and it ranges over the whole of imperial history rather than focusing on India alone. It begins with a defence of intellectual history or political thought, as he calls it, against the tendency to dismiss ideology as a force in political history which was in full spate with the 'Namierite deluge' of the 1950s and 1960s. Even if Herbert Butterfield's strictures on Namier's view of the eighteenth century lacked force (and they probably did not), Stokes argued, one could not 'take the mind out of the history' of the later nineteenth century when 'classes open to intellectual influences had a much closer hold on political power'.[68] Despite this rejection of Namierism, Stokes remained fascinated at some level by the notion of political faction and the politics of rational economic man. He was to see the heresy emerge once again in the so-called Cambridge school of Indian political history of Anil Seal and John Gallagher ten years later and often quixotically denounced his own earlier work on ideology as the history of 'one clerk talking to another'. Yet it was this capacity to tack between the politics of ideology and those of practical reason which made Stokes such an interesting historian.

In the *Political Ideas of English Imperialism* Stokes was also reacting against the highly abstract and academic history of political theory represented by the tradition of Bradley, Hobhouse, Sidgwick, and others whose reflections on politics had been removed form the active world of politics to 'the quiet of the College cloister'. His stress on the need to contextualize the work of prominent thinkers in wider and deeper currents of thought echoed the approach of Michael Oakeshott and anticipated, in a minor way, the approach of Quentin skinner.

In his inaugural lecture, Stokes tried to demonstrate the influence of the idealist thought of T.H. Green and S.R. Bosanquet on imperial ideology. It was ironic, he argued, that most of those latter-day Hegelians who articulated the notion of state and society as organic entities girded by sentiment and tradition were liberals in politics, uneasy about imperial expansion (this was, indeed, a description of his own views). Idealist thought was, nevertheless, an important influence on figures such as Lionel Curtis and the Round Table group who, before the First World War, had sought to refound the British Empire on an ideal of trusteeship and insist on the moral basis of imperial power. Aspects of this line of thought were later taken up by Stokes's Ph.D. student, Clive Dewey, who discerned idealist strains in the later nineteenth-century discourse among British Indian officials on the ideal of 'village community' and the paternalist traditions of the Punjab Commision.[69]

Stokes also provided some clues as to how he would have developed the history of Utilitarian and 'liberal imperialist' tradition which had been analysed in the *English Utilitarians*. This tradition, more calculating and devoid of sentiment than the idealist one, but equally prone to accept the use of force in the interests of progress was propelled into the later nineteenth century by thinkers such as James Fitzjames Stephen and Lords Cromer and Milner who applied the 'policy of thorough' to African government. Stokes saw this tradition bifurcating towards, on the one hand, the ideology of the 'high imperialism' of the 1890s and 1900s, and towards the scientific, eugenicist, and authoritarian socialism of the Webbs and other radicals, on the other. Both these traditions subscribed to national efficiency, though the earlier utilitarian emphasis on the individual being was now supplanted by an emphasis on the individual race.

Two other features of the inaugural lecture were of interest. First, Stokes revealed his deep sympathy with Rudyard Kipling, a topic to which he was to return in his inaugural lecture in Cambridge in 1974. He resented the tendency of the post-War anti-imperialist age to denounce Kipling as a mediocre artist and a mindless chauvinist. In both these lectures he sought to show, as more recent and level-headed literary critics have done, that Kipling's views on race and empire were both more nuanced and more ambiguous than superficial readings suggest. Britain's Empire in this reading was as evanescent as all other despotisms; East did ultimately meet West, but in ways neither intended.

In Rhodesia in 1961 Stokes gave a series of talks on the meaning of university education, alerted to the topic by the teething troubles of the new African universities and colleges. He was also conscious of the debate raging in Britain associated with C.P. Snow's (another Christ's man) thesis about the 'two cultures'. Stokes's theme was the need to support humane teaching and learning in an era when the demand in both advanced and developing societies was for technocrats and specialists.[70] He turned back to Sir Walter Moberley's, *The Crisis of the University* (1947) which also argued against over-specialization. Stokes thought that one great advantage of the University College of Rhodesia and Nyasaland was that it was still intimate enough to remain a community of learning. Stokes also drew upon Cardinal Newman's *On the Scope and Nature of University Education* to argue that 'while liberal knowledge must be morally neutral', each scholar or scientist must comprehend this learning in the light of 'private belief and faith'. The student need not be ashamed to hold fast to 'instinctive truths and elemental loves', even though he dimly perceived their true rationality. Ten years before in Singapore Stokes had argued that the Western intellectual tradition derived its dynamism precisely from its rootedness in the security of 'moral and religious agency'.[71] The problem was that the ancient faiths of Asia were being subverted or abandoned, freeing the intellect as a pure principle of power. The danger of the divorce of reason from morality also faced the new African societies. Here again, in Salisbury, the influence of Christian idealism broke surface from under the calm of Stokes's rationalism.

More mundane educational issues, however, divided members of the Salisbury staff. The University College's high admission standards had the inevitable effect of keeping African participation at a minimum. Opinion was divided between those members of staff who argued for a reduction of standards to promote racial integration of the student body and others who felt that this was wrong and that high academic standards were the best gift for London University to bequeath to its African offshoots.[72] While tending to the latter view, Stokes's combination of humour and moral seriousness as Chairman of the Faculty of Arts and

Social Sciences averted a damaging personal rift in the midst of these passionate arguments. The issue was later resolved by the institution of a pre-A-level course for African students, funded and taught by the University.

Stokes summed up his lived experience of nationalism in India, South-East Asia, and Africa when he wrote for a Rhodesia talk 'a democracy cannot hold down another community against its will . . . a prolonged effort at coercion drives the nationalist movement into the hands of the extremists, so that the final solution is always worse than the one which might have been obtained by negotiation at the beginning'.[73] To today's audience this may seem self-evident; to the Salisbury audience of 1962, it was far from so. Milnerism fitted here too. Stokes interpreted Milner as a late embodiment of that utilitarian tradition, welfare-orientated but authoritarian, whose first experiments had been carried out in India in the 1830s. Milner's austere 'priest-like' devotion to duty and the state both attracted and repelled Stokes.[74] Milner argued that the Boer Republics were hangovers of the medieval world trying to impede the development of the modern. But it was in his time. Stokes thought, that the 'ideal of imperialism' (a term Stokes used in a specific sense) was 'tested and defeated'. The High Commissioner had forgotten the limitations to state action that did not rest on the popular will.

This, however, was not a lesson that had been learned by the white ruling class in Southern Rhodesia. Though Stokes had greatly enjoyed his years at Salisbury and regarded them as a period of service to the broader ideal of a racially blind Commonwealth, he had already begun to look for positions in British universities which were poised to expand once again. In 1960 for instance, he was in discussion with University College London about a Readership there[75] and had also been approached by J.S. Galbraith about a position in the University of California. By 1963 he was determined to return to Britain.

Political uncertainty in Africa was a major concern. It was clear to Stokes that the racial tensions of Central and Southern Africa could not be resolved without major conflagrations now that Kenya, Uganda, Nyasaland, and Northern Rhodesia were independent, majority-ruled republics, while the white Rhodesian expatriates clung resolutely to power in Salisbury. The University College, founded to create a cohesive multi-racial ruling elite for Central Africa as a whole could not possibly work when nationalism and racism were tearing apart the political environment in which it had developed. As Stokes wrote to Sir Alexander Carr-

Saunders (Director of the London School of Economics, 1937-56. Vice-Chancellor, London University) of the deportation by the Federal Government of Terence Ranger, who was regarded as a dangerous radical, 'Terry's expulsion has merely brought to a head the long-gathering crisis. With the Rhodesian Front Victory, the impending break-up of the Federation, and our unpopularity in the [African-ruled] North, the College is now looking into the mouth of that dark tunnel through which, as you expressively said to me, it needs must pass.'[76]

Stokes's attitude to the College's Principal, Walter Adams was ambivalent, but he certainly doubted the wisdom of Adams's 'Napoleonic principle: when in doubt expand'. This was because 'a University cannot operate like a resistance movement and must be in an effective working relationship with the Government of the day',[77] a view that also divided him from his more radical younger colleagues.[78] The real tragedy, according to Stokes, was that 'the multi-racial ideal on which the College was founded has been rejected—at least in the political sense—by black and white alike'.[79] The College Council remained, apart from one silent African, completely white and, in effect dominated by the Salisbury European members. The student body was still overwhelmingly white. The result was the spread of a 'quiet despair about the future' among the staff.

The danger Stokes saw was of the fragmentation of university education in Central and East Africa into a devalued system in the black north, cut off from its London links, and an embattled white core in Salisbury. The solution which Stokes (and Ranger) proposed was that the College at Lusaka (Northern Rhodesia–Zambia) should be taken into direct communication with London University once the Federation broke up in order to preserve its quality of education. Stokes also felt that the rapid development of a law school in Salisbury might help to recruit able young Africans and preserve 'the British conception of higher education in Central Africa'.[80] In the event, 'quiet despair' was to be a more appropriate emotion; all the institutions in contention would be battered by economic collapse and revolutionary war in the 1970s.

The Stokeses' decision to return to the UK was also determined by family concerns. The perennial problems of securing a good education for four daughters loomed again. In 1963, therefore, Stokes applied for the position of Lecturer in History at the University of Cambridge and was appointed as a University Lecturer in Colonial Studies from 1 October 1963 to the retiring age.[81] Since he had left the University in 1949, he had kept in close touch with it through his friend Charles

Parkin, besides entertaining visiting luminaries such as Ronald Robinson.

Cambridge was unusual among British universities at this time in that its History Faculty regarded Commonwealth and 'extra-European' history as a staple of undergraduate teaching. To the older generation of historians of the Commonwealth and Empire such as Nicholas Mansergh and E.E. Rich was now added the dynamic pair of Robinson and Gallagher, whose *Africa and the Victorians* Stokes had both welcomed and critiqued several years before. It was Rich, however, a historian of Canada and Master of St Catharine's College, who proved Stokes's strongest supporter and it was to Rich's College that he returned in the Michaelmas Term of 1963. Stokes followed Oliver MacDonagh as Director of Studies in History and went through the usual *cursus honorum* of College office and committees. Such committees were particularly active as the College engaged in a large and contentious rebuilding programme, expanded its Fellowship and, ultimately, admitted women.

Stokes, though sceptical and impish in his attitude to established authority, had always venerated the ideal of Cambridge from afar, 'the sense of generation on generation, the beauty of ancient buildings, the grace of ceremony, the peace of College courts' as he saw it from Singapore in 1952.[82] Now ensconced in the Fenland town struggling to slough off, in the early 1960s, its Victorian carapace, the romance tarnished somewhat.

Stokes kept in touch with his Rhodesian colleagues, particularly during the events which followed the Unilateral Declaration of Independence in 1965. He continued to be involved in Asian and African issues at the national level as a result of his membership of the Inter-University Council for Higher Education (1972-9), the Indian Committee of the British Council, the Cambridge Livingstone Trust and membership of the Governing Body of the School of Oriental and African Studies. His many research and lecture trips to India also kept him abreast of events in the subcontinent, and on one of these, in 1977, he became an Honorary D.Litt. of the University of Mysore.

Yet Stokes's life undoubtedly became more sedate and domestic than it had been in the colonies. A moderate reformer as ever, he was more favourable than most of his peers to demands for student representation and an end to formal dining in college halls. With four academic daughters and resolute wife, he resented the manner in which female guests were excluded from high table and women were denied access to the older colleges. Even at the height of the generally tame student demonstrations which marked the Vietnam era in Cambridge, he urged the Governing

Body of St Catharine's 'not to hate the undergraduate'. On the other hand, he was no libertarian. He was hostile to the casual sexual permissiveness which was another feature of this period, believing that it damaged family life, which he greatly valued.

Stokes was elected in 1970 to the Smuts Chair of Commonwealth History in succession to Professor P.N. Mansergh and in 1977 he became Chairman of the History Faculty. His main concern in College and Faculty committees was to promote talent and work for some change in the rather hidebound Historical Tripos. The fact that Stokes was a proficient political theorist greatly aided his attempts to promote extra-European history, as 'intellectual historians' then regarded themselves as the elite of the Cambridge Faculty. Stokes attracted an international body of graduate students who mostly worked with him on Indian agrarian issues in contrast to the so-called 'Cambridge school' of political historians of India grouped around Anil Seal and John Gallagher. Several of these went on to make major contributions to Indian agrarian history through the sort of detailed studies of rent, revenue, and demographic change which he had pioneered.[83] As a supervisor, Stokes was supportive and kind, but definitely of the old school in that he viewed the writing of a dissertation as the personal act of a mature scholar, not as an exercise in teaching, or 'training', as the rubric now has it. His graduate students appreciated their visits to the Stokeses' house in south Cambridge. For many of them, their strongest memories of Eric Stokes were of his impish humour and capacity to puncture academic pomposity even while chairing meetings in Commonwealth History.

At Cambridge, Eric Stokes's intellectual life developed in two main directions which had already been foreshadowed in Malaya and Africa, towards theories of imperialism and Indian social history. Lecturing for the Part I Tripos paper, the 'Expansion of Europe' and the new paper he had helped to establish, 'The West and the "Third World" since the First World War', he tried to maintain the broad overview of imperial ideology and practice which had informed *The English Utilitarians*. Much of his intellectual effort here was spent in responding to Robinson and Gallagher's challenge to the field, while reserving a space for the intellectual history of empire. He expanded the critique of *Africa and the Victorians* which he had published in Rhodesia[84] in a series of articles and lectures. This was the most acute and also the most sympathetic of the large number of reviews, comments, and even multi-volume works attempting to turn back their 'historiographical revolution'. Ronald

Robinson admitted as much when he remarked 'Old Stokey, was the only one who ever really understood us'.

While he certainly drew on earlier responses of Colin Newbury and David Fieldhouse, Stokes anticipated practically every lineament of the critique of *Africa and the Victorians* which the field later painfully developed. Essentially, his argument was that their emphasis on the supreme importance of the British occupation of Egypt in triggering the Partition of Africa was overdone. The French were already seeking to advance in West Africa as early as 1878, while the movement forward of chartered companies, individual entrepreneurs, anti-slavers, and others could not be reduced to the Egyptian question.

Whereas Robinson and Gallagher's understanding of contemporary Suez and South African crises in the 1940s and 1950s shaped their view of the Scramble for Africa, Stokes's personal experience of the working of sub-imperial agents and colonial capital in South-East Asia and Africa gave him a more complex view of that history. It was ironic, he thought, that despite Robinson and Gallagher's apparent emphasis on African agency, they reduced Central Africa to a passive victim of colonial expansion from north and south, while the Muslim *jihads* of French West Africa became, for them, epiphenomena of European expansion.

It is notable also that, rather than tackling the Robinson and Gallagher thesis at the level of the ideology of empire, he chided their apparent diminution of the economic factor in British territorial expansion. Lenin and Hobson continued to play a (reduced) part in Stokes's scheme, while they had been rejected with derision by Robinson and Gallagher. European capitalism did change its form about 1900, Stokes thought, but Lenin's view of 'imperialism the highest stage of capitalism' had to be understood as an argument directed more to developments in European government and finance than African and Asian ones. If one read what Lenin really wrote about Africa during the period of the Scramble, it was much the same as what Robinson and Gallagher said, he concluded mischievously.[85]

Stokes genuinely admired Robinson and Gallagher, the 'great artificers' of the new imperial history, and he always eschewed the point scoring and idle comparisons between the virtues of the Smuts Professor, the Beit Professor, and the Vere Harmsworth Professor, which some of their less stellar followers indulged in. It was remarkable indeed that all this talent was circulating between Oxford and Cambridge in the same short span of years. Normally dull seminars on 'imperial and Commonwealth history' at the two places were temporarily galvanized by Stokes's iconoclasm and the ironic detachment of Robinson or Gallagher. But one reason why Stokes admired his comperes was that they had 'turned the field' by a single stroke of insight. Since the *English Utilitarians*, he had felt himself unable to do that, once gloomily remarking that scholars produce only two truly original books, if they are lucky, one impelled by the hunger of youth, the other by intimations of mortality.

Stokes's difficulty was that the complexity of his understanding of history was in absolute antithesis to his view that the field responded to the one brilliant idea. In the circumstances, he could not have found a more difficult terrain to work on than Indian agrarian history of the early nineteenth century. It is easy to see why the topic appealed to him, of course. Indigenous resistance had become a scholarly industry and Stokes was highly responsive to the interest in resistance of the clever young Indians who now came to study Ph.Ds under him in increasing numbers. Stokes's early essays on the Mutiny–Rebellion of 1857 referred back to the work done by his Africanist colleagues on the link between 'primary' anti-colonial resistance and later 'proto-nationalist' movements. With Mau Mau ten years behind, the Vietnamese revolution in its final bloody stages, and peasant revolutions breaking out in Latin America, Western capitalism seemed about to bury itself in the mud of peasant resistance. This was a romantic delusion, as we now know, but compelling at the time.

Stokes also felt the pull of British and European historiography and, more circumspectly, anthropology. The agrarian history of M.M. Postan, Joan Thirsk, and Eric Hobsbawm was mirrored in Europe by the grand syntheses of Fernand Braudel and Emmanuel le Roy Ladurie. Indian anthropology and history now seemed set on an upward path in Europe, North America, and India. More practically, the Indian rebellion of 1857 was a topic that could be mined for sources in Cambridge itself and had considerable potential for undergraduate and graduate research in the University.

Stokes was elected a Fellow of the British academy in 1980, but, sadly, was unable to attend any meetings. He died tragically young at the age of fifty-six. It is difficult to know whether he would have produced the other 'big book' on agrarian history or ventured back into the terrain of the history of imperial ideas. The two volumes of essays on Indian agrarian history. *The Peasant and the Raj* (Cambridge, 1978) and *The Peasant Armed* (New Delhi, 1986) are considerable achievements in their own right, if inevitably unfinished and difficult for non-specialists to penetrate. His own work and that of his colleagues on African political systems and resistance movements made it clear to him how primitive Indian agrarian historiography was even in the early 1960s when he was searching for a new topic. A simplistic argument that the 1857 Rebellion was merely a mutiny was confronted by the equally simplistic view that it was the 'first war of independence'. The Marxist argument, that the 'landlords' betrayed the people to the British in the course of the struggle, seemed complex by comparison.

Using the detailed British records of the Rebellion and official rent-rate and land-revenue settlement reports of the 1870s and 1880s, Stokes began to show how the particular forms of the pre-existing Indian political systems combined with the impact of British agrarian taxation to create very different outcomes in different parts of north India. This was very much the work of a 'splitter' rather than a 'lumper'. He distanced himself from the view promoted at that time by T.R. Metcalf, *The Aftermath of Revolt* (Berkeley, 1966) that the Rebellion was determined by the degree of penetration of indigenous capitalism in the form of the moneylender or *bania*. Instead, he found that the weight of land-revenue and access to commercial opportunities was a more accurate 'predictor' of the propensity to rebel than were the depredations of the moneylender. He also retreated from his own early view that simple caste affiliations were the mainspring of revolt.

Much of this work was very austere; its generalizations were delicately moulded and never exaggerated. One Indian historian, Gyanendra Pandey, argued that this was constraining empirical history, unable to take seriously the reality of popular resistance and revolt.[86] More recently, Rajat Ray has implied that Stokes underplayed the element of 'traditional patriotism' and by inference religious feeling in the Rebellion.[87] Both views have some truth in them. Stokes made little use of indigenous sources (even in translation) and he steered clear of religion and culture as an issue in his analysis. It is noteworthy that only one of the ninety or more undergraduate long essays that he assigned for his Cambridge documentary-based Special Subject on 1857 in the early 1970s concerned religion and ideology. Most of these student papers were set as detailed district or subdivisional studies of tenurial forms, such as he was carrying out himself.

This was partly because Stokes had become suspicious of the tendency of the contemporary American 'ethnohistory' to reify 'culture' as a social given. His wary but admiring relationship with British social anthropology did not extend to French structuralism or American debates about historical metanarratives. Indeed, he specifically warned one of his graduate students not to waste time reading about the anthropology of religion. His views may also have reflected the hard, positivistic stance taken by both the right and the left in Cambridge at that time, with Geoffrey Elton lauding the mythical historian who entered the archives with a mind like a *tabula rasa*, while Peter Laslett urged his followers to retool with statistics or be relegated. Yet Stokes's stance remains a puzzle, given his own stated conviction that religion was the fundamental aspect of human experience. The result was that it seemed in Stokes's later historical writings that Europeans continued to have ideology and religion (though he now saw these as largely ineffectual in practice), while Asians or Africans merely had tenurial systems and the structures of everyday economic life.

The only break in a socio-economic history as dead-level as the great north Indian plain itself were the first two remarkable chapters of his posthumous work. *The Peasant Armed* which deal with the British and Indian soldiers of the Bengal Army, and subjectively drew on his experience as a young man in the Indian Mountain Artillery. The stylistic excellence of this work was reminiscent of the articles on literature and empire which he regularly wrote for the *Times Literary Supplement*, to finance new dresses for his daughters, or so he claimed, and his inaugural lecture 'Kipling: the Voice of the Hooligan', published in the Festschrift for J.H. Plumb. This imaginative piece of writing played on the tension between the sense of an idealized agrarian past and the onset of modern industrialization in Kipling's work, especially *Kim.* Stokes argued that the agrarian historian was trying to do something similar in his attempt to capture the reality of that past before its memory was entirely eclipsed.

Eric Stokes regarded all his work on the agrarian history of India as provisional, and often said so. When he died of lung cancer on 5 February 1981 (never having smoked a cigarette in his life), his work on the Mutiny book was palpably incomplete. Whether he would ever have attempted to reintegrate the history of political thought with economic and social history, and the history of the British colonizers with that of indigenous society, remains unclear. My view is that paradox, scepticism, and a fundamental honesty about the limits of historical explanation would always have impeded him from bundling up his ideas on this subject in an appropriately dramatic form. He was also acutely aware that there is a right time for an idea in the development of historiography. The high tide of 'area studies' and local history in the 1970s had swept himself and many others into the creeks of the Ganges, the Jumna or the Limpopo, as he once memorably put it. But the tide was now receding and there was a danger that a whole generation of historians would be beached on the sands of these distant rivers.

Eric Stokes's work and teaching on Britain, India, and Africa nevertheless remain a vital intellectual influence in universities throughout the world, not least in India and Africa themselves. His own life and writings also stand as a memorial to a time now only forty years past, but seemingly of the deepest antiquity, when educated, middle-class Britons played a significant, and sometimes, as in Stokes's case, humane role on the World Stage.

NOTES

* I am deeply grateful to Mrs Florence Stokes for making this memoir possible by patiently answering my many questions and by supplying me with Professor Stokes's correspondence and papers. Mrs Jessie Muirhead kindly made available ETS letters from India 1944-6. Others who have provided invaluable help are Professor Frank Spooner, Professor Terence Ranger and Dr C.R. Whittaker, and Dr Richard Brown. I have benefited from the comments of Dr S.B. Bayly, Dr John Lonsdale, Dr N. Gupta, Dr T.N. Harper, Dr John Thompson, and Professor Lynn Zastoupil. Manuscript references are to the Stokes papers except when otherwise indicated.

1. Cambridge University *Reporter*, 24 Dec. 1941.

Proceedings of the British Academy, 97, 467-98 © The British Academy, 1998.

2. 'The Voice of the Hooligan: Kipling and the Commonwealth Experience', in N. McKendrick (ed.), *Historical Perspectives. Studies in English thought and Society in honour of J.H. Plumb* (London, 1974), p. 286.
3. Ibid.
4. Ibid., p. 287.
5. E.T. Stokes [ETS] to Jessie Muirhead [JM], 1 Aug. 1944.
6. ETS to JM, 21 May 1945.
7. Ibid.
8. ETS to JM, 1 Oct. 1944.
9. Letter in romanized Urdu to ETS in London from an Indian NCO (illegible), 1946.
10. ETS to JM, 15 Dec. 1944.
11. ETS to JM, 24 June 1945.
12. Ibid.
13. Ibid.
14. ETS to JM, 3 April 1946.
15. ETS to JM, 15 Dec. 1944.

16. Ibid.
17. ETS to JM, 8 May 1945.
18. ETS to JM, 8 Feb. 1946.
19. Eric Stokes, *The Peasant and the Raj*: *Studies in agrarian society and peasant rebellion in colonial India* (Cambridge, 1978), preface; cf. pp. 140-84.
20. Ibid.
21. ETS to JM, 8 Feb. 1946.
22. ETS to JM, 15 Aug. 1945.
23. ETS to JM, 8 Feb. 1946.
24. P. Spear to ETS, 21 Feb. 1953.
25. Student Statistics, *Magazine of the Students Union, University of Malaya, 1950-52 edn.*, p. 120.
26. Edwin Lee and Tan Tai Yong, *Beyond Degrees*: *The making of the National University of Singapore* (Singapore, 1996), pp. 81-95; cf. minute, 9 Jan. 1948, 'Higher education salaries, Malaya' Colonial Office Records, 117/160/1, Public Record Office, London.
27. Foreword, *Magazine of the Students' Union, University of Malaya, 1950-2 edn.*
28. D. Fryer to ETS, 27 May 1950.
29. *Singapore*: *An illustrated history, 1941-1984* (Information Division, Ministry of Culture, Singapore, 1984), pp. 132-3. Maria Hertogh was a Dutch Catholic girl who had been brought up during the War by a Muslim family. Following a lawsuit over her custody, she was sent to a Catholic orphanage, an event which sparked off mass protests during which eighteen people were killed, signalling growing tension between the colony's different ethnic and religious groups.
30. Stokes to unidentified correspondent, 25 May 1952.
31. E. Thio to Stokes, 20 Feb. 1953.
32. 'Malayan Students compared with others, ISS Conference 1952', MS.
33. 'Basis of a Malay Nation', MS, Nov. 1952.
34. 'Malaya and the Colonial Question in Asia', 1954, MS.
35. 'Political Disunity; the historical background', MS.
36. Ibid.
37. 'not sent', 1951.
38. 'Malaya and the Colonial Question in Asia', MS.
39. 'Can History be Objective?', *Magazine of the Students Union, University of Malaya Sessions 1950-51 and 1951-52*, pp. 56-65.
40. Wang Gungwu to ETS, 1 July 1952.
41. John Bastin to ETS, 29 July 1958 and clipping.
42. P. Spear to ETS, 21 Feb. 1953.
43. MSS, 1954.
44. ETS to Charles Parkin, 23 May 1956.

45. ETS to Parkin, Boxing Day 1956.
46. Ibid.
47. ETS to Parkin, 25 May 1956, not sent?
48. F. Rosen, 'Eric Stokes and the English Utilitarians' forthcoming.
49. Peter Penner, *The Patronage Bureaucracy in North India. The Robert M. Bird and James Thomason School, 1820-70* (Delhi, 1986).
50. Lynn Zastoupil, *John Stuart Mill and India* (Stanford, 1994).
51. F. Rosen, 'Stokes and Utilitarians'.
52. See, e.g., Anthony Verrier, *The Road to Zimbabwe, 1890-1980* (London, 1986).
53. ETS to Editor, *Evening Standard*. Salisbury, 1 Dec. 1959.
54. 'The Meaning of Democracy: Another View', MS, apparently published in the *Central African Examiner*, a journal which catered to 'the less-unprogressive white intelligentsia' of Salisbury (Dr Richard Brown, personal communication).
55. 'Political Messianism in Africa', *The Central African Examiner*, 17 Dec. 1960, p. 20; cf. 'Alarums-and-Excursions', ibid., Dec. 1962, pp. 25-6.
56. ETS to Parkin, 2 July 1957.
57. 'East Africa', MS.
58. Personal communication from Dr. C.R. Whittaker, 9 January 1997.
59. ETS, review of A.J. Hanna, *The Story of Rhodesia and Nyasaland* (London, 1960) MS, 17 Aug. 1960.
60. 'Zambesian History', MS.
61. Personal communication from Professor Ranger, 8 Jan. 1997.
62. 'Zambesian History', p. 4.
63. Parkin to ETS, 9 Dec. 1949.
64. 'History as taught and written at UCRN, 1957-63', *Rhodesian History*, 5, 1974, 1-3.
65. 'History as taught', ibid.
66. 'Indirect Rule: expediency or ideology', MS.
67. E.T. Stokes and R. Brown (eds.), *The Zambezian Past: Studies in Central African History* (Manchester, 1966), pp. 352-75.
68. *The Political Ideas of English Imperialism* (Salisbury, 1963), p. 7.
69. See, especially, C.J. Dewey, *Anglo-Indian Attitudes: The mind of the Indian Civil Service* (London, 1993), pp. 7-10.
70. 'The first year at the University', MS.
71. 'Malayan Students', MS.
72. Personal communication from Professor Terence Ranger, 19 March 1997.
73. 'Nationalism', MS.
74. 'Milner and Southern Africa', MS.
75. Ifor Evans to ETS, 5 Jan. 1960.
76. ETS to Sir Alexander Cart-Saunders, duplicate, 25 Jan. 1963.
77. Ibid.

78. Personal communication from Dr C.R. Whittaker, 9 Jan. 1997.
79. ETS to Carr-Saunders, 25 Jan. 1963, p. 2.
80. 'A Law School and the Future of Higher Education in Central Africa', draft MS., 1962-3?
81. *Reporter*, 31 July 1963, p. 2071.
82. 'Malayan Students' MS., 1952, p. 2.
83. For example, Professor Ernest Chew, Dr Clive Dewey, Dr Neil C. Charlesworth, Dr Ratnalekha Ray, Dr Chittabrata Palit, Dr Simon Commander, Dr Peter Musgrave, Professor Sugata Bose, Professor Sumit Guha, Dr Susan B. Bayly, however, turned towards the study of religion.
84. 'Historical Association of Rhodesia and Nyasaland', 1963.
85. E.T. Stokes, 'Late nineteenth-century colonial expansion and the attack on the theory of economic imperialism: a case of mistaken identity?', *Historical Journal*, 12, 2 (1969), 285-301.
86. G. Pandey, 'A view of the observable: A positivist "understanding" of agrarian society and political protest in colonial India', *Journal of Peasant Studies*, 7 (1970-80), 375-83.
87. R.K. Ray, 'Race, Religion and Realm: The political theory of "the Reigning India Crusade"', in Mushirul Hasan and Narayani Gupta (eds.), *India's Colonial Encounter: Essays in Memory of Eric Stokes* (Delhi, 1993), pp. 133-82.

Pre-Colonial Indian Merchants and Rationality

C. A. BAYLY

Introduction

This essay seeks to reopen the question of rationality, capitalism and pre-colonial Indian merchants by considering the relationship between merchant culture and north Indian society *as a whole* in the period 1700-1820. Many examples are taken from the merchants of the Benaras region in the immediate pre-colonial period or the first years of direct colonial rule. But the important issues seem to me to lie not in a minute examination of the rationality and 'methodicalness' of particular firms or even in the practices of particular commercial castes. They lie rather in the question of whether pre-colonial north India was generating or capable of generating a 'public culture' of rational, goal-oriented procedures, methods and regulations which could bring together its capitalists, literati and rulers into a single dynamic political economy. This essay therefore approaches issues which have been raised in recent debates over proto-capitalism in pre-colonial South Asia and the origins of the modern world system, but it draws attention to the area of the sociology of knowledge and is concerned with the issues of 'counting' and 'accounting'. These very English words raise key issues: all societies 'count': to count implies rational procedures. Not all societies developed systems of 'accountability', the capacity to 'count in', as it were, individuals, families, clans or castes into a wider public domain.

The essay argues that such a 'public culture ' was in fact coming to exist in pre-colonial India through the fusion of Islamic, specifically Mughal forms of rule-making, with the deeper and wider money and service ethic of Vaishya, Brahmin and the writer caste within Hindu society. Mughal culture became a kind of shelter which allowed the ethic of the Indian manager communities to penetrate more deeply into society. These developments took place alongside the more material manifestations of monetization, the development of markets and proto-capitalism. This was possible because certain expansive aspects of Brahmin and Vaishya culture were enhanced, in a sense unlocked, by the rule-making proclivities of the Mughal form of Islamic government. The amalgam which resulted—a kind of Islamic-Vaishya syncretism—provided in the late Mughal Indian world a culture of rationality. That this did not come to develop as an alternative form of modernity, comparable with that generated by European capitalism, must be put down to adventitious historical changes such as the military defeat of the Mughal states and their heirs by Central Asian invaders and westerners as much as to certain intrinsic instabilities in this synthesis.

The Literature

The debate in the literature about Weber and Indian merchants is rather misleading both because of the contradictions within Weber's own work and because of certain inherited nineteenth-century notions of the 'grasping' Indian bania dominated by caste and custom. Refuting these ideas has absorbed too much intellectual energy. The issue of the rationality of pre-colonial Indian merchants has still some mileage in it. But what is no longer really in question is the ability of Indian commercial people to adopt a rational, capitalist methodology *once India had been subjected by colonialism to the pressures of the capitalist world system and industrializm.* Notwithstanding Weber's own doubts about the success of industrializm and business management in India many observers, notably Singer (1967) and Morris (1967), have shown how caste values are modified, how Hindu religion of various different forms has contributed to the emergence of a specific form of business ethic and how Indian labour problems arose not from 'caste' or 'rural mentalities' but from certain specific features of the Indian labour market and capital formation (Chandavarkar, 1982). Singer, in a somewhat different context, argued that Brahmin and Sanskritic culture showed great adaptability over time and implied that this facilitated India's entrepreneurs' later encounter with industrial capitalism. While some anthropologists emerging from the Dumontian tradition continue to question the existence of a pure capitalist class in modern India and to assert that caste continues to encompass economy (Stern, 1971, see also Rudner, 1986), the existence of rational entrepreneurship in India is no longer really an issue.

Weber's doubts about the possible success of capitalism in India (Weber, 1973, p.61) are, however, less interesting and salient than two other sets of arguments he made. One is the explicit questioning in the *Religion of India* (Weber, 1958, pp. 73-75) of the rationality of Indian merchant capitalists themselves *in the historical past and before the onset of colonialism.* Secondly, a much more sophisticated set of ideas can be derived from Weber's work on European history and sociology and applied to India. These hold that *even if Indian merchants in the past were rational, they could never have generated a public culture to spread that rationality to the rest of this caste and lineage ridden society.* This essay will consider these two sets of ideas, more particularly the second.

The Intrinsic Rationality of Indigenous Indian Merchants

Weber's arguments on this issue are stated at various points in his essays on India and China. The proposition seems to be that Asian mercantile activity was 'sound and fury signifying nothing'. Thus of China (and implied of India), it is 'striking that out of this unceasing and intensive economic ado and much-bewailed crass materialism of the Chinese there failed to originate on the economic plane those great and methodical business conceptions which are rational in nature and presupposed by modern capitalism'. Such merchants were devoid of trust, tended to put money into land not capital accumulation because of status concerns, displayed a 'money hungry attitude', and so on. In India these broad Asian failings were compounded, even among 'pariah' merchants such as the Jains, by 'extreme asceticism' and notions of purity and pollution which limited the range of business activity. Thus 'the entire atmosphere of caste rebels against every form of cooperation'. Notions such as this were lineal descendants of orientalist critiques of the 'corruption' and 'domestic tyranny' of the Indian merchant (Tennant, 1804), and of the alleged failure of Indian merchants to honour oaths and refusal to invest for future gain. Even specialist publications of the present century continued to refer to 'queer' practices among Indian merchants (*U.P.Banking Enquiry Committee*, 1930, ii, 273) and to 'stagnant entrepreneurship'.

Because certain types of cultural history and anthropology appear to have revived or kept alive these notions in a more sophisticated form, it seems worthwhile confronting them at the outset with more recent findings. In the first place, in order to deal with each other across regional and local cultures, and most particularly to work as dubashes (*do bhasha*) for Europeans, Indian merchants must have been operating at that wider, universal level of rationality which Lukes isolates (Lukes, 1978). Secondly, it seems unlikely that the pious, religion-centred activity (rational in Lukes's second sense) impeded business activity even in historical Hindu society. 'Traditional' merchants elaborated many methods of bringing ritual and religious life into dynamic symbiosis with business life. There appears to have been no tension between these different ethics. Speaking of his grandfather's time, one of my informants stated that 'there could be harmony in caste and religion and very strong competition in business'. The realm of worship was clearly demarcated from that of business, though in different ways from those in modern society. For instance, the Benaras brass market in Chaukhambha was a huge exchange market for brass devotional figures. These were sold by weight, melted and recast; they were also objects of religious value. Merchants behave *both* in a pious and in a 'pharasaical' manner. There is no reason to believe that elaborate death ritual ceremonies (*Shraddhas*) were not seen as a road to salvation by Indian merchant people, yet at the same time commentators were, and are, aware that conspicuous piety and status battles helped to enhance the credit and trustworthiness of a family (notably, my informants insisted that whereas they—Purbiye Agrawals, for instance, endowed temples for god, 'the others'—Marwaris or cheap-jack Agarwals, according to them, merely did it to impress people). Countless pieces of information recorded in merchant adjudications and the sixteenth-century Jain merchant Banarsidas's *Ardhakathanak* suggest that restrained piety was seen as an ideal for living *and* as an appropriate code of conduct for a merchant. 'Expensive persons', those who indulged in luxurious life-styles, were spending their moral and material substance and were likely to invite default and debt. In this way the rationality of long-term business activity (the value-free sense of rationality) was adjusted to the rational pursuit of family righteousness and salvation (the 'closed' type) of rationality.

Anthropologists appear now to be moving away from a monolithic and hegemonic vision of culture (e.g., Fox, 1986). Drawing on the work of literary critics, and sometimes of historians, the emphasis is upon how people make culture, rather than *vice versa*. We have been urged to abandon the notion that 'castes' not persons are the actors in South Asian society, or that India is a peculiar dream-society, the social manifestation of the mystic and irrational in the human psyche (Inden, 1986). This fits with empirical work which has been done on Indian merchants over the last twenty years. Much of this material demonstrates how Indian businessmen in the past turned the specific features of Indian society (caste, lineage, religious practice) into advantages in their business world.

Thus merchants used caste and regional associations as a 'resource group' for pooling capital and resources, advancing young men in branch agencies and excluding opposition (Timberg, 1978). At the same time, business activities were not necessarily bounded by caste groups. Agencies were given to non-caste members; the use of money and the 'hand of the artisan' was held to be pure. Where a mixed merchant community was called upon to operate in setting prices, in controlling the market on adjudicating about individuals' credit, cross-caste *mahajans* and *sabhas* came into existence. These were often validated by appeals to common religious beliefs and symbols. Thus merchant people of several different castes were associated with the temple of Lalji in the old central quarter of Benaras. The joint support by merchants of this temple and its priests asserted a sort of commonality above the differences of caste and the conflicts of business which operated as a kind of wider 'opinion of the mart' when the whole community needed to adjudicate on bankruptcies or deal with rulers (Bayly, 1983).

Many of the apparently irrational acts of merchants from hoarding, through to the taking of 'excessive' levels of interest, can be reinterpreted as methodical and rational responses to circumstances. So hoarding was connected with the need to have different institutions of credit for different fields (Benaras merchants held Mughal gold mohurs, in case of problems with silver; they hoarded family jewels in the case of the death of the family head; they kept Mughal jewels for occasions of public display, and latterly they kept Company paper to be able to operate in the arenas of the East India Company). The holding of land was not apparently, as Weber argued, a lust for irrational status. Instead merchants ended up with land-rights unwillingly, often because debtors had collapsed, especially in the hard period of the early colonial regime. Pre-colonial merchants stated that they were unwilling to become too heavily involved in the direct management of agrarian resources because this might impinge on their creditworthy status as merchants.

A final aspect of the supposed irrationality of pre-colonial Indian merchants—one mentioned by Weber and constantly reiterated by colonial observers—was their tendency to take 'excessively' high rates of interest. Merchants were seen therefore as 'grasping', unable to plan and unconcerned with the future. Interest rates when examined more carefully look thoroughly reasonable, given the political and management costs likely to be encountered in eighteenth-century India, problems of security and recovery. They compare favourably with rates charged in the proto-capitalist economies of contemporary southern Europe. The persistence of high rates of interest into the colonial period were not necessarily a reflection of 'lag' or 'backwardness' among Indian merchants, simply the fact that colonial law made little difference especially in the context of rural society (Washbrook, 1981).

The consensus of recent investigators and more sensitive economic or cultural analyses of the practices of Indian merchants do not appear to discover the forms of irrationality and lack of long-term method perceived by Weber and mentioned by many eighteenth and nineteenth-century observers of the Indian scene. This is not to say that in their religious and social practices Indian merchants were 'pharasaical' or 'hypocritical', simply that the rationality of religious and social practice could be and was often brought to be congruent with the wider 'rationality' required for the practice of merchant life.

Merchant Rationality and the Spirit of Social Organization

It could be argued though, that Weber did not push through his own arguments. His generalizations about India (and China) appear to have been ill-informed and much less sophisticated than his broader understanding of European historical development. Just as the 'oriental' mode of production marked a decline from the quality of Marx's arguments about Europe, so Weber was led to unnecessarily general characterizations of Indian and Chinese religion (Eldridge, 1970). If we consider his European work, the implications of *The Protestant Ethic and the Rise of Capitalism* become rather clearer. It is no necessary part of Weber's argument to assert that merchant classes before the onset of capitalism were irrational. His materials make it quite clear that capitalism, in a more restricted sense, existed from the early middle ages in Europe, possibly even earlier. The merchants of the Italian city states were, for him, consummate, rational capitalists, but mercantile capitalists. Medieval usury laws could be circumvented; business activity was goal-orientated. What was critical was that, for him, *rational, goal-oriented economic activity had not infused, penetrated and motivated the whole society.* This was, in Weber's view, because irrational or magical notions permeated it in two particular senses. First, (as in Jainism) there was a preponderance of 'excessive' otherworldy asceticism, reflected in particular in the immobilization and misdirection of talent and resources within the monastic system. Second, activity and status was constrained by the irrational, magical and status bound forms of tribalism (the sib) and magical, 'feudal' lordship. Here in his work the abstract notions of irrationality take on much clearer institutional and social forms. This is where, in broad terms, Protestantism was so important. It emphasized this-worldly activity (bringing economic and religious goals into congruence); at the same time it penetrated through the whole organization of society. Protestantism was therefore able to 'seed', as it were, the whole of society with values which were congruent with the methodical and rational ethos of the merchant.

Weber's work on Europe can be applied to India in a much more powerful way and one which would bring it into line with the position adopted by Dumont and more possibly, Marriot and Inden (1974). The important point, it could be argued, was not the irrationality of Indian merchants, but the way in which their rational and methodical activities were limited by the demands of sib, asceticism and most notably by an 'extreme' form of the 'magical' or other worldly imperative reflected in the caste system. These were all features of the relationship between values and action in the wider society, and need hold no implication that the activity of merchant castes was *in itself* irrational, unmethodical or even non-capitalistic.

Let us then turn to the broader 'spirit' of the Hindu social order and the interaction between different castes at the level of *jati*. Here there is a clash between what is still the dominant 'Dumontian' interpretation of the supra-historical incorporating ideology of purity and pollution, on the one hand, and the material which has come out of research, particularly on seventeenth and eighteenth-century Indian social history, on the other. The picture we get from the latter is the capacity of Indian merchants and scribal people to refashion aspects of the wider ethic of caste and religion to turn them to advantage in periods when the subcontinent was experiencing internal economic and political growth and new demands from the 'world system'. A key ideological resource here was in the concept of *dharma* itself, so important to Weber. It has already been pointed out by Singer and others that the particularistic ethics of individual *varnas* could give rise, contra Weber, to an ameliorative this worldly ethic. But Weber could have objected that the ideological mindset of Hinduism as a whole made impossible the emergence of a broader, this worldly universalistic ethic. However, even at the scriptural level it is not at all clear that this is so. Within the concept of *apadharma* (a situation in which the laws of *dharma* do not apply) can be found a justification for the modification of castes and the slippage of caste life-styles. In this age of destruction (the *Kali yuga*) Brahmins devoid of patronage can take to agriculture and trade; Vaishyas to agricultural work and Shudras to polluting activities. There is some evidence that people actually used these ideas as a justification for working outside the hereditary occupational categories. Ironically, then, a notion of human and cosmic degeneration over time could provide a window of opportunity for entrepreneurship as wide as the idea of spiritual (later material) 'progress' in Christendom.

Hindu kingship of the medieval period also inherited a strong economic and entrepreneurial dimension from classical tradition represented in the *Artha Shastra*. As Reuven Kahane has argued (1984), the organization and resources of the royal treasury formed an important topic of debate for the *shastras*, and kings were ranked according to their wealth as much as by their piety to Brahmins. This tradition of raja as entrepreneur facilitated the further 'commercialization of Hindu kingship', possibly from the time of the south Indian Cholas and certainly following the development of a full cash-based revenue system over most of India by the fourteenth -century. This paper suggests, however, that the small-scale and segmentary nature of Hindu kingdoms limited the development of a broader public commercial culture such as emerged under the Mughals, other Muslim sultanates and the Hindu Vijaynagar rule which began to replicate them. Yet even participation in the limited entrepreneurial culture of the early Hindu kingdoms might improve the embodied rank of groups which could abandon labouring occupations or inferior service and become clerisy and merchants (Hall, 1985; Appadurai and Breckenridge, 1976). The case of the Kayasthas (a group apparently formed by the creation of clerical service between 1200 and 1600) and the Telis (who raised their status by moving from oil to money-trading in the pre-colonial era) gives an indication of this sort of mobility. It could be also that the reification of a more defined concept of 'sin' (*pap*) in Hindu devotional worship and the possibility of cleansing through *shraddha* and pilgrimage actually reduced the social penalties for transgressing social rules.

From an early period Hindu society witnessed the existence of a creative tension between a realm of ritual and a realm of business which had complementary sets of specialists drawn from the same broad caste background and operating similar types of skills. The 'Brahminization' of merchant practice into a set of closely guarded hieratical and rational skills went hand in hand with the commercialization of ritual. We can see this also perhaps in the emergence of a special category of *lokika* or 'worldly' Brahmins. Interestingly, *lokika* Brahmins who took part in the 'administration' of pre-colonial kingdoms (notably the Chitpavan and Deshashta Brahmins of western India, or the Telegu Brahmins of the Karnatic were held in higher esteem than some types of ritual Brahmins. It was less polluting to serve great kings than, for instance, to follow the practices of temple Brahmins who took money for service and demeaned their ritual status by such means. This drift towards statuses based upon this-wordly occupation cultures is demonstrated in pre-colonial Rajasthani documents where terms such as *poddar* (a merchant involved in the succour of kings), *mutsaddi* (a Persian word applied to a man of numbers and letters), *darbari* (a man of status because of appearance at court), *karori* (the wider term for local official) are used interchangeably for caste names and often seem to be viewed as parallel with caste communities. In the early colonial documents one finds many references to merchants, asked what their *jati* was, answering *mahajan* (great man = merchants) or *sahukar* (money-dealer).

We can suggest, therefore, that at the level of everyday understandings of status and respect there occurred a 'drift' which was gradually sharpening a perception of a category of high status based upon the deployment of managerial skills in the world. This development occurred parallel with and was related to the contemporary creation of a wider and more elaborate ritual domain through the integration of pilgrimage routes and the creation of large temples. The great temple at Tirupati, for instance, developed as a major centre after about 1500. It became a place of great sanctity for, among other groups, merchants from the whole of north India and Gujarat. But this very phenomenon is a recognition that people of merchant caste across such a wide geographical range had begun to operate together as a broader unity in worship. At an ideological level the distinction between merchant, priest and writer was capable of erosion, and was probably being eroded.

Not only could subtle changes in the meaning of caste provide ideological force for the creation of new ruling groups. It could also provide the force behind the creation of dependencies between different strata of society. We have already suggested that the incorporative ideology of the caste system could be used to generate a sense of 'belonging' of rights, shares and hence of participation both in a common religious community and in a common community of business and economic activity. In the same way the ritualized system of patronage (*jajmani* system) could operate both in the urban and rural environment as a method of controlling and subordinating labour, in some cases directly contributing to the emergence of a form of limited capitalism. Patronage-type relations were generated in the city out of concern for Brahmins, cattle and the poor. But they also maintained pools of dependents: sometimes artisans for work in the *karkhanas*; sometimes armed men for protection or runners for conveying credit notes, jewels or gold. Here again, the divisive, irrational aspect of caste relations has been somewhat exaggerated. In fact, what we know of caste in the seventeenth and eighteenth-century in the urban and rural bazaar environment and around emerging temple and pilgrimage complexes can be equally well interpreted as a methodical and rational ordering of people in a rapidly changing environment. Hindu kings required services of fort and bazaar building; caste in one aspect was a code for the procurement of labour and services through jobbing headmen. This style of caste was flexible, *ad hoc* and incorporative. Temples and festivals here provided a kind of paradigm for community building. 'Shares' could be sold or rented allowing for rapid changes consequent on physical or social mobility. It appears that it was colonial interpretations and uses of caste which emphasized its capacity to immobilize and restrict labour.

In a Weberian analysis, serfdom and the dominance of rural sibs was seen as the reification of the irrational and magical in society. Caste in pre-colonial rural India has often been seen in the same light, even by those who argue for the penetration of money and commercialization. Yet caste can as plausibly be seen as social institution with the flexibility to undermine the close control of rural warrior clan groups over labour. Thus eighteenth-century Rajasthani kings could use *ad hoc* bodies of dependent labourers (*chelas* or *halis*) to direct cultivation and circumvent tightly organized kin brotherhoods. In the countryside, merchant people who took over estates in the early nineteenth-century often recruited Chamars or men of very low caste status to work in their farms. The large ritual gap between merchant caste and untouchables could, therefore, operate as a kind of social control, which would have been much weaker in a situation where entrepreneurs hired workers of 'clean' agricultural castes. So the expected, ideal organization of patronage through caste interaction in Hindu society could always be mediated in such a way as to generate new and flexible economic relationships. It follows that the *jajmani* system of ritualized clientage which has been taken as a unitary scheme reflecting an underlying religious homology can often be reinterpreted as a loose bundle of relationships, some of which were *ad hoc* and temporary arrangements akin to 'piece rates'. In the same way, dependencies based on inferior ritual status as pools of field labour on expanding frontiers of the pre-colonial rice economy (Gyan Prakash, 1985).

One final aspect of the broader and more sophisticated Weberian interpretation of the caste system concerns 'other-wordly asceticism'. Weber implies that the predominance of this in both medieval European and in Asian cultures inhibited the development of a universalistic ethic compatible with the rational organization of everyday life. What is striking about pre-colonial Hindu ascetic organization as several commentators have pointed out (Cohn, 1964, J.N.Sarkar, 1947) is that Indian monasticism allowed the pooling of capital, the flexible switching of resources, from trade to land-control, to military entrepreneurship; and a system of political authority which transcended family. In many ways the Gosains and Bairagis *were* the most successful capitalists of the immediate pre-colonial period in India. The existence among them of a 'this-wordly' form of asceticism was recognized by the distinction between *grihasta* or *lokika* and 'withdrawn' sects and also between 'trading' and 'meditating' sanyasis. In this sense, eighteenth-century Gosains and Bairagis were different from Jain monks, the more austere Sufi *majdhubs* and Buddhist monks during periods when complete withdrawal from worldly business was in vogue.

Even if we take the broader argument that a fragmentation of entrepreneurial resources may have occurred as a result of the existence of a separate category of renouncers, the Weberian argument is suspect. In pre-colonial Allahabad, Benaras, Mirzapur and Nagpur, sanyasis were not only highly respected but very active members of a broad merchant society. *Atits* ('those without passion') were witnesses and adjudicators into intra-merchant disputes and combined with in-caste merchants in merchant organizations. They also provided a large pool of capital for merchants and artisans and they absorbed and transformed labour from all clean-caste groups by the practice of adoption. Even if merchants and rulers did not themselves become sanyasis in large numbers, sanyasis provided an extensive network of organizations and a pattern of methodical business activity and investment which facilitated business culture. Much the same could be said for the guru-pupil organization of organized *bhakti* sects such as the Ramanandis, Vallabhacharyas, Charandasis or Satya Narayanis. Devotional sects tended to emphasize community and a sober ethic of work and worship. Patterns of allegiance to gurus commonly drew together people from a variety of different caste backgrounds. This transformed such sects into powerful magnets for commercial association which attracted and gave stability to other groups of merchant people. But it is probably incorrect to overstress bhakti sects in order to make an analogy with Weber's Protestantism. As has been suggested, more ritualized forms of temple-based worship could also provide the basis for a methodical and routinized style of worship and business life. In fact, those sectarian groups who were prominent in business in eighteenth and nineteenth-century north India had already passed from the expansive devotional form of bhakti to a more institutionalized form which had usually incorporated aspects of hierarchy and of temple-worship.

Interestingly, Randall Collins in a recent book on Weberian historical sociology (Collins, 1986) has taken a similar line with regard to the role of the Church and monasticism in medieval Europe, and monasticism in medieval China. He argues that the Church was the ultimate capitalistic and rational bureaucracy of medieval Europe and it was the rule-making proclivities of the Church which made possible Europe's rapid development of new institutional and mercantile forms in the early modern period. Weber's distinction between this-wordly asceticism and other-wordly asceticism (which he associated with monasticism) is shown once more to be misplaced and to have aborted a much more interesting argument which he was beginning to deploy, but was deflected by his emphasis on the unique features of Protestantism.

Weber's broader point would still have virtue if one considered the rather slow penetration of this type of commercial culture into the great warrior and landholder clans of the Hindu interior and the absence of a common system of law, legal status and legal remedy during much of pre-colonial Indian history. While there is no doubt of the relative differences here between late medieval Europe and India, this paper would wish to argue that such a rule-making generalizing capacity had, in fact, been generated by the rational structures of Mughal rule and late Islamic political ideology. The failure of that culture either to transform India or to 'save' it from colonialism should not be regarded as evidence of its lack of dynamism. Rather it achieved a remarkable amount of change given the short period of Mughal supremacy in the subcontinent.

Before moving on to the Mughal synthesis, however, a final point needs to be raised about caste and entrepreneurship. This follows from Rudner's contention (1986) that caste (in the sense of *jati*) should not simply be interpreted as a passive resource group for entrepreneurs (as this paper has tended to do) but as an active unit of entrepreneurship in itself. This relates to his further point that some recent literature has appeared to take the individual entrepreneur as the focus of study and set up an artificial antithesis between individual and community. This, I think, is a fair point. Castes such as the Nattukotai Chettiars in the South and Maheshwari Marwaris in north India can certainly be regarded as corporate units of entrepreneurship which were sometimes seen sacrificing the interests of individual merchant families in the pursuit of commercial objectives.

However, it is important to distinguish between different uses of the term 'caste' and in particular to consider the internal ritual and kinship organization of different communities. Whereas Nattukotais appear to have had close-knit and localized patterns of marriage and social relations this was by no means true of the broad merchant caste categories of north India. The key unit of merchant organization among Khattris and Agarwals was likely to be a small group of families representing a three generational span from a common ancestor. These units cannot really be seen as 'castes' so much as family groups. Such were the famous Jagat Seths of eighteenth-century Bengal or the Purbiye Agarwal family of Bhaiaram Gopal Das of Benaras. If we cannot speak of individualistic entrepreneurs we can certainly speak of small caste fragments or large families (and it even seems unlikely if the 'pure', individualistic merchant existed even in the European context). It seems possible that quite apart from the rather looser structure of merchant caste organization among the great merchant caste groups of the north, the impact of Mughal rule was important here. The association of particular families with Mughal revenue systems and the households of Muslim nobles tended to favour the entrepreneurship of family groups rather than 'castes', however defined. This is one important aspect of the broadening of scale achieved by Mughal rule in the north.

Islam and Rationality: An Overview

The classic treatment here is Maxime Rodinson (Rodinson,1966). Rodinson argued that the supposed Islamic antipathy to capitalism was in fact a misperception based on exaggerated interpretations of the Quranic opposition to *riba* (interest, or usurious interest) and the quasi-socialist element of the thought of some modernizing reformers. In fact, the Quran and the *Sunna* both praise merchants and the performance of the Islamic life-style breeds method, order and planning. Indeed, 'Le Coran, est un livre sacre ou la rationalite tient un tres grande place' .... Allah ne cesse d'y argumenter, d'y raisoner'. Islam was no 'enchanted place' and if was it was merely the persistence of pre-Islamic beliefs, including those, ironically for Weberians, of eastern Christianity. Moreover, Islamic Law and the enormous corpus of *fiqh* was a prime example of systematized, unified and rationalized prescriptions for behaviour. If the bourgeosie failed to take a significant share of power (as opposed to taking an important role in the organization of the economy) this was because of the weakness of the state and ecological features of the arid zone.

Rodinson attracted a certain amount of criticizm because of his failure to consider the possibility that belief systems did in more subtle senses impede the development of a capitalist rationality *which could infuse the whole of society.* One line of reasoning which is important here is the notion (see e.g., Ruthven,1986) that Islam did not encourage the emergence of a state-level bourgeoisie because it ignored or disapproved of the existence of alternative centres of power within society. The *shariat* was essentially individualistic; the *umma* was a tightly knit group of individuals and there could be little in common between the individual (or lineage) and the Sultan or Khalifa (Hourani and Stern, 1970). This was in contrast to the Christian European tradition where, ironically, the magical notion of the Body of Christ, the *corpus mysticum* was progressively secularized into city corporations and ultimately into mercantile companies, which could provide a secure base from which commercial planning could operate throughout the whole society. The law of corporations (a rational system for the pursuit of gain) could operate within a quasi-mystical body to provide a shelter from the intrusive state and residual power of the Church. It was the very flexibility of this system which provided the dynamism of the European economy, somewhat before the Calvinist breakaway. The only exception to the relative inflexibility in Islam was the *waqf* or mortmain benefice to religious institution or lineage. But Rodinson's critics were thinking very much of early medieval Islam here. In the later Muslim Middle Ages Sultans and Padishahs effectively recognized the *de facto* independence of corporations of Christian, Armenian, Jewish and Hindu merchants as well as the entrepreneurial activities of groups of Muslim merchants themselves. Late Islam, like late Christendom, could be said to have generated a corporate life which modified the nature of the state and its ideologies. One such example is that of India after Akbar.

Mughal India: A Flexible Islamic System and a Universalized Hindu Ethic

In addition to the more general West Asian inheritance of rational legalism, later Muslim sultanates in India and the Mughals in particular had developed certain features of organization which facilitated entrepreneurship. The fact that the Mughal ruling class was a polyglot amalgam of individual magnates, often distant from their kin, and paid on the basis of assignments of a cash revenue, encouraged notions of public accountability which transcended personal loyalty to the emperor. Mughal rank was based on counting troops and the value of *jagir*, not on seniority of lineage. From the very earliest period, also, the practice of 'farming out' the revenue and other royal rights to men of capital on the basis of bids was associated with the practice of Islamic kingship. In India, insecurity and the presence of a huge 'underworld' of Hindu commerce encouraged these practices.

Indian historians have written much about the religious syncretism of the high Mughal period. The argument has tended to become an idyllic exercise in folklore studies. This is because the emphasis has never shifted from religion, because the changes in knowledge systems implied by such syncretism have rarely been examined, and because the synthesis is seen as the creation of an ancien regime with little dynamic power. Religious syncretism was in fact simply one aspect of a wider amalgamation of different systems of knowledge which had considerable implications in the sphere of economic management. What happened in effect was that Hindu systems of numerical counting and classification —'accountancy'—came into contact with and were generalized by Mughal notions of 'accountability' of testimony, audit and positive, universalistic law. Such syntheses also came to exist in areas as diverse as medicine (the fusion of Ayurvedic medical 'archive' with the classifying rationalism of Greek Yunani medicine), music, astrology and architecture.

At the highest political level, the *Ain-i-Akbari*, Akbar's great inventory or domesday book of the Mughal Empire (c.1590) is a good example of the synthesis. The work is both an explanation of the duties of officers and an account of the economy of India which pays particular attention to the life and geography of the Hindu population. This work and many other 'revenue manuals' circulated thereafter should probably not be regarded as objective accounts of a revenue system (as historians have tended to see them), but as mediating political documents bringing into the same plane the concerns of the emperor, with those of his subordinate accounting officials (the *karori* or *mutsaddis*), and the vast culture of Hindu commercial society which was the oil of the whole fiscal and commercial system. The books provided a picture of the ideological synthesis of these two systems; the royal mints and the emergence of a tri-metallic coinage was the physical manifestation of the merging of 'accounts' with accountability.

The full system of Hindu accounting represented in the five different types of *bahi khata* (account books) is much more than an exercise in recording debits and credits in double account. To a remarkable degree the books provided a map of the relationships between the family firm and the economy as a whole. It was possible to trace the consequences of an individual transaction in several different spheres and to guard against future drains on liquidity (*the nakad bahi*). Merchants also employed clerks learned in the methods of Persian letter-writing to mediate their activities with the state. The state, in turn, issued them with badges of recognition, and even in some cases with Mughal ranks and honours.

In order to generalize this new, syncretic knowledge there flourished in the seventeenth and eighteenth-century a branch of Indo-Persian literature—which is hardly mentioned in the standard works- called *Ilm-us-Siyaq* or the science of accountancy, expounding both principles of accounts drawn from the arithmetical and fractional systems of the Hindu merchants and the analysis of procedures and officials which appear to come from the Mughal and Iranian systems. Interestingly, two of these documents are known to have been written by members of Hindu commercial castes (Khattris) living in commercial towns (notably the 'Science of Accounts' of Shiv Das of Kara). *Siyaqnamahs* were clearly a device for facilitating the interaction of subordinate state officials with the *diwans*, *khazanchis* and *mutsaddis*—men of business connected with armies, noble households and courts, who were drawn from the commercial communities. And the educational excercise was extremely successful.

The most extensive records of seventeenth-century India were those of Rajasthan (Dilbagh Singh, 1975; Bajekal and Chaudhuri, 1986). What is striking about the pargana-level revenue documents of this area (where Mughal rule was at best indirect) is the fact that 'state' revenue accounts are set out in precisely the same terms of double entries, profit and loss, and in many of the same units of account, as the extant private records of Indian merchants from that period (e.g., the book of Sarakhji of Jaipur). It is worth recording here that much of the organization of public accounting had been taken over even in areas of India which were formally 'Hindu' or outside the Mughal purview. The Maratha states in the Deccan (Perlin, 1979, 1985) and Tanjore with its 'ministers', 'shares' and 'revenue brahmins' adapted and streamlined much of the apparatus, even if in Tamil Nadu revenues were still formally paid in kind.

The vitality of this commercial culture is echoed in the private records and inventories of the eighteenth-century merchants of Benaras, a notably Hindu commercial and artisan city. Merchant traditions, for instance, specifically record that the form of account books used right up to this day in family businesses was standardized by the Mughal Empire, represented in their stories by the figure of the Hindu Khattri finance minister, Todar Mall. Many of their legends also related to their interactions with the Mughal jurisconsul—the *kazi* —who could act as a registrar and judge for mercantile disputes which could not be compromised within caste councils or commercial institutions. Benaras merchants had the benefit of *de facto* corporations (supposedly absent from Muslim societies) but also appeal to external judicial authorities and systems of accounting represented by the Mughal system of commercial and commercialized justice. Moreover much of the credit which circulated in the Benaras bazars in the eighteenth-century was in the form of *dakhillas* which were promissory notes on advances of the state's revenue, guaranteed by double and triple sureties. This again was an example of the deep penetration between 'state' and 'commercial' forms of accounting and accountability.

Notable here is the term 'custom' which appears in the English versions of now perished Persian originals and as *mamul* in the Persian records of some of the Hindu merchants. When I read of the 'custom of the merchants', I tended, at first, to think of arcane lore, those 'irrational' practices of the *mahajans* beloved of the colonial observers. In fact, however, the term custom seems usually to have meant 'systems of operations worked out by the merchants for dealing with representatives of outside authority', be they the Muslim courts, customs, or revenue which activities and problems were within the domain of the 'outside', which related to merchant arbitration, and which were matters for families. It was the tendency of early colonial officials to intervene in family matters, but to neglect some aspects of their 'public' role in arbitration which called forth many plaints and petitions from the merchants in the years 1770-90.

The 'public' commercial culture of late Mughal India penetrated quite deeply in the more accessible parts of the countryside. One indication of this is the very extensive records of sales, mortgages, complicated partition arrangements which have survived from the seventeenth-century for areas around small towns and on major routeways. These are evidence not only of 'commercializaton' but of the growing power of written records and record-keepers in the society and politics of the period. At the same time contemporary Hindustani is full of terms of accountancy, terms for the accountability of persons and terms which indicate arrangements for 'fractionizing' dignities, holdings, even the charisma of holy men and deities. Hundreds of folktales collected by colonial officials in the mid-nineteenth century (e.g., Fallon, 1879) refer to disputes over accounts, inventories and partitions.

Not surprisingly, there is also evidence of further modification of the status and life style of social groups in India as a result of this developing public culture. The *lokika* Brahmin and the Kayastha writer have already been mentioned. Another group of great importance were the Khattris, particularly the Pacchim Khattris of western Hindustan and Punjab. Todar Mall, the Mughal finance minister, was a Khattri; Khattris are by far the most prominent Hindu caste group working in Mughal administrative offices, and even in their commercial lines they appear to have been favoured by the Mughal rulers. Pacchim Khattris, moreover, were known to have adopted a Mughly life-style, and relations with Muslim governors (often concerning the defilement of women) are common in their family histories. What is interesting is how difficult nineteenth-century Hindus (Khattris included) found to classify Khattris. They preserved some features of the ruling charisma of the Rajput (Kshatriya) warrior. At the same time they were less than warrior caste by virtue of their association with penmanship and with Muslim practices. Like the Kayasthas, they seem to represent a different and historically more recent type of caste-formation in that occupational culture and relationship to a non-Hindu state was essential to their incorporation as a social group, and status in respect to Vedic themes is of secondary importance. These two groups, it can be argued, as seen in the nineteenth-century, were the creations of an aborted social change which had been taking place under the Mughals. This was the emergence of a syncretic managerial elite.

By the eighteenth-century the synthesis of public commercial culture appears to have been expanding rapidly. Revenue farming had been greatly expanded, and the economic imperative seemed to be beginning to undermine the very rule-preserving features of Mughal practice which had facilitated its expansion. This lies behind the plaints of Mughal chroniclers and poets that the *Qazis* rights and other God-given offices were being leased out, that 'grocers' (*bakkals*) and low men, with nothing more than a minimal grasp of arithmetic, were achieving power (Shiv Das, Lucknawi c. 1706, 1980) and that Hindus and Shias were overturning the empire. As Andre Wink has shown (1986), the amalgamation of the 'lottery' of revenue-farming with the technique of state-building through revolt (*fitna*) created a dynamic, though conflict-ridden political economy, which the British superficially characterized as 'anarchy'. If the later Middle Ages in Europe had seen the emergence of a 'bastard feudalism', characterized by the operation of mercenary principles within the shell of feudal privileges, eighteenth-century India should be seen as a 'bastard sultanism'.

The Decline of the Mughal Managerial Culture

The archive-generating propensity of Hindu commercial culture had come together with the rule-making propensity and systems of accountability of Mughal political culture to create a dynamic synthesis. For eighteenth-century Asia this synthesis (and its equivalents in Arab-Coptic Egypt or Arab-Armenian Iraq) could be regarded as an alternative culture of modernity alongside the amalgam achieved by capitalism and the modern state in contemporary Europe. Moreover this Indian synthesis provided an important matrix within which was generated British colonialism, both bureaucratic and commercial. Features of this in the guise of institutions such as government trading corporations can perhaps be perceived in the principles underlying the activity of the Republic's state capitalism.

Nevertheless, the Mughal synthesis proved incapable of reproducing itself or providing the basis for an Asiatic modern state, even to the extent to which this occurred in other late Islamic states (under Muhammad Ali in Egypt, for instance). It would be perfectly in line with a Weberian type of argument to suggest that this was primarily the result of contingent events at the global level—the exponential development of Europe, and Britain in particular over the same period. The consequence of British colonialism was certainly to sever 'government' from 'commerce' once again. The British, seeking stability for their own commercial and fiscal operations, put a stop to revenue entrepreneurship and what they saw as 'corruption' in public life. This apparent stability took much of the dynamism out of the Indian political economy and relegated the commercial culture of the eighteenth-century to the closed corporations of the merchant castes, though it had once extended to the whole polity. The stereotypes of the 'grasping bania' and 'venal public officer' which still haunts some of our anthropology, and much more of our development economics, derive from a historical fragmentation of a world in which these two figures operated in symbiosis within an expanding domain of public culture.

At the same time, there is no doubt that the public culture we have been describing was subject to great internal strain and conflict. While *karori* or official and *mahajan* or commercial man had an ultimate interest in rational accounting and public accountability, in method and prediction, there were shorter-term contradictions between their modes of operation. The nature of the agricultural seasons and the timing of the military campaigning system, for instance, tended to bring official and merchant into severe conflict on a systematic basis. Merchants alone possessed capital all the year round, but needed trading capital in autumn and spring. The military elite needed large capital at the very same time in order to equip armies. While accommodation was generally achieved the persistence of damaging conflicts was evidenced in the constant complaints of 'looting' of merchants by state officials. At the same time, as we have suggested, the dynamic, accumulating aspects of revenue-farming conflicted quite seriously with the normative codes of jurisconsul and law-giver which had facilitated their expansion.

Finally, the development of public commercial culture occurred within a given political terrain, and it was extremely uneven. In many ways the warrior peasant class of the hinterland should also be seen as entrepreneurs. They too adopted and manipulated many of the new systems of accounting, revenue farming and accountability which emerged out of the Mughal synthesis (Gordon, 1978; Indu Banga, 1980). Yet in the medium-term, such developments weakened the central power by arming its enemies with new political methods; at the same time the older bases of allegiance were becoming redundant at the centre itself. Paradoxically the decline of the Mughals and the demise of the 'medieval Indian merchant' proceeded in part from the dangerous success of the public knowledge and culture they had forged.

This outcome also points up the fact that contradictions between the rational procedures appropriate to different social groups might, in the short-term, impede the development of a wider, incorporative rational social ethic. The emergence of new forms of knowledge had a dialectical form which involved conflict as well as accommodation. English capitalism was able to exploit the Indian conflict-accommodation because its own synthesis between merchant rationality and the state was firmer and had emerged out of conflict at an earlier historical period.

REFERENCES

Appadurai, A. and Breckenridge, C., 'The South Indian Temple', *Contributions to Indian Sociology*, n.s., x, 2., 1976.

Banking Enquiry Committee, Report of the U.P. Provincial Banking Enquiry Committee, 1929-30 (Delhi, 1930).

Banarsi Das, *Ardha Kathanak*, ed.& tr. R.S.Sharma, *Indica*, vii, 1970.

Banga, Indu, *The Agrarian System of the Sikhs*, (Delhi, 1978).

Bayly, C.A., *Rulers, Townsmen and Bazaars. North Indian Society in the Age of British Expansion, 1770-1870* (Cambridge, 1983).

Chandavarkar, R.S., 'Labour and Politics in Bombay, 1920-36 unpub. Ph.D. diss., Cambridge University, 1982.

Chaudhuri, K.N. and Bajekal, M., 'Quantitative Study of Rajasthan Land Records. A proposal', SOAS, London, 1986.

Cohn, B.S., 'The role of the Gosains in the economy of eighteenth and nineteenth-century Upper India', *IESHR*, 1, 1, 1964.

Collins, R., *Weberian Sociological Theory* (Cambridge, 1986).

Commander, S.J. 'The jajmani system in north India', *MAS*, xvii, 2, 1983.

Dilbagh Singh, ' Local and Land revenue administration of... Jaipur', Ph.D., JNU, 1975.

Dumont, L., *Homo Hierarchicus*: An Essay on the Caste System, translated by Mark Sainsbury (Chicago, 1970).

Eldrige, M., *From Max Weber*, (London, 1970).

Fallon.S., *A New Hindustani Dictionary* (London, 1879).

Fox, R., *Lions of the Punjab* (Berkeley, 1985).

Gordon, S., 'The Slow Conquest. Administrative integration of Malwa into the Maratha Expire', *MAS*, xi, 2, 1986.

Gyan Prakash, 'Reproducing inequality. Spirit cults and labour relations in colonial eastern India', *MAS*, xx, 2, 1986.

Habib, I. and Raychaudhuri, T.(eds.), *The Cambridge Economic History of India*, vol. 1, (Cambridge, 1982).

Hall, K. R., *Maritime Trade and State Development in early south east Asia*, (Honolulu, 1985).

Hourani, A. and Stern, S.M.(eds.), *The Islamis City*, (Oxford, 1970).

Inden, R., 'Orientalist Constructions of India', *MAS*, xx, 2, 1986.

Kahane, R., Eisenstadt, S.N., and Shulam, D., *Heterodoxy and Dissent in India* (Berlin, 1984).

Lukes, S., *Rationality* (London, 1978).

Marriott. M. and Inden R., 'Caste Systems', *The Encyclopaedia Britannica*, 15th ed., iii, 1974, pp. 982-91.

Morris, M.D., 'Values as an obstacle in growth in South Asia,' *JEHist*, xxvii, 1967.

Nayeem, M.A., *Mughal Administration of the Deccan under Nizamul Mulk Asaf Jah* (Hyderabad, 1985).

Perlin, F., 'State Formation reconsidered', *MAS*, 19,3, 1985.

Rodinson, M., *Islam et capitalisme*, Paris, 1966; English trans. *Islam* and *Capitalism* (London, 1974).

Sarkar, J.N. and Nirad Bhusan Roy, *A History of the Dasmani Naga Sanyasis* (Allahabad, 1959).

Schluchter, W., *The Rise of Western Rationalism* (Berkeley, 1981).

Singer, M., *When a Great Tradition Modernises* (Princeton, 1967).

Stern, H., 'Religion et Societe en Inde selon Max Weber', *Information sur les Sciences Sociales*, x, 6, 1971, Paris.

Tennant, W., *Indian Recreations* (London, 1804).

Timberg, T., *The Marwaris: From Traders to Industrialists* (Delhi, 1978).

Washbrook, D., 'Law, State and Agrarian society in colonial India', *MAS*, xv, 3, 1981.

Weber, M., *The Religion of China*, tr. H. H. Gerth (New York, 1951).

Weber, M., *The Religion of India*, tr. H. H. Gerth and D. Martindale (New York, 1958).

Weber, M., *The Protestant Ethic and the Spirit of Capitalism*, tr. Talcott Parsons (London, 1930).

Weber, M., *Economy and Society*, tr. K. Wittich and G. Roth (New York, 1968).

Wink, A., *Land and Sovereignty in India* (Cambridge, 1986).

India and Henry Maine

GORDON JOHNSON

Henry Maine was the Legal Member of the Council of the Governor-General of India from 1862 to 1869. The appointment involved serving in India and throwing into appropriate legislative form the policy decisions of the Viceroy and his Council. Although Maine had doubted whether his health would stand up to extended residence in India (in fact illness had prevented him from accepting the job when it was first offered to him in 1861), the climate and the work suited him extremely well, and his friends were delighted to see how fit he was when he returned to Europe on leave in 1865.

The office of Law Member was a very attractive one for Maine. He had found that the openings for an academic lawyer in Britain were limited for one who could not withstand the rigours of practising at the bar and at a time when legal studies in the universities were unrewarding both intellectually and financially. The appointment was well paid (Macaulay received £10,000 a year when he held the office in the 1830s) and, following the success of his first major publication (*Ancient Law*) in early 1861, Maine lobbied his political friends to secure him some such well-remunerated public position. His wife was unable to accompany him to Calcutta and so accordingly, as Mountstuart Grant Duff tells us 'He lived . . . the life of a bachelor; but of a very hospitable member of that brotherhood. His breakfasts, over which a lady whose many gifts have made her well known in London, as of old in Calcutta society, usually presided, were especially famous'.

The service he rendered in India, for which he was rewarded by being created a Knight Commander of the Star of India in 1871, continued after his return to England upon his appointment to a place on the India Council, a body which advised the Secretary of State for India on Indian matters. Maine's election to the Mastership of Trinity Hall 'gave him a dignified position and a pleasant occasional home at Cambridge, without burdening him with duties sufficiently serious to interfere with his work as a Member of the Council of India.'[2]

The overwhelming impression one has from contemporary records is that Maine's work in its Indian context constituted an important public service and that in the exercise of his duties he was restrained and conservative in his approach. 'Like all sensible men in India', Grant Duff wrote, 'Maine was anxious, whenever he could, to support the man who had to bear the greatest weight of responsibility for all the decisions, and he carried the same habit to the India Office, having as little of the *frondeur* in him as any man I have ever known'.[3] Maine's uncertain social background, together with his dazzling academic success at Cambridge and his subsequent achievement in making a place for himself in English society, had provided him with a set of political attitudes characterized by Professor Burrow as 'hard-headed Peelite elitism varied by a taste for Burkean rhetoric'.[4] Why was it that such a temperament, combined with Maine's considerable academic prowess and his undoubted legal skills, found such a congenial niche in mid-nineteenth-century India?

The question is not an easy one to answer, for India in the 1860s has been rather neglected by the historian. It is difficult to think of any important event which took place during the decade, and impossible to recall the Viceroys. Lord Canning, who presided over the mutiny in 1857 and dealt with its immediate aftermath gave way to Lord Elgin, who died in the hills. At the end of the decade, Lord Mayo arrived, soon to be assassinated by a prisoner during his tour of the penal settlements on the Andaman Islands. In between Elgin and Mayo, and thus during most of Maine's tenure of office, the Viceroy was Sir John Lawrence, an appointment notable perhaps for the lack of enthusiasm with which it was made, since Lawrence, having served long and successfully in Punjab possessed a qualification which was universally held to bar a man from being Viceroy: actual knowledge of India itself. Lawrence was associated—indeed was an essential part of—an approach to Indian administration which stressed direct personal and discretionary rule, and who, in the light of his experience in Punjab, believed very much in patriarchal government on the spot without too many regulations and without much interference from superiors. Although his government had to stir itself to secure peace on the north-west frontier, on the face of it he was determined to do as little as possible. If it was not necessary to do something, then it was absolutely necessary not to do it.

In part, the apparently conservative pragmatism which so marked the policies of the 1860s, was made easily explicable by reference to the mutiny. As Maine himself put it 'a nervous fear of altering native custom has, ever since the terrible events of 1857, taken possession of Indian administrators'.[5] It was necessary, therefore, to be cautious and to avoid taking all possible risks. But, although the prevailing ethos might appear hostile to change, it is arguable that in the 1860s India underwent a sea-change. In formal terms, the crown had succeeded the East India Company as government, and there was a lot of detailed tidying up to be done to see the change through. Then the structure of the government of India itself began to move off in ways which made its administration decidedly more modern and uniform in appearance. Both politically and economically, India began to stand in a different relationship to Britain. The extraction of revenue through the operation of revenue systems and the exercise of fiscal and commercial monopolies, together with the indirect trading patterns of the early nineteenth century whereby Indian goods financed Britain's trade with the Far East, gave way, in importance, to growing bilateral trade, increasing British investment in India, the development of new Indian exports, not only to Asia but to Europe and North America as well, and massive use of India for the purposes of imperial defence. The 1860s ushered in the glorious years of the Empire: the next half-century were to be the truly untroubled decades of British rule in the subcontinent. Such a profound transformation during a period of overt conservatism and caution requires fuller explanation.

Early British government in India depended for its success on a hectic blend of force and political influence. Armed might and subtler politics combined to extract goods and money from a large and, on the whole poor, agrarian economy. This was in the great tradition of Indian government, and the Company simply built upon and improved the native institutions which it found. The British in India (in marked contrast to economic policies at home) continued and strengthened state monopolies, and they worked with those social elites who were best able to squeeze money from the rural economy. The Company used its army, on a regular basis, to collect a revenue demand pitched high and in cash (thus also ensuring that commodities needed for trade came on to the market), and it reinforced and developed ways of tying labour to the land and of preventing the free movement of cultivators (particularly important at a time when land was plentiful and labour was not). Success in these hazardous enterprises depended upon securing a reliable army and operating a revenue-collecting system which provided privilege and protection for important elements in society.

The precise nature of this organization varied enormously across the different parts of India, Dr Washbrook argues:

> it could be characterized as consisting of corporate, kin-related patterns of land settlement shaped over a long period by the attempts of the state to reduce their autonomy and by a penetration of the caste-system, both of which created internal social and political differentiation. The Company state, following its predecessors, tried to latch on to this differentiation, where it could find it, and turn it into the dominance which could be used to extract surplus. The early raj reinforced the authority of local leaderships (headmen, vatandars, small zamindars, single-family mirasidars, malguzars, etc.) and subvented caste-based privileges (through inams and differential rates of assessments). In some cases, it failed to find significant differentiation within the kin-body but was obliged to elevate it in its entirety to privilege over outsiders (bhaiachara, co-sharing mirasi tenure etc.). The key feature of the process, however, was that although the state partially drew out these elements of potential dominance, it neither controlled nor created the context from which they came and in which they remained half-situated. In consequence, actual rights to possess and use the land remained part-conditioned by this context and dependent on the customs and norms of the local agrarian community. These customs and norms (institutionalised in the authority of panchayats, lineage leaders, caste and religious deference, etc.) played at least as large a role in determining the relationship of society to the land as did the granting of state privilege in the first place.[6]

Although the Company had some leverage in rural society, it was never strong enough to fully control local leaderships, far less to redesign the social context from which they came. Thus government was in a perpetual struggle with strong elements in rural society to control the economy and share in its profits. The fact that both army and police, as well as all levels of lower or local administration were part and parcel of the same social network, further hampered the freedom of action of the policy-makers. The same argument applies in other areas of society as well: the Company was heavily dependent upon the indigenous commercial and banking elites to achieve its fiscal and trading objectives, and it had perforce to draw upon the traditionally literate to staff its administrative offices at the higher levels. The Company's needs were met by the application of force but in a lively political arena where its wishes were mediated through semi-autonomous social groups and institutions over which the British had no final control. Thus, India exhibited not a series of small, simple archaic societies, but extremely complex sets of social networks which were very difficult to manage. From the earliest governmental experiments in Bengal, fundamental contradictions underlay the Company's rule: while on the one hand it, and some of its Indian supporters, could set out clear, cogent policies for reform, progress and development, on the other, care had to be taken to see that such change was compatible with the maintenance of a perceived status quo and would accommodate local customs and tradition. Hence also the long-standing paradox in Indian law that while, from the eighteenth century, there was a trend to legislate in order to encourage and safeguard the freedom of the individual and his or her rights in property, there was a simultaneous development of personal law which entrenched ascriptive (caste, religions and familial) status as the basis of individuals in a world of amoral marker relations and of individuals inextricably trapped in joint-families or other communal organizations.

Far from being a static or isolated society, India had come under tremendous pressures, both domestically and internationally, in the late eighteenth and early nineteenth-centuries. Natural disaster and the fragile environment for agriculture had led to shortages, famine and large-scale depopulation in the closing decades of the eighteenth-century. Internal political turmoil and rapidly changing governments marked the politics of the period. At the same time, various parts of the Indian economy were linked in new ways to international markets, providing both opportunity and enhanced vulnerability to changes over which Indian producers had no control. In ways in which historians are only just beginning to fathom, the East India Company and dynamic Indian groups in alliance with it, began to provide a more stable political and economic context from the early nineteenth-century. The emergence of the new state of things was slow in coming and very uneven, geographically and socially, in its impact. Hence it would be fair to characterize much of the early part of the nineteenth-century as a period in which the Company's rule was never totally secure (despite its virtual monopoly of force from about 1820 onwards), and during which it faced chronic unrest in the Indian country-side. There was hardly a year in which the Company was not at war, either on its shifting and seemingly ever-expanding frontiers, or against its own recalcitrant subjects, constantly tussling with the new overlord for shares in resources. In this context, the mutiny of a part of the Indian army in

1857 and the serious and widespread disturbances, with significant loss of governmental control which followed hard on the initial rebellion at Meerut, were the last, albeit perhaps the grandest, attempt at resistance to the new social and economic order which had been a century in the making.

The events of 1857-59 hit British confidence so hard not so much because in objective terms the revolts were impossible to deal with but because loss of control had been so sudden and the close connection between rural society and the army had been underlined in such a striking way. If there was a moral to the tale, it was to err on the side of caution. But, in fact, there was another side to the coin. Most of India, after all, did not revolt. Punjab, the most recently acquired of the provinces, and the one which had attracted the most by way of scarce government resources to develop its economy, remained firm, already benefiting from a decade of economic growth. Elsewhere, improved communications in the form of road, canal and, most lately, railway, together with renewed attempts to encourage irrigation, were also beginning to have an effect. There was an increase in the number of schools and in the establishment of the first Indian colleges and universities, Most importantly, groups in the countryside which had become established through the operation of the revenue systems, were now launched in a period of unprecedented prosperity: the population increased (thus making labour easier to control), acres of farmland expanded, marginal areas were brought under cultivation, new foreign markets were opening up, and, in real terms, the burden of the land revenue demand everywhere began to fall. In some areas, the economic gains were very striking indeed, and, although benefits were far from being evenly distributed, it could not be denied that they were there. Even the government found itself better off than before as inflation and the increased areas under production brought more rupees into the exchequer.

Such developments were not, however, without strain. The government needed to exercise constant vigilance in its management of the changing situation. As before, it was forced to follow policies riddled with paradox and contradiction: in this sense there is no marked change of policy or of process at mid-century. But whereas the earlier nineteenth-century may perhaps have trumpeted reform and change to mask its fundamentally conservative activities, in the second half of the century the prevailing ethos was to hide change under concern for tradition. Thus virtue was made of protecting under-tenants and 'poor' peasants while quietly strengthening the legal and economic position of dominant cultivators. 'Moneylenders' became a much abused class, discriminated against in peculiar ways (for example, by preventing certain specified social groups from buying more land outside of towns), but the position of creditors was also improved; a fetish was made of leaving religious and social customs well alone, unless it happened established usages were so flagrantly opposed to British ideas of right and wrong (such as particular marriage customs or the consequences for ownership of property arising from them) in which case the government stepped briskly forward, irrespective of the critical outcry. And, underneath the policy statements and the laws, there was the continual quest to find those groups in Indian society which could best serve the purposes of the raj. This was a delicate political task, society being so open to change. But the invention of social anthropology and the rise of the sociologist in government made men bold. Society was analysed and classified and labels placed unerringly upon the social categories which were deemed reliable or dangerous. Hence the late-nineteenth century view of Indian society as coherent groups, which could be used as building-blocks in the political game: 'peasants', 'proprietors', 'princes', 'Muslims', 'criminal tribes', 'moneylenders' and a myriad of other social descriptions which, whatever their actual justification, became live political categories.

This, then, was the India to which Maine came and he was wonderfully fitted to serve it well. Not only did he perform valuable services in his professional character as a lawyer, but he made the whole country, and the problems of governing it, seem intelligible to his contemporaries, and he did so in such a way as to give intellectual respectability to the courses of action upon which the government was set.

As Law Member, Maine passed no striking laws, and much of the legislation which was approved in his time was recast before the century was over. Although he was responsible for over two hundred separate Acts, his colleagues are remarkably unanimous in their welcome for his low key approach. Sir Richard Strachey found that Maine's virtue lay in that 'he limited himself to the actual requirements of his time'[7] while Courtenay Ilbert, who was later to prove an extremely controversial Law Member, praised Maine for abstaining 'from passing a great many measures of doubtful utility'.[8] Here was no adventurous law-giver, as Macaulay had been thirty years before, nor, it might be argued, as confident a legislator as James Fitzjames Stephen was to prove immediately after him. But his technical skills were without equal, and he established the highest professional standards possible for his Department. This high level of technical competence also allowed him to play an influential role as a mediator between conflicting demands made upon the law. The Acts passed through the Council between 1862 and 1869 are various: some applied to India in a very straightforward way the law as it already existed in England and these, particularly, benefited commercial activity and the easy recourse to the courts in support of property and contracts. Others gave legislative form to the civil usages and religious practices of particular groups of Indians, and here, while there were some notable exceptions particularly as regards marriage, the overall tendency was to put into statute form customary laws and to do so in ways which were prevalent at the time. This gave a specious authenticity to particular versions of Hindu law and, in a sense, worked against the trend of more secular contract-type relations in the society. Maine also saw that the new government of India must rule through laws passed by the legislature rather than by rulings handed down by the courts or by regulations issued by executive authority. His opinion, therefore, was on the side of developing centralized government and of dividing the functions of government into clearly separated departments. But with a Viceroy who in the districts had combined revenue, police and judicial powers all in his own person such a development was not likely to be welcomed. Maine conceded, therefore, that while the former was to a large degree inevitable ways might be found of discovering expedients whereby the tendency of legislation to hamper discretion could be minimised. Maine also saw that, given the size and variety of India, an important feature of law-making in India in the future would be provision for all the regions to be empowered to frame their own provincial legislation (at that time only Bengal, Bombay and Madras could make their own local laws).

Much of the work of the law department was on the further codification of Indian laws. Here Maine had to negotiate the results with a law commission sitting in London, and the evidence suggests that for much of the time the two bodies worked at cross-purposes. But for Maine codification did not provide an opportunity for a fundamental reconstruction of Indian law (which is what lawyers in London would have liked) but simply an attempt to 'set forth fundamental principles with as much simplicity as was compatible with accuracy'.[9] Again, the practicalities of the Indian situation were to temper the force of reform. Finally, Maine employed a great piece of legal casuistry to show, from established precedents in international law, that sovereignty could be divided and that, varying as they did in their actual relationship with the British crown, the princely states in India were, in legality, quite distinct and separate from British India and must be treated as such. Politically, this laid the foundation for the use of princely India as a block on constitutional reform and it signalled an end to the continued absorption of Indian states into the British raj. Perhaps Sir Alfred Lyall best summed up Maine's legal contribution by pointing out 'he stood between ancient and modern ideas — between the opinions of Europe and India, and had to find a *modus vivendi* that reconciled both'.[10]

Of course, all Maine's contemporaries recognized that his influence spread far beyond the making of laws. His serious writing—particularly *Ancient Law* and *Village Communities East and West* — had a profound effect on how Indian society was observed and understood. Here his talent for imposing order on chaos and for lucidly setting out complex matters, made him compelling reading. 'Many books had been written about India, but most of them were unreadable'. Maine 'divided the essential principles of Indian institutions and he clothed his description of them in language of consummate literary art'.[11] In some respects, Maine cannot lay claim to be a particularly original thinker. Before he had ever set foot in India, Grant Duff tells us, 'he had written admirable papers about the Indian village system'.[12] Baden-Powell pointed out that Maine had had 'no opportunity for "camping out" and personal enquiry on the spot' and hence it was the case that all his knowledge was 'gathered from reading and conversation; he saw with the eyes of others'.[13] In fact, Maine drew upon an enormous range of early nineteenth-century writing about India—prominent, no doubt, being works like those of James Mill, Elphinstone, Metcalf, Malcolm and Tod, together with the voluminous published records of the East India Company, particularly revealing for revenue arrangements in Bengal and Madras. He combined these with fashionable ideas from the German historical school: he took a whole mass of incoherent facts and by applying social theory to it gave it form and shape. 'His mind seemed like a sun shooting forth rays of light which bridged over great intervals of space and time, which brought Indian village communities into relation with village communities in Russia, and associated Rajpootana society today with the society of the Homeric age. His writings were luminous, stimulating and suggestive'.[14] The last -quarter of the nineteenth-century saw a tremendous flowering of social studies in India. Census and settlement reports contained miniature ethnographic surveys, and minute enquiry was encouraged into the structure and working of Indian society—its castes, its cultures, its religions and its economies. For the very best minds who applied themselves to the daunting task of observing, recording and explaining India, it is remarkable how often Maine is the point of departure, even when the new work sets out to modify or to disagree with his own arguments. For lesser minds, the ordinary revenue officer who had read Maine's books as his preparation for government in India, it was easy to pluck from Maine's prose a comforting phrase or paragraph about the true nature of Indian society. Such information would usually be of a conservative nature and would seem to point towards the fineness of simple archaic society and to justify conserving it against change.

Although it would be easy to portray Maine as representing a rather bland conservatism and lending his academic authority to a counter-revolution, it would be a mistake to do so. Besides being an extremely lucid thinker, Maine was also sophisticated. The brilliant prose is not only coherent and compelling but it is also ambivalent and ambiguous. He falls into none of the traps that beset the unwary. He knew that Indian society was not, and never had been, static; he saw clearly that 'the natives of India are not so wedded to their usages that they are not ready to surrender them for tangible advantage'.[15] He argued strongly against there being any uniform or clearly stated set of Indian law: rather the whole was a mess of shifting customs which varied from place to place and over time. He had no truck with the popular impression that 'Indian society is divided...into a number of horizontal strata, each representing a caste'. He told students at Oxford:

> This is an entire mistake. It is extremely doubtful whether the Brahminical theory of caste upon caste was ever true except of the two highest castes; and it is even likely that more importance has been attached to it in modern than ever was in ancient times. The real India contains one priestly caste, which in a certain, though a very limited, sense is the highest of all, and there are, besides, some princely houses and a certain number of tribes, village communities, and guilds, which still in our day advance a claim, considered by many good authorities extremely doubtful, to belong to the second or third of the castes recognised by the Brahminical writers. But otherwise, caste is merely a name for trade or occupation, and the sole tangible effect of the Brahminical theory is that it creates a religious sanction for what is really a primitive and natural distribution of classes. The true view of India is that, as a whole, it is divided into a vast number of independent, self-acting, organised social groups — trading, manufacturing, cultivating.[16]

Earlier, in *Ancient Law*, he had encapsulated the Indian village community in a formulation both persuasive and fraught with difficulty. The village community, in reality, was 'at once an organized patriarchal society and an assembly of co-proprietors'.[17] As Lyall, no mean scholar himself, told a meeting of the Society of Arts, Maine had not made so many original discoveries as had been supposed.

> Other people had the facts, and knew what they wanted to do, but they did not know how to do it, nor how to justify it; but when they produced their case, Maine found exactly the formula which explained everything. If you put before him a set of facts, or a certain number of ideas and suggestions, which most Anglo-Indians had stumbled upon in a confused, unfinished way, he would suddenly set them all in order by one of his weird and wide generalizations, and they discovered that they had been right all along.[18]

In the surviving literature, not least that which he wrote himself, Maine appears as a decidedly ambiguous figure. Sir Frederick Pollock praised 'the great practical wisdom displayed in everything Maine did, and perhaps also in several things he refrained from doing'.[19] His books were so influential because their clarity stands not in the way of many interpretations of their content. Conservative in attitude he may have been, but he was historically sensitive and this lent an ambivalence to his thought. Perhaps this is why Maine provides a good way of looking at the wider questions of India and its government in the later nineteenth-century. That society and its administration was shot throughout with contradictions too. But what seems to have been happening was that, from the early 1860s a new balance was struck between British and Indian interests: British rule was re-established after the difficulties of the 1840s and 1850s, on a new basis, and India settled in to a new and profitable relationship with Britain. Economic development, reform of the political and administrative structures, a definite move into the international economy all took place within an ideologically conservationist ethos. Those British interests primarily connected with India did well, while significant social groups within India benefited from the economic consequences of rising population, expanded agriculture, growing exports, lessening taxation and increased opportunities for new employment outside their traditional sectors. It was, therefore, an ideal time to be seen to be doing nothing very much and letting nature take its course. The contradictions in society, in the economy and in the political structure did not obtrude. It was perfectly possible, and agreeable, to back both the dynamic and the static; to allow change while protecting an old order; to maintain a fundamentally inefficient order of agricultural production while building canals and railways; to build up native rulers as real princes and to look with pride on colleges and universities.

In the longer term, difficulties would make themselves felt. The social and economic orders were neither efficient enough nor flexible enough to respond to further pressures from within—such as continued growth of population—or to change from without—like new competitors entering the world's market places. The balance achieved in the second part of the century would be destroyed by increased social conflict and economic stratification. There would be no easy evolution of Indian society from the archaic to the modern, and it would be as difficult for a nationalist movement as for an imperial government to put in order Indian societies as they buckled under the pressures of the twentieth century.

In retrospect, the later nineteenth-century may seem to have been a time of lost opportunity: just when the raj could, perhaps, have pushed ahead and re-ordered itself on the backs of the more dynamic and entrepreneurial of India's social elites, and given a boost to individual freedoms by attacking more vigorously the mediating social institutions which ensnared men and women in communal and kin associations, it hedged its bets. It felt the need to support and protect a status quo, ever driven by the realization that no government, even the most despotic, can outlast its beneficiaries. And so it balanced the old and the new; it reined back development when it was believed to threaten the stability of order as a whole. It was wisest to play safe. Maine puts the argument into clearer form:

> I have said that there are many different countries in the remarkable dominion which we call India. But on all of them a double current of influences may be seen to be playing. One of these currents is of foreign origin, and it has done much to shape the mental condition of a relatively small minority, characterized by aspirations with which it is impossible for Englishmen not to sympathize, but too apt to take its opinions from what are called schools of advanced thought, an expression to which I hope I do no injustice by suggesting that it means thought which has shaken itself free from the restraints of human nature and historical fact. The other current arises in India itself, engendered amid a dense and dark vegetation of primitive

> opinion, stubbornly rooted in the *debris* of the past. It feeds the minds of a majority so large that its very vastness makes it irresistible. I have quoted elsewhere the saying of an eminent Anglo-Indian, that the British rulers of India are like men bound to make their watches keep time in two longitudes at once. Nevertheless, I added, this paradoxical position must be accepted. If they are too slow, there will be no improvement; if they are too fast, there will be no security. The British dominion in India is much too wonderful a creation for despair to be justifiable, but a man must have a very superficial conception of what Indian government is if he thinks that it has been made easier by the necessity for reconciling these two conditions.[20]

NOTES

This paper was prepared for a seminar held at Trinity Hall, Cambridge, in September 1988 to mark the centenary of the death of Sir Henry Maine who had been Master of the College. An early life of Maine is by Mountstuart Grant Duff : *Sir Henry Maine: A Brief Memoir of his Life by the Right Hon.Sir M.E. Grant Duff G.C.S.I. With some of his Indian Speeches and Minutes*, selected and edited by Whitley Stokes (London, 1892). The standard modern biography is George Feaver, *From Status to Contract: A Biography of Sir Henry Maine 1822-1888* (London, 1969). An important recent study is Raymond J.C. Cocks, *Sir Henry Maine: A Study in Victorian Jurisprudence* (Cambridge, 1988). A selection of the papers presented at the Trinity Hall symposium is to be edited by A. Diamond and published by Cambridge University Press. An important source for this article has been Charles Lewis Tupper, 'India and Sir Henry Maine', presented to the Society of Arts, 10 March 1898, together with a report of the discussion following, *Journal of the Society of Arts*, volume XLVI, London, 1898. Three other essays have been of great value to me: J.W.Burrow, 'The Village Community and the Uses of History in Late Nineteenth-Century England', in *Historical Perspectives: Studies in English Thought and Society in Honour of J.H. Plumb*, edited by Neil McKendrick (London, 1974), pp. 255-84; J.Duncan Derrett, 'Sir Henry Maine at Law in India : 1858-1958', *The Juridicial Review : The Law Journal of the Scottish Universities*, vol. iv, 1959, pp. 40-55; and C. J. Dewey, 'Images of the Village Community : A Study in Anglo-Indian Ideology', in *Modern Asian Studies*, vol. 6, part 3, 1972, pp. 291 - 328.

I have also drawn upon J.W.Burrow, *Evolution and Society: A Study in Victorian Social Theory* (Cambridge, 1970), B.S.Cohn, 'From Indian Status to British Contract', *Economic History*, vol. XXI, pp. 613-28 and Louis Dumont, 'The Village Community from Munro to Maine', *Contributions to Indian Sociology*, vol. IX, 1966, pp. 67-89. But in some respects my essay is little more than a commentary on part of the stimulating and important article by D.A.

Washbrook, 'Law, State and Agrarian Society in Colonial India', *Modern Asian Studies*, vol. 15, part 3, 1981, pp. 649-721.

1. Grant Duff, *Memoir*, p. 31.
2. Ibid., p. 48.
3. Ibid. p. 23.
4. Burrow, 'The Village Community ...', p. 255.
5. H.S. Maine, *Village Communities in the East and West* (4th edition, London,1881), pp. 38-39.
6. Washbrook, 'Law, State and Agrarian Society....', *MAS*, *op.cit.*, pp. 663-64.
7. *Journal of the Society of Arts*, XLVI, 1898, p. 391.
8. Ibid., p. 402.
9. Ibid., p. 393.
10. Ibid, p. 402.
11. Ilbert's comment, ibid. p. 403.
12. Ibid., p. 399.
13. Ibid., p. 455.
14. Ilbert's comment, ibid., p. 403.
15. Maine, *Village Communities*, p. 39.
16. Ibid., pp. 56-57.
17. H.S.Maine, *Ancient Law: Its Connection with the Early History of Society, and its relation to Modern Ideas* (4th edition, London, 1870), p. 260.
18. *Journal of the Society of Arts*, XLVI, 1898, p. 402.
19. Ibid., p. 401.
20. 'India' in T. H Ward (ed.), *The Reign of Queen Victoria: A Survey of Fifty Years of Progress* (London,1887), vol. 1, pp. 527-58.

Resistance and Acquiescence in North India: Muslim Responses to the West

MUSHIRUL HASAN

When I reflect on the want of energy and the indolent dispositions of my countrymen, and the many erroneous customs which exist in all Mohammedan countries and among all ranks of Mussulmans, I am fearful that my exertions will be thrown away. . . . It may consequently be concluded, that as they will find no pleasure in reading a book which contains a number of foreign names, treats [*sic*] on uncommon subjects, and alludes to other matters which cannot be understood at the first glance, but require little time for consideration, they will, under pretence of zeal for their religion, entirely abstain and refrain from perusing it.

MIRZA ABU TALIB KHAN, *Travels of Mirza Abü Taleb Khan in Asia, Africa, and Europe during the years 1797 to 1803*

Decadence has brought us to a sorry pass; adversity far and wide lays us low. Our honour has long since vanished from the world, and no hope of revival is in sight. One hope alone sustains us now we are laid low; we live on in the expectation of paradise after death.

Too inept to travel, too spineless to journey, we know nothing of what God's creation holds. The four walls of our home which we see before our eyes are for us the limits of human habitation—like fish in a tank, for whom its limits bound their whole world.

ALTAF HUSAIN HALI, *Mussadas-i maddo-jazr-i Islam (Mussadas-i Hali)*

Any number of scholarly works delineate the responses of the Muslim aristocracy, the ulama and the literati to the first major incursion of a European power into India.[1] The late Aziz Ahmad was the first to dwell on this theme in his seminal study of *Islamic Modernism in India and Pakistan*. Muhammad Mujeeb, former vice-chancellor of Delhi's Jamia Millia Islamia, added fresh insights through his lucid analysis of, among others, Mirza Abu Talib 'Londony's' *Masir-i Talibi fi Bilad-i Afrangi*, Lutfullah's (b. 1802) *Autobiography*, and Mirza Ihtisamuddin's *Shigurf Nama-i Velayet*.[2] In this paper, my concerns are twofold. First, to shift the focus from 'revivalist' and 'fundamentalist' trends in the first-half of the nineteenth-century—extensively covered in secondary literature—to the presence of alternative currents of thought. This may provide a corrective to the essentialist view, which was part of the colonial stereotype, that Muslims were so steeped in their religion and so firmly anchored in Islamic traditions that anything Western or modern was inimical to their world view. Secondly, I wish to underline both the elements of continuity as well as the variety of responses to the West. This places in perspective the ongoing debates on identity politics in the nineteenth century.

I

Most thinking Muslims of the late nineteenth and early twentieth-centuries looked at the events of the past hundred years as a historical catastrophe for their religion. The notion of *umma*, resting on the utopian concept of a unified belief system and ritualistic structure, lost its validity as the house of Islam stood hopelessly fragmented and doctrinally polarized. As the colonial powers established their political hegemony, the beleagured Ottoman sultan remained the sole surviving symbol of resistance to Western imperialism. Many educated Indian Muslims, swayed by the pan-Islamic ferment, rose to defend the sultan and his empire. By the time their passions cooled, the khilafat bubble had burst, the empire had withered away, and the khalifa/sultan was far removed from Constantinople. '*Chhak kar di Turk-i Nadaan ne khilafat ki Qaba*' (Alas, the naive Turk has cut to pieces the khilafat robe), wrote a distraught Muhammad Iqbal.[3]

The trauma of decline, a recurrent theme in world-wide Islamic literature, was expressed in a variety of ways. In some places it was manifested in militant assertions of Islamic identity, a stricter conformity to the Koran and the *Sunna*, and a call for a return to the pristine Islam of the early days of the orthodox khalifas. In other places, most notably in West and North Africa, there was greater consciousness of the internal degeneration of Muslim society and an awareness of the positive lines of reconstruction through an integration of modern ideas and institutions with the bases of Islam.[4] In advocating such a course, early Islamic modernism encouraged the import of Western thought and educational initiatives, and offered partial justification for the Western intellectual influences that were already there and were bound to come anyway.

In the Indian subcontinent, early reformist trends were either dormant or suffered from ambiguity until Saiyid Ahmad Khan advocated, in the tradition of his Egyptian counterpart Muhammad Abduh, integrating the modern scientific world view with the injunctions of the Koran. The theme of decline mattered to him a great deal, though his own discourse was remarkably free of ceaseless lamentations over the eclipse of Muslim power and the declining Muslim civilization. Others did so with unfailing regularity and with great effect. Altaf Husain Hali, acutely sensitive to the departed glory of Islam and its followers, wrote: 'We have eclipsed,' he bemoaned, 'the fame of our ancestors' name. Wherever we set one foot our countrymen are ashamed of us. We have squandered the high honour that our ancestors won, and have lost the nobility of our Arab forbears.'[5] 'With my unskilful mirrors', he stated in his preface to a book, 'I have built a house of mirrors, in which our people can see their face and form reflected.'

There was, in addition, a good deal of soul-searching, and many earnest attempts to ask what had gone wrong, a question Shah Waliullah had raised amid the ruins of the Mughal empire. Few could claim to have the right answers. And fewer still, when faced with the reality of foreign rule, could decide on how best to cope with the colonial encounter, withstand the ideological assault of the Christian West, and acquire the strength to confront Europe and become part of the modern world. There were varied responses, each one being seriously debated. When the poet Mirza Ghalib reached Delhi in 1810 he found the conflict between the 'traditionalists' in religion and the 'radical' reformers 'raging vigorously'.[6] When maulvi Karimuddin (b. 1821) of Panipat visited Delhi he found 'the fountain of knowledge' flowing in every direction.[7] He referred to the setting up of new printing presses in Delhi. These gave spurt to publications and stimulated interest in contemporary social and political issues.

Early responses to colonial rule were, predictably, mixed. Nineteenth-century historical literature is replete with instances of resistance to and rebellion against the 'infidels'. Some tangible expressions of opposition to the new symbols of authority was the *fatwa* of Shah Abdul Aziz, eldest of Waliullah's son, the adventurist campaigns of the *mujahidins* in the Frontier region, the Faraizi movement of Haji Shariat-Allah in Bengal, and the involvement of some prominent ulama in the 1857 revolt. Islam provided a ready-made conceptual framework for such wide-ranging reactions.

Equally intense was the stubborn resistance to the proselytizing activities of Christian missionaries and their denigration of Islam and its Prophet, to the influx of unorthodox ideas which threatened to undermine religious beliefs, and to what Abu Talib described as 'that overbearing insolence which characterizes the vulgar part of the English in their conduct of Orientals'. There was, moreover, strong and pungent criticism of unabashed British expansionist designs. Like so many others his generation, Ghalib's sense of pride was wounded by the annexation of Awadh. 'Although I am a stranger to Awadh and its affair,' he wrote on 23 February 1857, 'the destruction of the state depressed me all the more, and I maintain that no Indian who was not devoid of all sense of justice could have felt otherwise.'[8] 'No doubt,' observed Saiyid Ahmad a year later, 'men of all classes were irritated at its (Awadh) annexation, all agreed in thinking that the Honourable East India Company had acted in defiance of its treaties, and in contempt of the word which it had pledged.'[9]

Nineteenth-century movements of revivalism and reform symbolized anger and indignation against political subordination and the cultural hegemony of the 'outsiders'. They were grounded in the belief that the Islamic community enjoyed an autonomy of its own requiring no mediation. Thus, Islam in India had to be purged of Hindu accretions, and its followers to be equipped to combat the pernicious influence of the West through the unchanging social and religious codes enunciated in the Koran and the *Hadith*. The conception of community, still in its embryonic form, had to be revitalized and its lost pride restored through a carefully devised educational scheme. Such was the rationale behind the founding of the Dar al-ulum at Deoband. The institution inspired by the ideas of Waliullahi school and conforming to Hanafi codes, delivered hundreds of rulings (*fatawa*) a year to guide the faithful and maintain a close vigil on their social and religious conduct.[10] On a lesser scale, Lucknow's Firangi Mahal, the seminary founded in Aurangzeb's reign (1658-1707), performed the same role. These interventions were designed to bring about an uniformity of belief and practice, rejuvenate and revitalize the slackening faith of the believers, define the place and status of the Muslims in a Western-dominated cultural and intellectual milieu, and cement the bonds of unity in an otherwise stratified community.

Saiyid Ahmad spurned the 'traditionalist' world view. In his generation, he was among the few to recognize the presence of a powerful colonial force in the subcontinent, and, for that reason, laid stress on *ijtehad* (interpretation) and not *taqlid* (conformity), on innovation, reforms and change rather than on unquestioning adherence to the *Shariat*. Drawing upon the Islamic intellectual heritage and his own reading of the contemporary political scene, he endeavoured to convince the British that the Muslims were loyal subjects. Importantly, he told his co-religionists that they would gain much more by cooperating with the government and learning from them than they would by carrying on with futile resistance or withdrawing into a sulk They were not to live as the British themselves lived, but to carve out a place for themselves within the establishment. To do this, they were not required to adopt nineteenth-century British liberalism, but only to accept some of its values as at least a second-best substitute for the vanished Muslim glories.[11]

Muslim theologians found this a bitter pill to swallow. Denouncing the Aligarh reformer, they called him a *nechari* and an apostate. But Saiyid Ahmad ignored such blunt criticism and the rude *fatawa*. At the end of the day, the grand old man of Aligarh emerged a clean winner and his message embodied, in large part, the *ijma* (consensus) of succeeding Muslim generations in the subcontinent. His interpretation of Islam became part of the mental frame of educated Muslims, including those trained and tutored in the traditional centres of learning. Those who condemned him had to eat their words. Those who chided him sent their own children to the college he founded at Aligarh, a town (also known as Koil) in western Uttar Pradesh (hereafter UP), situated 79 miles south of Delhi. 'The world has seen,' stated Hali in a moving tribute to his intellectual mentor, 'how one man has aroused a whole land, one man saved a caravan from destruction, and small boats sinking ships to the shore . . . Hidden among the gravel there are pearls to be found; and mingled in the sand are particles of gold.'[12]

As the nineteenth-century wore on, it became increasingly clear that there was little prospect of successful military resistance, and little hope of fulfilling the dream of establishing a *Dar al-Islam*. Just as the collapse of the Mughal empire had upset the uncertainties of the previous era, the coming of the British created eddies of uncertainty in certain circles. Yet, a broad consensus existed in favour of an Anglo-Muslim rapprochement as opposed to the repudiation of everything Western.

Much before Saiyid Ahmad, the *sajjada nashin* of certain Sufi shrines in Punjab had assisted the British during the siege of Multan in 1848-9.[13] Nor did the Muslims of Bengal stir, a fact noted by Canning (1812-62), the governor-general at the time of the 1857 upheaval. In Punjab, they joined with Sikhs and the tribesmen of Kohat to form part of the reinforcements for the British troops on the Ridge outside Delhi. In the North-Western Provinces, 'the Mahomedans have, I think, behaved better than might have been expected . . . and that the result, far from bringing to light a chronic Mahomedan conspiracy, has been to show that we have not in that class of our subjects that formidable danger that has been sometimes apprehended'.[14] The historian Eric Stokes explained how the economic and political ties of members of Muslim learned families helped moderate their response to cries for *jihad*. Only in the vicinity of Thana Bhawan, north of Delhi, did the poverty of the petty gentry and a strong ideological impulse from local religious leaders, who later helped set up the Dar al-ulum in Deoband, forge a 'truly' Islamic response.[15] The heroics supposedly performed by the ulama, catalogued in *Ulama-i Hind Ka Shandar Maazi*, was no more than a latter-day idealized construction.[16]

New generations grew up for whom foreign rule was an unchanging fact of life, whether they liked it or not. For some time, since the British perpetuated the administrative patterns of the Mughals, including the use of Persian as official tongue, the presence of a handful of Britishers at the top made relatively little difference in day-to-day routine. In judicial and revenue employ, except in the highest posts, Muslims held their own in Bengal until the middle of nineteenth-century, in the region of modern UP for a generation thereafter. Likewise, while the landed classes proved vulnerable to British-induced changes in some areas, it was not so in others. In Bengal, Muslims did not become as insignificant a proportion of the new landed class as their numbers among the population might suggest. In UP, the 'Islamic gentry' in the *qasbahs* remained well-entrenched in the lower levels of the British service during the early nineteenth-century; the Muslim landlord class exercised an influence and power that persisted well into the next century.[17]

Some Muslims quickly sensed that their community could no longer live in a stable and self-sufficient system of inherited culture: their need was now to generate the strength to survive in a world dominated by 'Others'. A large number of them explained the reasons for the strength of Europe to demonstrate that Muslims could adopt European concepts and methods without being untrue to their belief. Although this realization eventually diluted opposition to and softened hostility towards the British, the earliest signs of change is broadly reflected in the careers of Mirza Abu Talib and Lutfullah (1802-74), the two outstanding representatives of early nineteenth-century north India.

II

Abu Talib spent his early years in Murshidabad at the court of Muzaffar Jung. With the accession of Asaf al-Daula (r. 1775-97) he returned to Awadh as *amildar* of Etawah and other districts. He also served as a revenue official under Colonel Alexander Hanny in Gorakhpur, and spiritedly defended his revenue administration in *Tafzih al-Ghafilin*, a history of Awadh under Asaf al-Daula. Later employed by Nathaniel Middleton, the English Resident (1773-82), and connected with Richard Johnson in managing the confiscated jagirs of the Begums of Awadh, his superiors were impressed with his robust attitude to life, his scholarly disposition, and his sensitivity to the winds of change blowing in the areas under Company rule. A Scotsman, Captain David Richardson, recognized these traits in his personality and arranged for his travel to Europe.[18]

On 7 February 1799, Abu Talib sailed from Calcutta to Europe where he visited England, France, Turkey, and other countries, returning to India in August 1803. He reached London on 21 January 1800, the starting point of his trip to other parts of England. He set out on his return journey on 7 June 1802, travelling through France, Constantinople, Baghdad, Karbala, Najaf and the Persian Gulf to 'describe the curiosities and wonders . . . (and) give some account of the manners and customs of the various nations (he) visited, all of which was little known to the Asiatics'.[19]

The Mirza was received with warmth and courtesy. He had an audience with George III and Queen Charlotte, met the old colonial hands—Warren Hastings (1754-1826), Cornwallis (1738-1805) and Charles Metcalf (1785-1846)—and interacted with literary figures and artists. Known as 'The Persian Prince', the press followed him everywhere. 'I declare', he wrote, 'I never assumed the title; but I was so much better known by it than by my own name, that I found it in vain to contend with my godfather.'[20] He was courted, entertained lavishly, and his wit and repartees were apparently the subject of conversation in the politest circles.[21] He was perfectly at ease in such circles, enjoying 'every luxury my heart could desire', drinking 'exquisite' wines, and visiting operas in the company of 'ladies of quality'. He viewed the visit to playhouses as an 'employment of sensuality', and detailed the arrangement of the stage, seats, spectacles, and spectators. He even drew a blueprint of the playhouse in Dublin. He was taken in by the beauty of the women, and their grace in dancing; his senses 'charmed' by the variety and melody of their music. Exhilarated by the coolness of the climate and devoid of all care, the Mirza wrote about how he 'gave' himself 'up to love and gaiety'.[22] On his return journey home he visited the shrines of the Shia *imams*, Hazrat Ali, Imam Husain, and his son Imam Zainul-Abidin, and sought their forgiveness for his sins in Europe. He also composed two elegies in praise of Ali and his son Imam Hasan.

Returning to Calcutta on 4 August 1803, Abu Talib put together his notes and diaries to write a truly 'monumental assessment' of Anglo-Saxon civilization.[23] Written nearly a quarter of a century before the impressions of the Egyptian scholar-educationist Rifa al-Tahtawi, *The Travels of Mirza Abu Taleb Khan* was one of the first introductions to modern Western civilization. 'I believe this is the first time,' wrote Abu Talib's translator, 'the genuine opinions of an Asiatic, respecting the institutions of Europe, have appeared in the English languages.'[24] Translated by Charles Stewart, Professor of Oriental Languages in the East India Company's college at Hertford, the *Masir-i Talibi fi Bilad-i Afrangi* was published in 1810, in two volumes, by Boxbourne, London. A French translation (*Voyages du Prince Persan Mirza Abul Taleb Khan*) appeared in Paris in 1812, the year when the Persian text was published by his son Mirza Husain Ali; its second version a year later. The same year a German translation was out in Vienna.[25]

Lutfullah, who visited England nearly half a century later,[26] agreed with some of Abu Talib's impressions of the West. Both were struck by the progress in mechanical inventions, the tangible benefits of the industrial revolution, and by the organization and functioning of mills, iron foundries and hydraulic machines. 'On entering one of the extensive manufactories in England,' recorded Abu Talib, 'the mind is at first bewildered by the number and variety of articles displayed therein; but, after recovering from this first impression, and having coolly surveyed all the objects around, every thing appears conducted with so much regularity and precision, that a person is induced to suppose one of the meanest capacity might superintend and direct the whole process.'[27] In fact, the 'sixth excellence' of the English people, according to him, 'is a passion for mechanism, and their numerous contrivances for facilitating labour and industry'.[28] He was fascinated by the fire extinguishing 'machines',[29] and by the art of printing, 'the utility of which may not appear at first sight to be Asiatic'.[30] Likewise, Lutfullah admired the bridges in London:

> The first objects that engaged our attention were the enormous bridges in the city, especially the iron bridge, and the swinging bridge. It astonished us greatly to see large masses of cast iron regularly fixed and nicely cemented together in these useful fabrics. The country, we felt convinced, must have some inexhaustible mines of this metal, which is so necessary for man; for, besides these bridges, iron appears to be used profusely. No house seemed to be without iron railings, iron bars, and some houses are even roofed with iron, and some gardens hedged with iron bars.[31]

Consider, too, Abu Talib's description of Woolwich:

> I there saw several large ships on the stocks; and such stores of timber, iron canvas etc. that had the war (Anglo-French) continued for ten years longer, they would not have required a fresh supply. I was particularly attracted by the mode of casting the cannon-balls and shells; also by the manner of boring and shaping the exterior surface of the guns at the same time, all done by the motion of a wheel turned by a steam-engine, which so facilitated the work, that an old woman or a child might have performed the rest of the operation.[32]

Clearly, the impact and potentialities of the industrial revolution sensitized Abu Talib to its implications. Attributing Britain's economic superiority over the Napoleanic empire to industrial technology and its military success to the navy, he stated: 'The great perfection to which the English have brought their navy is, doubtless, the chief cause of their prosperity, and the principal source of all their wealth.'[33] Likewise, he attributed Britain's conquest of Egypt and other colonies to 'the prowess of their own arms', and to their being formidable on shore as at sea. In this way he thus recognized the importance of sea-power more than eighty years before the publication of Mahan's classical work on the subject.[34]

Abu Talib attributed Britain's industrial revolution to the system of government, to the country's vibrant social and cultural ethos, and to the 'national character' of its people. He commended the unwritten British constitution underlining its monarchical, aristocratic and democratic character, and the respect for individual freedom protected by the British Law; 'liberty may be considered as the idol or tutelary deity of the English; and I think the common people here enjoy more *freedom* and equality than in any other well-regulated government of the world'.[35]

During his stay he went several times to the Houses of Parliament, and was astonished to discover that this was a legislative assembly, with the duty of enacting laws to regulate both civil and criminal matters. The English, he explained to his readers, unlike the Muslims, did not accept any divinely revealed holy law to guide them and regulate their lives in those matters and were therefore reduced to the pitiable expedient of making their own laws 'in accordance with the exigencies of the time, their own dispositions, and the experience of their judges'.

Abu Talib took great interest in the education of English women and their freedom. He mentioned six spheres where the liberty of the Asian women appeared 'less than that of Europeans', though he also pointed to those spheres where they had more rights. Likewise, Mirza Ihtisamuddin (Mirza Itesa Modeen, *Shigurf namah-i-Valaet, or, Excellent intelligence concerning Europe*: *being the travels of Mirza Itesa Modeen in Great Britain and France-e Velaet*, translated by James Edward Alexander, London, 1872), who visited England in 1765, praised the status of women, their devotion to education, and their quest for knowledge. 'They are not like the people of this country,' he wrote, 'who repeat Hindi and Persian poems in praise of a mistress's face, or descriptive of the qualities of the wine, of the goblet, and of the cup-bearer, and who pretend to be in love.' He was, moreover, impressed with women unveiled in the public sphere, and attracted to the spectacle of male-female intimacy in public parks. This is how he describes the scenes near the Queen's palace in London:

> On Sunday, men, women, and youths, poor and rich, travelers and natives resort here. This park enlivens the heart, and people overcome with sorrow, repairing thither, are entertained in a heavenly manner, and grieved hearts, from seeing that place of amusement, are gladdened against their will. On every side females with silver forms, resembling peacocks, walk about, and at every corner fairy-faced ravishers of hearts move with a thousand blandishments and coquetries; the plain of the earth becomes a paradise from the resplendent foreheads, and heaven (itself) hangs down its head for shame at seeing the beauty of the loves. There lovers meet without fear of the police or of rivals, and gallants obtain a sight of rosy

cheeks without restraints. When I viewed this heavenly place I involuntarily exclaimed:

If there is a paradise on earth,
It is this, oh! It is this.

(*Gar firdows bur ru-ye zamin ast*
hamin ast va hamin ast va hamin ast)

At the same time, Abu Talib noticed widespread poverty, social inequalities, the disparities between the rich and poor, and the effects of a high cost of living,[36] rates of taxation on the common people, and the enormous national debt.[37] He criticized the unsavoury role of commercial magnates and proprietors of joint stock firms enjoying large extra-constitutional powers. He found, much to his dismay, that the privileged sections of society were 'puffed up with their power and good fortune for the last fifty years',[38] and had no idea of how the 'flame, though . . . smothered by a heap of fuel thrown on it, breaks out in the sequel with the greatest violence'.[39] Concerned that no attempt was being made to alleviate the sufferings of those people in London who had 'assembled in mobs on account of the great increase of taxes and high price of provision, and were nearly in a state of insurrection', he opined that this attitude 'betrays a blind confidence'.[40] Instead of meeting the 'danger' and preventing disaffection, the English people waited for the misfortune to arrive: 'such was the case with the late King of France, who took no step to oppose the Revolution, till it was too late.'[41]

In delineating the features of the British 'national character', both Abu Talib and Lutfullah highlighted their sense of honour and prestige, their concern for and recognition of merit, and their cautious, law-abiding, disciplined, and courteous nature.[42] He mentioned, with implied approval, that instead of rushing ahead with changes the British proceeded slowly and cautiously. Yet, he castigated them for their 'want of chastity',[43] criticized the want of faith in religion,[44] and upbraided the upper classes for being complacent and haughty. Contemptuous of their passion for wealth and their preoccupation with worldly affairs,[45] he disapproved of their insularity, their contempt for the customs of other nations, and the preference they gave to their own.[46] He reminiscenced how

in London, I was frequently attacked on the apparent unreasonableness and childishness of some of the Mohammedan customs; but as, from my knowledge of the English character, I was convinced it would

> be a folly to argue the point philosophically with them, I contended myself with parrying the subject. Thus, when they attempted to turn into ridicule the ceremonies used by the pilgrims on their arrival in Mecca, I asked them, why they supposed the ceremony of baptism, by a clergyman, requisite for the salvation of a child, who could not possibly be sensible [*sic*] what he was about. When they reproached us for eating with our hands; I replied, 'There is by this mode no danger of cutting yourself or your neighbours; and it is an old and a true proverb, 'The nearer the bone, the sweeter the meat': but, exclusive of these advantages, a man's own hands are surely cleaner than the feet of a *baker's boy*: for it is well-known, that half the bread in London is kneaded by the feet. By this mode of argument I, completely silenced all my adversaries, and frequently turned the laugh against them, when they expected to have refuted me and made me appear ridiculous.[47]

Although receptive to some of the new ideas, Abu Talib distanced himself philosophically from the West and found much that was of enduring quality in his own intellectual traditions. Rooted in his own soil, he derived inspiration and strength from the values he had inherited and imbibed in late eighteenth-century Awadh society without, of course, sharing the scepticism of some of his own contemporaries towards Western ideas and institutions. He noticed the social transformation taking place in the industrialized nations of Europe, and commented on its world-wide impact.

Abu Talib's religious identity was unassailable; it was a major component of his ideological orientation. But he did not find religious categories of much help when it came to understanding either Awadh society or delineating the contours of Western polities, economy and society. If anything, he attached importance to the diverse economic forces moulding attitudes and shaping the destiny of humankind. Thus, in analysing the ancien régime in France and his contemporary Awadh society, he referred to the growing disparities between various classes and to the widening economic disparaties. Implicit in his narrative is the view that the key factor leading to the collapse of the ancien régime was the exacerbation of class differentiation. He wondered why such an upheaval had not occurred in Awadh in spite of excessive taxation, the tyranny of the landlords, the impoverishment of the peasantry, a fall in production, and in land revenue realization. It is not without significance that he attributed the passivity of the oppressed to the role of religion, and to

British policies which buttressed the wazir and averted the immediate collapse of his kingdom.

Abu Talib belonged to a declining aristocracy. But, like so many people of his social background, he tried to make the best of the opportunities available under the Company's dispensation. This was a pointer to his generation of Muslims, as indeed to the generations thereafter, who were faced with an inescapable dilemma *vis-a-vis* British rule. Eschewing a defiant posture towards the colonizers, he acknowledged the inevitability of change and the necessity of softening belligerent attitudes towards foreign rule. For this reason he adhered to his resolve, despite fears of being villified and ridiculed, to inform his countrymen about the political and economic conditions, the industry, and the social and cultural life of the British who had come to preside over India's destiny. He hoped that many of 'the customs, inventions, sciences, and ordinances of Europe, the good effects of which are apparent in their countries, might with great advantage be initiated by Mohammedans'.[48] In this respect, at least, he was a forerunner of the ideas of Saiyid Ahmad Khan, the major catalyst of social and educational reforms among India's Muslims in the last-quarter of the nineteenth-century.

III

Representing the scribal class—those serving the regional and local bureaucracies under the Mughals and their British successors—Abu Talib and Lutfullah were not the only ones favouring rapprochement with the British in India or seeking government patronage. Muhammad Khan of Bilgram joined the foreign department of the governor-general in the early days of Company rule.[49] Ghalib's uncle, Nasrullah Beg Khan, served the Company in the Anglo-Maratha war of 1802-3 as commander of a contingent and received a life jagir from the British commander-in-chief, Lord Lake.[50] The father of nawab Mustafa Khan Shefta (b. 1806), Ghalib's fellow-poet, received estates for resolving the disputes between Lord Lake and the Maratha commanders.[51] In this way, the British continued with the Mughal traditions of granting jagirs and *inam* lands for political loyalty and military services. For thirty years after the Maratha war of 1802-3, the holders of such grants were left relatively undisturbed. For a generation after 1803, a gentlemanly existence in something like the old style was thus possible in upper India for those Muslims who were ready to serve the British as auxiliary cavalry and as subordinate revenue and judicial officers.[52] Bishop Heber's *Narrative* for 15 September 1824 contains a British collector's impression of 'a new order rising from the middling classes' to replace that of 'very many ancient families . . . gone to decay'.[53]

The 'middling classes' were drawn from those enterprising groups who were prepared to make the most of what little there was. They were, to begin with, small in numbers. Yet, they formed a major component of what was, until the last-quarter of the nineteenth-century, the Muslim intelligentsia in north India, the harbinger of reforms and social change. They contributed, as in the case of their counterparts in Bengal and Maharashtra, to the efflorescence of modern learning, which C.F. Andrews described as the 'Delhi Renaissance'.[54] They pioneered the Aligarh movement, where the first generation of students and teachers set the tone and tenor of powerful intellectual ideas in the twentieth century.[55] They were also the first to promote Western education and the learning of sciences among Muslims through organizations—the Anjuman-i Himayat-i Islam in Punjab, the Muhammadan Literary and Scientific Society, and the Central National Mohammedan Association in Bengal. Hali would have had them in mind when he spoke of 'men of feeling', 'men of sympathy', 'men of worth'. 'Amongst these heedless sleepers,' he wrote, 'some are awake'. 'In the taverns are some who are still sober. These are men who are not like the rest of their group. Among the worthless are still some men of worth.'[56]

Education was the key to success, a passport to government service. Though most Muslims defiantly stayed away from British schools and colleges, there were others who acquainted themselves with Western languages and literature, philosophy and science. As early as 1775-6, Mirza Ihtisamuddin, who travelled to Europe in the year of the Treaty of Allahabad between Clive (1724-74) and Shah Alam (1759-1806),[57] visited the laboratories and observatories in London. 'In England,' he wrote, 'it would be extraordinary if the arts and sciences did not flourish (from their being encouraged). Now in India, if a person by a long course of study were to acquire knowledge, so as to excel the world, yet he would remain despised and contemned [*sic*]: he would neither acquire honour nor respect, and in the end misfortune and misery would overtake him.'[58] In 1788, Tipu Sultan (r. 1783-99), the ruler of Mysore, wanted one of his sons to be educated in France. The French authorities approved of the idea, but suggested that the prince should learn to read and write French, learn a little calculus and some arithmetic before leaving for Paris.[59] In

1794, Mirza Ahmad Khan of Broach, a town in Gujarat, reached Paris, learnt French in three months, and translated *The Declaration of the Rights of Man* into Persian. He then presented his work to the Committee of Public Safety, which had it deposited in the *Bibliotheque Nationale*. This translation was the first in any oriental language.[60] Such works were channels through which knowledge of the new world of Europe travelled to India.

Tafazzul Husain Khan (d. 1800), long associated with the Company as well as the Awadh nawabs, compiled important mathematical works, and translated into Persian Newton's *Principia*. Officials in Calcutta commended his command over the English language, and his knowledge of European literature and philosophy.[61] His successor, Saadat Ali Khan (r. 1798-1814), founded an observatory in Lucknow. Both Ghaziuddin Haider (r. 1814-27) and Nasiruddin Haider (r. 1827-37) patronized Western and Oriental philological studies. According to Bishop Heber, the former had 'a strong taste for mechanics and chemistry' and constructed a laboratory in Lucknow.[62] Speaking of a breakfast at the Residency at which Ghaziuddin Haider was present, Heber (who visited Lucknow in 1824) noted that the King talked about steam engines and a new device, invented by an English engineer in his pay, of propelling ships by a spiral wheel at the bottom of the vessel. He also explained his acquaintance with English books read to him in Hindustani by his aides-de-camp.[63] Nasiruddin, inheriting such scientific and artistic tastes, hired an English tutor to make himself at home in English culture. He built an observatory in the charge of an English Astronomer-Royal, a colonel Wilcox.

Finally, the Fort William College in Calcutta encouraged literary and scientific learning all over India. A resident of the city, Mansher Khesumul Riya, wrote to the *Calcutta Journal* on 13 April 1820:

> I am a Mooslem of this city, who by early instruction in the English language, have acquired access to the general literature with which that tongue is adorned, and am enabled to enjoy the numerous publications which advocate the cause of liberty.

Lutfullah wrote his *Autobiography* in English, 'the first (and) almost the best autobiography by an Indian in English'. He had read Gibbon, a Latin book on the customs and institutions of the Turks, and a *Universal History* by some Dr Philip Prince.[64] A lesser known person, Abdur Rahim Dahri (1785-1850), travelled from Gorakhpur in eastern UP to acquire proficiency in English at the Fort William College. He wrote widely, including a pamphlet on the virtue of studying the English language and disseminating Western thought. He insisted, in a memorandum submitted to Warren Hastings, that modern education be introduced through the medium of English. Abdur Rahim spent the last years of an extraordinary career as an English teacher at Fort William College.[65] For him the civilization of the West did not appear wholly alien; Muslims could move towards it without any sense of being untrue to themselves or their faith.

The Madrasa Aliyah flourished in Calcutta. Among its beneficiaries were Saiyid Ameer Ali, author-historian, and Abdur Rahim, a judge turned politician. The Delhi College, an early and significant enterprise in secular education, was established in 1825 with two branches: an English branch where English language and literature and modern European sciences were taught and an Oriental branch in which not only Arabic, Persian and Sanskrit were taught but geography, mathematics and sciences as well.[66] By far the most popular side of the education offered in Old Delhi College was that which dealt with science. Maulvi Zakaullah, in his old age, used to tell C.F. Andrews 'with kindling eyes how eagerly these scientific lectures were followed'.[67] The doctrines of ancient philosophy taught through the medium of Arabic were 'thus cast in the shade before the more reasonable and experimental theories of modern science. The old dogma . . . that the earth is the fixed centre of the universe was generally laughed at by the higher students of the Oriental as well as by those of the English Department of the college.'[68]

The Delhi College was the nucleus of a group which tried re-evaluating inherited doctrines and beliefs. Take maulvi Karimuddin, whose book provided the basis of Farhatullah Beg's modern Urdu classic, *Delhi ki Akhri Shama* (The Last Mushairah of Delhi). He belonged to a family of maulvis, left his home town Panipat to join Delhi College in 1839, and set up a printing press to meet the growing demand of writers trying to express, in Urdu and English, their consciousness of themselves and their place in the modern world.[69] Consider, too, the career of Munshi Shafaqatullah, an English teacher in Bareilly. He translated Chamber's introduction to the sciences, as also a well-known work on astronomy, natural philosophy, geology, and other sciences. It was entitled *Khulsatul-Ulum.*

There was another noticeable trend: influential groups in various regions, especially those needing a fresh imprimatur from each ruling power, made the colonial government work. Thus, many *sajjada nashins* in rural Punjab agreed to be incorporated into the framework of the British administration, often playing leading roles as *ziladars*, honorary magistrates, and district board members. By early twentieth-century, they had become an integral part of the class of rural intermediaries on whom British rule rested in the area.[70] In Sind, the British constructed a political system hinging on the cooperation of landed elites, of whom the pirs made up a sizeable proportion. Sarah Ansari has established how both sides took advantage of the system and how the pirs, in particular, discovered new ways of increasing their power and prestige. The very section of the élite which, in theory, had most to lose from being too closely associated with the administration, found that there was much to gain from maintaining a good working relationship with their new 'infidel' rulers. They managed to retain an aura of spiritual aloofness at the same time as making the most of the benefits of cooperation. In the long run, their willingness to participate in the colonial system helped endow pir families with the resilience needed to cope with British rule.[71]

The British realized, particularly after 1857, that the crucial task in maintaining their rule was to be able to react quickly and sensitively as power flowed from one group to another in response to processes of economic, social, or even ideological change. The imposing edifice of colonial government rested on delicate political relationships with powerful and influential groups in a myriad localities.[72] Though wary and distrustful of the Muslims, the British co-opted some of them into administrative and bureaucratic structures. They were to form the pillar of the raj during the inter-War years during the twentieth century.

Some ulama, following an old established tradition of pliancy and conformism, accepted British rule. Some others were, however, made of sterner stuff, falling into the colonial stereotype of being bigoted, fanatical and intransigent. Shah Abdul Aziz had declared India as *Dar al-harb*; so the Friday and Id prayers could not be performed as congregational prayers. 'From here (Delhi) to Calcutta,' he announced, 'the Christians are in complete control.' This pronouncement sustained Saiyid Ahmad Shaheed's exertions against the British, and legitimized other nineteenth-century movements against their rule, even though the *fatwa*, read in its totality, conveyed different meanings to different people and was, therefore, subject to diverse interpretations. Muhammad Ismail, the nephew of Abdul Aziz, recommended a *modus vivendi* with the British as long as they did not interfere with the religious freedom of the Muslims.

In the early days of Company rule, such positions may well have prompted Fazl-i Rasul Budauni, Mufti Sadruddin, Fazl-i Haq Khayrabadi and a section of the Firangi Mahal family to serve the Company, take up jobs in institutions, and accept government titles. There were many more Muslim divines in the nineteenth-century who held the view that India was *Dar al-aman* (land of peace) as the British allowed the Islamic Personal Law to be applied to the Muslims in cases of inheritance, succession, gifts, *auqaf*, marriage, divorce, parentage, guardianship, and maintenance. They invoked the Koranic verse—'Obey God, obey His Prophet, and obey those in authority over you'—to argue that the duty of obedience to a legitimate authority was not merely one of political expediency but a religious obligation. The ulama availed of the opportunities either left by the British policy of non-interference with religion, or created by the development of communications, printing and the press. This enabled them to propagate their teachings more widely and, with their considerable resources and knowledge of Islamic traditions, confront Christian missionaries and the forces inimical to Islam. Saiyid Ahmad Shaheed's *Siral al-Mustaqim* (The Sacred Path) and Muhammad Ismail's *Taqwiyat al-Iman* (Strengthening the Faith) were printed in lithographic editions thus receiving wider circulation than had hitherto been possible.

Nineteenth-century Indian Islam did not produce scholars like Rifa Badawi, Rafi al-Ṭahtawi, Khayar al-Din, or Abduh, who reinterpreted the Islamic Law in the direction of conformity with modern needs and endeavoured to adapt the *Shariat* to new circumstances. Yet, India's ulama, while jealously guarding their exclusive right as guardians of a fixed and established tradition, grudgingly came to terms with British rule. In the aftermath of the 1857 revolt, in particular, they acquiesced in rather than repudiated Pax Britannica. Deoband's Dar al-ulum, founded in a spirit of compromise rather than opposition to colonial rule, rested on an unstated principle: if living in the nineteenth-century world demanded changes in the Islamic ways of life, the ulama must try to make them while remaining true to themselves and their faith.

IV

Hali's repeated pleas and exhortations, couched in his *Mussadas*, summed up a major strand in the thinking patterns of the north Indian literate Muslims in the nineteenth century. He wrote:

> No man wishes evil to your faith and religion. No man attacks the

Traditions and the Koran. No man seeks to harm the pillars of your community. No man seeks to prohibit you from the commands of the Holy Law. Say your prayers without fear in your places of worship, and let the call to prayer ring out in your mosques.

The roads to travel and trade lie open. None blocks the roads to crafts and industry. The roads to the acquisition of learning are lighted. The roads to the gaining of wealth are made level. . . .

Know the words of this peace and freedom. For the paths to advancement have been cleared in every direction, and the age is the friend of all who would travel upon them. The cry comes persistently from every side, 'There is no enemy to dread, no highway robber to fear: come out and take the road, for the roads are safe!'

Many caravans have long been on the move. Many more are loading up their burdens. Many are in agitation at the movement all round them. . . . You alone amongst them are still sunk in heedless sleep. Take care, lest in your heedlessness you fail to reach your goal![73]

Ghalib announced the tidings of the dawn and pointed the way to the light of the sun.

The harp player, when he strikes the chord
One can see what he is after,
Happiness lies concealed behind the veil of sorrow,
Not for wrath does the washerman beat the cloth.[74]

NOTES

1. A. Yusuf Ali, 'Muslim Culture and Religious Thought', in L.S.S. O'Malley (ed.), *Modern India and the West: A Study of the Interaction of their Civilization*, Oxford, 1941; Muhammad Mujeeb, 'First Impressions of Western Culture on Indian Muslims', in H. Rao (ed.), *South Asian Studies I*, New Delhi, 1965; Aziz Ahmad, *Islamic Modernism in India and Pakistan, 1857-1964*, Cambridge, 1967; Muhammad Mujeeb, *The Indian Muslims*, London, 1967; S.A.A. Rizvi, 'The Breakdown of Traditional Society', *The Cambridge History of Islam*, vol. 2, Cambridge, 1970; Peter Hardy, *The Muslims of British India*, Cambridge, 1972; Mujeeb Ashraf, *Muslim Attitudes towards British Rule and Western Culture*, New Delhi, 1982; Peter Hardy, 'Islam in South Asia', in Raphael Israel (ed.), *The Crescent in the East: Islam in Asia Major*, New Delhi, 1985, rpt.
2. Mujeeb, *Indian Muslims*, pp. 491-501.

3. Mushirul Hasan, *Nationalism and Communal Politics in India, 1885-1930*, Delhi, 1991; Mushirul Hasan, *A Nationalist Conscience: M.A. Ansari, the Congress and the Raj*, New Delhi, 1987.
4. On these themes, Albert Hourani, *A History of the Arab Peoples*, London, 1991, and his *Arabic Thought in the Liberal Age, 1798-1939*, London, 1962; Fazlur Rahman, *Islam*, London, 1966; Deliar Noer, *The Modernist Muslim Movement in Indonesia, 1900-1942*, London, 1973; Wilhelm Halbfass, *India and Europe: An Essay in Understanding*, State University of New York Press, 1990; Edward Mortimore, *Faith and Power: The Politics of Islam*, London, 1982.
5. *Musaddas-i Hali*, pp. 43-4, in Aziz Ahmad and Grunebaum (eds.), *Muslim Self-Statement*, p. 95.
6. Ralph Russell and Khurshidul Islam, *Ghalib 1797-1869*, vol. I: *Life and Letters*, London, 1969, p. 31.
7. Akhtar Qamber, *The Last Mushairah of Delhi*, New Delhi, 1979, p. 39.
8. Russell and Khurshidul Islam, *Ghalib*, p. 134.
9. Saiyid Ahmad Khan, *History of Bijnor Rebellion*, translated with notes and introduction by Hafeez Malik and Morris Dembo, New Delhi, 1982, p. 15.
10. For Muslim revivalist movements in the nineteenth and early twentieth centuries, see Mohiuddin Ahmad, *Saiyid Ahmad Shahid*, Lucknow, 1975; S.A.A. Rizvi, *Shah Abdul Aziz and his Times*, Australia, 1983; Qeyamuddin Ahmad, *The Wahhabi Movement in India*, revd. edn., New Delhi, 1992; Rafiuddin Ahmed, *Bengal Muslims 1871-1906: A Quest for Identity*, New Delhi, 1981; Asim Roy, *The Islamic Syncretistic Tradition in Bengal*, Princeton, N.J., 1983. For Deoband, see Barbara Daly Metcalf, *Islamic Revival in British India: Deoband, 1860-1900*, Princeton, N.J., 1982.
11. Marshall G.S. Hodgson, *The Venture of Islam: The Gunpowder Empires and Modern Times*, vol. 3, Chicago, 1974, p. 335, and C.W. Troll, *Sayyid Ahmad Khan: A Reinterpretation of Muslim Theology*, New Delhi, 1978.
12. *Musaddas-i Hali*, pp. 83-5, quoted in Ahmad and Grunebaum (eds.), p. 98.
13. David Gilmartin, *Empire and Islam: Punjab and the Making of Pakistan*, Berkeley, 1988.
14. Hardy, *Muslims of British India*, pp. 67-9.
15. Eric Stokes, *The Peasant Armed: The Indian Rebellion of 1857*, edited by C.A. Bayly, Oxford, 1986, p. 240.
16. Mushir U. Haq, *Muslim Politics in Modern India, 1857-1947*, Meerut, 1970, and Metcalf, *Islamic Revival in British India*, pp. 81-5.
17. Anil Seal, *The Emergence of Indian Nationalism: Competition and Collaboration in the Later Nineteenth Century*, Cambridge, 1968, Chap. 7; Francis Robinson, *Separatism among Indian Muslims: The Politics of United Provinces' Muslims, 1860-1923*, Cambridge, 1975; Hardy, *Muslims of British India*, pp. 36-50; Mushirul Hasan, *Nationalism and Communal Politics*, pp. 12-20; C.A. Bayly, *Rulers, Townsmen and Bazaars: North Indian Society*

in the Age of British Expansion, 1770-1870, Cambridge, 1983, pp. 190-1.

18. Abu Talib was the son of Haji Muhammad Beg, who fled from Tabriz in his youth, lived in Isfahan in order to escape the tyrannies of Nadir Shah, and settled in Lucknow. The Haji led a troubled life until his death at Murshidabad in 1768. Misfortune also struck his son who, after some years of service in Etawah and Gorakhpur, became a victim of the machinations of his detractors in the Awadh court. He lost his job and his yearly allowance. From 1787 to 1797 he journeyed to Calcutta thrice and sought the help and intervention of senior Company officials into his affair. He met the governor-general, Cornwallis, and his successor John Shore. 'During the three years of expectation which I passed in Calcutta', wrote Abu Talib, 'all my dependents and adherents, seeing my distress, left me; and even some of my children, and the domestics brought up in my father's family, abandoned me'. For biographical information, T.W. Beale, *An Oriental Biographical Dictionary*, London, 1894, p. 32; Colin C. Davies, *Encyclopaedia of Islam*, new edn., p. 152; Mujeeb, *Indian Muslims*, pp. 491-2; Humayun Kabir, *Mirza Abu Talib Khan*, Patna: The Russell Lecture, Patna College, 1961.
19. *Travels*, p. xiv.
20. Ibid., p. 111. Wherever he went, Abu Talib aroused interest and curiosity. Nearly half a century before him, Mirza Ihtisamuddin had similar experiences during his stay in England. People were attracted by his robe and turban, the sash tied around his waist and the dagger in his belt. 'Whenever I attempted to go abroad, crowds accompanied me, and the people in the houses of the bazars thrust their heads out of the windows and gazed at me with wonder.' Mirza Ihtisamuddin, *Shigurf Nama-i Velayet*, translated from the original Persian by James Edward Alexander, London, 1827, p. 40.
21. *Travels*, p. 75.
22. Ibid. Notice his description of a party hosted by the Mayor of London, where he spent 'one of the most delightful nights I ever passed'. He was 'gazing all the time on the angelic charms of Miss Combe, who sat in that assemblage of beauties like the bright moon surrounded with brilliant stars'. Ibid., p. 155.
23. Ahmad, *Islamic Modernism*, pp. 6-7.
24. Charles Stewart, in *Travels*, p. xiii.
25. In 1791, Abu Talib produced an edition of *Diwan-i Hafiz*, and shortly after, a compendium account of ancient and contemporary poets (*Khulasat al-Afkaar*). He was himself a poet and there is a manuscript of his *Diwan* in the Bodleian. His collection of poems were edited and translated into English by George Swinton. It was published in 1807 under the title *Poems of Mirza Abu Talib Khan*. He also composed a *mathnawi*, available in the Edinburgh University Library, a medical treatise (*Miraj al-Tauhid*) on astronomy with a prose commentary, a book entitled *Lubb al-Siyar*, and *Tafzih al-Ghafilin* (English translation by W. Hoey, 1888), a history of Awadh under Asaf al-Daula, an important source for the careers of Hyder Beg and the various English residents.

26. Lutfullah belonged to a distinguished Sufi family of Malwa. But the fortunes of the family dwindled to such an extent that 'we sold all we had, and sometimes starved for a day or so, after which we obtained but some food through our own hard labour'. The family travelled to Baroda, Ujjain, Gwalior, and Agra until it reached Delhi in early 1817. Soon thereafter, Lutfullah found odd jobs in the course of his extensive travels. He developed his reputation as a teacher of Arabic, Persian and some Indian languages, notably Marathi, and was *en rapport* with young Britishers of the ICS. In March 1844, he accompanied Mir Jafar Ali Khan, son-in-law of the nawab of Surat, to England. His *Autobiography*, acclaimed in England, was written in 1854 and dedicated to colonel W.H. Sykes. It was later edited by Edward B. Eastwick and published in London, in 1857.

His first reaction on reaching London was:

> Here (7, Sloane Street) we settled after our long voyage from the middle of the globe to the end of the world, where the sun appears, far to the south, as weak as the moon, and the polar star nearly vertical; where the country all over is fertile, and the people ingenious, civil and active; where the language, customs, and manners are entirely different from our own; where, in fine, the destiny of our sweet native land lies in the hand of some twenty-five great men (Directors of the East India Company). It cannot be, I am sure, without the will of that one Supreme Being that this island, which seems on the globe like a mole on the body of a man, should command the greater part of the world, and keep the rest in awe.

Autobiography, p. 406. Reprinted in India under the title *Autobiography of Lutfullah: An Indian's Perception of the West*, with an introduction by S.A.I. Tirmizi (Delhi, 1985).

Equally interesting is his comment on a dissection taking place at the St. George's Hospital. He wrote:

> Here I became convinced that a great part of what I had studied in 'Galen's Anatomy' in Persian and Arabic was founded upon fancy and conjecture, and that it was impossible for anybody to acquire a thorough knowledge of this most useful study for mankind, without the practical course of dissection.

Autobiography, p. 415.

27. *Travels*, p. 121.
28. Ibid., p. 182.
29. Ibid., p. 184.
30. Ibid., p. 110.
31. *Autobiography*, p. 407.
32. *Travels*, pp. 114-15.
33. Ibid., p. 112.
34. Mujeeb, *Indian Muslims*, p. 498; Kabir, *Mirza Abu Talib*, pp. 10, 24.

35. *Travels*, p. 129.
36. Abu Talib found that 'living is very expensive in England; and a good appetite is a serious evil to a poor man'. He listed the prices of meat and bread to illustrate his point. Ibid., p. 112.
37. It is remarkable that a man of his background and his limited experience of Awadh recognized the 'evil' of National Debt. 'Let the creditors of Government be assembled', he proposed, 'in the presence of the Parliament; and let the Minister, clearly and dispassionately, explain to them, that the state of affairs is arrived at such a crisis, that is impossible the nation can continue longer to pay the amount of the enormous taxes which oppress them; that a revolution is to be apprehended; that the first act of the leaders of the revolution certainly will be *to cancel the national debt*, and that the rich may consider themselves fortunate if left in possession of their real wealth; that the national debt, being thus cancelled, they, the creditors, will lose *the whole* of their property invested in the funds; and therefore it will be much wiser to enter into an immediate compromise, and relinquish a part'. Ibid., pp. 165-6.
38. Ibid., p. 168.
39. Ibid., p. 179.
40. Ibid., p. 168.
41. Ibid., p. 169.
42. Ibid., p. 181. Also, Lutfullah's comment, *Autobiography*, p. 433.
43. *Travels*, p. 175.
44. Ibid., p. 178.
45. Ibid., p. 169.
46. Ibid., p. 177.
47. Ibid., p. 178.
48. Ibid., p. xv.
49. Bayly, *Rulers, Townsmen and Bazaars*, p. 356.
50. Peter Hardy, 'Ghalib and the British', in Ralph Russell (ed.), *Ghalib: the poet and his age*, London, 1972, p. 56.
51. Russell and Khurshidul Islam, *Ghalib*, p. 67.
52. In an interesting observation, Andrews recorded that the intrusion of the West did not make much difference to maulvi Zakaullah's lifestyle. 'None of his outward manners and customs had been changed, and he remained outwardly the most conservative man in Delhi. His dress, his habits, his domestic life, his religious life—all that he valued most dearly—remained unalterably eastern.' C.F. Andrews, *Maulvi Zakaullah of Delhi*, New Delhi, 1928 edn., p. 118.
53. Hardy, 'Ghalib and the British', p. 55.
54. Andrews, *Zakaullah of Delhi*.
55. David Lelyveld, *Aligarh's First Generation: Muslim Solidarity in British India*, Princeton, N.J., 1978.
56. *Musaddas*, pp. 83-5, in Ahmad and Grunebaum (eds.), p. 100.

57. He travelled to Europe as a representative of Shah Alam, who wanted a British protective force at Allahabad. The identity of his companion, Captain 'S', is not known. Nor is there much information on Mirza Ihtisamuddin. What we know is that the sea voyage took them to Mauritius, and around the Cape of Good Hope to Europe where the Mirza stopped briefly in France. The book—*Shigurf Nama-i Velayet*—is a commentary on his travels and impression of England and Scotland written after his return to India. It was translated from Persian into English by James Edward Alexander and published in London in 1827.
58. *Shigurf Nama-i Velayet*, p. 70.
59. Mohibbul Hasan, *History of Tipu Sultan*, Calcutta, 1971, 2nd revd. and enlarged edn.
60. Mohibbul Hasan, 'An Indian Prince and the French Revolution', *Iran Society Silver Jubilee Souvenir*, 1968.
61. Michael H. Fisher, *A Clash of Cultures: Awadh, The British and the Mughals*, New Delhi, 1987, p. 70.
62. Yusuf Ali, 'Muslim Culture and Religious Thought', p. 391. See also Fisher, *A Clash of Cultures*, pp. 172-3.
63. Ibid., p. 397.
64. Mujeeb, *Indian Muslims*, p. 497.
65. For details of Abdur Rahim Dahri's life and career, see Ashraf, *Muslim Attitudes Towards British Rule*, pp. 190, 261.
66. Barbara Metcalf, *The Islamic Revival*, pp. 72-3.
67. Andrews, *Zakaullah of Delhi*, p. 42.
68. Ibid., pp. 38-40.
69. *The Last Mushairah*, pp. 39-40.
70. Francis Robinson, 'Ulama, Sufis and Colonial Rule in North India and Indonesia', in C.A. Bayly and D.H.A. Kolff (eds.), *Two Colonial Empires: Comparative Essays on the History of Indonesia in the Nineteenth-Century*, Dordrecht, 1986, p. 19.
71. Sarah F.D. Ansari, *Sufi Saints and State Power: The Pirs of Sindh, 1843-1947*, Cambridge, 1992, pp. 53-6.
72. Robinson, *Separatism Among Muslims*.
73. *Musaddas*, pp. 43-4, in Ahmad and Grunebaum (eds.), p. 96.
74. K.M. Ashraf, 'Ghalib and the Revolt of 1857', *Rebellion 1857: A Symposium*, New Delhi, 1957, p. 256.

Tribal Society in Transition: Eastern India, 1757-1920

BINAY BHUSHAN CHAUDHURI

The late Professor Eric Stokes had only a marginal interest in India's 'tribal society'. The theme of this essay is to examine, in the context of tribal history, some of his seminal ideas and of other historians, including his pupils at Cambridge, about the nature of the 'imperial impact' on rural society.

Stokes rejected the fairly widespread view that British rule subjected 'the immemorially stable and backward agrarian base to the disintegrative influences of modern legal relationships, usury capitalism and commercial agriculture'.[1] He also questioned the 'peasant stratification thesis', which describes the imperial impact on peasant society in terms of the emergence of sharply stratified groups with distinctive economic roles. In explaining the absence of an 'articulated class structure' he commented on the 'diffusion of economic roles and the obstinate refusal of the social and economic order to evolve on clear, determinate lines of class differentiation'.[2] The agrarian society, he concluded, was not 'blown apart by market forces'; instead, 'it was taken hold of and stretched out elastically from either extremity'. He borrowed a phrase from Clifford Geertz to describe the changes occurring therein: 'the advance towards vagueness'.[3]

Similarly, Neil Charlesworth, one of his pupils, argued that the traditional rural society absorbed the external influences without undergoing any structural change. He 'reasserts', with particular reference to the Bombay Presidency, 'the stability of the peasant mass',[4] differently interpreting the rural changes generally taken as indicators of 'peasant stratification'.[5] He cites a few instances. The phenomenon of 'growing expenditure on land, houses and agricultural facilities' has usually been associated with the rise of a rich peasantry. Such an expenditure, he argues, was not necessarily an evidence of 'elite control over such resources'. This, points to the 'diffusion of wealth', 'a general rise in the income levels throughout the agrarian society in the 1880s and in the early 1890s'. He admits the occurrence of an increase in tenancy, but argues that this alone did not signify a decline of the peasant proprietor. Tenancy, he concludes, 'was evidence, not of peasant decline, but of greater tenurial flexibility in a more commercialized economy, faced at the same time with a serious problem of land availability... In this situation peasants seeking to expand operations might often need to rent land, and tenancy, then, would become a natural response to economic stimuli'. Tenancy was, thus, not an indicator of stratification but of stabilization of the peasant society. Commercialization, Charlesworth agrees, created conditions apparently favourable to stratification, but also created a counter-mechanism, so that the benefits from commercialization did not wholly accrue to the dominant village groups, such as the rich peasantry and moneylenders, but tended to be diffused. 'Extensive labour requirements for cash-crop cultivation forced up some labourers' wages, and in the villages which produced widely for external markets opportunities for emigration and supplementing incomes outside agriculture became more known and utilized'. He concludes: 'The rule may be, then, that extensive agricultural commercialization tempers social stratification'.

C.A. Bayly, another pupil of Professor Stokes, agrees with the notion of the 'stability of the peasant mass'. With reference to early nineteenth-century, he explains how the period saw the 'consolidation of the Indian peasantry' and was 'critical in the creation of the modern Indian peasantry, its pattern of social divisions and its beliefs'.[6] The frontiers of the peasant society widened, with groups lying outside being gradually assimilated into it. An instance was the 'incorporation of tribal peoples into patterns of agrarian wage labour in the plains'.[7] Internally, too, the peasant society was becoming increasingly homogeneous. Agricultural commercialization, spread of money use, and the growth of population undermined 'distinctions based on personal status' and 'eroded tied, patronal relations', such as domestic and field serfdom for untouchable groups, 'a status...infused with ideas of religion and magic'. If 'some poor peasants' then lost land, 'there is evidence that persons of very low caste who had previously been debarred from holding land were themselves becoming poor peasants'.[8]

I

'Stability of the peasant mass', 'stabilization of the peasant position', 'consolidation of the Indian peasantry' are open-ended questions. We examine in this essay their appropriateness for studying the tribal society of colonial India. What exactly was the nature of the 'imperial impact'[9] on tribal society? Can we characterize the changes occurring therein as 'stabilization' and 'consolidation'?

The manner in which the theme of this essay is stated suggests the recognition of two distinct societies: the tribal and the peasant societies. The assumption is implicit in Bayly's argument that an element of the 'consolidation of the Indian peasantry' was the absorption of the part of the tribal labour force in peasant economy. He has not, however, specified the points of distinction between the two societies.[10]

A school of anthropological thought tends to regard them as distinct structural types and as universally valid categories. Andre Beteille demonstrated, with particular reference to India, the methodological inadequacy of this approach.[11] The criteria chosen for distinguishing 'tribe', he has argued, does not apply to some major Indian tribes. On the other hand, the characteristics usually attributed to 'peasantry' are also noticeable in several tribes: for instance, predominance of settled agriculture; its subsistence orientation; 'household economy' in the sense that the tribal family provides the required labour supply for agriculture, and the subordinate position, the 'underdog position', of the peasantry or their domination by outsiders. As regards tribes, Beteille has emphasized the last feature—'domination by outsiders'.[12] He admits that 'economic inequalities no doubt exist in these villages, but they are of a totally different order from the inequalities in villages where Brahmin or Rajput or Muslim landlords reside'.[13]

Beteille's personal experiences of some Oraon, Munda, Ho and Santal villages of Chotanagpur related to a fairly recent period, 1956-57. However, he did not regard 'domination by outsiders' merely as an aspect of the imperial impact. At least in the Munda country, he argued, 'landlords and moneylenders' were not 'completely unknown:...before the advent of British rule'. The Munda *Khuntkatti* village 'had begun to disintegrate during the period of Muslim rule'.[14] Thus 'what some would call the 'underdog position' of the Munda peasantry, or their exploitation by outsiders is at least three hundred years old'.[15]

While Beteille found 'tribe' and 'peasantry' in India nearly indistinguishable, Terence Ranger questioned the validity of the notion of 'tribe' itself.[16] 'Tribe', he argued, was merely a 'white creation' as well as 'black imagining'. 'Tribe' as an entity was non-existent; it was, argued Ranger, a construct of the colonial authority; on the other hand, the indigenous communities, thus inaccurately represented as tribes by their white masters, came to imagine their distinctive identity in the course of their encounters with them.

I agree with Beteille's his conclusion that 'tribe' and 'peasantry' are not distinct structural types. However, since I regard them as historically determined social formations, we need to look beyond their formal similarities which Beteille has pointed out, find out if they also had specificities, and if new attributes appeared over a long historical time, particularly during colonial rule.

I take two instances. Settled agriculture constituted, in Beteille's analysis, the foundation of the predominant economy in both the tribal and peasant regions. However, this structural similarity did admit of striking specificities in each case and the agricultural economy there developed new attributes under conditions associated with British rule, though not directly produced by its intervention in local society. Secondly, the tribals were as much involved as peasants in relationships with 'dominant' groups, with a wider political authority. However, the formally similar domination-subordination relationship may have varied because of its different origins in different cases. It may also have developed new characteristics under altogether new circumstances during British rule.

This essay follows this line of reasoning. It attempts to identify the distinctive elements of tribal societies chosen for this study in regard to the predominant mode of subsistence and the roots and forms of domination over them and to investigate if, in these respects, new attributes developed during the colonial period. This study also reflects on the social organization of the tribal groups, an aspect Beteille ignored.

The tribal groups of our choice belonged to Bengal and Bihar: the Santals, the Mundas and the Oraons. We have referred to other tribes of the Bengal Presidency, such as the Bhumij, in order to illustrate the complexities of the changes occurring in this part of India's tribal world.

II

I take up, first, the social organization, which was inseparably connected with the economic organization of a tribal village and its relations with the 'dominant' groups and describe a more or less typical social organization in a Munda village only marginally affected by the intrusion of outsiders connected with the process of 'State formation'.[17] While the Santal settlements, at least those on a large scale, had mostly occurred during the colonial period,[18] the settlements of the Mundas had gone on over a much longer period,[19] with the pace of reclamation probably slowing by the beginning of British rule. Hence the stronger roots of their social organization.

The settlers, mostly migrants, added to their arable land through reclamation of forests. The composition of the labour force considerably determined the form of social organization. Migrants to an unfamiliar tract presumably came in a sizeable group, and part of the initial reclamation was not possible without collective efforts. The large tract on which they settled was later divided into several portions, probably through mutual agreement. Cultivation then ceased to be a collective enterprise, with an individual family looking after the cultivation of the portion it received. The portion was, of course, much larger than the area the family could immediately reclaim with its resources, and besides the arable it included a considerable amount of forest land. Initially small, the family grew. So did cultivation. The village, with its recognized boundaries, thus came into existence.

This process itself determined to a considerable extent the social organization. A vital aspect was the institutional form of control exercised over the material resources of the village. In the Munda village this form was the first claim of the members of the village founder's family to these resources. The claim was confined to the descendants on the father's side, who were distinguished from those on the mother's side. The latter had no right to the village land and to forest resources. They cultivated only such lands as were given to them. While every member of the original founder's family could cut and take wood for domestic and agricultural purposes, their access to it was conditional upon the prior consent of the extended family.[20] The rationale behind this discrimination was the concern to maintain the solidarity of the original members of the village, since the mother's kins could be residents of another village.

The same concern explains why alienations to outsiders of village land by sale or in any other manner, were also forbidden; it could only be passed on through inheritance of the male descendants of the family. This sentiment of solidarity, based on a sense of exclusiveness of the tribal village, was reinforced by the absence of what may be called 'social stratification'. There, naturally, were differences between individual families in regard to wealth but these did not mean domination of one family over the other deriving from the former's control over land and other means of production.

Some of the functionaries having a crucial role in the village organization, such as the village headman, i.e., the *Munda* and the *Pahan*, did enjoy a superior status. This, however, was generally social in nature and did not involve any special position in regard to control over land. Grants of land, if any, were remuneration for services rendered which the tribal village considered vital for its continued existence and welfare. The headman may or may not have been connected with the foundation of the village; he was normally chosen from the families of village founders. Internally, he presided over vital activities of the village, such as communal rituals, religious ceremonies and festivals and settlement of disputes. Furthermore, he was the link with other villages or the external political power. Chosen by the village itself and looking after its vital interests, the headman was the symbol of its solidarity. Indeed, the village social organization was inseparable from him. One of the primary reasons of the gradual disintegration of the organization in later years was the replacement of headmen by persons of choice of the alien intruders, who misinterpreted the role of the headmen, denied its communal roots and argued that the headman was a mere collector of 'village rent', allegedly agreeing to hold over to the 'zamindar' a stipulated sum as rent and appropriating the rest. In fact, even where he was not replaced, he increasingly became dissociated from the communal and collective activities of the village, developing interest antagonistic to the village's welfare.

The Munda social organization was, however, firmly anchored in magico-religious beliefs — beliefs rooted in experiences at the level of material existence, i.e., the Munda confrontation with nature. In regard to origins, religion and magic constituted two separate domains. Religion is generally concerned with some deeper questions of the mystery of life, death and creation of the universe. Magic is more immediately connected with the day-to-day recurring experiences and with the means of coping with hostile forces, human as well as natural. However, religious concerns tended to shade off into magical practices in the context of the rudimentary state of the technology of Munda agriculture. Whatever the origins, the magico-religious practices and beliefs as also the associated myths tended to survive the changes in material existence.

Particularly notable here was the bearing on the social organization of the Munda beliefs in the existence of spirits (*bongas*, *Singbonga* being the lord of them all) and the Munda mortuary beliefs. In brief, *bongas*, the

Mundas believed, could influence for good or evil the course of human affairs. Though invisible, their existence was pervasive. Their abode was not somewhere in the 'world across yonder'; it could be the usual Munda habitat and also beyond. Spread of cultivation at the cost of forests, it was believed, must have disturbed the spirits. Hence the Munda practice of setting apart part of the forest area as sacred groves (*sarnas*), places where the spirits would live undisturbed. Even the worst food-scarcity would not persuade the Mundas to convert the *Sarnas* into cultivation. It was left to the key village functionary, the *Pahan*, to propitiate the spirits. 'No village can get on without this person...as he alone can possibly know how to appease the *bhuts* or spirits who delight in upsetting all mortal arrangements. The village is often spoken of as belonging to the *Pahan*, but the office is not always, though it is generally, hereditary'.[21] Pleasing the spirits was not just an act of piety by a lone individual. The whole community took part in the sacrifice offered by the *Pahan*, and 'all partook of the sacrificial meat'.[22] Part of the village resources was diverted for the purpose. The land the *Pahan* received as remuneration of his services was known as *pahani*.[23]

Mortuary beliefs, too, vitally affected social organization. Death, it was believed, did not just mean the end of material existence; it also marked the beginning of a new existence, a disembodied one—a spirit living on in his former home as the family's protector. Remembrance of him by his descendants was thus not a casual act, which might be ignored at times, but a ritual act, recurringly and systematically done according to prescribed rules. The ritual was placing a burial stone (*sasandiri*) over his grave. This was not a private family affair, the neighbours too participated as witnesses. The descendants thereby established not only a communion with the dead ancestor, but also an infallible proof of their membership of the family and of their right to a share in the village land. In case of a dispute over the title of the land which he claimed as his own, a Munda, when asked to furnish evidence about the basis of his claim, invariably pointed to the tomb-stone his family had put on the ancestor's grave. The British court often rejected the evidence as inadmissible, but the Munda stubbornly stood by his claim.

The Munda social solidarity had a broader territorial basis than a single village. This happened where growth in the number of families in the original village necessitated foundation of new villages. In such cases the common ancestor continued to be worshipped by all the families in the villages, belonging to the same clan (*kili*). Such villages were closely associated in social and administrative matters. This broader association (*parha* or *patti*) now became the domain of Munda solidarity.[24]

Elements of distinctiveness in the Munda social organization emphasized above relate to the institutional form of control over the material resources of the village and to the roots of communal solidarity in the village. Where the process of 'state formation'[25] had not yet seriously impaired the old order, control was exercised by the patrilineally descended members of the tribe. The patrilineal descent, to the extent that it fostered a sense of exclusiveness, also contributed to the sentiment of solidarity in the tribe. The sentiment was not restricted to a single village; it was shared by all the villages linked with a particular clan. Religious rituals, beliefs and practices and 'creation myths' of their own continually reinforced it. Individual tribals were thus being linked with the wider tradition of the tribe, because such rituals and practices were essentially communal in nature and organization. With growing links with other villages and the wider political authority, persons chosen by the tribe to maintain the links, such as the Mundas and *Pahans*, represented the tribe and thus symbolized this solidarity. The sense of separateness of the tribe from others was strengthened by the gradual intrusion into the tribal village of aliens connected with the process of 'state formation', aliens who, unlike the artisan communities having a vital role to play in the viability of the tribal economy, developed into a class of expropriators of the land and labour of the tribals. On the other hand, absence of social stratification in the Munda village strengthened this sense of solidarity.

In all these respects a typical non-tribal peasant society was condiderably different. Whatever the origins peasants here constituted, by about the beginning of British rule, a composite group. Partly because of this compositeness and partly of the generally more improved agricultural techniques, the role of magico-religious beliefs was often different. Such beliefs prevailed here too, but the practices connected with them were not communally organized and were, therefore, not a fundamental basis of social organization. By the beginning of British rule influence of such beliefs was still traceable in the village practice of setting apart portions of the peasant produce for astrologers and other groups having quasi-religious functions in society. However, the practice was mostly confined to Bihar districts where the system of produce rent continued to prevail. In general, the system of produce rent (distinguishable from the system of crop division in the case of crop-sharing arrangement) tended to disappear, and even where it survived, the existing rural practice did not necessarily provide for leaving a share in the village produce for astrologers, etc. Unlike the Munda village, as also most other tribal villages, the village headmen here had just a marginal role in the communally organized practices of the village. In fact the village headman had, by the beginning of British rule, nearly ceased to be a key functionary. It is striking how within a few years of the establishment of British political authority the headmen were, in most places, integrated into the machinery of rural control by zamindars. That a considerable number of headmen could then develop into affluent peasants was partly due to their ability to manipulate, with an eye to promotion of their own interests, and the distribution of the rent quantum fixed by zamindars on the village. On the other hand, from the point of view of social organization, the peasant community formed part of a stratified, essentially inegalitarian, Hindu social organization.

Dumont and Pocock argue that 'the village in India is only an architectural and demographic entity...it is caste that is sociologically real'.[26] Anthropologists, they assert, 'confer upon the village a kind of sociological reality which it does not possess'; lower castes do not possess a sense of loyalty to the village; 'they are clients of powerful patrons; obligations of clientship force them to act in ways which are misrepresented as arising out of village solidarity.[27] Srinivas disagreed with the conclusion. While admitting that 'the village was no doubt stratified along the lines of caste and land', he concludes that 'the productive forces made it an interlocking community', and that the inegalitarian social system was not incompatible with the existence of a sense of community, of communal solidarity.[28] It remains an open question whether 'inter-caste complementarity' in the hierarchical Hindu social organization constituted a firm basis for 'communal solidarity'. Even admitting that it did, we need to bear in mind that the roots of this solidarity were altogether different in nature from those in the tribal village.

III

I now return to the two questions formulated earlier,[29] relating to the predominant mode of tribal subsistence and the roots and forms of tribal subordination. I intend to argue that formal similarities, in regard to both, between the tribal and peasant societies, should not lead us to ignore either the significant differences between them or the altogether new attributes that began to appear during British rule in both these respects.

Growing alien domination constituted a decisive influence on tribal society. In fact, the nature of constraints on agricultural growth here is only partly explicable in terms of its specific ecological context. The normal difficulty in overcoming the ecologiclly derived constraints was considerably aggravated by the changing relations of power in tribal society. In explaining the continuing vulnerability of Chotanagpur agriculture to failure of rain, Detlef Schwerin has emphasized 'the socio-economic development of the region and the resulting institutional impediments to agricultural production'.[30]

I would, therefore, deal at greater length with the broad question of tribal subordination. It was here that striking changes occurred during British rule. Our brief note on the tribal economy would mainly indicate some of its peculiarities, some long-term changes in it and their implications for the tribal society.

Apart from settled cultivation, a distinctive aspect of the tribal economy of the regions included in this study was the greater degree of dependence on forest resources than in the usual non-tribal areas. The tribal economy was characterized by the close integration of cultivation with forest and pasture'.[31] The integration was not appreciably disturbed at the beginning of British rule. Things changed thereafter. One of the crucial changes occurring then was the diminishing access of the tribals to forest resources, partly due to conversion of forests into arables by the tribals themselves, but mostly due to altogether new forms of alien domination.

Beteille is right in pointing out that settled plough cultivation, distinguishable from the slash-and-burn type of farming, characterized the agricultural system both in our chosen tribal region and in the usual non-tribal area. The household nature of tribal agriculture was all the more striking because of the absence here of the caste ban on the employment of female labour in cultivation. Infertility of the soil did preclude in many places continuous cropping, necessitating short-term fallowing. This practice essentially differed from the non-utilization of a portion of the arable under the slash-and-burn type of farming. A variant of settled plough cultivation, the practice often resulted from the inefficiency of the technique of irrigation in use.

The agricultural system of the Santals, one of the most numerous communities in our chosen tribal belt, was essentially one of wet, settled agriculture. It was familiarity with plough cultivation and irrigation devices that largely accounted for the amazingly rapid Santal settlements, mostly occurring from about the last decade of the eighteenth-century, in the vast government-owned forest, Damin-i-Koh (literally skirt of the Hills, here the Rajmahal Hills). The Paharias, the tribe inhabiting the Rajmahal Hills and practising a kind of slash-and-burn type of cultivation (*Kurao*), could get, for the mere asking, the right to settle there, as the British Government was keen that they did so. For the government it was then primarily a law and order question. A change over from the *kurao* cultivation on the Hills to plough cultivation at their skirt, the government assumed, would ensure a bigger social surplus to the Paharias and thus persuade them to give up the occasional raids on the settled villages in the neighbourhood as a means of subsistence. The raids were all the more disruptive of local peace, because the Paharias did not carry them out on their own, but at the instance of powerful and greedy zamindars of the locality. The Paharias did not abandon their traditional mode of cultivation, while the Santals surged on. As migrants from the zamindari estates in Bhagalpur, Birbhum and Murshidabad, they had already been familiar with the art of forest reclamation.[32] Where zamindars had called in the Santals to reclaim the lands recently gone waste as a result of the large scale rural depopulation caused by the famines of 1769/70 and 1783, the migrants could partly rely on the techniques devised by the local peasant community.

The area under the slash-and-burn-type cultivation (*jhuming*) in the Munda/Oraon region was also negligible, at least by about the beginning of the twentieth-century. 'The practice', as Reid, Ranchi Settlement Officer, found, 'obtains only in the remote parts of the district, where the jungle trees are still of little or no economic value'.[33] The area under *jhuming* was perhaps larger by the beginning of British rule, though it is difficult to estimate it. Part of the reason for the impressive size of settled cultivation in this region was the length of time, even before British rule, over which the Munda/Oraon agricultural settlements had been taking place. Also notable was the role of the superior technique of cultivation which the skilled migrant agriculturists from the non-tribal tracts of Bihar had brought along with them.[34]

However, the organization of cultivation here had a distinctive element, compared to that in the usual peasant tract: limited utilization of existing land resources because of insecure water supply. The swiftness of the river current in the upland precluded deposit of fertilizing alluvium. Rain water, on which cultivators were obliged to depend, was not properly stored as a means of irrigation. Even by the beginning of the twentieth-century, as the Ranchi Settlement Officer found, 'there is very little artificial irrigation. Some of the zamindars construct occasionally tanks and bunds for the irrigation of their own *khas* (demesne) lands . . . but the great bulk of the cultivation is entirely dependent for its prosperity on the rainfall'.[35] The difficulties which ecology created in the way of artificial irrigation were reinforced by the negligible investment of landlords, tribals and government. Landlords preferred to invest only where they were certain of proper rewards for their efforts. The cultivators' means were too small for costly irrigation devices. The 'land improvement loans' provided by the government were normally negligible. The most important source of irrigation was, notably, wells (accounting for about 73% of the irrigation in Ranchi), which did not require any elaborate device for storing rain water.

The inadequate artificial irrigation explains the limited utilization of the available land resources. This is evident from the preponderance of low-value, inferior lands, locally called *Tanr* (upland), which, incapable of sufficiently keeping moisture, 'produce coarse rice and various rabi crops'. 'Large parts of *tanr*, which comprise approximately 30% of the total arable area, cannot be cultivated on a yearly basis but have periodically to lie fallow to recover'.[36] The *don*, the better quality land, occupying the hollows intervening between the continuous ridges of uplands, 'is levelled, embanked and is exclusively used to grow rice'. The *tanr* had in some places hardly any rental value, its cultivators being required to provide *begari* (unpaid labour) to the zamindars.

Population pressure obliged cultivators to produce more through converting the *tanr* into *don*. In the beginning of the 20th-century, of the total area of Ranchi district (of which 51% was cultivated), *don* accounted for 17% and *tanr* 34%. Again, of the *tanr* a considerable portion was not fertile enough to be annually cropped without a rest, and the converted *tanr* lands were, naturally, much less productive than the original *don*.

Some implications of the particular organization of the Munda/Oraon agriculture may now be indicated. The initial reclamation was inevitably an extremely labour-intensive process. On the other hand, stable labour supply for reclamation was hindered by the agricultural system, characterized by low productivity of most parts of the cultivation area, increasing dependence on monocropping and chronic uncertainty about output. Failure of rain tended to reduce to a precariously low point the small surplus the tribal agriculture could generate. Admittedly, the tribals were the worst sufferers during famines in Bengal and Bihar. Indeed, scarcities, causing severe subsistence crises for the tribals, deeply affected their cultural mores, occasionally producing an intense, pervasive emotional upsurge, which constituted the *immediate* background to several tribal revolts.[37] Most cases of violence against grain merchants during the famine of 1865/66 came from the chronically deficit tribal belt.

The difficulties created for Mundas/Oraons by their low-surplus agricultural economy were increasingly being compounded by the proliferation of 'uneconomic holdings'. The Ranchi Settlement Officer found an 'enormous number of raiyati holdings to be of this type . . . rents are paid not from the profits of the holdings, but from the wages derived from extraneous employments, some of them unconnected with agriculture'.

As a consequence, the Settlement Officer found, 'the only alternative is emigration'. According to his estimate, based on the 1901 census, 'the net loss by emigration from the district was more than twice as great as in other districts of the province with the possible exception of Bankura'. The intensity of the economic pressure forcing the tribals out of their villages is underscored by their persisting with culturally-determined attitudes to sustained association with their ancestral villages and to continued possession of their family holdings. 'It is not uncommon', observed the Ranchi Settlement Officer, 'to find that a Munda or an Uraon will persist in cultivating the ancestral lands long after he has been ejected from them by the courts, and I have known numerous cases in which individual aborigines underwent imprisonment five or six times for persisting in their attempts to get back to their ancestral lands'.[38]

Dependence of the tribals on forest resources, which constituted a vital aspect of their economy, was also being threatened. The causes were partly diminishing availability of the resources, and more importantly, diminishing accessibility of tribals to them. The diminishing availability was partly due to *jhuming*, 'indiscriminate grazing' by tribals and forest reclamation for actual cultivation. The Settlement Officer called the first two causes of 'deforestation' 'subsidiary'. The 'extent of complete deforestation due to reclamation' barely exceeded 'ten to eleven per cent' in some parts of the Chotanagpur Raj estate between 1884 and 1909. The decisive factor in the declining availability of forest resources for tribal use was the increasing restrictions imposed by dominant aliens on the traditional access of tribals to them. The Settlement Officer, writing in 1909/10, was firmly of the opinion that 'it is only within comparatively recent period that the jungle question arose'.[39] The Munda 'forest rights' largely survived in the 'intact *khuntkatti*' villages. In some cases the tribals were allowed to take wood for their personal use. In many more villages the tribals nearly lost even this right. At the time of his 'settlement' work (1902-1910) Reid found in existence some 'customary rights in jungle', such as the right to cut trees for building and repairing houses, for making ploughs and carts and for fuel.

The main reason why landlords found it increasingly worthwhile to restrict the tribal access to forest was the rising 'economic value' of forest products, particularly timber. Improving transport, facilitating wider exchanges between the tribal region and the neighbourhood then undergoing rapid urbanization and commercialization, stimulated the demand for forest products. The changes occurred mostly during British rule. Timber owed its increasing market value to the rapid growth of railways and of mining enterprises in the neighbourhood. Bradley-Birt noted how the railway 'entering Chotanagpur on three different sides, and 'slowly creeping towards the central plateau', was transforming the 'face of old Chutia Nagpur'.[40] 'Valuable jungle trees situated in a jungle hundred miles from the nearest railway', as Reid found in the first decade of the twentieth- century, 'are evidently of little or no commercial value'.[41]

IV

We now examine Beteille's proposition that, as the pre-British tribal society had been as much involved as the usual peasant society in a wider political authority, there was not much to distinguish between the two. Tribal societies did cease to be 'stateless' prior to British rule. The point to decide is whether encapsulation of small scale tribal societies into the new colonial policy and economy had any significant implications for them.

The process of involvement of tribal groups in a wider structure of political power before British rule had two major types. We come across the first type in the Munda/Oraon case: the emergence and consolidation of this authority from within. This was how the Nagbangshi Raj had evolved. The Raj developed within the still wider framework of Mughal suzerainty. The two were not incompatible, as they represented two levels of political authority: the Mughal authority only nominally exercised on the tribal tract and the Nagbangshi Raj more directly and immediately impinging on the Munda/Oraon society and economy. The new colonial authority gradually supplanted the Nagbangshi authority, but the pre-existing position of alien groups in the tribal village which the development of the Nagbangshi Raj had brought about,[42] constituted for long the matrix of the evolving rural power relations, increasingly propped by the colonial authority. The Santal case represented the second type. Search for new land made the Santals, a migrant community, move into the pre-existing authority of zamindars. Their first encounter with the colonial state resulted from the increasing diversion of their reclamation efforts from zamindari areas to the thinly-populated government estate—Damin-i-Koh.

I first take up the Santal case. The area of the Santal concentration, known since 1855 as the Santal Parganas, originally belonged to three districts: Birbhum, Bhagalpur and Murshidabad. The Santal migration was presumably encouraged by local zamindars as a device towards reclamation of wastes in their estates.

Santal settlements took place evidently outside the periphery of caste Hindu concentrations. So strong was the aversion of caste Hindus to any kind of social intercourse with the Santals that the latter were not even 'permitted to work the cow'. Buchanan tells us how when 'some impure Saungtars' (Santals) were first allowed to do so 'a most violent opposition was at first made to such an atrocious innovation'.[43] The aversion, however, seldom caused overt hostilities between Hindus and Santals. The Hindus were careful not to antagonize the Santals, believed to be 'powerful in witchcraft'. A more important reason perhaps was the demonstration of the Santal skill as waste reclaimers.

When exactly the Santal migration started is difficult to ascertain. However, its scale by the beginning of the nineteenth-century was big enough not to go unnoticed. It was obviously to the zamindar's interest that it continued. This, surely, was not true of all zamindars. In fact it was out of annoyance with zamindars that Santals in large numbers left their estates for the government estate, Damin-i-Koh, gradually marked off from the neighbourhood during the years 1824-1833.

It was this migration to the Damin that first involved the Santals in the apparatus of the colonial state. Not that the enterprising Santals just moved into a void, a wild waste, without any economic organization and political system. Had this been the case, the state, familiar with the industry and skill of the Santals as forest reclaimers, would surely have encouraged this migration. This was not done till about the 1830s. This hesitation was largely due to the government's preoccupation with the bothersome 'Paharia question'— the acute problem of law and order that the economy of the Paharias (hillmen) created for the new state. The initial government attitude to the migrant Santals was influenced by a feeling that free access of the Santals to the Damin, which included the Paharia habitat, would aggravate the Paharia question. The question had much to do with the nature of the Paharia economy, mostly based on a variant of shifting cultivation (*kurao*) and hunting. The meagre surplus such an economy could produce often led the Paharias to carry on raids on the plains at the skirt of the Rajmahal Hills. The government felt unrestricted Santal access to the Damin would further weaken the Paharia economy, since the shifting cultivation of the Paharias, necessitating a continuous movement from one reclaimed area to another, ceased to be a meaningful proposition where encroachment by outsiders tended to diminish the possible zone of the Paharia movement. The government believed the Paharias would gradually change over to wet rice cultivation so that the roots of instability of the Paharia economy would be removed.

Disappointment of such expectations made the government change its attitude to the Santal migration to the Damin. An instruction from the government in 1837 emphasized that 'every encouragement should be given to the Santals in the work of clearing the jungle'. Once the government became tolerant of the Santals there was no stopping them. Between 1838 and 1851 the number of Santal settlers increased from 3000 to 83,000 and of Santal villages from 49 to 1437.[44] In fact the Paharias were ever on the retreat, presumably because they were no match for the Santals who were familiar with the technique of wet agriculture. The Paharia conservatism hardened. By about the end of the century the Paharias asked the government to protect their *kurao* rights, a plea rejected by the government on the ground that *kurao* was a wasteful agricultural practice.

The nearly virgin soil of the Damin thus lured an increasingly large number of Santals away from the zamindari sphere of influence. The nature of the dual authority structure as it evolved in the Damin and in the zamindari zone needs to be analysed. We first take up the Damin tract partly because till the Santal rebellion of 1855 it was here that the decisive development in this evolution occurred. Thereafter, a qualitative change took place in both spheres of power relations.

The manner in which the Santal involvement in the apparatus of the colonial state began scarcely presaged the later shape of the state role. The beginning was simple: obligation of the Santals to pay revenue to the government, unlike the Paharia case where the government was keen on preserving an archaic mode of agriculture. The revenue kept on increasing with the continuing Santal influx. Between 1837/38 and 1849/50 the demand increased by 582 per cent. The growth rate slowed thereafter, the percentage between 1849/50 and 1854/55 being about 33.[45]

Whatever the basis of the revenue demand, two things particularly aggravated its effects on the Santals: the level of agricultural prices and the arrangement for revenue collection. The 1840s was generally a period of depressed agricultural prices in the Bengal Presidency and elsewhere. In 1843, Pontet, Superintendent of the Damin, attributed his difficulty in collecting the revenue to the depressed grain market of the time. The second thing relates to the mechanism of colonial control at the village level, which was particularly true of the tribal belt. In order to secure a cheap administration the government left the exercise of its authority at this level to extremely ill-paid and ill-controlled indigenous agencies, mostly, aliens, called the *sezawal* and his deputies (*naib-sezawals*). Evidently, they exploited their official position to promote their private gains. The *sezawal's* position was considerably strengthened by his status as the police *darogah*. No wonder that Mohesh Dutt, the *sezawal*, was one of the first victims of Santal violence during the 1855 rebellion.

The Santals came to be more deeply encapsulated in the colonial authority as a result of their credit relations with alien moneylenders. Some interpretations of the origins of the credit relations seem misleading. We take two representative views, those of Bradley-Birt and George E. Somers.[46] We have chosen them because the official view on the question is nearly identical. The actual organization of Santal cultivation and the size of the surplus in the economy, it is argued, had not much to do with the credit needs of the Santals. 'Prosperity', 'abundance', 'pleasure principle' and availability of exotic goods created a demand for them among the Santals —such were the terms in which the origins and growth of Santal indebtedness have been explained. Bradley-Birt stressed an aspect of the Santal life-style: their 'happy-go-lucky disposition', their 'improvidence' and their lack of concern for saving against a rainy season'. Somers explicitly denies any role of 'moneyed capitalists' in the financing of Santal migration and attributes the origins of their credit needs to the so-called 'primitive' 'love of pleasure', making them thriftlessly spend on things of 'pleasure'. The more decisive factor, argues Somers, was the change in the traditional consumption pattern of Santals, with their 'unaccustomed prosperity' tempting them to spend on exotic commodities unconnected with their immediate subsistence.

Contemporary descriptions of the recent Santal agricultural settlements tell a different story. We take, for instance, the reports of Captain Sherwill, Revenue Surveyor in the region in the 1850s. His analysis of the composition of the Santal migrants, particularly those from Singbhum, and also of their typical economic exchanges, contradicts the assumptions of Bradley-Birt and Somers. The Santals, recalls Sherwill in 1855, 'arrive at the Damin from Singbhum and other Santal districts very poor, possessing literally nothing but a hatchet, a gourd for water and a leaf umbrella, one small piece of cloth round the waist. . . .'[47] Such utterly resourceless migrants could not, obviously, do without the 'moneyed capitalists'. In fact Somers' own admission that Santals depended on them for 'iron, draft oxen and seed grains' refutes his argument that organization of Santal agriculture had not much to do with this dependence. Sherwill's description in 1841 of the typical economic exchanges of the Santals clearly shows that it was the supply of these and other basic needs that necessitated their links with traders and moneylenders.[48] The forms of the creditors' appropriations at the time were also largely determined by the fact that the creditors were mostly traders, with local shopkeepers occasionally serving as links between them and the Santals. Until the 1855 rebellion the creditors rarely dispossessed indebted Santals of their lands. The cases of destitute Santals being reduced to 'bonded serfs' were not numerically significant either. The first form did not quite suit the major objective of the merchant-creditor: securing control over Santal agricultural produce as cheaply as possible and their transport to a relatively dear market nearby. Extortion of unpaid labour from a 'bonded' Santal did not, for the same reason, serve his purpose, particularly where he did not reside in the locality or did not have the right infrastructure for supervising the cultivation of widely dispersed Santal holdings. Making indebted Santals pay usurious interest charges promoted his interest far more than reducing them to landless labourers or 'bonded serfs'.

The increasing involvement of the Santals in the network of colonial authority was inseparable from the way the alien moneylenders sought to consolidate their position, and also from the Santal notion of the new state as the source of 'justice' and as their 'only protection', an attitude showing how the relative isolation of the Santal village had completely broken down by then.[49]

Moneylenders did occasionally rely on local law courts administering the 'ordinary' law relating to debt realization and obtained decrees 'ex parte in most cases' authorizing distress sales of the 'house and cattle' of the Santals. They, however, could do without recourse to the law, as their domination was largely ensured through their collusion with the village level representative of the Raj—particularly the police personnel. They could manipulate the police establishment, which, in fact, was made to appear as an instrument of terror to the disgruntled Santals. They could get away with such intrigues due to the indifference of the higher authority (in this case Pontet, Superintendent of the Damin) to the tales of Santal woes. True, the complicity of the police with the wily moneylenders severely disrupted the flow of information from the village to Pontet. However, as the enquiry into the origins of the 1855 rebellion revealed, Pontet did receive numerous petitions of Santals praying for protection against their tormentors. Evidently, he did not regard the complaints as exaggerated at all. 'Three villages absconded', says his report of August 1848, 'in consequence of the oppressions of the mehazuns . . .'[50]

While the local administration continued to tolerate the moneylenders, the Santals seeking to chastize them in their own way were severely punished. By about the middle of 1854 the Santals carried out a series of raids on the houses of some notorious moneylenders. The intention, obviously, was to frighten them into mending their ways. No property whatsoever was taken away. The government interpreted the raids as 'dacoities' and meted out harsh punishment which the criminal law provided for the offence. The Santals were, for the first time, subjected to organized state coercion. The bitter Santals invoked even then the 'protection' of the government. Increasing evidence of growing restiveness among the Santals made the government realize the folly of ignoring the danger signals. 'With such a spirit as this abroad among the Santals of the Damin', warned the Bhagalpur Magistrate, 'that district will soon become a most lawless one'.[51] A government 'order' in the beginning of 1855 'required' the mahajans to leave the 'detached villages' of the Santals and 'move into hats and bazaars', and provided for a daily penalty of five rupees for its violators. The local administration was not presumably energetic to enforce it systematically. Pontet did frighten the mahajans by citing the 'orders of the government prohibiting the settling of any others than Sonthals in the Damin' and 'threatening expulsion of mehajuns accused of oppression'. In no case was the threat carried out. On the other hand, Pontet exercised 'extraordinary powers' where the moneylenders' exactions jeopardized the collection of revenue. Significantly, nothing was done toward breaking the complicity of the local police with the 'crimes' of mahajans. The police increasingly colluded with them. The Santal insurrection of 1855 started when the police, obviously in deference to the wishes of moneylenders, then visibly alarmed at the growing unrest among the Santals, took the blatantly partisan step of seizing two of their ringleaders.[52]

The post-insurrection developments in the Santal region contradict a widespread assumption that the reformed administration called non-regulation system, tended to free the Santals from alien domination and to facilitate retreat into their old tribal insularity. Carstairs called the essence of the new system 'Man, not Machine', under which the formal body of laws ceased to apply and the deciding principle instead was the exercise of discretion by British officials.[53] Placing the Santal tract outside the usual Regulation system, it was assumed, would mean erection of a *cordon sanitaire* against the penetration of alien domination, which had over the years subverted the traditional Santal social order. 'The wrongs of the Santals', argued W.W. Hunter, 'proceeded from the inefficiency of the administration and they speedily disappeared after the revolt'.[54] 'In the years that immediately succeeded the rebellion', goes Bradley-Birt's confident assertion, 'prosperity returned to the long suffering Santal'. Their old enemies—police, the moneylender and the zamindar, were now, he thought, effectively controlled.[55] Both Hunter and Bradley-Birt regarded the new railways and the opportunity for emigration as liberating forces for the Santals. Employment provided by the railway, they argued, undermined the basis of agrestic serfdom and 'furnished the Santal with the wherewithal to start life again in his own land'. Somers, presumably influenced by their analysis, nearly repeated their conclusion: 'the result of the rebellion favoured the Santals and brought redress to many of the complaints which had prompted the violence'. He calls the post-insurrection Santal society an 'encapsulated society', in the sense in which F.G. Bailey uses the phrase, i.e., a 'political structure', 'partly independent of and partly regulated by, larger encapsulating structures'. 'While Santal peasants did not attempt to isolate themselves from the commerce of British India', concludes Somers, 'they did attempt to retain some power of self-determination in their economic decisions. Specifically, they could retain their ownership of land against all legal and commercial manipulation'.[56]

The developments in the Santal society and economy tend to contradict Somers' conclusion. A distinct trend in them was the steadily declining role of the Santal's 'own traditions'. The sense which the phrase 'encapsulated society' is intended to convey is, at the least, vague. The crucial point to decide is the relative strength of the two tendencies operating at the time: 'independence' or involvement in the wider power structure in the neighbourhood. A major trend in the post-1855 developments was the increasingly pronounced decisiveness of the second.

This was partly due to the particular manner of the suppression of the insurrection, aimed as much against the government as against other alien groups. Alarmed at its rapid growth over a large area the government sought to put it down with all its might and as quickly as possible. The characteristic stereotype of the official thinking that only 'wild savages' like the Santals were capable of the violence that marked the rebellion partly accounted for the severity of the repression for taming the 'savages'. The Bhagalpur Magistrate argued with a clear conscience: 'The entire extirpation of the Santhal tribe will be the only way to ensure peace ....'[57] With the declaration of Martial Law (10 November 1855) reassuring the army and the local administration, the rebels were exposed to more indiscriminate violence of the State. 'Capture in arms in open hostility to government...' was now an offence punishable by death. The usual means of making the defiant villages yield was wantonly burning up the ripening crops or the harvested grain. The movement of the ruthless army till the revocation of the Martial Law (3rd Jan., 1856) left a trail of destruction. Bradley-Birt estimated that about ten thousand Santals perished. Moreover, 'large bodies of Santals are abandoning their villages', reported an army colonel.[58] The Santals had to cope with successive strains on their economy: the sudden spurts in all sorts of commodity prices during the Mutiny hitting most the destitute vagrants who had not yet settled down to stable agriculture and the disastrous famine of 1865-66.

The Santal 'tradition' and 'autonomy' could scarcely survive such an unprecedented dislocation in the local economy. We take up the first major phase of renewed alien intrusion, 1855-1872, the latter years seeing the revival of the non-regulation system abandoned in 1863.

The recovery of the Santal economy necessitated, under the circumstances, restoration of the alien credit system which the 1855 insurrection had badly hit. Moneylenders, suffering most from the rebel violence, could before long dominate the Santal economy again. The real source of their strength was the non-existence of any alternative source of credit for the Santals in their hour of dire need. Nursing the nearly ruined Santal economy back to health necessitated a large capital input towards enabling the Santals to buy seeds, implements, cattle and to subsist till the next harvest, i.e., November-December, 1856. (The insurrection ended in January of that year). Realizing the enormity of the work of regenerating the economy, the government had no long-term plan for this. Its measures were mostly restricted to short-term relief, such as temporary suspension of the revenue demand in the Damin estate, 'postponing' collection of revenue dues from zamindars who 'did well' in helping 'resettlement' of destitute Santals, and construction of a few roads as a means of providing some purchasing power to needy Santals. The farthest limit to which the local administration could go was illustrated by the initiative of the Deputy-Commissioner of the Santal Parganas in the resettlement of the Santals of the Dumka subdivision, a fairly extensive tract containing about 800 villages, and admittedly the worst affected part of the Damin.[59] The modesty of the amount he asked the government to provide, Rs 1500, is indeed surprising. Even this small grant sanctioned by the government was conditional: contribution by the Santals themselves of half of the approved grant.

Official reports reveal that zamindars were even more niggardly. The sudden influx of Santals into their estates from the Damin made them less eager to show any kindness to their Santal *praja*, as scarcity of labour was not as acute here as in the Damin.

The only source of credit for the Santals was, therefore, the moneylender. The inflow of credit, all from alien sources, increased, too, with the gradual opening up of the Santal country, particularly after the Mutiny. The number of traders setting up shops and business houses, particularly in conveniently situated market places, considerably increased over the years. For instance, by January 1867, the number of 'mahajans and petty traders' in the Lohundia bazaar of Dumka rose from the pre-insurrection figure of 'ten to twelve' to eighty, the newcomers being principally hard-headed Bhojpuria Bhakats from Arrah of Sahabad district. The government policy till 1867-68 of 'farming' out bazaars to the highest bidders had something to do with the settlement of opulent traders in such bazaars. The successful bidder (*chowdhuri*) naturally preferred resourceful traders, because his main inducement in making the bid was the prospect of earning more from the ground rent (*basauri*) payable by the 'settlers' in the bazaar than the amount of his bid.

The increased availability of credit and the increased number of creditors did not evidently make for liberalization of the terms of credit. In the context of the Santal economy at the time the creditors had now, in fact, better opportunities of consolidating their control over the economy. The attitude of the state to the rural credit relations only encouraged the creditors. It is surprising how even during the critical days of the famine of 1865-66 the government declined to intervene in favour of the Santals who wanted it to ensure a 'fair market price' of their paddy and to reduce the usurious interest rates. The local administration ignored both the Santal pleas. As regards the first, the Assistant-Commissioner bluntly observed: 'Of course this I could not do'. The Commissioner thus defended his 'inaction' in regard to the second: 'This is not a matter which legislation can touch. The evil must work its own cure. Free trade in money must ultimately produce the same results as free trade in anything else; high profits must bring competition, and competition will lower prices'.[60] While on a similar occasion later the Commissioner arranged a compromise providing for postponement of grain-repayment by about fifty days, he threatened the Santals that 'their gathering together in large numbers to intimidate the mahajans would not be allowed, but would entail on them severe punishment and also render them responsible for any loss sustained by mahajans should the latter desert their houses and property in consequence of such intimidation'. The only bold step of the local administration in May 1867 was the eviction of some notorious moneylenders from the principal bazaars in the Damin. The step probably made some erring mahajans in sizeable bazaars mend their ways, but it scarcely affected their far-flung credit network in the Santal villages. Moreover, the eviction order did not apply to the traders 'whose residence in any place dates from before the insurrection'.[61]

The marginality of the role of the 'non-regulation' experiment in containing the increasing alien intrusion into the Santal Parganas is also evident from the way zamindars consolidated their power outside the Damin, a critical development from the point of view of the stability of the traditional Santal social organization. The new 'rent offensive' of zamindars directly impinged on this organization. Planning to secure a large increase in the rent demand, zamindars, rarely in direct contact with individual Santals and dependent on the mediation of the village headman (*manjhi*) for the distribution of the rent demand on the village, sought to devise new modes of control over the headman. They intended to turn him into an instrument of their will and, if he crossed their will, they would force him out, taking in a more pliant one. Either way the Santal village organization was vitally affected. The first meant distortion of the role of a key Santal institution; the second introduction of an alien element having no roots whatsoever in the Santal social and cultural traditions.

The consolidation of landlord control, points to the gradual breakdown of the old insularity of the Santal society and its exposure to altogether new forces. The fact that the change first occurred in the Hendwah estate, then under the Court of Wards[62] and managed by a European, Barns, is indicative of the new forces at work in Santal society. The government preferred Barns as manager as it regarded European management as a progressive force making for rational estate management and systematic development of economic resources of government estates. This faith in 'British energy and capital' reflected a growing sentiment after the Mutiny in favour of 'European settlement', i.e., investment of European enterprise, skill and capital as a factor in India's economic development.

The Commissioner of Santal Parganas explained the eagerness of Barns in taking over as the Hendwah estate manager in terms of its growing attractiveness to the gradual opening up of the Santal country. Characterizing the recent changes in the region as 'a state of transition', the Commissioner noted how 'the railway has created a vast demand for supplies of all kinds: food, fuel, timber, coals, labour etc.; money has consequently flowed into the people faster than they ever dreamt of ... the price of everything has consequently risen enormously'.[63] The manner of Barns' reorganization of the estate management also points to the influence of new ideas, particularly on the question of rent increase. The major influence on his plan of rent increase was the recent example set by European indigo planters in systematically using the Rent Act of 1859 during the 'indigo revolt' as a coercive device toward taming the defiant indigo cultivators. Barns concentrated on one of the permissible grounds of rent increase under the Act—increased cultivation—relying on careful measurement of individual Santal cultivations. Fixation of rent rates on this basis was a sharp break with tradition. Earlier, the Santal headman distributed the zamindar's rent demand among individual families on the basis of 'plough strength' of each family, the assumption being that a given plough strength could sustain a certain amount of cultivation. A similarly striking breach with tradition was Barns' plan to treat forest products as part of the Hendwah estate property and to encroach on the customary forest rights of Santals and even on their 'sacred groves', which their cultural tradition had regarded as inviolable.[64] His most daring innovation was in reinterpreting the source of the headman's authority, redefining his relationship with the estate owner and converting him into an instrument of his power. He found the attitude of the local administration greatly encouraging. The Assistant-Commissioner, Taylor, bluntly told the restive Santals that 'capabilities of the villages' actually justified a larger rent increase and sternly warned them that any 'riotous assembly' against Barns was 'not allowable'.[65] The official tolerance of his exacting methods partly explains how he could go as far as he actually did. In fact the compromise the local administration arranged to pacify rebel Santals did not question at all the propriety of his methods. It merely asked Barns to be content with an increase of 25 per cent in rent. Despite its obvious excessiveness under the circumstances the government regarded Barns' consent to it as evidence of his 'good feeling and liberal and benevolent spirit'.[66]

The initial non-regulation experiment (1856-1863) did not, therefore, mean any honest attempt on the part of the government to preserve the traditional Santal institutions. With the formal abandonment of the experiment (1863-1872) matters naturally worsened.

This was particularly evident from the deepening crisis in the Santal *manjhi* system originating from the persistent attempts of zamindars to build up a social base of their power by having a community of loyal headmen. Barns did not present a consistent theoretical defence of his step in this direction. The defence came later from European zamindars or managers. The petition (187.) of leading Santal Parganas zamindars was, notably, a reaction to what appeared to them as an ominous rethinking by the Government of Bengal on the Santal rent question and the actual status of the *manjhi*.[67] The central assumption of the defence was the indistinguishability of the *manjhi* from an *ijaradar* in zamindari estates elsewhere, i.e., a person temporarily entrusted with rent collection and the consequent justifiability of his replacement by persons of zamindars' choice. The petition did not deny the derivation of the status of a *manjhi* from his vital role in the Santal village organization, but argued that the old order had only marginally survived the developments following the 1855 insurrection, such as the death and flight of many a headman, their replacement by others, wholly dependent for their position on zamindars' favour, and the appreciable weakening of the Santal village organization in general.

The ruthless pacification measures of the state caused the death and the migration of very many Santals, including *manjhis*. However, with the restoration of 'order' many of them did gradually return. The systematic replacement of old *manjhis* on a considerable scale, at least in some particular estates, was more a result of the zamindar's rent offensive, occurring mostly in the 1860s, than of deaths and migration of *manjhis* during the rebellion of 1855.

The success of zamindars largely depended on the formal approval of their actions by the local administration. Indeed, its first crucial decisions on the *manjhi* question, mostly influenced by the zamindar's point of view, perpetuated the half-truths on which the pretensions of zamindars rested. In a rare moment of stern self-criticizm the government of Campbell (1871-74) admitted that 'the administration of the law' in the 1860s 'has been tinctured' by the strong pro-zamindar sentiments then prevailing in Bengal.[68]

The first major judgement (1862) on the *manjhi* question, that of Money, the Santal Parganas Commissioner, was not based on any enquiry into the complex question of the status of a Santal *manjhi*. One of his central assumptions was the non-existence of any community of interests and the absence of any bond between the *manjhi* and Santal cultivators. To him the *manjhi* was none other than a *mustajir*, holder of a short-term 'rent-farming' lease, whose primary motive in taking the lease was promotion of private gains. On the other hand, he argued, Santal cultivators were not obliged to share the increased rent demanded of the *manjhi* by the zamindar. That the cultivators behaved differently was attributed to their 'stupidity'. The Santals 'as a rule, consider their lot and the manjees' lot as bound up together'.[69] Having assumed the identity of a *manjhi* and a *mustajir*, Money concluded that the demand of increased rent by the zamindar was legitimate and went as far as to say that denial of the zamindar's right in this regard 'would be to perpetuate a mode of tenure which may in time prove unsuited to the improvement and progress of the country'.[70] This new trend in official perception was precisely the reaffirmation of the validity of the notion of Santal collectively, with the *manjhi* having an ascriptive role in it. 'When a Sonthal hive settles in the jungle to clear a location and establish a village', wrote Campbell, 'the manjee is to the Sonthal hive what the Queen Bee is to the hive of bees; they cannot get on without him'.[71] The Birbhum Magistrate, Allen, analysed the cultural implications of preserving this 'regularly organized community': 'it is almost entirely owing to the vitality of this system of village rule that the Sonthals have not been absorbed long ago amongst low-caste Hindoos'.[72]

The Santal history in the post-insurrection period till about 1871-72 thus shows how, contrary to the views of Hunter, Bradley-Birt, Carstairs, Somers and others, opportunities for the Santals to 'live according to their tradition' steadily diminished. The Santal society was being increasingly exposed to new economic and political forces, which tended to undermine their traditional institutions. When the non-regulation experiment was abandoned during 1863-1872, the government did not perhaps think it feasible to segregate artificially the Santal society from such adverse alien influences and contracts. Nor did it regard the Santal economy and society as an ideal organization to be preserved at any cost. As a result, the forces operating here were too powerful for the state to contain. Having only a marginal role in the economy, the state only occasionally sought to control and regulate social relations generated by the new economic forces. On the other hand, the initiative of the state was continually being hamstrung by its preconceptions about the limits of the permissible regulation, preconceptions formed out of its experiences in the non-tribal areas.

This was partly the reason why the revival of the non-regulation system[73] in 1872 failed to create the right conditions for the Santals 'to live according to their tradition'. By then, the alien domination was too firmly entrenched to be casually meddled with. The government did not opt for any radical plan of breaking away from the established order. Its measures were half-hearted from the beginning. The lost lands of Santals were not retrieved. Nor were the dispossessed *manjhis* reinstated. Nothing was done toward moderating the recent rent increases. This innate official conservatism, i.e., the reluctance to face the consequences of questioning the propriety of alien domination, prevented the government from looking beyond the immediate present. Indeed, the particular form of its intervention complicated matters for the Santals in respect of all the three major questions that deeply worried the government: rent, status of the *manjhi* and rural credit.

The government did admit the propriety of rent increase but merely sought to state the principle governing the increase in order to remove the prevailing uncertainty in this regard, which it attributed to lack of precise knowledge about the size and quality of family holdings. This uncertainty had much to do with the nature of Santal agricultural settlements. Santals, mostly migrants, were permitted by zamindars to reclaim wasteland in their estates, and rent was fixed on the entire block of new cultivation, without reference to the size of individual holdings and the quality of the lands included therein. Only an elaborate survey, the government felt, would remove the uncertainty. However, the survey, as later official reports revealed, was rather casually done. Apart from its 'extreme roughness',[74] the survey, later derided as 'survey at a glance' (*nazarpaimash*), worked on a basic premise that the existing rent quantum would by no means be reduced. The Santals suffered all the more because of the 'finality' of the survey, i.e., impermissibility of 'reopening' the rent question through local law courts.

The government intervention in the *manjhi* question was a positive step in that it rejected the interpretation of the status of a *manjhi* merely as that of a functionary of the zamindari bureaucracy and regarded a *manjhi* as an inseparable part of the Santal village organization. In practice the intervention only marginally repaired the damage done to *manjhis*. Dispossessed *manjhis* were rarely restored. Though appointments of headmen, all made by the government after 1872, were in principle restricted to 'village residents' and 'representative villagers', the norm could easily be evaded. It was enough for an outsider to have a minimal link with the village and yet qualify as a headman; his main 'artifice' was 'maintaining a house in the village and paying occasional visits to it'.[75] Even where 'representative villagers' were taken in the role they were now expected to perform, its context contributed a great deal to the process of deformity in the institution of headmanship. Now 'reckoned as a public official, under the control of the Deputy Commissioner', the headman was fast becoming a vital component of the authority of the colonial state slowly penetrating to the village level. The powers that the new system after 1872 created for the headman were unprecedented. The nature of the 'compensations' for the headman's role in the administration made him feel that he had a vital stake in holding on to his position. The traditional practice of the Santal village of allowing him control over a part of the village land (*manjhi man*) was continued. If he so chose, he could now rent at half the usual rates the land reclaimed by other Santals. Another of his 'chief prerogatives' now was the 'commission' of about 6.4 per cent of the rent collection from the village. The *manjhi* thus tended to develop interests which were not quite consistent with the interests of the village. As a measure of such 'vested interests' we may take the size of the village land actually controlled by headman in addition to the traditionally sanctioned *manjhi man*. While at about the beginning of the twentieth-century the proportion of the latter of the total village area was only 0.9 per cent, that of 'private holding' was 11.9 per cent.[76] Naturally, the headmen's families could not provide the necessary labour for the direct cultivation of the whole of the 'private' lands. Renting out part of them, therefore, involved the emergence of a kind of relationship of subordination within the Santal society itself. The headman's domination may not have been institutionalized in the form of definitive land control, but he could use his powers, particularly those deriving from his status as a 'government servant', to promote his personal interests.

In the light of this discussion we may now tentatively answer the question whether the headman could be regarded as an 'authority' or a 'leader'.[77] Authority is 'associated with a person holding a prestigious status or position in an organized setting in which structural relations of superordination and subordination have become institutionalized or habitual'. In this sense it does not apply to the Santal headman, despite the fact that his new powers and his 'prerogatives' as a lynchpin of the village-level authority of the Raj created a distance between him and the villagers. On the other hand, this sense of distance tended to take away from the headman's role as the traditional leader, the role being essentially one of fulfilling some well-understood communal norms.

It was the question of rural credit that the government found most baffling. The reasons are two-fold. The problem was part of the wider question of Santal agricultural organization, in which the government had only a marginal role. Still more negligible was its role in providing credit to needy Santals. On the other hand, it could do precious little towards containing the moneylenders' growing powers.

The intervention of the government was largely determined by the changing forms of moneylenders' appropriations in the 1870s and later: their increasing reliance on acquisition of Santal lands, the diminishing importance of extra-legal coercions and of exploitation of bonded labour as modes of debt realization. The 'settlement' of 1872[78] greatly stimulated land transfers, which rarely occurred earlier. Its definition of 'raiyati rights' made Santal landholding a commodity of considerable market value. A report of 1882 noted that 'the bazar traders of Dumka had gradually absorbed all the Sonthal settlements in the vicinity and that a considerable proportion of the lands of cultivators in the great *tuppah* of Handwe, with an area of 450 square miles, had passed into the hands of their creditors'.[79] Realizing as it did the implications of the phenomenon —'disruption of primitive communities, the loss of the position of village chiefs and the degradation of the raiyats' —the government hesitated to intervene. In 1883 it contemplated prohibition of 'all transfer of raiyati interest', but refrained from taking the final step. This indecisiveness on the part of government helped moneylenders consolidate their domination. Its firmness would surely have emboldened the Santals to question the legality of the transfers in the courts and deterred the moneylenders from going as far as they did. For instance, when Forbes, the impetuous Deputy Commissioner of Santal Parganas (1884-86), indiscriminately set aside the transfers on the assumption that 'all alienations of their lands by Sonthals were illegal', 'there was a rush all over the district to institute suits. Cattle, ornaments, household goods were sold to buy court stamps and thousands of plaints were filed'.[80] However, the Bengal government restrained Forbes before long, nullifying 'some of the orders founded on the new doctrine'. It only allowed the Deputy-Commissioner to exercise his discretion in annulling (1887) improper sales.

The strength of the moneylenders' position in the Santal village is evident from their reactions to this new threat. They did not directly flout the government decision, but had recourse to subterfuges. Transfers did take place but in other forms. The 'most common disguise' was a kind of mortgage. For the success of another strategem the village headman's complicity was crucial. The indebted Santal formally abandoned his holding to the headman, who, in collusion with the moneylender, 'resettled' it with him. 'Both of these were as good to the mahajan as outright sales?'[81] By about the end of the nineteenth-century McPherson, Settlement Officer of the Santal Parganas, thus described 'the result of all this continuous assault and encroachment on village lands': 'there are very few villages . . . in which the mahajan has not obtained a footing . . . the mahajan is now, in nine cases out of ten, the co-villager, and intending vendor and one knows how very little pressure is necessary on the part of the mahajan to convert an indebted raiyat into an intending vendor'.[82]

The increasingly assertive mood of the moneylenders resulting from their growing strength was reflected in their persistent clamour for removing all formal constraints on free sales of Santal lands. Some officers, presumably influenced by this plea, pointed out the untenability of the old assumption of the proponents of the non-regulation system that the Santal country could be insulated from the disruptive alien forces. Their major emphasis was on the fast changing demographic and economic scenes of the Santal Parganas. Bompas, Commissioner of the Bhagalpur Division and Santal Parganas, thus argued the point.

> . . . the population of the Sonthal Parganas is not composed solely of simple Santals and wily mahajans. The Sonthals number only one-third of the population....The considerable non-aboriginal population desires that *jotes* (landholdings) should be transferable not mainly out of the wicked desire to usurp their neighbour's lands, but because of the convenience of being able to realize money from property which has an actual money value in the market.[83]

The Bengal government disapproved of Bompas' plea for making Santal holdings freely salable. It did not argue that the proponents of free sales had misrepresented the nature of moneylenders' control over the Santal village. It felt the worst had yet to happen and that the damage done to the Santal society and economy by the intrusion of alien elements could still be repaired. The government stand also betrayed a feeling of nervousness in coping with the uncertainty created by exposing the Santal society to unrestricted market forces.

The post-insurrection administrative system, known as the non-regulation system, thus scarcely enabled the Santals to preserve their right to live by their own traditions and under their own leadership in a region they called their own.

The material conditions of the Santals were far worse in the Regulation area. This had much to do with the 'enclave' nature of the Santal agricultural settlements there, i.e., the fact that the Santals constituted here only a small segment of the total population, except in a few pockets of dense Santal habitation. This meant that the Santal economy came to be increasingly encapsulated before long in the wider economy of the region. As a consequence, the easier availability of at least a part of the required labour force in the immediate neighbourhood enabled zamindars and moneylenders to replace the Santals who were not willing to cultivate land on their terms. The universally communal nature of Santal settlements, i.e., concentration of Santals as an ethnic group in a cluster of villages and the rarity of dispersed Santal settlements also meant that alien domination affected them as a collectivity. The communal nature of the settlements determined the nature of an aspect of alien aggression on them: replacement, as far as possible, of Santal headmen by persons loyal to the alien zamindars, and the zamindars' success in this largely depended on the extent of breakdown of the headmen system (also known as *pradhani* or *mandali* in some places).

Numerous official reports provide ample evidence of the progressive disintegration of the system and the growing strength of moneylenders' control over the Santal society and economy. Only a bare mention of some of them is possible here because of considerations of space.

The first scathing exposure of the failure of the administration to protect the Santals came in 1871 from the Birbhum magistrate Allen.[84] He vividly describes the rapid decay of the Santal village system. The increasing destitution of the Santals struck him all the more because of the overwhelming evidence he came across of the decisiveness of the Santal enterprise in the growth of cultivation in the region. Convinced that the vitality of the village system would considerably counter the alien assaults on Santal villages he suggested its legal recognition, forcefully arguing that unless this was done Santals 'would altogether disappear as a distinct people, and become mere hewers of wood and drawers of water to the Hindoos tacked to the tail of the system in the very lowest caste'. The government was not at all enthusiastic about the suggestion. Investigations in Birbhum in 1907-08 showed that the process of loss of Santal lands had reached, nearly everywhere, a pretty advanced stage. While camping near Suri, the Birbhum Collector Foster 'spoke to a large number of Santals and found that most of them had lost their lands to moneylenders'.[85] A local missionary Skrefsrud, claiming familiarity with the Santals 'for more than forty years', also found that 'many Sonthals become' as a result '*kisanis* (day labourers) or *bhagdars* (sharecroppers) of their own lands'. Finding all sources of fresh loans closed 'they run away to Burdwan, to Murshidabad and become servants to Hindus and Mohammadans, go to Malda or Dinajpur district, where there are about 100,000 Sonthals settled during the last 25 years, and finally they go to the tea gardens and are lost'.[86]

The local missionaries particularly noted the significant communal implications of the increasing loss of land, showing how the loss tended to weaken the cultural basis of the feeling of communal solidarity, particularly where the loss cut the Santals adrift from an organized community and forced them to try their luck elsewhere, primarily as isolated individuals. The Reverend A.L. Kennan noted how the absence of 'the restraint of the village organization to which they have been accustomed is rapidly lowering the morals of the community'.[87] Skrefsurd found that Santals were now so "dead to exclusiveness' that they 'even intermix with *Domes* and Muhammadans in sexual inter-course'.[88]

McAlpin's *Report on the conditions of the Santals*...(1909) is far more authoritative. His enquiry covered the major Santal tracts outside the Santal Parganas and the information it provided had a fairly reliable statistical base. This is particularly true of his analysis of the question of the extent of survival of the village system. As an indicator of the continuity of the traditional village organization McAlpin considered the numerical strength of the 'intact' villages, i.e., villages where the old headmen still continued to pay rent to the zamindars, distinguishing them from 'broken' villages where 'the landlord ceases to take his rent through the manjhi and recognises each Sonthal as a separate raiyat...'[89] Of the 175 villages 'examined' in Birbhum 105 were found 'broken'. About 53 per cent of the Santal villages surveyed in Bankura then belonged to this category. In fact in several parts of the district 'the Sonthal headman system is merged in the Mandali system, *common to all castes and tribes*'.[90] In Midnapur he examined the extent of survival of *man* lands, i.e., rent-free lands allotted to Santal village functionaries, including the headman. 'In all the areas under report', he found, 'the existence of *man* land, except in isolated cases, is now practically defunct'.[91] Two major findings of McAlpin in regard to the origins of 'broken' villages were the recentness of the practice of removal of headmen and the crucial role of moneylenders in the process in very many places. The removals occurred mostly in the second half of the nineteenth century.

The process of decay of the village system in the Midnapur Zamindari Company's estate, the extensive Silda Pargana of Midnapur, was different primarily because of the distinctiveness of the estate management by the Company. A characteristic feature of the management was the pronounced 'business' orientation of the Company. Once a thriving commercial concern having a considerable investment in silk and indigo, the Company gradually transferred its capital to zamindari with the increasing unviability of the two commercial enterprises and primarily concentrated on securing as large a rental income as possible. This reorientation in the Company's objectives was reflected in the changing nature of the authority the Company became keen to exercise: change from its status as a mere *ijaradar* (temporary leaseholder) in parts of the Silda estate to that of a landed proprietor. The rather slow process of acquisition of the proprietary status was completed in 1908, when the Company purchased the whole of it at the public auction. The circumstances, such as the continuing squabbles in the old zamindari family, the resultant mismanagement of the estate and the crippled state of the zamindari finances, which helped the Company gradually fasten its stranglehold on the estate, also bore on its later plan of optimizing its rental income from it. The incompetent estate management by the old family precluded any coordinated efforts towards revision of the rent rates. The Company, called Messrs. Watson & Co. at the time it got its first *ijara* in the estate (1861), being primarily interested in promoting its silk and indigo manufacture, had generally ignored the question of rent revision. It was the depressed market of the two products that prompted it to find out means of increasing the rental income. It was encouraged in this by the considerable increase in cultivation since its arrival in the estate in the 1860s, due to the growing Santal population and the increasing commercial value of forest products following the growth of railways and the general widening of the market. Permissibility of rent increase under the Bengal Tenancy Act (1885) also helped the Company. It set about applying legal sanctions far more consistently in the case of '*mandali*' villages (which constituted the majority of the Santal villages here), where zamindars received rent through the mediation of mandals. The Company distinguished between a *manjhi* and a mandal, claiming that unlike the former, a mandal was essentially an enterprising middleman, entering into an agreement with the zamindar to reclaim a specified area of waste land and arranging for the reclamation by inducing fellow-Santals to migrate here, so that he regarded the Santal cultivators as his 'tenants'. The tenancy laws treated such a middleman as a 'tenureholder' and empowered the zamindar to redefine rent relations with him, leaving it to him to readjust his rent relations with the subordinate cultivators.

The Company exploited the laws to their utmost extent, removing the mandals if it suited its purpose, and taking in outsiders, partly Bengalis and partly *Kurmi* Mahatos and others. The Santal headmen questioned the interpretation that the mandali status was a purely personal one deriving from the mandal's role as a middleman in the reclamation process, arguing that Santal settlements had seldom occurred in this way. The exception—the emergence of a community of resourceful middlemen and the development of a 'dependent relationship' between them and the Santal migrants, was probably a later development, in the process of which the original role of headmen was distorted or altogether new people replaced the old Santali headmen.

V

We now try to answer, with reference to the Munda/Oraon society, the question we have indicated earlier: to what extent was this society, which had ceased to be stateless long before the beginning of British rule, affected by its increasing encapsulation in the new colonial polity and economy? Here again we would concentrate on the relations of power in the tribal village and examine if any new attributes had appeared during British rule.

In order to answer the question we first need to characterize the pre-colonial developments in this respect. The way the Munda political system, i.e., Nagbangshi Raj, had evolved did impinge on the tribal village society. However, the leading authorities on the Munda/Oraon history do not seem to have a clear idea of its nature.

An aspect of the process of consolidation of the Nagbangshi Raj is identifiable with reasonable certainty: association of the process with the intrusion into the tribal villages of non-tribal outsiders, who were gradually integrated into this authority structure. The attribution of the intrusion to the so-called 'Hinduization process'[92] encouraged by the Nagbangshi Raj, i.e., its conversion to Hinduism and increasing inclination to Hindu social and cultural values, is only partially valid. The Raj family, converted to Hinduism, did encourage settlement of Brahmins, but this was only partly motivated by considerations connected with Hinduization. It was essentially a device for building up a social base of the royal authority. Brahmins had also a role in inventing the appropriate tradition in order to bolster the pretensions of the Raj family to non-tribal descent. Apart from this distinctively political orientation of the cultural process of Hinduization, the coming of outsiders was also an inevitable result of the gradual consolidation of the Nagbangshi political authority, necessitating the creation of the usual apparatus of power: the army, the police and the bureaucracy. Once created, the apparatus tended to proliferate, and outsiders poured in increasing numbers. Since the political authority was vested in the royal family, maintaining the increasing number of its members involved diversion of a portion of the tribal village resources. Emulation by the Raj family of the culture of pomp and orientation from the Mughals and the resultant rise in the cost of its living inevitably increased the scale of this diversion. The outsiders, living in various ways off the surplus of the tribal village, also included dealers in items of luxury for the royal family, gradually developing into creditors, to whom the Raj family, unable to repay their loans from its cash resources, transferred part of its dues from specified villages. In fact in the absence of any effective centrally-controlled machinery for the mobilization of the 'tribute' from the villages, the manner of remunerating the services of other groups was similar: transfer to them of the royal family's claim to tribute.

While the components of the Raj political authority and the typical mode of paying for their services are identifiable, the way the entire process affected tribal society is still not well known. The crucial question is : How did the process affect the access of the tribals to the existing village resources and the old tribal social organization?

The divergent characterizations of the pre-British tribal order by the leading authorities on the Munda/Oraon history testify to their imperfect understanding. J. Reid argued that the arrival of outsiders in the tribal villages had completely disrupted the old tribal order even before the coming of the British.[93] Sarat Chandra Roy similarly analysed the implications of the alien intrusion in terms of the 'disintegration of the ancient land system of Chotanagpur'. He, however, argued that the process occurred first in the Oraon villages and that, on the whole, the Mundas suffered much less. This was attributed to 'the unbending conservatism of the more strong-willed Mundas'.[94] Fidelis de Sa, endorsing more or less Roy's view, emphasized the relatively greater loss suffered by the Oraons.[95] J.C. Jha concludes that the intrusion of outsiders 'inevitably led to the ruin of the tribesmen the original clearers of the land'. He approvingly cited the observation of a British official that, except in a few areas, the village headmen 'were entirely dispossessed and replaced by Suds (foreigners) or their villages taken by the Raja himself'.[96]

Curiously, the empirical part of such studies scarcely corroborates their own conclusions, and indeed, in some cases, contradicts them. Reid's elaborate analysis[97] of the developments affecting the tribal village organization during British rule clearly shows that, though the process of its disintegration did start earlier, it was far from complete by the beginning of this rule. The status of the original village founders (*bhuinhars*) was perceptibly disturbed, he concluded, mainly 'in the first half of the nineteenth-century'. He also admitted that it was only after the 'Kol insurrection' of 1831-32 that 'a considerable disturbance of peasant proprietary tenure undoubtedly occurred'. Roy's evidence, though richer than Reid's, is similarly inconclusive. The evidence concerns the timing of the 'land' grants (*jagirs*) to outsiders, their extent and their particular use by the grantees. Roy could not trace any grant earlier than 1676. Of the number of later grants and about their contents he had no firm data either. His impression in this regard is notable: 'The attacks on the land system of the Mundas and on their rights to the villages that they had themselves established, appear to have commenced in the eighteenth century.[98] His theme of 'disintegration' makes sense only on the assumption that the number of *jagir* grants and the 'attacks' on the tribal villages so abruptly increased during the first six decades of the eighteenth-century as to cause this 'disintegration'. Roy did not explicitly say so. He also pointed out how the 'Panch Parganas', only marginally controlled by the Nagbangshis, mostly lay outside the aliens' sway. Again, even where outsiders secured a firm foothold, concluded Roy, control over the village waste lay with the village community. Jha's contention is based solely on an official document, a 'table of grants' prepared by British officials during the enquiry into the origins of the 1831-32 rebellion. About the manner of the use of the grants by the grantees the document says nothing. If the grants simply meant transfer of the royal income from the villages concerned, they only marginally affected the structure of the tribal organization. A striking feature of Jha's Table is the small number of grants other than those made toward the subsistence of the royal family members and also of the beneficiaries of the Raj patronage of Hinduism, such as Brahmins. Only about 25 per cent of the villages included in the Table belonged to this category. This needs to be stressed in view of the admittedly decisive role of such jagirdars in initiating the 'attacks' on the tribal 'land system'. Jha does not clarify how many of these grants were actually made after the British take-over. K.S. Singh clearly distinguishes between the old grantees, belonging mostly to the royal family and the 'new class of alien jagirdars-zamindars, called *Dikus*, who were granted leases of villages in consideration of their civil, military or religious services, and the *thikadars*'.[99]

It has, thus, not been conclusively established that the evolution of the process of 'state formation, i.e., the evolution of the Nagbangshi political authority, had 'revolutionized' the old tribal 'land system'. However, major trends in the changes resulting from the process are identifiable. 'Hinduization', connected with process, had no impact whatsoever on the tribal culture. Hinduization did not affect tribal social organization either, at least to the extent that a system of rewards for culturally determined communal services (for instance, those of Mundas and *Pahans*) formed a vital part of this organization. Far more important were changes in the 'secular' sphere. Maintenance of the state apparatus necessitated diversion of part of the village resources. The diversion in the form of 'tribute' or 'rent' did not necessarily limit tribal access to such resources, as the tribals continued to control their use parting with only a portion of the product. The villages where this practice prevailed were called *rajhaus*. The villages where the diversion meant loss of this control and consequently impinged on the tribal economy were called *manjhihaus*. The size of *manjhihaus* land is not known. The 'theory' of the German missionaries that: 'The Mundas and Uraons freely gave up half of the fields of their villages for the maintenance of the Raja, when he was first elected' has been rejected by Reid, Ranchi Settlement Officer as: 'there is no evidence whatsoever in support of the theory'.[100] In view of the continuity of the unrestricted tribal access to 'village wastes'[101] the proportion of the *manjhihaus* of the total arable of the village perhaps declined on the assumption that growing population led to reclamation of the wastes. Such lands, again, were mostly cultivated for long by the local tribals. Influx of non-tribal labour, as K.S. Singh has pointed out, occurred mostly in the nineteenth century.[102] The royal family and the outsiders also occasionally requisitioned, without payment, labour of tribals. *Beth-begari*, as the practice was called, was then evidently only partly connected with the cultivation of *manjhihaus* lands. In general, the royal family or its local representatives demanded *begari* on distinctively 'state occasions' when they badly needed it, for instance, movement of the army when heavy baggages had to be carried from place to place. Demand for *begari* was also connected with purely personal needs.

Documentation for studying the changes in the Munda/Oraon society in the colonial period is far more satisfactory. Still, our imperfect understanding of the pre-colonial tribal order renders tentative our characterization of the changes. However, it is at least possible to indicate what had then actually happened.

The initial British intervention in this part of the tribal world only indirectly and marginally affected the tribal village. This is due to its particular background: factional strifes in the royal family, with one of the factions persuading the British to back it against other contenders. The British readily intervened, exacting a price for it — the promise of a much larger revenue payment by the beneficiary of their partisanship. For quite sometime, later interventions too primarily affected the political status of the Raj family.

The decisive British intervention in the tribal village mainly followed the insurrection of 1831-32. Its area continually widened with the intensification of the antagonisms between the tribals and the assorted community of 'aliens'. To the growth of this antagonism eventually exploding in the 1831-32 revolt some administrative and economic measures of the government contributed a great deal.

One was the police reorganization, which made for entry into the tribal village on an increasing number of aliens as police personnel, insufficiently paid and controlled by the local administration. Bitter complaints against their petty exactions were a commonplace of petitions of tribals to local officials. The widening of the 'economic frontier' of the colonial state affected the tribals far more directly and deeply. The state intervention here amounted primarily to regulation of the existing economic organization, entirely with a view to appropriating a portion of the income generated in the economy. Its adverse consequences for the tribals were aggravated by the role of the outsiders who constituted a vital component of the apparatus of this regulation.

Some aspects of this regulation, particularly the salt and opium monopolies, have been characterized by David Washbrook as essentially practices of a 'mercantilist state'.[103] The government believed that elimination of private traders and sales of the two commodities at fixed prices would ensure a sizeable increase in its income. A major implication of the salt monopoly, involving, at certain stages of the retail sale of salt, participation of alien traders, was a sharp rise in the retail prices, the rise being particularly pronounced in the tribal regions because of the absence of an effective marketing network. The opium monopoly adversely affected the Munda region mainly because of the government's drive, since about 1828, to increase opium cultivation as much as possible. Earlier the government was not normally keen on an increase as long as its monopoly ensured, in the context of the growing consumption of the commodity in China, a steady rise in prices in the Chinese market. The rise was inevitably reflected in the auction prices of opium in the Calcutta market, where the government sold all of its monopoly products. The higher the Calcutta auction prices, the greater the government's revenue income. The government had no worry over the matter as long as the monopoly system smoothly worked. The background to the government decision to increase opium cultivation was precisely an apprehension over the growing threat to the Bengal opium monopoly from a rival variety, Malwa opium produced in some 'native states' outside British political control.

In its desperate haste to maximize opium production within the shortest possible time the government was not often careful about choosing the right places for it. The choice of the Munda region was particularly unwise. The tribals here were not familiar with the extremely sophisticated art of opium cultivation, traditionally mostly confined to a particular community of skilled agriculturists, the Koeries. In fact the crop was hardly grown there, unsuitability of the soil being one of the reasons. Tribals now escaped the obligation of growing this exotic and presumably unremunerative crop by handsomely bribing the agencies entrusted with the execution of the government plan. Hence the bitterness of the Mundas with opium and the people seeking to force it on them.

An intervention of far greater significance in the economic organization of tribal villages was taxation of 'country liquor', *handiya*, made nearly in all Munda homes. The assumption behind the taxation was that the Munda produced it for sale and made profit. The taxation was also regarded as a means of reducing their 'drunkenness'. The assumption was wrong. *Handiya* was mostly domestically consumed. Apart from being a mode of relaxation after the day's hard toil, the drink had an important place in the cultural life of the tribal village. The tax was particularly galling because of the mode of its collection, wholly entrusted to outsiders. The collection, normally farmed out to the highest bidders, subjected the tribals to various extortions by the venal tax farmers, eager to make as much out of their office as possible. Munda protests led the government to replace the outsiders by Munda headmen and to abolish the tax where the government was convinced of the exclusively domestic use of *handiya*. The changes brought no real relief to the tribals. Making the headmen part of the imperial system of fiscal control tended to distort the traditional role of the headman and thereby strengthened this system of control. On the other hand, the tax continued to be collected despite its abolition in some special cases.

Currency reform, another instance of state intervention, was not motivated by the prospect of an immediate increase in government income. However, the way it worked in the tribal region involved a decisive role for alien moneylenders and facilitated their control over the local economy. The reform was designed to introduce a standard silver currency in place of the multiple local currencies. Transition to the new monetary system was naturally easier where the local economy had been closely linked with the wider market system. In the tribal regions, having such links only marginally, the non-silver local currencies continued to circulate as a medium of exchange. On the other hand, reduced availability of silver resulting from its reduced inflow, following the severe commercial depression of the time (1829-34), caused a considerable rise in the market price of silver and correspondingly reduced the exchange value of non-silver local currencies. Persons receiving their dues in such currencies subjected the Mundas to a *batta*. The alien moneylenders had a crucial role to play in all the exchange transactions. The depreciation in the exchange value of non-silver local currencies in relation to silver was a nearly universal phenomenon, but was far more pronounced in the Munda region because of the nature of the local economy.

We need to analyse other aspects of the antagonistic relations of power in the Munda village, which formed the background to the insurrection of 1831-32 necessitating the first decisive state intervention in these power relations.

We have indicated the composition of the alien intruders into the tribal village till the beginning of British rule. The rebel violence was, notably, not aimed against all. The worst sufferers, apart from the aliens connected with the British administrative bureaucracy, were a member of the royal family Kuar Harnath, and his 'creatures'. The Raja himself was largely spared. The only Raj property affected by rebel violence was the *bhandar* (directly managed) villages, since storing of village grains received as royal dues facilitated control of the local grain market by the people looking after the grain store, including non-local grain merchants. The control had disastrous consequences for the tribals during food scarcities. The activities of Harnath and his 'creatures' directly hit the relatively influential Mundas, the Mankis,[104] the village headmen and the common cultivators. Harnath replaced several Mankis and headmen and outsiders, mostly dealers in commodities for the royal family's consumption and a major source of credit at the time. The measure was presumably a desperate device for liquidating his accumulating debt to them. Official reports suggest that the practice did not perhaps occur prior to 1809, and the more flagrant cases of 'dispossession' of Mankis occurred after 1818. His financial stringency, which largely explains his desperation, was at least due to the ever-increasing diversion of the royal family's assests to revenue payment and to the maintenance of the new police system. Whatever the origins, Harnath's measure significantly differed from the usual practice of the Raj family in regard to grant of villages to its members and outsiders, which were often merely arrangements for transfer of the Raj dues from the villages to the grantees, and did not, therefore, interfere with the traditional position of Mankis and headmen. The manner in which his 'creatures', generally Hindu traders and Muslim 'revenue farmers', lorded it over the tribal villages worsened matters for them. The tribals particularly resented their coercions, such as seizure of their cattle and crops, outraging of the 'honour' of their wives and sisters and various kinds of public insults.

The origins of the insurrection of 1831-32 are thus unintelligible without an analysis of the *new* sources and types of conflict developing in the tribal villages. Of the framework of conflict, the old Nagbangshi political system did constitute a vital component. However, the conflict tended to develop altogether new attributes. This is illustrated by the particular origins of Harnath's land grants—grants to creditors towards liquidation of his debt or mobilization of resources for tiding over his financial stringency—and also by the manner in which the grantees hastened to remove the traditional Mankis and headmen.

While the rebel objective of eliminating the *Suds* (outsiders) utterly failed, the insurrection created conditions in which they consolidated their position and thereafter carried out fresh assaults on the traditional Munda preserve. British officials later admitted that the 1831-32 revolt was a turning point in this regard. 'It was then that the greatest disturbance of the peasant proprietary tenure occurred', concluded Dalton, Chotanagpur Commissioner.[105] Reid, the Ranchi Settlement Officer, also thought alike.

Initially, the decisive factor was the role of the state. It intervened on a massive scale to put down the revolt, but did little towards containing the counter-offensive of the enemies of the Mundas. Its ruthless pacification measures decisively turned the scale against the rebels: villages were recklessly destroyed, grain stores burnt and cattle driven off. Deaths and panicky flights of harassed Mundas undermined the Munda village system, which formed the foundation of their resistance. Their enemies adroitly exploited the army intervention to terrorize the Mundas. With the beginning of the counter-insurgency measures, as a British official later recalled, 'the zamindars gave out that all the Kols would be cut off or blown away. Many simple people believed, and thinking the government was a friend of the Hindus, fled into the jungles. For a year or two lands in many a village were left fallow for want of cultivation'.[106] The government did not dispel this mischievous rumour. It was at this vulnerable moment for the Mundas that their revengeful landlords 'retaliated severely. Many Kols who had abandoned the country returned in subsequent years; but . . . the *thiccadars* and proprietors refused to give them back their lands'.[107] Particularly vindictive was Harnath. On the other hand, the post-insurrection administrative measures of the government towards rectification of the wrongs suffered by the Mundas were perfunctory. Only the most recently dispossessed Mankis and headmen were reinstated, and nothing was done to make the tormentors of the Mundas mend their ways.

Paradoxically, later too, the Mundas suffered most after their abortive rebellions, with the state playing a similarly crucial role in the process.

The intensity and the scale of the 1831-32 revolt was not noticeable until the beginning of the Birsaite movement in the last week of December 1899. Yet the Munda unrest remained endemic, though till the 1850s we do not see any sign of organized protest. The break in the lull then had much to do with missionary activities among the Mundas and Oraons. While the missionary correspondence does not suggest any large scale movement, it points to a perceptible change in the Munda mentality, the growth of a 'spirit of independence' among the converts and a stubborn refusal to do the zamindars' bidding. An opportunity for zamindars to chastize the obdurate converts and their followers came with the temporary collapse of government authority following the outbreak of the Mutiny. The reckless manner of persecution of the converts points to zamindars' ulterior motive of intimidating them into submission. With the end of the Mutiny the tribals gradually retrieved part of the lost ground. The Christian brotherhood, severely disrupted during the Mutiny, reasserted its 'independence', the major objective being preservation of the communal village organization against the continuing aggression of zamindars. This essentially 'communal orientation' of the aims of the resistance struck contemporary officials and observers. 'They scout with contempt the idea of being actuated by any such notions (redress of individual grievances). They go in boldly to re-establish themselves and their pagan brethren in the position that tradition describes them as holding more than seventy generations ago, when, according to the legend, they first chose a raja to rule over them'.[108] Their toughest fight was for the recovery of the recently lost *bhuinhari* lands, and the battle over land was inevitably a battle over produce, often a violent resistance to the people zamindars had sent to cut and carry away the crops. The strong opposition to increased landlord demand for *begari* was a product of this struggle over land, particularly where zamindars, keen on the cultivation of the very lands they had filched from the tribals, largely depended on this requisitioned labour.

The 1870s saw a marked retreat from the strategy of this direct confrontation and return to the path of 'legal battle'. Its background was the so-called 'Bhuinhari Survey' (1869-80), an ambitious programme of the government to settle conclusively the conflicting claims to the lands called *bhuinhari*. The tribals sincerely believed the survey would help them in establishing their claim. However, despite some gains, they come to form an impression that the government had let them down, as they soon found out how the more resourceful zamindars had tricked them out of their just rights. The complete collapse of faith in the government as a source of justice sharpened the radical orientation of the aims of their movement, which came to be increasingly inspired by the idea that the only form of legitimate political authority was the Munda Raj. It was in such a climate that the charismatic leader Birsa could gradually mobilize the Mundas around the radical slogan of creating an independent Munda polity on the ruins of the existing political authority.

The tribal protest movement owes much to contacts with Christian missionaries. However they did not endorse, let alone actively encourage, it. Evangelical work did necessitate an intimate familiarity with the tribal way of life, but they were careful not to mix up religion with what they called the 'social movement' of the tribals. They were particularly wary where the anti-landlord movement also betrayed a pronounced anti-government stance. They did know of the involvement of some of their converts in such movements, but consistently asserted that such converts were not 'true Christians'. Paradoxically, they even disapproved of collective petitions to government against landlords. The Senior Missionary of the Chotanagpur Mission went as far as to say, in connection with such a petition, that the names of some converts as signatories 'disgrace the petition'.[109]

The usual emphasis on the role of missionaries in the tribal resistance tends to ignore the initiative of the tribals themselves, their perceptions and conscious will. For instance, while missionaries were merely critical of some of landlord practices, the tribals readily concluded that it would be a legitimate step to combine to stop the practices. Contacts with missionaries were all the more encouraging to the tribals as they had not come into contact with any other group of outsiders similarly questioning the legality of the practices. In fact the tribals had, admittedly, no honest religious motive in becoming Christians. They valued their association with the missionaries because of a conviction that they could persuade the British government in India to intervene in their favour. Moreover, since conversion did not mean a break with their old religious faith, it scarcely affected the solidarity of their social organization. Therefore, when the rebel converts sought to mobilize their 'pagan brethren' they did not have any cultural barriers to cross. The influence of Christian teachings on the Birsaite movement (1894-1900) was different in nature. A major source of Birsa's millennial vision was the Biblical notion of the 'second coming' of Christ, with which Birsa became familiar, presumably during the school days in a missionary institution. Here again his concentration on this notion, to the exclusion of many other aspects of Christian teachings, was a conscious choice of his own. It was Birsa who had integrated it into his central concept of a revolutionary change in the Munda world.

It is a misleading view that, if the government had erred at all in its policy decisions regarding tribal resistance, the reason was its ignorance of the complex tribal agrarian system. There is abundant evidence that though fully aware of the steady encroachments of outsiders on tribal lands, the local administration was reluctant to commit itself to any firm policy to counter such aggressions. The grounds on which it justified its stand varied from time to time. In general it feared that 'raking up the past' would be a hazardous step. The alien domination, ran the argument, was too firmly entrenched to be wished away; questioning its basis or its moral propriety might mean plunging the countryside in endless turmoil and violence, and, it was concluded, the government could ill-afford to see it happen. However, the government was half-hearted in redressing even the most recent wrongs suffered by the tribals, for which there was evidence. Here its argument shifted to a new assumption: if zamindars had filched tribal lands, the tribals themselves were not entirely guiltless; they had taken advantage of the confusion of the Mutiny days to appropriate portions of zamindars' demesne lands. The government thus tarred the tribals and the powerful zamindars with the same brush. This assumption of the government vitiated the much-vaunted 'Bhuinhari Survey'.

VI

The major trends in the changing power relations in the tribal society in the second-half of the 19th-century were: intensification of the landlord assaults on the traditional *khuntkatti/bhuinhari* villages; insistence on altogether new determinants of rent demand, which may be taken as an index to the nature of landlord control over non-demesne lands; effective exploitation of the vastly increased demesnes gradually necessitating a marked increase in the employment of the traditional *begari* in their cultivation, and restricted tribal access to forest products and village wastes.

We have analysed earlier the last trend. Here we deal with the rest. As regards the rapid erosion of the *khuntkatti/bhuinhari* status of the tribal villages, the findings of Reid's 'survey and settlement' in the first decade of the twentieth-century reveal the survival of the Mundari *Khunkatti* villages only in small pockets.[110] The size of the Bhuinhari lands, i.e., lands claimed by their present occupants as having been reclaimed by their ancestors, also steadily diminished. The process, evidently dating from pre-colonial times, admittedly quickened after the suppression of the 1831-32 revolt. The outbreak of the Mutiny saw fresh inroads on a large scale on *bhuinhari* villages. The 'law and order' measures of the government had a severely restrictive influence on tribal resistance, which, if prolonged, could have thwarted the inroads. The initiative of the government in 'registration' of *Bhuinhari* tenures greatly contributed, too, to the legitimization and stabilization of the landlord appopriations of such lands. The 'Bhuinhari Survey' scarcely did anything towards restricting the existing power relations in the village; it merely systematically described them. Its arbitrary exclusion of the cases of 'wrongful dispossessions' not occurring 'within the last 20 years' reassured the earlier intruders. Even the losses of tribals during the 20-year period were only partially retrieved. The assumption of the government that the *bhuinhars* were as much to blame as landlords for the recent spate of violence arising out of disputes over *bhuinhari* lands inevitably prejudiced their cause. Their interests were also considerably harmed by the arbitrary pronouncement of the government invalidating the old tribal custom, according to which absence of a tribal from his village, whatever its duration, did not affect his right to his own family holding. The firm decision of the government against the 'reopening' of the 'bhuinhari question' on the ground that it would keep alive the state of rural tension made matters worse. The Survey, therefore, not only legitimized landlord domination, but also perpetuated it. The decisions and findings of the 'Bhuinhari Commissioners' thus amounted to a new code, a corpus of unimpeachable evidence, having behind it the venerable and coercive authority of the state, much too overbearing for the tribals to defy, except under unusual stress.

The slowing of the pace of expansion of the demesnes, partly due to the Bhuinhar Survey and mostly due to the resurgence of tribal counter-offensive, led landlords to concentrate on stabilizing and increasing their income by modernizing the methods of rent increase and exploiting the existing demesnes more effectively. Landlords now adopted the relatively 'modern' grounds of rent increase provided by the Rent Act of 1859, the major justification of rent increase being an expansion of cultivation. This restricted the traditional tribal access to village resources, the arable and the wastes, because the landlords now clearly distinguished between the old and new cultivation. The new cultivation, liable to rent assessment, increasingly became a part of their domain of authority. The distinction was arbitrary as the new cultivation was as much a product of tribal labour as the old. The change was all the more harmful for the tribals as increasing population necessitated cultivation of the inferor and infertile high lands *(tanr)*.

The system of *betbegari* was also being gradually transformed. Two of its major stages were the intensification of the labour demand primarily in connection with the cultivation of demesnes and the increasing unworkability of this coercive system. Complaints of tribals and the official 'proclamations' seeking to control the operation of *begari* clearly show that *begari* was then being mainly employed in agriculture. The 'rules' the government now laid down regarding the optimal permissible amount of *begari* related to various agricultural operations.[111] The context of this striking change was the expansion of the demesnes, particularly since 1831-32, while only a small part of the labour force could be provided by non-tribal peasant migrants from the neighbouring districts. Tenancy, i.e., renting out of the demesnes on a regular basis, was practised on a small scale. Tenancy anyway was not compatible with the system of unpaid labour. Landlords could not avoid dependence on *begari* in the context of the diminishing availability of local labour because of its increasing migration to the mining areas of

Bihar and to the plantation districts of Bengal and Assam, with the recurring scarcities in the 1890s stimulating migration.

The tribals, however, increasingly resisted *begari*. Insistence by zamindars on its utilization in agriculture made the labour process far more demanding and exacting, because of the specific nature of agricultural operations which involved long hours of work, particularly during the sowing and harvesting seasons. The stiffening of the resistance to *begari*, particularly in the later years of the nineteenth-century, was inseparable from the broadening of the social base of the supply of *begari*. Originally, villagers patrilineally connected with the village founders' families were exempted from the labour service, which was mostly provided by the 'non-kin' villagers. In general, persons so obliged were provided with rent-free *betkheta* lands. This discrimination was now ignored. Zamindars now demanded *begari* from altogether new groups, not any longer regarding it as a purely personal service. They insisted that the labour service was part of the obligation connected with land holding.

Zamindars did not possess a coercive system which was efficient enough to enforce *begari* in the face of combined opposition. The only means open to them was the use of physical force. This, obviously, did not work where the whole community had resolved to defy their authority. Anyway, such coercions could not ensure the necessary labour supply for agricultural operations. This precisely was the background to the initiative of the government to commute the labour service into cash payment. Here again, as in the case of *bhuinhari* lands, state intervention amounted to legitimization of landlord appropriations, though in an altered form. This is striking, for the local administration itself was convinced of the 'baneful effects' of the system on agriculture and called it 'this relic of bygone feudal ages'.[112] The government did not end this anachronism but settled for a compromise, which did admit the legitimacy of the *begari* demand, if it was kept within 'limits'. For instance, the Chotanagpur Commissioner Grimley's 'Proclamation' (April 1890), issued at the time of a 'grave threat' to 'law and order', firmly told the tribals of their obligations to provide *begari* for the cultivation of landlords' demesnes, prescribing at the same time the optimal length of labour service. The later commutation scheme of the government was far more favourable to the landlords, as it was based on a computation of the money value of the services rendered at the time. If this partisan measure turned out to be unworkable, the reason was the quiet, determined opposition of the tribals.

VII

This essay has argued that despite its structural similarities with what is called the 'peasant society', the tribal society was distinctive in several ways, and that some elements of its distinctiveness were becoming more pronounced with its encapsulation in the wider political and economic systems during British rule. We have stressed the process of this encapsulation and the failure of the tribal society to adjust to the strains the process had generated. The increasing signs of the gradual disintegration of the old tribal village organization and the distortion of the roles of some of the key institutions and functionaries of the tribal society are taken as an index to this failure.

The emphasis on the distinctiveness of this historically determined social formation even before British rule leads to the conclusion that 'tribe' was neither a 'white construction', nor just a 'black imagining'. The colonial authority did not construct a non-existent entity, but merely described the existing one. For instance, British officials described the Santals as 'Saotars', 'Santars', presumably borrowing the local name for the group. Other features of the description are also notable: their skill as waste reclaimers and as practitioners of 'plough cultivation'; exclusiveness of their habitations in the village and their distance from caste Hindu concentrations; the 'communal' nature of their social organization, with the headman playing a crucial role in it; their animistic religious beliefs; alleged possession of the power of 'witchcraft' and the total absence of the hierarchical caste organization of the Hindus. Perhaps the only construct that continued to influence official judgement on the Santal culture was its 'inferiority' to the civilization of the Hindus.

The notion of 'tribe' was not the product of 'black imagining' either. The perception of this identity had distinct historical roots: memories of collective agricultural settlements, language, religious beliefs including 'creation myths' and folklore. However, the perception was scarcely static but was being enriched, particularly by the increasing awareness of the tribals about their adversaries and by the overriding need to build up an effective resistance against them. The growing sense of an ethnic identity was thus inseparable from the intensification of this collective protest movement.

NOTES

1. Eric Stokes, *The Peasant and the Raj: Studies in agrarian society and peasant rebellion in colonial India* (Cambridge Univ. Press, 1978), p. 65. For a detailed discussion of this trend in the historiography of agrarian changes in British India see B.B. Chaudhuri, 'Trends in the recent studies in the agrarian history of colonial India', in T. Banerjee (ed), *Indian Historical Research since Independence* (Naya Prakash. Calcutta, 1986), Part II, pp. 1-77.
2. E. Stokes, ibid., p. 262
3. C. Geertz, *Agricultural Involution: The Process of Ecological Change in Indonesia* (Berkeley, 1968) quoted in Stokes, ibid., p. 262.
4. Neil Charlesworth, *Peasants and Imperial Rule: Agriculture and agrarian society in the Bombay Presidency, 1850-1935* (Cambridge, 1985).
5. Ibid., ch. 6.
6. C.A. Bayly, *Indian Society and the Making of the British Empire* (The New Cambridge History of India, Cambridge, 1987), pp. 136-37.
7. Ibid., p. 140.
8. Ibid., p. 146. As causes of the loss he mentions: 'the pressures of the land revenue and of agricultural depression'.
9. The phrase is used here in a broad sense. The changes in the tribal region were not necessarily attributable to direct imperial intervention.
10. C.A. Bayly, *op. cit.*, pp. 142-44.
11. Andre Beteille, *Six Essays in Comparative Sociology* (Delhi, 1974), ch. 'Tribe and Peasantry'.
12. '...if there is any single category of Indian peasants who have been exploited from 'outside' for over a century, it is the Oraon, Munda, Santal villages of Chota Nagpur, and tribal agriculturists in India as a whole'. Ibid., p. 66.
13. Ibid., p. 66.
14. Ibid., p. 69. The tribals in control of a *khuntkatti* village were descendants in the male line of its founder.
15. Ibid., p. 71.
16. He has argued the point with reference to Africa. What follows is based on his lecture in the Department of History, Calcutta University, in February, 1990. In his essay 'The Invention of Tradition in Colonial Africa' Eric Hobsbawm and T. Ranger (eds.), *The Invention of Tradition*, Cambridge, 1983, Ch.6, Professor Ranger argues how the concept of empire, which was 'central to the process of inventing tradition within Europe itself' during the last three decades of the nineteenth century, took on, when deployed in Africa many parts of which became colonies of white settlement, a peculiar character'. p. 211.
17. This means the emergence of central authority which tribal villages, for various reasons, came to accept as a legitimate authority.
18. *Infra*, Section (V).

19. It is difficult to fix the periods of successive Munda settlements. See Sarat Chandra Roy, *The Mundas and their country* (Asia Publishing House, New York, 1970 edn., first edn., 1921), chs. III-IV.
20. Fidelis de Sa, *Crisis in Chotanagpur* (Bangalore, 1975, Redemptorist Publication), pp. 6-7; Sarat Chandra Roy, *op.cit.*, ch. 3.
21. *Papers Relating to Chotanagpur Agrarian Disputes* (Printed for official use), vol. 1, p. 47, para 52.
22. Fidelis de Sa, *op.cit*, p. 22.
23. See f.n. No 21, p. 46, para 36.
24. Sarat Chandra Roy, *op. cit.*, pp. 228-233.
25. *Infra*, Section (IV).
26. For a summary of the debate on the question between Louis Dumont and David Pocock on the one hand and M.N. Srinivas on the other, see M.N. Srinivas, *The Dominant Caste and other Essays* (Delhi, 1987), ch. 1, pp. 39-55.
27. Ibid., p. 40.
28. The effectiveness of this sense of solidarity, Srinivas argues, was contingent on two things: the dominant castes consistently followed certain common values and protected the interests of the village as a whole, and secondly, a general acceptance of caste, and of the idiom of caste in governing relationships between individuals and between groups'. Ibid., pp. 45, 57.
29. *Supra,* Section 2.
30. D. Schwerin, 'The control of land and labour in Chotanagpur, 1858-1908', D. Rothermund and D.C. Wadhwa (eds.), *Zamindars, Mines and Peasants* (New Delhi, 1978).
31. Ramachandra Guha, *The Unquiet Woods: Ecological change and Peasant resistance in the Himalaya* (Delhi, 1989), p. 28.
32. McPherson, H., *Final Report on the survey and settlement operations in district Santal Parganas* (Calcutta, 1907), paras 21-24.
33. J. Reid, *Final Report on the survey and settlement operation in district Ranchi* (Calcutta, 1910).
34. *Papers relating to Chotanagpur Agrarian Disputes*, 1, p. 23; Chotanagpur Commissioner to Government of Bengal, 23 Dec. 1871, para 15.
35. J. Reid, *op. cit.*, p. 4.
36. D. Schwerin, *op. cit.*, p. 29. J. Reid found that in some parts of the district 'the cultivation is sporadic and the yield uncertain. In the more remote and jungly area *tanr* lands are cultivated frequently only one in every two or even three years'.
37. For instance, the revolts in Tamar of Chotanagpur (1819-20), the Bhagirath movement (1874-75) in the Santal Parganas and the Birsa movement in Chotanagpur (1899-1900).
38. Ibid., para 20.
39. Reid carried out his 'settlement' work roughly in the first decade of the

twentieth century.

40. F.B. Bradley-Birt, *Chotanagpur, A little known Province of the Empire,* (London, 1910), p. 2.
41. Reid, *op. cit.*, para 295.
42. *Infra*, Section (VI).
43. Quoted in H. McPherson, *op. cit*, para 21, p. 31.
44. Ibid., para 25.
45. Bengal Judicial Progs., 14 Feb. 1856, No. 157. Final Report by Bidwell, Special Commissioner for the Suppression of the Santal Insurrection, 10 Dec., 1855.
46. F.B. Bradley-Birt, *The Story of an Indian Upland*, pp. 166-177; G. E. Somers, *The Dynamics of Santal Traditions in a Peasant Society* (New Delhi, 1977), ch. 3. The emphasis on the so-called 'pleasure principle' and 'gay life' of the tribals as the crucial factor in their credit ties is a commonplace of anthropological literature on tribal societies in India.
47. Bengal Judicial Progs. 14 Feb. 1856, No. 159; Captain Sherwill's letter to Bhagalpur Commissioner, 24 July 1855, para 4.
48. Ibid.
49. Ibid., 14 Feb. 1856, No 157.
50. Ibid.
51. Ibid., 9 Nov. 1854, No 85; Bhagalpur Commissioner's letter of 9 Aug. 1854 enclosing an extract from the Bhagalpur Magistrate's letter (para 5).
52. The incident probably took place on 7 or 8 July 1855.
53. R. Carstairs, *The Little World of an Indian District Officer* (London, 1912), book IV, ch. 2.
54. W.W. Hunter, *The Annals of Rural Bengal* (London, 1883); Reprint, (Calcutta, 1965), pp. 133-34.
55. Bradley-Birt, *The Story of an Indian Upland* etc., *op.cit.*, pp. 214-16.
56. Somers, *op. cit.*, p. 51.
57. Bengal Judicial Progs. 23 Aug. 1855, No. 150. The commissioner's 'Proclamation' arguing this point was dated 18 July 1855.
58. Ibid., 10 Jan. 1856, No. 58.
59. Ibid., 15 Aug. 1856, No. 178; Deputy-Commissioner's letter 26 June 1856.
60. Ibid., Santal Parganas Commissioner to Govt. of Bengal, 3 July 1865, para 39.
61. Bengal Land Rev. Progs. Dec. 1902, Nos. 5-6; H. McPherson, Settlement Officer, Santal Parganas to Director of Land Records and Agriculture, 7 July 1902, paras 5-6.
62. A large number of the estates coming under the control of the Court of Wards were financially embarrassed.
63. Bengal Judicial Progs. July 1861, No. 262; Offg.-Commissioner, Santal Parganas to Govt. of Bengal, 27 May 1861, para 6.
64. Ibid., May 1861, No 552; Examination of Soonder Manjhi by Deputy-

Commissioner; Santal parganas, 9 May 1861. Soonder was then the *Parganite* of Nowadee.

65. The Offg.-Commissioner of Burdwan called Soonder 'a notorious bad character'. Bengal Judicial Progs. May 1861, No. 544, Plowden, Offg. Commissioner of Burdwan, 7 May 1861.
66. Ibid., No. V 1861, No. 129; Secretary to the Govt. of India to Govt. of Bengal, 14 Nov. 1861, para 4.
67. Ibid., Dec. 1871, Nos. 159-160.
68. Ibid., July 1871, No. 158; Secretary to the Govt. of Bengal to Govt. of India, 1 July 1871, para 10.
69. Ibid., July 1871, No. 159; Demi-Official letter from Money, 21 June 1871, para 4.
70. Ibid., July 1871, No. 162, Commissioner's 'Order' on the case Pertoo Manjee Versus Ram Kamal; Appendix C of Bhagalpur Commissioner's letter, 26 June 1871.
71. Ibid., Dec. 1871, No. 161; Govt. of Bengal to Govt. of India, 6 Dec. 1871, para 16.
72. Ibid., May 1872. Allen's report of 23 Jan. 1872.
73. Its immediate background was the apprehension of a serious Santal uprising in July 1871. Ibid., July 1871, No 163; Wood, Dy.- Commissioner, Santal Parganas to Santal Parganas Commissioner, 4 July, 1871.
74. H. McPherson, *op. cit.*, para 57. Carstairs, entrusted later with the 'Revision Settlement' here, cut carping jokes at this survey. Carstairs, *op. cit.*, pp. 240-41.
75. McPherson, *op. cit.*, para 90.
76. Ibid., para 76.
77. G.E. Somers, *op. cit.*, pp. 100-101.
78. The Settlement followed the revival of the Non-Regulation system; it mostly concentrated on the rent and credit questions.
79. McPherson, *op. cit.*, para 37.
80. Carstairs, *op. cit.*, p. 262.
81. McPherson, *op. cit.*, para 39.
82. Bengal Land Rev. Progs., April 1904, Nos. 11-12; McPherson's letter to the Commissioner of Santal parganas and Bhagalpur, 30 July 1901, para 6.
83. Ibid., April 1908 Nos. 76-77; C.H. Bompas, Commissioner of Santal Parganas and Bhagalpur to the Govt. of Bengal, 28 Oct. 1907.
84. The background to his investigation was the 'vague rumours of discontent among the Santals' and a widespread fear among the 'Bengali traders and others who had been dealing with them'.
85. Bengal Rev. Progs. Nov. 1907, Nos. 90-91; Foster, Birbhum Collector, to Burdwan Commissioner, 15 March 1907, para 1.
86. Ibid., No. V 1908, Nos. 94-95; Skresfsur to Birbhum Collector, 28 Jan, 1908, para 2.
87. Ibid., Nov. 1907, No. 60; Kennan to Govt. of Bengal, 31 July 1906, para 2.

88. The *Doms* were a section of low-caste untouchable Hindus.
89. M. McAlpin, *Report on the condition of the Sonthals in Birbhum, Bankura, and North Balasore,* (Calcutta, 1909), para 41.
90. Ibid., para 54. Under the Mandali system the headman need not, therefore, necessarily have been a Santal.
91. Ibid., para 41.
92. J.C. Jha, The *Tribal Revolt of Chotanagpur, 1831-32* (Patna, 1987), pp. 130-31.
93. Reid supervised the elaborate 'settlement' work in the Ranchi district following the suppression of the Munda movement led by Birsa (1900).
94. *The Mundas and their Country, op. cit.*, p. 91.
95. *Crisis in Chotanagpur* (Bangalore, 1975, Redemptorist Publication), pp. 36, 37-38.
96. Jha, *op. cit.*, pp. 130-31 & 36.
97. Reid, *op. cit.*, para 80.
98. S.C. Roy, *op. cit.*, p. 97.
99. K.S. Singh, *Dust Storm and Hanging Mist: Story of Birsa Munda and his Movement* (Calcutta, 1966), p. 2.
100. Reid, *op. cit.*, para 80.
101. Roy, *op. cit.*, p. 95.
102. K.S. Singh, *op. cit.*, p. 2.
103. D.A. Washbrook, 'Law, State and Agrarian Society in Colonial India', C. Baker, G. Johnson and A. Seal (eds.), *Power, Profit and Politics* (Cambridge University Press, 1981), pp. 661-62.
104. A Manki was in charge of a cluster of villages, while a Munda was normally in charge of a village.
105. E.T. Dalton, Chotanagpur Commissioner to Govt. of Bengal, Rev. Dept. 23 Dec. 1871, para 5. *Papers Relating to Chotanagpur Agrarian Disputes Act*, vol. 1, p. 81.
106. Rakhal Das Haldar, 'An Account of the Village System of Chotanagpore', undated; (presumably written in the latter part of the 1870s). *Papers Relating* to etc. vol. 1, p. 105.
107. Reid, *op. cit.*, para 80.
108. India Legislative Progs., March 1869, No 18. Chotanagpur Commissioner to Govt. of Bengal, 30 Sept. 1868 para 2.
109. Ibid., Appendix B of Chotanagpur Commissioner's letter to Govt. of Bengal, 31 Jan. 1868 Letter of the Senior Missionary, 15 Nov. 1867, para 6.
110. Reid, *op.cit.*, para 189. *Khuntkatti* village meant a village where the descendants in the male line of the original founders of the village owned all the land included within its boundary.
111. Ibid., para 95.
112. *Papers Relating to etc.* vol. 1, p. 151: Dy. Commissioner of Lohardugga to Chotanagpur Commissioner, 31 Dec. 1889.

II

The Life of a Text and Its Meanings: Reflections on Sahajanand Saraswati's *Mera Jivan Sangharsh*

WALTER HAUSER

It all started in Chicago in the mid-1950s. As the son of German immigrant parents I found myself at the University of Chicago studying European history, concerned in some naïve but not unreasonable way with understanding my roots, to use the term Alex Haley would introduce into the American experience so powerfully two decades later.[1] It could and

* Earlier versions of this essay were presented in the Writing Lives Symposium of the Center for South Asian Studies at the University of Virginia, 23-4 April 1999; and at the Conference on South Asian Life-Histories of the School of Oriental and African Studies of the University of London, 15-17 May 2000. I want to thank the participants at both symposia for their critical responses and especially the organizers for their generous invitations, Professor Farzanah Milani at Virginia and Professors David Arnold and Stuart Blackburn at London. My friends and colleagues Griff Chaussee, Mushir Hasan, Kailash Jha, Phil McEldowney, Anne Monius, and Vijay Pinch have been equally generous with their time and ideas in reading earlier drafts. I am also pleased to thank Florence J. Hauser for her thoughtful reading of the final versions of this essay. Eric Stokes with whom I discussed some of the issues raised in this paper during a lively year at Cambridge in 1979-80, would have responded to Sahajanand's candour in representing peasant interests of the twentieth century with the same twinkle of approval he used so often in defining those interests for peasants of the Raj in the nineteenth century.

Finally, I must thank my wife of 51 years, who in the final stages of her last illness insisted that I be in London for the SOAS conference. Dedicating this essay to Rosemary's memory is a very small token of appreciation for her unambiguous involvement in the Sahajanand project from the beginning.

would have been an interesting project, I am sure. But a funny thing happened on the way to that Ph.D., namely, India, and its endlessly fascinating rural population. It turns out that I was seduced by the peasants of the subcontinent.[2]

My European teachers and teachers of European history were fine scholars, but for me also uninspiring interpreters of someone else's interpretation of the human experience, many times removed from the experience itself or its ethnographic description, whether in the field or in the archive. To be entirely fair, I suspect I was learning that I was not disposed to serious intellectual history, given what I would soon learn was a fascination I shared with others, in what our friend Bernard Cohn would come to call 'the new social history'.[3] Over time that social history would come to include for me the political, and as this essay and everything else I have written makes clear, how the people on the ground, the peasants of India, have expressed themselves in the arena of public affairs in the twentieth century. The fact that they were also the producers of India's food and substance, and not coincidentally the central constituents of its Freedom Movement, made my fascination that much more compelling.

The first turn in the road heading in that direction came when I encountered two fine British historians for whom social and political experience and its institutional structures and meanings were conveyed as powerfully in the classroom as on the printed page. Alan Simpson and Charles Mowat were uncommon teachers and wonderfully sensitive human beings who helped clarify the terms of academic engagement of a place like Chicago for a raw and inexperienced postgraduate student.

At about the same time, a young Robert Crane, with a fresh Ph.D. from Yale and a rough Marxist view of the colonial experience (then quaintly but accurately described as 'The Expansion of Europe' among the 'fields' available for study in the Department of History), began his brief tenure as a historian at Chicago before moving on to Michigan, then Duke, and finally Syracuse. Crane's critical reading of the imperial colonial connection, combined with a solid understanding of the agrarian base of Indian politics emerging from his Yale dissertation provided a new and even more revealing sense of the possibilities of scholarship beyond the limits imposed by the Eurocentric view of the world in which most of us then lived, certainly in Europe and the United States.

Viewed reflectively, however, it was the relaxed but rigorous intellectual ambiance of Robert Redfield's Wednesday afternoon Village India seminar at Chicago that was for me the defining influence in the serendipitous journey to India on which I was now embarking. I was most taken in by the fact that there were no grand pronouncements and no pretence in Redfield's seminar performance. It was rather an exercise in intellectual candour recognizing how little we knew about the social and political present of the subcontinent and its people. Redfield and his associates were more interested in raising questions about process and meaning in the lives of the people, the peasants of this Great Civilization, than in providing answers.[4] It was a compelling and wonderfully refreshing approach to the world of human experience that drew many of us into its ambit.[5]

That Redfield brought in regular participants from among the few American academics who had recently worked in India served to define and enrich the encounter in very immediate terms. These included Alan R. Beals, Bernard S. Cohn, Kathleen Gough, Oscar Lewis, David G. Mandelbaum, McKim Marriott, and Gitel P. Steed. M.N. Srinivas was also a participant, and his paper was examined in one of the weekly sessions, but he himself was unable to be at the seminar.[6] And quietly but forcefully in the background was Milton Singer, whose imagination and creative administrative skills would shape from these beginnings the Chicago South Asia programme.[7] If my journey started with the richly sensitive intellectual imagery of India conveyed by Robert Redfield and friends, it would be reinforced with a series of equally fortuitous encounters in India itself, which took me in 1957, 1958, and 1959 from Allahabad, to Calcutta, to Patna and the districts, towns and villages of Bihar where I would learn much that I know from the activists and the peasants themselves about their lives and efforts to achieve social and economic freedom, and, in the process, the larger freedom of the nation. It is a venture that has absorbed me from that day to this.

But studying peasants was not exactly the historical rage in 1957 whether in India, the United States, or elsewhere on the planet. Happily I had support from Bob Crane, even after he left Chicago in 1956, and most particularly from Barney Cohn, whom I had met during the Redfield seminar and got to know well in Allahabad in 1958 when he was doing his initial Banaras research. Cohn then returned to Chicago in 1959-60 on a one year visiting appointment when I was also back from India, and served as chair of my dissertation committee.[8] The other happy coincidence is that I overlapped briefly in India with Myron Weiner, whom I met in Delhi at the old Fulbright House on Curzon Road in October 1957. Myron was also back at Chicago in 1959-60 and served as the other member of my dissertation committee. For someone writing about peasant activism in India it was a remarkably fruitful critical engagement with two of the most sensitive academic scholars in the business.[9]

My wife and I landed in Bombay, coincidentally, on 4 July 1957 and entrained almost immediately across central India for Allahabad, where I had been assigned by Fulbright to the Department of History at that fine University. We were there in good time to celebrate India's tenth Independence Day, living in Tagore town, almost in the shadows of Swaraj Bhavan and Jawaharlal Nehru's Anand Bhavan.

Being at that place at that time was for me perhaps an entirely appropriate coincidence. As we all know, Nehru's shadow and those of the pantheon of Founders were cast very heavily over much of India's modern history. I was told in no uncertain terms at Allahabad and subsequently at Patna that 'modern history' was inevitably that of the anti-British 'nationalist' movement writ large, and less generously and somewhat grudgingly that in any event studying peasants fell in the domain of political science or anthropology, and not history.[10] After all, Sahajanand Saraswati of Bihar, the dominant player in the politics of peasant activism in the 1930s and the first President of the All India Kisan Sabha, had died only seven years before, in 1950. And N.G. Ranga of Andhra and Indulal Yagnik from Gujarat, and many others of Sahajanand's close associates in the 1930s and 1940s, were still very much alive. In the prevailing political and intellectual climate of the day, it was all supposed to be self-evident, and for me, in a very real sense, it was.

Clearly, if I was going to understand the nature of peasant activism I would first have to understand the social and cultural environment which gave that activism its meaning and the agrarian conditions that made it happen when it did. I was more and more convinced that these sensibilities would have to come from the peasants themselves and from the activists who were a part of their lives. Their politics, I reasoned, would thus be defined by that lived experience and not derived from a cultivated perception of the peasant environment, as was so often the case among many of the major players in India's movement for freedom.

No one was perhaps more candid in making this point of remote perception than Nehru, writing (in 1934) about the Awadh peasant movement of 1920, observing as he did on 'our total ignorance of this great agrarian movement'. 'I realized more than ever how cut off we were from our people,' Nehru wrote, 'and how we lived and worked and agitated in a little world [quite] apart from them.' The experience 'lifted the veil and disclosed a fundamental aspect of the Indian problem to me to which nationalists had paid hardly any attention'.[11]

Coming as it does from one of the most sensitive players in the politics of freedom, this observation tells us much about the many levels at which this politics was played out and the separation of awareness and expectation that fact imposed on the overarching movement for freedom and its many complex parts. It was in an effort to identify and understand what I apprehended to be among the most distinctive of these parts that I set out in 1957 to access the political experience of India's peasants. This was in the days before post-modern critics had raised questions about whether (or not) peasants had voices, so I was not inhibited in moving beyond the academy to talk with the peasants themselves and with the many activists from the 1930s and 1940s who could speak with and for them in the 1950s and 1960s.

Nehru would subsequently become President of the Indian National Congress, meeting at Lucknow in 1936, the same year and at the same place where Sahajanand was named the first President of the All India Kisan Sabha. Their encounter on that occasion was sympathetic as it would remain, given their deep ideological and populist commitment to the peasant cause and flowing from a mutual respect they had developed much earlier in prison.[12] By August 1940, Nehru would recognize that the 'agrarian problem was, after all, the major problem of India'.[13] While I was fortunate enough to meet Nehru (and his daughter Indira), indeed to spend an evening of relaxed conversation with them at Teen Murti with my small class of Fulbright fellows (in October 1957), regrettably I did not have an opportunity to discuss politics, peasants, or Sahajanand with Nehru in subsequent years and before his death in 1964, when I could have done so rather more intelligently.

As interesting as that would have been, I was determined to engage India at a more intimate and immediate level of social experience. As admired and loved as Nehru was by the people of India, he was nevertheless the remote intellectual, the didact explaining to the villagers of eastern UP, for example, how nuclear energy held for India both the potential for energy and for security.[14] I followed him more than once in 1957 and 1958 as he swept out of Anand Bhavan in his black, convertible Buick, moving swiftly to one of the neighbouring villages to engage the peasants, in the tens of thousands, about the meanings of the new India. It was always a magnetic moment to be sure, and that Nehru did it on some regular basis in the eight or nine months I was in Allahabad was in itself impressive, but the encounter always had, for the peasants certainly, something of a *darshan* quality.[15] This in itself told us much about the nature of the relationship, and about the quality of the Freedom Movement itself at this level of popular experience.

For me the critical moment in my journey to the social and political world inhabited by the peasants of Bihar occurred in late 1957. I have already mentioned having met Myron Weiner at Delhi in October that year. He had recently been to Bihar and the Shri Sitaram Ashram of Swami Sahajanand at Bihta in Patna district and felt that it might be worth a more serious visit. The Ashram, which served as Sahajanand's base from 1927 until the time of his death in 1950, then housed the boys Sanskrit School founded by the Swami.[16] But it had also served as the headquarters of the Bihar Provincial Kisan Sabha from 1929 on, and from 1936 as the office of the All India Kisan Sabha in those years when Sahajanand was its president or general secretary, which was often. Though the materials there had not been maintained since Sahajanand's death, nor were they a complete record, they were nevertheless an important point of departure for a study of the movement and its leading advocate. And critically, the Swami's library, comprised primarily of books from his Sanskrit, Kashi period in the teens of the century, did contain much of his published work, including his *Mera Jivan Sangharsh* [My Life Struggle] memoir, published in 1952, two years after his death. It was a life history that would absorb me in one way or another for much of the next forty-five years.

That Sahajanand had been a central player in the activism of the peasants, and Bihar the core site of that activism, was confirmed and reinforced for me only weeks after my encounter with Weiner. This was when I attended the fifteenth annual session of the All India Kisan Sabha (AIKS) at Bongaon in 24 Parganas district in West Bengal, hard on what was then the East Pakistan border. This was from 1-3 November 1957, and provided a remarkable opportunity to meet and interact with some of the luminaries of the Communist Party of India, many of whom had been active in the AIKS, especially from 1941 onwards. This included among others Muzaffar Ahmad; A.K. Gopalan, who was the re-elected president of the AIKS; E.M.S. Namboodiripad, the then Chief Minister of Kerala; Bhowani Sen; P.C. Joshi; Bankim Mukherjee; and Abdullah Rasul. It was the latter two—Mukherjee, who had been the general secretary of the AIKS on a number of occasions, and Rasul, who would become the historian of the AIKS—who were most supportive in urging me to pursue the movement in Bihar and the career of Sahajanand.[17] And that, of course, is what I did.

I went to Patna and Bihta after the Bongaon meeting, to confirm what my friends had proffered, and was more than convinced of the wisdom of their suggestions. This would mean shifting from Allahabad to Patna to work in the Bihar State Archives and at Bihta, and to interact with the peasants and the activists whose politics made the movement what it was, especially in the decades of the 1930s and 1940s. Of these, there were many, but among those who were crucial to the movement, and always generous with their time, the names I recall most easily are those of Jadunandan Sharma, Kishori Prasanna Singh, Awadeshwar Prasad Singh, Karyanand Sharma, Panchanan Sharma, and Karpoori Thakur. Among this number, all but Karpoori, who was a later activist and would become Chief Minister of Bihar, were associates of Sahajanand. But that is another story.

It is a story, however, that reinforced for me at every turn and at every moment the symbiotic oneness of Sahajanand, the district and local level cadres, and the peasants in the fields of conflict in their collective efforts to achieve for the *kisans* a life of justice and dignity. Their activism was and is the story, and Sahajanand was its quintessential spokesman. Through everything he said and wrote, it was he who gave expression to the voice of the people. And he spoke often and he wrote much, most often of course in the vernacular language of the people. The most luminous expression of his story and that of the peasants who literally created and defined it was his *Mera Jivan Sangharsh*. Their struggle for equity and justice was his struggle. I now turn to that life history, or perhaps more accurately, to those life histories.

The Idea of Autobiography

Sahajanand's personal and public struggle, as he defines the 'truth' he was seeking, is in fact deeply rooted in the social, cultural, and political realities of twentieth-century India, so the memoir is in every sense a powerful narrative of the self *and* that of the nation as he perceived it. But the personal and public statement Sahajanand makes in this text is, as I have already suggested, directed in some ultimate sense to achieving a life of dignity for the ordinary and marginal(ized) lives of the peasants of India and Bihar. So it both represents and speaks for those lives. Indeed, while the *Sangharsh* text is a remarkably elaborate and complex personal document, it is also the case that nearly 400 of its 570 pages are concerned in one way or another with the peasants and the activism and movements meant to relieve their exploitation. As I will say in the conclusion, their story and his became one, especially in the critical decade of the 1930s.

David Arnold has provided me a final point of departure for this inquiry with the argument developed in his November 1998, SOAS

Workshop paper on India's Prison Autobiographies, where he considers the self-images of Gandhi, M.N. Roy, Nehru, and Savarkar as defined by their prison experiences.[18] Arnold comes to these prison autobiographies as part of his larger project of writing a history of the colonial prison, much as I come to the Sahajanand memoir (and others) through my interest in the history of peasant activism.[19] But the common thread in most political autobiographies of the twentieth century, as Arnold points out, is for obvious reasons the prison experience.

So, much like Arnold's four subjects, Sahajanand spends considerable time reflecting on the prison experience, most notably on what it revealed about his fellow prisoners and their understanding and practice of the Gandhian idea, which was for him the central commitment initially drawing him (as so many others) to a career of service and politics. In fact, the prison experience becomes for Sahajanand one of the two primary bases for his subsequent critique of Gandhi, namely that of introducing religion and morality into the arena of politics. The other, of course, was the Swami's break with Gandhi on the degree of the Mahatma's understanding—or misunderstanding—of the peasant experience of exploitation. I will touch on each of these experiences in the life history of Sahajanand as reflected in his *Sangharsh* memoir (and much else that he wrote), in the pages following. Let me then turn first to Gandhi.

In the introduction to his important and well-known autobiography, the Mahatma allows that it is not his purpose 'to attempt a *real* autobiography. I simply want to tell the story of my numerous experiments with truth, and as my life consists of nothing but those experiments, it is true that the story will take the shape of an autobiography.' He goes on to say that he flatters himself 'with the belief, that a connected account of all these experiments will not be without benefit to the reader'.[20] Gandhi's purpose, therefore, is two-fold, first and primarily to identify his selfhood, or to use his words, to achieve 'what I have been striving and pining for these thirty years, i.e., self-realization, to see God face to face, to attain *Moksha*'.[21]

His second goal, if I understand what he was writing in the autobiography *and* doing and saying at the same time in the non-cooperation movement of the early 1920s, was an instructional one, or, at the risk of being indelicate, of converting Indians and India to his idea of *satyagraha*. This effort was directed not only to his most intimate and immediate followers but to the larger constituency of the Freedom Movement he was leading. The failure of that effort in Gandhi's perception is certainly one way of reading his reactions to the events of

4 February 1922 at Chauri-Chaura. (And similarly his apparent depression in the last days of his life immediately preceding his assassination on 30 January 1948.[22]) It will be recalled that the killing of 23 constables by the peasant villagers of eastern UP on that day (in 1922) moved Gandhi, among other reasons, to withdraw the movement and to undertake a fast to bring the people back to non-violence.[23]

I think everyone would agree that Gandhi's autobiography is a uniquely powerful narrative of the self. While this introspective examination of his inner being is at the heart of Gandhi's reflection and is the issue that has attracted the widest attention, my point is that the autobiography is at the same time much more. If Gandhi's reactions to the events at Chauri-Chaura tell us anything, it is that he saw himself deeply engaged in both a spiritual *and* a political journey. In other words the autobiography is as much a political document as it is a personal reflection. It is an idea Gandhi himself pursues, directly and indirectly, throughout the autobiography.

My point in this brief disquisition about Gandhi is that all his apprehensions and qualifications about writing his autobiography notwithstanding, writing an autobiography is in fact precisely what he did. Whether or not it had anything to do with his experience in the West, an impression he wanted to guard against, is not my concern here.[24] What he did was to write a powerfully distinctive autobiography, in the process revealing the Gandhian self in ways that most observers consider to be unique. But if, in that process, Gandhi was trying to devalue the political elements in his experiments with truth, I would argue that he failed in doing so. He himself tells us that for much of his life, however he may define it, politics was all-consuming, and that everyone, even in the 'civilized' world, was familiar with the nature and extent of his political involvement.[25] He was, indeed, a central player, if not *the* central player in the politics of freedom, what was inevitably the centrepiece of India's historical experience in the twentieth century.

What this means for me is that however venerated Gandhi was during (and after) the Freedom Movement (and he was almost always referred to in the honorific form, Gandhiji), his total if not absolute involvement in the politics of the day also opened him to critical examination, some of which went to the very core values of the Mahatma's truth experiments and their application to the movement for freedom. This is, of course, not a revelation to anyone even vaguely familiar with the history of twentieth-century India, where the names of B.R. Ambedkar, Subhas Chandra Bose, and M.N. Roy stand among the major participants in the politics of freedom *and* the most severe critics of the nature and logic of the Gandhian idea in that movement.[26] Nehru was, of course, a firm supporter of the Mahatma, one might say even a devotee, though not without deep intellectual doubts. Another admirer and then a severe critic was Sahajanand Saraswati, whose memoir I consider here as a window on the social and cultural experience of the Freedom Movement, not only as its author estimated Gandhi's person and politics in broadly general terms but most explicitly in its impact on the lives of India's peasants.

I will forego here the issue of how the autobiographies of each of these major players was influenced or not by the West and what they might have represented about the nature of India's nationhood.[27] I will turn briefly to that issue in my concluding reflections. It should, however, be noted that among the names I have invoked in the preceding paragraph, Sahajanand's experience is, in a very real sense, the most vernacular. He came from a peasant environment, then as a young *sannyasi*, a renunciate, Sahajanand searched for a guru at the major pilgrimage sites across much of north India.[28] This was followed by seven years of study and scholarship in the Shastrik tradition at Kashi and in Mithila, and his subsequent move to a life of social reform, Congress politics, and thence to a uniquely symbiotic encounter with the peasants of India and Bihar. My suggestion is that this personal and public experience gives Sahajanand's life history a particularly compelling cultural and political edge. That we know so little about the man is significantly a function of the fact that 98 per cent of his vast corpus of writing, including his political advocacy, was produced in Hindi, and very little of that material was either copublished or translated into English.[29]

Swami Sahajanand as Social and Political Critic

It is generally agreed, and I would certainly argue that Sahajanand Saraswati was the foremost peasant leader of twentieth-century India. His was by any definition a remarkable career, spanning the full gamut of Indian experience from the religious and cultural to that of social reform and political activism. Of Sahajanand's extensive corpus of literary reflection, none is perhaps more revealing of the man and the peasant movement he led, or the wider movement of political freedom of which ...s a fundamental part, than his *Mera Jivan Sangharsh*, that is, 'My ...ggle'. It is this memoir that I use as a point of departure in this reflection. It is a vernacular document describing a vernacular politics, in the process opening an interpretive window on the Freedom Movement from the cultural and political inside, so to speak. That Sahajanand was one of the movement's most intimate and outspoken participants means that there is perhaps no more penetrating and honest a consideration of the struggle for justice, equity, and decency in the lives of peasant India than is found in this document.

The representation I make here is that memoir and autobiography by definition provide us access to the lives of their authors. But even more compelling is the window they open on the life of the nation, specifically on the lives of the peasants of India who, in the end, were at the political base of the Freedom Movement and gave meaning to what the Nehrus, Gandhis, and Sahajanands were doing and saying in that movement. That they were also the producers of the food and fibre that sustained the movement confirms in my mind the power and importance of their politics, the politics of peasant activism. In order to understand the nature of that politics and the peasant voice it reveals, I will consider briefly how that politics and its movement intersected both positively and negatively with the person of Gandhi and the wider movement for India's political freedom that he led.

From his first meeting with Gandhi in 1920 to his death in 1950, Sahajanand was by any definition a major player in the events of the day. Few will know that from 1923 he was a member of the Uttar Pradesh Congress Committee (UPCC) and from 1924, at the age of 35, a member of the All India Congress Committee (AICC), or that in the 1930s when he was the central figure in the Bihar Provincial Kisan Sabha and the All India Kisan Sabha, he was at the same time a member of the Working Committee of the Bihar Provincial Congress Committee (BPCC). In all of these capacities and certainly by the middle thirties, he was universally recognized as India's foremost peasant leader.[30]

Viewed from this perspective, it is also important to explain that when he was writing in 1940 and 1941, Sahajanand was disillusioned with and critical of the Congress and especially of Congressmen. None of this of course prevented him from being even-handed in his admiration for Gandhi who drew him into the Freedom Movement, while ultimately raising fundamental questions about the Mahatma's approach to politics.[31] For us, the important point is that he was there, and when he provides observations on the politics of the day, whether at AICC meetings, or during elections, or while in jail, we are essentially getting a first-person account of what was happening. And (to put a present-day gloss on his critique) it is also my sense that when Sahajanand talks in critical terms about the Congress and Congressmen for being effectively un-Gandhian in their political behaviour, he is referring to political activists in a much broader and more inclusive sense than those of the Congress alone.[32]

In order to provide something of the flavour of the Freedom Movement as it was happening, I will quote passages from Sahajanand's *Sangharsh* text to make my point about the role of the peasants in the movement and the life of the nation. A subtext in this formulation is that, apart from the widely accepted generation of Founders, and certainly some among their equally committed followers, many others of those engaged in the effort were political players of a quite ordinary kind. It is this group of whom Sahajanand was most critical for being un-Gandhian in their failure to live by the precepts Gandhi set as the *sine qua non* of the movement, though he did occasionally include some of the more major players in his critical assessments as well.[33]

Gandhi as Shiva, the God of Destruction

I will provide four brief extracts from the *Sangharsh* text to give us a sense of the time, the people, and the ideas at work in the decades of the 1920s and 1930s. Two of these, the first and third, involve Sahajanand's personal encounter with Gandhi at his first meeting with the Mahatma late in 1920, and then in January 1934 at the time of the great Bihar earthquake. The other observations are Sahajanand's assessments of the un-Gandhian reactions of many Congressmen in prison, and finally the responses of leading Congressmen to the idea of mass support for the movement. The idea is to provide an image of Sahajanand's wider sense of the movement for freedom, that of the peasants, and ultimately in his view, that of the nation.

Sahajanand first met Gandhi at Patna in December 1920, and it was that encounter which confirmed his determination to 'plunge into politics, not because it would do any good for my country, but because it would be only then that I would realize the true meaning of service as a sannyasi'.[34] His impressions of that meeting were to be reinforced by Sahajanand's participation in the Nagpur Session of the Congress later that same month. Nagpur was in many ways the turning point in con-firming Gandhi's leadership and programme as the programme of the [Con]gress and the nation. Sahajanand's comment on Nagpur, though [in] retrospect, captured much of the quality of that session and the direction in which Sahajanand's own social and political views were developing.

It was at Nagpur, he wrote, that the Congress 'forsook the time-honoured procedure of begging for something . . . and instead took to the path of self-respect. For the first time it was decided that on the refusal of government to fulfil the rightful demands of the country, we should throw out a challenge, and thus a fresh lease on life was given to India.'[35] The same enthusiasm and excitement pervaded the Ahmedabad Session in 1921. 'No one can describe the great enthusiasm which pervaded the Congress', Sahajanand was to write, 'wave after wave of enthusiasm was visible.'[36] Again it was the Mahatma, who by his words and very presence, projected that universal sense of excitement and achievement that now infused the politics of freedom. 'I listened to Gandhiji's speech with rapt attention', Sahajanand wrote:

> Gandhiji was seated on a table as he spoke. His whole body, especially his face had a ruddy appearance. It seemed that some power in the garb of a demon was throwing a determined challenge to government and warning that it should be on its guard. He spoke for hours. There was pin drop silence. Never again did I see him speak with such emotion. Every word that came out of his mouth was like a thunderbolt against the government. It seemed that Shiva, the God of Destruction was raging and that soon the great deluge would follow.[37]

These were heady times in Indian politics, and Sahajanand threw himself into the effort with complete abandon. For the Swami politics had to be the politics of activism. He would write that 'by nature I have always favoured situations full of struggle. Whenever that was absent, I quickly became indifferent. But as soon as the Congress declared the resumption of the struggle in 1930, I at once suspended all other activities and prepared to plunge into the movement even by leaving the Kisan Sabha and the Sitaram Ashram to which I was so deeply attached.'[38]

But the prospect of an active renewal of the freedom movement was to end in disappointment for Sahajanand and would begin for him a sense of disillusion with individual Congressmen and Congress politics that he had already noted at the time of his first imprisonment. His enthusiasm and his disillusion were apparent in January 1930, when Sahajanand was ready to 'plunge into the movement'. while some of his Congress associates, especially in the Patna district seemed decidedly less so.

Whatever the problem may have been in 1930, the episode sharpened Sahajanand's anxieties about the Indian National Congress itself. He became more and more critical of what he described as the pretense and posturing of individual Congressmen, but ultimately he would fall out with Gandhi himself on the very nature and substance of the movement. It was that sense of disillusion that would turn Sahajanand to a firm posture of opposition to the Congress even while working within it. The opposition role was certainly one in which he felt more comfortable and in which he was clearly more effective. For him service to the people (*jan seva*) would ultimately be realized only when he could focus on a specific set of injustices. This would come to mean peasant politics, or as he called it, the politics of bread.

The transition to that politics, I am suggesting, was for Sahajanand a natural one. It would happen within the framework of the politics of freedom, developing with his work on behalf of the peasants of west Patna district, in and around the *ashram* in Bihta, to emerge full-blown in 1933 with the formation of the reorganized Bihar Provincial Kisan Sabha. From that time on, Sahajanand became totally absorbed in the effort to resolve the problems of social and economic exploitation among the peasants, and ultimately, by the late 1930s and early 1940s, the poorest of those peasants and the agricultural labourers, or *khet mazdoors* of India and Bihar. For Sahajanand, all other considerations were ultimately determined by this single overriding concern. In the process, he would become the foremost spokesman of peasant interests of his time.[39]

The Gandhi Idea in Practice: A View from the Prison

As a committed Gandhian in principle and practice, it was the breakdown between proclaimed belief on the one hand and the actions he observed in the conflict between supporters of C.R. Das and Gandhi, already at Nagpur, that most distressed Sahajanand. His growing pain and anxiety is apparent in the passages that follow, first with those who denied Gandhi's precepts in their actions and then gradually with Gandhi himself for allowing it to happen, and then for the very idea of combining morality, religion, and politics in the arena of the Freedom Movement. That there were doubts in Gandhi's own mind about the degree of commitment and achievement in his precepts of truth value is of course well known: witness his withdrawing the Non-Cooperation and Civil Disobedience Movements as he did. And those same doubts and anxieties of course were there in the minds of others as well, not least of all that of Rajendra Prasad, whose anxieties, especially with the un-Gandhian behaviour of political prisoners, Sahajanand refers to a number of times in the memoir.

It was, in fact, in the jail environment, common for most political activists during the Freedom Movement, that Sahajanand found the breakdown of Gandhian principles most persistent. He returns again and again to the theme in his *Sangharsh* memoir, from his first imprisonment in early 1922 at Ghazipur, then to jails in Faizabad, Banaras, Lucknow, and Hazaribagh.[40] I will cite extracts from those jail experiences in the early 1920s and early 1930s to make Sahajanand's point about how proclaimed belief and actual practice appeared to be out of phase, most often in defying jail rules, whatever form that defiance might take. Most commonly, as Sahajanand reports, this involved harassing jail authorities, breaking jail rules wherever and whenever possible, demanding first-class treatment and high quality food, and, on at least one occasion at Faizabad, setting fire to the jail premises on the occasion of Holi. Of these experiences he writes:

> I joined politics and the Congress as a committed follower of Gandhism. Therefore I accepted and followed all the prescriptions and commands of Gandhiji literally and made every effort to have others do the same. So I learned spinning and began a daily routine of working with the *charkha* and later also worked with the *takli* or small hand spindle. In this way I met the goal I had set for myself in the daily hand spinning of cotton thread. And of course I presumed that other educated and sensible people joining the Congress would certainly also follow the instructions and discipline of Gandhiji. But later, when I was in jail, I was much disillusioned in this regard.
>
> Many of the incidents I encountered in jail from the very beginning disturbed me greatly. I was astonished to see what was happening around me. Why were educated people disregarding Gandhiji's orders in this way? This utter defiance of Gandhiji's instructions side by side with the shouting of 'Gandhiji Ki Jai' caused me much pain.[41] It was not a good sign. Since then I found the same thing happening in other places as well. When I was jailed for the second time, in 1930 in the Hazaribagh jail, I found the same state of affairs. So far as observing jail regulations was concerned, Gandhiji's instructions had absolutely no meaning. Even political prisoners of the first or second class cared not one whit for Gandhiji's instructions although he was the leader of the country. Later he might have to run the government

of a free India. I found that even Rajendra Babu [Rajendra Prasad] was unable to prevail on the political prisoners in the Hazaribagh jail to accept Gandhiji's word. No one paid Rajen Babu any heed.[42]

In the [Banaras] jail I witnessed many examples of how those who had become votaries of Gandhism behaved. The decision of the government was that all first class political prisoners from the United Provinces were to be lodged at Banaras. This meant that only prisoners of that category were brought there. Their reactions would accordingly be a good indicator of the extent to which these political prisoners were abiding by Gandhiji's instructions and example. They harassed the jail authorities and demanded that inasmuch as we were not thieves or dacoits, but rather political prisoners, we should be provided fine food, including ghee, milk, and sweets, and in plentiful amounts, otherwise we would undertake a hunger strike. All of this was wrong and completely against the instructions given by Gandhiji.[43] But as I have already said, who cared for Gandhiji? For many of the prisoners the question was rather one of personal prestige and self-interest.

Hundreds of persons from every district of U.P. were in jail with us. Now if those of us who were first class prisoners began to talk about better food for ourselves, it would certainly have serious moral repercussions, most especially in the minds of the ordinary prisoners among us. They would think that if even before the achievement of freedom their own comrades were accepting special concessions from government, leaving them behind, then who would care for them once Independence was a reality? This thought came to me again and again, and it pained me greatly. To what extent would we be demeaning ourselves if we accepted such concessions? Why then did we give up our positions, legal practices, council memberships, etc.? After all these too were all government privileges. Accepting better quality food would be the same thing. There could be no justification for such a shameful act and the policy of government to divide us would be entirely successful because those of our comrades classed as ordinary prisoners would, in due course, leave us.[44] This whole sorry episode was for me a matter of surprise and much personal pain! Gandhiji's words were in fact being denied by his followers in actual practice.

During my eight to nine months' stay in the Lucknow jail I found a similar range of license and indiscipline. There was scarcely anyone who did not systematically disobey jail regulations. In place of good

> conduct, truth, and non-violence one finds in the Congress rather false pride, untruth, deceit, fraud, and violence. Strangely enough, candour seems to have no place in the party of Gandhiji and only hypocrites are found there! They have become the all in all! [pp. 198-254]

Sahajanand's next imprisonment was in April 1930, at the time of the Salt Satyagraha of April and May of that year. His reactions are unremitting in damning the followers of Gandhi, whom Sahajanand accuses of being followers in name but not in principle or spirit. He writes:

> I have written at length about my bitter experiences in jail in 1922. On reaching the Hazaribagh jail in April 1930, [for making salt] I found that no one seemed to be guided by the words of Gandhiji nor was he having any impact on most political prisoners. But I thought that over the last two years people might have learned to live up to his teachings. [That is since 1928, when the political movement more or less resumed.] On the matter of principle Gandhiji considered himself to be very strict. He said that he would forego freedom but would not forsake his principles. In these circumstances, before launching the struggle [of 1930], he must have felt that the people had overcome their shortcomings of an earlier time. That is presumably why he resumed the movement.
>
> With this background in view I had hoped that the general level of public morality would have improved and that Gandhiji's words and the discipline he prescribed would have been more fully observed. But in actual practice I found just the reverse to be true. in the years since 1922 things had actually gotten worse. It was a painful thing to observe. For people like me who were deeply committed to Gandhism, how could we accept this kind of decline? I came into politics from religion and with religious sensibilities, and what I found was dirt, jealousy, lying, and manipulation. I was shocked and felt deceived.
>
> What I experienced during my second term of imprisonment completely disillusioned me and confirmed my earlier views about jail life and political character. Everyone was essentially pursuing his personal interests. What Gandhiji had said about maintaining rules and regulations was totally ignored. It was as though no one was aware of what Gandhiji had said! No one seemed to be concerned about him. Gandhiji did not seem to be aware that all the rules and

regulations and codes of conduct were being systematically broken by political prisoners. There were at most three or four exceptions. It was indeed strange. I saw that Babu Rajendra Prasad was also anxious about what was happening, but no one listened to him; he too was helpless. Why then would they listen to anyone else?

Most of those who have now become political leaders and workers in many of the districts of Bihar, and indeed the whole province, were with me in the Hazaribagh jail. In the same way that I encountered hundreds of prominent persons of the United Provinces in the Faizabad, Lucknow, and Banaras jails, so too I came to know hundreds of friends from Bihar in Hazaribagh. Today they have all become prominent leaders. So I had the opportunity of observing at close hand both the manner in which they applied Gandhian principles in their personal lives and in their political behavior. I came to know both their minds and their hearts. Consequently, I cannot now accept them in terms of the high sounding principles in which they project themselves and their political ideas. [pp. 362-70]

Sahajanand was released from the Hazaribagh jail in September 1930. He was next jailed in mid-April 1940 following his call for immediate direct action against the British; this in his capacity as Chairman of the Reception Committee of the Anti-Compromise Conference organized by Subhas Chandra Bose. This was at Ramgarh in the Hazaribagh district of Bihar. Sahajanand repeated that call at the Palasa session of the All India Kisan Sabha of which he was General Secretary and then again during the agitations of the National Anti-Compromise Week.[45] He was released in March 1942. It was during that two-year jail period, again in the Hazaribagh Central jail, that he produced *Mera Jivan Sangharsh*, among many other books and tracts.

The Great Bihar Earthquake

In the afternoon of 15 January 1934, Bihar was rocked by a cataclysmic earthquake. The destruction was massive, especially in Bihar north of the Ganga. Sahajanand writes graphically of the human cost and the political consequences:

I saw that hundreds of thousands of peasants were ruined. Their hutments and houses had collapsed and the grain they had stored had literally fallen into the fissures which had opened in the earth. So too with grain that was lying in the open *khalihans* [i.e. outdoor threshing floors]. And the fields had become vast stretches of sand which destroyed many of the standing crops. So the *kisans* were literally searching for whatever grain they might find, wherever they might find it.

On top of this there was the ruthless realization of land rent by the *zamindars*. Whatever property of the *kisans* had not been destroyed or lost, whether *lota*, *thali*, goats, cows, buffalo, or oxen, the *zamindars* forced the peasants to sell these, to take loans, and thereby to pay the rent. And when they were given loans by the Earthquake Relief Committee or the government to remove the sand from their fields, immediately the agents of the *zamindars* would seize that money towards payment of the rent. I myself came across an order in which the *zamindar* had instructed his *amlas* forcibly to seize the loan money given to the *kisans* for reconstructing or repairing their houses or for removing sand from the fields. I had such a written order published in the newspapers. The *zamindars* saw the earthquake as an opportunity to realize the rent, whatever the circumstances, so it should not be missed.

So while we were helping the *kisans* on the one hand by giving them literally 2, 4, 10, or 20 rupees or a bit more, on the other hand the *zamindars* were perpetrating a vast deception by snatching this relief money from the *kisans* and forcing them to sell their animals and mortgage their land. All of this convinced me that unless we began to organize the *kisans* and agitate for their rights by holding *kisan sabhas*, their grievances would not be redressed. We had already seen that without an *andolan*, a movement, the rights of the *kisans* would not be recognized by the *zamindars*.

But the problem was that we were all too busy with relief to organize meetings of the *kisans*. Who would then do it? In the circumstances I felt that it would be good if we were to take the help of workers from the relief camps. But this required the assent of the relief leaders and Rajendra Babu clearly said that this could not be done without the express orders of Gandhiji. So I decided I needed to have a direct talk with Gandhiji and get his permission for this purpose. He is the servant of the poor, so he will happily give the order.[46] The date and time was fixed for our meeting at the office of the Bihar Relief Committee in the Pili Kothi [in Kadamkuan] in Patna where Gandhiji was staying.

In the end, my discussion with Gandhiji left me greatly disappointed. When I narrated to him what was happening, he said that no meetings could be held in view of a government ordinance against such meetings. He did not know that in the last two years we had been holding many meetings and creating serious problems for the *zamindars*! I said that we will hold the meetings and let us then see what the government does. He said that this should not happen quietly but that we should distribute notices of any meetings that might be held. I agreed. Yes, notices will be distributed and they will be distributed widely.

Then he said that only genuine complaints must be taken up. I replied that of course, why would false complaints be made or taken up? Actual complaints are so great in number that we cannot begin to consider all of them. Then he said, but each complaint should be thoroughly investigated, only then should action be taken.[47] I explained that these inquiries would be conducted by the workers and they would keep us informed. Gandhiji said but they might commit mistakes. I replied that there were hundreds of thousands, literally lakhs and lakhs of complaints. And if we were to be concerned about the ultimate truth, and needed to get involved in each complaint to assure that it was genuine, it would be impossible for us to proceed. In such a situation we would be unable to help the *kisans*. Ultimately one has to have faith and trust in the workers. [p. 426]

Gandhiji then said that if these complaints were brought to the notice of the Maharaja of Darbhanga (I had mentioned the Maharaja's name earlier in our conversation), he [Gandhi] had faith that the Maharaja would remove and redress the grievances. His manager, Shri Girindra Mohan Mishra, is a Congressman, Gandhiji said. I replied that I would look into it inasmuch I wanted that the complaints should be resolved. Then he suggested that instead of speaking in vague and general terms, the names of each and every *kisan* and their grievances must be submitted. I said that I could not do this because if the names of specific *kisans* were cited, instead of redressing their grievances the *zamindars* would terrorize them, and no *kisan* would ever talk to us again about complaints against any landlord. I know fully the ways and means by which the *zamindars* function. My talk with Gandhiji ended here.

This discussion gave me a rude shock. The experience opened my eyes. Gandhiji's suggestions that, 'the *zamindars* would redress the grievances of *kisans*', and that 'his manager is a Congressman and would therefore certainly remove the miseries of the *kisans*', was remarkable. Gandhiji's ignorance of the way in which the machinery of the *zamindars* worked was appalling! He had no knowledge as to how they crushed the *kisans*; he did not know at all! How can anyone, simply because he is a Congressman, change the whole *zamindar* apparatus of oppression? Such a person would be no more than a cog in that machinery of oppression. Even this basic fact Gandhiji did not understand.

I have watched thousands of Congressmen contributing to the ruin of the *kisans*. But Gandhiji seemed to be unaware of this. He was so much worried about the idea of truth that the work we proposed would be impossible. As soon as the *zamindar* or his *amla* came to know about a *kisan* who had complained he would literally pounce on him immediately. Even this ordinary thing Gandhiji did not seem to know. Those who have mercilessly plundered the *kisans*, kept them starving in order to enjoy their luxuries, they can never be expected to redress the grievances of the *kisans*. I was astonished at Gandhiji's implicit faith in the *zamindars*. My heart revolted at the thought. Is Gandhiji indeed the servant of the poor?

I am convinced that Gandhiji does not know one iota of these matters although he talks a great deal about his familiarity with them. After my conversation with him on that day I lost all respect for Gandhiji and from that day I parted company with him forever. This was another mental earthquake after that first physical earthquake for me. Afterwards I learned that while Gandhiji was at Madhubani to attend a meeting, when people of that place complained to him about the atrocities of the Maharaja of Darbhanga then Gandhiji gave the same reply which he had given me. Anyway whatever happened was good. On that day fourteen years of my devoted commitment to Gandhiji came to an end. [p. 427]

This extract speaks volumes about the nature of the Congress, certainly in Bihar, about the nature of the *zamindari* system in that place and about the varying roles of Gandhi as the dominant leader at the national level of politics, Rajendra Prasad at the regional or provincial level, and Sahajanand at the regional and local level. That these levels of involvement and responsibility demanded different kinds of responses to the circumstances posed by the vastness of physical destruction and social trauma of the earthquake is perhaps obvious. Less obvious is the fact that the Bihar Relief Committee was beholden to many of the major *zamindar* players in the events of 1934, not the least being the Maharaja of Darbhanga himself. Whether Sahajanand's charges against the

Mahatma were true (though all evidence would indicate that they were), or whether Gandhi knew more about what was happening than appears in this document, we cannot know. We do know that Gandhi and the Indian National Congress through the Bihar Relief Committee were not in a position to alienate Darbhanga and other *zamindars* for all the obvious reasons. Whether Sahajanand's doubts and anxieties both in this case and that of the jail experience reflected a degree of moral and political naivete, it is clear that he was now moving from a moral objection to the actions of fellow prisoners, to specific procedural objections to Gandhi's politics.

We also know that for Sahajanand and the Bihar Provincial Kisan Sabha, this was ultimately one of the critical issues that forced a process of peasant mobilization from compromise and accommodation to a more explicitly militant activism. The public world of Sahajanand's activism was now becoming explicitly political. Despite the 1934 break with Gandhi, however, Sahajanand continued to work within and in accommodation with the Congress, as the next extract shows, but the connections were growing increasingly strained.

A final observation suggested by Sahajanand's encounter with the Mahatma is that whatever Gandhi might or might not have known about ground-level realities in north Bihar, it seems clear that given their respective backgrounds and roles, that Gandhi's image of rural India at that village level was a perceived one, assiduously cultivated to be sure, but nevertheless one that did not emerge from a lifetime of lived experience. In Sahajanand's case just the opposite was true inasmuch as he emerged from a rural village environment and developed a level of intimacy with that environment as a peasant activist that was unparalleled in the history of twentieth-century India. His lived experience was that of peasant India.

The Peasant Masses as Mob

The final vignette I will cite in Sahajanand's consideration of Gandhi's ideas as they functioned in the ground-level experience of the peasants, has to do with Gandhi's reputation as a leader of the masses, or perhaps more accurately, in converting India's movement for freedom under the leadership of the Congress into a mass movement. In a relative sense that happened, and it was an image which Gandhi nurtured from the time of his return from South Africa in 1914, and then very explicitly at Champaran in Bihar, Bardoli in Gujarat, and at the all-India level during the Non-

Cooperation Movement of the early 1920s, the Salt Satyagraha and Civil Disobedience Movement of the early 1930s, and after. Writing from Gandhi's inner circle at the time of his last imprisonment in late 1942, his close companion, Sushila Nayar, observes that 'Gandhiji had identified himself with the masses. To ensure the freedom of the common man and eliminate exploitation of the weak by the strong, he felt that decentralization of political and economic power was necessary.'[48]

It turns out that there were many countervailing influences in the Gandhi schema of social reform and political freedom that militated against the reality of 'eliminating exploitation of the common man and the weak'. Among these influences was Gandhi's concept of trusteeship, which was not unrelated to the larger question of attracting and maintaining the financial and political support of landlord interests in the freedom movement. No place in India perhaps saw so dramatic a juxtaposition of a committed Gandhian leadership on the one hand, and a dominant and a controlling landlord community on the other, as did Bihar. Rajendra Prasad, subsequently India's first President, was in the 1930s and 1940s the major Indian National Congress figure in Bihar, and widely considered both then and subsequently to be the quintessential Gandhian.[49] In the circumstances it is perhaps not surprising that there would be a collision between the agrarian policies that the Congress party did or did not implement when it assumed office in 1937 and the interests and expectations of the peasants as mobilized in the Bihar Provincial Kisan Sabha under the leadership of Sahajanand.

The specific encounter I cite here, the first among many, happened shortly after the Congress accepted office in late July 1937. The issue involved a range of tenancy reform that had emerged out of the Faizpur Agrarian Programme of the Indian National Congress and that became the focus of the election campaign in late 1936, which the Congress party won with the massive support of peasant interests, specifically that of the Bihar Provincial Kisan Sabha and Sahajanand himself. It was this background which raised expectations that serious legislative change would be forthcoming.

Describing some of the massive rallies and demonstrations of peasants in Patna and Gaya meant to bring pressure on the Congress party in the Bihar Legislative Assembly, Sahajanand writes about the changing perceptions among prominent Gandhian Congressmen to the nature of peasant support:

There was an interesting incident which occurred at about this time

> which helped me understand the views of our Congress ministers. Shortly after several big *kisan* rallies involving lakhs of *kisans* had taken place in Patna, I happened to meet the Prime Minister.[50] [This was Shri Krishna Singh, the head of government and another committed Gandhian. The office is now designated as that of chief minister.] In the course of our conversation he warned me to beware of the mob: 'Swamiji, beware of this mob!' I listened quietly! But I thought within myself that there was a time when these ministers referred to large gatherings of the *kisans* as the masses. But today they have become a mob! These *kisan* rallies were mobs earlier as well, but then it was expedient for the peasants to be referred to as the masses! And now what was a mob in fact, has again become a mob in name! Perhaps these leaders no longer need the *kisans* and so they have become the mob! The [British] government always referred to the peasants as a mob, and now our [Congress] ministers have become the government! Which is perhaps why they have adopted the same epithet! What a piece of irony! [p. 490]

It is a level of irony that perhaps serves as a more-than-adequate conclusion to this brief disquisition on the value of Sahajanand's memoir as a window on the social and political reality of the crucial decades of the 1920s and 1930s leading to political freedom in 1947. It was a freedom won with the sustained support of India's peasants. I think Sahajanand's point and my point is that peasant support was consistently forthcoming, while that of the Congress and the wider political establishment, in some reciprocal sense, to bring the story forward to the contemporary present, was less so. Therein lies the irony. It is a continuing process and a continuing story, which in the end, certainly from the perspective of the peasants of the 1970s, 1980s, and 1990s, reinforces the irony.[51] And the events in Bihar of March and April 2000, with the Indian National Congress, firmly condemning ten years of Laloo Raj in the Assembly elections of February and then suddenly entering into a coalition with the ruling Rashtriya Janata Dal of Laloo Prasad Yadav, confirms the irony more powerfully than anything I can write.

Reflections on Meanings

I am convinced that David Arnold, Mattison Mimes, and Andre Beteille have it right when they tell us that the individual lives of the many players in India's (political) history are significant for what they obviously reveal about themselves and so too about the social, cultural, and political qualities of the nation.[52] But neither Indians nor those of us who think about their individual and social lives live in an either/or world. In other words, focusing on Indian life histories does not mean that those lives are inevitably irreconcilable with ideas of hierarchy, kinship, family, and religion. What it does mean, however, is that we must go beyond the commonly accepted-wisdom that the notion of the individual and the self is somehow outside the pale of Indian experience.

That Sahajanand was dramatically conscious of his individual selfhood to the point of persistent and consistent rebellion is revealed on every page of his *Mera Jivan Sangharsh*. That process of struggle with the prevailing orthodoxies—whether personal, social, cultural, religious, or political—is what defined each of the overlapping phases of the Swami's life history from the very beginning in the Deva village of his birth in Ghazipur. It was that individual sensibility that moved him, despite a brilliant school career, to fly in the face of his family's expectations, to take the vows of *sannyas* in 1907, and then to confront the world of religion, of caste dominance, and hence to a life of service in politics. But there, too, if reality fell short of his expectations, he was prepared to engage and take issue not only with the dominant Congress, but with the Mahatma himself, moving ultimately, as I have suggested in the preceding pages, to adopt the cause of the poorest of the poor. If we accept Andre Beteille's formulation of seeking values in the context of behaviour, then the case for Sahajanand's identity as his own person is clear.

It was for Sahajanand a personal and public identity that was constantly being redefined and reconceptualized in his transforming and transformed selfhood. His was a career always on the leading edge of cultural, social, and political change. For him that change had to be transformational. I would argue that Sahajanand uses the *Sangharsh* text to identify his selfhood and to define the transformations through which it evolves to a new, modern, political Sahajanand. In the end the text reveals what this transformational process means for him and the political world in which he chooses to work, and most particularly for the peasants whose cause he takes as his own, and in that process the cause of the nation. In the end Sahajanand's life history, his struggle, is a reflection of his engagement with and transformation of his Jujhautiya Brahmin self in the arena of the modern political and ultimately with the social, agrarian, and political world of the peasants, and thereby to achieve a symbiotic union of the personal, the social/agrarian, and the political/national.

In that symbiotic engagement on the ground, and specifically in the

Sangharsh text, Sahajanand conflates the historical and the popular, or what Ajay Skaria refers to as the national historical and the national popular.[53] Without pursuing Skaria's interesting argument, my point essentially is that throughout the *Sangharsh* text, Sahajanand consciously explains (and justifies) his autobiographical effort by telling us that the *andolan*, the movement of the peasants for justice and equity as reflected in the Bihar Provincial Kisan Sabha, was a movement and an activism of 'historic importance', and it is incumbent on him (as its central player) to record that history for posterity.[54] That he does this through a vision and with a passion inspired by the peasants of Bihar and of India gives the effort a popular edge and a depth of meaning, significant beyond most such efforts. His *Mera Jivan Sangharsh* is much more than the *Atmakatha* of a Rajendra Prasad, or even the *Atmakatha* of Indulal Yagnik, or the *Meri Jivan Yatra* of a Rahul Sankrityayana, that is the life story of a politically involved player, essentially reporting on that involvement, however determined it may have been. Sahajanand had a passionate commitment to his life and his politics that comes through with a compelling force on every page of the *Mera Jivan Sangharsh* text. It is that passion that makes the life and the *Sangharsh* memoir distinctive.

Epilogue

The Chicago experience with which I began this reflection happened many years ago, amazingly as I think about it, more than fifty. I arrived at Chicago in 1951, a year after Sahajanand's death, and a year before the publication of his *Mera Jivan Sangharsh*, with which I have been concerned in these pages. At that time of course, I was aware of neither, but as I have explained, that changed dramatically in 1957. In the meantime, there have also been many changes in the academy and in the study of South Asia, and equally so in how we perceive the social and political world of rural India. Reflectively, I have benefited in my understanding of that distance in time and its meanings. Personal circumstances have kept me away from this essay and the *Sangharsh* book project it considers for most of the two years since the SOAS Life-Histories Conference in May of 2000. Now, as I resume the reflection and the writing in May 2002, I am constrained to observe briefly on some of the things I have learned in this re-engagement.

So far as our perceptions of rural India are concerned, the first and most obvious comment is that some things have changed and others haven't. I am not surprised, for example, that among my current readers I heard the same question that was posed in the first seminar presentation

I did at Chicago on returning from India in 1959, namely, How do we account for the fact that a peasant movement was led by someone who was a Brahmin and not a peasant as commonly perceived?

I cannot in this brief space begin to examine the sociology of leadership, nor to retrace the remarkable career of Sahajanand that made him who he was and became, beyond what I have done in this paper and the half dozen other essays that have touched on the subject, all of which are cited in the endnotes. The whole point of this paper, and specifically the *Sangharsh* text of Sahajanand, is precisely that he was by no stretch of the imagination a 'traditional' elite. In each of the complex and overlapping phases of his career as a school student, a *sannyasi*, a Shastrik scholar, a caste activist, a Congress party activist, and finally a militant peasant mobilizer, he was always and inevitably in conflict with the prevailing establishment orthodoxies. It was precisely this quality which defined who he was and what he did. Sahajanand was a *sannyasi* to be sure, but in the end a *sannyasi* committed to the well-being of living men and women, the peasants of Bihar and of India. Everything that he said and did, so too his associates and co-workers, and most especially the peasants at all levels of experience who were a part of his life, testifies to the symbiotic nature of the *andolan*, the movement that bound them in their common struggle for equity and justice. That was the *sangharsh* of their collective lives.

It was this lived experience that was central to Sahajanand's understanding of the peasants of Bihar and of India then, just as it continues to be relevant today.[55] The issue has always been two-sided of course: first, Who is a peasant? (some will even question whether 'peasant' is a meaningful term); and second, What are the social and economic conditions that bring the peasants to their present circumstances? It is not my intention here to get involved in either a disciplinary or ideological contretemps with friends and colleagues in anthropology, history, or political science, or those on the left, right, or centre of the political-theoretical spectrum, modern or post-modern. For me the terms peasant (*kisan*) and agricultural labourer (*khet mazdoor*) emerge from the experience and language of the activists and peasants in the fields of conflict, then and now, exemplified in the words and vivid descriptions of Sahajanand and his co-workers, many of whom I have been privileged to know over the years and to observe in their politics and their activism.

I am of course fully aware, oftentimes painfully so, of the tensions and conflict generated by social, economic, or cultural differences on the land, whether these are a function of class, caste, or sectarian sensibilities. I am equally aware that those interests and identities have powerful meanings on the ground where the rural citizens of India live their lives, and that those commitments can and do lead to conflict and violence, not simply at the obvious level of exploitation, but where those identities and interests intrude one on the other.

In my understanding of Sahajanand, I have always been impressed that as his awareness and sensibilities of the village environment of rural India grew and became more subtle and complex, his effort was always to bridge these kinds of social and sectarian interests, and over time to represent the interests of those at the bottom of the social, economic, and cultural hierarchy. Later in his career he had more than a flirtation with the ideological left, but one of the reasons those encounters never became a long-term personal or political commitment had to do, in my view, with his deeply practical concern for what life was like on the ground. His descriptions of the conditions in which men and women lived their daily lives in the villages of rural India, from the earliest days of his spiritual wanderings, to his most militant days of peasant activism, are burned vividly into the mind's eye of anyone who has read them. For Sahajanand the politics of struggle and the politics of bread meant exactly that—bringing justice and equity to the lives of the peasants and labourers in the fields, and feeding hungry stomachs. For Sahajanand the meanings of those peasant lives came from a lifetime of experience. It was not a perception cultivated *a priori* either in politics or theory. If for him the peasants of India, all of them, came first, then by definition the nation too would benefit, either in achieving its political freedom from imperial rule, as it did, or in moving forward on the road of economic growth, which was then and is now a continuing process.

The good news is that in the end in a free and democratic society like that of India, it is the people—by and large peasants—who will decide their destiny. There will inevitably be victories and defeats, but it is in the process of engagement, in the movement (*andolan*) and the struggle (*sangharsh*) now as it was in the 1930s, that the result will be achieved. Vote banks of politicians and theories of armchair ideologues are not irrelevant, but that is not what drives peasant interest in the end. The peasants know better than anyone what their interests are, wherever in the social and political system those interests might be pursued. And in many ways that includes the Dalits, the depressed, downtrodden, and exploited, not because they do not need all the support they can get, but because they too possess an awareness of history and the lived experience that places them in the social and cultural niche defined as Untouchable. Gandhi referred to them as Harijans, or people of God. The term Dalit, or exploited and oppressed, is itself a more aggressively militant expression of the awareness of which I speak.

I conclude pointedly with a reflection about the Dalits, most often the poorest of the poor and the landless labourers in rural India, and Sahajanand, who used the term in 1941 in his *Khet Mazdoor* tract, decades before it came into common usage in the academic and political lexicon of India.[56] Sahajanand understood the meaning of exploitation and conflict. For him the term was struggle, or *sangharsh*. His and that of the peasants, whose lives he helped define, and who helped define his. It was my interest in understanding that phenomenon as an expression of Indian social experience that drew me to Bihar in 1957. It is an interest that continues forty-seven years later, for the same reason.

NOTES

1. Alex Haley, *Roots* (Garden City, NY: Doubleday, 1976).
2. Given the emerging trajectory of my interest in peasant activism at the time, there would be another coincidental confluence of a 'roots' nature with my father's family, who were in fact daily wage labourers, i.e. landless agricultural labourers in Indian terms, on a large landed estate in Galicia or Bukovina in the eastern part of what was then Austrian Poland. This was in the early years of the twentieth century before and during First World War and the Bolshevik Revolution.
3. 'Is There a New Indian History? Society and Social Change Under the Raj', *South Asian Review* 4:1 (October 1970); and in Bernard S. Cohn, *An Anthropologist Among the Historians and Other Essays* (Delhi: Oxford University Press, 1987), pp. 172-99.
4. See Robert Redfield, *Peasant Society and Culture: An Anthropological Approach to Civilization* (Chicago: University of Chicago Press, 1956). This essay was subsequently published together with Redfield's Gottesman Lectures delivered at the University of Uppsala in 1953 as *The Little Community and Peasant Society and Culture* (Chicago: University of Chicago Press, 1960). The Wednesday afternoon India seminar to which I refer was happening in the spring term of 1954. See McKim Marriott, ed., *Village India. Studies in the Little Community* (Chicago: University of Chicago Press, 1955), for the published versions of the papers presented in the Redfield seminar.

   Redfield was in India briefly from September to December 1955 pursuing his 'little tradition' interests, juxtaposed against Milton Singer's 'great tradition' scholarship. During that time he participated in the All India Conference of Anthropologists and Sociologists meeting at the University of Madras, 5-7 November 1955, with among others M.N. Srinivas, Nirmal Kumar Bose, A.M. Shah, I.P. Desai, Irawati Karve, and A. Aiyappan. For papers presented at the conference see Aiyappan and L.K. Bala Ratnam, eds., *Society in India* (Madras: A Social Science Association Publication, 1956). Subsequently, while in Calcutta, Redfield became ill and was advised to return immediately to Chicago where he was diagnosed with lymphatic leukemia. Redfield's plan to access Indian civilization from the perspective of an Orissa village was not to be. He died on 16 October 1958. I am grateful to Rosemary Witko Kaut for helping me with dates and reminiscing about Redfield (19 March 2000 at Charlottesville). Ms. Kaut was Redfield's secretary for two and one half years from 1953 to late 1955 and then briefly in 1958 before his death. For the Aiyappan reference and observations on the Madras conference, I am grateful to Pauline Kolenda, who was a participant to that conference (Personal communication, 31 March 2000).

5. There was no South Asia programme as such at the time at Chicago, but among fellow students working on India were Burton Stein and Brijen K. Gupta in history and Martin Orans in anthropology.
6. Time has dimmed my memory of other participants in the Redfield seminar, but if I am not mistaken, Morris Opler from the Cornell India Project was among them. And there were also visitors from among prominent figures in Indian public life who came to Chicago in those days as well. Perhaps because of my subsequent interest in Bihar and its people, the name of Jaipal Singh, the noted sports figure and political activist from Jharkhand is vividly embedded in my mind among those visitors.
7. Redfield was funded (in 1951) by the Ford Foundation for the Comparative Studies of Cultures and Civilizations seminars of which The Indian Village seminar of April and May 1954 was one. The South Asia programme at Chicago emerged from these beginnings, first with the inauguration of the Introduction to Indian Civilization course in the College in 1956, followed by an expansive transformation in 1958-9 which Ralph Nicholas describes as 'spectacular' (Personal communication, 27 March 2000). This history is recounted briefly in the Redfield and Singer Foreword to *Village India: Studies in the Little Community* (Chicago: University of Chicago Press, 1955), edited by McKim Marriott. As I have indicated, this volume includes the eight papers which were the subjects of the weekly seminar. For further details see Singer's portrait of Redfield in Edward A. Shils, ed., *Remembering the University of Chicago: Teachers, Scientists, and Scholars* (Chicago: University of Chicago Press, 1991), pp. 413-29.
8. To make this part of the story more complete, I should also say that I was named one of the teaching interns in the Introduction to Indian Civilization course in the College for the 1959-60 academic year, an internship supported, as I recall, with Carnegie dollars, though it may have been Ford funding. The course was administered by the Committee on Southern Asian Studies. It was appropriately cross-disciplinary involving most members of the humanities and social sciences faculty with the teaching interns meeting smaller groups of students in regular weekly sessions.
9. Barney Cohn went from the junior visiting appointment in history and anthropology at Chicago to facilitate the creation of a Department of

Anthropology at Rochester, and then returned to Chicago in 1964 and a joint appointment in anthropology and history, a position he held until his retirement in 1995. Myron Weiner was in the Department of Political Science at Chicago from 1956 to 1961 when he accepted an appointment at the Massachusetts Institute of Technology, a position he assumed in 1963. We were all saddened by Myron's death on 3 June 1999. I appreciate especially talking with Sheila Weiner (20 February 2000) and Barney and Rella Cohn (2 April 2000 and 25 October 2001) in helping me confirm relevant dates.

10. As example, the point was made to me on an early visit to Patna by the eminent historian of ancient India, R.C. Majumdar, who had himself only recently published one of the many histories of 1857 which the centenary of that event generated. It will surprise no one that additionally, on that tenth anniversary of Freedom, there were collections of documents and histories of the Freedom Movement being issued many decades before the ill-fated Towards Freedom project of the Indian Council of Historical Research, so much in the news in the early months of 2000. See for example, K.K. Datta, *History of the Freedom Movement in Bihar*, 3 vols. (Patna: Government of Bihar, 1957); Government of U.P., *Freedom Struggle in Uttar Pradesh: Source Material*, 3 vols. (Lucknow: U.P. Publications Bureau, 1957); and Government of Bombay, *Source Material for a History of the Freedom Movement in India* (Collected from Bombay Government Records), vols. 1 and 2 (Bombay: Government Central Press, 1957).
11. Jawaharlal Nehru, *An Autobiography* (London: Bodley Head, 1936). Reprinted with additional chapter, 1942, pp. 49, 54-5, 61, and 63.
12. Sahajanand and Nehru were both political prisoners in the Lucknow Jail in 1922, when they agreed to meet one day 'after the midday meal', in Sahajanand's quarters. Sahajanand recounts the occasion and his surprise and satisfaction that Nehru insisted on being the visitor and not the host as Sahajanand had proposed, given that this was during the hot summer season. See *Mera Jivan Sangharsh* [My Life Struggle] (Bihta: Shri Sitaram Ashram, 1952), p. 242.
13. Nehru, op. cit., p. 601.
14. On these early perceptions of Nehru and Homi Bhabha on issues of nuclear energy and security, see George Perkovich, *India's Nuclear Bomb: The Impact on Global Proliferation* (Berkeley: University of California Press, 1999), and especially the review by A.G. Noorani in *Frontline* (17 March 2000). Other relevant recent reviews of this title are those appearing in *Biblio: A Review of Books* (November-December 1999) and *The Times Literary Supplement* (21 January 2000). The Perkovich book is distributed in the UK by Wiley, and published in India by the Oxford University Press.
15. *Darshan* is from Sanskrit, literally the act of seeing, having sight of, being seen, in this case being in the presence of a respected public figure (or otherwise a deity) and gaining merit from that transaction. The idea was of course especially familiar in the case of Gandhi, as it was also certainly with Sahajanand in his role as a Dasnami Sannyasi, or Swami, from his early religious career. It

was a quality, however, that certainly carried over into his secular, political career.

16. For those readers unfamiliar with the complex trajectory of Sahajanand's career, I must make two points entirely clear at the outset, first, that swamis in politics are not at all uncommon in India. Without stretching the point very far, we need only cite the case of Gandhi the Mahatma in the political history of twentieth-century India. That Gandhi and Sahajanand intersected very directly at this political conjunction is one of the central issues in their very interesting relationship. The other point is that Sahajanand's career went through many very distinct phases which variously impinged or did not impinge on successive phases. I am suggesting that founding a Sanskrit school was not at all inconsistent with who Sahajanand was before, or more importantly, who he became after, the pre-eminent peasant activist of the twentieth century. For a consideration of some of these issues see my essay 'Sahajanand and the Politics of Social Reform', *The Indian Historical Review* 18:1-2 (July 1991-January 1992), pp. 59-75. The most detailed representation of Sahajanand's role in the social, cultural, and political history of India is contained in his *Mera Jivan Sangharsh* [My Life Struggle] memoir. I am presently completing an edited translation of this important document.
17. On the Bongaon meeting (and others), see, M.A. Rasul, *A History of the All India Kisan Sabha* (Calcutta: National Book Agency, 1989), pp. 195-204.
18. David Arnold, 'The Self and the Cell: India's Prison Autobiographies', presented in the Life Histories Workshop of the School of Oriental and African Studies, University of London, 6 November 1998. I wish to thank Dr Arnold for providing me an early draft of this paper.
19. Among the many other relevant autobiographies touching either on Bihar or peasant activism, or both are those of Rajendra Prasad, Rahul Sankrityayana, and Indulal Yagnik. Rajendra Prasad's original *Atmakatha* appeared in English as *Autobiography* (Bombay: Asia Publishing House, 1957); Indulal Yagnik's *Atmakatha* was published in Ahmedabad in six volumes between 1955 and 1973. Yagnik, a close associate of Sahajanand in the 1930s and 1940s died in 1971 while vol. 6 was in process, so that volume is incomplete and comes up to his involvement with the Maha-Gujarat movement. Rahul Sankrityayana's *Meri Jivan Yatra* was published in five volumes, the first in 1944 (reissued by Adhunik Pustak Bhavan, Calcutta in 1951), the second and most elaborate in 1950 (Allahabad: Kitab Mahal), and the remaining three volumes posthumously in 1967 (Delhi: Rajkamal Prakashan). Sankrityayana was an eminent Buddhologist, litterateur, political activist, and world traveller. He was member of the CPI from 1938 to 1948, and his peasant activism happened mainly in the late 1930s and primarily in Bihar. See pp. 494-549 of vol. 2 for this phase of his remarkable career and p. 543 for a brief characterization of Sahajanand. To my knowledge, none of these volumes have been translated into English. Yagnik's *Atmakatha* has been translated by Howard Spodek and his associates (in 1986) and I am grateful to Spodek for providing me a copy of that translation,

important sections of which touch on Yagnik's association with Sahajanand. On Yagnik see also the recent essay of Ajay Skaria, 'Homeless in Gujarat and India: On the Curious Love of Indulal Yagnik', *The Indian Economic and Social History Review*, 38:3 (June-September 2001), 271-97.

20. M.K. Gandhi, *An Autobiography,* or *The Story of My Experiments With Truth* (Ahmedabad: Navijivan Publishing House, 1958), p. xiii. The emphasis here is mine.
21. Ibid., p. xiv.
22. See Karen E. James, 'From Mohandas to Mahatma: The Spiritual Metamorphosis of Gandhi', *Essays in History*, vol. 28 (1984), pp. 5-20. *Essays* is published annually by the (postgraduate students of the Department of History of the University of Virginia. Karen James was a final year BA student in a Major's Seminar I taught that year on Gandhi, effectively in response to Attenborough's Gandhi film. Her essay was judged to be the best essay written that year on an Indian subject, and the best undergraduate essay on any subject, in the College, and hence published in *Essays in History*.
23. See Shahid Amin, *Event, Metaphor, Memory: Chauri-Chaura, 1922-1992* (Berkeley: University of California Press, 1995), and specifically p. 161 and following on Gandhi in Chauri-Chaura. Also note the Attenborough representation of the event in the film *Gandhi*.
24. While it is not directly relevant at this point, I think it is necessary to mention the recent work of the historian William R. Pinch on martial asceticism, and his effort, at least indirectly at this stage, to contextualize the idea and practice of Gandhi's nationalist asceticism in the wider historical experience of asceticism in the subcontinent. Among other things, Pinch's suggestion is likely to expand our understanding of the Gandhian idea beyond the Mahatma's psycho-civilizational dialogue with the West, which is so prominent in our effort to engage the man and his politics. See Pinch, 'Killing Ascetics in Indian History, ca. 1500-2000', NEH Grant Proposal, in *Political and Legal Anthropology Review* (Methodology Section) 23:2 (November 2000), 134-40. An earlier version of this essay was presented in the symposium on Asian Scholarship in Politically Charged Environments, Center for South Asian Studies, University of Virginia, 21-2 April 2000. An intersecting and related set of issues are considered by Joseph S. Alter in his *Gandhi's Body: Sex, Diet, and the Politics of Nationalism* (Philadelphia: University of Pennsylvania Press, 2000). Equally relevant to this conversation are the creative ideas of Ajay Skaria in his forthcoming book, *Gandhi's Neighbours: Liberalism and the Question of the Ashram.* I thank Professor Skaria for sharing with me parts of that manuscript in progress (23 April 2002).
25. Gandhi, *Autobiography*, p. xiii.
26. Many of the themes raised by Gandhi's social and political critics including Sahajanand, as cited in the later pages of this paper, were also explored in contemporary literature, especially that of south India. See for example, Raja Rao, *Kanthapura* (Bombay: Oxford University Press, 1947); and R.K. Narayan,

Waiting for the Mahatma (London: Methuen, 1955). I thank Anne Monius for reinforcing this very important point.

27. While it is not my direct concern in this paper, we can certainly say with confidence that autobiography and memoir are central to the intellectual experience of India and Indians, historically and in the contemporary present. David Arnold suggests that there are literally hundreds of examples, and I am familiar with dozens of life histories, some of which I have mentioned in note 19 above. And I cannot resist noting the remarkable seventeenth-century autobiography of Banarsidas, merchant, poet, and Jain religious figure. See his *Ardhakathanaka, Half a Tale: A Study in the Interrelationship Between Autobiography and History*. Translated, introduced, and annotated by Mukund Lath (Jaipur: Rajasthan Prakrit Bharati Sansthan, 1981). I thank Professor Sumit Guha for calling this important document to my attention.
28. That searching, as an eighteen year old yet impressionable *sannyasi* moving by foot across much of north India, exposed Sahajanand to many of the social and economic realities of the rural countryside. They were impressions that would last a lifetime and reinforce his sensibilities about what it meant to be hungry and poor. He did not forget.
29. I touch on this issue in my essay in the Sunil Sen memorial volume edited by Chittabrata Palit. See 'Peasants, Activists, and Scholars: A Late Twentieth Century Reflection on Definitions', in Palit, ed., *Political Economy and Protest in Colonial India* (Calcutta: Firma KLM, 1997), pp. 251-67. See also Shahid Amin and Gyan Pandey, eds., *Nimnavargiya Prasang* (New Delhi: Rajkamal Prakashan, 1995), a collection of essays from the Subaltern project, conveyed in Hindi, especially the introduction by the editors. Also relevant are the reviews of this title by Arvind Das in *Biblio*: II:1 (February 1996), and by Harish Trivedi in *The Book Review* XX:2-3 (February-March 1996).
30. For a reprise of Sahajanand's early career, especially in his pre-Kisan Sabha and pre-1930s religious and social reform phase, see my essay, 'Swami Sahajanand and the Politics of Social Reform', *The Indian Historical Review* 18:1-2 (July 1991-January 1992), pp. 59-75. Brief introductions to his political career can be found in Walter Hauser, ed., *Sahajanand on Agricultural Labour and the Rural Poor* (New Delhi: Manohar Publishers, 1994), pp. xiii-xix; and Hauser, ed., *Swami Sahajanand and the Peasants of Jharkhand: A View from 1941* (New Delhi: Manohar, 1995), pp. xvii-xxiii.
31. In his differences with Gandhi after 1934, as I have already suggested, Sahajanand was certainly not alone among the major political players of the day. The names of Subhas Chandra Bose, B.R. Ambedkar, and M.N. Roy come quickly to mind in this context, at least two of whom are inevitably included in the currently perceived pantheon of Founders.
32. For an elaboration of this idea comparing politics and politicians from the perceptions of 1997 and fifty years of freedom with the reality of Freedom Movement politics, see my essay, 'From the Freedom Movement to Freedom: On the Dilemma of Politics, Politicians, and the Political Classes, Circa 1920-

1997', presented initially at the international conference on Bihar in the World and the World in Bihar, 15-19 December 1997 at Patna. The Bihar conference was organized by Arvind Narayan Das, sponsored by the Asian Development Research Institute (ADRI) of Patna and supported in part by the European Science Foundation. We were all deeply saddened by Dr Das' untimely death in Amsterdam on 6 August 2000. He was editing the essays of the Bihar conference for publication at the time.

33. Please note that all extracts in this essay from Sahajanand's *Mera Jivan Sangharsh* are drawn from the original 1952 edition published at Bihta (Patna), by the Swami's Shri Sitaram Ashram. The book comes to 570 pages of Devanagri text. With the exception of a short epilogue section, this manuscript was written in 1940 and 1941 when Sahajanand was incarcerated in the Hazaribagh Central Jail. Because space does not permit me to include extended or continuous quotations from *Mera Jivan*, I have tried to convey Sahajanand's meanings by abstracting and collapsing his argument into a tighter representation while at the same time retaining the directness and candour of his style. Some material has also been reordered in the interest of continuity. The range of pages from which extracts are taken is shown in brackets at the end of each section of text material. There have been two subsequent Hindi editions of *Mera Jivan*, the first issued by the People's Publishing House, New Delhi, 1985, and the second edited by Awadhesh Pradhan and issued in Delhi by Granthshilpi in 2000. This new edition is supplemented by a series of additional essays by and about Sahajanand.
34. *Mera Jivan Sangharsh*, p. 185. In some very particular way this statement reflects for Sahajanand the melding in his mind and action of the person who was a renunciate and at the same time active in the world of public affairs. See my 'Swami Sahajanand and the Politics of Social Reform', *The Indian Historical Review* 18:1-2 (July 1991-January 1992), pp. 59-75, for a more detailed examination of this issue.
35. *Mera Jivan Sangharsh*, p. 187.
36. Ibid., p. 212.
37. Ibid., pp. 212-13.
38. Ibid., p. 349.
39. I touch on these transitions of Sahajanand as swami to Sahajanand as peasant activist in the 'Politics of Social Reform' essay (*IHR* 1991-2) cited in note 34 above. See also my edited translation of Sahajanand's *Khet Mazdoor* tract for his remarkable take on the world of the poorest of the poor. This is Hauser, ed., *Sahajanand on Agricultural Labour and Rural Poor* (New Delhi: Manohar, 1994). See esp., pp. 72-89.
40. Sahajanand was a political prisoner on three occasions. He was arrested at Ghazipur in January 1922, almost immediately on his return from Ahmedabad, as he was again in April 1930 in Bihar at the time of the Salt Satyagraha, each time for a year. And then from 1940 to 1942 Sahajanand was at the Hazaribagh Central Jail for a period of two years.

41. The slogan literally means, Victory to Gandhi, here as most commonly, in the honorific form Gandhiji.
42. The fascinating point that emerges in this paragraph and indeed this entire section, and which Sahajanand makes himself, is that there were many perceptions of who Gandhi was and what he meant, depending on what personal and political interests were being served. The point in this case is no different than what Shahid Amin has made with reference to the peasants of Gorakhpur and Chauri-Chaura, albeit the actors in the present instance were 'educated'. From the perspective of the argument I am making in this paper one might say that it was then as it is now and in most politics, a matter of self-interest. On Shahid Amin's argument see, for example 'Gandhi as Mahatma: Gorakhpur District, Eastern U.P., 1921-22', in *Subaltern Studies*, III, ed. Ranajit Guha (New Delhi: Oxford University Press, 1984), pp. 1-61; and *Event, Metaphor, Memory: Chauri Chaura, 1922-1992* (Berkeley: University of California Press, 1995).
43. Sahajanand captures here the intimate quality of the whole jail atmosphere of which he is so critical, i.e. the attitudes of many of the political prisoners assuming a Gandhian pose but ignoring the most basic elements of Gandhi's logic, the breaking of jail rules on the one hand while seeking the good life in jail on the other. Sahajanand suggests that with rare exception everyone was doing it; and one of those exceptions was obviously Rajendra Prasad.
44. Here Sahajanand's objections to the behaviour of his fellow prisoners is shifting from the moral to the strategic, opening the movement, in his view, to a divide and rule logic. His opposition to Gandhi would also increasingly shift to the explicitly political, as will be apparent in the next example.
45. Coincidentally, the president of the Palasa session of the AIKS was Rahul Sankrityayana, who was however already jailed and hence unable to serve. He was subsequently a 'special invitee' at the Bezwada session in 1944, when Sahajanand was again the president. See Rasul, *A History of the All India Kisan Sabha*, pp. 109-14.
46. Sahajanand provides here a less than veiled sarcasm in his retrospective reflection on this encounter with Gandhi.
47. Gandhi was obviously harking back here to his dramatically more limited encounter with the peasants of Champaran in north Bihar in 1917, where he succeeded in resolving that local problem by generating and providing specific individual instances of peasant tenant grievances. In that instance Gandhi made his case and the government responded.
48. Sushila Nayar, *Mahatma Gandhi's Last Imprisonment: The Inside Story* (New Delhi: Har-Anand Publications, 1996), p. 19.
49. On Rajendra Prasad's position of dominance in the Bihar Congress, see Jawaharlal Nehru, *An Autobiography*, pp. 488-9; and Walter Hauser, 'Changing Images of Caste and Politics', in *Seminar* 450, The State of Bihar: A Symposium on the Legacy of a Troubled State (February 1997), pp. 47-52.

50. A lakh is one hundred thousand.
51. On the politics of the these decades in Bihar see Walter Hauser, 'Violence, Agrarian Radicalism and Electoral Politics: Reflections on the Indian People's Front', *The Journal of Peasant Studies* 21:1 (October 1993), pp. 85-126.
52. See David Arnold, 'The Self and the Cell', SOAS Workshop Paper, 6 November 1998; Mattison Mines, 'Conceptualizing the Person: Hierarchical Society and Individual Autonomy in India', in R.T. Ames, ed., *Self as Person in Asian Theory and Practice* (Albany, SUNY Press, 1998); and Andre Beteille, 'Individualism and Equality', in *Current Anthropology* 27 (1986), pp. 121-34.
53. In a running series of personal conversations at Charlottesville in 1998 and 1999, and more specifically in the unpublished draft of Skaria's paper 'National, Historical, Popular: the Many Lives of Indulal Yagnik', presented in the Writing Lives Symposium of the Center for South Asian Studies of the University of Virginia, 23 and 24 April 1999. For the current version of that paper see Ajay Skaria, 'Homeless in Gujarat and India: On the Curious Love of Indulal Yagnik', *The Indian Economic and Social History Review*, 38:3 (June-September 2001), 271-97.
54. See for example his comments on this issue on p. 316 of *Mera Jivan Sangharsh.*
55. The suggestion is that as peasants in the year 2004 seek to achieve their goals of social and economic justice, many of them are aware, certainly in Bihar and more than fifty years after the fact, that Sahajanand set the tone. Few have read or know *Mera Jivan Sangharsh* as a text, but the history it tells is a shared story of struggle. It is an awareness that I encounter in the villages of Bihar now no less often than I did on my first visit in 1957 and 1958.
56. See Hauser, ed., *Sahajanand on Agricultural Labour and the Rural Poor* (New Delhi: Manohar, 1994), pp. 73, 81-2.

The Sepoy Mutinies Revisited

RUDRANGSHU MUKHERJEE

The revolt of 1857 or the Indian Mutiny, as it is still conveniently labelled in most of the western world, was spread over a large area covering from Delhi in the north-west to Bihar in the east, and from the foothills of the Himalayas to Jhansi. There were scattered instances of revolt outside this area. Within the area, again, the region north of the river Yamuna right upto Awadh seems to have been the core where the sepoy mutinies were clustered and the rebellion most popular and intense.

This paper concentrates, against the current fashion, on the sepoy mutinies: on the *sipahi* and his activities. There are reasons for looking at the sepoy mutinies separately. In the literature on 1857, rich as it is, this is a neglected aspect. In the nineteenth-century, in the high noon of British imperialism, when the great narratives of the 'Mutiny' were written, the activities of the sepoys were written about as something disorderly and chaotic: the work of disloyal soldiery. This could give rise to ambiguities. For example, J.W. Kaye called his account, *The History of the Sepoy War, 1857-58*. For him, the events of 1857 were nothing more than the work of sepoys, a very small section of the population; yet, he called it a 'war', a term that implies the involvement of a large section of the population and also more importantly, a degree of planning, co-ordination and organization. More recently, Eric Stokes has drawn attention to the military tactics of the sepoys.[1] But, for him, the mutinies were 'the work of a small minority'; the mutinies were the product of 'designing men'; a conspiring few substituted for collective action.[2] In nationalist historiography, prone as it is to prove that 1857 was much more than a mere mutiny, the tendency is to gloss over the activities of the sepoys. Thus, in the writings of S.B. Chaudhuri, the activities of the sepoys are not discussed; he writes only about the civil rebellions which, to him, were important.[3] This paper will attempt to show that these approaches are flawed: they fundamentally misunderstand the nature of sepoy action, thereby also missing the crucial interconnections between the sepoy mutinies and the popular rebellion.

I have argued elsewhere[4] that a chronological survey of the mutinies suggests a certain pattern. The first outbreak takes place on 10 May at Meerut. There the soldiers having mutinied sped off towards Delhi. It is significant that between 10 and 14 May there were no mutinies in any of the garrisons of north India. It is only after the sepoys in Delhi had mutinied (11-12 May) that the other garrisons in north India follow suit as if in chain reaction: 20 May-Aligarh, 23 May-Etwah, and Mainpuri, 27 May-Etah, 30 May-Lucknow, 4 June-Kanpur and so on. There is here a contagion of movement facilitated by the fact that there was a degree of communication between the sepoy lines. Often, such communication could be direct. The 7th Awadh Irregular Infantry, who had refused to take the cartridges in early May, wrote to the 48th Native Infantry that 'they had acted for the faith and awaited the 48th orders'.[5] Men moved from one cantonment to another carrying the message of mutiny: in Kaye's words these were the 'emissaries of evil'.[6] Sepoys came from Benaras to Lucknow, British officers reported, 'to corrupt the troops'.[7] The sepoy lines in Fyzabad were swarming with mutinous sepoys from neighbouring Azamgarh and Jaunpur.[8] In Salon, the mutiny occurred only when mutineers from Allahabad, Sultanpur and Partapgarh had come there and 'goaded' the troops in Salon to rise.[9]

Edwards, the Magistrate of Budaun, noted that the 10th N.I. in Fatehgarh would mutiny depending on the movements of other mutinous corps with whom they were in daily correspondence.[10] In the context of communication of the message of revolt, the experience of Francois Sisten, a native Christian police inspector in Sitapur, is revealing. He had gone to pay his respects to the joint magistrate of Saharanpur and was dressed and seated like an Indian. A Muslim *tahsildar* of Bijnor entered and asked Sisten where he was from. On hearing that the latter was from Awadh, the *tahsildar* said, 'What news from Awadh? How does the work progress, brother?' Sisten replied, 'If we have work in Awadh your highness will know it well.' The *tahsildar* interpreting this as caution said: 'Depend upon it, we will succeed this time, the direction of the business is in able hands.' People were thus planning and talking of the uprising. In fact, the *tahsildar* was later to be the chief rebel leader of Bijnor.[11]

There were others instances, too, of communication through non-military sources. The official narrative for Meerut noted that

> one of the many emissaries who were moving about the country, appeared at Meerut in April, ostensibly as a fukeer, riding on an elephant with the follower and having with him horses and native carriages. The frequent visits of the men of the native regiments to him attracted attention and he was ordered through the police to leave the place. He apparently complied, but it is said, he stayed some time in the lines of the 20th N I.[12]

Lucknow, too, immediately after the annexation of Awadh, was full of religious leaders and self-styled prophets all preaching the destruction of British rule.[13] The outbreak of the mutinies was not chaotic or disorderly. On the contrary, the *sipahis* showed a remarkable degree of planning and co-ordination in the way the mutinies were carried out. The mutinies began at a preappointed signal: in Bareilly, Lucknow and Meerut the signal was the firing of the evening gun. In Fyzabad, it was the sounding of the bugle at 10.00 p.m.[14] In Kanpur, the sounding of the bugle was the signal for the massacre to begin at Satichaurpura Ghat.[15] The execution of the mutiny, in most places, was well-planned. In Fyzabad, for example, as the bugle sounded the troops quickly organized themselves: they stopped the gunners from touching their guns and under the direction of a *risaidar* (an Indian infantry officer) the English officers of the 22nd and 6th were placed with the Quarter Guard. The *sawars* patrolled all roads and approaches to the cantonment.[16]

Such instances indicate planning and suggest a decision-making body which laid down the plan of action. The crucial question is, of course, what were such bodies, and how and when they were formed. Unfortunately, no direct answers to these questions can be provided. But from two events one can get clues as to how the mutinies came to be so well-organized. The first is the experience of Captain Hearsey of the Awadh Military Police. During the mutiny he had been given protection by his Indian subordinates. The 41st Native Infantry, stationed in the same place, insisted that as they had murdered all their officers it was necessary for the military police to do the same or deliver Hearsey up as prisoner to the 41st. The Military Police refused to do either and so it was decided to settle the matter by refering it to a *panchayat*, i.e., a collective body composed of native officers drawn from each regiment.[17] Ball in his *The History of the Indian Mutiny* noted that *panchayats* were a nightly occurrence in the Kanpur sepoy lines.[18] There is a suggestion here that matters were decided collectively and given the character of the sepoy lines it is not difficult to imagine sepoys sitting together to decide their own future.

The other piece of evidence is a little more vivid. It concerns the Mangal Pandey episode. This is one of the better documented episodes of the Revolt and its origins. The investigations revealed that before Mangal Pandey decided to act there had been midnight meetings in Barrackpore which had been attended by sepoys from different regiments. And, on that fateful afternoon when he opened fire on his officers none except one of his fellow sepoys, all of whom had gathered around, tried to stop him. The only exception was Sheikh Paltu. In fact the other sepoys displayed a complicity, for while Mangal Pandey drew his sword and slashed and wounded Lieutenant Baugh, an unidentified sepoy hit Sgt.-Major Hewson from behind. During his trial, Mangal Pandey steadfastly refused, in a remarkable show of solidarity, to name the sepoys who were implicated. He had only one answer that he had acted on his own. His reiteration of his own responsibility for his own actions can be read as an attempt to shield the reality which was the exact opposite of an individual acting on his own. The collective aspect was again made evident when sepoys of the 34th, Mangal Pandey's regiment trampled their caps on the ground when they were disarmed. A gesture of protest carried out collectively which would in a month's time transform itself to more violent and concrete forms.[19]

The sepoys were thus the makers of their own rebellion: they did not undertake to challenge the might of the Company Bahadur in a fit of absent-mindedness. They were conscious agents and their acts were marked by deliberation and planning. This needs emphasis because all too often in the literature on the subject their actions are described as 'spontaneous', i.e., lacking a coherent programme and plan. As Gramsci wrote, it is only a 'scholastic and academic historico-political outlook which sees as real and worthwhile only such movements of revolt as are one hundred per cent conscious, i.e., movements that are governed by plans worked out in advance to the last detail or in line with abstract theory.' Indeed, as Gramsci would have it, ' "pure" spontaneity does not exist in history.' The sepoys had a consciousness which was framed, one could say following Gramsci, 'through everyday experience illuminated by "common sense"'.[20] As conscious agents the sepoys chose to destroy. Direct action, that commonest form of popular protest, informed the sepoys' moment of insurgency. In each and every station the commencement of the mutiny was marked by extensive arson and plunder. The official narrative from Meerut described the ferocity of the destruction,

> the inveterate animosity with which the work of destruction was carried out . . . may be judged of by the fact, that houses built entirely of masonary, with nothing inflammable, except the doors and beams which a considerable height from the ground supported the roof formed of cement, resting on kiln-burnt bricks, were as effectually destroyed as the thatched bungalows. Property, which the miscreants could not carry off, was thrown out and smashed into fragments, evidently pounded to pieces with heavy clubs.[21]

The mutinies were signalled by arson. Kaye noted this:

> What meetings and conspiracies and oath-takings there may have been in the sipahi's quarter...can only be conjectured; but one form of expression in which the feelings declared themselves, was patent to all. It was written in characters of fire and blazed out of the darkness of the night. From the verandahs of their houses the European officers saw these significant illuminations and knew what they portended.[22]

As W.H. Carey put it, 'And thus the Fire King began to demonstrate an inkling of what was in store for almost every station in the North-Western Provinces.'[23]

The destruction was not indiscriminate. Property owned, used or lived by the British were always the first to be attacked. Thus the bungalows in which the Europeans lived, alien to any kind of Indian residence, were always the first to be attacked and burnt. Buildings identified with the British, their institutions, the symbols of their power were invariably destroyed. Thus, in Aligarh one large indigo factory, the property of an European, went up in flames. Similarly, 'the records of the Suddur Cutcherry and those of four out of eight Tehseels were destroyed.'[24] Invariably, the government offices were the object of rebel wrath. In Etawah, the *kachahri*, the sessions court house, the post office—all symbols of alien domination—were victims of incendiary attacks.[25] Almost always the records of the tahsil were destroyed in a symbolic rejection of all that a foreign power had enshrined in its records. For the rebel the mark of enmity was unmistakable. The enmity could also be extended through association. Friends of the British became enemies of the sepoys. Thus, the Bengalis who were seen as the next thing to a Christian, were plundered and forced to swear allegiance to the 'native' government. Bholanath Chunder, a Bengali, wrote,

> The Bengalis cowered in fear, and awaited within closed doors to have their throats cut. The women raised a dolorous cry at the near prospect of death from massacring their officers, and plundering the Treasury, and letting open the gaol-bird, the sipahis spread through the town to loot the inhabitants. Our friend, as well as his other neighbours were soon eased of all their valuables, but were spared their lives on promise of allegiance to their (the Native) Government.[26]

To most north Indians Bengalis at this time were an object of ridicule; as one of them put it, the Bengalis were only good for being attorneys or for teaching Milton and Shakespeare.[27]

By this logic of extension those that had gained from British rule became targets of rebel fury. Dunlop described vividly one such attack:

> ...many of the prisoners released had enemies in the district, mostly Bunyahs who had brought suits in our courts and the arrival of a period of anarchy was at once seized on by them to wreak a summary revenge on almost all the Bunyah caste. Thus at the village of Bhojpore, the best house, a large brick building with a courtyard in the centre and massive wooden portals, belonged to the family of a Mahajun or Bunyah, by name Beharee Lall, who was a four Biswa (or one fifth) sharer of that village; one of the other shareholders, a Jat, was at the time of the outbreak in prison, confined for debt under the Civil court decree at the suit of the Bunyah. He arrived during the light of the 11th at Bhojpore with a few of his fellow prisoners and at daylight the villagers were collected for an attack on the Bunyah house.[28]

What began as an individual vendetta soon transformed itself into an entire village's fury against an oppressor and led to the latter's destruction.

As the above quotations make evident, one of the obvious targets of destruction was the jail. One of the first things the mutineers did was to break open the jails. It appeared to them to be the epitome of domination of an alien legal system. In Meerut, the mutineers rushed to the new jail, 'dug out of the wall the gratings of some of the windows of the ward...and took their comrades away' and in the jail 'about 300 or 400 sipahees released the convicts.'[29]

Through the previous one hundred years of colonial rule the sepoys had been kicked, flogged and brutalized: they had seen comrades blown from the mouth of canons. In their own movements against their quondam masters they replicated that violence on the master's property and on the master's body. 'Troopers and sipahees' the official narrative of the Meerut outbreak noted, 'were plundering, burning and destroying in every direction and savagely hunting to death every European, every Christian, man, woman or child they could find.'[30] Such replication is, of course, not uncommon. George Rude in his study of the eighteenth-century crowd in Paris and London wrote, 'The eighteenth-century crowd...could hardly fail to be corrupted by the example set them by their social betters. It was an era of brutal floggings, torture of prisoners and public executions.'[31] Again, Richard Cobb in his study of French popular protest juxtaposed the violence of the *sans cullottes* with the violence of the ruling class of the *ancien regime*.[32]

The springboard of this violence was the common hatred of all things British. But this hatred, itself, grew from or was aggravated by two interrelated factors. I have discussed already the contagion of the mutiny in its spread from one sepoy line to another. A similar transmission was noticeable in the rumours that circulated in north India in the summer of 1857. There were rumours about greased cartridges, about flours polluted by the bone-dust of cows and pigs, about the intentions of the British to disarm the sepoys, about forcible conversions to Christianity and about the inevitable end of British rule at the centenary of Plassey.[33] All these rumours circulating at the same time aggregated into one gigantic rumour. Untraceable in their origin and unverifiable in their import, the rumours moved in a powerful current touching on issues that were profoundly close to indigenous sentiments. Like the great fear of 1789 in rural France which Lefebvre analysed, there spread in north India the alarm of a deliberate British plot to despoil the religion of Hindus and Muslims. One British officer stationed in Awadh wrote graphically about it:

> Government it was said had sent up cartloads and boatloads of bone-dust, which was to be mixed with the flour and sweetmeats sold in the bazaar, whereby the whole population would lose their caste. The public mind became greatly excited. On one day, at Sultanpur, it was spread over the station that a boat had reached a certain ghaut on the river Gomtee laden with bone-dust, and the sepoys were hardly restrained from outbreak. A few days later, at the station of Salone,

> two camels, laden with ammunition, arrived at the house of Captain Thompson, the commandant. It was rumoured that the packages contained bone-dust and a panic spread through station. Not only the sepoys in their lines, but the domestic servants about their officers' bungalows, and the villagers and zemindars attending court, hastily flung away, untasted, the food which they had cooked and fasted for the day. At Lucknow, the rumours which were whispered about were perpetual, and the public mind was never allowed to rest. Now it was at one shop, the next day in another bazaar, that despatches of bone-dust had, it was asserted, been received. It was in vain that facts were opposed to this prevailing panic.[34]

The people were convinced that there was a move afoot to destroy their caste and religion. The programme of reform and westernization so eagerly pursued and propagated by a generation of British administrators only fuelled such a belief. Rumours brought men together, stoked their suspicions and engendered a common hatred and thereby led to common action.

There was one theme in all these rumours: a threat to religion. The sepoys saw their action as being in defence of their religion. In Meerut, 'small parties of cavalry troopers with cries of "Yah Ullah" and "Deen Deen" rushed into the city and called upon the people to join in a religious war against the infidels.'[35] A group of sepoys captured in 1858 were individually asked before the execution why they had taken to arms, each one of them individually replied, 'The slaughter of the English was required by our religion.'[36] In this context, the experiences of Ranjit Singh Bissein, a former *havaldar* of the 63rd N.I. is of some relevance. He was coming into Lucknow on May 24 when he passed a police outpost,

> ...the police [Ranjit Singh reported]...were lounging on the charpoys. They called him to come and sit down and talk. They said they were new levies stationed there. He asked what duty was assigned to them. They said that they were to oppose any of the Sepoys...and fight them. But they added, we shall not fight them. Kala kala admee sab eyk hyn. Deen kee bat hyn. Hum log kahi ko beydhuram ho." All black men are one. It is a matter of religion. Why should we lose our religion.)[37]

Religion served as the source of solidarity and fraternity. Religion for them was something that was imbricated with their entire life: it informed their world-view, it was their fountain of knowledge, it provided them with a practical code of ethics; it was, one could say, following Marx their *point d' honneur*.[38] British rule was seen as a challenge to an entire way of life. Thus the division of sepoys into Hindus and Muslims did not serve, contrary to British expectations, to disunite the rebels. In Lucknow, the sepoys could hail Birjis Qadr as their Krishna.[39] The British, and Christianity, by extension, were identified as the common threat to a cherished and familiar way of life. In Sitapur, the name of the Commissioner, Mr. Christian, became identified with the religion, increasing the wrath and fury of the rebels.[40]

I have been trying so far to draw out some of the general characteristics that informed the actions of the sepoys. These are briefly, collectivity as revealed in the planning and co-ordination, a destruction that discriminated and extended itself by the logic of association, a violence whose chief modality was arson and direct actions which were spurred on by rumours. In short, the mutinies were informed by a consciousness of a project of power, most obviously manifest in the singular way the sepoys wanted to destroy their dominators. All these features have parallels with the general features of peasant insurgency in the colonial period.[41] The sepoys were, in fact, behaving in exactly the same way as the peasants behaved when they took to arms time and again, against the dominant triad of *sarkar*, *sahukar* and *zamindar*.

This similarity is not surprising. All data that we have of the recruitment of the sepoys of the Bengal Army show that they were mostly drawn from the agricultural families of southern Awadh and eastern U.P.[42] This common background explains the easy communication across sepoy lines in north India and also the similar reaction of the sepoys to rumours. The sepoys were, to use a cliche, 'peasants in uniform' and so when they rebelled they did so in exactly the same manner as their brothers in the villages did. This similarity also explains another thing. It puts into perspective the transformation of the mutinies into popular insurgency. Once the mutinies had struck and British administration had collapsed, in the words of one British officer, 'like a house made of cards',[43] the rebellion spread rapidly in the countryside and among the common people. The common people were waiting for the mutinies to initiate the uprising. In Meerut, to quote the official narrative again:

> Before a shot was fired, the inhabitants of the Sudder Bazar went out, armed with swords, spears, clubs, any weapon they could lay hands on, collected in crowds in every lane and alley, at every outlet of the bazars; and the residents of the wretched hamlets ... were to be seen

> similarly armed, pouring out to share in what they evidently knew was going to happen.[44]

They used these arms, as we have seen, against government property, against the white man, the zamindar and the moneylender. In Kanpur, Nanak Chand described in his diary the plunder of all the houses of the mahajans and the rich.[45] What began as a mutiny transformed itself into a peasant rebellion. The sepoy-peasant continuum explains why the features of the mutiny were so similar to the features of peasant rebellion and also why the sepoys' actions found such a direct and immediate echo in the countryside.

The sepoy, when he revolted, shed his uniform. In Meerut, most of the mutineers were in undress and 'they went to Delhi not, in military array, but in straggling disorder.'[46] In Kanpur, the sepoys broke out of their lines and tore off their regimental colours.[47] In short, the sepoys were rejecting the regimentation that had been imposed on them. The one thing they refused to surrender from their days in the Bengal Army was, of course, their arms. The peasant in uniform became the peasant with arms.

The rejection of the uniform and regimentation also has, perhaps, a greater significance. The act of mutiny was an act of negation, an act to eliminate individuals and a form of government that was seen as a threat to the social order. But this negation even if it replicated the violence of the masters was not a mere inversion, an empty act of imitation. In the rejection of the uniform, the regimentation, the colours—all those various signs by which an alien order had tried to separate the sepoy from his peasant brethren—there is the quest, however faint or groping, of an alternative identity which was perhaps entrenched in the shared common world of the peasantry. The alternative lay in that commonality and it was that sense of collectivity that provided the uprising with its ultimate source of strength.

NOTES

1. Eric Stokes, *The Peasant Armed: The Indian Revolt of 1857*, edited by C.A. Bayly (Oxford, 1986), Ch. 2.
2. Ibid., pp. 50 and 54.
3. S.B. Chaudhuri, *Civil Rebellion in the Indian Mutinies, 1857-59* (Calcutta, 1957).
4. R. Mukherjee, *Awadh in Revolt, 1857-58: a study of popular resistance* (Delhi, 1984), p. 65.

5. National Archives of India (NAI): Foreign Dept., Secret Consultations, 18, Dec., 1857, No. 565: Henry Lawrence to Canning, 2 May 1857.
6. J.W. Kaye, *History of the Sepoy War, 1857-58*, 3 vols (London, 1880; Reprint, New Delhi, 1988), ii, p. 244.
7. S.A. Rizvi and M.L. Bhargava (eds.), *Freedom Struggle in Uttar Pradesh*, 6 vols. (Lucknow, 1957), ii, p. 14.
8. NAI: For. Dept., Secret Cons., 25 Sept. 1857, Cons. No 398: E.O. Bradford to Edmonstone, 2 July 1857.
9. Barrow's narrative in G. Hutchinson, *Narrative of the Mutinies in Oude*, (London, 1859), pp. 127ff.
10. W. Edwards, *Personal Adventures during the Indian Rebellion in Rohilcund, Futtehghur and Oude*, (1858; Reprint Allahabad, 1974), p. 65.
11. R.H.W. Dunlop, *Service and Adventure with the khakee ressalah or Meerut Volunteer Force, during the Mutiniess of 1857-58*, (1858; Reprint Allahabad, 1974), pp. 153-54.
12. *Narratives of Events attending the outbreak of disturbances and the Restoration of Authority* (Calcutta, 1858), Meerut, p. 250, para 152.
13. Mukherjee, *Awadh in Revolt*, pp. 36-37.
14. Ibid., p. 68 and note 19.
15. The massacre at Satichaura Ghat is analysed and reconstructed in R. Mukherjee, '"Satan let loose upon earth": the massacres in Kanpur in the Revolt of 1857', in *Past and Present*, Aug. 1990.
16. Mukherjee, *Awadh in Revolt*, p. 70.
17. Hearsey's narrative in Hutchinson, *Narrative*, p. 97.
18. C. Ball, *The History of the Indian Mutiny*, 2 vols. (London, n.d.), pp. 299-300.
19. The evidence for this paragraph is taken from C. Hibbert, *The Great Mutiny: India 1857* (Harmondsworth, 1978), pp 65, 69, 70 and 72. In reconstructing the episode Hibbert draws on G.W. Forrest, *Selections from letters, despatches and state papers in the Military Department of the Govt. of India 1857-58*, 4 Vols. (Calcutta, 1893-1912).
20. See Antonio Gramsci, *Selections from the Prison Notebooks*, edited and translated by Quintin Hoare and Geoffrey Nowell Smith (New York, 1971), pp. 196-200.
21. *Narrative of Events*, Meerut, *op.cit.*, p. 253, para 192.
22. Kaye, *Sepoy War*, ii, p. 46.
23. W.H. Carey, *The Mohammedan Rebellion* (Roorkee, 1857), p. 9: quoted in R. Guha, *Elementary Aspects of Peasant Insurgency in Colonial India* (Delhi, 1983), p. 141.
24. *Narrative of Events*, Aligarh, p. 217, paras 36 and 37
25. R. Guha, *Elementary Aspects*, p. 141.
26. Quoted in Kaye, *Sepoy War*, ii, p. 258.
27. S.N. Sen, *1857* (Delhi, 1957), p. 29.
28. Dunlop, *Service and Adventure...during the Mutinies of 1857-58*, p. 36.
29. *Narrative of Events*, Meerut, p. 251, para 169; p. 252 para 171.

30. Ibid., p. 252, para 172.
31. G. Rude, *Paris and London in the 18th Century* (Reprint: London, 1974), p. 26.
32. R. Cobb, *The Police and the People:French Popular Protest 1789-1820* (Oxford, 1972), pp. 88-89.
33. For rumours see Mukherjee, *Awadh in Revolt*, pp. 72-76; for a general discussion on rumours in peasant insurgency see Guha, *Elementary Aspects*, pp. 251-77.
34. M. Gubbins, *An Account of the Mutiness in Oude and the Seige of the Lucknow Residency* (London, 1858), p. 86.
35. *Narrative of Events*, Meerut, p. 251, para 170.
36. Ball, *History of the Indian Mutiny*, ii, p. 242.
37. NAI: For Dept., Secret Consultations, 26 June 1857, Nos., 52-4: Gubbins to Couper, 27 May 1857.
38. K. Marx, '*A Contribution to the Critique of Hegel's Philosophy of Right, Introduction*, in Marx, *Early Writings*, edited by L. Colletti (Harmondsworth, 1975), p. 244.
39. Mukherjee, *Awadh in Revolt*, p. 87.
40. Kaye, *Sepoy War*, iii, p. 456.
41. Guha, *Elementary Aspects*.
42. Mukherjee, *Awadh in Revolt*, pp. 76-79.
43. Gubbins, *Mutinies* p. 118.
44. *Narrative of Events*, Meerut, p. 251, para 165.
45. Nanak Chand's diary of events in Kanpur: printed as 'Translation of a Narrative of Events of Cawnpore', in *Narrative of Events in the NWP in 1857-58* (Calcutta, n.d.).
46. *Narrative of Events*, Meerut, p. 253, para 184.
47. 'Synopsis of the Evidence of the Cawnpore Mutiny', in *Narrative of Events*, Kanpur; see also G.W. Forrest, *Selections from Letters*, ii, Intro, pp. 156-58.

Race, Religion and Realm: The Political Theory of 'The Reigning Indian Crusade', 1857

RAJAT KANTA RAY

The political theory of the Mutiny, a term coined many years ago by the missionary F.W. Buckler ('The Political Theory of the Indian Mutiny', reprinted in A.T. Embree, ed., *1857 in India*, Boston, 1963), hardly amounted to any systematic political philosophy. The mutineers had neither time nor inclination to develop a theory of the order propounded earlier by Saiyid Ghulam Husain Khan, that theorist of the Later Mughal Empire in whose view the Hindus and Muslims of the Empire were brothers from the one and same mother. Nor of course could they envisage the conjoined Indian nation as later conceptualized by Mohandas Karamchand Gandhi, who harnessed the Indian struggle of 1920-1922 to the combined visions of Ram Raj and Khilafat. Yet 'the reigning Indian Crusade', as the men of 1857 viewed their own struggle, may be placed midstream in a flow of notions that go back to the Saiyid and move on to the Mahatma. In the scores of Mutiny proclamations, orders, letters and slogans now available in print, there lurk several inchoate ideas, hardly amounting to a political ideology as such, that, upon close observation, may be seen to fit into an identifiable view of the country and its people.

Perhaps the most significant of these, in terms of the continuum hinted at above, is the idea embedded in the term, 'the Hindus and Musalmans of Hindustan', an expression made repeatedly in the proclamations. The term was not used in the loose sense of common parlance, indicating the two major communities of the subcontinent, but was on the contrary a sort of constructed political term, such as the United States of America in the Declaration of Independence, or the

Indian Federation in the Constitution of 1935 (but neither so articulate nor so well defined). It is here that the Mutiny made perhaps its most original contribution to developing the political theory of the Indian struggle.

The idea was not simply communal harmony (in fact there was a good deal of disharmony in 1857), but something more, or rather, something different: a confederation of two separate peoples tied into one political unit by the social perception of Hindustan as one land. There were Muslims in Afghanistan and Hindus in Nepal, but these, as one can see in the mutual correspondence of the mutineers and the Nepal Darbar, were not parts of the political community spelt out as 'the Hindus and Musalmans of Hindustan'. The Nepal Darbar, as we shall see, realized that the Indian mutineers were using the term as a specific political category, and the Nepal Darbar in turn used it in the same sense, denoting the people of Hindustan as one nationality. There are several distinct implications in the use of the formula: (a) the Hindus and Muslims remain two separate peoples (*qaums*) based on two separate creeds; (b) they are co-sharers of the realm of Hindustan, and as such one people, and two peoples, at one and the same time; (c) there is no question, at this stage, of a single secular national community of Hindustanis, nor of their being bonded together, independently of 'deen' and 'dharma', by secular political sentiments alone; d) what in fact bonds them together is the united struggle for the 'deen' of the Muslims and the 'dharma' of the Hindus; (e) what unites the struggle is the threat posed by the alien and aggressive British presence to the two *qaums* based on 'deen' and 'dharma' respectively; (f) what distinguishes them from other *qaums* beyond the land, even those external *quams* that belong to one or the other creed, is the land itself; (g) in the social and cultural perspective, the land is one; (h) 'the Hindus and Musalmans of Hindustan' is a term taken by the mutineers, in a political sense, to cover the whole of its population.

These are not the same ideas as the later idea of the Indian nation. At the heart of these notions lie religious sentiments: 'deen' and 'dharma' are to be the joint basis of a whole reconstruction of the political universe, one in which the land would be purged of the alien race that threatens its population with the loss of their identity. One can distinguish three basic sentiments in the shaping of this violent political mass: race, religion, and realm. These are closely intertwined, essential constituents of the religious-patriotic consciousness that charged and activated this mass. Racial humiliation, in its crude physical form, is bound up with an incomparably more violent fear of spiritual enslavement—conversion to the religion of the master race and the loss of cherished beliefs and practices. Associated with all this is a sense of the land being lost at all sorts of levels—ranging from the loss of the hereditary possession of the peasant, the zamindar and the prince to the alienation of the indivisible sovereign realm of Hindustan which belongs rightfully to 'the King of Delhi, the bona fide ruler of Hindoostan who is the shadow and representative of God'. The Mutiny is, in essence, an outburst of outrage—a defensive and punitive reaction against the fear, and reality, of outrageous aggression at all levels, physical, spiritual, material, by the trespassing white rulers.

I

'If niggers have souls, they're not the same as ours.'[1] Such was the prevailing attitude in the English camp which confronted the mutineers of 1857. It was an attitude that created a single new category ('natives'; 'niggers') out of an entire population, and invested it, willy nilly, with an existence and mind of its own. 'Here', wrote W.H. Russell, 'we had not only a servile war and a sort of jacquerie combined, but we had a war of religion, a war of race, and a war of revenge, of hope, of some national promptings, to shake off the yoke of a stranger, and to establish the full power of the native chiefs, and the full sway of the native religions.'[2]

It was not, however, the rebels who put the struggle in terms of a war between the races: that was, distinctively, the language of the masters.[3] The rebels themselves clothed the underlying race war in the ideological vision of a struggle of the Hindus and Muslims against the Nazarenes. The joint brotherhood of the two principal religions of the land expressed, in so far as they were capable of expressing it, the instinctive feeling that the native subject race constituted one people as against the white Christian rulers. The inchoate sense of the nation embedded in the mass psychology had no terms to express itself except through the formula, 'the Hindus and Musalmans of Hindustan,'[4] joined together in what a leader of the struggle described as 'the reigning Indian crusade'.[5]

Conceptually, then, the Mutiny is a peculiarly difficult phenomenon to define: a war of the races that was not a race war because the subject race conceived it as a war of religion; a religious war that cannot be called truly and purely a war of religion because what was being opposed was not so much the creed of the master race as their political dominion; as such, then, neither a war of race, nor a war of religion, but a patriotic war of the Hindu-Muslim brotherhood, or the inchoate social nationality of Hindustan; yet not a national war either. It was all these things, therefore none of them.

By waging a brutal war to put an 'inferior race' in its place, the British imparted to the struggle a predominantly racial character; but it must not be forgotten that from the point of view of the rebels, the governing motive was 'religion'.[6] Even in an act of overt racial animosity like the massacre of the whites, the rationale behind the action, as captured sepoys consistently maintained when cross-examined, was this—'the slaughter of the British was required by our religion'.[7] This was so right from the beginning of the outbreak at Meerut, where the men of the 3rd cavalry broke out with the cry, 'our fight is for the cause of religion'.[8] 'Brothers, Hindoos, and Musalmans', cried a sawar galloping towards the jail with sword unleashed, 'we are going to a religious war. Be assured we will not harm those who join us, but fight only against the Government'.[9] As the sawars rushed, riding without saddle, bare-headed, armed with drawn swords and pistols, pausing here and there to cry out: 'Babas, this war is in the cause of religion, whoever likes to join, come along with us'; and soon enough they were followed by the Muslim weighmen from the *bazaar* and butchers armed with stones, crying, 'Yah Ali! Ali!.'[10]

'This day orders have been given to the whole force to turn out and plunder the English and to remember that the war is one of religion.'[11] Here, the primary racial impulse to hit out at the whites is converted into a religious struggle against the infidels enjoined by one's inner sense of duty, a process reminiscent, in some respects, of the Freudian transition from the id to the super-ego. Racial antagonism—the primary impulse—is of course too elemental not to break through: 'the yellow faced and narrow minded people', exults Nana Sahib, 'have been sent to hell';[12] 'these people with white skins and dark fortunes', promises a minor Muslim nobleman to Bahadur Shah, would be totally exterminated in three days if command of the operations were to be given to him;[13] and an armed Rajput retainer, pointing a matchlock at one Mr. Corridon's breast, says in less ornamented language that it 'made his blood boil to see a Feringhee'.[14] But the injunction laid by religion upon every mutineer's conscience was so far internalized that the enemy, instead of being perceived in stark terms of colour, was more usually referred to as 'kafir'[15]—an unclean infidel on naming whom 'a man's mouth became impure (for) forty days'.[16] Thus a trooper and some townsmen of Meerut, chasing a white man, cry out, '*Māro kāfir ko*' (kill the infidel) even as they manage to sever his head. Joseph

Henry Jones trembles as he hears a party of insurgents led by some policemen exclaim: '*Ali Ali, aj marlia hai kafiron ko*' (Ali, Ali, we have finished off the infidels today), and is gleefully informed by a native: '...the sepoys are killing the European soldiers, and no Feringhee will be allowed to exist on earth.'[17]

Race and religion were thus fused into an explosive psychological compound. A group of disaffected policemen lounging on the charpoy on the eve of the outbreak in Lucknow put the matter simply: 'Kala kala admee sab eyk hai. Deen kee bat hai. Hum log kahe ko be-dhurm ho' (All black people are one. It is a matter of religion. Why should we incur loss of faith?'[18]) The matter was debated at somewhat greater length between Vishnubhat Godase, travelling north to Hindustan, and a Marathi-speaking sepoy who was making his way back to Goa from the scene of the Mutiny. On being urged by the fleeing sepoy to go back, the Brahmin reflected that he, as a mendicant, had nothing to fear from a war of religion by the assembly of blacks. 'We are not, after all, involved as fighting men. I am a poor begging Brahmin (Gharib Bhikshuk Brāhmin āhon). I have nothing at all to fear from black people getting together to fight for the sake of religion (Kāle log ekatra hoon dharmakaritā bhāṇḍarāt tar āpanyās bhaya nāhin)'. Further up he encountered a group of threatening sepoys, and managed to conciliate them by putting forth the same argument: 'O sepoy sons! I am a poor begging Brahmin...I have, however, no fear. Because a poor scripture-trained mendicant like me has nothing at all to fear from black people uniting to fight for the sake of religion' (Kāran kāle lok jar dharmasāṭhi bhāṇḍanār tar āmhā vedasāstrasampanna garib bhikshukāngsa bilkul bhaya nahin).[19] The heart of the matter—the root of what Shahzada Feroz Shah called 'the bitterest enmity between the natives and the English'—was the perceived intention of 'these wicked Christian kafirs' to spread Christianity by violence and 'to do away with the religion of Hindoos and Mussulmans'.[20] That is why all subjects who did not wish to become Christians were urged to unite with the sepoys and not to leave 'the seed of these devils anywhere'.[21] The 'unclean infidels', in their 'pride', had committed the ultimate excess—a transgression that must be made to recoil totally upon itself by the traceless elimination of the perpetrators.[22]

One of the many minor outbreaks that set the pattern of the Mutiny has as its protagonist an unknown and forgotten Brahmin, caught in the act of carrying messages from some disaffected villagers to sepoys at Aligarh. The English had good reason to believe till then that the sepoys would be 'true to their salt'. Scarcely had the man been hanged in the presence of the troops than one of them stepped out and shouted to his comrades: 'Behold a martyr to our faith:'[23] That is how the ranks that broke out immediately into mutiny perceived the man—a martyr to faith rather than a patriot sacrificing himself for the nation. Again, the Charkhari Raja, a loyalist, was upbraided by the mutinied troops of the Gwalior contingent, not for being a traitor to the country, but for 'being regardless of the next world'.[24] What we seem to have here is a collective super-ego that pitted the rebellious people of Hindustan against the infidels as a matter of religious duty—apparently with no overt injunction from the 'higher self' to fight for the country as such.[25] The pervasive religiosity of the Mutiny, then, seems on the surface to preclude the people's awareness of themselves as a political nation.[26] We must, however, look below the surface. Unless we do so, we shall not plumb that inarticulate subconscious in which a nation was in the making, nor shall we interpret correctly what lies behind the signs of religious symbolism.

Religion, constituting as it did the very basis of the community in 1857, was an immensely complex phenomenon with many different shades of meaning in that society—alternate senses that contained in consequence the possibility of vital encounters and resolutions within its own parameters, and which cannot be grasped if the deceptively easy formula of a 'war of religion' is seen as a self-explanatory theorem precluding deeper investigations into its multiple inner dynamics.[27] To start with some of the simpler variations on the theme, Muslim women in Delhi taught their children to pray for the success of their faith during the Muharram of 1857, and their own fervent prayers were 'generally accompanied by execrations against the English'.[28] The Hindus, with whom it was not so straightforward a matter of creed,[29] were thought by one Christian prisoner of the Red Fort to be less averse to the Company's Government than the Muslims.[30] What he meant, perhaps, was that the grievances of the former had less doctrinal a form:[31] as Sindhia and his prime minister assured the English, 'Banaras, Gya, and the other centres of Hindu opinion, to which all had looked, had abstained from sanctioning any religious pretext' for the revolt.[32] Passages from the Quran, however, were quoted time and again to set out the grounds on which it was obligatory for the Muslims to oppose the Christians.[33]

One miscellaneous group that joined in the Mutiny—the misnamed 'Wahabis' (more correctly, the men of the Waliullahi tradition going back to Shah Waliullah of Delhi (1703-1762)—had been long active in preaching *jehad*. The widely circulated tract *Risalah Jehad*, composed some thirty years earlier by Maulvi Mohammad Ismail and translated into the Hindustani language in 1850, was to be found in Delhi, Lucknow and Kanpur on the eve of the Mutiny, exhorting the Muslims to attain heaven 'by dying in Battle with the Infidel.'[34] No sooner had the mutinies broken out in the cantonments than bands of Ghazis (or Mujahidin) appeared in Delhi from Tonk, Gwalior, Bareilly and other places—fine looking fellows, 'grizzlybearded elderly men for the most part,' with green turbans and cumerbands and every one of them wearing a silver signet ring with a long text from the Quran finely engraved upon it. Men without fear, they would come on 'with their heads down below their shields, and their tulwars flashing as they whirled them over their heads, shouting "Deen! Deen" and dancing like madmen'—only to be shot between their eyes by white soldiers stepping out with their Enfield rifles.[35] To all appearance, they were the same sort of men Saiyid Ahmad Khan of Rae Bareilly had led in *jehad* against the Sikhs in Punjab, and who had appeared even more recently at the imagined birth place of Rama, 'with a fanatic molovee at their head...resolved to enter the Hindoo shrine or die.'[36] But in consequence of a dramatic realignment of forces, *Jehadis* were transformed in 1857, fighting shoulder to shoulder with the Purbeah Hindu sepoys against the British batteries mounted on the Ridge outside Delhi.

The new *Risala Fath-i Islam*, one of the pamphlets that appeared during the Mutiny calling upon the Muslims to wage holy war upon the infidel, also carried an *ishtihar* (proclamation) 'meant for the Hindus and the Muslims of India, so that they should think over, and should prepare themselves for the slaughter of the English in order to protect their deen and dharam.'[37] There could be no clearer manifestation of the Mujahidin conscious acceptance of the altered context of holy war. Deen—the use of the word now dramatically extended—became a political rallying cry for both Muslims and Hindus amidst the din of battle.[38] But there were still more dramatic transformations of deen. Its remarkable shift from one meaning to another—from a code of personal conduct to a matter of public duty—transformed the lives of some remarkable Muslim women who appeared in Delhi as *mujahida*: women who, if they had abided by the conventional sense of religion, should have stayed back at home to do their duty and contented themselves with a daily prayer for the defeat of the infidel.

Colonel Keith Young, encamped on the Ridge, wrote to his wife, who was in Simla, on 29 July 1857: 'Did I tell you that they took a woman prisoner the other day, who they made out was leading a charge of Cavalry and who killed two of our men with her own hand? I believe the greater part of this to be fiction, and she is old and ugly, not much romance attaches to her, though she is wounded.'[39] The dour Civil Commissioner in the camp, H.H. Greathead, to whom the elderly *Jehadin* was taken in captivity, made a more exact mention of the event:'A Joan of Arc was made prisoner yesterday; she is said to have shot one of our men, and to have fought desperately. She is a Jehadin, a religious fanatic, sports a green turban, and was probably thought to be inspired. She is to be sent prisoner to Umballa.'[40] History does not record who these elderly women were, how they were displaced from home, and what were the circumstances that drove them into the war, but we have one indigenous record of the impression they made on the rebel camp in Delhi.

The police chief of rebel Delhi (the second in succession) recalled later: 'Frequently two old withered Muslim women from Rampur led the rebels, going far in advance with naked swords and bitterly taunting the sepoys when they held back, calling them cowards and shouting to them to see how women went in front where they dared not follow-'we go on without flinching among the showers of grape while you flee away'. The sepoys would excuse themselves saying: 'We go to fetch ammunition', but the women would reply: 'You stop and fight and we will get your ammunition for you'. These women frequently did bring supplies of cartridges to the men in the batteries and walked fearlessly in perfect showers of grape, but by the will of God were never hit. At length one of them was taken prisoner and brought before Mr. Greathead, the Commissioner, who after enquiring into the state of the city and the rebel army gave her five rupees and released her, at the same time issuing strict orders that no men should molest her. As she never returned to the mutineers she was considered by many to be a British spy. When the band of ghazis moved off to assault the women invariably went in advance of all.'[41]

The more well-known career of the Rani of Jhansi illustrates the same shift from one meaning to another with regard to the use of the word 'dharma'—a transcendence her own words on one occasion capture unconsciously. The incident is related by Vishnubhat Godase. On the way to Kalpi the poor pilgrim was resting by the shade of a well when the young Rani, riding away from a disastrous encounter with the English at Charkhari, came up with four or five sawars who were then her only attendants. Here is the pilgrim's account of the encounter.

> She was dressed from head to foot as a Pathan and her body was full of dust. Her face was slightly flushed and she looked a bit pale

> and dejected. Seized by extreme thirst she got down from the horse and, coming up to me she asked: 'Who are you?" Stepping quickly forward I said with folded hands, 'I am a Brahmin'...As I started lowering the earthen vessel into the well, the Bai Saheb interrupted: 'You are a learned Brahmin (tumhi vidvān Brāhmin), please don't draw water for me. Let me draw it up myself:. As I listened to these generous words, I felt so bad, but being helpless I put the ropes and earthen vessel down. The Bai Saheb, drawing the water up, quenched her thirst by drinking with cupped hands from that earthen vessel (Bāi Sāhebani pāni kāṭun tyā mrinmaya pātrātun onjaline piyun trishā haran keli). Strange are the ways of providence. Thereupon she said with an acute expression of despondence: 'I am entitled to half a seer of rice alone (mi ardhā sher tāṇḍulāchi dhanin): I need not have given up the common widow's dharma and taken up all these enterprises (majlā randmuṅḍesa vidhabādharma sorun hā udyog karanyāchi kāhi jarur nābbhati), nevertheless I have set my hands to these endeavours to uplift the honour of the Hindu dharma (parantu hindudharmāchā abhimān dharun yā karmāsa pravritta jhāle), and to this end I have given up everything - the hope of riches, of life, of all things on earth (wa yājakarita vittachi, jivitāchi, sarvāchi āshā sorali)".[42]

The unconscious shift in the meaning of dharma, from 'the common husbandless woman's widow religion' (rañḍmuñḍesa vidhbā dharma) to the mounted warrior woman's 'proud Hindu religion' (hindudharmāchā abhimān), bears the traces of a remarkable transfiguration that lived on in the popular memory. More than half a century after the event, William Crooke recorded a Mutiny song by the village muse, Rameshwar Diyali Mishra, who still remembered it after the lapse of fifty-three years:

> She fought well, that brave one, the Rani of Jhansi,
> There were guns in the towers, and the magic shells were fired.
> O the Rani of Jhansi, how well she fought that brave one.
> Her soldiers were fed on sweetmeats but she took only coarse sugar and rice.
> O Rani of Jhansi, how well she fought, that brave one.[43]

What was the passion in the breast of the young Rani, and those elderly *mujahida*, that drove them to these deeds? Undoubtedly it was the passion of martyrdom for the faith, for faith alone could have moved women so intensely in that age. And yet the feeling itself, as recorded in folksong, is indistinguishable from patriotism, for all intense feelings are alike when they reach the ultimate pitch of transfiguring a person. Crusader or patriot—what does it matter? The same word, *Shaheed* (martyr), describes both in the Hindustani language of today and the shift from one to the other is too elusive to track. That the assimilation of the two is not a later development, but on the contrary a contemporary one, seems to be indicated by an utterance attributed to Nana Sahib during his retreat from Kanpur: An effort will have to be made once again for the sake of the Hindu religion and the Hindu realm'. (*Hindudharmakaritā punhā ekbār jhatle pāije*).[44] As realm and religion are even more closely tied together in the Islamic faith, not surprisingly the implications for the country's governance were no less clearly articulated in the proclamations of *jehad* in 1857. Thus Maulvi Liaqat Ali exhorted his co-religionists: 'O my Mussulman brethren! as soon as you hear the above glad tidings prepare yourself for Jehad, come to Allahabad, subdue and put to sword the besieged Christians there, and then rule the country according to Laws and Institutions of Mohammad'.[45]

The question may now arise as to how these apparerntly conflicting Muslim and Hindu visions of realizing the Sacred Realm were to be resolved in the actual sphere of governance. It is here that the mutineers made a striking contribution to the development of political concepts. Though original, these concepts were profoundly embedded in the past. A clue to these not so well-articulated conceptions is found in the words of an unknown Muslim nobleman whom a native Christian heard conversing on the verandah of the Bijnor Collector's bungalow six weeks before the Mutiny. The company consisted of the Muslim nobleman whom the Collector's chaprasi addressed respectively as Nawab (he apparently had a brother who was tahsildar in the district), another Muslim who was serving as Jamadar in the Canal department, and the native Christian, Francis Shester. 'The Nawab commenced the conversation by observing that two regiments to the eastward had taken their discharge, because the Kafirs had mixed pigs' and cows' fat with the new cartridges, that the Kafirs had determined to take away the castes of all Mohammadans and Hindoos, and that these infidels should not be allowed to remain in India, or there should be no difference between Mahomedans and Hindoos, and whatever they said, we should have to do.'[46]

Note the Nawab's unstated commitment, a value attached unconsciously as it were, to 'the difference between Mohamedans and

Hindoos' (which lay at the very heart of the traditional Indian social and political system),[47] the destruction of which he knows, instinctively, would result in all of them being obliged to do whatever 'they', the foreign masters, would have them do. The Nawab was only voicing a thought then in the mind of every sepoy, and indeed the entire population. Just one day before the Mutiny Henry Lawrence heard a trusted sepoy in Lucknow say: 'That is just it. You want us all to eat what you like that we may be stronger, and go everywhere.'[48] And Captain Martineau, posted at Ambala, heard a belief then current that the people of Hindustan 'should be all compelled to eat the same food', which was taken to be a token that 'they would likewise be compelled to embrace one faith, or as they termed it, 'one food and one faith''.[49] As the Mutiny broke out, the instinctive and subconscious commitment to the fundamental principle of Indian society, unity in diversity, took firmer ideological shape. That ideology was most articulately set out in the justly celebrated proclamation of Khan Bahadur Khan, the rebel Nawab of Rohilkhand, to the Hindu rajas and zamindars of Hindustan, which the English prosecutor produced in extenso in the trial of Emperor Bahadur Shah:

Proclamation[50]

'With the approving sanction of God, the Lord of the Nation[51]
'Exposition of a letter written regarding the victory of the faith

All you Rajahs are famed for your virtues, noble qualities, and liberality, and are moreover the protectors of your own faith and of the faith of others. Keeping your welfare in view, I humbly submit that God has given you your bodily existence to establish his different religions and requires you severally to learn the tenets of your own different religions, institutions, and forms, and you accordingly continue firm in them. God has moreover sent you into the world in your elevated position, and given you dominion and Government, that you may destroy those who harm your religion. It is incumbent, therefore, on such of you as have the power, to kill those who may harm your religion, and on such as have not, to engage heartily in devising means for the same end, and thus protect your faith; for it is written in your scriptures that *martyrdom is preferable to adopting the religion of another* (italics mine, a quotation from the *Bhagavad Gita*). This is exactly what God has said, and what is evident to everybody. The English are people who overthrow all religions.... It is now my firm conviction that if these English continue in Hindoostan they will kill everyone in the country, and will utterly overthrow our religions....Under these circumstances, I would ask what course have you decided on to protect your lives and faith? Were your views and mine the same, we might destroy them entirely with a very little trouble; and if we do so, we shall protect our religions and save the country. And as these ideas have been cherished and considered merely from a concern for the protection of the religions and lives of all you Hindoos, and Mussulmans of this country, this letter is printed for your information. All you Hindoos are solemnly adjured, by your faith in the Ganges, Tulsi and Saligram; and all you Mussulmans, by your belief in God and the Kuran, as these English are the common enemy of both, that you unite in considering their slaughter extremely expedient, for by this alone will the lives and faith of both be saved. It is expedient, then, that you should coalesce and slay them.

Khan Bahadur Khan's proclamation brought out the central principle of the Indian social system—coexistence and compartmentalization of the religions in their respective social spheres. Under the system, the parts were dependent on the whole in the sense that no religion would be secure in its demarcated sphere if the accommodation of doctrinal diversity were to come under threat. The patriotic commitment of the proclamation lay in the commitment to the social system evolved in Hindustan over the centuries. The argument was developed with a remarkable grasp of the mind and doctrines of the Hindus as set out in the *Bhagavad Gitā*, for Khan Bahadur Khan translated almost word for word Lord Krishna's exhortation to Arjuna in the Kurukshetra war: *svadharme nidhanam shreyah, paradharmo bhayāvadah* (it is better to die for one's own faith, for adopting the faith of another is too terrible to contemplate). It is no coincidence that the same principle is enunciated by quoting the same *sloka* in the parallel proclamation of Rani Lakshmibai:

The Shastra declares that it is best to follow one's own religion, and not to adopt another's, and God himself has so declared; but it is evident to all men that these English are perverters of all men's religion. From time immemorial have they endeavoured to contaminate the Hindoo and Mahomedan religions by the production and circulation of religious books through the medium of missionaries, and by extirpating such books as afford arguments against them.

In an age when the mentality of the people was steeped in profound religiosity, it may be historically misleading to try and isolate the patriotic feelings that have come to stand on their own in the course of later developments. No doubt such feelings were embedded in the *jehad* that erupted in many parts of the Islamic world, including Hindustan, but the historian must not forget that in the people's own consciousness these were wars of religion. The Mutiny, however, while including a prominent element of *mujahida*, must, as Khan Bahadur Khan's proclamation makes it clear, stand in a category by itself. It has no exact parallel anywhere else. In those countries where one people and one religion have made possible an indissoluble blend of faith and patriotism, national identity itself must in some measure be a matter of religion. The situation was far more complex in India in 1857. Here was a country consisting of two communities striving to construct their respective sacred realms by ousting the common enemy, and at the same time profoundly moved by a sense of the land as one indivisible whole. What joined the two communities together was not just mutual opposition to 'the common enemy of both' but, as Khan Bahadur Khan's proclamation also stressed, the country itself to which they belonged, and where both enjoyed the mutually recognized right to set up the appropriate sacred realms. Note the words—'we shall protect our religions and save the country': the latter was the common link and in that sense stood outside of the two religions.

As to the mechanics of the accommodation between the two, the proclamation was vague, and had nothing to say except that the Muslim rulers and Hindu rajas were naturally the protectors of their own faith 'and of the faith of others' (not an inappropriate description considering the rulers of eighteenth-century India). The same vague conception reappeared in the popular notions of Ram Raj and Khilafat in the Indian struggle of 1920-22. The *ulama* of Deoband and the Ali Brothers articulated a vision of the Indian destiny not altogether dissimilar: one country with two realms, two nationalities within one people (a solution that might well have been realized if the confederation envisaged by the Cabinet Mission had not been rejected by Jawaharlal Nehru in his single-minded pursuit of the secular nation).[52]

The rebels were up in arms not because they objected to the rulers' doctrines as such, though on one occasion they were provoked by Queen Victoria's assertion of 'the truth of Christianity'[53] to pour scorn on the doctrine of Trinity.[54] But as Begum Hazrat Mahal put it in her rejoinder: 'What has the administration of justice to do with the truth or falsehood of a religion?' The people were driven to 'mortal desperation' (in the Begum's phrase 'murta kya na karta'—a dying man will do anything), not so much because of missionary propaganda in favour of the 'false' doctrine of Trinity, nor because of the subtle undermining effects of the spread of English education[55] (which they were perfectly confident of coping with and taking advantage of), but because they were convinced that the government was maturing in secret the terrible master plan—kill or convert.[56] The 'alarms' of 1857 had reference 'to the Government alone—to its news, its decisions and its designs'. The terror that gripped their minds was the completion of the physical and spiritual domination of the alien masters, the final enslavement of their very souls by means of the extinction of the native religions of Hindustan, and the loss of the identity of the people rooted in the cherished differences of their social system. The psychological 'defensive reaction' against the feared result was translated into the rhetoric and language, not of national resistance to the imperial aggrandizer (a language then being born in the Presidency towns of Calcutta, Bombay and Madras but altogether unknown in the heart of Hindustan) but of the confederate alliance of the Hindus and Muslims against the 'firangi' or 'kafir', expressions indicative of the twin unlovely characteristics of the enemy looming large in the minds of the people.[57]

The manner in which the people perceived and defined themselves was most strikingly evident in these descriptions of the enemy. 'They' were sometimes addressed as 'firangis'; 'we' being by implication the Hindustanis, or the inhabitants of Hindustan; more frequently 'infidels', 'Christians' or 'Nazarenes' were set against 'the Hindus and Musalmans' in the rebel language. The commonest term by far was 'kafir' (infidel),[58] an expression covering not merely the English, but also the native and half blood Christians (Nazarenes'). The Englishmen were 'accursed Christians',[59] enemies of religion and accursed 'vilaitis' (foreigners),[60] unbelieving Nazarenes' who must be despatched to hell.[61] The NWP Police Commissioner's *Synopsis* of the Kanpur evidence tells us:'...the troopers...were indefatigable in their search of Christians'.[62] That the latter category also included non-whites comes out in the evidence of an opium gumashtah who was in Kanpur on leave: 'Many merchants expected that the sepoys would spare their property and that they would consequently be able to carry on business under the new government. The sepoys however murdered every

Christian they found, and also fired at every person they saw wearing English garments.'[63] In Lucknow, Christians, half-breeds and 'Keranees' (literally clerks, a term indicating the Eurasian employees of the government) were kept in a separate prison and some of them were put to death along with the 'Sahib Logue'.[64]

The warlike instincts impelling the people to deeds of violence would appear to have consisted of two akin emotions—hatred of the whites and dislike and distrust towards all others whom they instinctively associated with white domination. One aspect of that domination was perceived to be spiritual and religious, and several missionaries, computed by Reverend Alexander Duff to be 37 in all, were killed. But missionaries were not specially singled out. They were dealt with in precisely the same way as all other Europeans, and, as Dr Duff himself pointed out at the time, all persons 'identified by the rebels with the governing class' were made to suffer, Bengali babus no less than native Christians and Eurasian clerks.[65] There would appear to have been some sort of instinctive gradation of the victims according to the severity of the punishment they deserved. Each European was singled out and slaughtered in Hamirpur, whether he be a high government official or a private landholder and merchant. The native catechist of the Church Missionary Society, Jeremiah, was also murdered with his wife and four children. But Bengali babus, while relieved of everything they possessed, were all able to beg successfully for life. The half-breed judicial clerk, Bunter, and his wife, were also given their lives on promising to become Muslims, but later the couple was cut down by the infuriated mutineers when Bunter inadvisedly came out and bowed to the European magistrate and joint magistrate as they were being marched out to the firing squad at the Cutcherry.[66]

Nothing revealed the alignments in the Mutiny more clearly than the consensus of people who took refuge in the Agra Fort when the town fell into the hands of the mutineers. Charles Raikes observed in the motley six thousand-strong assemblage 'unwilling delegates from many parts of Europe and America', for what mattered was colour, and next to it creed, not distinctions of nationality. 'Nuns from the banks of the Garonne and the Loire, priests from Sicily and Rome, missionaries from Ohio and Basle, mixed with rope-dancers from Paris, and pedlars from America. Besides these we had Calcutta Baboos and Parsee merchants. Although all the Christians alike were driven by the mutinous legions into the Fort, the circumstances of the multitude were as various as their races.'[67] The Parsees and Bengalis were, of course, neither whites nor Christians, but the Mutineers could hardly have overlooked the fact that there were Parsee merchants on the Ridge outside Delhi supplying wines, spirits and beer to the English camp,[68] and cowering Bengalis in Kanpur, suspected of sending messages to the English force marching up from Allahabad. Orders were issued by Nana Sahib that 'the baboos of the city, and every individual who could read or write English, should have their right hands and noses cut off', but the timely arrival of British troops saved them.[69]

Such were the spontaneous impulses of a population smelling out and identifying the enemy. In seeking to put these feelings into ideological terms, however, they adopted the only universal definitions familiar to them—those derived from the phraseology of religion with its opposed categories of *kafir* and *mujahid*.[70] So deep was the impression of these categories on the popular mind that those natives who were prepared to help the English were denounced as Christians and Pariahs,[71] while the Christians themselves were recognized to have a right to protection on abandoning their infidel Nasri doctrines and embracing the true faith. From the standpoint of the secular nationalist India of 1885-1947, these redefinitions might have appeared embedded in false consciousness, but to the rebels of 1857 and their ways of articulate thinking, the categories were real enough.

Thus the diary of the Nannhe Nawab, at first a reluctant and then an enthusiastic rebel nobleman of Kanpur, opens with two common troopers taunting him in the following manner: 'As I had not joined with the men of *Jhunda* (Muslim flag), two troopers were sent by the Nana to fetch me, saying that they have waited long for me, how it was that I did not join the *Jhunda*, it appears that I was not a Mahomedan but a Christian (an expression of contempt), I had better soon attend the Nana's Court, or they have orders to take my head to the Nana.'[72] The obverse side of the same logic is illustrated in the following petition of the vacillating Raja of Ballabhgarh to Emperor Bahadur Shah: 'Further I heard from some persons who had requests to make to me, that it has been represented to Your Majesty, that the Chief of Ballabhgarh has secreted two Englishmen, with their wives and children. God is witness that this is entirely a false and unfounded calumny. How could your slave dare to commit an act of the kind, without Your Majesty's wishes and orders. A native, however, who was formerly a Christian, had been twelve years in my service; but I put even him away, fearing Your Majesty's displeasure. This man has now discarded Christianity and embraced the Mahomedan religion, and he is accordingly deserving of mercy and forgiveness.'[73] It would appear from the tone of the letter that Europeans were not supposed to be allowed the same dispensation. But we have on record from the rebel police chief of Delhi the following instance of the logic of the doctrine being pushed to its furthest extent by General Bakht Khan, who is said to have been a 'Wahabi':

> A European sergeant whom they called Abdullah was with the Bareilly brigade, as well as two or three Christians, half castes of the poorest class. John Powell, son of Powell of Saharanpur, whom they had seized and brought from Moradabad, was also with them but under surveillance. The 29th Native Infantry were favourably disposed to these persons and would let no one molest them, saying they had made them Moslems. The regiment indeed took considerable care of them, provided their wants and would not permit sepoys of the other corps or the townpeople to approach them.[74]

A slightly different version by another rebel police chief of Delhi (a predecessor), makes it clear that Abdullah played an active role in the defence of Delhi against the British. According to this version, he was a discharged European soldier of the 17th Foot at Meerut: he turned Muslim and as Abdullah Beg became leader and adviser to the mutineers in Delhi.[75] The incident, too well authenticated to be doubted, forms a curious instance of the impulse of race animosity being overlaid by the ideology of religious solidarity, and in the process the particular definition of the rebellious native race or nation itself being superseded by the universal category of the brotherhood of faith.

No wonder the rhetoric of religion preponderates in the scores of mutiny proclamations and letters recovered by the patient researches of the archivist and historian; and unless we suppose that the feelings of patriotism are concealed and embedded within those religious sentiments, we look in vain for any patriotic rhetoric in the numerous specimens of mutiny language now available in print. Consider, for instance, a proclamation discovered as far afield as Hyderabad, in which patriotic solidarity, if at all to be looked for, must be taken to be a function of religious ex-communication:

> A Muslim who resolves to kill a Kafir, i.e., a Christian, and delays will be cut off from the society and called a descendant of the pariah caste, of a pig, and of a dog. He will be a descendant of Yazeed and Shimar. It is an oath on God to a Muslim whether he is rich or poor, or the Dewan, or spiritual head, or Moulvi, Kazi, Mufti, Suba or Kootwal, to participate in the task and get the blessings of

> God. If he succeeds he will be called a victor (*Ghazi*). If he dies he will be counted among those who died in the holy wars and will get a place in Bliss.[76]

The only hint—a negative one—that this is not a pure Islamic *Jehad* in Shah Saiyid Ahmad Barelvi's style is the implicit exclusion of the Hindus from the definition of *Kafir*. The infidel, it is taken care to define, is a Christian. Negative though it is, the hint is all the same vital. For behind it lies an underlying commitment to the caste-bound social system of the country into which the Muslim had been integrated for several centuries. If he does not spring to its defence, it is made clear that he will be made a pariah.

If the infidel is by definition a Christian, the extension of the same logic points to the Hindus and Muslims as the faithful: therein lies the inchoate, inarticulate notion of the nation, embedded and absorbed in the matrix of religion.[77] While sensing out the unformed outlines of that phoetus may be an interesting exercise, it may lead the investigator astray if he looks upon the enveloping corpus of *deen* and *dharma* as a mere veneer concealing the real thing. The notions that sustained the rebels till the last hour of doom derived from faith. One who assisted at their systematic hanging in Kanpur was constrained to observe:

> As a rule, those who had to die died with extraordinary, I was going to say courage, but composure is the word; the Mahomedans, with a hauteur and an angry kind of scorn; and the Hindoos with an apparent indifference altogether astonishing...Some of the Hindoos treated death almost as if it were a journey.[78]

Convictions that helped them face death helped them also to fight for what they cherished. The things they cherished would not have appealed much to the men who were to gather in the Indian National Congress in 1885, and were indeed repugnant to the men who were even then assembled in the British Indian Association, the Bombay Association and the Madras Native Association. What a gulf lay between these alternative versions of patriotism! The Hindu pandits who served the Purbeah sepoys in Delhi used to sing what an English officer dismissed as 'wild rhapsodies', a description the nationalists already articulate in Calcutta, Bombay and Madras would not have disagreed with. Take this specimen:

> No white face can move out

Therefore advance your batteries without fear.
The camp shall be destroyed like Lanka by fire;
Increase the number of your guns.
By the grace of Bulbhudder and Ramchander
The Camp shall be annihilated
Fight without intermission day and night;
Protect from injury our mother the cow
Offer sacrificial food to the Joala Maee and Bhovanee
And distribute it among the Brahmans
Present daily an offering of fourteen cows.[79]

The abstract concept of Mother India had already been formed by the English-educated Indians of the Presidency towns. But the mutineers of Hindustan, when referring to the mother, thought more readily of the real animal that sustained life in their villages. In a fast moving world that challenged them to look forward, they cast glances continually backward. And yet, there was something novel in their constructions, especially in one phrase repeated again and again in the language of the Mutiny. This was the word 'Hindus-and-Mussalmans of Hindustan', which was as much a political construct as the term 'Indian nation'. Even considered separately, these terms—Hindus and Muslims—were made-up categories in view of the numerous divisions of tribe, caste and region agglomerated in each. Taken together, they were of course a more strikingly novel agglomeration. In what sense were the Hindus and Muslims *both* entitled to the distinction of fidelity, as against 'kufr' and 'shirk'? Certainly in no doctrinal sense—there were far less serious differences between the peoples of the Book (Muslims, Christians and Jews) than between these and the idolators. The fidelity fusing the Hindus and Muslims as one confederate body was a concept born of the exigencies of political circumstances. They were linked together by the country to which they had a birthright, the country which the aliens had appropriated and were now threatening to destroy by undermining its characteristic social system.

In addresses meant for themselves and the people, the rebel leaders used the term 'Hindus and Muslims' unthinkingly. But as soon as the sphere shifted to correspondence between themselves and the Nepal Darbar, seeking to detach the latter from the British, the connotation of the term began to assume clearer outline. The Nepal Darbar, although Hindu, was understood to be outside the political system of Hindustan. Like the Kabul Darbar, it was 'foreign'. It required correspondence with a foreign power to bring out the concealed national significance of the term 'Hindus and Mussalmans'. Thus Birjis Qadr explained to the Maharaja of Nepal:

> The British, some time ago, attempted to interfere with the faith of both the Hindoos and Mohammedans, by preparing cartridges with cow's grease for the Hindoos, and that of pigs for the Mohammedans, and ordering them to bite them with their teeth. The sepoys refused, and were ordered by the British to be blown away from guns, on the parade ground. This is the cause of the war breaking out, and you are probably acquainted with it.

The boy prince's ambassador, therefore, professed it 'astonishing that you should have sided with the impure infidels, who are tyrants and enemies of the religion, both of Hindoos and Mohammedans, and have fought against the army of the faithful'. In his reply, acknowledging but rejecting the message from Awadh that 'the British are bent on the destruction of the society, religion and faith, of both Hindoos and Mohammedans', the Jang Bahadur posed the question : 'What grounds can we have for connecting ourselves with the Hindoos and Mohammedans of Hindustan?' He left the answer in no doubt: 'As the Hindoos and Mohammedans have been guilty of ingratitude and perfidy, neither the Nepaul government nor I can side with them'. Mindful of the fact that the Hindus and Muslims of Hindustan were strangers despite sharing at least one religion with Nepal, the Jang Bahadur rejected Birjis Qadr's appeal that 'it is proper for us to band together in the cause of religion', and harshly reminded the fugitive prince of Lucknow: 'Be it also known, that had I in any way been inclined to cultivate the friendship and intimacy of the Hindoo and Mohammedan tribes, should I have massacred nearly 5 (5,000) or 6,000 of them on my way to Lucknow'?[80]

What emerges from the correspondence is an alternative conception of what the Congress were to conceive later as the political nation: the confederated body of the 'faithful', acknowledged in neighbouring countries as the Hindus and Muslims of Hindustan, distinct on the one hand from Hindu Nepal and on the other from Muslim Afghanistan, and united in their opposition to the 'tyrants and enemies of religion' (in a manner the same thing but in another respect not quite so). These vague, half-articulate conceptions survived in the consciousness of the Indian population, powering the struggle for Gandhi's Ram Raj and the Ali Brothers' Khilafat three generations later, when once again the two nations joined together as one confederate nation. The formation of these conceptions is thus of sufficient historical importance to try and trace in some detail.

In the common parlance of the day the Muslims were a 'qaum' (people, race, community or nation), and so, in their eyes, were the Hindus. Acutely aware of each other's separateness, yet compelled to reckon with their oneness, they had come to regard themselves as two nations within one by the end of the eighteenth-century. As late as that the high-born Muslims of the country still regarded themselves, like the newly ascendant Englishmen, as conquerors from outside, but their difference with the English, as a Mughal nobleman and chronicler of keen insight put it, lay in the fact that the Muslim conquerors had decided 'to fix the foot of residence and permanence' in the conquered country. 'Their immediate successors having learned the language of the country, behaved to its inhabitants as brothers of one mother and one language.' Writing in the twilight of the Mughal Empire, under the shadow of Plassey and Buxar, he, Saiyid Ghulam Husain Khan, observed, in well chosen, justly celebrated words:

> And although the Gentoos seem to be a generation apart and distinct from the rest of mankind, and they are swayed by such differences in religion, tenets, and rites, as will necessarily render all Mussulmans aliens and profane, in their eyes; and although they keep up a strangeness of ideas and practices, which beget a wide difference in customs and actions; yet in the process of time, they drew nearer and nearer, and as soon as fear and aversion had worn away, we see this dissimilarity and alienation have terminated in friendship and union, and the two nations have come to coalesce together into one whole, like milk and sugar that have received a simmering. In one word we have seen them promote heartily each other's welfare, have common ideas, like brothers from one and the same mother, and feel for each other, as children of the same family.[81]

Perhaps Saiyid Ghulam Husain spoke a little too wishfully (although we may observe that his carefully chosen simile refers to one mother, the country, but not one father, the faith). But the process of assimilation was certainly carried a stage further in his day by common subjection to the English:'...such is the aversion which the English show for the company of natives, and such the disdain they openly betray for them, that no love, and no coalition...can take root between the conquerors and the conquered.'[82] The twin characteristics of the

Englishmen that impressed themselves on his mind were the transitory character of their stay in the country and their single-minded devotion to 'scraping together as much money in this country as they can, and carrying it in immense sums to the kingdom of England.'[83]

A century of sharing the common experience of racial humiliation would certainly have blurred the psychological distinction Saiyid Ghulam Husain made in his day between the Muslims and the Hindus as the conquerors and the conquered. Folk historical memory, however, carried a residue of bitterness and distrust that exhibited itself in the trouble over Hanumangarhi at Ayodhya just two years before the Mutiny.[84] The year 1857 witnessed this antagonistic religious distinction being transcended by the dramatic redefining of 'fidelity' that emerged from the dispute over the cartridge. 'Hindus and Musalmans' emerged all at once as a term of reference for the people of the country, fighting together for a common heritage of faith felt to be threatened from a single malign quarter. Pronouncing them together meant speaking of the entire native population, minus the section that had lost fidelity (i.e., native Christian). The 'other' of 'infidels' formed a collectivity not yet defined as the political nation, yet sufficiently formed in the consciousness of contemporaries for the *Risala Fath-i-Islam* to urge:

> A proclamation should be issued both to the troops and people of Bengal if possible, or if otherwise, as far as possible at present, to the effect that the people of every city, whether Hindoos or Mahomedans, should be unanimous in attacking simultaneously this accursed nation (by the appointment of a leader in each city).[85]

The people of Hindustan were now a people at war, in a sense no less definite than the Hellenes, divided up in many a small polis, had been a nation at war during the Persian invasion.[86] Consider the following proclamations by their chiefs, using again and again the characteristic expression connoting the nation being born:

(Khan Bahadur Khan): *Proclamation for the religious and faithful promulgated by authority.*

> Let it be known at present it is indispensable for both the *Hindoos and Mahomedans* to direct their united efforts to the extermination of the Christians—enemies of lives and faith.[87]

(Mirza Feroz Shah Shahzada): To all *Hindoos and Mahommedans of Hindoostan* who are faithful to their religion know that sovereignty is one of God's chief boons, one which a deceitful tyrant is never allowed to retain. For several years the English have been committing all kinds of excesses and tyrannies being desirous of converting all men to Christianity by force, and of subverting and doing away with the religion of *Hindoos and Mahommedans*. When God saw this fact, He so altered the hearts of the inhabitants of Hindoostan, that they have been doing their best to get rid of the English themselves; now the Feringhees have been destroyed, but still they overrun the country to its destruction, and persevere in their vain endeavours. Soon they will have been, by the grace of God, so utterly exterminated, that no traces of them will remain. Know that *all Hindoos and Mussalmans* have become so hateful to them, that they will not suffer any to live with honour.[88]

(Unnamed grandson of Bahadur Shah): It is well known to all that in this age *the people of Hindoostan*, both *Hindoos and Mohammedans*, are being ruined under the tyranny and oppression of the infidel and treacherous English. It is therefore the bounden duty of all the wealthy people of India, especially those who have any sort of connection with any of the Mohammedan royal families, and are considered the pastors and masters of their people, to stake their lives and property for the well being of the public...I who am the grandson of Abul Muzuffer Serajuddin Bahadur Shah Ghazee, King of India, having in the course of circuit come here [Azamgarh] to extirpate the infidels residing in the eastern part of the country, and to liberate and protect the poor helpless people now groaning under their iron rule, have, by the aid of the Majahdeens, or religious fanatics, erected the standard of Mohammad, and persuaded the orthodox Hindoos who had been subject to my ancestors, and have been and are still accessories to the destruction of the English, to raise the standard of Mahavir.

Several of the Hindoo and Mussulman chiefs, who have long since quitted their homes for the preservation of their religion, and have been trying their best to root out the English in India, have presented themselves to me, and taken part in the reigning Indian crusade, and it is more than probable that I shall very shortly receive succours from the West.[89]

In characteristic Mutiny language, the loyal Thakur of Kethyaree was addressed by a Muslim theologian as: 'To Hardeo Buksh of Kethyaree, Christian of Farruckabad'. He was admonished for 'your having deserted your kinsmen and brethren (both Hindoos and Mahommedans)' and upbraided for his 'shamelessness, worthlessness and dishonesty.' He was warned: 'Even should victory smile on the cause of the English, you will be shunned by your brethren.'[90] The 'reigning Indian crusade' thus produced its own categories of patriots and traitors. Calling perdition upon the 'infidel' chief of Charkhari, the 'Peshwa' enjoined upon all officers, Soobadars, Sirdars and Sepoys to consider him 'as an Englishman' and 'send him to hell.'[91]

What was to be the basis of the patriotic alliance between the Hindus and Muslims, or 'the reigning Indian crusade', as the unnamed Shahzada put it at Azamgarh? One popular argument, with intellectual precedents going back to the *Majma ul Bahrain* of Dara Shikoh[92] and the syncretic cults of the medieval saints, was thus put in a secret letter from the mutinous 51st Native Infantry at Peshawar to two disaffected regiments stationed at Shubkudder on 18 May 1857: 'O brother! the religion of Hindoos and Mahomedans is all one - Therefore all you soldiers should know this.'[93] That this was not mere casuistry, but had genuine feeling behind it, is shown by the real regard the Muslim sepoys showed for the religion of the Hindu sepoys over the issue of the greased cartridge. As Khan Bahadur Khan's celebrated proclamation pointed out: 'The Mussulman soldiers perceived that by this expedient the religion of the Brahmins and Hindoos alone was in danger, but nevertheless they also refused to bite them.'[94] The same mutual regard, intellectually based on the Indian dictum 'Svadharme Nidham Shreyah', quoted time and again, formed the ground of the *Risala Fath-i Islam*'s enunciation: 'The Hindoos will remain steadfast to their religion, while we will also retain ours. Aid and protection will be offered by us to each other.'[95]

That is all very well, a sceptic like Raja Man Singh of Shahganj (the commonly accepted protector of the so-called birthplace of Rama) might have asked, but what about the sharing of the realm? Maulvi Ahmadullah Shah's answer to this was not likely to satisfy him: 'The Hindoos should join the (appointed Muslim) chief...in as much as formerly the Mahomedan Kings protected (as they felt it incumbent on them to do) the lives and property of the Hindoos with their children in the same manner as protected those of the Mahomedans, and all the Hindoos with heart and soul were obedient and loyal to the Mahomedan

Kings.'[96] The assumption implicit here about the sharing of the realm—'commonsense and a regard for faith point out that servitude under the Mahomedan Chiefs and such Rajahs as are dependents of the Mahomedan Kings is infinitely better than that, under the infidel Victoria and the English'[97]—is unlikely to have appealed to a Raja who only two years ago was commonly believed to have declared, during the Hanumangarhi dispute that but for the support the Nawab was sure to receive from the English, 'he would have marched to Lucknow, destroyed the Mahomedan dynasty, and established a Hindoo Government in its place.'[98] Only a month before he joined the mutineers at Lucknow with his levy, convinced by Havelock's precipitate retreat that the British were the losing side, the Raja was writing in a letter to the brother taluqdars of Awadh:[99]

> It is also surprising that people should aid and put into power those very Mussulmans who, on invading India, destroyed all our Hindoo temples, forcibly converted the natives to Mohammedanism, massacred whole cities, seized upon Hindoo females and made them concubines, prevented Brahmins from saying prayers, burnt their religious books, and levied taxes upon every Hindoo.
>
> They are those very Mussulmans who prided themselves on calling us infidels, and in subjecting us to all sorts of humiliation.
>
> If any person will reflect on their former deeds, it will make his hair stand on end, cause such disgust that the very sight even of a Mohamedan will be abhorrent.
>
> What is more surprising still, is that the people should consider it a religious deed to kill those very persons who permitted the establishment of the decayed religion, and allowed all temples and places of worship to be rebuilt, and all religious ceremonies to be performed without any hindrance whatsoever.
>
> We should consider how much we suffered in the time of the Mahomedan kings of Oude.[100]

Man Singh voiced a part of the Hindu folk memory that undoubtedly co-existed with fonder memories, such as the cherished remembrance of the magnificent Nawab Asaf al-Daula of Lucknow in whose name every Hindu shopkeeper of the city would intone as he took his seat in his shop: 'Jis ko na de Maula, Us ko de Asif-ud-Daulah' (To whom the Lord does not give, Asaf al-Daula will)[101]. The rebel leaders were acutely aware of the problem of Hindu-Muslim conflict and the Muslim chiefs took particularly vigorous action to counteract it. A compact banning cow slaughter, initiated by Emperor Bahadur Shah during Bakr Id in Delhi,[102] was arrived at with the Hindu Rajas and sepoys:

> The slaughter of kine is regarded by the Hindoos as a great insult to their religion. To prevent this, a solemn compact and agreement has been entered into by all the Mahommedan chiefs of Hindoostan, binding themselves that if the Hindoos will come forward to slay the English, the Mahommedans will, from that very day put a stop to the slaughter of cows, and those of them who will not do so will be considered to have abjured the Quran, and such of them as will eat beef will be regarded as though they had eaten pork: but if the Hindoos will not gird their loins to kill the English, but will try to save them, they will be as guilty in the sight of God as though they had committed sins of killing cows....[103]

The true extent of concession under this national compact can hardly be grasped unless we keep in mind the degree to which Indian Islam had become symbolically and emotionally bound to the ceremonial sacrifice of the cow over the centuries. How important the compact was politically is briefly glimpsed in the communication from the English officers on the Ridge. As Id day approached, Keith Young wrote expectantly on the basis of reports received from spies: 'Some of the Mahomedan fanatics have declared their fixed intention of killing a cow as customary on that day at the Jumma Musjid. It is hoped that they will religiously adhere to their determination, and there is then sure to be a row between the Mahomedans and Hindoos.' On the day after the Id, he wrote in a disappointed tone to his wife:

> Our hopes of a grand row in the city yesterday at the Eed Festival have not, apparently, been fulfilled—at least the only newsletter received from the city alludes to nothing of the kind. The King issued strict orders against killing cows, or even goats, in the city, and this, if acted upon, must have satisfied the Hindoos; and instead of fighting among themselves they all joined together to make a

vigorous attack to destroy us and utterly sweep us from the face of the earth.[104]

Rohilkhand, where Khan Bahadur Khan enforced the compact scrupulously, was tense with potential conflict. After a riot occurred at night in Bareilly, a special ceremony was staged by the Nawab in the town:

He resolved to put a large flag or holy dhvaj for the Hindus and a Muhammadi Jhanda, i.e., holy flag, for the Muslims, and to call together the principal Hindus and Musalmans under those flags. Having made this resolve the Nawab proceeded through the town that afternoon with some Brahmans, Sobhram, Gokulanand, Newalanand, etc., and some Kayasths, Ganesh Rai, Harsukh Rai etc. Needless to say, the Hindus moved along by their dhvaj; the Musalmans proceeded under the Muhammadi Jhanda. The Nawab himself went round town with great pomp on an elephant. The cry rose every now and then: *Hindu Musalman ek—Ram Rahim ek—Shrikrishna Allah ek*, and it was also proclaimed: 'Those who are strong and adult among the Hindus, go to the Hindu dhvaj with arms, Musalmans assemble under the Muhammadi Jhanda, and all swear to extirpate the English.' Many spectators gathered round—such a crowd as one could hardly make his way through it. Amidst tumultuous sounds, the holy dhvaj of the Hindus was planted on the bank of the Ramganga, and on the same day the Muhammadi Jhanda was planted in a garden near town. Diwan Sobha Ram distributed food according to Hindu ritual - Luchis, Sandesh, Khir - on the bank of Ramganga. *Kalia, Kababs, Korma*, were being distributed in the garden.[105]

Earlier the same sort of ceremony had taken place under the aegis of Nana Sahib in Kanpur, where the green Muhammadi Jhanda had been set up, as well as a Mahavir Jhanda, calling upon the people to attack the entrenchment commanded by General Wheeler.[106]

The 'reigning Indian crusade', with battle cries of 'Deen Deen' and 'Har Har Mahadeo' accompanying the unfurling of the green and saffron flags of Muhammad and Mahavir, struck the *Hindoo Patriot*, which belonged squarely to the other category of nationalism, as a movement that, despite all its limitations, reflected the 'national feelings' of 'martyrs to a holy cause', who had been led to believe 'their national religion' to be in danger.[107] A proclamation from Charkhari some time later practically echoed the same words: 'I am desirous to extirpate Infidel Christians and preserve the national religion.'[108] A Rajput Pardesee peon sentenced to death for fomenting mutiny in Satara cried to the spectators from the scaffold that his own countrymen had betrayed him to the English and hanged him. Now was the time to strike: 'if they were sons of Hindoos and Mussulmans they would rise, if the offspring of Christians, they would remain quite.'[109]

Interspersed with these continual exhortations to the 'Hindus and Musalmans' there are such occasional references to the country and the countrymen; but they are hard to come by. In the absence of a clear political concept of the nation, the divisions within the population loomed large in the rebel language and consciousness. The written order of the Emperor to the chief police officer of Delhi, dated 6 September 1857, reads:

> You are directed to have proclaimed throughout the city by beat of drum that this is a religious war, and is being prosecuted on account of the faith, and that it behoves all Hindu and Mussulman residents of the imperial city, or of the villages out in the country, as well as those natives of Hindoostan who are arrayed against us on the ridge, or anywhere employed on the side of the armies of the English, whether they be men of the eastern provinces [Purbeahs], or Sikhs, or foreigners,[110] or natives of the Himalaya Hills, or Nepalese, to continue true to their faith and creeds, and to slay the English and their servants : and you are directed to have it further proclaimed that, those who are now present with the English force on the ridge, whether they be people of Hindustan, or foreigners or Hillmen,[111] or Sikhs,[112] or whatever country they may be natives of, or whether they be Mahomedans, or Hindus born in Hindustan, they are not to entertain any fears or dread of the enemy.[113]

These various categories stood sharply outlined in moments of fear: on 4 August there was a scare in town that the Pathans were coming from Swat, recruited by the English, to fight and kill the Purbeas;[114] and the next day the Sikh sepoys in Delhi complained to the Emperor that the Purbeahs were not helping them in attacks on the English entrenchments, and requested that a regiment of Sikhs be formed from amongst the regiments in Delhi to attack the English.[115] As for the citizens of Delhi, they looked upon the Purbeah soldiers as uncouth strangers,[116] and the latter were both disliked as the occupation army and abused for cowardice in facing the British on the Ridge (for fear of the Goras coming lay like a pall on the town).[117]

Fear, however, also fused the people into one mass psychologically, and knowledge of the common fate awaiting the natives—Neill's savage, unsparing, promiscuous butchery all the way from Allahabad to Kanpur was known by this time—lent weight to the Emperor's exhortations to 'the people of Hindustan' to unite. Impelled by the subconscious mass conviction that the Hindus and Muslims had become so 'hateful' to the English that 'they will not suffer any to live with honour', and that 'the padres and wise men amongst them, alarmed at the mutiny, the anarchy and the slaughter of the Europeans', had concocted a secret, devious scheme for the extinction of the very identity of the people of Hindustan,[118] Shahzada Feroz Shah said, 'Oh Hindustanee Brethren! you have heard what measures they had resolved to carry out. You must now wash your hands, and becoming their enemies exert yourselves in exterminating them for the sake of your religion and your lives.'[119] All at once, raw panic defined the opposed national identities in simple and unconscious words put into the mouth of the enemy: 'if all misconduct among the Hindustanis is punished, then the English rule will remain established for thousands of years.'[120] Voicing the same sort of mass panic and using the same coalesced expression of national identity, Nana Sahib circulated the following rumour:

> A traveller just arrived at Cawnpore from Calcutta states that before the cartridges were distributed a Council was held for the purpose of taking away the religion and rites of the people of Hindustan. The Members of the Council came to the conclusion that as the matter was one affecting religion seven or eight thousand Europeans would be required and it would cost the lives of fifty thousand Hindustanis but that at this cost all the natives of Hindoostan would became Christians.[121]

With such unmistakable expressions of nationality—'O Hindustanee Brethren', 'the people of Hindustan', 'the Hindustanis', 'the whole country of Hindustan'—now transforming the political climate in the country, no wonder the language of patriotic war broke through even the crusading maulvi's rhetoric of *jehad*:

> Mussulmans of India being destitute of resources, having no ammunition, Guns, or Army, have been all along in a helpless

> condition, but the Gracious God who has strengthened the religion of Islam internally has for the encouragement of weak creatures like ourselves, furnished us with the resources formerly enjoyed by the unsuccessful and unprincipled Christians without any attempt being made by us. Our being backed by a large Army of Infantry, Cavalry, and Artillery, our having obtained an immense treasure, the arrival of the letter from the King of Delhi, the bonafide ruler of Hindoostan who is the shadow and representative of God (May his Dominions ever extend!), our alliance with the Rajah(s) of the province of Oudh and the State adjacent to Allahabad, and the union which prevails throughout Hindoostan, notwithstanding the people are of different persuasions and tribes, are clear proofs that the people are determined to extirpate these rebel Christians now. O my Mussulman Brethren! as soon as you hear the above glad tidings prepare yourselves for Jehad, come to Allahabad, subdue and put to the sword the besieged Christians there, and try to expel the remnant of their body from this country, and then rule the country according to the Laws and Institutions of Mohammed.[122]

The triumph and tragedy of Hindustani patriotism in 1857 lies summed up in these words of Maulvi Liaqat Ali, weaver turned schoolteacher, who is exhilarated by 'the union which prevails throughout Hindoostan, notwithstanding the people are of different persuasions and tribes'; yet, innocent of any notion of the political nation, deeply commited to the *deen* that still encapsulates his universe in its totality, what can the maulvi conceive as the outcome of the struggle but the *dar al-Islam*? But surely if religion provides the ideological framework of the Mutiny, the totality of the emotional experince goes beyond it. Why is it that Bakht Khan explodes when the indispensable commissariat clerk of the *Risala* refuses the offer of a thousand rupee job with the Bareilly mutineers: 'Namakharam! Baiman! Hazar rupaiyāh tankhā bhi qabool nahi karte!' ('Traitor! Disloyal man! You refuse to serve even for a thousand rupee salary!')? What 'namak' (salt) does he refer to? What 'iman' (loyalty) has he in mind? His own furious words leave the meaning in no doubt:

'Āngrez aur Bāngāli sab ek hai, tumko nahi mālum hai, ki ham abhi tumhārā gardan katne ka hukum de sakte hain...Khub malum hai ki Āngrezon ke sath tumhāri sāzish hai' (Englishmen and Bengalis are all the same, you don't understand that I can order your head to be cut off right now... I know very well that you are in cahoots with the English).[123]

The concept of 'salt' has, by now, undergone a dramatic alteration among the sepoys: 'Company ka namak haram' (the salt of the Company is impure), cries the sentry on guard, and fires off his gun sounding off the outbreak at Azamgarh.[124] Without this reordering of loyalties, the fleeing Tantia Tope could hardly have exclaimed: 'This is the country of my grand-father and great-grandfather, and yet no one gives me supplies. All the people of my country, Hindoos and Mussulmen, have become Christian.'[125] At the back of this ordering of obligations in the rebel mind, lies the feeling that the English are 'trespassers'—a feeling greatly intensified among the Purbeah sepoys since the takeover of their homeland Awadh.[126] Coming as it did as the climax to an alarming chain of annexations in violation of treaty obligations, the latest appropriation strengthened the impression that these 'accursed vilaitis' were past masters in trickery—*daghabazi*, as Nana Sahib put it[127]—and would leave nothing to the princes and the people.[128]

Such were perceptions that awakened the patriotic feelings lying dormant in the breasts of princes, noblemen and people. The concept of the sovereign national state being unformed, the passionate attachment to hereditary possessions provided the focus to these expressions of patriotism. The Begum of Awadh exclaimed in her rejoinder to Queen Victoria:

> If our people were discontented with our royal predecessor, Wajid Ali Shah, how come it they are content with us? And no ruler ever enjoyed such loyalty and devotion of goods and life as we have done. What, then is wanting that they do not restore our country? Further, it is written [in the proclamation of Queen Victoria], that they want no increase of territory, but yet they cannot refrain from annexation. If the Queen has assumed the government, why does not Her Majesty restore our country to us when our people wish it?[129]

Begum Hazrat Mahal's pronouncement on the loyalty of her subjects is echoed in their own voice, as will be evident, for instance, from the noble resolve of her faithful servant, the Governor of Gorakhpur, 'hereafter to fight and die in the tenets of my faith and in the cause of my illustrious sovereign.' Governor Muhammad Hasan Khan added in the same letter to an acquaintance:[130]

> The British have exceeded all bounds in their breaking of promises—this is notorious—(witness the treaties) between them and the Raja of Lahore, the Peishwa and other Princes too numerous to mention. My business is with the King of Oude. All the world knows of the binding engagements and treaties which existed between those two exalted Powers, the King of Oude and the English Government...Kingdom has been wrested perfidiously from a dynasty which never opposed and which always conciliated the English Government, all kinds of tyranny have been perpetrated. No one now puts any trust in the British. I may sum up with the proverb 'Who has not received the reward of his deeds?" The Princes and people of Hindostan, witnessing this perfidious oppression, took the opportunity of the revolt of the army (the result also of the English government's own conduct) and the outbreak took place, involving the slaughter and plunder of thousands of innocent servants of God.

What the Lucknow nobleman's words reflect is a sense of the country focused on but going beyond hereditary possession. The same range of obligations finds expression in Hanwant Singh's parting words to Barrow, whom he conducts to safety. At their parting, when the Englishman expresses a hope that the taluqdar would join in suppressing the revolt, the dispossessed chief stands erect and replies:

> Sahib, your countrymen came into this country and drove out our king. You sent your officers round the districts to examine the titles to the estates. At one blow you took from me lands which from time immemorial have been in my family. I submitted. Suddenly misfortune fell upon you. You come to me whom you despoiled. I have saved you. But now, - now I march at the head of my retainers to Lukhnao to try and drive you from the country.[131]

The race of natives—that inchoate nation lacking the concept of the sovereign national state—is constricted to express its identity in the older and more familiar terms of realm[132] and religion.[133] But who can mistake the spontaneous sense of identity that forms the bedrock? A party of Europeans fleeing from Fatehpur to Allahabad narrowly escape massacre by the cleverness of a lady who had the presence of mind to put out of her palanquin a fair hand on which she had taken care to put on *choorees* or Indian bangles. Seeing them the surrounding *sawars* exclaimed: 'O Bhaee! They are our own people; let them pass.'[134]

Unshakable commitments, passing through whatever ideological channel, must issue ultimately from the spontaneous emotion. Compare the following statements, one by a Muslim bookbinder of Patna hanged by the British, the other by a Hindu prince from Bithoor driven to the pestilential terai of Nepal:

> [Pir Ali, 'heavily fettered, his soiled garment deeply stained in blood,' on being asked whether he had any information to give that might induce Government to spare his life]:
>
> There are some cases in which it is good to save life—others in which it is better to lose it.
>
> [He denounced the oppression of the British and added]
>
> You may hang me, or such as me, every day, but thousands will rise in my place, and your object will never be gained.[135]
>
> [Nana Sahib, from his Nepal hideout, on being asked to surrender]
> If you wish it, the thing can only be done in this way [by French mediation], and to this I consent. If not, life must be given up some day. Why then should I die dishonoured? There will be war between me and you as long as I have life, whether I be killed or imprisoned or hanged, and whatever I do will be done with the sword only.
> [He was heard of no more].[136]

Faith or patriotism, the heart-felt emotion behind it is the very same. The raw mass emotions that form the substance of nationalism must by their nature precede the intellectual concepts that give it definition. The emotions that went into the making of Indian nationalism later on—its psychological raw materials, so to say—are visible in the expressions of antagonism to the British in 1857, though the inchoate sense of nationality had not yet taken the conceptual form of the modern political nation. What the emotionally charged collectivity felt in 1921—the raw antagonistic impulse itself[137] as also the vague yearning for Ram Raj and Khilafat—would appear to bear a certain generic resemblance to the rebel expressions we encounter in

1857: the singling out of the members of the ruling race as well as those mentally associated with them by the people, the waging of a combined war in support of the mutually acknowledged claims of the Hindus and Muslims to establish their respective sacred realms upon the soil of Hindustan, above all the two-in-one formula of 'the Hindus and Musalmans of Hindustan,' two *qaums* based upon two different religions, but constituting a confederate people bent upon purging the land of an alien and impure presence.

Was there, then, a true sense in which the Mutiny could be called, as indeed Jawaharlal Nehru (and thirty years before him, V.D. Savarkar) called it, 'a war of Indian Independence?' Why did he say this despite his careful qualification that 'Nationalism of a modern type was yet to come?'[138] It must be remembered, for the clarity of the argument here, that patriotism is a far older phenomenon than modern day nationalism. The resistance of the Greek city states to the Persian invasion, the crusade of Joan of Arc against the aliens from across the English Channel, and the uprising of the people of Delhi against the Iranian troopers of Nadir Shah, all exhibit patriotism in various antique forms.[139] Patriotism signifies that spontaneous desire for independence from alien rule which, in all human societies, must long precede the modern concept of national unity embodied in the sovereign national state. The patriotism of those who mutinied in 1857 expressed itself in the specific form of a combined religious crusade.

Unlike the members of the Indian National Congress of 1885, or even the contemporary members of the British Indian Association who denounced the Mutiny so vehemently, the rebels of 1857 belonged to a society that had no notion of national sovereignty. Devoid of that notion, they were thrown back upon 'the full power of the native chiefs, and the full sway of the native religions.' And yet it would be to simplify matters unduly to dwell on the chiefs and religions alone; for the people's power that surged through these old methods of rallying round invested the apparent restoration of the chiefs with a content that was no longer the true substance of the old regime. And what the Congress leaders later called 'the Indian Nation', the rebel leaders already spoke of distinctly as 'the Hindus and Musalmans of Hindustan.'[140]

NOTES

1. W.H. Russell, *My Indian Diary*, ed. M. Edwards (London, 1857), p. 86.
2. Ibid., pp. 29-30.
3. Russell records in his *Diary*, 4 March 1858: 'Had a large party at mess, many of whom had been in recent 'dours', and I heard, a good deal of 'potting pandies' and 'polishing-off niggers". Ibid., p.67.
4. Proclamation of *jehad* by Maulvi Liaqat Ali, *Freedom Struggle in Uttar Pradesh Source Material* (Publications Bureau, UP 1957-) Hence *FSUP*, Vol. I, p. 447.
5. *FSUP*, I, pp. 453-4.
6. That is how the contemporary English documents render 'Deen' and 'Dharma', and for want of a better term the historian must perforce put it thus.
7. Charles Ball, *History of the Indian Mutiny* (London, n.d.), vol. 2, p. 242. It must be borne in mind that the sepoys said this when their death was certain and they had nothing to gain from lying. They met death, moreover, with that extraordinary composure which only faith could have inspired. Lt. Col. F.C. Maude, *Memories of the Mutiny: with which is incorporated the personal narration of John Walter Sherer* (London, 1894), vol. 1, pp. 251-52.
8. Meerut depositions, statement of Bhagwan Das, resident of Sadar Bazar, *Narrative of Events Regarding the Mutiny in India 1857-58 and the Restoration of Authority* (hence *NE*) (Calcutta, 1881), vol. 1, p. 341.
9. Statement of Gunga Fershaud, tahsildar of Meerut, *NE*, I. p. 308. Note the spontaneous resort to the joint formula, Brothers, Hindus and Musalmans', right at the start of the outbreak, illuminating the Mutiny's inarticulate and subconscious conceptions of the nation.
10. Statement of Hurnam Singh, mahajan, *NE*, I, p. 337. Sepoys, crowds and chiefs alike repeated the same idea throughout the Mutiny, and the Begum of Awadh s rejoinder to Queen Victoria's proclamation of 1858 reiterated: 'The rebellion began with religion, and for it, millions of men have been killed.' *FSUP*, II, p. 530.
11. Secret news from Lucknow, 2.12.1857, *FSUP*, II, p. 257.
12. Proclamation of Nana Sahib, 1 July 1857, *FSUP*, IV, p. 602. In an earlier message to officers at Sitapur and Sikandra, dated 27 June 1857, Nana Sahib wrote: 'Here (Cawnpore) this day 4th Zihad (27th June), the white faces fought with us. The whole of them, by the grace of God, and the destroying fortune of the King, have entered hell.' Proclamations and correspondence of Nana Sahib, printed in J.H. Kaye, *A History of the Great Revolt* (reprint, Delhi, 1988), vol II, p. 673.

13. Petition of Amir Ali Khan, son of the Nawab of Khurajpura, to the Emperor, 12 July 1857, *The Trial of Muhammed Bahadur Shah*, ed. H.L.O. Garrett (Govt. of Punjab, 1932), p. 245.
14. *NE*, I, Allahabad, narrative of Corridon, p. 20.
15. See, for instance, Liakat Ali's proclamation of *jehad* against the English at Allahabad, never once mentioning them as Europeans, but invariably as 'Christians'. *FSUP*, I, pp. 445-48. Some of the less complementary expressions used by the Maulvi against the English were 'Kufroh Fujruh Nisara (fraudulent Christian Infidels)', Kooffar Nabukar Nisara Bad Utwar (useless and misconducting Christian Infidels)' and 'Taghee Baghee Nisaras (fraudulent and mutinous Christian Infidels)'. Proclamation of Liaqat Ali under seal of Birjis Qadar, ibid., IV, pp. 614-15. By far the two most common expressions of contempt for the English in the Mutiny proclamations are Kafirs and Nazarenes. Proclamation of Feroz Shah, ibid., I, p. 462; Rana Beni Baksh Singh's petition to the Vazier, 21 July 1858, ibid., II, p. 454.
16. Deposition of John Fitchett, quoted by Rudrangshu Mukherjee, 'Satan Let Loose Upon Earth": The Massacres in Kanpur in the Revolt of 1857 in India', unpublished paper. So strong was the identification of sin with the physical presence of the British in the Mutineers' mind that the terms '*kufr*' and '*shirk*', denoting the abstract sin of lack of faith, was used by them to denote the English race. 'By God's grace Kufr and Shirk (the rule of the heathens) have been purged from Hindustan and Islam has been established,' ran an imperial proclamation. Ibid., I, p.320.
17. Meerut Depositions, statement of J.H. Jones, *NE*, I, pp. 334-35.
18. Rudrangshu Mukherjee, *Awadh in Revolt 1857-1858. A Study of Popular Resistance* (Delhi, 1984), p. 67. *Din* is derived by Arabic philologists from *dāna li*—...(submit to), hence 'corpus of obligatory prescriptions,' or more commonly, religion, in the sense of 'obligations which God imposes on His reasoning creatures.' *Encyclopaedia of Islam* (New Eds., B. Lewis, Ch. Pellat, J. Schacht, Leiden, 1965). The term *be-dharam*, a compound of the Persian negative *be*', ('lacking') and the Sanskrit *dharma* ('that which holds together') is peculiarly difficult to translate exactly: to render it as 'irreligious' would be to miss a subtle point. Since *dharma*, is, technically speaking, duty, understood in the context of social and religious prescriptions, *be-dharam* may be rendered as both undutiful and faithless.
19. Vishnubhat Godase, *Majha Pravas*, ed. B.B.C.V. Vaidya (Pune, 1948; 1st ed., 1907).
20. Proclamation of Feroz Shah, 18 February 1858, *FSUP*, V, p. 376.
21. Delhi Proclamation, May 1857, ibid., I, p. 438. Cf. Proclamation of the High Court of the Nawab, Ruler of the Province of Kutehur: 'To all

high and low, be it manifest as the sun at noonday. That the English are the enemies of the life, the property, and the religion alike of the Moosulmans and Hindoos, and being puffed up with self-conceit, forgetting themselves in their pride, have thought to make the people of God converts to the Christian religion. By the will of God, who abhors pride, whose displeasure they have incurred, these infidels have in many places been put to death, and sent down to hell...Let all take notice of this Proclamation and so exert themselves that no trace of the unclean infidels be left in this province.' Ibid., V, pp. 605-06.

22. Note the following words in the above proclamation: 'the will of God, who abhors pride, whose displeasure they have incurred'; 'this (killing of Englishmen) will be an act of merit'; 'If any one in this religious fight jehad, suffers martyrdom he will go to heaven;' 'no trace of the unclean infidels be left.' A sense of doom, of ultimate sin, of God's wrath, of hubris and nemesis, of the duty and merit of meting out punishment, of *jehad* by the *Ghazi*, of the attaining of heaven by the *Shaheed*, pervade the mentality behind the proclamation.

23. Kaye, III, p. 213.

24. Letter from Icha Singh, Chatta Singh, Shumsere Khan and Sheodeen Singh, Subadars and other officers in the Gwalior Contingent, to the Subadars and other officers in the service of the Raja of Churkuree, 31 January 1858: 'It was not becoming in your master to oppose us in our recent outbreak being regardless of the next world.' *FSUP*, III, p. 229.

25. In the English record of the event, General Neill, the butcher of Kanpur, is invariably portrayed as a man driven by a sense of religious duty. Curiously, in the indigenous Marathi record of the event, Nana Sahib, his counterpart, is also remembered in the same light, with the words 'Har, Har' (invocation to Siva) on his lips, making the following resolve upon his defeat at Kanpur: 'All my endeavours till today for the sake of the Hindu religion (Hindudharmakaritān) have been in vain (vyartha jāun), but if it be the wish of Mother Ganga, I give up even the hope of life (jivitāchihi āshā āmhi sorali āhe). *Majha Pravas*, p. 35. Apparently it does not occur to Nana Sahib to put in a word about the country, as distinct from religion. The conception of martyrdom for the country as such must, it seems, await the coming of Tilak and the Chapekars. Their predecessors of 1857, the patriotic Maratha Brahmins who issued a proclamation from Kalpi on 11 April 1858, are unable to conceive anything beyond faith.' Ibid., p. 356.

26. Consider the various Islamic calls for *jehad* in 1857. Thus Liaqat Ali: 'You all should act according to the following precept quoted from Quran, 'The real paradise lies beneath the strokes of swords". You will then obtain salvation and the honour of martyrdom, which is eternal life.' And Birjis Qadar: 'When death comes upon a man, who can save

him? In every place and country, thousands of men die from cholera, pestilence, and other diseases. No one knows whether they died in their senses or without senses, nor can it be known whether they died with their faith firm or not. To die in battle with the English for the sake of religion is glorious, and he who falls thus is sure to become a martyr.' Ibid., I, pp. 446, 447.

27. It is useful by way of analogy to bear in mind the importance of religion in fostering opposition to imperialism in the lands of Islam, and, in particular, in stoking Arab nationalism. India, of course, stands in a category by itself as Islam was a minority religion here.

28. Testimony of Mrs. Aldwell, 1.2.1858, *Trial of Bahadur Shah*, p. 158. She was the one white woman, among the European prisoners of the palace, who escaped with her life. She pretended to be a Muslim woman from Kashmir, and took care to teach her children the Muslim prayer. During her stay in beseiged Delhi she noticed that 'the Mahomedans always seemed glad that mutiny had taken place, and during the Muharram festival I heard the Mohamedan women praying, and teaching their children to pray, for the success of their faith...'

29. The *dharma* of the Hindus, after all, was never, like Islam, a defined creed, but was rather a righteous social order, and their grievances related instead to the fear of losing caste and the oppressive rule of the English.

30. Testimony of John Everett, *Trial of Bahadur Shah*, p. 198:

    Question: From what you know, were the Hindus in Delhi, or the Musalmans most averse to the Company's Government?

    Answer : The Mussalmans.

    The English had the same impression in Gwalior: 'With great exceptions and limitations, the Mahomedans cooperated with the revolt; the Hindus wished it well, but, having no religious grievance, while their civil grievances were inadequate to move them arms unled by their chiefs, they did not rise, and protected the lives of defenceless Europeans'. Report of S.C. Macpherson, Political Agent, Gwalior, 10 February 1858, *FSUP*, III, p. 202.

31. The Gwalior Darbar's view of the Hindu discontent, as conveyed to the Political Agent, was that the religious issue was inextricably mixed up in their case with other matters. Macpherson's report, ibid., III, p. 175.

32. Ibid.

33. Birjis Qadr's proclamation to the Mohamedans of the Territory of Oudh, Kosheya, Rompore, Moradabad etc: ~The Almighty God has enjoined thus in Holy Quran, 'O ye, the people who follow the religion! do not make the Jews and the Christians your friends. He who forms friendship with them becomes positively one of them, inasmuch as the friend of a Jew is a Jew and that of a Christian, a Christian. Certainly God doth not guide the tyrants, i.e., the infidels

in the path of righteousness". This sacred text plainly shows that the forming of friendship with the Christians is an act of infidelity and that consequently he who is on friendly terms with them is not at all a Mahomedan.' Ibid., II, p. 123.

34. Ibid., I, p. 302. 'The Resuscitation of such dangerous and unauthorised Doctrines, not generally participated by respectable Mahomedans, however, bigoted in India, was to some extent occasioned by feuds with Hindoos in Oudh regarding the site of a temple at Awud...' Significantly, the tract was translated in 1855, just after the 1854-55 communal disturbances at the so-called Ramjanambhumi near Fyzabad. A band of Muslims had gathered on that occasion under a maulvi to march on 'Ayodhya' and to take the place or die in the attempt. Raja Man Singh, later a rebel leader, had on the same occasion, raised a large body of men to resist the march. The British Resident persuaded the Nawab to prevent an encounter between the two forces. Martin Gubbins, *The Mutinies in Oudh* (Patna, 1978), p. 292. The Mutiny obviously brought about a dramatic realignment of religious divisions by channelizing these forces in a new direction.
35. Russell, *Dairy,* 5 May 1858, p. 146. Cf. the account by the police chief of rebel Delhi, Syed Mubarak Shah, prepared by the order of an English collector after his surrender. Narrative of Syed Mubarak Shah, printed in Michael Edwardes, *Red Year. The Indian Rebellion of 1857* (London, 1973), appendix 5, pp. 220-21. Also see Gwalior Report of S.C. Macpherson, *FSUP,* III, p. 184.
36. The Rajputs and the Hindu population would have fought the Muslims but for the fact that the Lucknow Nawab's troops came and dispersed the maulvi's rabble. Gubbins alleges that Man Singh, the leader of the Hindus, had declared his intention before this to march on Lucknow, destroy the Muslim dynasty, and instal a Hindu government in its place. *The Mutinies in Oudh,* pp. 292-93.
37. Partial translation from the original by Saiyid Zahir Jafri, 'The Profile of a Saintly Rebel - Ahmadullah Shah', Seminar on the Rebellion of 1857, Aligarh, 1988.
38. The outbreak of the predominantly Hindu Gwalior contingent is an instance to the point: 'He [the loyalist Maharaja of Gwalior who was trying to stem the tide] then, it is said, called for the Bodyguard, and it moved towards the left, I know not whither, but soon thereafter to the rear. Scindia's right was carried by a single sepoy who ran up to it waving his sword and shouting "Deen". No one would fire at him. The mass of the rebels now came on. They and Scindia's men shouted "Deen" together, while many congratulated and embraced, and very many went off to eat water melons in the bed of Morar.' Gwalior report of Macpherson, *FSUP*, III, p. 454.

39. *Delhi 1857. The Siege Assault and Capture As Given in the Diary and correspondence of the late Colonel Keith Young, C.B. Judge Advocate-General, Bengal*, ed. General Sir Henry Wylie Norman, 21 July 1857, p. 143.
40. H.M. Greathead, *Letters Written during the Siege of Delhi*, ed. by his widow (London, 1858), letter dated 19 July 1857, p. 130.
41. Narrative of Syed Mubarak Shah, *Red Year*, p. 221. The narrative is inaccurate in one respect: the *Jehadin*, as we learn from Greathead's letter, was not released, but sent prisoner to Ambala.
42. *Majha Pravas*, p. 95.
43. *Indian Antiquary*, vol. XL, 1911. Above translation by M. Edwardes, *Red Year*, p. 182.
44. *Majha Pravas*, p. 37. The striving for a Hindu realm was compatible, in Nana Sahib's view (as indeed in the view of his great ancestor Baji Rao), with the acceptance of Mughal sovereignty.
45. Liaqat Ali's proclamation for Jehad, *FSUP*, I, p. 447. Although Liaqat Ali spoke of a *dar al-Islam*, he was fully convinced that this would accommodate the non-Muslim population of Hindustan and their interests. He specifically mentioned the services to the cause by the Hindu rajas of Awadh and Allahabad and the unity of the people of different persuasions throughout Hindustan.
46. Meerut depositions, statement of Francis Shester, ibid., I, p. 301.
47. The Muslim rulers had long given up the thought of converting the Hindu population, and the Hindus would not convert non-Hindus anyway. The social and political system was one that rested on the difference, permitting each sect to exercise its own concerns autonomously.
48. Kaye, I, p. 593.
49. Evidence of Captain Martineau, *Trial of Bahadur Shah*, p. 171. That is how the people around Ambala interpreted the mysterious circulation of the chapatis—a British plot to impose the same food and the same religion, i.e., Christianity, and no difference to remain between the various castes, and between the Hindus and Muslims.
50. *FSUP*, I, pp. 442-43. Cf. Jhansi Rani's circular 'Victory of Religion', 14 February 1858, *FSUP*, II, p. 225, from which the next extract is given. Both proclamations were published by Maulvi Syud Kootub Shah at the Bahaduree Press in Bareilly.
51. The continuity of feeling that has gone into the formation of the modern Indian nation is reflected in the curious fact that Rabindranath Tagore, almost echoing Khan Bahadur Khan's invocation to 'God, the Lord of the Nation,' opened the national anthem of India with the line 'Jana-gana-mana-adhinayaka ....Bharata-bhagya-bidhata' (Lord of the hearts of the people...arbiter of India's destiny, i.e., God.).

52. It is customary to note Jawaharlal Nehru's judgement on the social and political notions of 1857 as backward-looking and 'fedual'. Vinayak Damodar Savarkar, whose views Nehru quoted, was instinctively closer to the notions of 1857. This is not a matter of surprise, considering that he was not a secular patriot like the writer of the *Discovery of India*. Savarkar grasped the mentality of the Mutiny far too closely for the comfort of the British government, which immediately proscribed the book (1909) in view of the impact it might have not on Indian soldiers.
53. Queen Victoria's proclamation of 1858: 'Firmly relying ourselves on the truth of Christianity and acknowledging with gratitude the solace of religion, we disclaim alike the right and the desire to impose our convictions on any of our subjects. '*FSUP*, II, p. 526.
54. The Begum of Awadh's rejoinder to above: 'In the proclamation it is written, that the Christian religion is true,...That religion is true which acknowledges one God and knows no other. Where there are three Gods in religion, neither Mussalmans nor Hindoos, nay, not even Jews, sun-worshippers, or fire-worshippers can believe it true.' Ibid., II, p. 530.
55. *The Times*: 'The natives do not seem to resent or apprehend the results of individual conversion, nor to object, as far as we understand, to the probable influences of general education. Their alarms appear to have reference to Government alone—to its news, its decisions and its designs....Under ordinary circumstances these apprehensions lie dormant and produce little or no effect, but at intervals they burst forth in paroxysms of terror, and then the smallest incident is magnified into a warrant for alarm and violence.' Ibid., I, p. 350.
56. Delhi Proclamation, May 1857. 'In fact it is the absolute order of the Governor General to serve our cartridges made up with swine and beef fat: if there be ten thousand who resist this, to blow them up: if fifty thousand, to disband them.' Ibid., I, p. 438.
57. For the expression 'holy warriors' (Ghazis) being counterpoised to the expression 'Kafirs and firengis', see ibid., V, p. 55. Walidad Khan to Bahadur Shah, 11 June 1857.
58. Although it was a technical term of the Islamic religion (derived from *Kufr* or lack of faith), Nana Sahib and other Hindu leaders used it frequently. Nana Sahib to Dhiraj Singh, 14 May 1858, ibid., III, p. 374. The term became so common as to become a political term indicating lack of loyalty, as is clear from the fact that the loyalist Maharaja Ratan Singh used it against the rebel forces under Deshpat in Bundelkhand ('I lack in adequate means to enlist a force fit to oppose 20,000 Kafirs'). ibid., III, p. 625.
59. Proclamation for *Jehad* by Liaqat Ali: 'Every Mussulman well knows and it is a notorious fact that the accursed Christians have been

awfully tyrannising over the whole country of Hindoostan, especially over the District of Allahabad.' ibid., I, pp. 445-46.

60. Hukumnama of Birjis Qadar, 4 August 1858, ibid., IV, p. 126. Vilaitis meant two different things in 1857: Afghan mercenaries in India, and foreigners (Englishmen).
61. Nana Sahib to the officer of the Army, 7 July 1857, Kaye II, p. 674. Occasionally there is a more specific reference to race in Nana Sahib's letters. 'The European has been sent to hell, thus adding to my satisfaction.' Ibid, p. 675.
62. Kaye, II, p. 314n.
63. M.H. Court to G.F. Edmonstone, 21 st July 1857, enclosing diary of events by the opium gumashtah, ibid., IV, p. 507.
64. 'The Rajah, Jeylal, ordered me to send all the Christians together with a list of their names with the Chobdar to Mummoo Khan. I picked out 15 individuals and on the 2nd day after this I heard that they had been murdered with the Sahib Ligue, the day after they were sent.' '...the prisioners - Christians, half castes &c. were put into Golam Hussain's mukan under the latter.' 'The Rajah used to move about to collect loot, and to seize Govt. servants and Keranees.' ibid., II, pp. 94, 98, 100.
65. Dr. Duff's letter, 6 October 1857, ibid., I, p. 486n.
66. *Mutiny Narrative*, Hamirpur, *FSUP*, ibid., pp. 114-17. For the pattern of victimization in Allahabad, see Kaye II, p. 258. Here the Bengalis 'were soon eased of all their valuables, but were spared their lives on promise of allegience to their (the Native) Government'. Bholanauth Chunder, *The Travels of a Hindoo*, quoted in ibid, p. 258n.
67. Kaye, III, p. 395n.
68. Young to wife 18 August 1857, *Delhi 1857*, p. 217.
69. Shephered's report, 29 August 1857, FSUP, IV, p. 588. According to the information of the Bengalis themselves, they were to be[illegible]lled next morning as several spies had been caught with letter[illegible] their possession, which, it was suspected, the Babus had wri[illegible] to the English, giving them information. *Hindoo Patriot*, 27 [illegible]ust 1857, ibid., IV, p. 684.
70. ibid., V, p. 127. 'Consequently *Mujahids* from the [illegible]ous villages and countryside have collected here [Thana Bhawan]. For fear that the *Kafirs* might do harm to the villages in the countryside, their protection will be provided in two ways.'
71. The sepoys after mutinying in Farrukhabad resolved 'to proceed next morning to attack the English at the Futtehgurh fort and would consider any one that did not join them as Christians and would kill him and loot their house.' The sepoy officers threatened to apply the label to the Nawab of Farrukhabad, who was vacillating at the time of outbreak. ibid., V, p. 733.

72. Translation of the diary of the Nunna (the correct spelling, Nanhe, implies young) Nawab, a native gentleman residing in Kanpur, containing an account of the occurences from June 5th to July 2nd 1857. Extracts given in appendix A, *Selections from the letters, Despatches and other State Papers Preserved in the Military Department of the Government of India,* ed. G.W. Forrest, vol. II (Calcutta, Military Department Press, 1902), p.xi. The diary was written by the young Nawab from memory during his captivity for trial by the British. At a less elevated place in society we have the example of three loyal sepoys who were captured in the Kanpur entrenchment along with the Europeans by Nana Sahib's troops, who 'abused us; and said we were Christians,' and told them 'we ought to have been killed and not taken prisoners; we had become Christians.' Cawnpore despositions, statement of Gobind Singh, Sheik Elahee Buksh and Ghouse Mahomed, Forrest, *Selections*, vol. III, pp. CXIIICXIV.
73. *Trial of Bahadur Shah*, p. 49. It would appear, however, that apostacy was no certain means of saving one's life. Three Christians clerks brought from Bareilly to Delhi by General Bakht Khan were kept under guard by the *ghazis* and were killed in the fighting that took place when the English stormed the city - it is not known by which side, but presumed to be the British. Narrative of Syed Mubarak Shah, *Red Year*, p. 231; Kaye, III, pp. 264-650.
74. ibid., p. 209. Syed Mubarak Shah was told by Bakht Khan that Powell had been made a Muslim and that his life was not in danger. Ibid, pp. 222-23.
75. Narrative of Moinodin, *Two Narratives of the Mutiny in Delhi*, trans. C.T. Metcalfe (London, 1898), p. 60.
76. *The Freedom Struggle in Hyderabad (A connected account)*, vol II (1857-1885) (Hyderabad State Committee, Hyderabad, 1956), p. 10. Text of Izaharnamah from Mss. Central Record Office, Hyderabad.
77. Nana Sahib to Raja of Rewa, 23 April 1858: 'Seeing the faith perishing I have gird my lions to defend it, and I have suffered much more for it. But this is no man's doing. It is God's design: I have done my utmost; as I have already written to you, the faith is the faith of us all. I have endeavoured to support and defend it; all chiefs, and monarchs, Hindoo or Mussulman who assist the English, the destroyers of the faith, destroy their religion with their own hands.' *FSUP*, III, p. 367.
78. Francis Cornwallis Maude, *Memories of the Mutiny With which is incorporated the Personal Narrative of John Walter Sherer*, 2 vols. (London, 1894), vol 1, pp. 251-52.
79. Federic Cooper, *Crisis in Punjab from the 10th of May until the Fall of Delhi* (1858, Reprint Delhi, 1977), p. 111.

80. The correspondence between the Oudh and Nepal Darbars is printed in *FSUP*, II, p. 44 ff.
81. Seid-Gholam Hossein Khan, *The Seir Mutaqherin* (around 1788, trans. reprint Delhi 1986), vol. III, pp. 188-89.
82. Ibid, pp. 161-62.
83. Ibid, p. 194.
84. See Raja Man Singh's letter to the Awadh taluqdars, 20 July 1857, referring bitterly to the Hanumangarhi incident at Ayodhya and many other past-incidents over the centuries. Printed in McLeod Innes, *Lucknow and Oude in the Mutiny* (London, 1895), appendix XII.
85. *FSUP*, II, p. 156.
86. Cf. the illuminating discussion of Hellenic nationality in the opening chapter of Thucydides, *The History of Peloponnesian War*.
87. No date. *FSUP*, V, p. 349.
88. No date. ibid., I, pp 459-60.
89. Azamgarh proclamation, 25 August 1857. ibid., I, pp. 453-54. Italics mine.
90. Hokoom-nameh addressed to Hurdeo Buksh by Shahunshan Mehral Shah Kubendur, 6 June 1857, *FSUP*, I, pp. 439-40.
91. Proclamation by Peshwa, dated Charkhari, 26 February 1858, ibid., I, p. 464. The Peshwa of the proclamation was Nana Sahib's younger brother. Nana Sahib himself had assumed the title Pant Pradhan.
92. After enquiring into the doctrines of the Sufis and the Upanishads, Prince Dara Shikoh maintained that 'he did not find any difference, except verbal, in the way in which they sought and comprehended Truth.' *Majma-ul-Bahrain or The Mingling of the Two Oceans*, trans. M. Mahfuz-ul-Haq (Calcutta, 1982), p. 38.
93. The letter, carried by a Brahman who was subsequently hanged, was headed with 'obeisance' to Brahmins and 'salutation' to Mussulmans. *FSUP*, I, pp. 353-54.
94. Ibid., p. 443. Evidence as to the ground of the Muslim objection to grease, rumoured to be mixed with pig fat, is somewhat conflicting. The speech of the sepoys before Bahadur Shah put the question, 'God only knows as to which were those animals whose fats were used. The Hindoos pleaded that they belonged to high castes—Brahmin and Kshatriyas etc. and that they did not take meat at all. The Muslims also objected saying that they did not take the meat of those animals which were not killed in accordance with the Muslim religious rites.' ibid., I, p. 405. Captain Martineau, posted in Ambala at the time, maintained in cross examination at the trial of Bahadur Shah: 'Yes, as far as the cartridge question went the Mahomedan sepoys laughed at it; it was only the Hindus that made the complaints in references to losing caste.' *Trial of Bahadur Shah*, p. 172.
95. Ibid., I, pp. 155-56.

96. Ibid., I, p. 155. *The Risala Fath-i-Islam* is recognized to be a work prepared under the aegis of Maulvi Ahmadullah Shah.
97. Ibid.
98. Gubbins, *Mutinies*, pp. 292-93.
99. Raja Maun Singh to the Talookdars, 20 July 1857, Innes, *Lucknow and Oude*, p. 336.
100. In this connection Man Singh did not fail to remind the Hindu taluqdars about the recent incident at Ayodhya. 'This is a place of great antiquity, and reputed to be of the highest sanctity among the Hindoos, and is distant from Fyzabad three miles, on the banks of the Ghogra. The Mahomedan aggression was secretly favoured by the bigoted and imbecile Court at Lucknow. A great convulsion appeared to be imminent; for the Mussulmans, with a fanatic molovee at their head, were marching on Adjooddea, resolved to enter the Hindoo shrine or die; while the Rajpoots and Hindoos of all the country around were flocking to defend their sanctuary. At this time Man Singh took the lead and placed themselves at their head, becoming the acknowledged leader of the Hindoo party. He raised a large body of men, with whom he took post at the Shiwala, or temple which he had built at his private cost, among the numerous convents and temples which crowd the deeply-shaded dells and ravines of Adjooddea. Fortunately the British resident's interposition prevented an encounter between the hostile parties. The King's troops attacked and dispersed the Mussulmans.' Gubbins, *Mutinies*, p. 292.
101. *FSUP*, I, p. 636. Man Singh's own family, it may be noted, owed everything to the Nawabs of Awadh, in whose service they rose to power and wealth from obscure origins. Man Singh himself was an influential man at the Lucknow court prior to annexation and gave loyal service except upon the occasion mentioned. It is to be noted also that the Nawab's troops came to his rescue at Ayodhya against the embattled *Mujahidin*—of course under the British Resident's influence.
102. On Id day, Emperor Bahadur Shah sacrificed a sheep instead of cow at the Juma Masjid. Diary of Munshi Jiwan Lal, 2 August 1857, *Two Narratives*, p. 176.
103. Proclamation of Khan Bahadur Khan, *FSUP*, I, pp. 443-44.
104. Young, *Delhi 1857*, pp. 158, 171.
105. Durgadas Bandyopadhyay, *Āmār Jivana-Charit* (reprinted in *Atma-Katha*, vol 3 (Calcutta, 1985); first published in the magazine *Janmabhumi* in 1891-1896), pp. 344-45. This Bengali memoir was dictated by Babu Durgadas, who had been a clerk of the cavalry at Bareilly at the time of the Mutiny. He fled to Naini Tal, where the English had gone, after a precarious stay in town. The above news was brought to him by a native spy in town. The spy added caustically: 'Nawab Khan Bahadur came home after completing all

this work at one prahar at night. But it does not seem as if it bore much fruit. I believe Hindu-Muslim cordiality did not increase one bit.' (āmar vishvās, Hindu-Musalmān sadbhāv ek karāo vriddhi hoila nā)).

106. Diary of Nunna Nawab, Forrest, *Selections*, III, p. xi; Translation of Narrative of Events at Cawnpoor by Nanakchand, mahajan of Cawnpore, 7 June 1857, ibid, p. ccc; Pratul Chandra Gupta, *Nana Sahib and the Rising at Cawnpore* (Oxford, 1963), p, 81. Azizan, a courtesan popular among the sepoys, was present at the scene and her evidence at court makes it clear that the people were cautious about the exhortations of the leaders asking them to attack the entrenchment. 'The sowars collected all the people, and took them to a house near the canal and they took me also. There were about 1,000 persons, men and women collected there. The Nana and Azeem Oollah [Nana Sahib's secretary, supposed to be his illegitimate Muslim half-brother] ordered the people to attack the entrenchments. Moulvie Sulamut Oollah [who had been dragged against his will] and the people said, 'You first attack them, then we will." They then sent the people away and I also returned home.' Deposition of Azeezun, ibid., IV, p. 600.

107. *Hindu Patriot*, 21 May 1857, ibid., I, p. 483.

108. Peshwa's proclamation, Chirkhari 26 February 1858, ibid., p. 464. The original expression from which 'national religion' has been derived is not given in the translation. It should be borne in mind that the Indo-Aryan languages do not contain any exact equivalent to the world 'national' or 'nation'.

109. Magistrate of Satara to Bombay Government, 7 July 1857, ibid., I, p. 363.

110. Original of the translated expression 'foreigners' is not given. If *Vilaitis* (lit.: men of the province or country), which meant either the British foreigners or the Afghan mercenaries from the Hindukush, then Bahadur Shah probably meant the Swat Pathans the English were rumoured to have brought. The Afghans referred to their home as *Vilait* and had come to be known in Hindustan and Malwa as the *Vilaitis*. They were greatly prized as able and fierce fighters and Rani Lakshmi Bai, who had such a corps devoted to her, had adopted their dress.

111. The joint expression 'foreigners or hillmen' makes it almost certain that Bahadur Shah meant the Afghans—certainly he could not have meant by 'foreigners', the British. The specific references to Hillmen seems to distinguish the category from 'the people of Hindustan', an expression apparently used in a dual sense here: i.e., (1) the residents of the Ganges-Jumna valley up to the borders of Bengal (2) the Hindustanis, or the Indians, among whom, of course, the hillmen, too

would be counted, but not the 'Nepalese' who are separately mentioned in the previous sentence.

112. Interestingly, 'Sikhs' are mentioned separately from 'people of Hindustan', and in the same breath as 'the Mahamedans, or Hindus born in Hindustan.' We are to understand, then, that the Sikhs and the residents of the land of Hindi are separate peoples, and while the latter are certainly an integral part of 'Mahomedans, or Hindus born in Hindustan,' i.e., the nation at large, the Sikhs are only loosely associated with it, in the sense that they, too, would be part of the 'natives of Hindustan...whether they be men of the eastern provinces, or Sikhs...'

113. *Trial of Bahadur Shah*, pp. 248-49.

114. Munshi Jiwan Lal's diary, 4 August 1857, *Two Narratives*, p. 180.

115. Ibid., 5 August 1857, p. 183. The Emperor had no intention of acceding to the dangerous proposal, for the native troops fighting on the Ridge shoulder to shoulder with the English were Sikhs, and those in town might defect. He soothed the sepoys, encouraged them, told them not to despair of victory.

116. Note the way the police chief of rebel Delhi, Moinuddin Hasan Khan, refers, in his memoirs, to the sepoys, who might be aliens for practically all purposes: 'Oude was the birthplace of the Purbeah race, and these feelings of dissatisfaction affected the whole Purbeah race in the service of the British Government' (the translated term race, however, may unduly accentuate the sense of their foreign character). A truer perspective of the distance between them and the Delhi resident occurs elsewhere in Moinuddin's narrative: '...this feeling was intensified on the annexation of the province of Oude. Thence first arose dissatisfaction among the native troops, most of whom were natives of that province.' Narrative of Moinuddin, *Two Narratives*, pp. 37, 31.

117. Signs of the latent antagonism between the resident citizens and the stranger sepoys occur continually in Munshi Jivan Lal's diary. Thus, on 30 May the Delhi Hindus, who were mostly traders, expressed joy at the sepoys' defeat at the Hindan river, for they had suffered much since their arrival. Again on 9 June, the city people, who had anxiously mounted on to the roofs of their houses to see the outcome of the battle of Badli ki Sarai, poured volleys of abuse upon the returning mutineers, accusing them of cowardice (for they knew their own fate would be sealed if the British were to storm the town). ibid., pp. 108, 118.

118. One part of the concocted plan to extinguish the identity of the Hindustanis was believed to be bribing and intimidation into marriage with the Europeans, 'that they may in a short time become the same as they'; another part, none but their doctors 'to be

permitted to assist at the confinement of Hindoo and Mussulman women.' Proclamation of Feroz Shah, *FSUP*, I, pp. 460-61.

119. And again using the same form of address: 'O Hindustanee brethren! thus put on your guard against their subversive determinations, leave them to their folly, and all uniting break their head.' Ibid, pp. 460-61.
120. Ibid, p. 461. The pronouncement was attributed to 'their' wise men in secret conclave.
121. Proclamation by the Nana Dunder Punt, 6 July 1857, ibid., I, pp. 451-52.
122. Proclamation for Jehad by Leeaqut Ali, ibid., pp. 446-47.
123. Durgadas Bandyopadhyay, *Āmār Jivan-Charit*, p. 86.
124. Statement of Quarter Master Sergeant Lewis, late of 17th Native Infantry, *FSUP*, IV, p. 94.
125. Letter of Agent Governor-General for Central India, Indore, 24 November, 1858, ibid., III, p. 530. As Tantia Tope was in Mootye in Jabalpur territory when he said this, the reference to the 'country' is not to his native place, but the country at large.
126. Narrative of Moinodin, *Two Narratives*, p. 31.
127. Nana Sahib's letter to the British from Nepal, 26 April 1859: 'Why should I join you knowing all the *dagabazi* perpetrated by you in Hindoostan?' Sen, *Eighteen Fifty-Seven,* appendix III, pp. 395-96.
128. Rani Lakshmi Bai's circular letter, 'Victory of Religion', 14 February 1858: 'These are the stratagems by which the Europeans deprive us of our thrones and wealth, for instance I refer to Nagpore and Lucknow.' *FSUP*, III, p. 226. Her own heart-felt words in 1854 - 'Mera Jhansi nahin dengee' - are now on every school child's lips, magnified into a sense of the sovereign national republic of India. John Lang, *Wanderings in India* (London, 1859), extract pp. 84-96 in *FSUP*, I, p. 64.
129. Begum of Awadh's proclamation, ibid., I, p. 466. That the Begum did not have in mind her own possession alone, but was impelled by a sense of English aggrandizement in the whole country, is clear from her preceding words: 'The Company has seized the whole of Hindoostan ... The company professed to treat the chief of Bhurtpore as a son, and then took his territory; the chief of Lahore was carried off to London, and it has not fallen to his lot to return; the Nawab Shamshoodeen Khan, on one side, they hanged and, on the other side, they salaamed to him; the Peishwa they expelled from Poona Sitara, and imprisoned for life in Bithoor; their breach of faith with Sultan Tipoo is well known; the Raja of Benares they imprisoned in Agra. Under pretence of administering the country of the chief of Gwalior, they introduced English customs; they have left no names or traces of the Chiefs of Behar, Orissa and Bengal; they gave the Rao of Farruckabad a small monthly allowance, and took his territory.

130. Mahommed Hussun Khan to Kyrooddeen, 16th Rubee ool Sanee, Sen, *Eighteen Fifty-Seven*, appendix II, pp. 386-89.
131. G.B. Malleson, *History of the Indian Mutiny* (London, 1878), pp. 407-8 n.
132. Mahommed Hussun Khan to Kyrooddeen, 16th Rabee ool Sanee: 'The meaning of all I have written is this. We servants and dependents of the King of Oudh consider it essential to our prosperity in both worlds to display devotion in protecting the Kingdom and opposing the efforts of invaders who seek a footing in it. If we fail in doing so we are traitors and will have our faces blackened in both worlds.' Sen, *Eighteen Fifty-Seven*, appendix II, pp. 386-9.
133. Nana Sahib's exhortation to an unnamed (possibly Rewa) Rajah to act honourably, 'this being a religious warfare, in which antecedents or consequences are not to be considered.' Letter from Nanah to Dhir Singh, 23 April 1858, *FSUP*, III, p. 368. Feroz Shah's proclamation: 'Placing my trust in God; devoting myself solely to God's service; observing the precepts of religion; strengthening my determination; clothing myself in; my sword taken in my hand, the sword of religious zeal, I arise in the name of God': *FSUP*, I, p. 463.
134. *NE*, I, Allahabad, p. 18.
135. *Kaye*, III, pp. 85-86.
136. Nana Sahib's last letter, 26 April 1859, Sen, *Eighteen Fifty-Seven*, p. 396.
137. Thus, in a notable repetition of the scenes of 1857, the Bombay hartal of 17 November 1921, in protest against the jailing of the Ali Brothers, saw the Maharashtrian mill hands and the Muslims attacking whites, Christians, anglicized Parsees and sometimes anyone wearing Western clothes. Sumit Sarkar, *Modern India, 1885-1947* (Delhi, 1984), p. 212. The targets of hostility, an unfailing indicator of the mass emotions, remained the very same.
138. Referring to the support the British received from the Sikhs, Jawaharlal Nehru remarked that, 'there was a lack of nationalist feeling which might have bound the people of India together.' Clearly, Nehru, in full awareness of the complexities of 1857, carefully chose the words 'a popular rebellion and a war of Indian independence.' Jawaharlal Nehru, *The Discovery of India* (Calcutta, 3rd ed. 1947), pp. 268-69.
139. Cf. Susobhan Sarkar, 'View on 1857', in *On the Bengal Renaissance* (Calcutta, 1979).
140. The point here is not about the unity and harmony between the two communities. As noted above, there was much tension between them. The point is the naming of the two communities together as a political category. 'The Hindus and Musalmans of Hindustan' is a novel category of thought, a technical term in the vocabulary of the new politics that erupted so suddenly and so violently in 1857. It is a

groping expression of national identity. Behind the category lies an inchoate political theory, or rather, a mentality that might, in more favourable circumstances, have crystalized into such a theory. Eric Stokes, the author of *The English Utilitarians and India*, had a natural interest in the subject, though he had no time to explore it in his unfinished book on the Mutiny. A glimpse of his ideas on the mentality behind the Mutiny may be had in his seminal essay, 'Traditional Resistance Movements and Afro-Asian nationalism: the context of the 1857 Mutiny Rebellion,' in *The Peasant and the Raj. studies in agrarian society and peasant rebellion in colonial India* (Cambridge, 1978).

The Muslims of Upper India and the Shock of the Mutiny

Rustkhez-i beja

FRANCIS ROBINSON

'In our ancient capitals once so well-known, so rich, so great and so flourishing', declared Saiyid Ahmad Khan to the Muhammadan Literary Society of Calcutta in 1863, 'nothing is now to be seen or heard save a few bones strewn amongst the ruins or the human-like cry of the jackal.[2] He was reminding the Muslims assembled at the house of Nawab Abdul-Latif that, five years after the end of the Mutiny uprising, Delhi and Lucknow, the two great centres of Muslim culture in Upper India, the London and Paris of their milieu, were, in large part, deserted. In doing so he draws our attention to the shock, the protracted shock, which the uprising and its brutal suppression brought to the Muslims of Upper India.

The impact of the Mutiny uprising on the British is well understood. No other event in British imperial history has attracted as much attention, and certainly, for the hundred years that followed, discussion of it might begin 'as every schoolboy knows...' The meaning of the event for British policy is also widely understood. Dalhousian self-confidence was replaced by caution and conciliation; policies towards the army, finance, the States and the landlords were changed; it was recognized that the government could not transform India willy-nilly in the light of western values and that it must make a point of listening to, indeed, taking the advice of, the powerful in Indian society.

The impact of the events of the Mutiny years on Muslims is not quite

'Unseasonable tumult', chronogram by Ghalib =1273 AH/1857[1]

so well understood. Among the reasons for this must be counted, some notable exceptions apart, the silence on the subject which many contemporaries observed, some for fear of further British retribution, others because they sought refuge from the trauma of the times in a collective amnesia. This said, it is widely accepted that the Mutiny uprising and its aftermath forms a watershed in the development of the ideas and attitudes of the Muslims of Upper India in the nineteenth-century. Before the great upheaval they did not appear to take seriously into account either the challenge of Western civilization or the meaning of British power. After it they were increasingly concerned to discover how best they could be Muslim under the new dispensation, whether it meant building ideological and institutional bridges between Islam and the West, or developing systems which could enable them largly to ignore Western civilization and the colonial state, or making a point of defending Islam wherever it was threatened in India and the world.

We have some knowledge of the Mutiny experiences of those who were to take the lead in these initiatives in Muslim life. We propose that there is value is drawing together these experiences and the wider contexts in which they took place. For it is in their shattering nature that we find some of the origins both of the realization that new Muslim approaches were needed and of the urgency which lay behind the great outpouring of Muslim creativity that resulted. In this light we shall examine three sets of people; the 'modernists' who coalesced around the Muhammadan Anglo-Oriental College at Aligarh, the 'reformers', a somewhat more disparate group whose most notable institution was the *Dar al-ulum* at Deoband, and the learned and holy men of the great Lucknow family of Firangi Mahal.

It is striking how many of those who were to play leading roles in the attempts to build bridges between north Indian Muslims and the West were caught up amongst the events of 1857 in and around Delhi. Of the leaders of the Aligarh movement, only Chiragh Ali (1844-95) and Nawab Mushtaq Husain (1841-1917) do not appear to have been involved in any way.

Saiyid Ahmad Khan is, of course, the outstanding figure in the group. Scion of a distinguished Mughal service family, noted writer on religious, historical and archaeological matters, when the Mutiny broke out he had served the British for nineteen years. Because he wrote his own history of the rebellion in Bijnor and because the period is well-covered in Hali's great biography of the Saiyid we know more of his experiences than those of anyone else apart from the poet, Ghalib. There is his rescue of the European population of Bijnor district and his assumption of its administration until he was forced to flee to Meerut by the forces of Nawab Mahmud Khan. There is his journey to Delhi, after hearing that his family property had been ransacked by government troops and his uncle and cousin murdered, to find his mother and her companion in desperate straits. There is the death of his mother a few days later in Meerut, which meant the premature passing of the woman who had almost total charge of his upbringing and education, on whose behalf he had lived in Delhi from 1846 to 1856, and for whom he had enormous respect. Looking back on these years in 1889, Saiyid Ahmad declared that he contemplated leaving India: 'for some time I wrestled with my grief and, believe me, it made an old man of me. My hair turned white'. He grieved in part over his personal losses and in large part over the appalling condition of his community.[3]

Khwaja Altaf Husain (1837-1914), who is better known under his *takhullus* 'Hali', poet and biographer of the Aligarh movement, came from the famed Ansari family of the qasbah Panipat on the banks of the Yamuna, some fifty-five miles north of Delhi. In 1854 he had run away from the limited opportunities and stifling atmosphere of the qasbah to seek his fortune in the Mughal capital. It was not long before his exploits in the *mushairas* drew his family's attention to where he was and he was brought back to meet his obligations in Panipat and to find a job as a clerk in a government office in Hissar. On the outbreak of the Mutiny he fled back to Panipat being robbed of all he had on the way save a Quran tied in a scarf around his neck. The experience left him physically ill and in a state of shock. He did not work again until he took up a position in 1861 as tutor to the sons of Nawab Mustafa Khan 'Shefta'.[4]

The ancestors of Munshi Zakaullah (1832-1910) were, for many generations, tutors to the Mughal royal family. The Munshi himself was the schoolteacher of the Aligarh movement; he taught at Agra College, Muir Central College, Allahabad, and was the headmaster of Delhi Normal School. His great achievement was the writing and also the translation into Urdu of many textbooks in mathematics, physics, history, geography and ethics. During the Mutiny uprising he was deeply affected when English friends, and notably Mr. Taylor, the principal of Delhi College, were killed by the rebels. But he was particularly affected when the man 'whom he loved and revered most in the world', Maulvi Imam Baksh Sahbai, saintly cherisher of the learning of the Delhi renaissance and assistant to Saiyid Ahmad Khan in his work for *Asar us-Sanadid*, was murdered along with his family by government troops.

'This deed of blood', he told C.F. Andrews half a century later, 'can never be forgotten.'[5] After the capture of Delhi he and his family were forced out of their house and had to seek refuge among the tombs of Nizamuddin Auliya, some three miles from the city wall. The family property, which lay between the Jama Masjid and the royal palace, was demolished and no compensation paid. 'For a long time', Zakaullah told Andrews, 'the shock of those last Mutiny days was beyond all bearing. The torturing thoughts of his mind drove him at last to a melancholy that bordered on despair.'[6]

Three further figures in the Aligarh movement were caught up in the events of the uprising. Saiyid Mehdi Ali Khan (1837-1907), who succeeded Saiyid Ahmad as the effective leader of the movement, apparently performed useful services during the disturbances as an officer under A.O. Hume in the Etawah collectorate. Maulvi Nazir Ahmad (1830-1912), who came from Bijnor, was a contemporary of Zakaullah at Delhi College and later British government servant and novelist of the movement. He was appointed a deputy-inspector of schools for saving the life of an Englishwoman during the disturbance in Delhi. Then, there was Maulvi Samiullah Khan (1834-1908), Zakaullah's closest childhood friend and product of a scholarly and noble family of Delhi. A successful government servant on the judicial side, he was Saiyid Ahmad's righthand man in the early development of Aligarh. During the sack of Delhi he saved Saiyid Ahmad's wife and family, escorting them to Nizamuddin; afterwards, like so many others, he suffered from shock.[7]

One further individual deserves at least partial inclusion in this group, the editor and literary critic, Muhammad Husain Azad (1830-1910). A contemporary of Zakaullah and Nazir Ahmad at Delhi College, his father was a pioneer of Urdu journalism. Devoted pupil of Zauq, the penultimate Mughal poet laureate, much of his working life was spent in the Punjab education service where he wrote textbooks for schools. In the aftermath of the Mutiny his father, although he had tried to give shelter to the principal of Delhi College, was executed for treason and his property confiscated. Azad only succeeded in escaping from Delhi in disguise, his one comfort being that he managed to take with him, as he was being driven from his home, the unpublished ghazals of Zauq. In 1885, he began to show signs of mental disturbance; by 1890 he had lost his mind.[8]

With regard to our second group, the 'reformers', we have details of their experience in the Mutiny uprising, but less personal ones. We do not know how they thought about the great upheaval, either at the time or subsequently; we must judge them by their actions. Five out of six of the group had been educated in Delhi: some in the ambience of Delhi College, and they shared teachers and acquaintances with Aligarh 'modernists' such as Saiyid Ahmad Khan, Nazir Ahmad, Zakaullah and Samiullah Khan. Three of the group, Haji Imdadullah (1817-99), both the spiritual director of Islamic reform and the spiritual guide of hundreds of South Asian Muslims in the second half of the nineteenth century, Muhammad Qasim Nanautawi (1833-77) and Rashid Ahmad Gangohi (1829-1905), the developers of the key institutional frameworks of Islamic reform in the *Dar al-ulum* at Deoband and its off-shoots, were all educated in the traditions of the great eighteenth-century reformer Shah Waliullah of Delhi. Haji Imdadullah studied briefly under Maulana Mamluk Ali of Delhi College, a great sustainer of the Waliullahi tradition until his death in 1851, and then found his vocation as a sufi. Muhammad Qasim and Rashid Ahmad, on the other hand, were star pupils both of Mamluk Ali and Maulvi Abdul-Ghani Naqshbandi, the successor of Shah Muhammad Ishaq, the great grandson of Shah Waliullah.[9] A direct contemporary of these two young tyros, Siddiq Hasan Khan (1832-1890), a leading figure amongst the Ahl-i Hadith and the husband of the Begum of Bhopal, studied under Sadruddin Azurdah, a much respected scholar of mid-nineteenth-century Delhi and the leading pupil of Shah Abdul-Aziz, son of Shah Waliullah.[10] Rahmatullah Kairanawi (1818-1990), the major force in the first Muslim defence in modern times against Christianity at Agra in 1854, and later the author of an attack upon it, studied in Delhi under Imam Baksh Sahba at Maulana Muhammad Hayat's madrasa by the Red Fort. And finally there is the odd man out, Dr Wazir Khan, the key supporter of Kairanawi in his controversies with Christian missionaries, who was very active in the Mutiny uprising. Kairanawi's background is relatively unknown but for his birth in Bihar, his attending an English-medium school in Murshidabad, his further education at the Medical College in Calcutta and subsequently his further studies in London in the 1830s.[11]

It has been suggested that at least some of this group had actually formed an organization to rid India of the British. According to the Deobandi, Ubaidullah-Sindhi, who wrote in the twentieth-century, there had been a continuous *jehad* movement in India going back to the time of Shah Abdul-Aziz. This had reached its peak in the *jehad* of Saiyid Ahmad Shahid (1826-31) but continued in an organized form after his death, first under the leadership of Shah Muhammad Ishaq, a great-grandson of Shah Waliullah, and, after his departure for the Hijaz in 1341, under Maulana

Mamluk Ali, and, after his death ten years later, under Haji Imdadullah. Indeed, we are given the impression that in the 1840s and 1850s there was a fully-fledged organization in existence with committees and so on. However, the claims of Sindhi apart, there is no hard evidence for this level of organization, and Farhan Nizami sums up the probabilities well when he suggests that the case for ideological continuity is reasonable but that for organizational continuity rather far-fetched.[12]

It has also been suggested that some of these same 'reformers' played a major role in one of the more important incidents of the Mutiny uprising, the *jehad* raised in the qasbah of Thana Bhawan (Muzaffarnagar district) in the early autumn of 1857. The story goes that Haji Imdadullah was the Amir of the *jehadis*; Muhammad Qasim, the commander-in-chief; Rashid Ahmad, the qazi; and Rahmatullah, a leading figure. There are detailed descriptions of how Rahmatullah went twice to Delhi to assess developments, of how the decision to launch the *jehad* was taken, of how the tahsil at Shamli was captured, of how Thana Bhawan was defended, and indeed of how Muhammad Qasim used a school playground trick to enable him to cut a Sikh sepoy in two, and of how Rahmatullah felt the pebbles which spurted up from the hooves of his pursuers' horses as he hid in a field to escape capture.[13] The one problem with this story is that there is no evidence for much of it before the 'reformist' tradition entered its nationalist phase in 1920. Indeed, earlier descriptions of events in Muzaffarnagar, one of which is by an eyewitness and friend of Muhammad Qasim, Muhammad Yaqub Nanautawi, are concerned to indicate how small the involvement of Muhammad Qasim in these events had been. Defenders of the post-1920 version, however, urge that their's is the oral tradition of the 'reformers' and that, if publication of this was suppressed for sixty years, it was to avoid the attention of the colonial powers.[14]

Fortunately, we do not have to adjudicate the truth of these matters. It is enough that the 'reformers' were caught up in events to some extent. Of the following facts there is little doubt: that Haji Imdadullah was in Thana Bhawan when the *jehad* was declared and thereafter migrated to Mecca; that Muhammad Qasim and Rashid Ahmad were in Thana Bhawan with their spiritual director in August and September 1857; that Rahmatullah made at least one visit to Delhi to see how the uprising fared and later migrated to Mecca; that Muhammad Qasim lived in hiding until the general amnesty of 1859; and that in the same year Rashid Ahmad was arrested on suspicion of involvement in the uprising but released six months later for lack of evidence.[15]

Turning to our two remaining 'reformers', Rahmatullah's partner in the Agra debates, Dr Wazir Khan, became governor of Agra for a brief moment while the British were driven into its fort, and later seems to have been active in several places: with the Maulvi of Fyzabad, Feroze Shah, son of the last Mughal Emperor, and in supervising the casting of a cannon in Bareilly. Afterwards he migrated to the Hijaz.[16] Then, finally, there is Siddiq Hasan Khan who, when the uprising took place, returned to his family in Kanauj only to have his entire village razed to the ground. For nearly two years he and his family lived the life of nomads, sheltering in the houses of friends, until the Begum of Bhopal asked him to write the history of her state and he was set on the road of becoming one of nineteenth-century India's more upwardly mobile Muslims.[17]

For the 'reformers', whether they were active participants, sucked into events unwillingly, or just victims of the moment, the uprising and its aftermath could have been nothing less than a time of loss, of shattered dreams, and of lessons harshly learned. Three of the six in our group chose to leave India permanently, either for fear of British retribution or because they could no longer bear to live under British domination they were not the only Muslims to take this path. Two lived lives of some uncertainty in the years after the uprising and had to do so without the comforting presence of their sufi shaikh, which was no mean loss for pious mystics. One saw his home destroyed, all possessions lost, and lived a life of much privation. In the suppression of the uprising the weight of British power had been made abundantly clear, not to mention their willingness to use it without mercy. It was now evident that a *jehad* of a military kind had no real chance of success.

Our third group, the learned and holy men of Firangi Mahal, is somewhat different. It is less a group formed by one common ideological theme than by blood and memory. The family dates its existence in Lucknow back to the early 1690s when emperor Aurangzeb granted the Firangi Mahal, the confiscated property of a European indigo merchant, to the four sons of Mulla Qutbuddin Sihalwi, a prominent scholar who had been murdered in a squabble over land. The descendants of the Mulla made Firangi Mahal into the leading centre of learning in Upper India. They created a new Islamic syllabus, the *Dars-i Nizamiyya*, and spread it throughout the subcontinent and beyond, its popularity deriving 'not least from the fact that it both strengthened students' intellectual faculties and enabled them to learn more quickly. They were also devout sufis, moderate supporters of Ibn al-Arabi's *wahdat al-wujud*, and three affiliations passed down the family generations—Chishti-Nizami, Chishti-

Sabiri and Qadri-Razzaqi. Quintessentially representatives of an Islamic culture which had grown under the wings of Muslim power, they stood apart from the Waliullahi reforming tradition which was designed to help Muslims survive without power. As Sunnis their relations with the Shia government of Awadh had not always been easy; one of the most gifted members of the family was forced to leave Lucknow because of the Shia-Sunni strife, while the biography of a noted family saint records several brushes with the Court over religious matters. The years immediately before the Mutiny uprising, nevertheless, find the family well-placed: Maulvi Waliullah had recently retired from Awadh service loaded with honours, Mufti Muhammad Yusuf was the Sunni *mufti* at the Court, Maulana Hafizullah was darogah of Fyzabad, Maulanas Naimatullah and Naimullah were well-placed in the Awadh administration. More generally the family continued its work of teaching, scholarship and spiritual leadership in Lucknow and beyond. Firangi Mahalis were to be found throughout northern India from Panipat to Calcutta, and in outposts further south such as Hyderabad and Madras. Wherever possible they served Muslim princes and Muslim institutions.[18]

In the Firangi Mahali mind the Mutiny disaster began two years before the events of May 1857 with what has come to be known as the Hanumangarhi *jehad*, an earlier round in the 'Babri Masjid' affair of the 1980s, in which Muslims campaigned to protect a supposed mosque at Ayodhya, which they claimed dated from Babur's time, against Hindu insistence that the building was the birthplace of Rama. The affair began in February 1855 when one Shah Ghulam Husain tried to oust a group of Hindu mahants who had taken possession of the building. A battle took place between large groups of Hindus and Muslims in which the latter were outnumbered and defeated. The Awadh court set up a three-man commission to investigate the matter which reported that no mosque had ever existed on the site. The king, Wajid Ali, tried to reach a compromise on the findings of the commission by suggesting that a mosque be built along the wall of the building. The Hindus refused to compromise. The Muslims, Sunnis almost to a man and now led by Amir Ali of Amethi, declared *jehad* against the occupiers of the 'mosque'. Wajid Ali warned Amir Ali to stop, his Shia *mujtahid* and Sunni *mufti* issued *fatawa* denying that *jehad* was appropriate in this case, and they also went out to preach to the *jehadis*. Amir Ali, although he lost much support as a result of the king's action, persisted in his course; on 7 November nearly 400 *jehadis* died in front of the guns of the Awadh army.[19]

Firangi Mahalis were involved in most stages of this affair. Maulana

Hafizullah, as darogah of Fyzabad, provided evidence for the three-man commission regarding the history of the alleged mosque, although it was dismissed as too strongly supporting the Muslim cause. Maulana Abdur-Razzaq, the leading spiritual force in Firangi Mahal at the time, supported Amir Ali's declaration of *jehad* along with his cousin Burhan ul-Haq, and then left Lucknow to join the *jehadis* with Hisam ul-Haq and Amin ul-Haq. However, because Amir Ali deputed him to negotiate a compromise with the Court in October, he missed the fateful battle of 7 November. Then, it was Mufti Muhammad Yusuf who gave the *fatwa* against the *jehad*, and both Maulvi Khadim Ahmad of Firangi Mahal and the *Mufti* reached out to the *jehadis* at different times to dissuade them. Other leading members of the family, such as Naimatullah and the saintly Abdul Wali, were expected, by government at least, to play a similar role. It is clear that the affair divided the family; it was not forgotten how Muhammad Yusuf and Khadim Ahmad had worked against the cause.[20] Abdur-Razzaq, on the other hand had to live with the memory that when the critical moment of the *jehad* came he was absent, a fact which his biographer in the 1920s worked hard to explain. There was also the belief, which was in part correct, that the *jehad* precipitated Britain's annexation of Awadh in the following year, an event which, amongst other disadvantages, had a crippling impact on the fortunes of all those Firangi Mahalis in the Awadh administration.[21]

The Mutiny uprising, therefore, came on top of two disastrous years for the family. Moreover, it brought further family division. Abdur-Razzaq presented his turban to the 'mutineers' as a banner, and found support in the family for his determination to crush the infidel.[22] Others, however, saw the affair, in retrospect at least, as lawlessness in which not only did the Europeans suffer at the hands of Indians, but Hindus at the hands of Hindus and Muslims at those of Muslims.[23] In July 1857 the family was driven out of its mohullah in the Chauk by the fighting to Saadatganj on the outskirts of the city, and later to the qasbahs beyond. Lives were lost; houses and possessions destroyed. All were forced to face, what most had hitherto managed to avoid, the fact of British domination in their world. 'Up to now', declared Muhammad Yusuf as, in tears, he explained why he had left the job of registrar found for him by the Chief Commissioner of Awadh, 'I have been signing fatawa relating to God and His Prophet, and now I am expected to sign fatawa relating to interest.'[24] 'Although his feet tread the ground' said Abdur-Razzaq of a disciple who came to him wearing English boots, 'I feel they tread on my heart.'[25]

On top of what were often ghastly personal experiences, there was the fate of Delhi and of Lucknow, for so many the acme of cultivation, the centres of their civilized existence. Both cities were sacked. In Delhi, according to one estimate, almost 30,000 were killed, most of them indiscriminately. Those left alive were herded out of the city, the Muslims amongst them not being permitted to return till many months had passed. Much of their property was auctioned off by prize agents. Meanwhile the British set about reshaping the cities in the best interest of colonial control, stamping on them the imprint of their industrial civilization.

For those who go through troubled times it helps if loved homes, comfortable streets, accustomed vistas remain, as reminders at least, of the folkways in which they were brought up, and of the values they were taught to cherish. At the same time, it helps if great buildings, symbols of their community's achievements in the past, and of the possibility of the continuance of its thread of existence into the future, are regarded with respect, indeed survive. The citizens of Delhi and Lucknow found no such comfort.. The bricks and mortar, stone and marble, carapace of Indo-Persian civilization, which had so long stood proud against the oncoming tide from Britain, was either blown up or abused.

The British revenge on Delhi was terrible. Indeed, for a time they considered demolishing the city altogether. Fortunately, less drastic counsel prevailed. In June 1858 Hindus were permitted to return and in August 1859 Muslims, although the overall numbers of inhabitants within the walled city did not reach the 1857 mark until 1900. Poets, most notably Ghalib, took to composing elegies on the death of the city, a genre of Urdu verse known as *Shahr-e-Ashub*. His letters recount week by week the humiliation and the destruction of the Mughal capital. For five years the Jama Masjid was used as a barrack for Sikh soldiers. The greater part of the second largest mosque, Fatehpuri, was sold to a Hindu, and was restored by Viceroy Lytton only twenty years later. The Zeenatul Masjid, the 'Ornament of Mosques' was used as a bakery until restored by Viceroy Curzon almost fifty years later. Most of the structures within the Red Fort were flattened, and of those that survived, the Mughal Hall of Public Audience became a hospital and the buildings to the south of the Hall of Private Audience a barrack. All houses, mosques and bazars within 448 yards of the walls of the Fort were razed. 'Here it seems the whole city is being demolished', wrote Ghalib to a friend in September 1860, 'some of the biggest and most famous bazars—Khas Bazar, Urdu Bazar—each of which was practically a small town, have gone without trace. You cannot even tell where they were. Householders and shopkeepers cannot point out to you where their houses and shops used to stand.'[26] Further demolitions took place to make way for the cantonment which was to cover the eastern third of the city, its parade ground placed insolently between the Red Fort and the Jama Masjid. Then, the railway line from Calcutta was punched through the northern walls of the old Mughal palace and a path nearly four hundred yards wide was laid waste as it made its way through the city to the Lahore Gate. By means of the confiscation of land from those who could not prove their innocence there was a great transfer of property from Muslims into the hands of Hindu bankers. The character of the citizens also changed: "Delhi People" now means Hindus, or artisans, or soldiers, or Panjabis or Englishmen' - Mughal Delhi was gone. .'By God', wailed Ghalib in 1861, 'Delhi is no more a city, but a camp, a cantonment. No Fort, no city, no bazars, no watercourses....'[27]

Muslims who returned to Delhi after the general amnesty of 1859 entered a nightmarish world. For all those in our first two groups, whether they were to become 'modernists' or 'reformers', the places of their youth, of their learning, of their spiritual development—the very nurseries of their civilization were gone. Saiyid Ahmad Khan, who had lived close to the world of the Red Fort, will have noted how complete was the assertion of British over Mughal past down to the renaming of the palace gates after Victoria and Alexandria. Saiyid Ahmad Khan, the historian, will have seen just how many of the monuments he had recorded in his *Asar us-Sanadid* had been wiped away. Zakaullah, the scholar, will have bemoaned the loss, as we all do, of the city's great libraries, that of the Imperial household, of Shah Waliullah's descendants, of Shaikh Abdul-Haq Muhaddith's descendants, of Mufti Sadruddin, and of Nawab Ziauddin Ahmad Khan of Loharu which had supplied the manuscripts from which Sir Henry Elliot had compiled his eight volumes of translated excerpts on the history of India. Zakaullah, the man, as he visited the site of his Kuchah-i Chilan Mohalla around which many of the intellectual and cultivated families traditionally lived, must have shivered at the memory of the 1400 people who were butchered there as British bloodlust ran wild. Those 'reformers' who stayed in India, Rashid Ahmad Gangohi or Siddiq Hasan Khan, if they picked their way through the ruins which were strewn through their old haunts from Kashmiri Gate to Daryaganj, will have noted the palaces of the nobility destroyed, for instance Jhajjar, Ballabgarh, Farrucknagar and Bahadurgarh, the palaces of the mind that had gone, for instance, the Akbarabadi Mosque where the reforming tradition had been long sustained by the descendants of Shah Waliullah, and the palaces of the spirit that were no more, for instance, the *Khanqah* of the progenitor of the Chishti revival, Shah Kalimullah, and that of the sustainer of the Naqshbandi revival, Mirza Jan-i Janan. 'Harken to me', Hali told his *mushaira* audience in 1874 'do not go into the ruins of Delhi. At every step priceless pearls lie buried beneath the dust...times have changed as they can never change again.'[28]

The fate of Lucknow was little better. It was the largest pre-colonial city in South Asia with a population of 400,000, the 'Baghdad of India' as Ghalib called it,[29] whose buildings were much admired by European visitors. Bishop Heber on seeing the Rumi Darwaza and Asaf al-Daula Imambarah in October 1825 compared it to the Kremlin, but thought it was better.[30] W.H. Russell, correspondent of the *Times*, wrote in March 1858 of 'a vision of palaces, minars, domes azure and golden, cupolas, colonnades, long facades of fair perspective in pillar and column terraced roofs - all rising up amid a calm still ocean of the brightest verdure. Look for miles and miles away, and still the ocean spreads, and the towers of the fairy-city gleam in its midst.'[31] Within weeks of Russell sending this despatch from the newly conquered city the razed demolition squads had set to work. Two-fifths of the city buildings were as a great swathe four miles long and half a mile wide was cleared along the river Gomti from Ghaziuddin Haidar's canal to well beyond the Jama Masjid, and wide straight roads were driven through the city, as Haussman had done in Paris, to enable troops to move easily to curb a turbulent citizenry. The Jama Masjid was turned into a barrack, as was Asaf al-Daula's Imambarah, and fifty or so mohulla mosques were seized and for two decades put to other purposes, some most demeaning. Fifteen years after the Mutiny uprising the population of the city was little more than 280,000.[32]

In the 1860s, as the Firangi Mahalis began to raise their heads to look about them, the magnitude of the changes and the shape of the new colonial world must have been clear. One great wide straight road, Victoria Street, swept by the edge of their mohulla; if they thought about it they were fortunate to hang on to Aurangzeb's gift at all. Should they wish to pray in the Jama Masjid they now had to cross an open plateau full of rubble to do so; the focal point of the Islamic city was now an island on the outskirts. To the southeast, where once there had been the country residences of the king and the nobility, there was now the cantonment and the civil station, a world of straight-lined sameness so different from the mohulla arabesques of the city. As in Delhi, moreover, the railway was driven through the tight-packed mohullas until it reached a station, in this case fortified, on the far side of the city.[33] Those few words we hear the

Firangi Mahalis utter in these years, whether in *Karnamah*, the newspaper edited by Muhammad Yaqub, a member of the family, or in the *malfuzat* recorded in the biography of Abdur-Razzaq, are ones of suppressed rage.[34]

The extent of the shock of the Mutiny uprising and its aftermath is clear. To the 'modernists', who came from or were associated with the old elite of Delhi, it was evident that there was no future in the Mughal way; it was in a phrase Saiyid Ahmad used of the emperor himself 'a mouldering skin stuffed with straw'.[35] The events of these years had given a sharp and dramatic demonstration of how the basis of power had changed; to repeat the words of Hali, 'times have changed as they can never change again'. It was evident too to these men of the *sharif* class, who felt that power and privilege was their's by right, that they must build a bridge between their world and that of British power if they were to maintain their status. The Aligarh movement, the fervour for things Europeans it meant, the cultural sacrifices it represented, the sense of urgency which accompanied it, had their psychological origins in these years. 'I could not even bear to contemplate the miserable state of my people', Saiyid Ahmad told the Muslim Educational Conference in 1889 as it celebrated the anniversary of the founding of Aligarh College; 'it was my duty to share its misfortunes and do all in my power to dispel them.'[36]

To the 'reformers', conscious sustainers of the Waliullahi tradition of Delhi, the lessons of these years, at least to those who remained in India, were no less clear. Dreams of a military *jehad* must be abandoned. Now was the time for a *jehad* of the pen and the tongue. Moreover, because British power seemed so durable and so transforming, and because the qasbahs to which they had retreated were so evidently in decline, it became a matter of the utmost urgency to find ways of sustaining Islamic life outside the framework of the colonial state. It is against this background that the creativity of the Deoband movement, of which Muhammad Qasim and Rashid Ahmad were the founders, should be understood. We think of the new bureaucratically organized madrasa with the capacity both to survive its founders and to give birth to fresh madrasas, of the dependence of the organization on the subscriptions of the community at large rather than on grants from the government or the nobility, of the missionary impulse to spread Islamic knowledge as widely as possible both by printed word and by word of mouth. We also think of the 'protestant' style of Islam it helped to fashion, in which the sanctions which brought Muslims to follow the *sharia* were not those of the law, in part at least imposed by the state, but those of the individual

Muslim conscience. This personal responsibility for sustaining Islamic society was taken yet further by the 'reformer' of our group who stayed in India, Siddiq Hasan Khan, a leading figure in the Ahl-i Hadith movement. Furthermore, the crucial role of personal responsibility in religion must be understood. It explains, for instance, the intensity of the 'reformers' quarrels with the followers of Ahmad Reza Khan Barelwi; whose beliefs in the intercessionary powers of the Prophet and of saints undermined that very foundation of human will on which the 'reformers' aimed to sustain Islamic society under British rule.[37]

To the learned and holy men of Firangi Mahal, the events of the Mutiny era brought division. Some freely cast in their lot with the colonial government. Others, particularly those in the circle of Maulana Abdur-Razzaq, who was, it should be noted a Chishti shaikh, did not. The Hanumangarhi *jehad* and the Mutiny uprising, it was felt, had been great tests for Muslims and they had been found wanting. 'The weakness displayed by the Muslims in the Mutiny', Abdur-Razzaq declared at the time of the Russo-Turkish war of 1878, 'resulted in the calamities that followed. If you want to compensate for these and to be rescued from the calamities, you should help Islam and an Islamic country. Thus it is possible that Allah will forgive your past mistakes.'[38] So he founded the *Majlis Muid ul-Islam* in order to support the Ottoman Empire, toured India to raise funds, wrote articles and issued *fatawa* urging donations to the cause as a *jehad.* This same organization contributed to the early stages of the family's striking efforts for the defence of Islam from 1911 through to the early 1920s; this same spirit was present throughout. Family members worked for Islam at home in matters such as the Kanpur mosque affair and Council reform, and abroad, as the Ottoman empire went into terminal stages, the holy places were threatened and the Khilafat moved towards its end.[39] To place all this remarkable activity at the door of the family's Mutiny experiences would be going too far, but it had certainly helped to spur Abdur-Razzaq into establishing their tradition of public effort for Islamic causes which reached a peak in those twentieth-century organizations it either founded or played a part in founding: the Anjuman-i Khuddam-i Kaaba, the Khilafat Committee, the Jamiyat al-Ulama-i Hind and the Anjuman-i Khuddam-i Haramain. Maulana Abdul-Bari, Abdur-Razzaq's grandson, was the leading Firangi Mahali involved in all these ventures, and it was he too who, in dictating his grandfather's biography to Altafur-Rahman Qidwai, drew the connection between their work for Islam in the twentieth-century and the shock of the Mutiny years.[40]

NOTES

1. Ghalib produced this chronogram in *Dastambu*, his diary of the events of the Mutiny which was published in Agra in November 1858. See Khwaja Ahmad Faruqi trans., *Dastanbuy: a Diary of the Indian Revolt of 1857* (London, 1970) pp. 30-31. The translation offered here is that of Ralph Russell and Khurshidul Islam. They note that 'rustkhez' means 'Judgement Day' as well as any great tumult or upheaval such as that caused by the stunning impact of a woman's beauty or the sudden news of a friend's death. Ralph Russell and Khurshidul Islam, *Ghalib. Life and Letters* (London, 1969), p. 247.
2. Quoted in the introduction to Hafeez Malik and Morris Dembo trans., *Sir Sayyid Ahmad Khan's History of the Bijnor Rebellion* (East Lansing, 1972), p.x.
3. Altaf Husain Hali, *Hayat-i Javed*, K.H. Qadri and David J. Matthews trans. (Delhi, 1979), p. 56.
4. For the life and work of Hali see: Gail Minault trans., *Voices of Silence* (Delhi, 1986), pp. 3-30, and Laurel Steele, 'Hali and his *Muqaddamah*: the creation of a literary attitude in nineteenth century India' in *Annual of Urdu Studies*, I, 1981, pp. 1-45.
5. C.F. Andrews, *Zakaullah of Delhi* (Lahore, 1976), p. 60.
6. Ibid., p. 75.
7. S. Moinul Haq, 'Samiullah Khan and Mohsin-ul-Mulk' in *A History of the Freedom Movement*, vol. II, Part II (Karachi, 1961), pp. 533-43.
8. Muhammad Sadiq, *A History of Urdu Literature*, (2nd edition, Delhi, 1984), pp. 375-78.
9. For the Delhi world of the 'reformers' see Barbara Daly Metcalf, *Islamic Revival in British India: Deoband, 1860-1900* (Princeton N.J., 1982), pp. 46-86.
10. For the life of Siddiq Hasan Khan see: Saeedullah, *The Life and Works of Muhammad Siddiq Hasan Khan Nawab of Bhopal (1248-1307/1832-1890)* (Lahore, 1973), pp. 21-53.
11. A.A. Powell, 'Maulana Rahmat Allah Kairanawi and Muslim-Christian Controversy in India in the Mid-19th Century' in *Journal of the Royal Asiatic Society*, No 1 (1976), pp. 42-63.
12. Farhan Ahmad Nizami, 'Madrasahs, Scholars and Saints: Muslim Response to the British Presence in Delhi and the Upper Doab 1803-1857', unpublished D.Phil., Oxford University, 1983, p. 214.
13. Among the main promoters of this account are Muhammad Mian in his *Ulama-i Hind Ka Shandar Maazi* (Delhi, 1963), whose argument is reflected in I.H. Qureshi, *Ulama in Politics* (Karachi, 1972), pp. 200-2. The most recent discussion along these lines is in Saiyid Tahzibul Hasnain Rizvi, 'Life and Works of Haji Imdadullah Muhajir-i-Makki', Thesis submitted for the degree of Ph.D. in the University of Calcutta, 1984, pp. 101-53.

14. The most thorough critique of the twentieth-century historigraphy of the Deoband school is in Mushir U.Haq, *Muslim Politics in Modern India 1857-1947* (Meerut, 1970), pp. 4-19. Metcalf, *Islamic Revival*, pp. 82-83, is also sceptical of the claims made by twentieth-century writers, as is Powell, 'Maulana Rahmatullah', pp. 58-61.
15. *Idem.*
16. S.A.A. Rizvi, *Freedom Struggle in Uttar Pradesh*, vols. I-IV (Lucknow, 1957-61), II, pp. 145-49; V, pp. 381, 437; Nizami, 'Madrasahs', p. 218.
17. Saeedullah, *Siddiq Hasan Khan*, pp. 38-53.
18. Francis Robinson, 'The Ulama of Farangi Mahall and their adab', in B. Metcalf ed., *Moral Conduct and Authority: the Place of Adab in South Asian Islam* (Berkeley, 1984), pp. 152-83; 'Problems in the History of the Firangi Mahall Family of Learned and Holy Men', in N.J. Allen *et al.* eds., *Oxford University Papers on India*, vol. I, Part 2 (Delhi, 1987), pp. 1-27; 'Frangi Mahall' in B.Lewis *et al.* eds., *Encyclopaedia of Islam*, 2nd. ed., supplement, 292-94.
19. For a clear description of the complicated development of this affair see Michael H. Fisher, *A Clash of Cultures: Awadh, the British and the Mughals* (Delhi, 1987), pp 227-34. From the government point of view it is covered in a remarkable file, Foreign & Political Consultations, 28 December 1855, National Archives of India; and from the Firangi Mahal point of view a version is offered in Altaf ur-Rahman Qidwai, *Anwar-i Razzaqiyya* (Lucknow, n.d.), pp. 23-29.
20. For Firangi Mahal involvement in the affair see: Foreign & Political Consultations, 28 December 1855, nos. 355-56, 389, 422, 429-34; Qidwai, *Anwar-i Razzaqiyya*, pp. 23-29; Maulvi Rahman Ali, *Tazkira-i Ulama-i Hind*, edited by Muhammad Ayub Qadri (Karachi, 1961), pp, 74, 177-78, 485-86; Maulvi Inayatullah, *Tazkira-i Ulama-i Farangi Mahall* (Lucknow, 1928), pp, 53-54, 96-99. For criticism of the actions of Mufti Muhammad Yusuf and Khadim Ahmad see: Qidwai, *Anwar-i Razzaqiyya*, p. 27 and Rahman Ali, *Tazkira*, pp. 177-78, 485-86.
21. Qidwai, *Anwar-i Razzaqiyya*, pp. 27-28.
22. Ibid., pp. 29-30.
23. Muhammad Abd ul-Khaliq, *Salah Falah* (Lucknow, 1909), pp. 26-29.
24. Inayatullah, *Tazkira*, p. 209.
25. Qidwai, *Anwar-i Razzaqiyya*, p. 59.
26. Russell and Islam, *Ghalib*, p. 244.
27. Ibid., p. 252; the fullest analysis of the post-Mutiny changes in Delhi is to be found in Narayani Gupta, *Delhi Between Two Empires 1803-1931: Society, Government and Urban Growth* (Delhi, 1981), pp. 1-69; there is further coverage in Percival Spear, *Twilight of the Mughals: Studies in Late Mughal Delhi* (Cambridge, 1951), pp. 218-28.
28. Froma *marsiya* entitled 'The Devastation of Delhi' recited by Hali at a mushaira in Lahore in 1874, Gupta, *Delhi*, pp. xviii-xix.

29. This falls in a passage by Ghalib bemoanig the fate of Lucknow: 'What praise was too high for Lucknow? It was the Baghdad of India, and its court - may God be praised! - a mint of rich men. A man could come there penniless and become wealthy. Alas that autumn should come to such a Garden.' Russell and Islam, *Ghalib*, p. 241.
30. Reginald Heber, *Narrative of a Journey through the Upper Provinces of India from Calcutta to Bombay, 1824-1825* (London, 1828), Vol. I, p. 386.
31. W.H. Russell, *My Indian Mutiny Diary*, ed. Michael Edwardes (London, 1957), pp. 57-58.
32. For an analysis of the post-Mutiny changes made by the British in Lucknow see Veena Talwar Oldenburg, *The Making of Colonial Lucknow, 1856-1877* (Princeton N.J., 1984).
33. Ibid., especially pp 27-61.
34. Ibid., pp. 34, 111, 114, 121, 145; Qidwai, *Anwar-i Razzaqiyya*, p. 59.
35. Hali, *Hayat-i Javed*, p. 61.
36. Ibid., p. 56.
37. Metcalf, *Islamic Revival*, pp. 87-260.
38. Qidwai, *Anwar-i Razzaqiyya*, p. 30.
39. Francis Robinson, *Separatism Among Indian Muslims: The Politics of the United Provinces' Muslims 1860-1923* (Cambridge, 1974), pp. 262-356, 419-20; and Inayatullah's biography of Abdul-Bari, Maulana Maulvi Muhammad Inayatullah, *Risala-i Hasrat al-afaq ba wafat majmua al-akhlaq* (Lucknow, 1348/1929-30).
40. Qidwai, *Anwar-i Razzaqiyya*, p. 30. Lest it appear that we argue nineteenth century action from twentieth century sources, it should be clear that our understanding of Firangi Mahali attitudes during the Mutiny and afterwards does not rest purely on the Abdul-Bari/Qidwai biography of Abdur-Razzaq but amongst other sources, on the file Foreign and Political Consultations 28 December 1855, the records of the Majlis Muid ul-Islam for the late nineteenth-century, Rahman Ali's *Tazkira*, and the Vernacular Newspaper Reports.

III

Colonial Urban Transformation in India

MEERA KOSAMBI

The universal recognition of the British colonial impact on India's urban configurations remains, unfortunately, unaccompanied by an in-depth analysis of the exact nature and extent of this impact or its theoretical interpretation. Into this largely uncharted territory, the present essay ventures to enter for a preliminary exploration. It seeks to demonstrate that the colonial impingement inhered structural changes leading to a total urban transformation, and further that the same basic process of transformation was replicated, with local variations, in the three regions which were pivotal to India's colonization: Western India (which came to constitute the Bombay Presidency), Eastern India (Bengal Presidency), and South India (Madras Presidency)[1]. The time-frame for this analysis stretches from the early seventeenth to the end of the nineteenth century, encompassing the complete unfolding of the process.

The Context

The body of literature on colonial urbanism being addressed here stems mainly from sociology, geography, and related disciplines, with a contribution also from history. Broadly speaking, this literature has been informed by two ideological perspectives — or, rather, paradigms— whose diametric opposition hinges on their interpretations of the nature of the Indo-British interaction and its urban repercussions. The paradigm projecting the British influence on Indian urbanism as a positive contribution has been dominant over the last four decades, and rests upon the premise that: 'For good or ill, colonialism has been the primary channel through which the ideas and techniques, the spiritual and material forces of the West, have impinged upon the rest of mankind' (Emerson 1968:5). It views the current Indian urban patterns as the natural culmination of historical trends, further enriched by a significant British urban component. The alternative paradigm stressing that the indigenous evolutionary trends have been considerably distorted due to colonial intervention has only recently been gaining ground.

Integral to the dominant paradigm is a tendency to posit a precolonial-colonial urban dichotomy in various garbs (such as Asian-Western, preindustrial-industrial, etc.) with stereotypes of both, and a certain looseness in the conceptualization of the 'colonial' city. It has originated chiefly from three complementary sets of generalizations, authored by Murphey, Redfield & Singer, and Sjoberg in the 1950s and 60s; and has continued tenaciously to mould even current thinking on the subject, both in India and the West.[2] It is characterized also by a Euro-centric and essentially ahistorical approach, despite its claim to identify urban 'traditions' and trace historical evolution.[3]

Probably the most pervasive statement of the Asian-Western urban dichotomy remains that presented by Murphey (1956, repr. 1972). Here the traditional Asian city is identified as 'predominantly a political and cultural phenomenon', located inland for its effective functioning 'primarily as administrative, ceremonial, and symbolic centres rather than as a base for trade' (1972:62). In contrast, the Western type of city in India was usually a port city built for overseas trade by European merchants, located allegedly at carefully chosen and advantageous coastal sites which were hitherto neglected by the builders of traditional cities, unconcerned as they were with maritime trade. Predictably this reading of Indian history leads to the conclusion that such port cities were 'largely new to Asia, which had traditionally lacked both the economic and institutional infrastructure for the kind of commercial enterprise which Europeans built' (1972:63).

The same cleavage surfaces in Redfield and Singer's (1954) world-wide analysis of the cultural role of cities. Their typology of cities, derived by combining the temporal variable (before and after the Industrial Revolution and Western expansion) with the functional variable (political and economic), yields four city types: the indigenous administrative-cultural cities (such as Allahabad in India), and cities of native commerce (no example from India); as well as the West-influenced metropolitan cities of the new world economy (e.g. Bombay), and cities of modern administration (e.g. New Delhi). The thesis presented is that the indigenous administrative cities carry forward old traditions and introduce 'orthogenetic' cultural change or the development of traditional cultures into new forms; while the other three types of cities, because of their contact with alien cultures, generate 'heterogenetic' change by creating new traditions and new cultural modes. The absence of an example of the indigenous Indian commercial centre in this whole scheme is symptomatic of the ideology which assumes, implicitly or explicitly, that such cities in fact did not exist. By implication it also translates the indigenous-Western contrast into the parallel orthogenetic-heterogenetic contrast.[4]

Sjoberg's universal construct of the 'preindustrial city', that is, the city generated by all societies at the pre-industrial level of technology, is basically a political centre geared to administration and/or military functions. Its antithesis, the 'industrial city', is the creation of Western societies in the industrial stage of technology, and, by definition, intended for economic functions (1960:87). Later, Sjoberg (1967) has attempted to convert this dichotomy into a continuum by introducing an intermediate or transitional category, namely, the 'industrializing city', to accommodate products of Western colonial rule, such as Calcutta. Theoretically, however, this category obfuscates rather than clarifies the issue. Obviously, a city like Calcutta, though a British colonial creation, began its career basically as a pre-industrial city— to employ Sjoberg's scheme—and its current status can best be described as an industrial city in an industrializing society.

A broad consensus of opinion among 'urbanists' thus favours the image of the indigenous Indian city as a governmental centre founded for territorial control and administration, and the contrasting image of the European city in India as a maritime port and therefore a Western innovation. This line of thinking runs like a red thread through much of the subsequent writings on the subject, as for example, Lewandowsky (1975: 41); King who contrasts the traditional South Asian city, 'primarily concerned with religious, political or administrative functions', with its contemporary counterpart, 'essentially Western in nature and function, dominated by trade and manufacture' (1980:4); and in a more diffuse manner, Bradnock (1984). A more extreme expression of the same ideological stance comes from Breese: 'In most newly developing countries there is only a brief history of indigenous urbanization. Rather, most of the existing urbanization appears to have begun under colonial interests and sponsorship'; consequently, in the case of India which lacked 'a national tradition of urbanization, it was natural that Western forms and ways of doing things would be imitated' (1966: 47, 54).

The alternative paradigm, though not altogether missing, was somewhat muted in the beginning. For example, Crane (1955) has traced the careers of the indigenous Indian administrative centres, handicrafts centres, and trade emporia; and has analysed the reasons for their decline due to the operation of different aspects of the colonial dynamic. Although this analysis failed to make inroads into the mainstream thinking, in recent years, the 'de-urbanization' thesis has been advanced in clearer terms by, among others, Bhattacharya (1984: 277-9), and formulated more emphatically by Habib (1985:364-8).

The issue of colonial urbanism has been further complicated by the diffuseness and ambiguity surrounding the concept of the 'colonial city'. Two illustrations will suffice as a substantiation. McGee (1967:51-2), in tracing the influence of colonialism on the Southeast Asian city—basically parallel to its Indian counterpart—reserves the term 'the true colonial city' only for the city which emerged during the rapid industrialization of the nineteenth-century, the prime example being the colonial port city. In the context of India, King (1976) subsumes under the term 'colonial urban area' only the civil-military cantonments and hill stations, but not the Indo-British port cities which were colonial cities *par excellence*; however, later, in a complete reversal of this position, King (1990) treats the Indo-British (and other colonial) port cities as the pivots of global colonial urbanism.[5]

The intellectual and ideological shifts in the social sciences during the last few decades have also affected the connotation of the terms 'colony' and 'colonialism', as judged by the two landmarks— the Encyclopaedia of the Social Sciences (1930) and the International Encyclopaedia of the Social Sciences (1968). The first publication defines the term 'colony' as 'a transplanted fragment of a human society', with a specific political connotation as 'a settlement of the subjects of a state beyond its frontiers', or 'a territorial unit geographically separated from a state owing allegiance to it in some specific and tangible way'. Such a colony could also be an instrument of exploitation. This 'exploitation colony' is understood as 'a small group of business men, administrators, soldiers, or all three, thrust into conditions quite different from those of their home country. The region may be densely populated by natives and possessed of a mature civilization' (Knight 1930:653). In the latter publication, 'colonialism' is still defined as 'the establishment and maintenance, for an extended time, of rule over an alien people that is separate from and subordinate to the ruling power'. But it has veered away from the term 'colonization' as understood earlier, and acquired a specific ethnic slant:

'Colonialism has now come to be identified with rule over peoples of a different race inhabiting lands separated by salt water from the imperial center; more particularly, it signifies direct political control of European states or states settled by Europeans as the United States or Australia, over people of other races, notably over Asians and Africans'. From this follow certain distinctive socio-cultural and economic features of the 'colonial situation', namely, 'domination of an alien minority, asserting racial and cultural superiority over a materially inferior native majority; contrast between a machine oriented civilization with Christian origins, a powerful economy and a rapid rhythm of life and non-Christian civilization that lacks machines and is marked by a backward economy and a slow rhythm of life; and the imposition of the first civilization upon the second' (Emerson 1968:1). This definition or its component elements are acknowledged as the basis of the recent and current thinking on urban development in India (e.g. King 1976:17, 1980:7, 1990:15,47) and elsewhere in Asia (McGee 1967: 51:52).

Evidently, the very complexity of the concept of colonialism demands a more elaborate analysis, since the equation of colonialism with its industrial phase restricts its scope unjustifiably. In the Indian case, this amounts to ignoring two centuries (c. 1612 to 1813) of British presence, British commercial and political domination, and urban activity before industrialization in Britain impinged upon the Indian economy and polity. That industrial colonialism was only one phase in the progression of British colonial rule (exercised first by the English East India Company and after 1858 by the British Crown) is most conspicuously seen in the case of Western India. The establishment of British territorial control in this region in 1818 was long predated by significant economic and urban changes which were colonial in nature and which had far-reaching repercussions. The need to conceptualize this phenomenon of pre-colonial domination has suggested the coining of the term 'proto-colonial' to indicate the inter-related complex of naval, economic and other types of domination which had nascent colonial overtones but which ante-dated direct political control. In short, this initial phase of proto-colonialism paralleled the later phenomenon of neo-colonialism: the former preceded the full-fledged colonial stage just as the latter has succeeded it.[6]

The second phase involved direct political domination and was initiated in the subcontinent in a piecemeal fashion in the wake of territorial conquest and expansion: in 1757 in Bengal, in 1800 in South India, and in 1818 in Western India. It was still a case of pre-industrial colonialism, most clearly in Bengal where it set in well before the Industrial Revolution in Britain had advanced sufficiently enough to make its effects felt.

The third phase began about 1813 when the Company's monopoly of India's trade was abolished and India was exposed to the full force of industrialization in Britain; and it ushered in the era of industrial colonialism (as described by Emerson mentioned above). At the outset it witnessed a reversal of the existing trade patterns to India's disadvantage, and later the transfer of modern industrial technology to India. Each of these component developments effected its own set of urban changes which are commonly associated with colonial urban development.[7]

Thus, conceptually, British colonial domination in India needs to be analysed in terms of three distinct and broadly successive (though partially overlapping) phases: proto-colonial, pre-industrial colonial, and industrial colonial. Each phase was propelled by its own dynamic which rendered certain urban changes imperative. The complete conceptual model is outlined below.

The Model of Colonial Urban Transformation

1. The Proto-Colonial Phase

The tentative foundations of proto-colonial domination were laid when the English East India Company established trading stations or 'factories' at major Indian seaports, as convenient entry points into the existing network of Asian maritime trade.

As a second step, the Company obtained small, independent, and largely undeveloped coastal sites and equipped them with fortified factories, later elevated to the status of 'Presidency towns'.[8] The chief pre-requisites of these sites were: insularity and strategic location; defensibility; a minimum of harbour facilities; and efficient links with neighbouring major Indian seaport and, preferably, also with inland areas producing goods for export (especially textiles). In the interest of these pre-requisites, handicaps of the actual site (e.g. absence of existing trade, unhealthy climate, marshy land) could be, and were, condoned.

Thirdly, from the Presidency towns used as coastal bases, the Company captured the maritime trade in the region by capitalizing on superior naval and commercial strength, and sometime by exerting political pressure derived from such strength. This established the supremacy of the Company's ports (i.e., Presidency towns) at the cost of older and larger indigenous ports.

Finally, the Company's combined naval and commercial supremacy was utilized also for effecting intervention into the domestic politics of the region, paving the way for territorial conquest.

2. The Pre-industrial Colonial Phase

The Company's political power was consolidated by constituting the conquered territories into large provinces known as Presidencies which were governed from the Presidency towns which logically became the new political capitals. The inevitable result was the devastation of indigenous governmental centres.

Secondly, the creation of new British urban centres was necessitated by the exigencies of administrative and military control (civil-military cantonments) and by climatic conditions (hill stations).

Thirdly, new routes were laid out in a radial fashion from the Presidency towns to reach major inland cities. This new route network, superimposed on the old one, endowed the hitherto peripheral coastal Presidency towns with a new centrality and accessibility *vis-a-vis* the interior region.

3. The Industrial Colonial Phase

In the wake of the Industrial Revolution in Britain, the existing pattern of trade between India and Britain was reversed to India's detriment. The long-established export of Indian textiles was converted into that of raw cotton, while cheaper mill-made piece-goods imported from Britain flooded the Indian market. Predictably, the very foundations of the indigenous textile centres were eroded, leading to their 'de-industrialization' and general decay.

Shortly thereafter, industrial technology began to be applied in India, primarily at the Presidency towns which also became the new industrial centres.

Simultaneously, a railway network was constructed so as to converge on the Presidency towns, and strengthen their newly achieved centrality. This inevitably led to the emergence of railway towns at important junctions, and to the decline of old towns which were bypassed by the railway.

Finally, the predominance of the Presidency towns as regional 'primate cities' became evident in terms of size and of the concentration of all important urban functions, and was accentuated by the related depopulation or 'de-urbanization' of indigenous towns.

The model having been presented, some clarifications are in order. First, while these three major phases can be conceptually separated, in reality there was a considerable chronological overlap and also considerable regional variation. Nor did they synchronize temporally in all three regions. The proto-colonial phase was seen in its most emphatic and extended form in Western India (1612 to 1817). The pre-industrial colonial phase was most evident in Eastern India (1757 to about 1813) where political conquest pre-dated full industrial expansion in Britain, whereas this phase occurred almost simultaneously with the industrial colonial phase in South India (1818 onward). In spite of this overlap, however, the urban repercussions of the different phases can be distinctly identified.

Secondly, the rise and fall of cities is in no way assumed to be a solely colonial phenomenon; it has formed an integral part of urbanization since the earliest times. For example, changes in inland political alignments and/or natural causes (such as the silting of the harbour) have been advanced as reasons for the successive decline of the ports of Broach and Cambay in Gujarat prior to the rise of Surat. The chequered careers of the successive cities of Delhi are legendary, and the vacillating fortunes of Mughal Delhi (Shahjahanbad) and Agra contingent upon royal patronage are equally well-known. Our primary concern in the present essay is to outline the over-all framework of urban transformation, within which to analyse the vicissitudes of specific types of Indian and Indo-British cities as the inevitable outcome of colonial domination.

The Proto-Colonial Phase

The English Company's exclusively maritime orientation and desire to utilize naval superiority for extracting commercial privileges were a logical perpetuation of the Portuguese prototype. The Portuguese maritime hegemony had been successfully imposed on the strength of their mandatory 'cartaz' system which involved the sale of passes to Indian (or generally non-European) ships for protection on the seas, and the levy of customs on these ships both on their outward and return journeys at one or more of the string of Portuguese ports along the coast (Pearson 1976). The British ambitions to supplant the Portuguese as the 'Lords of the Sea' and inherit their system of naval domination were expressed by Sir Thomas Roe as early as in 1618 (*The English Factories in India* [hereafter EFI] 1618-1621: xii-xiii), and were soon fulfilled.[9]

The British maritime expansion in the Indian waters was a step towards founding a sea-based empire; and trading posts, preferably at independent coastal ports, were acquired in order to forge oceanic links. This design became manifest by the mid-seventeenth-century when the English Company's Surat factory was given charge of the English factories from Bandar Abbas (or Gombroon) and Isfahan in Persia to Tatta in Sind; and the Madras factory controlled the English establishments at Balassore in Orissa, Masulipatam on the Coromandel coast, Bantam in Java, Jambi in Sumatra, Macassar in Celebes, Syriam in Pegu, and Camboja in Indo-China (EFI 1655-1660 7).

The strategy of acquiring independent ports also had a strong financial angle—it was the sole and sure means of escaping the customs duties levied at indigenous ports (which was usually a source of friction) and of augmenting the Company's own revenues by charging higher customs. This also was a replication of the precedent set by the Portuguese whose revenues in India accrued largely (up to 55%) from customs receipts (Pearson 1981:76).The rate of customs charged at indigenous and European ports differed significantly. In the late seventeenth-century, Surat charged two and a half per cent on both exports and imports (with bullion exempted), but reduced the levy to two per cent as a concession to European merchants (EFI 1661-64:314). At Karwar the English merchants obtained a customs reduction to one and a half per cent on imported goods, treasure being duty free (EFI 1665-67: 108-9). The English Company itself charged three and a half per cent on both imports and exports at Bombay in the mid-1670s, and eight per cent on specific commodities (GBCI I:406-7). The Portuguese had charged from four and a half to six and a half per cent in customs at Goa in the late sixteenth and early seventeenth-centuries (Pearson 1981:75), and five per cent at Diu in the late seventeenth-century (EFI 1668-69:203).

Bombay and Western India

The English East India Company's early trade with the Indian subcontinent pivoted on Surat on the Gujarat coast. As the largest Indian port for maritime trade, Surat was a magnet for all foreign traders, equipped as it was with a well-developed commercial infrastructure, linkages extending from cotton-growers and weavers through middlemen to merchants and bankers; access to inland markets; as well as harbour and shipping facilities (Das Gupta 1970). On obtaining a licence from the

Mughal Emperor, the English Company set up a factory at Surat in 1612 to tap the rich textile trade of Gujarat and supplement it in a small way with spices from Malabar. The Dutch and French Companies followed in the same footsteps later in the seventeenth-century.[10]

Surat's numerous and obvious advantages were offset, from the English Company's perspective, by a few but weighty disadvantages, including the presence of rival European mercantile companies. The initial handicaps, however, concerned mainly the payment of the local customs duties which had the dual effect of imposing indirect trade controls and cutting into the profits. An additional concern was the physical insecurity due to the ban on foreign fortifications in Mughal territories. The need for defence became a major preoccupation as early as 1625 (EFI 1624-29:xxi), and was sorely aggravated due to European hostilities, especially the Dutch wars in the 1650s.

The English Company was compelled to launch a search for an independent coastal site which could be turned into a fortified port 'as that wee might call our owne' (EFI 1650-54:xv). In response to the Surat factors' appeal, the Company's Directors empowered them 'to treate for the obteyning of' a port 'fitt for securing of our shipping, and that hath a good inlett into the countrie and trade, and such other convenience and accommodations as are necessarie for a settlement' (EFI 1655-60:151). Although the subsequent screening of the west coast ports proved unfruitful, Bombay island, off the Konkan coast, eventually came into the Company's possession by a fortunate accident. It formed a part of the royal Portuguese presents to Britain's Charles II to seal a matrimonial and military alliance in 1661; it was ceded to the British Crown in 1665, and transferred to the Company two years later. As the Company's territorial possession, Bombay qualified to be its headquarters in Western India, and the shift from Surat was duly accomplished in 1687; however, Bombay remained commercially dependent upon and overshadowed by Surat until the mid-eighteenth-century.

Bombay's location was somewhat problematic in that its lifeline extended through coastal shipping to Surat and the rest of Gujarat which formed its commercial hinterland. At the same time, Bombay was cut off from most of its geographical hinterland— the region of Maharashtra — both by the massive Sahyadrian range which barred the way to the inland Deccan plateau, and by political hostility of the Marathas, Mughals, and the Portuguese. Consequently, Bombay's capture of the commercial and political spheres was successive rather than simultaneous (Kosambi 1985), and the proto-colonial phase in Western India was far more pronounced and protracted than in the other two regions under consideration.

The struggle for Bombay's commercial survival lasted almost for a century. Even the maximum utilization of its chief assets—insularity, proximity to Surat, territorial possession facilitating adequate fortification, and an excellent natural harbour sheltered by its situation between the eastern shore of the island and the west coast of the mainland—was hardly sufficient to make up for its total deficiency in merchandise for trade and a mercantile community. In addition, the largely rocky and barren island possessed an unhealthy climate fatal for Europeans, as summed up in the proverb 'Two Mussouns are the Age of a Man'. The only way to develop Bombay into a viable trading station was to induce the merchants of Gujarat, by offering commercial and other privileges, to settle there and to handle the merchandise for export. The latter consisted mainly of textiles, also imported from Gujarat through the Surat factory and known as 'Surat goods'. These were then transhipped to Europe from Bombay port which thus started its career as an entrepôt. In addition, the Company's naval strength supported the system of issuing 'passes' to Indian ships, which proved to be a lucrative source of revenue (Grose 1757:67:8).

It was only after Surat's decline in the mid-eighteenth-century that Bombay's trade finally picked up. The initial constriction of Surat's trade has been attributed to the simultaneous collapse of the Mughal peace resulting in the disturbed conditions in the interior, and the power struggles in Persia and the Red Sea region, leading to the loss of crucial markets in those areas. Thus, although Surat's decline was not caused by Bombay, Bombay could grow only after, and because, Surat had declined (Das Gupta 1979:8). The process of erosion was further hastened by the English Company's application of its by now considerable commercial and political force. After 1759 the English Company shared political power with the Nawab of Surat, and commanded the city's castle and fleet. Soon Surat's maritime trade was inexorably diverted to Bombay (Surat Gazetteer, ii:128).

Surat's reduction to the status of a coastal port feeding Bombay with export goods boosted Bombay's rise as an international port of considerable size—a development which was reinforced by the shift of the ship-building industry from Surat to Bombay. Trade statistics show a continuation of this trend during the following century. In 1802-3, Surat's seaborne trade was valued at £ 988, 388 and about 21 per cent of it was with Bombay; in 1815-16 this proportion had increased to 41 per cent. In

1875 Surat's seaborne trade was further reduced to £ 507, 866 due to the introduction of the railways as an alternative mode of transport in 1868 (Surat Gaz.: 166-69). This economic decay inevitably resulted in depopulation. According to one (though by no means the only available) set of estimates, the city's inhabitants numbered over half a million at the close of the eighteenth-century, were reduced to about 250,000 in 1811, and to 80,000 in 1847 (The Imperial Gazetteer XXIII:164).

The eighteenth-century ended with the English Company in possession of very restricted territorial authority in Western India, but able to exert a commercial-political domination over, and to generate significant urban changes within, a much wider area. Part of the proto-colonial phase, involving maritime commercial domination, was completed and the stage was set for political initiatives.

Until the mid-eighteenth-century Bombay's position as an isolated British possession in Western India made it insecure and vulnerable to attack, especially from the Marathas under the powerful Peshwa of Pune. The general perception was that 'certainly Bombay...ceases to be tenable, that instant that the Marattas determinedly resolve the conquest of it' (Grose 1757: 155). But by the 1770s the Company was poised to enter the Maratha political arena, and a series of military confrontations culminated in its final conquest of the Peshwa's dominions in 1818.

Madras and South India

On the Coromandel Coast, the English commercial interests were anchored primarily to the spice trade of Malabar for which the Portuguese, Dutch and English were competing in the early seventeenth-century, and also to the renowned printed fabrics or 'payntings' of the area. The earliest English settlements on the coast were at Nizampatam and Masulipatam, created in 1611. In 1619 the English Company gained a foothold at Pulicat where the Dutch Company had a settlement (besides Sadras and other places), but was driven out by trade rivalries the very next year. In 1625 a small factory was set at Armagaon. However, the Masulipatam factory continued as the 'principal mart' on the coast, being located at a safe distance from the 'invetterate and most mallitious enemys', the Dutch (Madras Census: 17; Ranson 1938:7; IG XVI:250-51).

English trade at these factories was impeded by the rivalry with the Dutch; friction with the local chieftains, especially over customs duties; and distance from the major weaving and dyeing centres which lay further south. The search for a new suitable location led to the discovery of Madraspatam (two miles north of Portuguese San Thome) where the local chief or Naik welcomed the English Company with 'very fayre proffers' including a lease of land for building a fort. Work on the fortified factory (later named Fort St. George) was started at once in 1640, and an application was sent to the Company's Directors in London for permission. By the time the Company's dispatch arrived two years later, refusing permission for the enterprise, the Madras factory had already started functioning as a substitute for the hastily dismantled Armagaon factory (Madras Census: 17:18; Newell 1919:12-15). In 1641 the Company's headquarters on the Coromandel Coast was shifted from Masulipatam to Madras; in 1653 Madras was raised to the rank of a Presidency, independent of Bantam; and in 1658 the factories in Bengal were placed under its orders (IG XVI:369-9). At the end of the seventeenth-century the subsidiary English factories on this coast included Fort St. David near Cuddalore, Porto Novo, Madapollam, and Vizagapatam (IG XVI:251).

The site of Madras, on a small hill protected on the west by the Cooum river, was handicapped by the lack of a natural harbour, so that ships had to anchor in the open road-stead about two miles from the shore while cargo and passengers were transported in small *masula* boats in a precarious operation. (This state of affairs lasted until 1862, when the first artificial harbour was built.) Thus the choice of 'an unfavoured and uncompromising tract of bare, sandy shore, almost completely devoid of natural advantage' for the English factory was 'fortuitous rather than deliberate and governed by political rather than geographical considerations' (Ranson 1938:7), the political considerations being insularity and defensibility.

The town's chequered political career involved military confrontations with both European and Indian powers. The French, from their stronghold at Pondicherry, attacked Madras and its vicinity repeatedly in 1672, 1746 (occupying the town until 1749) and in 1759. It was only after the retaliatory English attack on Pondicherry in 1761 that the French were subdued and the English Company became the strongest European power in South India. The tussle with the Indian powers—the Muslims under the Nizam of the Deccan, the Nawab of the Carnatic, Mysore under Haider Ali (and later his son Tipu Sultan), and the Marathas— lasted until 1799 when the Company either defeated or negotiated with all of them and established its political hegemony in the region (IG XVI:251-55, 369-70; Newell 1919:27-32).

The commercial rise of Madras was far from being dramatic, and the result probably of the general decline of the Coromandel ports due to 'internal factors and the dynamics of Asian trade', as in the case of Surat (Arasaratnam 1986:354-5) coupled with its ultimate political-military superiority. However, by the end of the nineteenth-century, Madras single-handedly claimed nearly half of the Presidency's maritime trade; Tuticorin and Cochin trailed far behind with about a one-tenth share of the total trade each; followed by Calicut, Mangalore, Cocanada, Tellicherry, and Negapatam (IG XVI: 297).

Calcutta and Eastern India

Calcutta, the last-comer which won the race for political power, was founded to tap the rich trade of the Gangetic valley and of Bengal, especially the silks and muslins of Murshidabad and Dacca, with a special interest in Bihar's saltpetre essential for the manufacture of gunpowder in Europe.

In the early and mid-eighteenth-century, Murshidabad had dominated Bengal's urban scene as the administrative capital of the Nawab, as a silk manufacturing centre, and a major river port. Its focal position in the Bengal silk trade had attracted several European factories to its administrative jurisdiction—the English at Qasimbazar, the French at Saidabad, and the Dutch as Kalkapur. The English Company, starting with a commercial base in Orissa in the 1630s, obtained permission in 1652 to open trade in Bengal with a customs exemption. A factory was permitted at Hugly town in 1658, and subordinate agencies were maintained at Patna, Balassore, and Qasimbazar. Hugly was a Mughal imperial port and garrison town on the river Hugly (a branch of the Ganga) about a hundred miles from the Bay of Bengal. The Portuguese had established trade here in 1540; while a string of European factories—Dutch Chinsura, French Chandernagore, and Danish Serampore—stretched southward along the same, or west, bank of the Hugly river. The shifting currents of the river, however, posed severe navigational problems, so that the first English ship was able to sail up as late as in 1678 (Calcutta Census: 14, 113-4; Mohsin 1980:72-80).

A major setback was the eviction of the English factors from Bengal in 1686 after defying the Mughal Government and ransacking Hugly town. They were allowed to return in 1690 to Sutanuti, a village which, together with those of Kalikata and Govindpur, formed modern Calcutta. This site lay further south and on the east bank of the Hugly river, on a strip of raised ground enclosed by swamp. The unhealthy site provided physical security as its greatest asset, because the river separated it from Hugly town and the nearby European factories. Bypassing the earlier imperial orders expressly forbidding the fortification of European factories, the English Company obtained a tacit consent, during a local rebellion in 1696, to the construction of Fort William (Calcutta Census:16-17).

The locational advantages of Calcutta also were strategic rather than commercial, because the English factors 'needed a fortified settlement like Madras or Bombay, near the mouth of the Hugli, in which they could take shelter in case of need and from which they could exert pressure on the Mughal officials by blocking the estuary' (Furber 1976:96). Calcutta's commercial rise was considerably boosted by its position closer to the Bay of Bengal than the existing ports on the Hugly, making it the only seaport available for the maritime export of the Gangetic valley and Eastern India.

A crucial event in Calcutta's life was the attack, followed by military occupation, by the Nawab of Bengal in 1756. The next year he was defeated by his rival at the battle of Plassey, with help from the English Company which not only re-occupied Calcutta, but was also rewarded with a grant of additional territories.

The Pre-Industrial Colonial Phase

Concentration of Political Power

Essential for the sustenance of the newly acquired territorial control was the British monopoly of the region's political power which had earlier been distributed amongst separate kingdoms and principalities. This political power resulted in the creation of three Presidencies within which some indigenous semi-autonomous princely enclaves were allowed to remain under the control of the British Political Agent, an arrangement continued even after 1858 when the government of the English East India Company's territories passed to the British Crown. A logical expression of the British political hegemony was the concentration of political power in the Presidency towns, and the resultant disintegration of the older governmental centres.

The Company tasted political power first in Bengal, and its urban repercussions were not slow in manifesting themselves. In 1765 the Company acquired the rights of revenue administration in Bengal, Bihar and Orissa, and became the real power in the region. In 1777 Calcutta was made the seat of the Company's Governor Generalship, and invested with control of all the Indian possessions of the Company. The transfer of governmental functions to Calcutta sealed the fate of Murshidabd. In the mid-eighteenth-century Murshidabad was, in Clive's words, 'as extensive, populous,and rich as the city of London', and estimated to contain 600,000 people. In 1794 its extent 'might still be compared with that of London, but its population was certainly much less, not exceeding...200,000...In *wealth* the falling off since the British conquest...was undoubtedly still greater' (Twining 1893:107). The depletion continued throughout the nineteenth-century. An estimate of 1837 recorded a population of 124,807; the Census of 1872 recorded only 46,182; and the Census of 1901 a meagre 28,558 (including 13,385 in Azimganj with which it was bracketed). A part of this decline was also due to the fall in commerce, since the trade of Murshidabad as a river port and commercial centre was deliberately stunted by the East India Company by applying administrative pressures for commercial objectives; and the effects were aggravated by natural calamities such as severe famines (Mohsin 1980). In other words, Calcutta's commercial and political rise occurred simultaneously, and at the cost of Murshidabad as a riverport and as a governmental centre in the pre-industrial colonial phase.

In Western India, Bombay's commercial rise had been contingent upon Surat's decline in the proto-colonial phase, and its political rise upon usurping Pune's functions during the pre-industrial colonial phase. The conquest of the Peshwa's territories in 1818 was followed within a few years by the annexation of Gujarat and Sind; and together they were constituted into the Bombay Presidency, to be governed from Bombay city as its administrative capital. Pune, the region's erstwhile political focus, suffered visibly in the aftermath of the British conquest. In the words of Elphinstone (1821:5): 'Poona may be reckoned to contain about 110,000 inhabitants, having lost from a tenth to a fifth since the removal of Baji Row (Peshwa) with his Court and Army'. The decline continued unabated for the next three decades. In 1851 Pune city contained only 70,000 residents, with the adjacent British civil and military station adding another 15,000 (Kosambi 1980:183,194).

The pattern for Madras's political rise was similar. In 1799 Tipu Sultan was defeated and killed, Mysore proper was restored to a representative of its original Hindu dynasty, and Tipu's territories were divided between the Nizam and the British. Also in 1799 the Maratha Raja of the principality of Tanjore, who had received help from the British to regain his throne, resigned the administration of his kingdom to the

Company in return for an annual payment. A treaty was concluded with the Nawab of Carnatic in 1801 under which he also resigned to the Company the government of his territories while retaining his titles and a stipend. Thus most of the region of the Madras Presidency (with Madras city as its administrative focus) was under British possession in the opening years of the nineteenth-century, though its final limits were fixed in 1862.

New Urban Areas

The settlement types which qualify as British innovations were the civil-military cantonments and hill stations. They merit special notice not only because they introduced urban concepts and entities new to India, but also because they supported a wide network of colonial settlements to which the British presence in India was anchored.

Cantonments and Civil Stations

Initially, troop encampments had grown as an integral part of the three Presidency towns, housed in Fort William and Alipore in Calcutta, Fort St. George and St. Thomas's Mount in Madras, and Colaba in Bombay. After territorial expansion, the continuation of British presence on Indian soil could be guaranteed only by a network of permanent army camps. Perhaps the clearest statement of the exigencies of military control came from Elphinstone (1819:12) immediately after the conquest of the Peshwa's dominions: 'It is on the strength of our military establishments that the tranquility of the country and the security of our possession of it must principally depend...[I]t must be remembered that after so great a revolution as has taken place in India, it is dangerous too soon to calculate on undisturbed possession, and to cease to be prepared for unforeseen contingencies'.

All major towns (including the seats of the 'Native Princes') therefore came to be controlled and their lines of communication guarded by the adjacent military camps. Similar army camps were also situated at existing forts and other military strongholds (which usually commanded all strategic locations), and at or near the scene of a decisive battle. Occasionally, the decision regarding the exact site was influenced by the factor of pleasant climate (in addition to the special hill stations for convalescent troops).

The military cantonments attached to indigenous cities were usually accompanied by civil stations, responsible for urban administration. The juxtaposition of this combined British settlement with the indigenous city left a permanent stamp of the Indo-British dual structure (which is clearly visible even today underneath the urban sprawl engulfing both). The planned spacious layout and distinctive built environment of the former contrasted sharply with the latter's congested and haphazard appearance. The planning of the military cantonment was a matter of adhering to the standard blueprint which allotted spaces to sets of barracks for the troops (segregated along racial lines), lines of bungalows for the officers, garrison bazaars, hospitals, churches, and typical military areas such as the arsenal and the rifle range. A section of the cantonment known as the Sadar Bazar was demarcated for the Indian civilian population catering to the needs of the army. The civil station was less standardized in appearance but usually grew around the Collector's residence as its nucleus, and provided important services such as the post and telegraph offices, and cultural institutions integral to the British lifestyle, such as clubs and gymkhanas (i.e. clubs with outdoor recreation facilities).[11]

The earliest military cantonments were constructed in Bengal in the aftermath of territorial conquest. The largest was Berhampore outside Murshidabad (and close to Plassey). According to a Company civil servant who visited the place in 1794: 'The vicinity of Mooshedabad, doubtless, led to the choice of this spot for a military cantonment, and for the same reason a considerable division of our army is always stationed here'. The same motive prompted the creation of a large military station at Dinapur, ten miles from Patna: '[t]he practice of fixing our troops so near the principal cities seems to indicate some distrust of our native subjects...' (Twining 1893:107,139). The strong and extensive fortress of Monghyr, which commanded the entrance to Bengal from Bihar, was turned into a military station with a depot of military stores and a powder magazine (Twining 1893: 127). The cantonment of Barrackpur, established in 1772 on the east bank of the Hugly 15 miles above Calcutta, grew within fifty years to be a 'very pretty...large village inhabited by soldiers, with bungalows for the European officers and other white inhabitants'; and had a population of about 10,000 in 1901 (Heber 1873, I:33-4; IG VII:86). The nearby Dum-Dum was 'the principal European artillery cantonment in India' (Heber 1873, I:36). In the strategic boundary area of the lower Himalayas were situated the cantonments of Darjeeling and Lebong; Buxa which commanded one of the principal passes leading into Bhutan; and Gangtok in Sikkim.

The military complexion of Western India was radically altered when the British cantonments succeeded the hills forts as the region's military strongholds. On the hill forts had rested the establishment and sustenance of Maratha power from the mid-seventeenth to the early nineteenth-century; they had also protected the unwalled Maratha cities which lay under their shelter. At the time of the British conquest, these hill forts numbered about 200, 'all exceedingly strong', so that a regular army would be required to reduce them if occupied by insurgents. The British solution was, therefore, to demolish the forts which had no direct utility. 'All forts that are of military or political importance, or that without being formidable to our troops, would afford a refuge to the people of the country in case of invasion, are to be preserved, and all the rest destroyed'; and the policy was implemented with immediate effect (Elphinstone 1819:15). Predictably, Pune was the natural choice for the region's most important British cantonment. As the former political capital and a potential centre for insurrection, the city had to be kept under close watch and control. Also its central inland location and communication links facilitated troops movements (Elphinstone 1819:13). Close to Pune (on the way to Bombay) was established another cantonment at Kirkee—the site of the last and decisive battle between the Peshwa and the British. Other military cantonments in Bombay presidency were located at Ahmednagar, Sholapur, Nashik (at Deolali and Igatpuri), as well as Satara and Kolhapur in the Deccan; Belgaum in Karnataka; Ahmedabad, Surat and Deesa (Palanpur) in Gujarat; at Karachi, Hyderabad, and Jacobabad in Sind; and at isolated sites such as Mhow (Census of Bombay Presidency 1872:241). Dapoli in the Konkan was 'the site of a convalescent hospital for the European garrison of Bombay' in the 1820s (Heber 1873, II:142-3).

The Madras Presidency's military network consisted of, among others, the cantonments of Poonamallee (a convalescent centre for European troops) and Pallavaram near Madras city; Bellary, Trichinolopoly, Wellington, Vizagapatam, and Trivandrum. Several cantonments had been abandoned due to hot weather, incidence of malaria, or other similar problems: these included Ellore, Arni, Chittoor, Cuddapah, Ranipet, and Cochin. The largest cantonment in the Presidency was at Bangalore, established in 1809 when the British garrison was removed here from Seringapatam (the scene of the British defeat of Tipu Sultan) which proved to be unhealthy for the troops. This cantonment, later the 'Civil and Military Station', adjoined Bangalore city (which was under the Mysore State) and occupied an 'assigned tract' under British administration, through the Resident at Mysore. The importance of the civil and military station relative to the city is seen from the populations of both in 1901: the former contained 89,599, and the latter 69,447) (IG VI: 368-70).

Hill Stations

For the foreign rulers from the cold British climate, the summer heat of the coast and the inland plains was a major ordeal. Relief was therefore provided by creating hill stations which attracted a European exodus (with a sprinkling of the Indian elite) from the surrounding summer-scorched region. The phenomenon of the hill station dates from the 1820s when large tracts of the Indian subcontinent had come under direct British possession, facilitating the exploration of the mountains for suitable sites fulfilling the climatic and scenic requisites. Most of these sites were difficult of access, especially with the existing preindustrial modes of transportation; and the introduction of the railway half a century later was to affect the accessibility, and consequently also the popularity, of individual hill stations.

Although basically a variant of the newly popular summer resort town in Britain (King 1976:160-2), the hill station was more than a mere luxury; it was a physical necessity especially for the British troops whose health problems were aggravated by the harsh climate. This led to a categorization of hill stations into three major types: the official hill station patronized by the Governor of the Presidency and his staff; the military sanatoria or 'convalescent depots' for troops; and hill stations built by private European initiative (Mitchell 1972)12.

That the hill station was as much a cultural as a climatic need was evident from the special efforts expended on reproducing a European environment as far as was compatible with Indian conditions. The main attraction of the hill stations was the cool weather, varying between 60 to 70°F, usually found at an elevation of 6,000 to 7,000 ft. above sea level. Scenic beauty and greenery were an essential feature; and, in addition, cold weather flowering plants and shrubs were specially cultivated. In this setting were laid out long riding paths and carriage drives, race courses, and artificial lakes for boating. The British settlement was usually located at the highest points, with the bazaars and the Indian settlements at a separate and lower site[13]. Predictably, there was a considerable seasonal fluctuation in the population which swelled during the summer.

The Bombay Presidency's official hill station or the 'retreat of the Governor of Bombay and the chief officials of his Government' from

March to June was Mahabaleshwar in the Western Ghats, established in 1828 (IG XVI: 424-6). the journey from Bombay was usually made by steamer, boat, and horse-carriage to the foot of the hill, and up the steep and winding ascent in a palanquin (Falkland 1857, I: 132-44, 161). Matheran, 'discovered' a few years later, was also reached by the inevitable steamer trip to the mainland, a ride in a horse-carriage, and the final ascent managed either on horseback or in chairs carried by bearers. Matheran's proximity to Bombay ensured its popularity, especially when a good road was made to link it with Neral station on the Bombay-Pune railway, making it a serious rival to Mahabaleshwar (Oliver 1905:6-20). (Later, a special track was laid for a small train from Neral up to Matheran). On the Bombay-Pune road (and later railway), were developed the twin towns of Lonavla and Khandala at the top of the Borghat pass, the latter as a military sanatorium for the Poona Divison of the Western Command (IG XV 223-4). The hill forts near Pune were also pressed into service as hill stations — Sinhgad being patronized by European civilians, and Purandar by convalescent troops.

Darjeeling, acquired in 1835, became the summer headquarters of the Governor of Bengal and the favourite summer retreat of the Presidency officials. Situated in the lower Himalayas, the town varied in height between 6,000 ft. to about 7,800 ft. above sea level. Its regular population numbered only 3,157 in 1872; increased greatly after the construction of the railway; and reached 10,924 (including the cantonments) in 1901, with the summer influx inflating it to 23,852 (IG XI: 178-80). The nearby Kurseong, located at a lower elevation, was less popular as a hill station; but being situated on the Darjeeling-Himalayan Railway, it served as a centre of the tea trade (IG XVI: 54).

The Madras Presidency's most popular cluster of hill stations — Ootacamund, Coonoor, Wellington, and Kotagiri — nestled in the Nilgiris. Ootacamund was formally established in 1827 as the chief hill station, at a distance of 356 miles from Madras city, and acquired 18,596 permanent residents by 1901 (IG XIX: 238-9). The ascent of 7,500 feet up to this 'extremely pretty' and 'fashionable resort' was accomplished in a 'tonga' or a two-wheeled horse-cart, zigzagging up the wooded mountainside, past the Wellington barracks 'used for convalescent soldiers sent here from the low country' (Caird 1884:142-3) Among the numerous other hill stations of the Presidency, Kodaikanal in the Palni Hills enjoyed popularity because of its proximity to Madurai and the southern region, a relatively moderate rainfall, and perennial water supply (Mitchell 1972:93).

Route Patterns

Inland routes acquired a new and urgent significance as soon as the Presidency towns turned into the pivots of administrative-military control. Their coastal location had provided convenient access to sea routes at the cost of inland communications. This initial inaccessibility to and from the interior was partly deliberate, as a defence measure, party unavoidable due to political barriers, and partly unimportant because of the Company's heavy reliance on local commercial agents. The advent of territorial expansion suddenly invested inland transportation routes with a high priority.

In Western India, Bombay's problem of meagre inland communications was considerably aggravated by the massive Sahyadrian range which separated the coastal Konkan strip from the inland Deccan plateau, and which could be penetrated only through a few negotiable gaps or *ghats*. The conquest of the Peshwa territories made it imperative to improve Bombay's links with Pune, in order to keep it under close watch and to facilitate rapid deployment of troops and goods throughout the conquered territory. A road was therefore led up the difficult Borghat incline in 1830, on which was started a mail cart service between Bombay and Pune, the first of its kind in India (Poona Gaz. II:144).

Bombay thus provides an excellent example of a peripheral (or 'ex-centric', in geographical terminology) location being transformed into a central one through the creation of a new road network. The existing route pattern in this region consisted of an arterial north-south route in the Deccan being connected by east-west access routes from the Konkan coast through the *ghats*. This network did not service Bombay; upon it therefore was super-imposed a new network radiating outward from Bombay (Kosambi 1988).

In an entirely different topographical region, Calcutta faced its own transportation problems. Its initial strategic advantage lay in being located on the east bank of the Hugly,so that the river itself formed a part of its defences. Conversely, the city's access to the rich Gangetic valley and most of North India was minimized. Inland routes from the west, therefore, had to be made to converge on Howrah on the west bank of the river, from which a ferry service, and later a floating pontoon bridge, led across to Calcutta. Towards the east, Calcutta was connected with the Brahmaputra river system by means of a network of improved natural channels supplemented by artificial canals on which small river craft could ply (IG VII: 279:80).

The Industrial Colonial Phase

Reversal of Trade Patterns and 'De-industrialization'

The major upheaval in India's trade with Britain was occasioned by the Charter Act of 1813 which abolished the East India Company's monopoly of Indian trade and opened the country to the textile (and other industrial) manufactures of Britain which undersold domestic handwoven fabrics, so that India's export of textiles was rapidly substituted by that of raw cotton. The twin processes of industrialization in Britain and 'de-industrialization' in India (most marked in the case of textile manufacture, but also in ship-building) were accomplished largely through protective tariffs in Britain.

The East India Company's Directors, in the 1820s, preferred to emphasize the superiority of the British machine technology (an argument popular with the apologists of British rule in India), but were forced to admit the injustice of the protective taxation: 'The silk manufactures [of India], and its piece goods made of silk and cotton intermixed, have long since been excluded altogether from our markets; and, of late, partly in consequence of the operation of a duty of 67 per cent, but chiefly from the effect of superior machinery, the cotton fabrics which heretofore constituted the staple of India, have not only been displaced in this country, but we actually export our cotton manufactures to supply a part of the consumption of our Asiatic possessions' (cited in Digby 1901:89). This policy, while undercutting the manufacture of domestic textiles, also strangled the old and famous textile centres of India.

In Bengal, Calcutta's early commercial viability had rested largely on the export of Murshidabad silks and muslins (which was now replaced by the export of jute and tes; 16 1x : 269—70) The classic example of de-industrialization and the resultant de-urbanization was Deccan. Its famed muslins, patronized by the Mughal Court and introduced into Europe about 1670, were exported to the tune of between 30 to 40 lakh rupees annually until the end of the eighteenth-century; they fell radically in value to eight and a half lakhs in 1807, and practically ceased after 1817. This trend was paralleled by Dacca's depopulation: of its 200,000 inhabitants in 1801, only about 67,000 remained in 1830 (IG XI: 110-11, 116). A British visitor in 1824 found Dacca to be 'merely the wreck of its ancient grandeur. Its trade is reduced to the sixtieth part of what it was, and overgrown with jungle. ...The cotton produced in this district is mostly sent to England raw, and the manufactures of England are preferred by the people of Dacca themselves for their cheapness' (Heber 1873, I:92).

The English trade with South India had hinged partly on cotton fabrics, especially muslins, printed cloth, and white calicoes (deriving their name from Calicut). At the end of the eighteenth-century, the export of cotton fabrics from India to Britain formed one-third of the total of all Indian exports. After a hundred years, in 1902, Madras exported fabrics worth 59 lakhs and imported foreign machine-made fabrics worth 171 lakhs. Hardest hit were the cotton-printing industry of Masulipatam and the silk weaving industry of Madurai (IG XV: 229-7;291).

In Western India, the Company's commercial interests were tied to the cloth-weaving centres of Gujarat, chiefly Ahmedabad and Surat. Ahmedabad's prosperity, according to a local proverb, hung on three threads—gold, silk, and cotton. All three were severed by the British competition. It was a testimony to Ahmedabad's resilience that it was later able to adopt modern industrial technology and successfully fight Manchester with its own weapons (Gillion 1968). Surat, unable to accomplish a similar transition, sustained a severe loss of its textile manufacture, in addition to its earlier loss of port functions and ship-building industry. By 1825 the trade of Surat, according to an eye-witness account, was 'of very trifling consequence, consisting of little but raw cotton, which is shipped in boats for Bombay. All the manufactured goods of the country are undersold by the English, except kincob and shawls, for which there is very little demand; a dismal decay has consequently taken place in the circumstances of the native merchants' (Heber 1873, II:123).

Introduction of Industrial Technology in India

The logical recipients of the modern industrial technology were also the Presidency towns. The pioneering cotton mill in India was erected on the banks of the Hugly in 1818, although textile manufacture gravitated later to Bombay (GBCI, I: 486). Calcutta's industry, supported by European capital and enterprise, was concentrated at the more accessible Howrah city stretching in a seven-mile strip along the river, lined with 54 factories, employing 51,000 hands in 1901. While the primary emphasis was on jute processing (done in 9 jute mills, 7 jute presses, and 4 rope works), there was a considerable diversification of manufacture, which included six cotton mills, five railway workshops, four engineering workshops, and four iron foundries (IG XII: 209-10, 213-15).

But the country's premier industrial centre was Bombay. Its first cotton mill became operational in 1854, and the combination of indigenous enterprise and capital, coupled with easy availability of raw cotton and cheap labour, led to rapid proliferation. The end of the century found Bombay firmly entrenched as the unrivalled textile centre of the country, with 76 out of its total of 138 factories in 1901 being cotton mills; and Ahmedabad had captured the second position. By 1908, half of Bombay's 166 factories were cotton mills; there were also 16 printing presses and 15 iron works and foundries. Together these factories employed 107,739 men, 23,767 women, and 4,157 children (GBCI I:485-6).

Only in Madras, and in South India in general, did industry fail to take root, and the development of factories remained insignificant in the nineteenth-century. In 1903 there were only 12 cotton-spinning and weaving mills in the Presidency, employing 12,000 hands daily (IG XVI:294-5).

Construction of Railway Networks

The other significant application of industrial technology was the construction of railways which revolutionalized transportation. As with the earlier British route system, the railways were made to converge on the Presidency towns, and soon superseded the existing roads, navigable rivers, and coastal shipping for the transportation of goods and passengers. The railway networks impacted the urban scene in three ways: the Presidency towns enjoyed additional advantages of centrality; the fates of existing towns were decided mainly by whether or not they were serviced by the railways; and all railway junction towns grew rapidly.

The first railway track in India was laid between Bombay and Thane in 1853 and the entire stretch up to Pune through the Borghat pass was completed in 1864. Soon Bombay was also connected with Gujarat, Central India and North India, as well as Calcutta and Madras (GBCI I: 344-7). Madras and Calcutta (or more accurately Howrah) were similarly made the regional focal points of the railway network.

The decline of old towns bypassed by the railway was seen in cases such as Satara in the Deccan, but most dramatically in the case of the river ports in the north. Farrukhabad on the Ganga (situated outside the Bengal Presidency) was 'an interesting example of a river port whose former importance has disappeared since the railways became the great arteries of trade'; the same fate was shared by other river ports, such as Mirzapur, Fyzabad, and Chapra (Stamp 1986: 322, 324-5).

Colonial 'Primacy' and Indigenous 'De-urbanization'

The indigenous regional urban networks were distinguished by, firstly, the dispersal of urban functions among specialized centres, such as those based on governmental, economic (both manufacturing and commercial), religious, and educational functions; and secondly, a relatively balanced hierarchy of towns by size. In sharp contrast, the inevitable result of British colonial rule was the concentration of all major urban functions in the Presidency towns which claimed disproportionate predominance.

In Western India, for example, indigenous textile manufacture had been concentrated at Ahmedabad and Surat, the former being also the centre for inland trade and the latter for maritime trade and ship-building. The political power centres in Gujarat included Ahmedabad under the Mughals, and Baroda under the Maratha Chief Gaekwad; while Maharashtra was dominated by Pune which was the seat of the Peshwas with a considerable reputation as a centre of learning, by Satara, and Kolhapur. Among the principal religious centres were included Dwarka and Somnath in Gujarat; and Nashik, Kolhapur, and Pandharpur in Maharashtra. However, by the mid-nineteenth-century, Bombay had become the region's principal maritime commercial centre, largest port equipped with its own dockyards and ship-building, military and naval stronghold, administrative capital, and premier centre for Western education (as well as the focus of Protestant Christianity, being the seat of the Anglican and other Protestant bishops). Soon it also became the largest industrial centre not only in Western India but in the whole subcontinent.

Eastern India had earlier exhibited a mild tendency for functional concentration, with Murshidabad serving as a political capital, a commercial centre and major river port, as well as a silk weaving centre of importance. However, many of these functions were shared by other cities, notably Dacca. British Calcutta inherited these important political, commercial, and port functions, and later added to them also modern industrial manufacture.

The indigenous functional dispersal in South India had resulted in the printed and other cotton manufacture being concentrated at Masulipatam, Walajapet and Calicut; while the major seaports were Masulipatam, Calicut and Cochin; and the seats of government were Mysore and

Tanjore. Of these, the governmental and maritime functions were chiefly attracted to Madras.

The multi-functional character of the three Presidency towns was mirrored in their distinctive spatial structure (Kosambi & Brush 1988a, 1988b). The nucleus of these cities was the fortified factory turned later into a military-administrative citadel—Fort William in Calcutta, Fort St. George in Madras, and Bombay Castle in Bombay. The fort was surrounded by an esplanade, originally intended to provide a clear range of fire from the fort, and later preserved as a recreational open space.[14] Beyond, the semi-circular city fanned out in two broad ethnic sectors, with the British and other Europeans (invariably but without apparent reason) in the south and the Indians in the north. Within the Indian sector (initially labelled the Native or Black Town), commercial and residential land uses were mixed, while in the British sector (originally the European or White Town) the commercial zone acquired the character of the Central Business District of Western cities, and the residential population tended to move away centrifugally to 'garden houses' in the suburbs. The two sectors were largely the mirror images of each other, with some major deviations: the military cantonment was located in the British sector (indicating the priority of defence concerns), and the industrial zone (with its noise, pollution, and workers' colonies) grew along the periphery of the Indian sector.

The functional concentration in the Presidency towns was reflected also in their enormous population size, which raised them to the status of 'primate cities' in their respective regions, far outdistancing the next largest cities. The phenomenon was considerably aided by the steady depopulation of major indigenous metropolises. The successive maritime commercial, political, and industrial rise of the Presidency towns spelled the doom of indigenous seaports, governmental centres, and manufacturing towns. The effects of the colonial pressures were sometimes aggravated by natural disasters. The phenomenon of de-urbanization (discussed in detail in Bhattacharya 1984: 277-9; and Habib 1985:364-7) was as devastating as the growth of the Presidency towns was spectacular.[15] Probably the worst case of urban decay was Murshidabad which, from an estimated size of 200,000 in the mid-eighteenth-century, plummeted to 46,182 at the first Presidency census of 1872. Neighbouring Dacca, also estimated to contain 200,000 people in 1630, registered 69,212 in 1872. In the south, the population of Masulipatam, said to approximate 200,00 in 1672, sank to 36,188 exactly two centuries later. In Western India, Ahmedabad in the early seventeenth and Surat in the late seventeenth-century accommodated between 100,000 and 200,000 people; after a subsequent period of depression, however, they were able to register a recovery in 1872, with their respective populations (including the cantonments) recorded at 119,672 and 107,855 (Habib 1984; Census 1901). Pune, from an estimated 130,000 in 1815 fell to 70,000 in 1851, rising gradually to 118,868 in 1872 almost entirely thanks to the presence of the adjacent British civil-military station (Kosambi 1980).

In sharp contrast, the three Presidency towns which were struggling for survival at the end of the seventeenth-century, were firmly embedded as the regional primate cities two centuries later. In the Bombay Presidency, the Census of 1901 showed Bombay city (776,006) to be 4.2 times larger than Ahmedabad city-cantonment (185-889), 5.1 times larger than Pune city-cantonment (153,320), and 6 times larger than Surat (119,366). In the Madras Presidency, Madras (509,346) was respectively 4.8 and 4.9 times larger than Madurai (105,984) and Trichinopoly (104,721). (Bangalore, though larger than these two cities, was not part of the British area of the Presidency at this time; and its rapid growth in the twentieth-century has substantially reduced the primacy of Madras in South India). The classic case of primacy, however, was and remains, Calcutta. In 1901, Calcutta (847,796) was 5.4 times larger than Howrah (157,594) which was counted as a separate town, and 6.3 times larger than Patna (134,785) which was then part of the Bengal Presidency. With the inclusion of Howrah and the suburbs, Calcutta's population in 1901 shot up to 1,106,738, which earned it a rank among the ten largest cities in the world (IG IX: 261). In the twentieth-century, Calcutta has continued to tower over all other cities in the entire region of Eastern India.

As the phenomenon of regional primacy continues in a large measure today, so do most of the other urban trends introduced by the British colonial domination.

NOTES

[This article is a revised version of the paper presented at the Seminar on 'Aspects of Structural Changes in the Colonial Indian Economy' organized jointly by the History Department of Jamia Millia Islamia and Nehru Memorial Museum & Library, at New Delhi in March 1989.]

1. The model of this process of colonial urban transformation, already described in the context of Western India (Kosambi 1987), is sought to be

refined in this essay, and the claim of its replication in the other major regions of Indian substantiated.

2. A possible objection that outdated writings of little current relevance are being resurrected here can be easily dispelled by browsing through the social science literature on 'Urbanization in India' during the last decade. This exercise was undertaken by the present author for an exhaustive trend report on the subject, recently submitted to the Indian Council of Social Science Research.
3. A concise statement by Pearson (1976:5) identifies the two prominent biases in historical writing on India as 'whiggishness' and 'Euro-centricity'—'the former reading back from the present to find the significance of the past, the latter looking at things Indian through European spectacles'.
4. The correlation between types of cultural change and the indigenous-Western dichotomy is additionally problematic in the Indian case because of the several centuries of intervening Muslim political and cultural domination. This raises the complex question of whether to treat the Muslim cities as 'orthogenetic' (being non-Western) or as 'heterogenetic' (being originally foreign). The nature and extent of the Muslim impact on Indian society is appraised, within the context of the 'modernization' debate, by Singh (1986:60-84).
5. For an extensive review of King (1990), see Kosambi (1990).
6. The term 'proto-colonialism' was coined by the present author in 1986 while analysing colonial urban changes in Western India (and used in Kosambi 1987). It was subsequently discovered from Basu (1985) that the same term had already been introduced at a conference on the colonial port cities of Asia held some years earlier in the USA. From this volume, however, it appears that the term was used rather loosely at this conference, more as a tentative suggestion than as a conceptual tool. This impression was strengthened by the fact that some of the conference participants, with whom the present author had an opportunity to discuss the subject, were not familiar with the term.
7. In his book *Colonial Urban Development* (1976) King characterizes the colonial urban areas such as cantonments and hill stations as the products of industrial colonialism. This seems questionable, because these colonial settlement types arose from the exigencies of military control and the need (coupled with the opportunity) to create summer resorts. In terms of the colonial dynamic, they follow territorial conquest (and are connected with the second phase) and predate industrial development (or the third phase in our scheme). It was a matter of accident that in the case of Delhi, on which King has focussed, the phase of military conquest was delayed until after the advent of industrialization.
8. The port cities of Bombay, Calcutta, and Madras are often described as 'Presidency towns' (e.g. Brush 1970). The term seems to be used in two senses: as the seats of the English East India Company's Presidents or

Governors, and as the administrative capitals of the subsequently established Presidencies. The same practice is followed here. Elsewhere we have used the terms 'Indo-British ports' or 'colonial port cities in India' to indicate the three cities (e.g. Kosambi 1986, Kosambi & Brush 1988a, 1988b).

9. For details, see Kosambi (1987).
10. This brief account of the rise of Bombay draws heavily on Kosambi (1980, 1985, and 1987). Separate references are therefore kept to a minimum.
11. For a general description of the British cantonment-civil station complex, see Brush (1962). Examples of detailed case studies are: King (1976) for Delhi, and Kosambi (1980) for Pune.
12. See Mitchell (1972) also for a detailed analysis of the rationale, location, and distribution of hill stations in India as a backdrop for her study of Kodaikanal.
13. Height possessed a physical as well as symbolic significance, as summed up in a telling comment on the structure of Shimla, the country's premier hill station: 'There can be few places in the world where the upper ten was so literally upper; the Viceroy and the Commander-in-Chief had naturally the best peaks' (Spate & Learmonth 1967: 218).
14. In the case of Bombay, the entire old town or 'Fort', rather than only Bombay Castle, was surrounded by a wall and esplanade. The residential extensions of the Fort leapfrogged over the esplanade.
15. The following population figures are taken from Habib (1984) and Census 1901. There is an unavoidable discrepancy between the pre-census population estimates given here and those cited elsewhere in the text.

REFERENCES

Arasaratnam, Sinnapah. *Merchants, Companies and Commerce on the Coromandel Coast 1650-1740* (Delhi, 1986).

Bhattacharya, S. 'Eastern India [Regional Economy (1957-1857)]' in *The Cambridge Economic History of India*, vol. 2, ed. by Dharma Kumar (1984), pp. 270-332.

Bradnock, Robert W. *Urbanization in India* (London: John Murray, 1984).

Breese, Gerald. *Urbanization in Newly Developing Countries* (Englewood Cliffs, NJ: Prentice Hall, 1966).

Brush, John E. 'The Morphology of Indian Cities' in *India's Urban Future*, ed by Roy Turner (California, 1962), pp. 57-70.

_______ 'The Growth of the Presidency Towns' in *Urban India: Society, Space and Images*, ed. by R.G. Fox (Durham, N.C., 1970), pp. 91-114.

Caird, Sir James. *India, The Land and The People*. 3rd ed. (London, 1884).

Census of India, 1901. 1903. vol. I-A India, Part II-Tables. Calcutta.

Census of India, 1901. 1902. vol. VII-Calcutta, Town and Suburbs. Part I-A Short

History of Calcutta.

Census of the Bombay Presidency, 1872, 1875. General Reports and Tables. Part II. Bombay.

Census of the Town of Madras, 1871.

Crane, R.I. 'Urbanism in India'. *American Journal of Sociology*, vol. 60, no. 5 (March 1955), pp. 463-470.

Das Gupta, Ashin. 'The Merchants of Surat, c. 1700-1750' in *Elites in South Asia*, ed. by E. Leach and S.N. Mukherjee, (Cambridge, 1970).

_______ *Indian merchants and the Decline of Surat*, c. 1700-1750 (Wiesbaden: Franz Steiner Verlag, 1979).

Digby, William. '*Prosperous*' *British India; A Revelation from Official Records* (London, 1901).

Elphinstone, Mountstuart. 1819. *Report*. Appendix to Chaplin's *Report... of Administration, Introduced into the Conquered Territory...*, 1824, reprinted 1838.

_______ *Report on the Territories Conquered from the Peishwa*. 2nd ed. Calcutta. (Reprinted, Bombay, 1838).

Emerson, R. 'Colonialism'. *International Encyclopaedia of the Social Sciences*, ed. by D.L. Sills (Macmillan & Free Press, 1968), vol. 3. pp. 1-6.

The English factories in India, ed. by *W. Forster* (Oxford, 1911-27).

Falkland (The Viscountess). *Chow-Chow; being Selections from a Journal kept in India*... 2 Vols. (London, 1857).

Furber, Holden. *Rival Empires of Trade in the Orient, 1600-1800* (Minneapolis, 1976).

The Gazetteer of Bombay City and Island, (1909), 3 vols. (Bombay: Govt. of Maharashtra, 1977).

Gazetteer of the Bombay Presidency, vol. II. Gujarat: Surat and Broach (Bombay: Government Central Press, 1877).

Gazetteer of the Bombay Presidency, vol. XVIII. Poona. 3 parts (Bombay: Government Central Press, 1885).

Gillion, K.L. *Ahmedabad: A Study in Indian Urban History* (California, 1968).

Grose, John-Henry. *A Voyage to the East Indies* (London, 1757).

Habib, Irfan. 'Population [c.1500-1750]' in *The Cambridge Economic History of India*. vol. 1 ed. by Tapan Raychaudhuri and Irfan Habib, pp. 163-171.

_______ 'Studying a Colonial Economy— Without Perceiving Colonialism'. *Modern Asian Studies*, vol. 19, no. 13, 1985 pp. 355-381.

Heber, Reginald. *Narrative of a Journey through the Upper Provinces of India, from Calcutta to Bombay, 1824-1825*. 2 vols (1873, new edn. London: John Murray).

The Imperial Gazetteer of India. 1907-9. New edn. 26 vols.

King, A.D. *Colonial Urban Development*, (London, 1976).

_______ 'Colonialism and the Development of the modern Asian City; Some Theoretical Considerations' in *The City in South Asia, Pre-Modern and*

Modern, ed. by K. Ballhatchet & J. Harrison (London, 1980), pp. 1-19.

_______ *Urbanism, Colonialism, and the World Economy* (London & New York, 1990).

Knight, M.M. 'Colonies'. *Encyclopedia of the Social Sciences* ed. by E.R.A. Seligman. vol. III, (New York, 1930), pp. 653-663.

Kosambi, Meera. *Bombay and Poona: A Socio-Ecological Study of Two Indian Cities, 1650-1900*. Stockholm University: Dept. of Sociology (printed Ph.D. thesis, 1980).

_______ 'Commerce, Conquest and the Colonial City: The Role of Locational Factors in the Rise of Bombay'. *Economic & Political Weekly*, vol. 20, no. 1 (5 January 1985), pp. 32-37.

_______ 'Colonial Urban Transformation in Maharashtra' (to be published in the proceedings of the Second International Conference on Maharashtra: Culture and Society, held at Poona University in January 1987).

_______ 'Indigenous and Colonial Urban Development in Western Maharashtra', *City, Contryside and Society in Maharashtra* ed. by D.W. Attwood, M. Israel, & N.K. Wagle (eds.), University of Toronto: Centre for South Asian Studies, 1988), pp. 1-34.

_______ 'The Colonial City in Its Global Niche' (Review Article). *Economic & Political Weekly*, vol. 25, no. 51 (22 Dec. 1990), pp. 2775-81.

Kosambi, Meera and Brush, John E. 'Three Colonial Port Cities in India'. *Geographical Review*, vol. 78, no. 1 (January 1988), pp. 34-37.

_______ 'Early European Suburbanization in the Indo-British Port Cities' in *Asian Urbanization: Problems and Processes,* edited by Frank J. Costa et al. (Stuttgart: Gebruder Borntraeger, 1988b), pp. 9-23.

Lewandowsky, Susan J. 'Urban Gwoth and Municipal Development in the Colonial City of Madras, 1860-1900'. *Journal of Asian Studies*, vol. 34, no. 2 (February 1975). pp. 341-360.

McGee, T.G. *The Southeast Asian City*. London: Bell, 1967).

Mitchell, Nora. *The Indian Hill Station: Kodaikanal* (University of Chicago: Dept. of Geography. Research Paper No. 141, 1972).

Mohsin, K.M. 'Murshidabad in the Eighteenth-century' in *The City in South Asia,* ed. by K. Ballhatchet & J. Harrison, (London, 1980), pp. 69-87.

Murphey, Rhodes. 'Urbanization in Asia' in *The City in Newly Developing Countries*, ed. by G. Breese (London, 1972), pp. 58-73.

Newell, H.A. *Madras: The Birth Place of British India.*, (Madras, 1919).

Oliver, A.K. *The Hill Station of Matheran* (Bombay: Times of India Press, 1905).

Pearson, M.N. *Merchants and Rulers in Gujarat: The Response of the Portuguese in the Sixteenth Century* (California, 1976).

_______ *Coastal Western India: Studies from the Portuguese Records* (New Delhi, 1981).

Ranson, C.W. *A City in Transition: Studies in the Social Life of Madras* (Madras: The Christian Literature Society for India, 1938).

Redfield, Robert and Singer, Milton. 'The Cultural Role of Cities'. *Economic*

Development & Cultural Change, vol. 4, no. 1 (October 1954), pp. 53-73.

Singh, Yogendra. *Modernization of Indian Tradition* (Jaipur, 1986).

Sjoberg, G. *The Preindustrial City*, (Glencoe, Free Press, 1960).

_______ 'Cities in Developing and in Industrial Societies : A Cross-Cultural Analysis' in *The Study of Urbanization*, edited by P.M. Hauser & L.F. Schnore (New York, 1965), pp. 213-263.

Spate, O.H.K. and Learmonth, A.T.A. *India and Pakistan: A General and Regional Geography*. 3rd rev. edn. (London: Methuen & Co., 1967).

Stamp, Dudley. *Asia: A Regional and Economic Geography* (First Indian edn. New Delhi, 1986).

Twining, Thomas. *Travels in India A Hundred Tears Ago* edited by W. H. G. Twining (London, 1893).

The British Town-Planners and India: A Postscript to Eric Stokes' *The English Utilitarians and India*

NARAYANI GUPTA

> It is the undue attention to formal statements of policy aims that . . . . has grossly misled historians about the working practice of British rule. For these both unduly anticipate the introduction of modernising administration and exaggerate its power to alter society. Colonial rule is peculiarly subject to the distortions of bureaucratic structures, which mistake the report for the bullet, the plan for action, and what one clerk says to another for history.[1]

Social engineering in British India in the 1830s, inspired partly by Utilitarian principles and partly by pragmatic considerations, touched on many aspects of policy but not that of urban regulation. The beginning of interventionism in towns occurred as a consequence of the Revolt of 1857, when for a few months the towns of Delhi, Kanpur and Lucknow broke loose from official control. From that time, the regulation of urban areas became an aspect of policy*. The components of such regulation were control of public space, some control in the allocation of private space, concern for public health and for the security of the European inhabitants.

Much of modern Indian town-planning is received wisdom and it is therefore necessary to sketch the course of the town-planning

* By policy I mean principles spelt out by the Government based on considerations of state necessity and on recommendatons of commissions, disscussions with interest-groups and the views of individual officials. In varying degrees these reflected, diverged from or anticipated policies adopted in Britain.

'movement' in Britain. Town-planning, as distinct from town-building, is a concern noticeable from the 1830s, following on the British industrial revolution and the attendant pressures of population in towns.[2] The anti-urbanism reflected in the poetry of Blake and Wordsworth[3] was specific to the English; in Edinburgh the notion of the 'City beautiful' was seen as early as 1767 when an extensive 'New Town' had been laid out. The term 'town-planning' is used sometimes in a general and sometimes in a very specific sense. It implies intervention by official agencies through urban and regional management; such intervention affects social relations, the quality of life and the content of politics. In the 1830s officials in Britain (as in India two decades later) were anxious to check disease, avert social conflict and to improve the aesthetic quality of their towns. The cholera epidemic of 1830, the jerry-built industrial towns, the swelling urban populations with large colonies of Irish and European refugees, and the warning tremors of the Chartist agitation added up to an urban crisis. The writings of Dickens and Engels forced people to take a hard look at the industrial towns instead of merely dreaming of escaping to the countryside. Three elements of urban regulation were introduced by law—town surveys (on the suggestion of the Royal Commission on the State of Large Towns, 1844), control of city extensions (through municipal competitions for designs for town-extensions in the 1850s) and health safeguards (by the Public Health Act, 1875). A fourth element was the architectural one-showpiece areas of the towns proclaimed the triumphant industrial city, outlined in the massive facades of the town-hall and the railway station.

By the 1880s it had become obvious that all these regulations had a class-bias, and ignored the 'other nation' (Disraeli's term for the poor). The scathing and well-researched work of Charles Booth and the Webbs made the policymakers realize the travails of the poor[4]. As regards services, the European Conference on Demography and Hygeine (1891) showed the British how efficiently the Germans were coping with newly industrializing towns through zoning and population regulation. From the 1860s, many schemes for rehousing 'artisans and labourers' were worked out; it was quickly realized that while acquiring and rebuilding would be expensive, building houses in the suburbs on the outskirts of towns was relatively cheaper. 'Improvement Trusts' were created with powers to demolish old houses, widen roads and open up new suburbs (again Scotland scored a first, since the earliest Trusts were in Glasgow and Edinburgh).[5] The Housing Act of 1923 was concerned with new areas outside towns as part of a long-term plan to decentralize industrial populations. The Garden City plan of Ebenezer Howard, begun at the turn of the century, was a modification of the concept of suburbanization; it was proposed to buy agricultural land and develop part of it into a complete town for 30,000 people. When the population grew beyond this, another 'garden city' would be laid out. The Town-Planning Act of 1909 (modified in 1919 to become the Town and Country Planning Act) aimed to co-ordinate planned spatial growth, housing and health. The Town-Planning Institute, set up in 1913, did not see planning in terms of such social policy, but as an exercise in architecture and urban design. Thus, by the time the British polity was under stress because of the First World War, 'town-planning' was a widely-used term, used to mean any or all of the following—city extension, housing for the poor, sanitary and environmental regulations, architectural design.

Debates on various aspects of town-planning were transferred to India very soon after their being aired in Britain. This does not, however, mean that urban space had been left to the play of market-forces till then. From the early 19th-century, the social geometry of the grid in cantonments and civil lines had provided graded housing to the transient British officials.[6] The Sanitary Commission of 1864 laid down guidelines to keep the 'British' areas free from infection. A calculated distance from the areas where Indians lived, a bifurcation in the water-supply lines and *cordons sanitaires* of gardens, all ensured, it was believed, clean air and freedom from infections. The 1857 Revolt led to rebuilding of large areas in Lucknow and Delhi but the imperatives were different from those after the London fire of 1666, for that of racial segregation and security were uppermost.[7] Exactly contemporary with Haussmann in Paris, but with no evidence of being influenced by his ruthless 'planning', which cut boulevards through a city as congested as Delhi or Lucknow, were the measures which were taken to enable swift military deployment in these towns. Organic links between different areas were snapped by driving roads and railways through city centres, and by clearing shooting-ranges. The unity of older towns was irretrievably lost, and haphazard, often demoralized, suburbanization occurred. The railway traveller did not have to see much of this—the architectural showpieces created in the late 19th-century gave an impression of prosperity and stability as successfully as they concealed the squalor.[8]

Urban India grew behind the facade of the townhalls and museums, and along the railway-lines. The three Presidency towns resembled London; they were sprawling, multifunctional, primate cities. The provincial capitals, the 50 cantonment-towns, the 30-odd 'hill-stations', 'railway and industrial towns, also grew in size, though all this did not add up to 'urbanization'. The late nineteenth-century which saw many important Royal Commissions, could well have had one on towns, but urban problems were not considered to be in need of urgent remedies. In Britain, as we have seen, urbanism was treated not in a holistic, but a fragmented, fashion. In India local officials were more powerful than in Britain, because of the limited role of the 'elected' element in municipalities.[9] Some municipalities were also well-endowed in terms of land (the municipal boundaries of the Presidency towns had been thrown out well beyond the settled areas, and in old Mughal towns like Delhi and Agra vast areas of former royal properties had been taken over by the municipalities). In terms of finances they were, however, far poorer than the British ones.[10] The power of the officials was not matched by imaginative policy, and the wealth was not backed with vigilance. The path of local government in British India, therefore, was strewn with the pebbles of petty disputes and overrun with the undergrowth of encroachments.

Officials reported not the untidy growth, but the increasing numbers of town-dwellers. 'Growing' towns was a matter for self-congratulation for census-enumerators. Instead of recognizing much of it as the product of 'distress-migration' from an impoverished countryside, they explained it as caused by the growth of industries, thus making it appear as parallel to Britain's demographic history of a century earlier.[11] But complacency gave way to alarm when the demographic curve of the 1890s became transformed into the politics of crowded streets and battles over public space, and to rampant epidemic. The plague (1896-1907) did what the cholera epidemic of 1830 had done in Britain; it acted as the great leveller that did not discriminate between various areas of the town. The fallacy of the growth-fetish was seen in Bombay, where the epidemic began; while 'there was an absolute qualitative expansion in economic activity and comparable growth in total employment, the incomes of the majority of Bombay's inhabitants fell in real terms, environmental and ecological conditions worsened and an ordeal of death tainted the development process'.[12] Likewise in Calcutta when the city was 'surveyed' in 1913, the disastrous effects of 'fifty years of neglect' were evident.[13] The population of the city was fast outstripping its holding capacity.

There was a market for local, casual labour, which explained how immigrants were allowed to carve out bustees on plots sublet by wealthy Indian landlords.[14] In theory officials were agreed that people from crowded neighbourhoods should be moved to new areas beyond the town.

But such a measure was risky in the urban India of the 1890s where an aggressively nationalist and populist politics was growing, reminiscent for Britons of the Hungry' Forties and the Chartist agitation. Policy had to walk a delicate tightrope between intervention in the name of public health and callousness in the name of laissez-faire.

Since 'Improvement Trusts' were an article of faith in 19th-century Britain, they were set up in India too (Bombay, in 1898, scoring a first).[15] E. P. Richards, doing a survey for Calcutta Improvement Trust in 1913, was unambiguous in his recommendation that only by giving the Trust the powers of a town-planning authority could the congestion and the chaotic housing be relieved. If in Britain the difficulties were the cost of land and the problem of changing land-use, in India the squatter's strength was that there were no clear records of ownership rights (by contrast to the meticulous records in agricultural land rights). It was also difficult to adopt a Haussmann-type policy combining short-term ruthlessness with long-term benefits in Indian towns, where there were no clearcut class-based neighbourhoods, so that 'clearances' would mow down not only slums but also middle-class housing.

The three decades from 1914 were a crucial period for urban policy. The town-planning Acts in India after 1915 (the Bombay Act being the first) followed British laws and bye-laws faithfully. British policy was incremental and gradualist, but the attraction of the one grand solution never quite disappeared. In 1916 the Indian Industrial Commission looked optimistically to towns in India as 'possible centres for modernizing Indian society' whatever that might mean. To officials, town-planning implied three things in order of priority—a good traffic system, the development of city extensions and housing for the poor. A limited sense of social responsibility was shown by Bombay Corporation and the Calcutta Jute Mills in the 1920s, when they provided some houses for their workers.

One solution to the problem of towns exceeding their holding capacity was to build new towns, as the USSR did in the 1920s. The Town and Country Planning Act in Britain (1932) drew attention to the need for Regional Planning and the Barlow Commission on the Distribution of Industrial Population (1939) assumed that the main concern of town-planners should be that of distributing the population in the country evenly. The British Indian government, however, had no policy to establish new towns. This exercise was to be launched later, in the 1950s, as part of Nehruvian economics.

Urban management in India from the 1850s till the early 1900s had been concerned with limited aims—security and health essentially for the 'British' areas. City extension schemes, like Lahore's Model Town and Delhi's Western Extension Area, were also partly political measures, intended to reduce congestion and tension-points in the older cities. From the early 1900s Indians were offered the model of more holistic planning. A. E. Mirams, speaking to the Poona municipality about the Bombay Town-Planning Act, said that 'It was not desired to force the Act on the people but rather to give them an opportunity of asking for it to be applied'.[17] The most enthusiastic response came not from British India but from the Indian princes, who were also spending lavishly on monumental architecture. Geddes noticed that 'To the feudal princes Lanchester (H.V. Lanchester) has given a fresh constructional impulse, respect for Indian architecture, craftsmanship and way of life'.[18] The architect-planner Fayazuddin (in Hyderabad, Bhopal and Bahawalpur) and Mirza Ismail (in Jaipur, Mysore, Hyderabad and Bangalore) were able to implement many 'Improvements'. In Hyderabad, where a town-planning policy was adopted as early as 1908, 'there was not that divorce between government and municipal agencies which has been responsible for the failure of so many local government institutions in British India'.[20] Kolhapur set up a 'city Development Ministry' in 1921.[21] In Travancore the Town-Planning Act (1933) was superceded by a Town and Country Planning Act in 1945. The German-British architect-planner Otto Koenigsberger was to recall 'I accepted a post with the Government of Mysore, at the time a very active and progressive state... As government Architect and Planning Officer I had the widest possible scope, ranging from furniture design to the planning of several new towns. There were no other architects either in public service or in private practice'.[22]

Town-planning, then, was one of the many stars to which officials hitched their wagons after the trauma of the First War. But its utility —or rather, the utility of town-planning as the officials understood it— was questioned by Patrick Geddes, the Scottish sociologist who believed that planning should do the minimum necessary and not the maximum possible, and that each town should be seen in itself, and not subjected to patent remedies. People should be taught 'to distinguish between a city's heritage and its burden'.[23] In India, he was excited to discern a rich heritage of town-building. Indian monumental architecture had been long admired; its historic town-planning traditions were appreciated only in the 1920s and 30s, thanks to Geddes and to the 'discovery' of Mohenjodaro. Geddes fired a generation of Indians with enthusiasm for their history and with a sense of mission. ('City planning is always part of imperial policy. But people in all cities are asking-where do we come in?' - Geddes[24]). Apart from translations of Indian texts on town-planning, a manual on town-planning was written by Linton Bogle which recalled old prescriptions and suggested remedies for modern urban problems [25] It is significant that the fifty reports on Indian towns which Geddes prepared were literally shelved, lost and forgotten[26] and Indian planning practice later often came uncomfortably close to doing what he had feared British planners would do: become prone to fads, and create a melange of a German town extension, a Paris boulevard, an English garden village and an American civic centre.

A bold attempt at total town-planning was the exercise of building a new capital in Delhi. This was the era of new imperial capitals, Pretoria and Canberra being the others. Later Indian planning ideology was to be heavily influenced by the form of New Delhi. In spite of being built between the outbreak of War and the Depression (1914-31) which naturally made for many economies, Lutyens' city was a landmark, a defiant break with Indian town-building practices. While its monumental architecture was in line with older Indian town-building traditions, the hierarchical zoning (the principle seen earlier on a much smaller scale in civil lines and cantonments, and was to be repeated in Chandigarh) marked a break with the north Indian mohulla-pattern. The new planned area of Patna and the industrial town of Jamshedpur had points of resemblance with New Delhi in their townscapes, with formal zoning laid out by foreign architects.[27] In India no one made any harsh indictment like Ingrams did about West Asia. 'A town-planner had far better keep his town-planning to his own country. When European architects and town-planners get together in 'embellishing' purely Eastern towns the results are often even more deplorable than when the Arab builds in European style'.[28] Claude Batley in 1946 deplored the fact that 'Modern buildings and location and town-planning copy the west, forgetting Indian tradition'.[29] Koenigsberger, looking back on his 'Indian days', recalled that the first generation of Western planners that went out to help the poor countries of the Third World thought they had a lot to teach. 'They did not realize that their ideas were specific to the West and therefore irrelevant. The early attempts to introduce British development plans into India did little to help India and a great deal to harm the reputation of the planning profession'.[30]

In the literature on urbanism, it is the voices of planners that can be heard most clearly. Indians were not critical of Western planning theory, nor did they, after the spurt of writing inspired by Geddes, show any disquiet at the growing crisis in their towns, nor for that matter were there poets or novelists who celebrated the city as Tamil Sangam poets or Urdu writers had done earlier. There is neither a Charles Booth nor a John Betjeman in modern urban India. Percival Griffiths in his *Better Towns: A study of Urban Reconstruction* (1945)[31] urged Indian soldiers returning from the War to set up Better Living Leagues to improve towns with military efficiency. B.C. Ghose's *Industrial Location for Towns* (also published in 1945) was concerned with a balanced distribution of new towns.[32] The Congress Planning Committee in the 1940s prepared a study on 'National Housing', emphasizing the need for subsidized houses.[33]

The impact of British ideology on Indian urban policy was far greater after Independence than before. This was because 'Town Planning' became a subject of study at the undergraduate level. It also acquired an institutional framework (The Bhore Health Survey Committee in 1946 had recommended a ministry of housing and town-planning for every province). The first generation of Indian planners, in the 1950s, studied urban issues on an all-India level, or on the basis of the new linguistic provinces, disregarding regional geographical differences. The Report of the Environmental Hygiene Committee (1949) recommended regional planning. But the 'small and medium towns' strategy never got off the ground, chiefly because of poor communications. Many new towns did come into being. The new provinces needed capitals. Chandigarh, Gandhi Nagar and Bhubaneswar (in Punjab, Gujarat and Orissa respectively) were designed by foreign architects.[34] Many towns were established as an emergency measure to cope with the influx of refugees after Partition.[35]

What got sidelined was regional planning. Courses of 'Town and Country Planning' remained confined to town-planning. The Master Plan drawn up for Delhi (1957-1962) sometimes reminds one of Geddes' taunt of the 'catholicity' of views among his fellow-planners. Chicago and London were among the dominant influences on the Delhi Development Authority. ('Why did these people never speak about the piece of land on which they lived and breathed?[36]) The Delhi Plan has been the model for the master-plans drawn up between 1960 and 1975 for as many as 200 Indians towns.[37]

Overcrowding and inadequate housing have been perhaps the most serious problems in Indian towns. In the zeal for 'slum clearance' there has been a mindless acceptance of the Western definition of a slum, which is based on population density. As a result centuries-old urban areas and decades-old shanty-towns are both categorized as 'slums'. There has been an absence of sensitivity in handling overcrowded areas and squatters' territories, largely because planners work at the drawing-board and do not live in the slum, as Geddes did in Edinburgh or, more recently, Gunter Heliges in Bombay. Because the European-trained engineer in India has a pedigree that goes back to the 1840s, whereas architects with diplomas from RIBA appeared only from the 1920s, there is a generation-gap crisis of communication between the two professions.[38] At the same time, since both of them label themselves 'modern', there is a culture-gap between them and the 'traditional' craftsman. Only very recently has it been recognized that India is exceptionally fortunate in having both types of skills present simultaneously.[39] It is as if alongside the *grands travaux* being executed by hightech methods in Paris a team of workers were raising, slowly and durably, another Chartres Cathedral.

The transmission of ideas from Britain and the USA to India, and the absence of information (or curiosity) about how the USSR and China have dealt with urbanism and population distribution, strengthened the myth that 'town-planning' was a western art (science?) which had been unknown in India. It is in the fitness of things that it is yet another Scotsman, Laurie Baker, who has urged Indian architects to learn from the 'traditional' craftsman.[40] As for town-planning, a systematic body of knowledge about Indian towns is needed, on the lines of Geoffrey Payne's excellent analysis of the shanty-towns in Delhi.[41] Geddes can be faulted for being over-romantic and Nehru for putting too much faith in his notion of 'modernization'. But the fire of enthusiasm in both men has to be used to light the dull expanse of reports and statistics, and to lift the discussion above minutiae as well as to bring it down from the clouds of generalization. Colin Rosser unkindly but accurately identified one of the weaknesses in Indian discussions. 'The search for all- India solutions seems to be one of India's most common development blind alleys'.[42] What Eric Stokes wrote about British Indian government holds true for Independent India too— 'Formal statements of policy aims...both unduly anticipate the introduction of modernizing administration and exaggerate its power to alter society'.

What then? Geddes speaks again, through the anthropologist Nirmal Kumar Bose. 'A weakness of our urban development in recent times has been that the citizens... do not have a hand at any stage in the making of plans. Plans are drawn up by experts... The only reason why plans are described as products of democracy is that certain representatives of the people are associated with them. The central point about Gandhiji's constructive work was that both plan as well as execution were to depend on people's own labour and organization. In the improvement of a congested part of a town, the citizens involved in the process should share actively in the making of the plan. Each *para* or *muhalla* should be developed with a sense of pride in itself. It is thus that democracy can be built up from a concern about civic problems which affect everyone's life'[43] Also what Geddes called 'folk-planning' should be given the same respectability as is enjoyed by folk music, folk-art and folk-stories. Only by demystifing 'planning' and by recognizing its local indigenous variants can towns in India hope to have a viable future.

NOTES

1. E. Stokes, *The Peasant and the Raj: Studies in agrarian society and peasant rebellion in colonial India* (Cambridge, 1978), p. 30.
2. L. Benevolo, *The History of the City* (London, 1980), p. 755.
3. R. Williams, *The Country and the City* (London, 1985), ch.13.
4. C. Booth, *Life and Labour of the People in London* (London, 1903), B. Webb, *Our Partnership* (London, 1948).
5. A. Sutcliffe, *Towards the Planned City* (Oxford, 1981), p.168.
6. A. D. King, *Colonial Urban Development: Culture, Social Power and Environment* (London, 1976).
7. V.T. Oldenberg, *The Making of Colonial Lucknow 1856-1877* (Princeton, 1984), N. Gupta, *Delhi Between Two Empires 1803-1931* (Delhi, 1981).
8. N. Evenson, *The Indian Metropolis* (Delhi, 1989).
9. H. Tinker, *Foundations of Local Self-government in India, Pakistan and Burma* (Bombay, 1967).
10. N. Gupta, op.cit. for Delhi; S.M. Nield 'Colonial urbanism: the development of Madras City in the 18th and 19th centuries', *Modern Asian Studies*, 13, 2, 1979
11. Cf. Introduction to *Census of India*, 1891.
12. I. Klein 'Urban Development and Death in Bombay City 1870-1914', *Modern Asian Studies*, 20, 4, 1986.
13. E.P. Richards, *Report on the Request of the Improvement Trust on the condition, improvement and Town Planning of the City of Calcutta* (Calcutta, 1914).
14. C. Furedy 'Whose Responsibility? Dilemmas of Calcutta's Bustee Police in the 19th Century', *South Asia*, 1982.
15. H.E. Meller, 'Urbanization and the Introduction of Modern Town Planning Ideas in India. 1900-1925' in C. Dewey and K. N. Chaudhuri (eds.), *Economy and Society* (Delhi, 1979), pp. 330-350.
16. *Report of the Indian Industrial Commission 1916-18*, Parliamentary Paper, XVII, 1919.
17. A.E. Mirams, *An Address to the Members of the Municipality and the*

Citizens of Poona on the Bombay Town Planning Act of 1915 (Poona, 1916).

18. S. Geddes, *Cities in Evolution* (London, 1915), p. 240.
19. M.V.S. Prasada Rau, *Gazetteer of District of Hyderabad* (Hyderabad, 1980), p.181 ff.
20. *Report on Town Planning in the Nizam's Dominions* (1944).
21. *Maharashtra State Gazetteer*, Kolhapur District (Bombay, 1966), p. 813 ff.
22. Interview of O. Koenigsberger, *Architectural Journal* (London), July 1982.
23. P. Geddes, 'Two steps in Civics', *Town-Planning Review*, July 1913, p. 2.
24. P. Geddes, *Cities in Evolution* (London, 1915), p. 240.
25. J.M.L. Bogle, *Town Planning in India* (Bombay, 1929).
26. H. Meller, *Patrick Geddes: Social revolutionist and city planner* (London, 1990), Chapter 8.
27. R. G. Irving, *Indian Summer: Lutyens, Baker and Imperial Delhi* (Yale, 1981); Maya Dutta, *Jamshedpur, The Growth of the City and the Region* (Calcutta, 1977).
28. H. Ingrams, *Arabia and the Isles* (London, 1942).
29. Claude Batley, *Architecture* (Calcutta, 1946).
30. O. Koenigsberger in Foreword to A. Turner (ed). *The Cities of the Poor* (London, 1980).
31. P. Griffiths, *Better Towns: A study of Urban Reconstruction in India* (Allahabad, 1945).
32. Bimal C. Ghose, *Industrial Location for Towns* (Oxford Pamphlets on Indian Affairs, no.32, 1945).
33. K.T. Shah (ed), *National Housing* (National Planning Commitee Series) (Bombay, 1948) and E.A.J. Johnson, *Organisation of Space in Developing Countries* (Harvard, 1970).
34. G. Rosen, *Western Economists and Eastern Societies* (Delhi, 1985) Chapter 3.
35. R.K. Wishwakarma and G. Jha, *Integrated Development of Small and Medium Towns* (Delhi, 1983).
36. Sadat Hasan Manto, *Partition* (New Delhi, 1991).
37. Ved Prakash, *New Towns in India* (Duke University monograph no. 8, 1969).
38. Most houses in India are built without the luxury of an architect, and many subsidised houses and public buildings are the work of engineers.
39. Craft-skills continue to be hived off in 'Craft Museums' and are not, as they used to be, an integral part of architecture, though journals like *Architecture + Design* do publish articles on older towns, under the heading 'Heritage'.
40. G.Bhatia, *Laurie Baker: Life, Work and Writings* (Delhi, 1991).
41. G.K. Payne, *Urban Housing in the Third World* (London, 1977).
42. C. Rosser, 'Urbanization in India' (Mimeo, 1972), p. 93.
43. Nirmal Kumar Bose, 'Some Problems of Urbanization', *Man in India*, Oct-Dec. 1962, 42, 4, p. 259.

Structural Change in the Industrial Base of Colonial Cities: The Calcutta Hinterland 1881-1921

ATIYA HABEEB KIDWAI

An analysis of the urban economy is essential for a comprehensive understanding of the process of development or underdevelopment which beset national or regional systems at given moments in history because cities are the foci where the essential properties of larger systems are 'grossly concentrated and intensified' (Abrams, 1978, p. 10). They are reflective of the politico-economic and spatial relationships which govern a system and are a crystallized expression of the society in which they appear (McGee, 1971, p. 31; Harvey, 1973, p. 246; Roberts, 1978, p. 8; Smith and Feagin, 1987, p. 37). Moreover, macroeconomic constraints can be better understood when we see their impact on smaller entities (Bagchi, 1987, p. 247). In this paper it is proposed, therefore, to investigate into some aspects of the 'industrial' structure of selected cities in the hinterland of Calcutta during the last phase of colonial rule in the country with a view to highlighting some of the structural changes which characterized the Indian economy during this period.

The analysis presented in this paper is restricted empirically, spatially and temporally. Only ten cities in the hinterland of Calcutta, for which consistent time-series data on some indices of industrialization were available, have been analysed between the period 1881 and 1921. It is, however, hoped that these restrictions, imposed on the universe of the study for analytical convenience, will not denude the discussion of relevance because received historical research indicates that the wider hinterland of Calcutta was the prime arena for the interplay of British purposes in India and the period under analysis witnessed the final restructuring of colonial policies. It is also conceded that the analysis presents only an overview of 'trends observed' and suffers from lack of rigour and a comprehensive treatment of historical events which unfolded during the period under investigation. This paper is no more than an exploratory attempt to provide an interdisciplinary methodology of looking at the economy of Indian cities in a historical perspective.

The paper has been divided into four sections. In section I, an attempt has been made to place the 'industrial'[1] structure of the selected cities within the broader framework of the industrialization or de-industrialization processes which characterized the country and, more specifically, the hinterland of Calcutta. In section II, the long term sectoral trends in these cities are indicated in order to assess the importance of the 'secondary'[2] sector in the overall economy of these cities. In section III, the data on labour force available in the Census of India is put to a rigorous analysis so that the structure of industries in the selected cities can be comprehensively understood. The data on industrial establishments reported in the Census of India is also discussed to buttress or question the conclusions that emerge from the analysis of labour force data.

I: The Industrialization Process and its Impact on Urban Industries

Pioneered by Romesh Dutt, D.R. Gadgil, D. Buchanan and Rajni Palme Dutt, the controversies about Indian industrialization have been debated by almost all subsequent generations of historians. The debate has, from its outset, been characterized by both a problem-oriented and a comparative dimension (Simmons, 1985, p. 611). Consequently, as Simmons has pointed out, two kinds of questions have been asked. First, how can we account for the decline or the 'de-industrialization', and second, what were the reasons for the relatively slow pace of industrialization. The explanations offered also fall into two sets. Amongst the earlier writers, those subcribing to the apologist school, assigned responsibility on the 'unpropitous socio-cultural environment' and the nationalist school on the 'non-interventionism of the colonial state'. The more recent works have focused on the 'intrinsic supply side weaknesses and/or the deficiencies of aggregate demand as a consequence of the slow or negative rate of agricultural growth which had a 'dragging effect'. In the various regions of India these factors became relatively more significant during the different phases of colonial rule. It would be worthwhile to integrate these factors into a detailed study of the colonial urban economy.

It would also be useful to situate the process of urban industrialization or de-industrialization in terms of the different phases of industrial development in the country during the second half of nineteenth and the first-quarter of the twentieth-century. This period witnessed an extended involvement of British capital and enterprise in the industrial activities in India. Gadgil (1944) in his comprehensive analysis of the evolution of industries in the country divided this period into four phases. The evolution of industries specific to the hinterland of Calcutta is discussed here in terms of the periodization given by Gadgil.

The first phase, which lasted between 1860-80, witnessed a rapid decline of the indigenous urban handicrafts as a result of the disappearance of the old clientele. The new class of buyers that emerged, i.e., the European officials and traders, had only a limited demand for Indian products which by now had also declined in their artistic value (Vera Antsey, 1929, p.106). However, a new phase in the evolution of Indian industries was triggered off by two distant wars. The Crimean War had cut off hemp supplies to Dundee and had created a great demand for raw jute; and the American Civil War, in its turn, had created an inflated demand for raw cotton. 'With money pouring in and fibres pouring out it would have been strange indeed had no body turned his mind to local manufacture' (Spate, 1954, p. 309). Jute and cotton mills, mostly urban based, were therefore established to meet this demand. A large number of railway workshops were also opened to cater to the needs of railway construction. These again were urban based.

During the second phase (1880-95), cotton, jute, tea and coal mining industries made steady progress. The development of these industries led to the industrial growth of some cities but their impact was localized. The direct impact of these industries was confined to the commercialization of agricultural crops. Their growth did not materially change the profile of secondary production in the country. Coal mining led to the growth of some coal towns, but they did not develop into industrial centres, as some towns in the coal belt of contemporary England had done, because in India the development of metallurgy remained insignificant during this period.

The third phase (1895-1914) started with the severe famines of 1896-97, the impact of which lasted until 1905 and checked the industrial development of the country. Simultaneously the Swadeshi movement which meant a boycott of foreign goods, gathered momentum and strengthened nationalist feelings (Bipan Chandra, 1966, pp. 122-41). This gave a new spurt to the development of consumer goods industries like soap, hairoil, household drugs, enamel ware and chinaware. Some of these industries were set up in urban areas though many of them developed in rural areas to cater to the rural markets. Indian leaders had, by now, also become aware of the necessity of the development of machine industries as well as banking services for the industrial expansion in the country. Consequently the first pig iron flowed into the Jamshedpur moulds in 1911. Voices were also raised against the free trade policy, which, from the Indian point of view, was decidely illiberal (Spate, 1954, p. 310). Bagchi characterized this period as 'the most hopeful...for the growth of the Indian industry in a colonial context' (Bagchi, 1972, p. 77).

The last phase (1914-20) commenced with the First World War. The War highlighted a number of weaknesses in the industrial structure of the country. The most apparent was an almost complete lack of machines to make machines. While the untaxed import of machinery contributed to the growth of consumption industries, it seriously inhibited the development of production goods industries. The economy also paid heavily for the governmental policy of purchasing stores in England, a policy 'at once discriminatory and lacking discrimination' (Spate, 1954, p. 31). These policies imposed serious constraints under which Indian industries had to operate.

A significant development during the period under discussion was the uneven regional distribution of private investment in modern manufacturing industry (Bagchi, 1972, p.83). The relative level of investment in Western India was more than in Eastern India. Consequently, the overall industrial growth of Bengal was drastically reduced despite the setting up of metallurgical industry at Jamshedpur. There was a general decline in the industries of the United Provinces (the eastern half of which fell within the extended hinterland of Calcutta) as well. The only industries to have developed here were those connected with leather goods and iron tools. An increasing demand for the former was created by the War and for the latter by the expanding need for agricultural implements (Hyde, 1921, p. 162). A few units to manufacture sugar and cement were also set up in the Province.

It may, however, be noted that in terms of industrial development the second-half of the nineteenth-century was qualitatively different from the first-half in two major respects. First, the investments which had hitherto been geared almost exclusively to external trade were diverted to import substituting investment in cotton textiles and later to some extent in steel; second, indigenous enterprise which had remained dormant until now emerged as a significant force (Bhagwati, 1970, p. 16). By the end of the nineteenth-century though India had been able to develop an expanded industrial base, its industries were not diversified. Its industrial base was distorted principally towards light manufacturing with very weak development in the decisive heavy industries, a situation that characterized all colonial countries (Amin, 1974, p. 170). Cotton and jute industries continued to dominate in Western and Eastern India respectively (Bagchi, 1972, p. 84). These industries, however, did not make a significant impact on the economic growth of the country (Bhagwati, 1970, p. 30).

However, the economics of industrial location tells us that no matter how limited or fluctuating the process of industrialization, it strengthens the economy of urban settlements since these are the preferred sites for industrial location. In urban settlements economies of scale and juxtaposition can be reaped to great advantage. This thesis, it is expected, should have been specifically true for urban settlements in the hitherland of Calcutta, not only because these settlements were the location for factories established by foreign enterprise in the initial phase of industrial development but also because most of the British private investment was concentrated in the Presidency of Bengal. The sectoral distribution of the working population should have been significantly altered in these settlements in favour of the secondary sector. In order to assess what actually happened in these cities the long term trends in the secondary sector are indicated for the selected cities in the hinterland of Calcutta in the following section.

II: Long term sectoral trends

The empirical analysis that follows employs two data sets published in the Imperial Census of India. The data on which the analysis relies most heavily are those pertaining to the 'Means of Livelihood' of the urban population. Data on establishments and means of power used are also analysed. The classificatory schemes employed to categorize the occupations of urban workers changed in terms of minor details from census to census between 1872 and 1921. However, the general format remained the same wherein occupations were grouped under a few 'classes' which included broad categories like agriculture, industry, trade, professions, etc. These classes were also disaggregated hierarchically in terms of 'orders', 'sub-orders' and 'groups'. The Census of 1881 indicated 480 groups which were gradually merged in the subsequent censuses until, in

1921, only 191 groups were identified. Since changes in the classificatory schemes were usually instituted at all levels, several adjustments had to be made in the data in order to make it amenable to cross sectional time series analysis. The occupational 'groups' were further classified in terms of categories not specified in the census in order to analyse the structural change that was taking place within the sector. It was also observed that several of the groups included in the 'industrial' class in the census belonged to the tertiary sector (such as sweepers, scavengers, etc.). The data were cleared of such anomalies by making adjustments at the level of 'groups' (see also Bagchi, 1976; Krishnamurty, 1977; and Vicziany, 1979).

The empirical analysis is divided into three parts. We begin with a quantification of the sectoral distribution of the working population for ten cities (for which data is available) in the hinterland of Calcutta, here taken to include the British Provinces of Bengal, Bihar and Orissa, the eastern half of the United Provinces, Central Provinces and Berar (Kidwai, 1979, p. 24). In order to compare the sectoral trends between colonial and 'capitalist' cities, the sectoral distribution in the twelve largest cities in contemporary England and Wales are also given.

The sectoral structure of an economy is usually analysed in terms of the distribution of the working population in the various sectors.[2] As the main concern of this paper is with the relative magnitude of these sectors in the colonial cities, absolute values (i.e., numbers employed in each sector) have not been used. Instead, the percentage share of the principal sectors in the work force has been calculated relative to the total working population—the share of the primary sector being denoted by L_P of the secondary sector by L_S and that of the tertiary by L_T (Sabolo, 1975, p. 5). In order to establish the relative absorption of labour in the secondary and tertiary sectors, the index of tertiarization given by Sabolo (1975) has also been calculated as follows:

$$L_T = (L_T/L_S)\,100$$

The data on the long term trends in the sectoral distribution of the selected cities, summarily reproduced in Tables 1 and 2, indicate that almost all cities in England and Wales had a well developed industrial base as early as in 1871, even before the modern phase of industrialization had set in at the close of the First World War. Industrial cities like Birmingham, Sheffield, Manchester and Leicester had already more than 60 per cent of their workers in the secondary sector and primary activities in all cities

Table 1

Sectoral Distribution of the Working Population in the Cities of England and Wales: - 1881 and 1921
(Figures indicate rounded percentage shares)

City/Year	L_P	L_S	L_T	City/Year	L_P	L_S	L_T	City/Year	L_P	L_S	L_T
London				Liverpool				Birmingham			
1881	2	43	55	1881	1	42	57	1881	1	64	35
1921	1	44	55	1921	1	40	59	1921	1	69	30
Manchester				Sheffield				Leicester			
1881	1	59	40	1881	1	68	31	1881	1	72	27
1921	1	56	43	1921	4	62	34	1921	1	69	30
Portsmouth				Sunderland				Huddersfield			
1881	2	49	49	1881	2	56	42	1881	2	71	27
1921	1	44	55	1921	1	61	38	1921	3	63	34
Southampton				Cardiff				Swansea			
1881	1	32	67	1881	1	40	59	1881	1	48	51
1921	1	42	57	1921	2	39	59	1921	3	50	47

Table 2

Sectoral Distribution of the Working Population in the cities in the Hinterland of Calcutta : 1881 and 1921
(figures indicate rounded percentage shares)

City/Year	L_P	L_S	L_T	City/Year	L_P	L_S	L_T	City/Year	L_P	L_S	L_T
Calcutta				Howrah				Lucknow			
1881	2	14	84	1881	NA	NA	NA	1881	10	37	53
1921	4	25	71	1921	5	39	56	1921	6	18	76
Kanpur				Benaras				Allahabad			
1881	8	44	48	1881	5	46	49	1881	12	41	47
1921	5	23	72	1921	15	39	46	1921	9	18	73
Gorakhpur				Fyzabad				Mirzapur			
1881	21	43	36	1881	20	31	49	1881	19	35	46
1921	35	20	45	1921	45	10	45	1921	79	11	10
Jaunpur				Jabalpur				Nagpur			
1881	24	35	41	1881	12	43	45	1881	5	50	45
1921	43	25	32	1921	33	24	43	1921	6	37	57

had become negligible. The tertiary sector was substantial but not dominant. There was little change in the sectoral distribution of population between 1871-1921. Both L_S and L_T values maintained their relative shares.

In terms of the proportion of tertiary workers to secondary workers as measured by L_T values these cities can be put into two groups as indicated in Table 3. The comparison of the L_T values for 1881 and 1921 shows that although no characteristic trend is noticed, tertiarization of the urban economy was not a universal phenomena. It may, however, be noted that the industrial cities, mentioned earlier, showed a definite increase in their L_T values.

In the colonial cities in India, on the other hand, the proportion of workers in the secondary sector remained very low throughout the period under investigation (Table 2). The highest L_S values recorded for the Indian cities were comparable to the lowest recorded for the cities in England and Wales, i.e., Jaunpur, 38 per cent and Portsmouth, 34.40 per cent, respectively. Within the Indian cities there was also a wide variation in the L_S values (the variation for 1871 ranged from 9.4 per cent (Mirzapur) to 34.38 per cent (Jaunpur) and for 1921 from 10.38 per cent (Fyzabad) to 38.75 per cent (Benaras)). The proportion of workers in the tertiary sector remained constantly very high. The L_T values increased quite substantially in seven out of the ten cities and decreased only in Calcutta, Howrah, Benaras and Jabalpur (Table 3). It can, therefore, be concluded that the tertiary sector made an appearance in the Indian cities and grew to imposing dimensions much before the emergence of a modernized secondary sector.

On the basis of this analysis it can be concluded that the urban economy of colonial cities was characterized by a secondary sector which was not only constricted to begin with, but which in most cities was further depressed with time. The tertiary sector proliferated and the primary sector tended to persist and in some cities even expanded. The general trend in the cities of England and Wales was for the secondary sector, which was already substantial, to increase and for the primary and tertiary sectors to decrease. In some of these cities the Clark (1940; pp. 6-7) and Fisher (1952; p. 822) hypothesis was beginning to hold true as the share of the secondary sector in their working population was declining in favour of the tertiary sector. This implies that the increments in the working population of these cities were initially absorbed in the secondary sector until it reached a position of dominance in the urban economy. In the colonial cities in India, on the other hand, the incremental workers entered directly into the tertiary sector.

Table 3
I_T Values for cities of England and Wales - 1881 and 1921 (I_T values are given in parenthesis)

Group	1871		1911	
1. I_T<100	Sunderland	(70)	Swansea	(95)
	Birmingham	(45)	Manchester	(76)
	Manchester	(44)	Sunderland	(61)
	Leicester	(41)	Sheffield	(56)
	Sheffield	(40)	Huddersfield	(55)
	Huddersfield	(39)	Birmingham	(44)
			Leicester	(43)
2. IT>100	Southampton	(189)	Cardiff	(151)
	Portsmouth	(184)	Liverpool	(150)
	Cardiff	(160)	Southampton	(138)
	Liverpool	(139)	London	(127)
	London	(113)	Portsmouth (	123)
	Swansea	(103)	-	

I_T Values for cities in the hinterland of Calcutta: 1881, 1901 and 1921 (I_T values are given in parenthesis)

Group	1881		1901		1921	
1. I_T<100	No city falls in this group					
2. I_T>100	Lucknow	(356)	Allahabad	(364)	Mirzapur	(1040)
	Allahabad (324)		Lucknow	(324)	Lucknow	(793)
	Fyzabad	(300)	Fyzabad	(316)	Fyzabad	(734)
	Kanpur	(257)	Jaunpur	(310)	Kanpur	(641)
	Calcutta	(250)	Kanpur	(284)	Allahabad	(516)
	Mirzapur	(243)	Calcutta	(250)	Gorakhpur (428)	
	Jaunpur	(213)	Mirzapur	(232)	Jaunpur	(217)
	Benaras	(173)	Gorakhpur	(207)	Calcutta	(207)
	Gorakhpur	(171)	Jabalpur	(208)	Jabalpur	(205)
	-		Howrah	(157)	Howrah	(147)
			Benaras	(148)	Benaras	(136)

Source: Derived from data on sectoral distribution of the working population given in the Census of England and Wales (1871, 1911), vol. I Part II, and Census of India (1881, 1901, 1921) Provincial Tables.

III. Structural Characteristics of Urban Industries in Colonial Cities

By the middle of the nineteenth-century, when Britain had already become the 'Chimney of the World' and its desire to have 'the world for its workshop and the world for its customer' (Briggs 1963, p.105) had been largely satiated, the Indian industries lay prostrate and dismayed (Venketasumbiah, 1940; Gadgil, 1944; Singh, 1965 Bagchi, 1976). The handicraft industries of the rural areas had rapidly decayed and the finer urban crafts, once patronized by the courts and the urban rich, had been reduced to insignificance.As mentioned earlier, British enterprise and capital had been extended to sugar manufacturing, rice and flour mills, indigo and tea plantations, cotton presses, shipbuilding and to similar activities geared to the growing external trade with Britain. Traditional indigenous enterprise had either collapsed or was reduced to a subsidiary position in the process. This pattern of industrial evolution was quite significant for the urban economy. In a period when cities in the metropolitan countries were being sought as the prime location for industries, where economies of agglomeration could be reaped and friction of distance reduced, Indian cities were still languishing in a pre-industrial phase.

The industrial structure of the selected cities will be analysed in this section in terms of the industrial workforce and establishment data. It may be mentioned here that the industrial structure is best understood when variables like value added, capital investment and share of industries in GDP are taken into consideration. But in the absence of such information for colonial cities, workforce data has been taken as an indicator of the significance of an economic activity in the total economy and also of the occupational status the participants share. This indicator is considered quite useful by many economic historians (Kuznets, 1971, p. 201).

III. (a) Consumer-Oriented, Service-based Industrial Structure of Colonial Cities

An analysis of workers engaged in the various types of industries in the selected colonial cities indicates that the majority of them were producing indigenous consumer goods, such as textiles, leather products, metal products and food and luxury items (Tables 4(a) and (b)). In contrast to the Indian cities, a similar analysis shows that the contemporary cities of England and Wales had developed a considerable degree of industrial specialization. About 40 per cent of the industrial workers in

Birmingham and Sheffield were engaged in metallurgical engineering; Manchester, Leicester and Oldham had the same percentage in textiles and readymade clothing. Sheffield and Birmingham also had a well-developed art and mechanical production industry.

In the cities of colonial India these indigenous service-based handicrafts which had survived the onslaught of imported goods from Europe either met the daily needs of the population or had a market 'sheltered by poverty' and dealt with raw materials not worth processing by modern methods (Spate, 1954, p. 306). They also included a small array of luxury goods.

The textile industry in towns like Jaunpur, Gorakhpur and Fyzabad, wherein 10 to 15 per cent of the industrial workers were engaged produced a coarse cloth called *gaji* or *garha* for the local market (*Gazetteer*, 1908, p.114). Benaras specialized in silk weaving. Modern textile industry, developed to some extent only in Kanpur. The hide and skin industry, employing between 2 and 10 per cent of the industrial workers, mainly produced half tanned 'kipps' from crude vats and catered to a market for cheap products (Buchanan, 1934; p. 94). The food industries, which employed between 4 and 20 per cent of the industrial workers, consisted of pounders, huskers, grinders, parchers, all dealing with raw material in small quantities for the city population and performing functions which would have been carried out in rural areas. The building industry consisted of excavators, brick-layers, lime-burners and well-sinkers.

The metal, wood and ceramic industries, though absorbed a significant proportion of the industrial workers, were rather unimportant in terms of their total product. The majority of the smiths and carpenters were really 'fixers' than 'makers' (Buchanan, 1934, p. 96). Most of the blacksmiths did nothing but forge crude iron (Martin, 1838, p. 255). Very few vessels of copper, brass or bell metal were made and workmen were chiefly employed to mend those imported from Murshidabad (Martin, 1838, p. 258). No factory process was used in the ceramic industry except in a limited way in Calcutta.

III (b). The Predominance of Elementary Processing Industries

After the industrial revolution cities in Europe began to specialize in secondary processing activities, i.e., they were producing final goods using skilled labour and mechanized methods of production and employed a high level of industrial organization. In the cities in colonial

Table 4(a)

Industrial Structure of Cities in the Hinterland of Calcutta (Average 1872-1921)

(Percentages are in terms of total industrial workers)

	Calcutta	Howrah	Lucknow	Kanpur	Benaras	Allahabad	Gorakhpur	Fyzabad		Mirzapur	Jaunpur
% Industrial to total workers	21.42	36.84	28.16	2.93	37.73	23.60	31.97	25.01	23.34	29.61	
1. Textiles	17.16	57.49	7.66	15.97	33.59	6.32	10.92	8.66		9.28	12.14
2. Hides	1.25	1.22	1.52	7.30	1.81	1.99	10.91	3.25		7.98	5.43
3. Wood	7.16	6.35	7.20	6.17	3.95	4.67	10.63	7.55		1.39	3.68
4. Metals	6.53	7.22	6.65	7.27	7.51	5.65	3.05	6.43		5.25	8.08
5. Ceramics	1.45	1.08	2.60	2.91	2.59	4.90	4.00	4.34		4.38	5.77
6. Chemicals	2.28	1.10	1.89	2.14	1.70	3.00	3.96	3.75		7.88	10.56
7. Dress Toilet	6.11	3.18	6.84	8.57	4.33	5.15	4.98	4.09		2.24	-
8. Food	7.84	3.68	14.78	10.03	8.99	9.63	8.19	19.68	13.21	9.67	
9. Furniture	0.47	-	0.55	0.55	0.29	2.20	0.06	0.13		0.12	-
10. Building	11.39	8.06	8.29	3.85	7.98	6.86	5.83	6.41		7.38	4.33
11. Gas water	2.42	0.12	0.15	0.11	0.04	0.58	-	0.03		-	-
12. Luxury	11.78	2.82	7.98	7.51	9.64	12.17	4.86	4.40		4.36	7.15

Note: Percentages do not add up to 100 as service occupations such as sweeping, scavenging etc included in the census in industrial category are excluded here.

Table 4(b)

Industrial Structure of Cities in England and Wales (Average 1872-1921)
(Percentages are in terms of total industrial workers)

	London	Birmingham	Liverpool	Manchester	Sheffield	Portsmouth	Leicester	Oldham	Norwich	Cardiff
% industrial to total workers	43.91	65.74	39.89	57.76	64.49	41.51	70.28	78.25	56.86	39.03
1. Textiles	4.88	1.26	3.98	20.83	1.00	1.62	11.03	58.22	5.61	7:65
2. Dress	25.64	12.35	18.73	20.65	8.48	29.39	53.43	4.86	43.01	16.10
3. Food	16.62	8.30	16.32	10.42	8.22	17.69	8.93	3.65	11.24	16.63
4. Construction	14.40	9.31	17.95	11.48	9.90	15.47	8.40	6.28	13.40	21.48
5. Chemicals	2.15	1.77	3.49	3.23	0.96	1.30	1.46	0.47	3.06	1.06
6. Minerals Met.	12.58	38.28	13.17	15.96	38.29	11.76	5.63	15.87	8.50	18.78
7. Art and Mech.	11.49	21.63	18.32	11.30	29.28	19.71	7.21	8.72	10.13	13.39
8. Hides	2.85	1.89	1.07	0.94	1.18	0.45	0.80	0.24	2.10	0.41
9. Wood	9.39	5.21	6.97	5.19	2.78	2.61	3.11	1.69	3.04	4.50

Source: Same as in Table 3

India, elementary processing activities continued to dominate. These activities dealt directly with raw material, did not always produce final goods, were not mechanized and employed low levels of skill. In essence, these industries were not necessarily 'urban' and if proximity to the market had not been profitable they could have been located in the rural areas.

In the analysis that follows we have divided the industrial workers into two categories, namely, those engaged in elementary or in secondary processing, these activities being defined according to the criteria mentioned above. To arrive at this categorization the 'orders' included in the industrial workforce, which ranged from 58 to 382 in the various censuses, were made comparable to the 58 'orders' listed in the 1921 census. These were then differentiated into elementary and secondary processing activities. The proportional share of workers in these two processes were subsequently calculated and indicated in Table 5.

The analysis shows that in no city, except Howrah, did the proportion of workers in secondary processing exceed that of elementary processing. Even in Kanpur which had developed a number of factory industries during this period, the share of secondary processing did not exceed 32 per cent. In Lucknow it remained as low as 17 per cent. It ranged around 30 per cent in other cities.

It should also be pointed out that not only was the share of secondary processing low, it declined in four out of the ten cities considered, i.e., in Gorakhpur, Fyzabad, Jaunpur and Mirzapur. The decline of industries in Mirzapur is well documented (Hamilton, 1828, p. 233; Thornton, 1854, p. 478; Hunter, 1881, p. 396; Bayly, 1982, p. 437). Industrial activities of a rural or semi-rural type continued to characterize the industrial structure of colonial cities.

The reasons for this were, first, the competition meted out by imported piecegoods and second, a change in consumer tastes and demands. Native consumer goods industries were practically stamped out by cheap imported goods within the range of the railways (Gait, 1911, p. 145; Roy, 1922, p. 46; Buchanan, 1934, p. 274; Dutt, 1940, p. 119). The market for both cheap and luxury goods which once belonged to the local craftsmen were gradually usurped by imported goods. As was rightly remarked, 'It was a hopeless task to try to drive Indian-made *dhoties* at Re. 1.8 down the throats or rather round the waists of cultivators and labourers to whom every anna is a consideration, when they could get a Manchester *dhoti* for Re. 1.4' (Blunt, 1911, p. 403). Even the Swadeshi movement could not effectively counteract this damage.

Table 5

Distribution of the Industrial Workers (exclusive of the tertiary component) into Elementary and Secondary processing (percentages are in terms of total industrial workers)

	Calcutta		Howrah	
	Elementary	Secondary	Elementary	Secondary
1876	62.35	37.65	-	-
1881	58.97	41.03	-	-
1891	61.99	38.01	-	-
1901	55.31	44.69	30.21	69.79
1911	55.98	44.02	29.82	70.18
1921	57.75	42.25	24.12	75.87
Average	58.72	41.28	28.05	71.95
	Lucknow		Kanpur	
1881	88.49	11.51	68.63	31.37
1901	80.72	19.28	66.38	33.62
1911	81.76	18.24	63.66	36.34
1921	83.15	16.85	73.39	26.41
Average	83.30	16.70	68.06	31.94
	Benaras		Allahabad	
1881	48.32	51.68	76.95	23.04
1901	42.04	57.96	75.07	24.93
1911	46.01	53.99	67.43	32.56
1921	50.05	49.95	70.78	29.22
Average	64.60	35.40	72.55	27.45
	Gorakhpur		Fyzabad	
1881	76.27	23.72	72.50	27.50
1901	79.07	20.93	82.25	17.75
1911	75.01	24.99	78.87	21.13
1921	87.65	12.35	92.19	7.81
Average	79.50	20.50	81.45	18.55
	Mirzapur		Jaunpur	
1881	74.90	25.10	54.50	45.50
1901	71.17	28.83	71.58	28.42
1911	66.44	33.56	68.08	31.92
1921	66.32	33.68	78.52	21.48
Average	69.70	30.30	68.17	31.83

Source: Derived from data on sectoral distribution of the working population given in the Census of India (1881-1921), Provincial Tables.

III (c). Elementary Levels of Industrial organization

We can safely follow Buchanan (1934, p.97) and analyse the level of organization of urban industries in India in terms of the stages of industrial organization which he adapted from Grass (1930) whereby he traced the evolution of industrial organization through four stages:

i. Usufacture: based on consumers, materials, home products, outside labour and capital;
ii. Retail handicraft: based on craftsman's material and catering either to the customer's orders or producing for chance sale;
iii. Wholesale handicraft: producing for bulk sale initially through an independent and later dependent phase;
iv. Centralized production: placed either in a central workshop or a factory.

The levels of industrial organization in colonial India, even in the urban areas, cannot be neatly placed in any of these categories because they were a complex of hybrid types. We will, however, attempt to keep the analysis as specific as is possible.

In the first stage can be included the work of some artisans who used the consumers' materials, at times provided capital and eventually produced personal services, such as the work of tailors. Bakers and washermen also fall in this category but they have been excluded from the secondary sector in this study, though the census enumerated them under industrial workers.

The second stage of industrial organization, i.e., the retail handicraft stage characterized most of the specialized handicraft industries of urban areas such as shoemaking, furniture, hardware, a large segment of cloth-weaving and the chemical and food industries.

The independent, i.e., the first phase, of the third stage, wherein the entrepreneur financed his venture was rare and confined to the larger cities and to foreign enterprises (Buchanan, 1939, p.103; Bagchi, 1972, pp.186-88). The first jute mill to be entirely sponsored and managed by Indians was Birla Jute Mills which was built as late as in 1919. The first iron and steel mill initiated by Indian enterprise came up in 1911 at Jamshedpur. The dependent phase of the third stage was, however, prevalent and was operationalized either through the finance and order system, specially in the brass and cloth industry or through the putting-out system where work was carried out at piece rates. The putting-out system was most common in the consumer goods industries that were operated on a considerably large scale like the leather industry in Kanpur, the carpet industry in Mirzapur and the weaving industry in Benaras (Buchanan, 1934, pp.144-49). The artisans usually used their own tools; there was no supervision and direction of work or regulation of labour. Wages were paid on piece rates and mechanization was at a very low level (Buchanan, p.114). A similar situation existed in many of the engineering works as well (Buchanan, p.115).

The fourth phase was perhaps present only in Calcutta, Howrah, Kanpur, Allahabad and Lucknow. It may, however, be noted that the factories represented an imported imposition rather than an advanced stage in the evolution of indigenous industrial organization and technology (Buchanan, p.119). Moreover, this phase was confined to the export-oriented and foreign-owned enterprises which were operated under the managing agency system. Outside of the Calcutta-Howrah industrial node, Kanpur had the largest concentration of factories (see Table 6). Allahabad was next in importance but the only important 'factories' of the town were the stone works and government printing presses. Lucknow had a miscellaneous assortment of industrial establishments. It also had the only major car works and paper mill in the Province.

Table 6

Factories in the Cities of United Provinces of Agra & Oudh (1911)

Industry	Kanpur	Allahabad	Lucknow
1. Cotton	8	-	-
2. Jute	1	1	-
3. Leather	13	-	-
4. Wood	1	2	1
5. Metals	5	5	1
6. Glass	5	2	1
7. Chemicals	6	4	2
8. Food	11	3	-
9. Building	4	15	7
10. Luxury	7	12	6
Total	61	44	18

Source: *Census of United Provinces and Oudh (1911)*, Part I, p. 407.

III (d). Low Levels of Industrial Technology and High Labour Intensity

The process of displacement of labour intensive techniques by the capital intensive power driven techniques which characterized the contemporary cities of England and Wales did not take place in India. The data base for the quantitative assessment of the level of industrial technology in the cities in the hinterland of Calcutta is very restricted. Except for a few stray observations in the Gazetteers, administrative reports and the sporadic reports published by the Industrial Enquiry Committees, consistent time-series data is non-existent, particularly for the nineteenth-century. Industrial statistics for selected cities was published for the first time only in 1911 in the Census reports. For the region under consideration this information is available only for the city and suburbs of Calcutta. Aggregated information at provincial level is, however, available for all the provinces included in the study. This information has been used to identify the provincial trends. Constraints of the data base has permitted the analysis of the level of industrial technology only in terms of the following criteria:

i. ratio of mechanized to non-mechanized establishments,
ii. the nature of power utilized, and,
iii. the ratio of technical to non-technical staff in the registered factories.

Table 7 summarizes the data on mechanized and non-mechanized establishments in Calcutta and its suburbs which employed more than 20 workers in 1911 and more than 10 workers in 1921. It is indicated in the table that the production processes in more than half the registered factories in the city were non-mechanized. The only mechanized industries were the export-oriented, British owned jute presses and mills as well as the government owned foundries and printing presses. The chemical industries were also mechanized but these included a substantial number of oil *ghunees* (60 in 1911 and 64 in 1921). Bagchi notes that there were no major changes in the technology either of the jute and cotton textile industry or in the chemical and paper industry (Bagchi, 1972, p. 82).

The level of industrial technology in the cities of the hinterland was still lower. The reasons are not far to seek. Few export-oriented or government sponsored industrial establishments had been set up there,

Table 7
Mechanized and Non-mechanized Industrial Establishments in Calcutta (1911 & 1921)

		1911				1921			
		Mechanized		Non-Mechanized		Mechanized		Non-Mechanized	
		Total	%	Total	%	Total	%	Total	%
1.	Textiles	40	13.03	8	3.02	51	10.99	26	4.78
	Jute presses	-	-			29		1	
	Jute mills	-	-			13		-	
	Rope	-	-			5		19	
2.	Leather	6	1.95	9	3.39	4	0.86	23	4.27
3.	Wood	3	0.97	6	2.26	15	3.23	32	5.89
4.	Chemicals	72	23.46	48	18.12	70	15.09	35	6.45
5.	Metals	43	14.01	22	8.30	48	10.34	27	4.97
6.	Food	36	11.73	35	13.22	64	13.79	36	6.63
7.	Press	1	0.33	20	7.56	6	1.29	103	18.97
8.	Transport	16	5.21	13	4.96	33	7.11	29	5.34
9.	Luxury	72	23.45	69	26.94	116	25.02	120	22.09
10.	Others	18	5.86	35	12.23	57	12.28	112	20.61
	Total	307	100.00	265	100.00	511	100.00	563	100.00

Source: *Census of the City of Calcutta (1911)*, Part II, Table XVE, pp. 98-112. 1921, Table XXII, Part I, pp. 110-127.

and as we have just noted, it was this category of establishments which were generally considered suitable for mechanization. The carpet industry of Mirzapur was the only industry that had a substantial foreign market. The trade was entirely controlled by the British exporting firms. The other enterprises in the United Provinces which were patterned on the western factory system, and used modern machinery and aimed at the distribution of their products to distant markets were the flour, cotton, woollen and leather industries.

Moreover, since large scale capital investment was not forthcoming and since bulk supplies were usually not required indigenous methods of production which were less capital intensive and produced smaller quantities, proved adequate and continued to linger on. Even at Kanpur, which had the largest number of factory industries amongst the cities of United Provinces, mechanization was only partial (op.cit. pp. 185-88). Buchanan gives a very interesting account of a shoe factory in Kanpur which employed the latest model of the American shoe machinery and was operated with elaborate division of labour by men on monthly wages.

But 'just beside these machines and under the same roof and management', Buchanan writes, 'were Indian cobblers, each performing all the processes of making pairs of shoes by hand at so much per pair'. (Buchanan, 1934, p.124) He also cites the case of a large woollen mill where there were 'spinning wheels, handlooms, both hand and power knitting-machines and elaborate power machinery for producing and making up high grade cloth for almost every possible type of woollen clothing'. This establishment which produced for bulk orders was at the same time prepared to operate on a small scale and turn wool direct from the sheep into a suit for a lady or a gentleman - tailored in the latest fashion'. Its proprietors were ready to cater to individual requirements as willingly as they were prepared to outfit a police force or an army.

Most of the processing activities in the urban industries were operated by draught animals or human power (Buchanan, 1934, pp. 96, 127). Steam power was employed only by the larger establishments in a few cities. Another important characteristic of the industrial establishments was that they employed more unskilled and non-technical workers than trained ones (*Census of the City of Calcutta*, 1911, pp. 110-27). About half of the skilled workers in Calcutta were non-technical. The situation in the provinces in the hinterland of Calcutta was no better. Except in Bengal, workers in organized factories constituted a very small proportion of the total industrial workers. Out of these about half were unskilled, a considerable proportion of them consisting of child labour (*Census of the United Provinces*, 1921, p. 416). Most of the skilled workers are accounted for by railway workshops. In contrast to the Indian cities, a large proportion of the labour force in the cities in England was skilled and earned good wages (Briggs, 1968, p. 186). In terms of the regional concentration of factory employment, Bengal had a much larger share as compared to the other provinces since this province had been the initial focus for the development of factory industry.

IV

During the second-half of the nineteenth-century, when industries had acquired a position of eminence in most of the cities of Victorian England, when British towns were labelled as Cottonopolis (Manchester) Worstedopolis (Bradford) and Metalopolis (Sheffield), when poets lamented at the loss of the individual identity of British towns ('Can this be Manchester? or is it Leeds?' —William Osborne) the cities in India continued to remain within the pre-industrial framework. The shock phases of industrial stagnation which had occasionally punctuated the evolution of Victorian cities had become a way of life in the contemporary cities of India. The urban economy had been fossilized under the impact of alien interests, and towns were still generally designated as state capitals, pilgrim centres or trading outposts. The analysis in this paper conclusively indicates that:

1. The process of de-industrialization that had characterized the Indian economy in the nineteenth-century had significantly affected the economy of colonial cities. Subsequent spurts in industrial investment had also failed to bring about a transformation of the urban economy and had not been able to make a dent in their traditional occupational structure. The reasons are not far to seek. First, the industries that developed during this period were generally raw-material oriented and did not necessarily seek an urban location. Second, the essentially urban-based industries that did come up, were elementary forms of engineering establishments, which could not significantly alter the sectoral distribution of the working population in favour of the secondary sector by throwing out chains of multiplier effects.

2. A major part of the industrial workers in the colonial cities were engaged either in indigenous, service-based handicrafts which met the daily needs of the urban population or were involved in the production of a limited range of luxury goods. The development of even these industries was marked by fluctuations. As a consequence, the colonial cities did not exhibit a trend towards industrial specialization. This was in direct contrast to what was happening in the cities in contemporary England and Wales.

3. The industrial production patterns in colonial cities were more or less an extension of rural production patterns and techniques. There was a predominance of elementary processing activities which directly dealt with raw materials or produced consumption goods requiring low levels of skill. The secondary processing activities, i.e., activities producing final goods and using higher levels of skill, instead of expanding and establishing a firm industrial base, actually declined. This happened for two reasons: First, Indian handicrafts had to compete both in terms of quality and cost with the products of a comparatively more

developed form of industry. Second, the demand pattern of consumers—both urban and rural—changed in favour of imported goods.

4. Industrial production in the colonial cities involved low levels of industrial technology characterized by high labour intensity. The ratio of mechanized to non-mechanized establishments was quite low because the type of industrial establishments that had developed in the cities were generally considered to be unsuitable for mechanization. Large scale capital investment for the purpose was also not forthcoming. Most of the processing activities in urban industries were operated by draught animals. Steam power was employed only by the larger establishments in a few cities. The chief users of power were the export oriented British-owned establishments. The ratio of technical to non-technical staff in the industrial establishments was quite low. Most of the industrial production was carried on by unskilled workers.

5. The level of industrial organization in the urban industries was quite primitive and inefficient. Most of the handicraft industries in the cities produced for chance sale. The finance and order system operated only in the specialized goods industries which were organized on a considerably large scale. There was usually no supervision or direction of work and no regulation of labour or wages. Factory industries had come up only in a few larger towns.

The almost complete control of the dynamic sectors of urban industry by foreign capital, coupled with the absence of a diversified urban industrial base, further reduced the chance of industrial development in the colonial cities and by implication also failed to create productive jobs in the other sectors of the economy. In economistic terms, the multiplier mechanisms were transferred or, to put it more aptly, 'exported' to the metropolitan country. As a result, very few traces of industrial development were found in the colonial cities in India.

NOTES

1. The terms 'industry' and 'secondary sector' are put in inverted commas because, as Simmons (1985, 593) has pointed out, these terms are ambiguous when used in the context of non-western economies. Here it is used to denote a 'disparate range of activities including both the "organized" and "unorganized" subsectors which may be weakly differentiated from "primary" and "tertiary" pursuits—but only as a first, and really unsatisfactory approximation' (Simmons, p.594).
2. For the present study we have adopted the classification given by the United Nations.

(i) Primary—agriculture, hunting, forestry, fishing.
(ii) Secondary—mining, quarrying, manufacturing, electricity.
(iii) Tertiary—financing, insurance, real estate, business services, community, social and personal services, activities not adequately defined.

In the present analysis mining and quarrying was included in the primary sector. See Department of Economic and Social Affairs, Statistical Office of the United Nations, 'International Standard Industrial Classification of all Economic Activities'. *Statistical Papers* (1968), Series M, No. 4, Rev. 2.

REFERENCES

Abrams, P., 'Towns and Economic Growth' in P. Abrams and E.A. Wrigley, *Towns in Societies*, (Cambridge University Press, 1978).

Amin, S., *Accumulation of Capital on a World Scale*, (Monthly Review Press, 1974), vol. I.

Antsey, V., *The Economic Development of India,* (London, 1952 edn.).

Bagchi, A.K., *Private Investment in India, 1900-1939*, (Delhi, 1975 edn.).

Bagchi, A.K., 'De-industrialization in India in the Nineteenth Century: Some Theoretical Implications' in *The Journal of Development Studies*, vol. 12, January 1976, no. 2, pp. 135-64.

———: *North Indian Society in the Age of British Expansion, 1770-1870.*

Bayly, C. A., *Rulers, Townsmen, and Bazaars,* (Cambridge, 1983).

Beauchamp, J., *British Imperialism in India,* (London, 1935).

Bhagwati, J. and P. Desai., *India: Planning for Industrialization*, (Delhi, 1970).

Blunt, E.A.H. (1911), *Census of United Provinces and Oudh,* vol. XV, Part I, *Report*.

Briggs, A. (1963), *Victorian Cities*, (London, 1968 edn.).

Buchanan, D.H., *The Development of Capitalist Enterprise in India*, (New York, 1934).

Chandra, B., *Rise and Growth of Economic Nationalism in India*, (Delhi, 1966).

Clark, C., *The Conditions of Economic Progress*, (London, 1940).

Dutt, R.C., *The Economic History of India*, (London, 1903).

Fisher, A.G.B., 'A Note by Tertiary Production', *Economic Journal*, 1952, vol. LXII, pp. 820-29.

Gait, E.A., *Census of India*, 1911, vol. I, part I.

Gadgil, D.R., *The Industrial Evolution of India*, (Bombay, 1944).

Grass, N.S.B., *Industrial Evolution*, (Harvard, 1930).

Hamilton, Walter., *The East India Gazetteer*, vol. II., (London, 1828 edn.).

Harvey, D., *Social Justice and the City*, (London, 1973).

Hunter, W.W., *Imperial Gazetteer of India*, vol. VI (London, 1881 edn.).

Hyde, E.H.H., *Census of the United Provinces*, 1921, Part I.

Kidwai, Atiya H., 'Urban Growth in India: A Historical Perspective', in P. Venettier (ed.), *Problems de Croissance Urbaine*, (CEGET, Bordeaux, France).

Krishnamurty, J., 'Changes in the Composition of the Working Force in Manufacturing, 1901-51: A Theoretical and Empirical Analysis', *Indian Economic and Social History Review*, vol. IV, no. 1, March 1967, pp. 1-16.

Kuznets, S., *Economic Growth of Nations: Total Output and Production Structure*, (Harvard, 1971).

Martin, M., *Eastern India*, 1838, vol. II.

McGee, T.G., *The Urbanization Process in the Third World: Explorations in Search of a Theory*, (London, 1976).

Roberts, B.R., *Cities of Peasants: The Political Economy of Urbanization in the Third World*, (London, 1978).

Roy, M.N., *India in Transition*, (Bombay, 1922).

Sabolo, Yves, *The Service Industries*, ILO, Geneva, 1975.

Simmons, C., 'De-industrialization', Industrialization and the Indian Economy, c. 1850-1947', *Modern Asian Studies*, vol. 19, no. 3, 1985, pp. 593-622.

Spate, O.H.K. and A.T.A. Learmoth, *India and Pakistan: A General and Regional Geography*, (Methuen & Co., Suffolk, 1967 edn.).

Thorner, D., 'De-industrialization in India, 1881-1931' in D. Thorner and A. Thorner, *Land and Labour in India*, (Bombay, 1962).

Thornton, E., *Gazetteer of the Territories Under the Government of the East India Company*, 1854, vol. III.

Venketasubbiah, H., *The Structural Basis of the Indian Economy*, (Calcutta, 1940).

Vicziany, M., 'The Deindustrialization of India in the Nineteenth Century: A Methodological Critique of Amiya Kumar Bagchi', *Indian Economic and Social History Review*, vol. XVI, no. 2, 1979, pp. 105-161.

Agricultural Rents in India c.1900-1960

SUMIT GUHA

Professor Stokes made major contributions to the study of the agrarian history of India. His comprehensive approach extended from the minutiae of land distribution and social structure to the motives and patterns of rural conflicts and uprisings. Among other things, he also carried out one of the few long period analyses of the nature and levels of rents in northern India over the nineteenth and twentieth-centuries. He was thus able to trace the gradual transformation of what had often been customary tributes to market-determined rents, and the twentieth-century ossification of some of these into 'a controlled ground rent'. As a consequence, he noted, 'the only point at which full economic benefit could be derived from control of land as a scarce resource was where subordinate cultivators enjoyed no protection, i.e., where labourers or shikmis paying labour and grain rents could be employed'.[1]

This paper takes up a single aspect of Stokes' many-sided, analysis, and examines the changes in the levels (and, it transpires, the forms) of unprotected tenant or 'free market' rents in a number of districts between (very approximately) the turn of the century and the 1950s. Some tentative explanations of the observed changes are also proffered. The data are summarized in Table 1, which shows the levels of rents and prices, as also the periods to which they refer. It will be evident that the periods differ considerably in different districts, depending on the availability of sources. The early sources also vary in quality: the Settlement Reports are probably the best, as the data were gathered by careful local enquiry over a period of years. The information on districts in the old Madras Presidency also seems to have been carefully collected, but unfortunately relates to only a single year, 1917-18.

The least reliable information is that for the districts of Twenty-Four Parganas and Hugli, culled from Hunter's *Statistical Accounts*. Belief in its authenticity is, however, bolstered by the concordance between Hunter's figures and the results of the more careful enquiry made by the Land Revenue Commission of 1940. So much for the initial period. As regards the later period, we are faced with a decline in the amount and quality of information resulting from the concealment of tenures due to actual or apprehended land reform measures after Independence. For this period I have used the various *Studies in the Economics of Farm Management*[2] carried out in the 1950s and 1960s, taking data from the Cost Accounting sample farms only. The data for these farms were collected week by week for a period of two to three years, reducing the chances of misreporting or concealment. The data on rentals would presumably have been supplied by tenants as a part of the listing of expenses of all sorts, and therefore should be fairly accurate.

It should be noted that the *Studies* always include an estimate of the rental values of owned and self-cultivated land in the costs of production. This value was not calculated on a uniform basis in the different districts. Thus in the districts of Salem and Coimbatore it was calculated on the basis of the actually prevailing cash rents for similar qualities of land, while in Punjab rents in kind were included, but the value set by reference to actual rents. On the other hand, in Deoria, rental value was fixed at 5 or 6 per cent of the notional value of the land, and in Ahmadnagar at 7 per cent. In Akola and Amraoti (Berar), the value of rent in kind on sharecropped land was used to fix the rental values of all land, so that rental value exceed the actual rent paid on some of the tenanted land. On the other hand, in some cases rental value seems to have been put at arbitrarily low levels, as in Cuttack, where rent plus rental value for local paddy were shown as being only Rs. 186 per Ha. while Rs. 502 was actually paid on leased land under this crop. In view of these problems, I have always calculated the rent rates from the actually paid rents, and ignored the estimates of rental value. The exceptions to this are the two pairs of districts in Punjab and Madras studied in 1955-57. In these cases it was difficult to separate the rents paid from rental values, and the careful calculation of the latter has made their use less hazardous than it would be elsewhere.

Another feature of the Farm Management Studies is that they relate to a sample of farms in a particular region, and to a rather small sample at that: generally 150 or 200 farms. In areas where agricultural conditions are variable, it is possible that variation over space may be mistaken for change over time. The comparison of rent rates in Surat district has, for instance, been excluded because of this possibility, as almost all the cases of renting occurred in one agro-climatic zone. As a further check on distortions of this sort, I have, where possible, calculated the rents as multiples of the land revenue assessment, thus minimizing variation caused by location and land quality. This was particularly necessary in peninsular India, where the difference between irrigated and dry land can be enormous. Where the land revenue had been revised between the periods compared, an adjustment has been made to cover the usual enhancement in the assessment.

Finally, the comparison also needed to allow for the changes in prices—here the most satisfactory solution seemed to take the price of a region's principal agricultural product as the deflator. Indian agriculture used few inputs from other sectors before the 1960s, and the prices of most agricultural products were found to change by much the same amount in the period under consideration. The only exception, cotton vs millet, was found in Maharashtra, and will be discussed more fully.

So far the discussion has referred to the sources and presentation of the data, but we should also consider what it is that we are trying to measure. No one can read the early reports without realizing that many different kinds of payment went by the name of rent. Essential to any argument that puts forward an economic explanation of rental levels is the assumption that there existed some identificable rent rate determined by market forces rather than law or custom, and that landlords were able, in at least some cases, to take full advantage of their bargaining position, and raise rents as high as the market would bear. It then becomes plausible to regard the market rate as that paid by unprotected tenants or sub-tenants in the early twentieth-century. As far as the *Studies* are concerned, the problem is much less serious: most of the erstwhile protected tenants were either ejected or became *de facto* proprietors. As the Monghyr *Study* put it: 'With the abolition of Zemindaries, it is this [sharecropper] class of cultivators who remain on the land as tenants. The other classes, though legally known as tenants, enjoy in reality, considerable degrees of ownership.'[3] So we are comparing tenants in similar situations at the two points in time.

The results of the comparison are to be found in Table 1. It must be obvious from the foregoing discussion that the results are only approximate, but despite this certain conclusions may safely be drawn. The most robust of them is clearly that various regions differed considerably from each other, and that generalization about India as a whole is quite unsound. Secondly, as far as Table 1 goes, a clear division appears to exist between northern and peninsular India: districts showing large increases in lie in the former, while those showing stability or slight decline are in the latter.

Table 1
Changes in rents and prices, c. 1900-1960

District	Ratio of F.M.S. rent to old rent	Ratio of old product price to new price	Years of comparison
1. Ferozepur	12.4	5.5	1912-1955
2. Amritsar	7.8	5.5	1912-1955
3. Deoria	116	13.4	1914-1967
4. Shahabad	9.5	6.4	1912-1962
5. Hugli	16.1	13.2	1872-1955
6. Twenty-four Parganas	14.6	13.2	1872-1955
7. Cuttack (Share Crop)	22.0	18.9	1895-1968
8. Godavari	5.0	3.7	1918-1958
9. Coimbatore	2.4	3.7	1918-1955
10.Salem	3.0	3.7	1918-1955
11.Ahmednagar	3.8	4.0	1910-1955
12.Nasik	4.0	4.0	1910-1955
13.Berar region	1.4	2.0	1920-1956

N.B. 1 to 7 have been calculated on the basis of cash rent rates per acre; 8 to 13 the cash rates have been converted into multiples of land revenue, and then compared.

Sources:

S.No.1. *Farm Management Study, Punjab*, 1954-57; *Final Report on the Revised Settlement of the Ferozepore District 1910-14* (Lahore, 1915).

2. *F.M.S. Punjab* 1954-57; *Final Report on the Fourth Regular Settlement of the Amritsar District 1910-14* (Lahore, 1914).

3. *F.M.S. Deoria* 1967-68; *Final Report on the Revision of the Settlement in the Gorakhpur District of the United Provinces (Padrauna, Hata and Deoria)* (Allahabad, 1920); *Prices and Wages In India 1914*.

4. *F.M.S. Bihar* 1961-63; *Final Report on Survey and Settlement Operations in the District of Shahabad 1907-16* (Patna, 1918).

5. *F.M.S. West Bengal* 1954-57; *W.W. Hunter A Statistical Account of*

Bengal (Reprint, 1973) vol. III *Midnapur and Hugli*.

6. *F.M.S. West Bengal* 1954-57; Hunter *ibid.*, vol. I, *Twenty-four Parganas*.
7. *F.M.S. Orissa* 1967-70; *Final Report on the Survey and Settlement of the Province of Orissa (Temporarily Settled Areas) 1890-1900 A.D.*, vol. I (Calcutta, 1900).
8. *F.M.S. West Godavari* 1957-60; *Report of the Special Officer for the Investigation of Land Tenures on the Proposals on Land Revenue Reform* (Madras, 1950) Appendix IV; *Agricultural Prices in India* 1959.
9. *F.M.S. Madras* 1954-57; *Report of the Special Officer* Appendix IV; *District Gazetteer Coimbatore 1935* (for prices).
10. *F.M.S. Madras* 1954-57; *Report of the Special Officer* Appendix IV; *District Gazetteer Salem 1933* (for prices).
11. *F.M.S. Bombay* 1954-57; earlier rent data relate to four talukas of Ahmadnagar: Nevasa, Shevgaon, Nagar and Rahuri, from *Selection from the Records of the Records of the Bombay Government* No. 588 - *Papers Relating to the Second Revision Survey Settlement of the Nevasa Taluka of the Ahmednagar Collectorate* (Bombay, 1922); prices from No. 12 below.
12. *F.M.S. Bombay*, 1954-57; Rent data refer to five talukas-Sinnar, Niphad, Yeola, Igatpuri, and Chandor—given in *Selection No. 541 - Papers relating to the Second Revision Settlements of the Nasik District* (Bombay, 1916); prices from *ibid.*
13. *F.M.S. Madhya Pradesh* 1954-57; earlier rent data refer to five talukas—Balapur, Jalgaon, Chikhli, Malkapur, Khamgaon—and are taken from

    i) Central Provinces Survey and Settlement Department Report: *Balapur Taluq of the Akola District* (Nagpur, 1926);

    ii) *Ibid.*: *Jalgaon Taluq of the Buldana District* (Nagpur, 1926);

    iii) *Assessment Group Rate Reports of the Second Revision Settlement of the Chikhli Taluq in the Buldana District* (Nagpur, 1926). Cotton prices 1916-25 from (i). In the 1950s prices ceilings wre imposed on cotton, but they were occasionally evaded; in order to allow for this I have taken the price 1954-57 to be Rs. 800 a candy on the basis of the *Annual Reports of the Indian Central Cotton Committee* for the relevant years. The 1916-25 average price was Rs. 408.

However, even within the northern belt, there are enormous differences as between the huge increase in Deoria and the modest one in the Twenty-Four Parganas or Cuttack. It may be well, therefore, to develop explanations on a case by case basis.

To begin with Deoria: its settlement report, compiled during the First World War, found rent rates 'astonishingly low' at Rs. 4 per acre for non-occupancy tenants. Nazrana and irregular levies were also sometimes made, but the basic reason for the low level of rent was that the region was one of recent settlement with cultivable land still available across the frontier in Nepal serving to keep down landlord demands. It was definitely not due to the legal or other powers of tenants: 'Most of the zamindars, big and small, have still a firm hold over their tenants,' and have been enabled to get pretty much what they pleased by way of rent without resort to the Courts...'[4] Other indications of this are that the rate for occupancy tenants was marginally higher than that for non-occupancy—Rs. 4.2 and Rs. 4—and that there was little rent in kind.

On the other hand, when the *Study* was conducted (1966-69), 'crop sharing and kind renting are the common practices....Fixed kind rents are also settled by a few farmers. The practice is also to supply seeds, manures and fertilizers and settle a portion of produce after adding proportionate cost of supplies, or to lease out land and settle one-third to one-half of the total produce without providing any input'.[5]

In 1967-68 the gross value of output on a cultivated acre was Rs. 895, and share rent charged on this would clearly result in a large increase over the earlier level. Here changes in productivity also become relevant. Reliable data are not available for 1916, but in 1933-36 the ICAR studied a group of farms in Gorakhpur,[6] and we can compare the yields they found to those of the *Study* in 1966-69. Since the ICAR chose its farms purposively, and perhaps with a tendency to over-represent the larger holdings, I have taken the median rather than the mean yield per acre. For the later period the means have been used.

The yield of wheat and sugarcane would appear to have increased, and that of paddy to have stagnated or declined slightly. In the aggregate, land productivity may well have increased. That by itself, however, need not increase rents, if the input costs rise by an amount equal or nearly equal to the increment in output. But the increase in wheat is likely to be the result of the partial introduction of HYV technology in the area, and the landlords could appropriate the gains by the device of paying and then recouping the extra input cost which is mentioned in the above quotation. But even allowing for productivity change, it seems indubitable that rents rose sharply here, and that they rose due to the mounting population pressure in the district. Share rents in the 1960s were then at the level—one-third or half the crop—that they had reached other parts of eastern India at the beginning of this century itself.

Table 2
Yields per acre of Crops in Gorakhpur/Deoria (lbs.)

	1933-36	1966-69
Wheat	469	1432
Early paddy	1035	1057
Late paddy	749	639
Planted sugarcane	22026	36784

Source: *Cost of Production of Crops for* 1933-36, and *Combined Report 1966-69, Deoria.*

In addition to the change in the level of rent, its' form seems to have changed as well, with rent in kind replacing cash rent. This, of course, is associated with the massive institutional change brought about by zamindari abolition, whereby most of the old tenants now became owners, and as a rule, only the smaller landlords remained. Often these would be men of the type described by the Collector of Ballia, H.T. Lane in 1946:[7]

> If it is thought that only zamindars "oppress" tenants, I would point out that in this district far more genuine "oppression" is done to the "tiller of the soil" by big fixed-rate tenants than is done even in Oudh by taluqdars. Some fixed-rate tenants (including many Congress Netas) hold up to 200 acres of land at Rs. 2 per acre and have sub-let all of it at rates ranging between Rs. 60 and Rs. 90 per acre.

At a later date, when most tenants had become owners it would be only landlords of this type who could conceal tenancy and enforce crop share. This tendency would be present everywhere, and would also tend to an increase in rent rates.

After Deoria, the next largest increase is observed in Ferozepur district in Punjab (125 per cent) with a smaller, but not insignificant increase in Amritsar (42 per cent). Agricultural conditions had also changed in the period: in 1955, 86 per cent of the cultivated area was irrigated in Amritsar, and 65 per cent in Ferozepur. The rental value of irrigated land in both districts, as calculated in the *Study*, was over twice that of unirrigated. Around 1912, only 63 per cent of cultivated land in Amritsar, and 35 per cent in Ferozepur had been irrigated. This would send up rents, the more so if irrigation charges from the predominant source—government canals—did not keep up with inflation. C.E. Pray has re-examined the agricultural statistics of British Punjab, and concludes that output was growing at about 1 per cent per annum 1907-46, with about 74 per cent of this attributable to the spread of irrigation. Since population was growing more rapidly than output, any fall in the real charges for irrigation as a consequence of the War and post-War inflation would probably accrue to the landlords. Another 10 to 15 per cent of the growth is attributed to improved strains of crop[8]—this would reduce costs per unit of product, and again, in the circumstances of excess demand for land, send up the rent. Finally, as regards the difference between the districts, Amritsar at the beginning of the century was already densely settled and cultivated while Ferozepur like Deoria, still had some of the characteristics of a frontier zone. The increase in Amritsar may almost wholly be accounted for by the irrigation factor allied with a say 10 per cent cost reduction due to better seeds.

Shahabad district in Bihar also shows a distinct increase. 75 per cent of its net sown area was irrigated in 1961 as against 45 per cent in 1913.[9] This district was settled by the statistically-minded J.A. Hubback in 1907-16, and he estimated the yield of paddy to be 11.5 maunds an acre. In 1960-63 it had risen to 21 maunds, or by over 80 per cent.[10] Rent in kind was quite widespread, and Hubback reckoned that the landlord received, after deductions, about a third of the crop. In the 1960s the stipulated rent was 10 maunds of paddy (average yield being 21 maunds) or half the crop. It would seem, therefore, that a considerable increase in productivity occurred, with a large resultant gain to the landlords. They may have been contributing towards costs however, since 10 maunds of paddy should have been worth at least Rs. 100, while the realized rent was Rs. 51.50 according to the *Farm Management Study*.

Increases in rent rates are to be seen in the West Bengal districts of Hugli and Twenty-Four Parganas as well, and in the latter case are small enough to be sensitive to the price taken as a deflator. The early rent rates themselves are calculated from Hunter's *Statistical Accounts*. These give the range of subdivisional rates for different types of land. The predominant crop being winter paddy, I have taken the mid-point of the range for paddy for each subdivision, and then the mean of the mid-points in order to produce a district figure. The result was a figure of Rs. 7.50 for Hugli, and Rs. 5.61 for Twenty-four Parganas. Now, it is known that ryoti rents in Bengal proper tended to ossify at the late nineteenth-century levels, and our confidence in above calculation is considerably increased by the closeness of the estimates to the actuals found by the Floud Commission in 1939. These were Rs. 7.43 for Hugli, and Rs. 5.81 for Twenty-four Parganas; under tenants by then paid Rs. 14 and Rs. 11 respectively.[11]

If we use the under-tenant rents, and take the price of paddy in 1939 to be Rs. 2 a maund, the increase in real rent 1939-56 is larger than that shown Table 1. It amounts to 54 per cent for Hugli and 32 per cent for Twenty-four Parganas. So there is an increase, whether measured over a longer or the shorter period. The agricultural statistics of eastern India were rightly suspect, and we have no usable data on late nineteen century yields. However, the yield of Aman paddy seems to have changed little from the 1930s to the 1950s (Table 3)

Table 3
Yields of Aman Paddy in lbs. per Acre

District	1932-37	1944-45	1954-57
Hugli	1415	1302	1451
24 Parganas	1380	1507	1296

Sources: Col. 1 from *Report of the Land Revenue Commission*, vol. II, p. 89; col. 2 from *Agricultural Statistics by Plot to Plot Enumeration 1944-45* (Calcutta, 1946) p.120; and col. 3 *Study, West Bengal*, Table A-17.

We may be reasonably sure then, that productivity had not changed significantly. But there is one change that we need to consider—the earlier data all relate to cash rents while the later set relate wholly to rent in kind. The West Bengal *Study* states:[12]

> Cash renting is very rare; the most common practice is to pay a certain specified share - usually half - of the crop and the by-product. Occasionally, the quantity of the crop to be paid as rent after harvest may be fixed in advance irrespective of the final production.

This was not a new practice; Hunter describes it in 1873 for Hugli: 'In the case of paddy lands, these rayats cultivate the land at their own expense and by their own labour, and divide the produce equally with the party who pays the rent for the land'.[13] Similarly in the Twenty-four Parganas, Brahmins, Kayasthas and others leased out on *bhag* 'a tenure under which the cultivator finds all the expenses of tillage, etc., and gives the owner of the land one-half of the crop.'[14] Reforms after Independence established many or most cash-paying tenants as virtual proprietors, and only share-tenancy survived. The area under tenancy shrank, but the rents of the remaining tenants rose.

This argument is supported by some evidence from the district of Howrah, which was resettled in 1934-39. If even cash paying under-tenants were paying less than what the sharecroppers paid, the holder of such a tenure enjoyed some fraction of the rent, which should make his tenure, if at all secure, a saleable one. And this is what we observe in Howrah.

Table 4
Approximate Prices of Rice Land Under Different Tenures

Tenure	(Rupees per Acre)
Raiyati	225 to 300
Under-Raiyati	150 to 225
Rent-free	375 to 525

Source: *Final Report on the Survey and Settlement Operations in the District of Howrah 1934-39* (Calcutta, 1940), p. 56.

The issue of the relation between cash and kind rents will be discussed more fully below.

As regards the last of the districts studied in eastern India, Cuttack, it has been possible to compare the cash and kind rent for the same crop at both points in time. The Settlement Officer estimated in the 1890s that a landlord leasing out on *bhag* received half the crop and by-products. This share he calculated at 8 maunds or 3 quintals of paddy, worth between Rs. 8 and 10. The share for paddy was still 50 per cent in the late 1960s, and with an average yield of 16.6 maunds or 6.2 quintals an acre, the landlord's rent would be practically unchanged. The small increase that appears in Table 1 may be explained by the inclusion of the value of straw at the later date--an item ignored by the Settlement Report. On the other hand, under-ryots paying cash in the earlier period paid Rs. 3.10 per acre, or one-third of the kind rent.[15]

The West Godavari district also shows an increase. As this district was separated from East Godavari in the 1920s, the data for 1917-18 relate to the undivided district. The two, however, were very similar in their agricultural conditions, so this should not seriously affect the result. As regards yields, our data are shaky. The *best* wet land (Class IV-1) was calculated for settlement purposes to produce 900 Madras measures or 2070 lbs. of paddy per acre. However, in 1955-56 the district yield of rice was 1203 lbs., and the average (not highest) yield found in the holdings studied was 1993 lbs. of paddy per gross cropped acre in the two seasons.[16] If payments for paddy land are converted into paddy equivalents, tenants in 1957-60 paid nearly 1,000 lbs. per acre. Some increase in average yields may have occured since 1918, and the rise in rents may reflect this.

No such increase appears in Coimbatore district - at least on the basis of a comparison of the ICAR and the *Study* data. These are set out in Table 5.

The rent rate here seems to have declined by one-third, but this may partly be due to the deflation being done with paddy prices—a comparison with-cotton would show a lesser decline. A slight decline in rent is also visible in Salem—perhaps associated with a fall in yield as in Coimbatore—but I have no direct evidence of this.

Table 5
Yields of Crops in lbs. per Acre: Coimbatore

	1933-36	1954-57
Cotton	658	544
Ragi	1726	1401
Paddy	2219	2003

Source: ICAR *Studies in the Cost of Production* and *Farm Management Study* 1970-73.

Then we come to the two Maharashtra districts of Ahmadnagar and Nasik, which show no change in rent rates. This result is not unexpected, as it has been found in a much more detailed study of the same region.[17] As regards yields, there is no direct evidence for these districts, but the balance of evidence seems to be against any increase. Table 4 shows the official Standard Yield multiplied by Condition Factors 1916-20 of the main millet crops in the two districts, as compared with actual yields (1952-53 to 1956-57).

It would be difficult to argue that yields rose in this region, and I would be inclined to reiterate my earlier conclusion that they either stagnated or declined.[18] The same may be said of the last case in the Table—the Berar (Varhad) region of easter Maharashtra. Cotton was the major commercial crop here, and its price ratio is given in column 3 of Table1.[19] The rents of the earlier period were recorded during a veritable cotton boom in the region, when very large profits were made by the cultivation of that crop and its productivity per acre also reached very high levels. By the 1950s, on the other hand, cotton prices had lagged behind foodgrain prices and yield levels were, for the Central Indian region as a whole, rather lower than in the 1920s though this comparison is complicated by the intervening varietal change. But a decline in the application of non-land inputs to cotton is suggested by the sharp fall in average yields that occurred with the crash in 1930—with yields falling to the levels that they were to maintain till the 1950s.[20] Rents and land prices also fell dramatically with the depression, suggesting that the decline or stagnation of rents in this region is related to the decline in the price of its staple commodity.

Table 6
Yields per acre in lbs.

	Ahmadnagar	Nasik
RABI JOWAR		
1916-20	335	364
1952-56	231	142
BAJRI		
1916-20	167	205
1952-56	174	232

Sources : Calculated from *Return of the Yield of Principal Crops and Season and Crop Reports*, Bombay. The crop years are 1916-17 to 1920-21, and 1952-53 to 1956-57.

One explanation of apparent increase in rent rates has surfaced several times in this discussion: this is that the change-over from cash to kind rents in eastern India resulted in a rise in average rent rates even though kind rents themselves remained unchanged at both points in time. This has been suggested for both Orissa and West Bengal. Implicit in this suggestion is the proposition that cash rents in these regions, were significantly lower than kind rents in the early twentieth-century. If we accept this, we have to explain why this was so and why the phenomenon was confined to this part of the country.

The answer, briefly put, is supervision costs. The Permanent Settlement in eastern India created a class of landlords with much bigger holdings than in the other regions studied, and they were unable to exercise the close supervision needed for the successful exaction of produce rent. Produce rent was therefore generally taken by small lessors, who were often tenants themselves, as Table 7 shows. Kind rent was more common in south Bihar, than in the north Bihar districts, being here related to the insecurity of yields on some land, and the zamindar's responsibility for providing irrigation on other lands.[21] However, Table 7 indicates that in the North tenants themselves strongly preferred to lease out on kind rent. The Monghyr Settlement Officer, trying to explain the variation in the incidence of produce rent saw supervision as the crucial factor:[22]

Table 7
Produce Rent Paying Area as Percentage of Land Held in each Tenure in Bihar Districts

District	Settled and Occupancy	Non-occupancy	Under-ryot
N. Monghyr	5	7	60
Darbhanga	3	7	53
Muzaffarpur	7	19	61
Saran	4	8	23
Champaran	4	22	65

Source: *Monghyr Settlement Report 1905-07*, p. 92.

> there is the fact that in these areas most landlords are petty and resident, they are better able to look after their interests in produce rent paying lands, and it was not uncommon to find lands which grow mainly the valuable crops, such as tobacco and chillies, paying a produce rent, which course brought in a very much larger profit to the landlord....

> On the other hand, in Gogri where the comparatively backward state of agriculture ought to have led one to expect a larger proportion of the area to be held on produce rent, the fact that the landlords are much bigger men with wider areas to look after, and the state of the country is such that communications are difficult, have successfully counteracted any tendency to settle the newly reclaimed areas on terms of produce rent.

Bengal landlords faced similar problems; the manager of a Burdwan estate said in 1880 that 'it is only when the gomasta [manager] is unable to let out the lands in money rent that he lets out the land in bhag'.[23] (share-crop). But cash rents had a strong tendency to ossify: thus the Floud Commission explained the high rent rates in western as contrasted to eastern Bengal in 1940 by referring to the fact that at[24]

> the time of the Permanent Settlement, western Bengal, and Burdwan in particular was more extensively cultivated than the rest of the province, where there were large areas of jungle and waste land which tenants had to be induced by preferential rates of rent to bring under cultivation.

Unable to check this process of ossification, the landlords increasingly resorted to the practice of taking *salami*, entry fee, on the occasion of transfers, rather than revising the rate of rent, effectively allowing an under-proprietary right to grow under them.[25] But even *salami* claims proved difficult to enforce. By 1925, the Inspector of Registration was writing that 'whatever the law may be on the subject, it is an established fact that occupancy rights are at present freely transferred without reference to and without the knowledge of the landlord'.[26] As regards the rate of *salami*, the Director of Land Records was 'convinced that a *salami* of 25 per cent is far too high. It is only very rarely that this amount is even demanded and 12 1/2 per cent would more nearly represent what is actually realised, though even this, I fancy, is higher than the average'.[27] Thus the problems of supervision and control worsened over time, and the gap between the grain rents taken by the petty landlord and the cash ones charged by the large zamindar widened.[28] Zamindari abolition swept away the latter but largely spared the former.

On the other hand, in areas characterized by small landlords such as Punjab, western India and most of Madras Presidency, the gap between kind and cash rents was not allowed to widen—even though a certain differential did exist. Thus in the 21 districts covered by T.E. Moir in 1917-18—a year of high prices—kind rents were 10 per cent higher than cash on single crop wet land, and 15 per cent higher on double crop land.[29] The cash-kind disparity was not as great in ryotwari as in zamindari areas.

With this we conclude the case analysis which the patchy and variegated nature of our information rendered necessary, and may review the findings. To begin with, the evidence strongly supports Professor Stokes' argument that over the twentieth-century 'the upper landholding elite were confronted not by a body of tenants...but by a mass of peasant sub-proprietors towards whom their relation tended to be increasingly that of absentee owners of a rent charge or ground rent'.[30] Our material also buttresses his view that the full profits of agricultural production could only be appropriated by those who were able to exercise direct control over sharecroppers or labourers.

Certain other conclusions also suggest themselves. Population growth, for instance, seems to bear no direct relation to changes in rents: it grew quite rapidly in every part of the country, but the rents show no uniform pattern of change. This is not surprising if we consider that the subsistence of the cultivator forms an obvious limit to the rent payable, and population pressure may push it towards this limit (the Ferozepur and Deoria cases), but not below it. If the income is already near this floor, then only an increase in production greater than the necessary increase in private costs could send rents higher. State investment in irrigation or seeds—as suggested for Punjab—could have such an effect. The benefits of a reduction in private costs would accrue to landowners.

The data on changes in productivity are poor, and relate to the average product of land, without considering the intensity of input use. Tentatively, however, it does seem possible to say that increases in rent rates are associated with increases in productivity and vice versa. If the two are, in fact associated, then landlords would seem to have a positive interest in productivity growth, particularly since they could not expect a secular rise in rents merely from population growth.

This argument, however, presupposes the existence of landlords with full control over the land, and thus capable of reaping the benefits of productivity increase or cost reduction. But land control was itself in dispute during this period, the issue being only definitively settled by the post-Independence legislation. Tenants may have been acquiring a measure of control, but the risk of reversal was always present. The situation was essentially a conflict ridden one, and these pervasive conflicts may well have contributed to the agrarian impasse that characterized rural India in the decades before Independence. It is also possible that their resolution through zamindari abolition and other reforms contributed to the surge of growth that marked the 1950s, as Stokes' 'peasant elite' finally came into its' own.

NOTES

1. Eric Stokes, 'Agrarian Relations: Northern and Central India', *The Cambridge Economic History of India*, ed. Dharma Kumar, vol. II (Cambridge, 1983), p. 84.
2. *Studies in the Economics of Farm Management* were all published by the Ministry of Agriculture, Government of India, at various times. They will be referred to by the abbreviation F.M.S.
3. *Monghyr F.M.S. Report 1957-58*, mimeo, p. 35.
4. *Gorakhpur Settlement Report*, pp. 10, 11, 3, 27, 9.
5. *F.M.S. Deoria Combined Report 1966-69*, p. 26.
6. Imperial Council of Agricultural Research: *Studies in the Cost of Production of Crops in Some of the Important Cotton and Sugarcane Tracts of India* (Calcutta, 1938, 1940).
7. *Report of the U.P. Zamindari Abolition Committee* (Allahabad, 1948), vol. III, p. 184.
8. C.E. Pray, 'Accuracy of the Official Agricultural Statistics and the Sources of Growth in Punjab 1907-1946', *Indian Economic and Social History Review*, XXI, 3 (1984).
9. *Agricultural Statistics of British India* 1912-13, and *F.M.S.* 1961-63.
10. *Shahabad Settlement Report* and *F.M.S.*
11. *Report of the Land Revenue Commission* (Calcutta, 1940), vol. II, p. 108.
12. *F.M.S. West Bengal*, p. 63.
13. Hunter, vol. III, p. 351.
14. Hunter, vol. I, p. 155.
15. *Orissa Settlement Report 1890-1900*, vol. I, pp. 233-4, 355-56.
16. *Report of the Special Officer for Land Tenures*, p. 39; and p. 47; and *F.M.S. West Godvari.*
17. See S. Guha, 'The Land Market in Upland Maharashtra 1820-1960', *Indian Economic and Social History Review*, XXIV, 3 (1987).
18. S. Guha, *The Agrarian Economy of the Bombay Deccan 1818-1941* (New Delhi, 1985), p. 124.
19. See also n. 13 to Table 1.
20. Cotton Yields in lbs. per acre: Central Provinces

1926-27 to 1929-30	107
1930-31 to 1935-36	71

1936-37 to 1939-40	75
1950-51 to 1954-55	75

Note: The calculation is only approximate, owing to boundary changes after Independence.

Sources: 1936-40 *The Bombay Cotton Annual*, various issues; 1950-55 *Estimates of Area and Production of Principal Crops in India* 1954-55, vol. I.

21. B.B. Chaudhuri, 'Movement of Rent', p. 309, *Indian Historical Review*, 1977.
22. *Monghyr Settlement Report*, p. 93.
23. *Report of the Government of Bengal on the Proposed Amendment of the Law of Landlord and Tenant* (Calcutta, 1883), vol. II, p. 177.
24. *Report of the Land Revenue Commission*, vol. I, p. 124.
25. Ibid.
26. Government of Bengal: *Collection of Opinions on the Bengal Tenancy (Amendment) Bill 1925*, p. 64.
27. Ibid., p. 61.
28. Subdivision of zamindaris by inheritance often created new sharers in the estate without a physical division of lands, thus worsening rather than easing the supervision problem.
29. *Report of the Special Officer Appendix* IV.
30. Eric Stokes, 'Agrarian Relations: Northern and Central India', p. 62 in *The Cambridge Economic History*, op. cit.

Agrarian Production and Colonial Policy in Punjab

J. S. GREWAL

Revenue from land was by far the most important source of income to the state when the British finally took over Punjab in 1849, and it remained the single most important source till the end of British rule in 1947.[1] This was one major reason why British economic policy in Punjab remained focused on land. The rate of assessment was, at least theoretically, supposed to be lenient,[2] whereas the realization of land-revenue was meant to be strict.[3] Periodic settlement of land-revenue was meant to ensure an increasing share for the state with the increase in agricultural production.[4]

In order to collect the land-revenue, it was necessary to decide with whom to make the settlement, or in other words, who should pay the sums assessed. All kinds of rights in land were examined to identify long term cultivators as well as proprietors with whom settlement could be made. Therefore, the settlement came to consist of two parts: the assessment of land revenue and the framing of a record of rights. Involved in this process was the determination of existing rights rather than the creation of new rights.[5] In the context of colonial rule, nonetheless, the formal recording of an individual's proprietary right and its legal recognition introduced an element of great significance. New laws rather than 'new rights' gave economic significance to proprietorship in land.[6]

Soon after the British annexation of Punjab, the area under cultivation began to increase. During the ten years after 1868, for instance, the area under cultivation increased from about 20 to over 23 million acres.[7] The proportion of the area under irrigation also began to increase, particularly due to the system of canals introduced by the new rulers.[8] In 1868, about 6 million acres of land were irrigated, mostly by wells. By 1900, the canals were irrigating over 5,000,000 acres.[9] Larger acreage under cultivation and irrigation increased agricultural production. It also meant increase in land-revenue.[10]

However, increase in land-revenue was not the only reason for which the colonial rulers encouraged agricultural production. An enormous incentive for higher production was provided by the new means of communications with which to reach a wider market. By the end of the nineteenth-century 4,000 miles of railways and metalled roads linked the cities and towns of Punjab with one another, and the region as a whole with-cities like Calcutta, Bombay and Karachi. In 1883, the railways carried away from Punjab nearly 10 million maunds of goods worth over Rs. 37 million. Twenty years later the corresponding figures were nearly 25 million maunds and over Rs. 115 million.[11] The most important item of export was wheat, followed by other grains and cotton. The increase in agricultural production was increasingly getting geared to markets outside Punjab. As a contemporary writer put it, the price of wheat in Punjab came to depend on its price in Liverpool.[12] The cultivator began to produce beyond his wants, and he was now a part of world trade. Punjab thus became an integral part of colonial economy, exporting food and raw materials and importing finished goods and precious metals.[13]

As the result of these developments, agricultural land became a valuable commodity.[14] In 1870 the average price of land was Rs. 10 rupees an acre but in 1891 it was more than Rs. 60.[15] Sales of land before 1857 were comparatively rare but their increasing volume was quite noticeable by 1872. From 79,000 acres sold in 1874-75, the number rose to 209,000 acres in 1884-85 and to 321,000 acres in 1894-95.[16] The figures for mortgage at these three points of time respectively were 204,000, 323,000 and 603,000 acres.[17] In the absence of industrial development, investment in landed property presented an unprecedented opportunity to those who possessed capital. The number of bankers and moneylenders began to increase at a rapid pace.[18] They belonged largely to the Punjab trading communities who were dominant in the civil administration and the courts as well. They were, indeed, a part of the urban middle class which was gaining great importance on the basis of its newly acquired wealth, education and influence.

The moneylenders and traders were not the only sections of society to gain from commercialization of agriculture. Some of the large landholders were successful in adjusting themselves to the new situation and in adding to their landed possessions through either state patronage or purchase. Many of them were descendants of former jagirdars and dharmarth grantees. They were looked upon as the 'natural leaders' of the society, and they were expected to use their influence in support of the empire and were thus patronized by the new rulers in several ways. Their importance, therefore, was out of all proportion to their numbers.[19] More numerous were the petty commodity producers, particularly in the canal colonies and the central districts, who produced for the outside markets on their holdings of 20 acres or more.[20]

Much more numerous than the large and middling landholders were the owners of small holdings and tenants. While the large and middling landholders could give land for cultivation to tenants, many of the small landholders had to take up land for cultivation as tenants. The marked increase in the number of tenants under colonial rule in Punjab was due both to fragmentation of holdings and to the fact that many an owner of land was becoming a tenant on his own land.[21] The majority of those who lost their lands to moneylenders and buyers were the small landholders who, though less indebted than the large or middling landholders, got more deeply into debt and were forced to part with their land.[22] By the end of the nineteenth-century, alienation of land was increasing at a rapid pace and a large number of transfers were in favour of the moneylending class.[23]

However, land alienation was not simply transfer of land from agriculturists to non-agriculturists.[24] Due to the differences of geography, systems of agriculture, character of the landholding groups and the outlook of the trading communities in Punjab there was enormous diversity in the pattern of mortgages and sales of land. In the southeastern districts, alienation of land was the least extensive. In the southwestern districts on the other hand, alienation was largely in favour of non-agriculturists, while in the upper districts of western Punjab, it was largely in favour of agriculturists. The semi-pastoral and high caste owners lost more than the settled agriculturists and the Jats. 'Then there were the Sikh Jats of central Punjab, not only able to keep outsiders at bay, but manifesting acquisitive and money-lending tendencies to a remarkable degree'.[25] Already by the close of the nineteenth-century the agriculturist moneylender had appeared on the scene.[26]

II

The Punjab Alienation of Land Act was passed in 1900 to become operative in the following year. Without 'unduly limiting the credit on which the peasants depend for the means of cultivation', the Act was meant to place restrictions on transfer of agricultural land 'with a view to checking its alienation from the agricultural to non-agricultural classes'.[27] Concern for agricultural production provided the grounds for economic argument in favour of this legislation.[28] The traditional owners of land, it was argued, were better cultivators than tenants and, since alienation in favour of non-agriculturists virtually meant larger and larger acreage under tenants, the prevailing process of alienation presented 'a serious political danger'.[29]

The awareness of this 'political danger' had been growing in the late nineteenth-century. The Commissioner of Multan in 1869 said that voluntary transfer of land was a 'political question of great importance'.[30] Justice Melville of the Chief Court of the Punjab, who asked the Punjab Government to revise the legal procedure connected with debt litigation and to place limitation on voluntary transfer of land, in 1872 expressed the view that a peasant without land becomes 'a disaffected and disloyal subject'.[31] In the 1880s, S.S. Thorburn, the author of the *Musalmans and Money-lenders in the Punjab*, underlined the political danger arising from the alienation of land in favour of non-agriculturists. According to him the peasantry in the 'sentinel districts' of the 'frontier province' of India, was being displaced by a class of men 'unconnected by tradition with the soil' and by no means 'too well disposed towards the Government'. Discontent among the peasantry was growing with the increasing alienation, and demanded timely action.[32] The problem of alienation in the last resort appeared to be linked with the future of colonial rule itself.

The political consideration tilted the balance against the doctrine of *laissez faire*. One of the ideals of British administration in Punjab had been to maintain as far as possible the integrity of village coparcenaries.[33] An unreasonable alienation could be set aside by the court. The rule of pre-emption was included in the Code of 1854. It was also the policy of the government not to resort to sale on account of arrears in revenue; compulsory sale on account of debt had to be referred first to the Commissioner, and subsequently to the Financial Commissioner. In the sphere of voluntary alienation *laissez faire* was allowed to operate. By the last decade of the nineteenth-century, however, many of the important administrators of Punjab had turned in favour of restriction on voluntary alienation.

In the interest of colonial rule, the British administrators eventually decided to look for support among the agrarian classes. At the outset of British rule in Punjab, when the middling class was of no great consequence, the theoretical possibility of making the former ruling class the main prop of British rule was discarded in favour of the more numerous small and middling proprietors and cultivators, so much so that the settlement officers made the long-term tenants hereditary (*maurusi*) mainly at the cost of the large landholders.[34] After the uprising of 1857-58, there was a definite change in favour of the rural aristocracy.[35] Consequently, the landholders in general came to be looked upon as the major political support for colonial rule.

'The matter was rendered the more serious by the fact that two-third of the Indian army was now recruited from the Punjab peasantry'.[36] The policy of recruiting Punjabis to the Indian army in large numbers had been formulated before the end of the nineteenth-century and it was systematically followed in the early twentieth. Contrary to the general impression, Punjabi Muslims rather than Sikhs were recruited to the army in the largest numbers.[37] In fact, from the viewpoint of recruitment, the Muslim dominated western districts were more important even than the central districts of the Punjab, just as the 'frontier province' as a whole was more important than any other province from the viewpoint of the defence of the empire.[38]

The social configuration of Punjab in the late nineteenth-century gave to the Alienation of Land Act a communal as well as a class complexion. Dominant among the Hindus in terms of wealth and influence was the urban middle class. Among the Muslims, the most important interests were represented by the landholders living in the countryside. The greatest gainers in the process of alienation were Hindus and the greatest losers were the Muslims. Opposition to the bill came largely from the moneylenders, traders, officials, lawyers and journalists who were overwhelmingly Hindus.[39] Support to the bill mainly came from some Muslim journalists and Muslim officials and professional men with a rural background. If the non-agriculturists found a spokesman in Harnam Singh Ahluwalia, the agriculturists got a spokesman in Muhammad Hayat Khan. The Indian National Congress dropped its opposition to the bill when its leaders discovered that it was gaining a communal complexion.[40]

There were racial as well as communal dimensions of the Act. It was left to the Punjab Government to notify 'agriculturists' and for this, the Punjab administrators adopted the relative importance of the landowning tribes and castes as the criterion for notification. Consequently many an actual owner or tiller of land was left out. In the districts of Amritsar and Gurdaspur, for example, Jats, Rajputs, Arrains, Gujjars, Dogras, Mughals, Pathans and Sayyids were notified in the very beginning. The Sainis were notified in Gurdaspur but not in Amrtitsar; while the Kambos were notified in Amritsar but not in Gurdaspur. Due to their increasing importance and pressure, new groups were notified in these two districts in 1906, 1907, 1909, 1914, 1933, 1937 and 1939. Classified as 'separate groups', Brahmins, Kakezais, Kumhars, Indian Christians, Sudras and Mazhabi Sikhs were also notified between 1908 and 1939.[41]

The communal and racial dimensions of the Act, painfully important in the eyes of those whose interests suffered a setback, remained subordinate to its class character. The urban middle classes included Sikhs and Muslims who were unhappy about the Act while the landholders in the countryside, including Sikhs and Hindus, were happy. If the urban middle classes looked upon the Act as a notice that they no longer enjoyed a favoured position in the eyes of their rulers, the landholders looked upon it as a charter of their rights.[42] The alienation of the urban middle classes from the colonial rulers and the support of the rural interests for colonial rule were the obverse and the reverse of the same political coin. The British administrators were aware of the growing importance of the urban middle class.[43] They espoused the cause of rural interests for their own self-interest.[44]

If the negative objective of the Alienation of Land Act was not to unduly limit credit, this objective was achieved. The average price of land fell from Rs. 78 per acre during the five years following it. In 1906, however it began to rise again, reaching 275 in 1919-20. Ten years later it was more than Rs. 400 per acre.[45] The average area sold also began to decrease in the early years of this century, but began to rise in the second decade largely due to the sale of government lands. What was more significant was the fact that the area sold by agriculturists was generally less than the area purchased by them. Also agricultural tribes were gaining by redemption and mortgage far more than they were losing by mortgage.[46] The agriculturist moneylender was gaining in numbers and importance.[47]

If the objective of the Act was to obviate transfer of land from agriculturists to non-agriculturists, this objective too was largely achieved. There were loopholes in the Act which were used by the non-agriculturist moneylenders to their advantage. But several of these loopholes were closed through later amendments. The importance, power and influence of the traditional moneylender did suffer a setback.[48] The plight of the small landholder did not diminish in spite of the cooperative movement and the programme of consolidation of holdings. If anything, differentiation among the landholders increased.[49] If the objective of the Act was to win rural support for the empire, this objective too was largely achieved.

But, for this political gain, British administrators had to work consistently during the early twentieth-century.

III

Writing towards the end of the nineteenth-century, James Douie observed that the old outlook which gave primacy to the political advantage of maintaining the traditional framework of society in the countryside was regaining importance after a lapse of few decades.[50] Nearly a decade after the Alienation of Land Act he reiterated rather explicitly that the bulk of the population of Punjab consisted of landowners and their dependents their contentment 'must always be the chief solicitude of its ruler'.[51] Michael O'Dwyer who became the Lieutenant Governor of Punjab a few years later, wrote in retrospect that throughout his term of office he did what he could 'to further the interests of the rural masses' who appeared to form 'the basis of stability and prosperity of the Province'.[52]

The British administrators of Punjab were consistent in their pro-rural policies during the early twentieth-century. In 1902, the Descent of Jagirs Act was passed to regulate succession in accordance with the principle of primogeniture. In the following year, the Court of Wards Act improved the legal position of the wards and created a single organization for all districts. In 1904 the Cooperative Societies Act was passed to enable landholders to borrow money on reasonable terms. In 1907, the Punjab Alienation of Land Act of 1900 was amended to remove the clause relating to 'statutory agriculturists', adversely affecting the interests of 'non-agriculturists' earlier treated as 'agriculturists'. In 1913, the Redemption of Mortgages Act provided for a summary method of redemption in all cases in which the principal money secured irrespective of the area involved was not more than Rs. 1,000.[53]

The anxiety of the British administrators to retain the support of the landed interests was reflected in their attitude to constitutional reforms. The principle of election was introduced in the province for the first time in the Act of 1909 and that too with a franchise that safeguarded the election of 'aristocrats' who were earlier brought to the Council through nomination.[54] In the Act of 1919, separate electorates for Muslims were retained and new ones were added for Sikhs; at the same time, separate electorates were introduced for the urban and rural areas. The members of 'agriculturist' tribes only were allowed to contest rural seats. The number of voters, not more than 3 per cent of the population, ensured the domination of the large landholders. All commissioned and non-commissioned officers of the army, jagirdars, zaildars, lambardars and safedposhes were enfranchized in addition to those proprietors and tenants who paid a yearly revenue of Rs.25 or more. Of the 500,000 voters, more than 420,000 belonged to the rural areas. The number of Hindu voters in the villages was more than three times their numbers in the cities; among the Muslims, it was seven times, and among the Sikhs, twenty times.[55] The preponderance of rural members in the Legislative Council of Punjab was the inevitable outcome of an institutionalized division between the cities and the villages.

By far the largest bulk of the rural members elected to the Punjab Legislative Council between 1919 and 1935 joined the Unionist Party which professed to safeguard and promote rural interests. The most eminent leaders of the Party, Mian Fazl-i-Husain, Sardar Sunder Singh Majithia and Chaudhary Chhotu Ram, presented a common front against trading and moneylending interests, though within the Party the interests of the large landholders in general and of Muslim landholders in particular were better served than the interests of the small landholders or the tenants. In 1924, the Unionists secured reduction in the enhancement proposed in the canal water rates; the rearranged budget increased urban taxation. In 1926, an amendment of the Alienation of Land Act closed certain loopholes revealed by the decisions of the High Court. The Land Revenue Act of 1928 gave certain concessions to landholders and cultivators. The Punjab Regulation of Accounts Act, passed in 1929 after a hot debate, was made operative in 1931, while another amendment of the Act of 1900 made an explicit provision that no piece of land belonging to a member of an agriculturist tribe could remain leased or farmed for a period exceeding 20 years. In 1936, yet another amendment included 'trees' in the 'land' over which they grew. The Debtors Protection Act of 1936 exempted standing crops other than cotton and sugarcane from attachment or sale due to the execution of a decree.[56]

The Government of India Act of 1935, which retained separate electorates and gave a large measure of autonomy to provinces, increased the number of voters without disturbing the Unionist hegemony. Only 250 thousand in 2 million voters belonged to cities. Landowners still dominated the electorate and non-agriculturists were not allowed to contest rural seats. The Unionist support for colonial rule appeared all the more important for the introduction of autonomy. The elections of 1937 brought them into undisputed power.[57] A six-year programme of rural uplift through model farms, schools, medical centres, and improved sanitation and drainage was launched in 1937. In the following year the 'golden' or 'black' Acts (depending upon one's viewpoint) were passed to obviate benami or false transactions of alienation of land, and to enable the indebted landholders to recover all lands which they had mortgaged before the Act of 1900 was passed, involving more than 700,000 acres of land. More than 200,000 Hindus and Sikhs had to give back land to its original mostly Muslim owners.[58]

After the outbreak of war in 1939, it became increasingly difficult for the Unionists to retain their support in the countryside. They supported the British in their war effort in all possible ways. The growing inflation, shortage of consumer goods, requisitioning of foodgrains and rationing, coercion in recruitment, and demobilization after the war enhanced discontet in the countryside which was exploited by the opponents of the Unionists. The demand for Pakistan and the knowledge that the British were to quit India in the near future led to disruption among the Unionists themselves. They were routed in the elections of 1946, fought essentially on the issue of Pakistan.[59] Due to the exigencies of the war, the British had ignored the political interests of the Unionists; after the war they were neither keen nor able to keep the Unionists in power. The reason for which the political system was raised in Punjab was gone with the prospect of Independence. The Unionists yielded place to the leaders of the All-India Muslim League, the Indian National Congress and the Shiromani Akali Dal. More significant, however, is the fact that the British administrators kept the League, the Congress and the Akalis at bay till nearly the end of British rule in India. The colonial authority, in collaboration with landed interests in Punjab, prolonged its economic exploitation for nearly half a century after the Punjab Alienation of Land Act of 1900.

NOTES

1. Some of the other important sources developed by the British were tax on water for irrigation, excise and taxation.
2. The stereotyped view of assessment is given by H. Calvert in his *Wealth and Welfare of the Punjab* (Lahore, 1936, first published in 1922), p. 250: 'Prior to 1848 there was little or no surplus produce to get hold of; but the British administrators reduced the revenue from the whole of the surplus to a theoretical half and practically about a quarter'. It is interesting to note, however, that if assessment was unacceptable to a proprietor the only

option he had was to forfeit his rights: ibid, p. 170.

3. The dates for the submission of revenue installments were fixed and strictly adhered to. 'Coercive' processes were used by the government to realize arrears. Many a cultivator was obliged to knock at the moneylender's door to pay the revenue in time.
4. The rate of assessment was reduced in some districts in the 1850s because the summary settlement made earlier appeared to be hard on the cultivators. During the rest of the nineteenth-century, however, assessment was increased at the time of new settlements. For the increasing rates of assessment, Calvert, *op. cit.*, p. 217.
5. It is generally believed that the British created proprietary rights in land for the first time in the history of Punjab. Hugh Kennedy Trevaskis, for instance, believed that the English concept of property in land as a transferable marketable commodity, absolutely owned and passing from hand to hand like any chattel, did not exist prior to British rule in Punjab: Hugh Kennedy Trevaskis, *The Punjab of Today: An Economic Survey of the Punjab* (Lahore, 1932), p. 3. Together with the rental value derived from British experience and theory, Dietmar Rothermud regards the new concept of landed property as the 'major innovation of British revenue administration: *Government, Landlord and Peasant in India, 1865-1935*, (Wiesbaden, 1978), p. 37. James Douie makes the position clear by stating that nowhere in Punjab did individual proprietary rights amount to full ownership: *Punjab Settlement Manual* (Lahore, 1899),p. 58. With similar limitations as well as the obligation to pay the revenue, proprietary rights in land had existed prior to the British rule in Punjab: B.N. Goswamy and J.S. Grewal, *The Mughal and Sikh Rulers and the Vaishnavas of Pindori* (Simla, 1969); J.S. Grewal, *In the Bylanes of History* (Simla, 1975); Indu Banga, *Agrarian System of the Sikhs: Late Eighteenth and Early Nineteenth Century* (Delhi, 1978).
6. The role of the courts in the process of alienation of land was emphasized by several contemporary administrators. Denzil Ibbetson, for instance, believed that 'our legal system not only offers facilities for enforcing alienations, but actually brings an unjust and onesided pressure to bear upon the peasant, which eventually forces him to part with the land': quoted, Norman G. Barrier, *The Punjab Alienation of Land Act of 1900*, Duke University, Monographs and Occasional Papers Series, no. 2, pp. 107-09.
7. Calvert, *The Wealth and Welfare of the Punjab*, p. 107. By 1917 the area under cultivation rose to over 29 millions acres: ibid., 121-22.
8. The system of canals changed the economic as well as the physical aspect of Punjab, making the new colonies the most prosperous region in British India: B.H. Dobson, *Final Report on the Chenab Colony Settlement* (Lahore, 1915); Richard G. Fox, *Lions of the Punjab: Culture in the Making* (Berkeley, 1985), pp. 52-62.

9. By 1917 the total area under irrigation was nearly 15 million acres and about 10 million acres were irrigated by canals. Calvert, pp. 121-22.
10. Enhancement of assessment was one reason of increase in land-revenue; increase in the area under cultivation was the other. In any case, it rose from about Rs. 20 millions in 1872-73 to nearly Rs. 43 millions in 1932-33: ibid., 107.
11. In 1919-20, the corresponding figures were over 41 million maunds and over Rs. 440 million. The railway mileage had increased to over 4,000: ibid., 107. Few places in Punjab were more than 25 miles away from the railway line, and each of its 660 stations served 50 villages on the average: ibid., pp. 109.
12. Calvert, *The Wealth and Welfare of the Punjab*, p. 35.
13. Ibid., pp. 34, 137, 156-57 & 280-81. Calvert was absolutely clear that revenue, agriculture and commerce in Punjab represented a single phenomenon: ibid., pp. 2-3. For a recent exposition of colonial economy in Punjab, Fox, *Lions of the Punjab: Culture in the Making, op. cit.*
14. Calvert mentions reduction of the revenue assessment, accurate record of rights and the legal protection accorded to these rights, together with the judicial system, as giving market value to land: ibid., p. 215. Elsewhere he refers to the net obtainable rental and new wealth seeking investment as the factors creating market for land: ibid., p. 158. At yet another place he mentions 'internal peace' as well: ibid., p. 13. The people themselves in the early twentieth-century gave a variety of reasons for the unprecedented rise in the price of land in terms not merely of government action but also of response from the Punjabis: ibid., pp. 236-37. The rapid and continuous rise in the price of agricultural land was one of 'the most conspicuous features in the economic history of the Punjab', with-consequences for the economic activities of its people: ibid., 211.
15. In 1900-01, the price of an acre was Rs. 77; in 1910-11, Rs. 124; in 1920-21, Rs. 345; and in 1930-31, Rs. 420: Calvert, *op. cit.*, p. 219.
16. Calvert, *op. cit.*, p. 214.
17. Barrier, *The Punjab Alienation of Land Act of 1900*, p. 103.
18. From less than 54.000 (including dependents) in 1868, the number of bankers and moneylanders rose to nearly 194,000 by 1911 (including agriculturists who lent money on interest without calling themselves money-lenders): H. Calvert, p. 254. Cf. Malcolm Darling, *The Punjab Peasant in Prosperity and Debt* (Delhi, 1977, first published, 1925), p.173. The moneylender did exist in Punjab before the British rule and did charge high interest on loans, but the state put restraints on his operations so that the proprietor or the cultivator was able to retain his land and the means to cultivate it. During the colonial period, the law and the legal system helped the moneylender rather than the peasant.

Calvert mentions the rigidity of land revenue collection as well the new legal system among the factors which accounted for indebtedness. The other factors, according to him, were the enhancement of credit and its abuse, famines and general mortality of of cattle: Calvert, pp. 259-60.

19. Lepel Griffin's *Punjab Chiefs*, published initially in the 1860s and revised subsequently as *Chiefs and Families of Note in the Punjab*, once in the late nineteenth and twice in the early twentieth-century, provides ample information on the changing fortunes of the descendants of the former *jagirdars* and large *dharmarth* grantees of the kingdom of Lahore.
20. For the petty commodity producers, Fox, *Lions of the Punjab, op. cit.*
21. Indu Banga in her *Agrarian System of the Sikhs* (Delhi, 1978) estimates the number of tenants at half that of the proprietors and the area cultivated by them as one-fourth of the total area under cultivation. In the last decade of the nineteenth-century, however, tenants were cultivating nearly 40 per cent of the area under cultivation, and this percentage increased to about 50 in the early twentieth-century.
22. Malcolm Darling developed the argument in detail in the early twentieth-century that though the larger proprietors were more highly indebted, the smaller owners were more heavily involved. Darling does not state explicitly that the more heavily involved small proprietors were mortgaging and selling lands, but this inference can be drawn from Calvert's statement that 'mortgages and sales are steadily adding to the number of fields cultivated under tenancy conditions': *The Wealth and Welfare of the Punjab*, p. 207. Cf. Darling, *The Punjab Peasant in Prosperity and Debt*, pp. 11-13. Elsewhere, however, Darling noted the plight of the small proprietor due to high prices which proved to be a boon for the large landholders who could produce for the market.
23. According to Malcolm Darling, the moneylenders succeeded in acquiring 1,179,000 acres of land in the Punjab during less than twenty years from 1875 to 1893. Ibid., p. 179.

    The land sold to moneylenders was 32,000 acres in 1874-75. The figures rose to 87,000 acres in 1884-85, but fell to 67,000 acres in 1894-95. The figures for mortgage in favour of money-lenders rose from 119,000 acres to 220.000 in 1884-85 and fell to 172.000 acres in 1894-95. Cf. Calvert, *op. cit.*, p. 219.
24. It was observed by Calvert that mortgages taking place in prosperous districts were mostly in favour of moneylenders, while sales in the precarious districts were mostly in favour of agriculturist. Ibid., p. 251.
25. P.H.M. van den Dungen, *The Punjab Tradition: Influence and Authority in Nineteenth Century India* (London, 1972), p. 38. Contemporary writings by British administrators contain frequent references to the characteristic attitudes of various agricultural tribes and castes, particularly from the viewpoint of cultivation. 'It is well known', says Calvert, 'that certain tribes have a greater reputation for good husbandry than others, that some succeed in extracting more from the soil, far more than their neighbours; that an Arain, for instance, is generally a better farmer than

a Jat Sikh, a Jat Sikh generally better than a Muslim Rajput while even a Muslim Rajput can usually show his fields with pride to a Baluch or Pathan of the Indus Valley'. Ibid., p. 24.

26. As early as 1876 there were agriculturist moneylenders in the Punjab. See Darling, *The Punjab Peasant in Prosperity and Debt*, p. 197.
27. 'Objects' of the Act quoted in Om Prakash Aggarwal (ed.), *Agrarian Legislation in the Punjab* (Lahore, 1940), vol. I, pp. 3-4.
28. This was a general assumption: for instance, Calvert *The Wealth and Welfare of the Punjab*, pp. 28, 202-03.
29. Text of the Act, C.H. Philips (ed.), *The Evolution of India and Pakistan 1858-1947* (Select Documents), (London, 1962), pp. 649-52.
30. P.H.M. van den Dungan, whose *The Punjab Tradition* is a detailed study of how and when Punjab administrators reacted to the problem of alienation, thinks of 1869 as the date with which we come upon the new idea that voluntary alienation could be restricted through executive action or legislation.
31. Barrier, *The Punjab Alienation of Land Act of 1900*, p. 17.
32. Ibid., pp. 104-06. Hugh Kennedy Trevaskis refers to the chilling of the peasant's loyalty because of alienation: *The Punjab Today*, II, pp. 26-27. Elsewhere he refers to political evils as more serious than the economic: ibid, pp. 339-40.
33. Government of India's instructions to the Punjab Board of Administration in 1849, quoted, P.H.M. van den Dungen, *The Punjab Tradition*, p. 42.
34. Strictly speaking there were no hereditary tenants in precolonial Punjab; no tenant had the legal right to remain on an owner's land, though in actual practice many a tenant had enjoyed long tenure without interruption or even left the land to his sons to cultivate as tenants. The occupancy' right was created by the British settlement officers. In Gurdaspur district, for example, the settlement officer used the criterion of 12 years uninterrupted occupancy for creating hereditary rights: *Report on the Settlement of Gurdaspur District* (Lahore, 1859), pp. 87-88.
35. P.H.M. van den Dungen misses the point that when Prinsep reopened the question of occupancy tenancy he was virtually trying to help mostly the large landholders who had given their lands to tenants for cultivation. There is substantial evidence in the *Punjab Chiefs* and *The Chiefs and Families of Note in the Punjab* in support of the view that British attitude towards the former ruling class of the kingdom of Lahore changed after most of them supported the British in 1857-58. In fact, most of the Muslim and Hindu jagirdars, and some of the Sikh jagirdars, had supported the British during the Anglo-Sikh War of 1848-49.
36. Trevaskis, *The Land of the Five Rivers*, p. 341.
37. M.S. Leigh, *The Punjab and the War* (Lahore, 1922), pp. 33-45. Cf. Ian Talbot, *Punjab and the Raj* (New Delhi, 1988); 41-45.

38. M.S. Leigh, ibid., p. 46; Ian Talbot, ibid., p. 38.
39. Barrier, *The Punjab Alienation of Land Act of 1900*, p. 65, n. 44.
40. Sumit Sarkar, *Modern India, 1885-1947* (Delhi, 1985, reprint), p. 93. For the Congress Resolution of 1899, Barrier, ibid., p. 110.
41. Aggarwal (ed.), *Agrarian Legislation in the Punjab*, pp. xxi-xxv. Khushwant Singh deplores that the Act split the Sikh community into three racial divisions: the Jats, the non-Jats and the untouchables: *A History of the Sikhs* (Delhi, 1986), vol. II, pp. 155-56.
42. According to Ravinder Kumar, the members of the urban middle class felt convinced that the British would support rural interests in the future as well, and they began to seek new avenues for the investment of their wealth in commercial and industrial enterprises: *Essays in the Social History of India* (Delhi, 1983), pp. 19, 110-11 & 165.

    The early twentieth-century leaders of the Punjabi Hindus did look upon the Act as a measure directed against the whole community, consciously equating the community with the urban middle class. This is evident from the letters published by Lal Chand in the *Panjabee* in 1909. That the Hindu trader was sore about the various pro-rural Acts was noticed by Macolm Lyall Darling, *Wisdom and Waste in the Punjab Village* (1934), p. 203 & n2. Calvert in the early 1920s was at pains to show that the Act did not discriminate 'unduly against Hindus' because the number of 'agriculturist' Hindus whose interest the Act protected was larger than the number of non-agriculturist Hindus (excluding the menials). The objection strictly came from the shopkeeping and moneylending classes, who were for the most part Hindu: *The Wealth and Welfare of the Punjab*, pp. 268-70, 273.

    Malcolm Darling observed that in the Punjab 'the peasant of today regards the Land Alienation Act as the Magna Carta of his freedom'. *The Punjab Peasant in Prosperity and Debt, op.cit.*, p. 229. Elsewhere he noticed that whereas the townsman viewed it as a serious disability and was inclined to convert it into a political grievance, the small peasant proprietor regarded it as the charter of his rights: Ibid., p. 156.
43. As the result of unprecedented prosperity, remarked Calvert, the commercial class had risen to 'wealth and importance': Ibid., p. 16. The context makes it clear that this class had gained the most from colonial rule.In a despatch of 1899, the Government of India anticipated a good deal of writing against the Land Alienation Bill in the vernacular newspapers 'for the classes which command the Native press are mostly those whose interests are on the side of the moneylenders': quoted, Barrier, *The Punjab Alienation of Land Act*, pp. 56-57.

    John Maynard, who was consistently opposed to the Bill and the Act thought that in the long run it would be necessary to deal with 'the educated man, the trader, and the townsman generally': quoted, P.H.M. van den Dungen, *The Punjab Tradition*, pp. 287-95.

44. The despatch mentioned in the previous note goes on to add that the agricultural community would recognize the bill if passed as a 'beneficial scheme': *The Punjab Alienation of Land Act of 1900*, p. 57. Curzon invoked the wider consideration of imperial security and referred to the duty of the Government to 'protect the agricultural population': he asked his Council to 'grasp the nettle' and face the inevitable agitation: Ibid., 59, n28.
45. Calvert, *The Wealth and Welfare of the Punjab*, p. 266.
46. Ibid., pp. 267-68. In certain areas the landowners were acquiring land through mortgage and purchase: Malcolm Lyall Darling, *Rusticus Loquitur or the Old Light and the New in the Punjab Villages* (OUP, 1930), pp. 286, 294; Darling, *The Punjab Peasant in Prosperity and Debt*, pp. 9-10, 14, 197-98 & 246-47.
47. Ibid., pp. 28-29, 255 256-57. If emigration, joining the army and high prices gave the agriculturist moneylender his means, the Alienation of Land Act gave him the opportunity. By the third decade of the twentieth-century, nearly half the total debt of the province was passing from the non-agriculturist to agriculturist moneylender. Malcolm Lyall Darling, *Rusticus Loquitur*, pp. 325-26.
48. The moneylender, according to Darling, was no longer the despot he had been; in parts of the central Punjab he was definitely beaten; but he was still indispensable. Ibid., pp. 174-76, 198 & n3.
49. Calvert, *The Wealth and Welfare of the Punjab*, p. 172. For the largest holdings, Talbot, *Punjab and the Raj*, p. 16.
50. Douie, *Punjab Settlement Manual*, p. 4.
51. Douie, *Punjab Land Administration Manual* (Lahore, 1908), p. 3.
52. Quoted in P.H.M. van den Dungen, *The Punjab Tradition*, p. 297. In 1918, Michael O' Dwyer had accepted the recommendation of a Commission for increase in agriculturists' representation among the Extra Assistant Commissioners, *tahsildars*, *naib-tahsildars* and *munsifs* and in the Irrigation Branch of the Public Works Department: Talbot, *Punjab and the Raj*, p. 57.
53. For texts of the various acts, Aggarwal (ed.), *Agrarian Legislation in the Punjab*.
54. Talbot, *Punjab and the Raj*, p. 63.
55. Ibid., pp. 77-78. K.C. Yadav, *Elections in the Punjab* (New Delhi, 1987, reprint).
56. Darling, *The Punjab Peasant in Prosperity and Debt*, p. 200; Talbot, *Punjab and the Raj*, pp. 80-97; Aggarwal (ed), *Agrarian Legislation in the Punjab*, for texts of the Acts. Talbot observes that the British continued to exert, through the Unionist Party, 'the same kind of local political control they had secured by informed alliances with the leading landowners', Talbot, p. 80.

57. Talbot, *op. cit.*, pp. 101-14; K.C. Yadav, *Elections in the Punjab, op. cit.*
58. Talbot, *op. cit.*, pp. 114-19.
59. Indu Banga, 'The Crisis of Sikh Politics (1940-1947)', *Sikh History and Religion in the Twentieth Century* (edited by Joseph T.O, Connell, Milton Israel, Willard G. Oxtoby, W.H. Mcleod and J.S. Grewal), (Toronto, 1988), pp. 233-55.

Aspects of Peasant Differentiation in Bihar in the Late Nineteenth and Early Twentieth Centuries

GYAN PRAKASH SHARMA

The term 'differentiation' brings to the mind dynamism and the metabolic process of the breaking up of the article into various subparticles of several sub-structures from one structure. This assumes two premise:

(a) The peasantry as a category remained undifferentiated and started undergoing change from a certain point of time.
(b) The peasantry was always a differentiated class but the extent of differentiation varied with time and place.

As far as the first premise is concerned, it is not valid because Indian history has been a witness to a process of differentiation from the very beginning[1] and at no point of time has the peasant remained undifferentiated.[2] There has always been a distinction between the prosperous and less prosperous peasantry, if not many other finer distinctions. However, differences start becoming appreciable with increasing monetization and greater operation of exchange. This brings us to the next premise which assumes that the peasantry was a stratified class comprising different sections, but this stratification remains incomplete until a polarization between the rich and the very poor takes place. Differentiation is this sense would then be a continuing process in which the middle peasantry, which formed a part of the segmented structure consisting of the rich, middle and poor, would be under stress and strain. This class would break up either into the rich or the poor.

Once it is accepted that differentiation is a continuing process, then one has to look at the dynamics which sustains this process. Does it have a dynamics of its own or is it guided by external factors or propelled by both internal and external factors?[3] Is it determined purely by economic causes or influenced by non-economic factors as well, or both?

It is often believed that the process of differentiation is intensified under extreme conditions of market economy. As Lenin pointed out, the crucial phase of differentiation begins only with the accentuation of the capitalist method of farming.[4] Perhaps he was right in making such a generalization, but this would not explain the process of differentiation in the backward areas. Here the process becomes complex due to the absence of any clear-cut path of historical development.[5] Some features we would like to associate with the process in the West are present in the Indian context but are rarely effective. Some specificities of the Indian case give it a unique character:

i) division of holdings instead of consolidation
ii) prevalence of rent in cash as well as kind
iii) widespread rural indebtedness based on usury
iv) less unified market structures leading to lack of uniformity in prices and dependence on intermediaries
v) social constraints in the form of caste and other social practices.

The enclosure movement, which epitomizes the high watermark of English capitalist farming signifying the consolidation of uneconomic small holdings into bigger ones, has few parallels in India.[6] On the contrary, subdivision of holdings on account of demographic expansion is more pronounced. The same was the case with the credit market with an extensive system of mortgages. Instead of fostering agricultural production it mainly aimed at appropriating agricultural surplus. Furthermore, lack of scientific methods of farming led to frequent famines and scarcities. The capitalist system operates through the appropriation of surplus through wage labour which indicates complete subordination of labour to capital.[7] Thus the profit-seeking machinery cannot sustain itself initially without the presence of a large labour force. The creation of such a labour market can only come about with an extreme degree of differentiation of the rural population and consequent impoverishment of the masses. It is this kind of situation which necessitates social legislation to alleviate declining standards of living as was the case in nineteenth-century England.[8]

The appropriation of surplus in precapitalist societies, however, took a different path. As there is no single predominant socio-economic system, this surplus is siphoned through a combination of various modes, namely, rent, usury, illegal exactions, forced labour, system of advance, etc.[9] These precapitalist modes of surplus extraction also play a crucial role in promoting differentiation.[10] However, the pace of this differentiation is slow and erratic. It is also uneven and, in some cases, localized.[11]

In our study we will take up two divisions of Bihar, namely, Patna (comprising Patna, Gaya and Shahabad districts) and Tirhut (comprising Saran, Champaran, Muzaffarpur and Darbhanga districts). The two divisions present altogether different topographies. The Patna division was endowed with certain physical characteristics which made it self-sufficient in irrigation. The entire land mass of this division is in the form of a slope from the south to the north which facilitated excellent flow of water in the rivers and streams, especially during the monsoon.[12] This enabled the peasant to store water in tanks throughout the year. The Son canal was another important source of irrigation in the division catering mainly to the needs of Shahabad and partly of Patna and Gaya districts.[13] This division was thus well-irrigated leading to stable agricultural production.

Compared to Patna, the Tirhut division's topography discouraged peasants from taking to any proper system of irrigation.[14] Its bowl- like shape, with a depression in the centre, allowed water to accumulate quickly. As such, during the monsoons rivers and streams tended to overflow their banks and flood the surrounding areas.[15] Since the region abounds in small rivers and streams it was annually threatened by floods.[16] Therefore there were frequent scarcity of foodgrains.

However, the topographical advantage of Patna division was undermined by the prevailing mode of surplus appropriation. In all the three districts of this division there prevailed a very high incidence of produce rent.[17] The total rent collected in Patna and Shahabad districts stood at 50 percent of the produce, and was even higher in Gaya district.

Payment of rent in produce had two adverse consequences. First, although theoretically the peasants possessed occupancy rights, in practice, they were denied these simply because they did not have any documentary evidence to prove their claim. Rent receipts were the only legally valid piece of evidence that could have helped in establishing their claim; but these were never issued.[18] There was also a general belief among the peasants that occupancy rights did not accrue in the produce rent paying lands.[19] the weak position of the peasants emboldened the landlords to increase rents periodically and evict tenants on the slightest pretext, with each new tenant being asked to pay a rent higher than the earlier one. Second, in the produce rent system the peasant had to surrender a large share of his produce amounting between 8/16 and 9/16 to the landlord.[20] This share was fixed in an arbitrary manner. The landlords or his agents first made a survey of the standing crop, estimated the output and then fixed the landlord's share. Thus the share of the landlord varied according to the outturn of the crop. This system was known as *danabandi* which was the most widely prevalent form of produce rent in the Patna division.[21] The landlords' position was further buttressed by their control over the irrigation system which was used as an instrument to coerce the peasants into paying a high rent.[22]

The peasant's plight was made worse by the fact that the big landlords mostly gave their land on lease to small landlords and rich peasants known as *thikadars*. As these leases were for a short term, the leaseholders tried to make the most out of their tenure.[23] In order to keep the lease intact for the succeeding term they often tried to please the landlords by frequently giving an inflated rent roll,[24] most of the rent burden being passed down to the primary producer. Added to these was the problem of illegal exactions which were collected in addition to the rent. According to H. Mcpherson, the tenant was protected against enhancement of cash rent by the Bengal Tenancy Act of 1859, but there was no such provision in the case of produce rent.[25]

An interesting example of the increasing share of the landlord was found in a complete set of papers produced in one of the villages of Patna district. According to these between 1788 and 1836 the rent was 20 seers *asal* (legal rent) and 1.5 see *dahyak* (a kind of illegal exaction).[26] In 1837 the *asal* was increased to 22.5 seers whereas the *dahyak* was raised to 2.5 seers. The rent was collected at this rate till 1897. From 1898 a rent of 26 seers in a maund was taken without any specific exclusion of illegal exaction. There was thus an enhancement of 1 seer over the rate of 1897.[27]

If high rent was a deterrent to the prosperity of the peasants in the Patna division it was equally damaging to the agricultural economy in the Tirhut division. The Tirhut division was largely characterized by cash rent. The prevalence of cash rent can be attributed to two factors. First, there was cultivation of high valued crops, such as indigo, sugarcane and tobacco which earned higher profits and led to high rent assessment. Second, as agricultural production was not secure in this region, the landlords collected rent in cash.[28] There was also a larger flow of cash in the region because of widespread cultivation of cash crops necessitating a larger credit network. Although occupancy rights accrued to the peasants, yet there was no guarantee against enhancement of rents. Hence rents were increased on various grounds, such as expansion in area under cultivation, increase in output, rise in price. However, most of the time it was done in total disregard of the above factors.[29]

In the beginning of the nineteenth-century the rent in Saran district of Tirhut division was over Re.1 per acre in the north of the district and Rs. 2 to 4 per acre in the rest of the district. Till around 1840-50 the rent remained more or less at Rs.2-6-0 per acre. In the 1870s the rate increased to Rs. 4-14-0 per acre. This was especially in the Hathwa Raj and was the result of the enhancement made between 1850 and 1870. Thus while the rent increased by 100 per cent, the rise in prices during the same period was not more than 30 per cent.[30] In Darbhanga district too, at the time of the Permanent Settlement (1793), the rent rate stood at slightly above Rs.2 per acre. In 1896, at the time of the first settlement operations, the rent went up to Rs. 3-9-5 per acre.[3]

Although rents tended to be on the higher side the actual rent demand depended on a number of factors, especially on the material strength of the tenant.[32] It was very often seen that the poor and the weaker peasants were mostly the worst victims of rack-renting. To the extent that they were not able to pay their rents they were constantly being pushed downwards. This was true both of Patna and Tirhut divisions.[33] In the former, land transfer did not take place formally because of the lack of such a tradition but it took the form of usufructuary land mortgage. The higher rates of mortgage in this division were due to the difficulty of getting such transfers registered. However, the mortgagee usually allowed the original tenant to continue cultivating the land at a rent which covered not only the rent due to the superior landlords but also the exorbitant interest due on the original loan.[34] So the fruits of his labour were mainly appropriated by the mortgagee and the landlord.

In the Saran district of Tirhut 35 per cent of sale of land was on account of arrears of rent.[35] In Darbhanga and Muzaffarpur districts, the partitioning of estates led to large scale suppression of tenants due to enhancement of rent. Almost each and every partition was followed by an increase in rent and in most cases the new proprietor favoured a change in the tenant because this facilitated the settlement at a higher rent.[36] It is not true that all sections of the peasantry yielded to the pressure of high rent demand; the upper caste tenants vigorously resisted such move.[37]

One comes across frequent references in the survey and settlement reports to caste prejudices in rent assessment which suggest that higher castes were favoured with lower rent and *vice versa*.[38]

Rural hierarchy consisted of several layers of intermediaries between the state and the primary producer.[39] As each component in this hierarchy occupied a privileged position in society, except for the primary producer, it meant that the latter had to share the bulk of the rent demand. The proportion of rent went on increasing at each successive stage, because the margin between what an intermediary collected and what he paid was his profit.[40] While the zamindars, leaseholders and occupancy tenants mostly came from the upper castes, the undertenants, tenants at will and agricultural labour mostly belonged to the lower castes.[41] Hence there was close corelation between caste and class.

Caste seems to have mattered very little when it came to collection of rent by the small landlords. Areas inhabited by petty proprietors witnessed a high incidence of rent. In both Patna and Tirhut divisions they had gained notoriety as the most oppressive rent collectors.[42] This is not surprising for they were caught in a dualism which explains their quest for higher rent.[43] As tenants of big landlords they were the victims of high rent assessment because they possessed the best land. As landlords they tried to match the living standards of the latter by spending lavishly in order to acquire prestige. As a result their expenses exceeded their incomes. Most of these landlords had small landed estates which did not yield much revenue. Therefore they had to take personal interest in matters of rent collection.[44] They insisted on collecting the actual rent in single payment and not in instalments. They mostly settled their lands with the low caste tenants who could be easily coerced, but they did not spare the high caste tenants either.[45] The concentration of small proprietors was in the south of the Tirhut division, particularly in Muzaffarpur and Darbhanga. In Patna division such proprietors were mostly in the Patna district.[46]

The entire gamut of relationships involving the three sections of the peasantry was, to a large extent, also influenced by the credit system. Rural indebtedness in Bihar was as widespread as anywhere else in India. Almost all sections of peasants borrowed money supplied by the well-off sections of the peasantry inside the village,[47] although the village mahajan did occasionally come to their help. Apparently, moneylending was more widespread in Tirhut than in Patna division. In Patna, the peasant had a remarkable capacity to withstand pressure from moneylenders. Peasants borrowed money but were able to repay these at the time of the harvest.[48] Such prompt repayments prevented them from falling into a perpetual debt trap. Thus land transfers did not take place on a large scale.[49] Whatever little transfer took place was mostly between the tenants suggesting the emergence of rich peasants.[50]

The Tirhut division, on the other hand, had a well organized credit market extending from the mofussil towns to villages.[51] The growth of the credit network in this divisions has to be viewed in the background of the basic infrastructure created by the European planters. They were concentrated in large numbers in this division.[52] From the days of opium cultivation, there was a steady flow of British planters into the region, which reached its climax during the indigo revolt in Bengal, when many planters shifted their area of operation to Bihar.[53] The arrival of the planters heralded an era of large scale cultivation of a variety of cash crops such as opium, indigo, sugarcane and tobacco.[54] Earlier, these crops had a limited market and hence were not cultivated widely. Later the English themselves were the major buyers, apart form the growing domestic market. In order to popularize the cultivation of cash crops, planters started a system of advances. The availability of ready cash, in an otherwise less developed money economy, made cultivation of such crops attractive and served as an inducement to the peasants.[55] But no sooner had the cultivation of cash crops picked up than the terms of advance became rigid. With the spread of commercial agriculture, there was greater demand for capital which brought more and more people into debt servicing and debt receiving. As far as the former was concerned, the new entrants were mostly the well off sections of the peasantry within the village whereas borrowing was mostly confined to small and medium peasants.[56]

The small peasant cultivators' position was more vulnerable in Tirhut division, where they were subjected to two-fold expropriation of the landlord and the moneylender. Unlike the Patna division, where the debt burden was not as large as rent, in Tirhut both were equal. The small peasant's miseries were compounded by crop failures either due to drought or excessive rainfall.[57] The vagaries of the monsoon placed severe constraints on the peasants' ability to save enough surplus to tide over difficult times. It eventually paved the way for the moneylenders' ascendancy over the small peasant economy.[58] An obvious outcome of this vicious circle of rural indebtedness was a thriving market in land and in crops. Land transfers were common in areas which remained outside the pale of a flourishing commercial nexus; but the Sadar areas or areas where the factories were located saw fewer land transfers. These include the northern parts of Muzaffarpur and Darbhanga districts. On the other hand, the backward areas within the region characterized by poor agriculture on account of less fertile soil[59] witnessed more transfers. Most of these took the shape of mortgage which the peasants found difficult to retrieve.[60] In such areas depeasantization took place in a systematic manner irrespective of social barriers like caste. Thus poor Brahmins were a common sight in the Darbhanga region. Many upper caste Bhumihar Brahmins were in a similar plight in north Muzaffarpur. They mostly became undertenants or tenants at will after losing their occupancy rights in land. Migrations from these areas to other parts of the province and to Calcutta were quite common.[61] A few of them who managed to secure a job were just about able to save their holdings.

There were certain other disadvantages from which the peasants of Tirhut division suffered: the size of their holdings and the density of population. The average size of holding in the Patna division was above 4 acres whereas in Tirhut it was between 3 and 3.5 acres.[62] It is often repeated in government reports that in advanced areas, like the ones closer to the commercial centres, the subsistence holding was 2.5 acres, e.g., in Hajipur it was 2.5 acres and in Sitamarhi below 3.5 acres.[63] However, when we move to other regions, especially the northern parts of the Tirhut division where the land is less fertile and agricultural crops not so secure, even an average size of 3 acres was neither enough as subsistence holding, nor could it ensure the survival of the small peasants. Supplementary income came from a variety of sources, such as animal husbandry. Cattle breeding was a profitable occupation and those who were enterprising and skilled were able to make a good profit. From an inquiry made in 1888 it was found that a buffalo gave a return of Rs.20, and a cow Rs.10 per annum.[64] However, unlike Patna, the quality of livestock in this division was not so good due to lack of fodder and grazing land. As expansion of cultivation had reached an optimum level by the 1890s, not much grazing land was left.[65] Moreover, frequent floods denuded the cattle population.

Another source of supplementary income came from various types of services rendered by the villagers which were linked to caste based occupations. However, certain odd jobs available included those of chaukidar (night watchman), barahil (landlord's muscleman), field labourer, etc. The first two were mostly cornered by those close to the affluent sections. The last one was available only during the sowing and harvesting seasons.[66]

The small peasants' debts may not have been enormous initially, because of their lower credit worthiness, but in course of time it assumed large proportions as the interest on the loan went on multiplying.[67] They were mostly indebted to the prosperous sections of the village because the scale of operation of the professional moneylenders was not large inside the village.[68] They also did not loan small sums on credit. The rich peasants on the other hand were willing to advance money, because they knew the methods of realizing their loan. They always had an eye on the holdings of hapless small peasants and waited for an opportune time to grab these.

The growing size of the peasant family and consequent pressure on land was another factor which explains the economic hardships of the small peasants and their disintegration in the Tirhut region. The average density of population was higher at 750 in Tirhut than in Patna where it was 515.[69]

Table 1
Mean density per square mile

District	1911	1901	1891	1881	1872
Saran	853	893	919	855	774
Champaran	540	507	527	488	408
Muzaffarpur	937	908	894	851	740
Darbhanga	875	870	837	786	638

Source: *Survey and Settlement Report, Saran district 1915-1921*

It is interesting to note that Tirhut had such a high density of population, despite the fact that it was worst affected by various natural calamities. While density caused fragmentation of holdings, natural calamities impoverished the peasantry. As the region was prone to periodic floods each monsoon brought in its trail untold misfortunes in the form of plague, cholera and other diseases. In a survey of selected villages of Muzaffarpur district it was found that 20 Koeri families were labouring cultivators or poor peasants and four were pure agricultural labourers. They were all pure cultivators or middle peasants at one time, but the death of their headman and some other calamities led to the loss of their land.[71]

Compared to the small peasants, the middle and rich peasants were in less debt. They borrowed mainly for non-agricultural purposes. Land disputes were quite common during those days. Since these were longdrawn legal battles, they proved to be a drain on monetary resources.[72] Children's education also led them to borrow. Transfer of land in the case of the well-off sections of the peasants occurred on account of litigations. Most of the loans had to be secured through mortgage of land. As the usufructuary rights lay with the lender, the peasant was unable to derive any benefits from the produce of the land.[73] In the backward areas of Tirhut division, the rich had to sell land even for their consumption needs. Since income from rent was not sufficient, the only course left open to them was the sale of land.

The operations of the credit market thus facilitated a two-way mobility, both in the upward as well as downward directions. It allowed all those who could afford to spare a little capital to indulge in moneylending and consolidate their economic position. However, in terms of actual numbers, such upward mobility would not be very large. On the other hand, impoverishment due to indebtedness accounted for a larger number of poor peasants and the landless.

Upward mobility amongst peasants was quite apparent in areas that lay close to the marketing centres, as was the case in Patna division and to a certain extent in Tirhut. This brings us to the third aspect of our discussion, namely, the mode of disposal of peasant surplus. But before taking up this question, I will briefly discuss the main currents of trade and commerce in the two divisions. This will show the extent to which the peasants participated in it and were influenced economically.

If we look at the balance of trade in Bihar, we find imports to be always higher than exports.[74] Nevertheless, the export performance was satisfactory till 1930, after which it started sagging. The leading items of export in 1893-94 were foodgrains followed by oil seeds, sugar and tobacco. Later in the twentieth century there was a decline in the export of foodgrains while the non-food crops showed an increase.[75]

Patna was the commercial depot of the entire province because of its strategic position at the junction of the three great rivers, Sone, Gandak and Ganga, where the traffic of North-west Province met with that of Bengal.[76] All the exports from Bihar had to be routed through Patna. This gave impetus to trading activities in the Patna division. Most of the big *vyaparis* or *goldars* (big traders) had their establishments (*golas*) in Patna city and they operated through their agents or the middlemen, *paikars* or peddlars.[77] In the north of Patna division were larger towns through which the East Indian Railway track ran. From Maner, in the extreme east of this stretch, ran an almost continuous narrow market through Danapore, Bankipore and Patna to Fatuah; from Fatuah on to Barh and again from Barh to Mokameh.[78] Large bazars and villages succeeded one another at short intervals. A branch line of the railway ran south from Bankipore (Patna) to Masaurhi to Gaya, and another from the same place to the river Ganga at Digha.[79] A light railway was started around 1900 along the metalled road from Bakhtiarpur on the East Indian Railway station to Rajgeer, Nalanda and Biharsharif.[80] The majority of the estates were within a few miles of a railway station; the remainder, with a few exceptions, were on or near the main roads which gave them easy access to big marts and railway stations.[81] The highly developed means of communication in the Patna division provided the peasants, especially the medium and small peasants, with a better opportunity to market their produce.

The prices generally remained uniform throughout Patna division. Even if the peasant decided to dispose of his crop at his doorstep, which in any case was the normal practice, the chances of getting an unremunerative price were less. Profits accruing to the peasants were definitely slightly less than what they would have been when taken to the market. When we move to the Tirhut division we find less developed means of communication and not such a wide network of smaller weekly markets. This can be explained by its relative isolation from the major commercial route. However, certain parts of north Bihar, such as Munger and Bhagalpur districts, were commercially more thriving than other districts because of their proximity to the railhead near Mokameh and Barahiya.[82] The river Ganga was also easily navigable at this point, and river ferries were used to carry goods from Mokameh across the Ganga to the collecting centres along the main rail route of the Patna division.

Communication was less developed in Tirhut division. This meant that there was less interaction between the peasants and the market which resulted in lesser profits for the former. There was a meter gauge rail service which ran through the region, one branch of which ran from Saran district along the periphery of Muzaffarpur touching Sonepur and Hajipur and then entering Darbhanga at Samastipur.[83] There was also a separate rail link between Champaran and Darbhanga. The disadvantage with this rail system was that the meter gauge railway could not carry bulk traffic and moved slowly. It is important to point out that these rail networks were meant primarily for the planters to carry raw materials to the factories,[84] and not to facilitate general trade. The railway traffic on the meter gauge was also not as frequent as in trunk route sections. The roads in the region were mostly unmetalled and, therefore, not usable during the monsoon months.[85]

The export performance of Tirhut division was, however, in no way behind the Patna division. In contrast to the Patna division, the consolidation of the economic position of the peasant on account of the process of commercialization in Tirhut became a remote possibility. The peasants in Patna division, due to their direct contact with a thriving export market, were able to derive better advantages with which they could improve their economic position.

The uneven development of colonialism in India gave rise to varied socio-economic structures in different parts of the country. Regions which were brought under colonial control earlier witnessed greater economic activity leading to distorted forms of capitalist production. In Bihar, too, we find a similar trend. Due to lack of development of full-fledged capitalist relations of production differentiation became a slow and long-drawn process. The very basis of capitalist production—the right to occupancy—was not guaranteed under the existing tenurial relationship during British rule. Theoretically, the peasants were granted occupancy rights but in practice these were largely eroded. The Tenancy Act did not provide enough protection to the tenant against eviction or enhancement of rent. He was not allowed to enjoy autonomy and thus advance economically. On the other hand, he was also not allowed to disintegrate because that would have deprived the landlords of the necessary resources required for the entire agricultural operations. Thus the middle category largely remained undifferentiated. The poor peasants were gradually reduced to landlessness, because they were unable to stand up to the vicissitudes of the market economy.

NOTES

1. R.S. Sharma, *Origin of the State in India*, (Bombay, 1989).
2. Irfan Habib, *The Peasant in History*, (Aligarh, 1982), p. 22.
3. Internal dynamism signifies an entire range of economic variables such as trends in price, market, credit, etc., which leads to greater monetization, thereby influencing the mode of surplus appropriation and promoting rural differentiation. The non-economic phenomenon mainly includes drought, food, epidemics and other natural calamities which have a bearing on economic life.
4. Lenin, *The Agrarian Question and the 'Critics of Marx'*, p. 105.
5. Barry Hindess and Paul Hirst, *Pre-Capitalist Modes of Production* (London, 1975), p. 263.
6. Christopher Hill, *Reformation to Industrial Revolution* (Middlesex, 1967), p. 65.
7. Eric Wolf, *Europe and the People Without History* (California, 1982), p. 78.
8. Wolfgang Abendroth, *A Short History of European Working Class* (London, 1972), pp. 28-30.
9. Amit Bhaduri, *The Economic Structure of Backward Agriculture* (Delhi, 1984), p. 9.
10. Ibid.
11. Due to uneven impact of the colonial rule development in different regions did not follow a uniform pattern. The British did not intend to develop India as an integrated whole. They concentrated on areas in and around the metropolis and developed these at the cost of the hinterland. Bihar was not

able to feel the full impact of commercialization in the same manner as Bengal, Bombay and Madras presidencies did.

12. J.F.W. James, *Surveys and Settlements Report*, Patna District, 1907-1912 (Patna, 1914), p. 2.
13. Ibid., p. 16.
14. Due to the depression in the land mass, water during the monsoon remained stagnant thus lending immense moisture to the soil. Wells could be easily dug in Tirhut division because of a higher water table.
15. J.H. Kerr, *Survey and Settlement Report*, Darbhanga District, 1896- 1903 (Patna, 1926), p. 9.
16. This is mostly true of the northern part where there are a large numbers of rivers and streams.
17. Revenue Department (Land Revenue) File S/140 of 1915, Nos. 55-58, p. 1.
18. Ibid.
19. James, *op.cit.*, p. 36.
20. Janak Kishore, *Selected Decisions of the Board of Revenue*. Bihar and Orissa, vol.II, 1923-27 (Patna, 1927), p. 47.
21. James, *op.cit.*, pp. 80-81.
22. Revenue Department (Land Revenue) File S/140 of 1915, Nos. 55-58, p. 2.
23. Revenue Department (Land Revenue), Government of Bengal, January 1888, 22-1/3, p. 31.
24. H. Coupland, *Survey and Settlement Report on the Deo Estate of Gaya District 1901-1904* (Calcutta, 1907), p. 15.
25. James, *op.cit.*, p. 93.
26. Ibid.
27. Ibid.
28. Another explanation for the wider prevalence of cash rent was the presence of big zamindaris like the Darbhanga Raj and the Hathwa Raj. In the big zamindaris it was not possible to supervise the collection of rents in produce because of the complex process of the fixation of respective shares of the landlord and the tenant. On the other hand we do find the prevalence of produce rents in the petty landed estates where the landlords could personally attend to their realization as was the case in the Dalsingsarai thana of Darbhanga and Hajipur thana of Muzaffarpur districts.
29. Revenue Department (Land Revenue), Government of Bengal, File No. 5M/1, 1 August 1894, p. 1037.
30. J.H. Kerr, *Survey and Settlement Report*, Saran District, 1893- 1901, Calcutta, p. 41.
31. J.H. Kerr, *Survey and Settlement Report*, Darbhanga District, 1896- 1916, p. 111.
34. Ibid., p. 12.
35. James, *op.cit.*, p. 103.
36. Ibid., p. 44. Their prosperity is also attested by the fact that they had the reputation of indulging in frequent litigation. They very of ten combined to

resist demands that they considered unjust. They were the major targets of high rent assessment because of their being skilled agriculturists specializing in high value crops.

37. J.H. Kerr, *op.cit.*, p. 51.
38. S. Moore, *Survey and Settlement Report*, Muzaffarpur District, p. 314.
39. Revenue Department (Land Revenue), Government of Bengal, January 1888, No. 22-1/3, p. 31.
40. Ibid.
41. J.H. Kerr, *op.cit.*, Darbhanga District, p. 38. Non-occupancy tenants mostly held land on produce rent and as a matter of belief did not enjoy any occupancy rights.
42. Revenue Departments (Land Revenue), Government of Bengal, January 1888, No.22-1/3, p. 22-23.
43. James, *op.cit.*, p. 104.
44. J.H. Kerr, *op.cit.*, p. 104.
45. Ibid., p. 55.
46. Ibid., p. 50.
47. *The Bihar and Orissa Provincial Banking Committee*, 1929-30, vol.II, (Patna, 1930), p. 193.
48. Revenue Department (Land Revenue), File S/140 of 1915, No. 55-58, p. 2.
49. James, *op.cit.*, p. 41. It must be pointed out here that in Patna division land was mostly mortgaged verbally to the lender who usually happened to be the welloff peasants and the zamindars. As rents were too exorbitant the inability of the raiyat to pay the rent led to accumulation of arrears. This arrear was treated as a loan on which interest was charged. Although the tenant continued to cultivate the land actually it was pledged to the landlord.
50. Ibid., p. 40.
51. L.S.S.O'Malley, *Saran District Gazetteer*, 1930, p. 110.
52. Stephen Henningham, *Peasant Movements in Colonial India, North Bihar 1917-1942* (Canberra, 1982), p. 37.
53. Ibid.
54. Revenue and Agriculture, Government of India File No. 35, June 1901. Report of the Committee appointed to enquire into the prospects of the cultivation of sugar by indigo planters in Bihar, p. 315.
55. Ibid., p. 313.
56. James, *op.cit.*, p. 40.
57. S. Moore, *op.cit.*, p. 257.
58. Natural calamities had always been one of the important agencies of differentiation. Losses occuring from such events tended to place heavy debt burden on the economically weaker peasants.
59. J.H. Kerr, *op.cit.*, Darbhanga District.
60. Revenue Department (Land Revenue), Government of Bengal File 6- A/8-1 of 1896, No. 56-57 p. 208.
61. J.H. Kerr, *op.cit.*, p. 12.

62. H. Coupland, *Survey and Settlement, Report of the Government and Temporary Settled Estates and of Certain Private Estate, Patna District,* 1901-1904, p. 7.
63. Ibid.
64. This sharp contrast between the cow and the buffalo continued till the 1950s when new high milk yielding breeds of cows were introduced.
65. LSS O'Malley, *op.cit.*, p. 67.
66. Most of the people did not adhere to their caste occupation because these were not enough to provide the necessary means of livelihood. Hence although the Brahmins in Darbhanga district were listed as a priestly caste, the majority of them earned their livelihood from agriculture. The same is true of people belonging to other castes. In Tirhut division between 84 to 90 per cent of the population depended on agriculture.
67. *Bihar and Orissa Provincial Banking Enquiry Committee Report 1929-30*, Evidence: Volume II, p. 70.
68. Ibid., pp. 402-03.
69. J.H. Kerr, *op.cit.*, Saran District, p. 2.
70. LSS O'Malley, *op.cit.*, p. 54.
    In a district like this which had a very dense population there were only 22 medical centres and most of these were run by charitable institutions.
71. Revenue Department (Land Revenue) Government of Bengal File 22 of of 1888, No 1-5, p. 44.
72. *Bihar and Orissa Provincial Banking Enquiry Committee Report 1929-30*, vol.II, p. 192.
73. Ibid.
74. *Report on the Trade carried by Rail and River in Bihar and Orissa in 1921-22* (Patna, 1923), p. 26.
75. Ibid.
76. *Report on the Internal Trade of Nepal, 1876-77* (Calcutta, 1877), p. 195.
77. H. Buchanan, *Patna-Gaya Report*, vol.II, p. 683.
78. H. Coupland, *op.cit.*, p. 3.
79. Ibid.
80. Ibid.
81. Due to the presence of a number of big zamindaris the communication, especially the road system, was quite developed. The general prosperity of the region also contributed to better communication networks.
82. This is not to suggest that there was no system of communication in Tirhut division. However, a well integrated system could not develop due to the presence of a large number of small rivers and streams. Despite these natural hurdles there was a thriving trans frontier trade with Nepal.
83. J.H. Kerr, *op.cit.*, Darbhanga District, p. 8.
84. J.H. Kerr, *op.cit.*, Saran District, p. 5.
85. Ibid., p. 4.

Towards an Understanding of Famine: Northern Madhya Pradesh, 1891-1901[1]

DAVID BAKER

In the late nineteenth-century, R.C. Dutt opened a debate on the origins of famine in India, contending that levels of revenue and the flow of capital from the country impoverished the peasantry, and so created famine. In the late twentieth-century, D.R. Gadgil and B.M. Bhatia also found assessment levels destructive. Irfan Habib added to the debate, claiming that railways constructed under British rule precipitated famine as they removed grain from deficit areas. Amartya Sen asserted that it was misleading to attribute famine to the non-availability of food—famine resulted when a section of the population was deprived of its entitlement to food because of inflation or unemployment. Recently, Michelle McAlpin has argued that there was no evidence that the initial or revised settlements impoverished raiyats.[2] She has denied that railways led to famine, but asserted that fewer famines occurred in the twentieth-century due to better communications. McAlpin contends that weather conditons were an important cause for famine. This study seeks to contribute to this debate.[3]

I

Between 1891-1901 two official famines and other unrecognized scarcities and famines occurred in northern Madhya Pradesh. This region comprised the districts of Sagar, Damoh, Jabalpur, Mandla, and Seoni in Jabalpur division; and Narsimhapur, Hoshangabad and Betul in the Narmada division. Ecological factors formed a background to the events of the

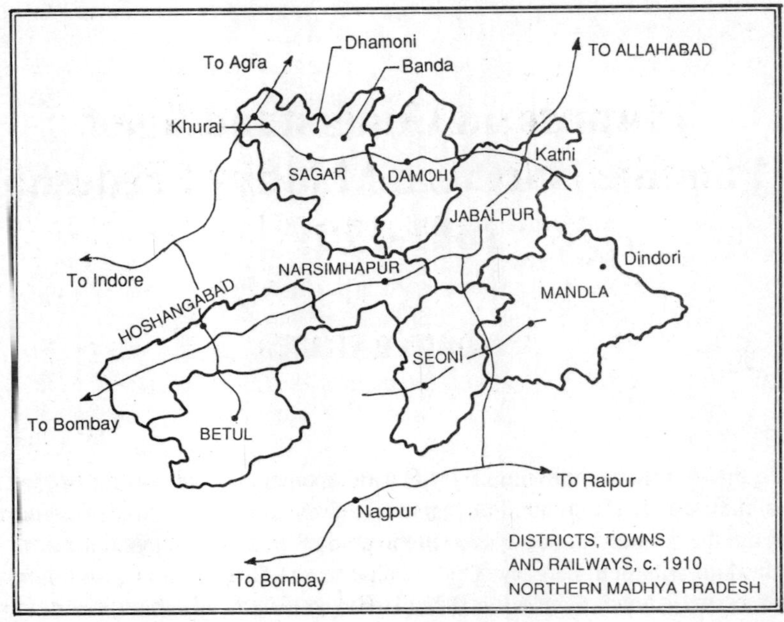

decade. For five years heavy monsoon rains and wet winters retarded crops; but from 1895-96 dry years had a similar effect. Declining production and the poor quality of grains curtailed the export trade, especially in wheat, to Britain and Europe that had developed since the seventies. Despite this officials permitted grain exports during the official famines and at other times as well. Poor harvests and low food stocks raised grain prices so that large numbers of people could not support themselves in what officials described as a 'famine of high prices'.[4] To relieve the situation the administration imported cheaper grains, which (with the decline in exports) reversed the provincial terms of trade for four years up to 1901. At the same time returns of land revenue from the region and province plummeted, pushing Madhya Pradesh towards bankruptcy.[5]

A more direct aspect of the famines was the loss of population. Between 1891-1901 the population of Madhya Pradesh declined by over nine lakhs, or 9.3 per cent, in a province ranking with Assam as the 'most thinly peopled part of India'.[6] The tribal population decreased more markedly, Gond numbers falling by 13 per cent. In Seoni, the tribal population fell by 17 per cent between 1872-1901. For the general population, Sagar lost 20.4 per cent of its population, the greatest loss of any district in the region.[7] In Khurai tahsil of Sagar the population fell by 26 per cent, and in Sagar tahsil by 24 per cent. Narsimhapur followed with a loss of 14.5 per cent, making its population in 1901 less than in 1866. The population of Damoh, Seoni and Betul dropped by about 12 per cent. Hoshangabad lost 10 per cent of its population after suffering partial or total failure of crops in six of the ten years. Only two districts lost fewer people than the provincial average. These were Jabalpur, which lost 8.7 per cent, and Mandla 6.5 per cent.

Part of the decline in population was due to emigration, though this itself was a product of scarcity and famine.[8] In 1894 large numbers of coolies left Narsimhapur in the rainy season for the tea gardens in Assam. Officials reported a similar movement from Seoni between 1895-98, when the district suffered from recurrent famine. Jabalpur, one of the districts hardest hit before the official famines, also formed a major source of labour emigrating to Assam. Officials estimated that one lakh people migrated from Madhya Pradesh during the decade, though the figure was probably understated. At the same time small scale immigration into the region took place from neighbouring states at times of famine, but the administration discouraged this trend, and by 1900 the princely states were supporting the needy from among their own populations during famine.

A more important factor in the loss of population was death from disease and starvation.[9] Although it is not possible to assess the proportion of deaths from either cause, both were connected as malnutrition made victims more susceptible to disease, apart from being a cause of death in itself. The most common diseases were cholera, fevers and small pox, and the incidence of these with accompanying mortality rose and fell between 1891-93. Another upward cycle commenenced from 1894 as conditions worsened in Sagar, Damoh and Jabalpur. In the official famine of 1896-97 starvation with widespread fever and cholera produced high mortality, and the provincial death rate rose to its highest level for six years. Births fell to their lowest level since 1881, giving Madhya Pradesh the second lowest birth rate in the country after Madras. The heaviest mortality in the region occurred in Damoh, which had four times as many deaths as births. In 1897 most districts had a death rate higher than the province's decennial average, the districts where mortality was heaviest being those where cholera was 'particularly fatal'.[10]

Two years of comparative respite from disease, starvation and accompanying mortality preceded the second official famine of 1899-1900, when heavy loss of life again occurred. In the meantime, however, Jabalpur recorded its first death from plague, which appeared in Bombay in 1896. The approach of famine in 1899 was heralded by a rising death rate, more deaths being due to fever than to any other disease. Crop failure and famine made 1900 the 'most unhealthy year in the province for 20 years' when over half a million people died.[11] Severe mortality persisted into 1901, which was the worst year for health in Madhya Pradesh since 1861.

While ascribing disease and death to gatherings and comunications, officials more readily linked them to current conditions, including famine.[12] In doing so they conceded that the market economy could not feed its population. The chief commissioner, Sir Charles Lyall, himself set the seal on such a view when he wrote in 1896-97 that, 'Famine conditions...followed...upon a succession of short harvests and seasons of agricultural distress, which had already exhausted the resources of people and reduced them to a condition in which they were ill able to resist the onset of privation and famine'.[13]

In the same manner, official reports blamed poor quality food for increased disease and mortality. The inferior, mildewed condition of grain eaten by the poor caused bowel deaths in the Narmada valley in 1894-95. In Mandla, cholera spread like 'wildfire' in 1897 among people who 'had their health ruined by an unwholesome diet of leaves, roots and toad-stools'.[14] The death rate was 'appalling'. Scarcity or famine in Jabalpur division for five years up to 1897 led people to eat quantities of vetch grain, thereby contracting a paralysis known as lathyrism, produced by poison in the grain. The affliction, which had no remedy, permanently incapacitated many labourers in Sagar, Damoh and Seoni.

Rising crime reflected the pressures on a population undergoing famine.[15] Between 1891-93 the levels of crime fluctuated, but rose thereafter to peak during the famine of 1896-97. During this period the incidence of burglary and theft increased in both divisions. In 1896 the Satpura districts were among the eight most criminal districts in the province due to the high rate of cattle theft. In 1897 levels of crime exceeded previous levels and jails became overcrowded, the most notable offence against property being petty theft, much of it grain theft, as in Mandla. The decade closed with a further spurt in crime between 1899-1900, distributed over all types of offences. That year Sagar had more dacoities than any district in the province.

Much of what officials described as crime arose from the want creating scarcity and famine. Officials themselves acknowledged this connection.[16] In 1891-92 they blamed an increase in petty offences, including theft, on the high prices caused by bad harvests and grain exports. Increased admissions to jails in 1894 were due to 'the scarcity amounting almost to famine' in the Jabalpur and Narmada divisions. Continuing scarcity in 1895 was 'aggravated in its effect on the poorer classes, who made the largest contribution to jail admission'. In the same year officials noted that dacoity occurred most often in districts suffering from poverty, and that the increasing offences against property or person in the wake of poor harvests were highest in the region's worst hit districts. In 1895, in Sagar prevailing want led to increased cattle theft by the 'half starved masses', who killed and ate the cattle they had stolen.

The official famine of 1896-97 made a devastating contribution to economic crime.[17] Administrators agreed that scarcity led to the large increase in recorded crime in 1896, jail admissions increasing due to 'agricultural distress'. Scarcity also fuelled rising crime in Narsimhapur, while dacoities in Jabalpur, Mandla and Seoni largely comprised the plunder of rural grain stores. In 1897 officials claimed that those who committed these dacoities were generally people suffering from scarcity, the dacoities often taking the form of grain thefts from men and women returning from the market. In Seoni scarcity and inflation set off waves of panic crime, in which 'the grain-dealing classes were the object of the greatest clamour. The ignorant masses condemned them as extortioners, and they incurred the odium of the more enlightened, including even some officers of the Government. There was doubtless unnecessary panic which raised prices higher than was justified...and individual dealers may have cheated the poor'.[18] Distress in Hoshangabad in 1896-97 issued in increased house breaking and theft. Officials also blamed famine for rising crime in Betul. In the same way official reports linked increased crime with the famine of 1899-1900, though the number of criminals was less than in 1896-97, possibly because the relief system was more efficient.

Sections of society most exposed to famine figured prominently in reports on crime.[19] While these included *malguzars* and landowners from the Bundela and Lodhi communities, they generally referred to lower social elements who found themselves outside the market economy and facing famine. Thus 'impoverished classes' of Mehras and Gonds committed the bulk of crimes in Betul between 1891-1901. In Betul, Banjaras with-communications biting into their carrying trade were prominent among cattle thieves. Gonds, Baigas, Kols and other poor classes were largely responsible for the increasing crime in Mandla during the decade. In 1895, it was the 'half starved classes' of Sagar who stole and ate cattle, and Gonds and Baigas who did so in 1896-97. That was the year when 'the ignorant masses' and 'famished people' attacked grain stores in Seoni to get the grain which was too expensive to buy. During the first famine, too, jails became 'poor houses' owing to the 'large number of paupers who had been driven to crime by distress'.

II

Let us examine the impact of famine on an agrarian community, the tribals of northern Madhya Pradesh. Comprising Gonds, Baigas, Kols and other tribes, the wider community ranged from *talukdars* and *malguzars* down through tenants to landless labourers, and formed a large section of society, especially in the hill districts of Mandla, Seoni and Betul. Official optimism apart, by 1891 observers maintained that the tribals' economic position had deteriorated since the settlements of the sixties.[20] As a result they were in no position to withstand a revised assessment or the rigours of famine.

By 1891 tribals exhibited a mixed pattern of agricultural practice.[21] Since 1861 the most notable development had been the transfer of shifting cultivation from the forests to village areas under the *malguzari* settlement, ostensibly within the market economy. This was the practice in the hill villages of Jabalpur division, though here and there in the plains tribals engaged in settled agriculture. In Sagar, tribals generally inhabited villages in jungle tracts fringing the district as small tenants or labourers with 'few resources and little or no credit'. In Damoh, too, Gonds lived in the hill regions practising 'indifferent agriculture'.

Gonds in Jabalpur engaged in shifting cultivation and settled agriculture, and were better off than tribals in the Satpura districts.[22] Some dwelt in or near jungles growing *kodon* and *kutki*, but in east Jabalpur they cultivated small holdings. Those practising shifting cultivation in the outer areas frequently worked as labourers in the *haveli* to supplement their income. But everywhere they were poor, cultivating with insufficient implements and hired bullocks, and paying produce rents. In Mandla, wherever Gonds were not *malguzars*, they comprised a 'roving and unsettled tenantry' or poor labourers. In Seoni Gonds mostly farmed the poor hill soils, supplementing their incomes with labour in the plains, though some had taken to settled cultivation there as well. Both groups were poorly off.

The same pattern was evident in tribal agriculture in the Narmada division. Where possible the hill tribes of Narsimhapur clung to shifting cultivation and resisted efforts to draw them into settled agriculture. Though indebted, Gonds and Korkus still held settled villages in the Hoshangabad hills, but their general position typified that of tribals throughout the region:

> The more energetic Hindu has ousted them from all the good land in the valley....The Gonds of the plains...have mostly sunk to the position of field labourers. They include a large number who are not cultivating tenants, but are recorded as such because the patch of ground attached to their houses has been entered as a holding. In the jungle villages they still form the bulk of the cultivators, but in the plains the number of real cultivators...is small. Those that regularly cultivate generally have small holdings. They form the poorest section of the agricultural community.[23]

Tribals in Betul lived in the same areas as in the sixties, though officials claimed that banning shifted cultivation in the forests had improved their lot.[24]

Administrative decisions worsened the position of tribals during the famine decade. In 1893 the administration finally closed the forests and introduced the principle of working plans. While this confirmed policy since 1861, it marked the end of shifting cultivation in the forests. More important were decisions relating to the Baigas.[25] From 1890 administrators made a final effort to force them into settled agriculture and the market economy. Having failed to contain them earlier, officials carved out a tract of hill country in Dindori tahsil, an inaccessible area in eastern Mandla, creating a *chak* or reservation. Outside the *chak* , *bewar*, the shifting cultivation of the Baigas, was forbidden; inside, it was tolerated, but officials showed their disapproval by taxing Baiga axes. Within the *chak* Baigas came under the purview of the forest department, which encouraged them to use the plough and found work in the forests for those who wanted it. To further induce Baigas to enter the *chak,* the administration agreed not to levy rent on leased plots for three years, and to give interest free loans for cattle and seed for seven years.

The Baigas' experience of the *chak* was unfortunate.[26] The areas where they could practise *bewar* were either too small or unsatisfactory, and officials were slow to honour their promises of aid. The experiment had already failed when the director of agriculture and settlements, J.B. Fuller, toured Mandla in 1893. Seeing the destitution of the Baigas, Fuller concluded that the administration could not force them to use the plough, and in 1895 officials retreated from this policy. As Baigas were not entering the *chak* in sufficient numbers, they allowed Gonds and other plough cultivators to settle there, making the Baigas even more insecure. As a result numbers in the *chak* fell, and by 1901 less than half of those who entered the reservation earlier in the decade remained.

The prospects for Baigas outside the *chak* were equally bleak.[27] Those wishing to retain their old ways migrated to the Pandaria zamindari in Bilaspur where 'indiscriminate *bewar*' was allowed. Officials dissuaded Baigas from leaving *malguzari* villages and settling in the *chak*, but where Baigas shifted to such villages, officials encouraged *malguzars* to induct them into plough cultivation by giving revenue concessions and acknowledging their help publicly. In such villages *bewar* was banned, and officials gave the Baigas no help in buying seed, ploughs or bullocks. These Baigas, too, could not find employment in forest villages.

Indebtedness compounded the hapless state of most tribals, whatever their background.[28] As they were already indebted by 1891, the enhanced revenues and rents of the revised settlements added to the problem. Most chiefs in Narsimhapur and Hoshangabad were in debt, and though the administration tried to place estates there and in other districts on a sound footing, debts were frequently so heavy that these measures did not help much. Gond *malguzars* suffered at the hands of moneylenders in Damoh and Jabalpur; in Mandla tribal *malguzars* were heavily in debt. During the nineties the debts of the Gond and Korku *malguzars* in Hoshangabad increased. Tribal tenants, too, suffered from debt, and their helpless state in Hoshangabad must have been typical of tenants in the other districts:

> they form the poorest section of the agricultural community...; they almost invariably borrow their seed grain and advances for food from the village money lender, who takes almost the whole of their crops. They are a careless, improvident people content to live from hand to mouth....They seem by constitution unable to adapt themselves to the changed circumstances under which they now live.[29]

Indebtedness led tribal chiefs, *malguzars* and tenants to transfer land on a large scale to moneylenders between 1891-1901.[30] Powerless to stem this process, officials at first blamed unscrupulous moneylenders for tempting tribal innocents into debt and seizing their lands. Thus, in Damoh smaller proprietors gave place to moneylenders in 'large numbers', the Kallar trader, Seth Dalchand, taking over many villages. Dalchand and other Kallars and Marwaris took advantage of Gond proprietors in Mandla as well, using any means to gain their land. Gond villages in the district dropped from 432 in 1868 to 144 by 1905. In Jabalpur, too, by 1909 Gonds possessed only a fraction of the villages they once held. Tribals in Seoni seemed unable to retain their land, and their villages and fields likewise passed to their creditors. By 1901 the smaller tribal *mulguzars* in Narsimhapur had 'practically all been ousted'; while in Hoshangabad officials noted uneasily that Hindus were still ousting Gonds and Korkus from their villages, and pushing tenants from cultivation to landless labour. Transfers were also reducing the estates of the old aboriginal rulers of the district. In Betul, banias 'snapped up' jungle villages belonging to tribals, whom officals described as 'submissive...(and) easily frightened'.

Drink was connected with tribal indebtedness and land transfers. Where *malguzars* and cultivators sold crops or utilised profits to buy drink, they had nothing to fall back on except credit from the moneylender. In some districts moneylenders themselves supplied drink in exchange for produce. Officials believed tribals to be grossly addicted to drink, so much so that even during famine starving Gonds bartered grain for drink.[31] They were aware, too, that liquor sellers were acquiring tribal land in Mandla. In Seoni, officials ascribed the chronic poverty among tribals to drink, which was part of their way of life. Officers also blamed the failure of cultivators in Hoshangabad on drink; and in Betul they condemned it as the 'great curse' of the tribes.[32]

Indebted, landless and addicted to drink, tribals in Mandla, Seoni and Betul reeled under scarcity and famine between 1891-1901. Even in better times they hovered on the brink of starvation, but during scarcity and famine they suffered added privation. When the administration finally conceded famine in 1896-97, the tribals' position everywhere was desperate. In February 1897, officials estimated that half the tribals in Mandla were 'without resources'.[33] There and in other districts they streamed from villages towards the nearest town or even distant Jabalpur or Nagpur. Many died on the way. Others disappeared into the jungles in a fruitless search for food. When the rains came, the diet of roots, damp leaves and toadstools engendered such diseases that many could not make the journey to a relief centre. As a contemporary noted:

> The great majority were hopelessly lost, and not a fourth of them will ever return to their homes. It is impossible to get any approximate idea of the mortality which has followed this migration from the hills, for many perished in the jungles and by the roadsides, and were devoured by jackles and vultures...the death rate has been steadily rising. . . . A large proportion of the Gond villages have been totally or partly deserted, and it is improbable that they will be taken up again for years, if ever, by the Gonds.[34]

Weak from destitution and starvation, one-sixth of the tribal population in Mandla died of fever. In Betul many succumbed to fever, cholera, dysentery and diarrhoea.

Official policies coupled with tribal attitudes worsened the latter's plight. Despite petitions from the Baigas, officials refused to permit them to reintroduce *bewar* to stave off tribal distress and so were unable to deal with the large numbers affected by famine.[35] When officials claimed that tribals did not come to relief works, critics urged that they needed relief in their villages as in the inoperative provincial code.[36] Officials replied that they had difficulty approaching villages, as Gonds and Baigas in Mandla,

> Always suspicious of strangers...took refuge in forests at the approach of a relieving officer, and refused to be tempted to the relief works, preferring to wring a scanty livelihood from the jungle than be forced to work at an uncongenial task in a remote and unknown region . . . . The authorities were hopelessly deceived.[37]

Not till February 1897 did the authorities discover that acute distress was prevailing in many tribal villages. Though relief centres and works were operating, they realised that unless they could get help to the villages many tribals would starve to death. This had already occurred in some places, where little mounds 'half buried in encroaching jungle were all that remained of the...village clearings'.[38] Elsewhere, as we have seen, tribals deserted villages en masse. In some villages disease and death stalled efforts to relieve distress. In Mandla, many Baigas died of starvation with relief at their doors, 'overlooked by their Gond and Hindu fellow villagers, and themselves afraid to apply'.[39] Numbers of tribals in Betul refused relief until they were past recovery. Despite these barriers the administration saved some of those left. In the monsoon,

> relieving officers forced their food supplies through deep jungles and

> flooded rivers, and penetrated into the inmost recesses of the hills. .. People ceased to die of starvation, but not to suffer from privation and want.[40]

Stung by the calamity and charges of inaction, the administration was better prepared for the subsequent famine. The famine commission sympathised with officials trying to stem tribal mortality in 1897, but suggested that the administration make tribal relief a special section of the famine code, and organise village relief in tribal districts.[41] Thus when famine occurred in 1899, officials were ready with relief works for tribals as they quit villages in Hoshangabad and other districts.

Famine and scarcity took a terrible toll of the tribal community in Madhya Pradesh. During the decade the tribal population declined by 11.8 per cent, a rate above that of the general population. Some of the decline was due to migration, as thousands of tribals left to work in the tea plantations of Assam. Others left their villages, dying by the way. Only the hardy survived. Levels of crime rose as tribals sought to appease their hunger in various ways. Even so some officials remained complacent about their suffering, as we see in the following: 'the high mortality...among the weaker members of society left a population purged of its weaker elements, and with its constitution improved both physically and morally by the trials it had gone through.'[42]

III

British officials bear clear responsibility for the famine in Madhya Pradesh between 1891-1901. At an administrative level, the post of the chief commissioner changed hands too often for the occupant to know the region or implement his policies. All chief commissioners were outsiders, except Arthur Fraser who was appointed as famine struck the region in 1899. As head of the agriculture department, Fuller remedied the shifting nature of provincial leadership to some extent, but his policies were harmful and the chief commissioners were not always strong enough to oppose him. The higher bureaucracy could not function effectively because it was understaffed; while the lower services were 'uneducated and inefficient beyond experience in other provinces'.[43] The Government of India added to these problems by seeking to reduce the strength of the administration in 1899-1900 for reasons of economy.

The administration's policy on the revised settlement was an important basis for the famine. Though Fuller was convinced that his method of assessing the revenue for different types of soil 'authoritatively proposed' the rents payable by each farmer,[44] in at least one district—Narsimhapur—officials wrongly classified soils, and in Damoh and Mandla, as in the province at large, they made errors in field and village measurements. A later chief commissioner criticised officers in Hoshangabad for relying too much on Fuller's 'arithmetical calculations in a matter which is so dependent on the seasons'.[45]

More serious than these lapses was the enhancement of revenue beyond the ability of the agriculturist to pay. In 1888, as the revision began, Fuller and the then chief commissioner, Alexander MacKenzie, pushed the percentage of assets taken by the state as high as 65 per cent, well above the 50 per cent imposed at the first settlement in order to reap the benefits of a supposed 'wheat boom' between 1861-90. Though later chief commissioners reduced the percentage, much of the increase remained and was defended as being 'lighter than in any other part of India'.[46]

Yet the revised assessments were excessive, given official policies and conditions in the region. During the first settlement *malguzars* and tenants had to pay full and often coerced exactions, which made no concession to crop damage, scarcity and famine in the form of suspensions, remissions or abatements. This led to high levels of debt and the transfer of villages and peasant plots to creditors. In every district therefore, many *malguzars* and tenants were in no position to pay the enhanced dues, and were more exposed to famine for attempting to do so. Officials later admitted that Sagar, Damoh, Jabalpur, Mandla, Narsimhapur, Hoshangabad and Betul, where officials enhanced the revenue 'shortly before or during the...scarcity' suffered most severely in the famine of 1896-97.[47] Moreover, Fuller reduced the duration of the revised settlement from 30 to 20 years to reap agricultural profits more frequently. Each district thus came on to a settlement roster. But to fill their correct place in the roster for the third settlement, some districts wre under revision for as little as eleven years. *Talukdari* estates were also settled in accordance with the roster for their district.

Talukdars, *malguzars* and tenants alike suffered from the revised assessments. From chiefs in Hoshangabad the administraton took the income formerly derived from excise, cattle pounds, unclaimed property and other sources, and enhanced their *takolis* up to 50 per cent of the assets, adding greatly to the revenues taken 30 years before. Fuller's abandonment of the half-assets rule told against the smaller and weaker *malguzars* in particular. To get its additional income, the administration levied home farms at a high rate and taxed permanent fallows and miscellaneous profits, cutting further into *malguzari* profits by directing settlement offficers to fix rents. As a result, in every district *malguzars'* profits declined on those of the first settlement, the highest loss being Rs. 3.68 lakhs in Hoshangabad.[48] In Jabalpur their loss was Rs. 3 lakhs, and in Narsimhapur R. 1.5 lakhs. To secure their assessments, officers also raised rents, frequently to levels which tenants could not pay. Though they did this by enhancing steeply the rents of privileged tenants, the mass of poor ordinary tenants in all districts bore part of the increased demand.

The administration also increased the revenue burden by coercing *malguzars* to pay their dues.[49] By pushing up revenue levels in this way, Fuller reduced agriculturists' capital and contributed to famine. Coercive processes comprised *dastaks* or notices to tardy payers, attachments of property, arrests and imprisonment, and their incidence generally increased as revenue payments fell during the first half of the decade. As rising balances showed, these measures did not succeed beyond a point. Officials coerced the revenue even in famine years, as in the years between the official famines. However, they eased the pressure in the hard-hit Jabalpur division as famine struck in 1899-1900 and provincial revenues recorded their first annual decline. In the Narmada division, where famine was more intense, officials used more savage coercion than in the better year of 1898-99. Rounding off a terrifying decade, in 1900-01 officials claimed near full collections in most districts, though they confessed that 'it was necessary to have recourse to the use of coercive processes in the collection of revenue to a much great extent than in the previous year....Arrests rose...and warrants of attachment....Backwardness in paying, was due to unwillingness to pay than to inability.'[50]

Other policies played a major part in stimulating famine. After the experience of the first settlement Fuller evolved a policy on suspending and remitting revenue as the famine decade began, but delayed implementing it. Despite a worsening situation Woodburn, the chief commissioner, did not suspend revenue until June 1894, while refusing to declare scarcity or famine, probably on the advice of Fuller who maintained that famine did not occur in Madhya Pradesh. The crop position in Sagar, Damoh and Jabalpur worsened in 1895, the outturns for both harvests for 1894-95 being less than one-third the average. Stocks of food were also low in the three districts, and agriculturists sold and mortgaged land and cashed savings and jewellery. Mandla reported scarcity and Seoni heavy mortality at the same time. Despite this, Woodburn refused the request for famine relief by a deputation from Sagar,[51] and abandoned relief works there, in Damoh, Narsimhapur and elsewhere as officials saw no starvation deaths, abandoned land, or emigration.[52]

The administration's policies in 1895-96 created the conditions for critical famine. The kharif crop was again poor in Jabalpur division, though Woodburn trusted that it would supply the lower classes with food.[53] He was reluctant to act, too, as he was to leave the province in December 1985 for a higher position. His successor, Sir Charles Lyall, also deferred declaring famine until the rabi harvest of 1896. In the meantime he instituted railway and road works, which mostly attracted people from neighbouring states. The Famine Commission unequivocally condemned Woodburn and Lyall:

> There seems to have been no sufficient reason for this hesitation....The history of the Central Provinces for 1895-96 shows the great danger of staking too much on the hope or chance of coming harvests turning out good....If regular relief operations had been begun early in 1896, not only would much distress have been alleviated, but the experience gained and the organisation perfected, would have been invaluable in enabling the local administration to deal properly with the general distress which followed the failure of harvests in 1896-97.[54]

As it happened drought destroyed the *rabi* crop of 1896, and at the same time conditions in the Narmada division began to resemble those in the districts to the north.

The administration's refusal to recognize scarcity or famine until too late intensified the famine and its effects.[55] Until December 1896 Lyall obeyed Fuller's dictum that famine could not occur anywhere in Madhya Pradesh. In May that year Fuller saw no point in drawing up a list of railway projects as famine works on the grounds that there was 'little need for famine relief in the province'. He also declaimed against famine test works as 'nobody went to them'. In September the administration characterized famine riots as criminal acts, had rioters whipped, and recommended the need for mounted police. By then the monsoon had failed, though Lyall deferred action until November, when he opened road works and poor houses in the Narmada division and relief centres in Jabalpur division. Yet during this time, merchants were exporting grains from the region for some six months.

In December 1896 when Lyall proclaimed famine, he abandoned the provincial famine code for that of the North Western Provinces.[56] Whereas the former emphasized small local or village works as the main form of relief, the latter gave first place to railway and large scale works, supplementing these with smaller operations. The Famine Commission condemned Lyall for the substitution, asserting that large works could not relieve the famine distressed, who could or would not join such works in great numbers.

The commission also attacked the administration's arrangements for relief other than large scale works. In place of local or village works, in November 1896 Lyall introduced relief centres to meet the 'emergent circumstances' created by large numbers of wandering poor, and to quieten mounting criticism in the press.[57] The centres were to provide relief for paupers unable to work and light labour for those unfit for regular tasks. From the outset Lyall stressed that these were temporary, and would close when other kinds of relief were operating. An official of the central government was closer to the truth when he claimed that the administration was using 'an exceptional and unauthorised expedient, because it was not ready'. Regular village relief in Sagar, Damoh and Jabalpur did not begin until February 1897, and then only 'to some extent'.

By May 1897 the relief centres and works programme were in difficulties, at a time of deep famine.[58] Officials were already disenchanted with the centres on the grounds that they did not attract people in 'absolute need', that workers were generally in a 'robust condition', and did not do a full day's work. The Famine Commission asserted that officials could not handle the crowds attending the centres, and that they failed to insist on adequate tasks. As a result the crowds at the centres grew until they became a 'mob doing a minimum of work'. The large works programme, too, was under a cloud.[59] The administration had discouraged minor works such as irrigation projects as the region offered 'least scope' for them. At the large works they maintained that people did not do work commensurate with the pay they received; though the Famine Commission held that the pay was not enough to maintain the health of the workers. Some roads built under this scheme were left incomplete; others 'were not really required'. Predictably, tribals did not 'take kindly' to such works.

To remedy defects in the relief programme Lyall decided to introduce piece work.[60] This decision coincided with a fall in the numbers on relief in May 1897, as people left works and centres for field labour before the monsoons. The administration thus decided to close down some works and presumably centres also as soon as the rains began, giving piece rates at relief venues for those still showing 'signs of deprivation'. This move was also calculated to push people back to the fields as the season opened. Though the decision once more departed from the provincial code, officials believed that piece work would be a better test of whether people genuinely needed famine relief or not as the rates were low. The Famine Commission held that the switch to piece rates dislocated relief, occurring as it did at the 'hardest time of the year, when the resources of the people were of necessity beginning to be most exhausted'.

The closure of some relief venues and the shift to piece rates had horrifying consequences.[61] Officers introduced the rates into districts hardest hit by famine, where workers were mostly tribals. The latter disliked the gang nature of the work, and the low pay made it difficult for them to support dependants. Even more distressing was the fact that as some relief centres closed, people returned to villages, but could find no work as there was no seed for crops and the land had been abandoned. They thus returned without warning to works and centres, causing the numbers seeking relief to rise astonishingly during June and July 1897. Mortality increased at the same time.

As mortality deepened and relief numbers swelled, officials became uncertain as to the the best course of action.[62] At this point it became evident that Fuller and Lyall were losing control over the famine administration. Some deputy commissioners opposed piece work and refused to introduce the scheme. In August, Lyall modified his orders in favour of a system of payment by results 'better suited to the last stages of the famine'. From applicants officials were to form separate gangs of infirm and able bodied. If each group did the tasks laid down, they received a minimum wage; but if less than the task, a lower wage. Protests from the Government of India compelled Lyall to modify the new scheme 'to some extent', but in most districts officials suspended the introduction of the modified scheme and switched back to task work. As they did so the death rate rose, especially among tribals, though the monsoon replenished food supplies, and the *rabi* of 1898 brought additional relief.

Some officials justified the mortality of the famine as inevitable.[63] For the Famine Commission it was inevitable, only if 'all methods and resources of...relief have been brought into play', which as we have seen was far from the case. Even so, the mortality was probably understated, as there were 'thousands whom relief of any kind could never and did never reach'. As an observer in Jabalpur pointed out: 'the official returns...cannot and will not embrace an enormous percentage of human beings who have simply sunk down under the distress uncounted and unaccounted for'.[64]

Further distress and mortality occurred in 1899-1900 as the resistance of ordinary folk crumbled before a famine more searing than that of 1896-97. This time, however, the administration under Fraser faced the situation with-confidence. With his officials the chief commissioner evolved a strategy that became standard practice in meeting subsequent disasters.[65] According to this strategy officers began village works, established kitchens and opened forests. At the same time the administration gave agriculturists funds to buy seed and cattle and to build tanks or make other improvements. In different parts of the region the public works department set up projects, each employing about 6,000 people. To avoid earlier charges of inertia and inefficiency, the administration imported engineers and non-commissioned officers to run the gigantic system, all works superintendents receiving twice the salary paid to overseers in 1896-97. Private charity supplemented the elaborate scheme, which cost two and a half times that spent in the previous famine and outran even the Government of India's more, economical views. The strategy, however, succeeded to some extent, where previous efforts had failed.

Yet the clamour for relief again underlined the serious nature of the famine. All sections of society sought aid, and they did so in large numbers.[66] Even during the famine's early stages, the crowds on relief were unprecedented, swollen by people from outside the province. Numbers rose even higher in 1900. In February that year 10 per cent of people in Sagar and Jabalpur were on relief. In Seoni the total reached 16 per cent. Towards the middle of the year as distress intensified and mortality rose, the administration relaxed the severity of the tests. In June more than 15 per cent of people in the province came onto relief; in July the number reached 20 per cent or 2 millions, 1.5 millions of whom received doles of some kind. Those on aid in Narsimhapur and Hoshangabad formed 25 per cent of the population, and in Betul a staggering 45 per cent. Numbers were even larger in August, with a total of 2.3 millions or 21 per cent of the provincial population in labour camps. The extent of famine can be further gauged from the fact that nearly half of the relief provided in India between 1899-1900 was concentrated in Madhya Pradesh.[67]

Though culpable, the administration disclaimed responsibility for the famines. To some extent it was the prisoner of district officers, who may have played down the extent of distress.[68] But Fuller at the helm of the agriculture department and commissioner for settlements must bear the chief responsibility for raising assessments and denying the reality of famine in Madhya Pradesh. Woodburn and Lyall did not oppose this view, and when Lyall did act he promulgated a famine code that did not suit conditions in the province. At some point, too, Fuller and Lyall lost the confidence of district officers in the region. Throughout, Lyall defended his policies, maintaining that the 'resisting power' of the people had increased 'during the past generation', and that cultivators had withstood famine with 'surprising firmness'.[69] He also asserted that a narrower section of people was destitute than in earlier decades.

However, it was the Famine Commission and the Government of India who had the last word. The government declared itself twice on the subject: the first when it defended Lyall against the Famine Commission's charge that he had not acted quickly enough to lessen distress and death. In a minute to the secretary of state in February 1899, the viceroy, Lord Elgin, claimed that the commission judged from knowledge acquired after the event.[70] On the second occasion, when Curzon became viceroy and interested officials urged a review of the commission's findings, the government's reaction was quite different. It declared 'that the Commission were on the whole the best judges of the evidence of this very difficult and complex subject; and that it is not incumbent on us to review their verdict.'[71] By then Lyall had quit the province for a position on the India council in Britain; and Fuller had become less influential as commissioner for Jabalpur.

IV

If British officials helped create famine, so, too, did those who supported and benefited from their policies. These were moneylenders who helped run the agrarian economy in the north. They included the smaller men, usually resident *malguzars*, who lent money to their villagers; and bania, Marwari and other urban moneylenders, who were absentee landlords of multiple estates. Both groups weakened agriculture by exploiting the constant need of *malguzars* and tenants for money between 1861-90, provided they could furnish security. Across forty years moneylenders realised many of their debts by seizing their clients' land—the moneylending *malguzar* within his own or neighbouring villages, and the professional moneylender larger acreages across one or several districts. Both groups thus spent their profits on gaining rather than improving land. Indebtedness and the transfer of property together with official policies created famine by leaving agriculturists without land, labour, cattle, money and food at a time when they needed them most.

The enhanced assessments of the revised settlements enabled moneylenders to drive a further wedge into the agrarian economy of northern Madhya Pradesh. Indebtedness was already high in 1891, and many if not most ordinary tenants in the region had difficulty with their rents, as suits to recover rent and rising sales of tenant land to realise rents or repay debts from 1891 bear witness. But such suits and sales also underlined the *malguzars'* difficulty in paying the revenue. As peasant resources dwindled and credit became difficult to raise, the gap between rent receipts and revenue payments widened. This enlarged the *malguzari* debt as proprietors borrowed to meet government demands. Inability to fulfil their obligations to the government or to their creditors led to the largest transfer of *malguzari* land since the province was formed. Indebtedness and the loss of land by *malguzars* and tenants prevented both from dealing with-crop failure, and exposed them to famine.

Let us examine the widening gap between rents collected and revenues paid by *malguzars* after 1891.[72] This will convey some idea of the dearth of capital among tenants and *malguzars*, who even so were dipping into reserves or borrowing against land to close the gap. As scarcity developed in 1894-95, *malguzars* in Jabalpur realised only half the demand, and were left with the profits of their *sir* land. The same year tenants in Narsimhapur could pay only half their rents, selling gold and cattle to do so. Yet the deputy commissioner collected the revenue in full, earning the administration s praise for doing so. Much the same situation occurred in Hoshangabad. The following year *malguzars* in Sagar realised 50 per cent of their rents; officials recovered 80 per cent of the demand. In Jabalpur *malguzars* paid revenues exceeding rents by some Rs 1.41 lakhs. *Malguzars* in Narsimhapur paid in full, though received 53 per cent of their rents. In the famine year collections in Jabalpur totalled 50 per cent, which was again in excess of the rents received.

Alarming gaps continued to appear in peasant and *malguzari* accounts for the remainder of the decade.[73] In 1897-98 revenue paid in Jabalpur exceeded rents by Rs. 1.3 lakhs. In Narsimhapur officials recovered the entire revenue and Rs. 2 lakhs in arrears, yet *malguzars* realised only 46 per cent of the demand and 39 per cent of the arrears from tenants. In all, between 1894-1900 the administration received 86 per cent of Narsimhapur's revenue, though the out-turn of crops was only 63 per cent of the normal, and rents must have been correspondingly low.[74] In Hoshangabad,

> during the period of bad years which have followed 1894, revenue collections have been most irregular. In 1897-98, the only year of the series when the outturns of the spring crops were not absolutely bad, great pressure was exercised, and the revenue collections did not fall very short of a full demand, but the payment of the sum was a heavy tax on the landlords, who managed to collect only about half their rents.[75]

Rent collections for 1897-98 in Sagar also lagged behind the revenue paid; while in the following year *malguzars* recovered only 41 per cent of the rents from tenants. In Narsimhapur *malguzars* paid half the demand, but gained 35 per cent of rents. The famine in 1899-1900 again threw revenue collection into confusion, before the administration secured near full collections from abated revenues in 1900-01.

Officials were aware of the rent-revenue gap and its effect on *malguzars*.[76] They admitted that *malguzari* debt rose between 1891-99 due to 'losses in cultivation and...rent collections'. As noted above, in 1898-99 a leading official described the position in Hoshangabad, where rents fell below the revenue, as a 'heavy tax' on *malguzars*. When recoveries from tenants in Hoshangabad in 1898 totalled only 41 per cent of the demand, the deputy commissioner confirmed that the district was bankrupt. It was common knowledge among officials in Jabalpur that rents fell into arrears and that *malguzars* often borrowed to pay the revenue. In Sagar with rents trailing revenues, in 1899 the deputy commissioner reported that most solvent *malguzars* had 'exhausted their resources and credit' to meet the demand. Non-official observers at the time also believed that part of the revenue was only paid with the help of moneylenders.

Borrowing from moneylenders to pay the revenue increased the *malguzari* debt between 1891-1901 and created the potential for famine.[77] In 1898 the Famine Commission noted that many old *malguzars* had 'fallen hopelessly into debt', while others were 'just' able to maintain themselves in prosperous years. Reports from the different districts substantiated this claim. By 1901 a majority of *malguzars* and peasants in Khurai tahsil, Sagar, were indebted in a district where landlords were the 'most encumbered' in the province. In Damoh the *malguzari* debt increased to 'an intolerable extent' during the decade.

Levels of debt in Jabalpur were also higher in 1901 than in 1893, as they were in Seoni. Settlement officers in Narsimhapur noted that some landowners were heavily indebted. In Hoshangabad they recorded the 'large amount of indebtedness among proprietors', particularly the Gonds and Korkus of the Satpura hills. In Betul, too, there was considerable debt among proprietors, which increased during the famines.

Debt was common among cultivators as among *malguzars*, leaving them exposed to scarcity and famine.[78] Indebtedness affected both privileged and ordinary tenants, as district reports bear witness. Everywhere during the decade tenants, already indebted, borrowed to pay rents and maintain cultivation because they had no capital of their own. Many without security could no longer rely on credit The situation in Hoshangabad typified the position elsewhere:

> In 1889 indebtedness was the normal condition of two-thirds of the population, so unprotected tenants had no reserves to meet the strain of famines. And these disastrous years left the bulk of the tenantry completely impoverished. Ten lakhs of revenue arrears accumulated in famine years.[79]

Non-officials confirmed this, reporting that cultivators in most tracts were 'simply bankrupts', with no money for seed or to buy or hire bullocks or ploughs. By 1901 the position would seem to have worsened. Fraser and other officials claimed that peasants throughout the province could not redeem their debts, because they had no capital and could get no credit. This changed them from being a 'prosperous and contented body of cultivators' into a 'position of practical serfdom'. When the seasons failed, these peasants were exposed to famine.

Heavy indebtedness, incurred before or after 1891, led *malguzars* to transfer their land on a large scale.[80] This deprived them of their basic resources and pushed them closer to famine. These transfers also demonstrated the exploitative nature of the system set up by British administrators and maintained largely by moneylenders. Between 1891-1903 *malguzars* in Sagar transferred a 'very large number of villages', including some of the 'largest estates'. Khurai was the scene of particularly heavy transfers. In Jabalpur *malguzars* transferred an unbelievable 1000 villages between 1899-1908. In Mandla 69 per cent of transfers between 1863-1904 occurred after 1895. More than one-seventh of villages in Seoni, a total of 215, changed hands between 1898-1905, the rate being three times as rapid as between 1868-98. 402 of 1110 villages in Narsimhapur were transferred between 1893-1904. *Malguzars* in Hoshangabad relinguished 384 villages or nearly 30 per cent of the total between 1893-1902. In Betul, 226 villages or 20 per cent of all villages in the district, were transferred between 1897-1906.

As during the first settlement, moneylenders were the largest beneficiaries from the transfer of property.[81] By 1895, one quarter of all proprietary land in the province had changed hands, and moneylenders were the most prominent recipients, the rate of transfers in their favour increasing towards the end of the century. Eric Stokes held that the major sweep of moneylenders into landholding, especially in the Narmada valley, occurred during this decade. In Sagar banias were the largest gainers, Khurai tahsil being dominated by several big moneylenders. More than half the villages transferred in Jabalpur between 1889-1907 went to moneylenders. Officials in Seoni claimed that increased indebtedness led to transfers of land to *mahajans*. Before 1897 the largest number of transfers in the Narmada division went to moneylenders. In Narsimhapur they took one-third of the villages transferred between 1894-1906; and in Hoshangabad there was

> not a single moneylender of importance, who has not, and is not, acquiring land. This has been intensified by two other causes, the increased consideration attached to landowners, and the accumulation of money formerly available for investment. These have been the principal causes which have induced a demand for the acquisition of land.[82]

In Betul moneylenders gained half of the 207 villages transferred between 1897-1904.

Indebted tenants also lost land in settlement of debt.[83] In Sagar and Damoh, protected tenants absconded or surrendered their lands between 1896-1916. Privileged holdings also fell in Jabalpur and Seoni, and in Hoshangabad many privileged tenants transferred their lands, the district being 'considerably affected' by enhanced rents. The contrasting growth of ordinary tenancy land during the decade masked the tragic condition of the bulk of the reigion's tenants.[84] Some of this growth occurred as privileged tenants became unprivileged or as *malguzars* and privileged tenants acquired the tenure after expelling the 'real' ordinary tenants or turning them into sub-tenants.

As *malguzars*, *malik maqbuzas* and tenants transferred land, moneylenders added to their property, at times on a princely scale. By 1901 this process had seriously distorted the society brought into being at the first settlement and the vision of the countryside it represented. In the villages moneylending *malguzars* continued to enlarge their home farms. More arresting was the class of banker *malguzars* who acquired large estates, intensifying a trend evident before 1891. The formation of such a class not only changed the compositon of the *malguzar* community, whereby Brahmins, banias and Marwaris displaced men of lower caste or tribal background.[85] It also signified the growing concentration of land and power in a small group of absentee landlords at the cost of widespread tenancy and landlessness. Such an economy fostered a low level of agricultural development, impoverished agriculturists, and left them unprotected against crop failure and famine.

For this phenomenon in the districts, observers in Sagar described a class of absentee landlords of mercantile background who vastly increased their estates during the decade.[86] Khurai tahsil was a byword for this type of landowner. In Jabalpur, too, moneylending landlords tended to concentrate their lands into large holdings. As early as 1893 a considerable proportion of villages in Mandla had gone to a few large proprietors. In Seoni, the settlement officer noted 'big landlords' in both tahsils during the decade. The same phenomenon was reported from Hoshangabad.

Harnetty, a modern historian, reported the concentration of property to be a dominant feature of the agrarian landscape, especially in Jabalpur division. There, assessments, coercion and poor seasons worked to the advantage of larger moneylenders, clustering from the eighteenth-century in the former capitals of Sagar and Jabalpur and adjacent towns, rather than in the far off, scattered urban setlements of the Narmada valley. As Harnetty commented,

> By the early twentieth-century the big landlords of the Central Provinces were now men like Dewan Bahadur Seth Bullubhdas of Jubbulpore, one of five big moneylenders, who between them held one-tenth of the villages of Saugor; he also had extensive holdings in Hoshangabad and lesser properties in the cotton districts....Seth Dalchand, a Kallar trader from Jubbulpore, bought villages in Damoh and Mandla, mainly from Gond proprietors.. .Raja Gokuldas continued to buy property all over the Central Provinces; he extended his holdings in Saugor at very little cost as a result of the famines of the 1890s, and at the time of his death in 1908 he owned 89 villages in

> Mandla. The largest landlord in Mandla was Jagannath Chowdhri,...a Kallar, who owned 156 villages or shares in villages....In Seoni, Rai Sahib Pandit Jiwan Lal owned 14 villages. Another to profit from the famine conditions of the last decade of the nineteenth-century was Sir Kasturchand Daga of Kamptee in Nagpur district, who became a large landowner in Saugor. Rao Sahib Seth Munnu Lal Chowdhri added to his extensive holdings in Jubbulpore by acquiring 45 whole villages in Balaghat.[87]

Nothing more eloquently expressed the bond between the administrations and moneylenders than official attitudes towards, them. Non-officials graphically pictured moneylenders tearing the proprietor from his land and leaving the 'fabric of Indian society and civilisation...a bleeding mass'.[88] By contrast, the administration came to accept and even suppport its partnership with moneylenders.[89] Even officials, who warned that once loyal chiefs and *malguzars* were turning against British rule after losing their land, were met with guarded claims that the administration aimed to prevent transfers to moneylenders 'as far as possible'. Fuller knew that 'a very large proportion' of villages was held by moneylenders, but did not regard transfers 'of much importance so long as the administration protected cultivators'. This it failed to do. In 1896-97, a famine year and one of especially heavy transfers, Lyall extended Fuller's view by asserting that

> we shall never teach mankind the lessons of social life, or leave room for progress in the future, except through practical experience of the results of improvidence and folly. It is right to protect the weak and simple as far as...possible.... But we must leave him the power of ruining himself if he deliberately chooses to do so.[90]

When applied to tribals this meant that if land could not be farmed 'efficiently', the weak must yield to the strong and the state should welcome and even expedite the process.[91]

Lyall's support for *laissez-faire* set the seal on the partnership that created famine in the region between 1891-1901. Before and after 1891, officials and moneylenders imposed on the region a system in which both maximised their share of rural wealth—the one in land and forest revenues and the benefits of trade, and the other in profits from moneylending, trade and rentier agriculture. By excessive revenue policies over the decades the administration deepened rural poverty and debt, while their Indian supporters lent money at a price, impoverishing agriculturists still further. Where the latter had no security, even credit failed. In the process moneylenders gained huge areas of agricultural land. Losing land and capital, rural society wilted before the onslaught of the seasons, its condition worsened by an inert and inefficient bureaucracy. Well might a non-official exclaim of Madhya Pradesh in 1899 that 'no other province in the whole Empire has suffered half so much'.[92]

V

The famines between 1891-1901 deeply affected Madhya Pradesh and its northern districts. Among the shorter term consequences was the abandonment of land. Famine, migration and death, together with debt, tore great holes in the agrarian economy as agriculturists deserted their lands. In 1899-1900 one observer calculated that the net cropped area in the province was 2,100 square miles short of normal.[93] As a modern geographer, W.H. Wake, noted:

> The period of...rapid expansion of gross cropped acreage came to an end, as a series of terrible crop failure and famines, coupled with epidemics, swept the State from 1894 to 1903. In 1896 alone the failure was so intense and widespread that only half the normal area was sown, and by 1901 the series of famines and epidemics had so decimated and demoralised the people that the net cropped area was nearly one million acres smaller than in 1893-94.[94]

In the north the removal of land from cultivation in all districts was widespread and continuous throughout the decade, particularly during the famines.[95] Throughout the region there was a consequent rise in fallows and the growth of *kans* grass on unused land.[96]

Another short term consequence of the famines was the abandonment of the revised settlement in all districts. This began when officials reluctantly suspended and remitted revenues from 1894-95, and concluded as they abated the enhanced assessments of the settlement.[97] The first abatements took place in Sagar where the settlement had 'hopelessly broken down'.[98] From 1897-98 the administration abated revenues of 424 villages in Khurai and in the Dhamoni pargana of Banda tahsil for up to five years on home farm and tenancy land in proportion to the decline in cropping. This proved insufficient, and officials later abated the revenues of 810 villages in the rest of the district. In 1901 the administration permanently abated the revenues of villages in Khurai and Dhamoni that missed out in 1899. Officials wielded the knife with a heavy hand, knowing the results of their actions:

> Partial and temporary revision is already being made in Saugor, and will be made next cold weather in a considerable portion of Damoh. Complete revision for the term of Settlement is now proposed for Hoshangabad. And every case in which relief assumes this form makes it more difficult to resist the demand for similar relief by other northern districts. . . . Narsinghpur . . . has now begun to press for it; and. . . Jubbulpore is busy framing an indictment against its Settlement on general grounds. . . . It is in any case a serious matter to re-open a Settlement within three years of its conclusion.[99]

Even so the process in Sagar remained incomplete. In 1910-11 officials re-imposed abated rents in 702 villages, and these held until settlement in 1916.

As they predicted, officials went on to abate revenues in the other districts of the region.[100] In Damoh abated revenues held until the third settlement got under way in 1909-10. In Jabalpur officials abated revenues in 618 of 1163 over-assessed villages, again until settlement operations began in 1909-10. Officials abated rents in 352 villages in Seoni. Revenues in Narsimhapur were abated from 1901, and these remained in force until the thrice postponed settlement between 1923-26. Hoshangabad's permanent abatements were over Rs. 2 lakhs, and continued in over 1000 villages until settlement in 1918 to give the district time to recover.

The main long-term result of the famine decade was economic stagnation in northern Madhya Pradesh. A basic factor was the strain which the events of the decade placed on the *malguzari* system, in addition to those experienced before 1891. The overseas wheat trade collapsed, and Punjab captured the Indian market for wheat. Many *malguzars* found that their resources could not withstand the pressure for revenue and they plunged further into debt, forfeiting their lands in the process. Without resources, many were ruined by crop failure and encountered famine. Indeed there was a consensus among officers that the famine of 1899-1900 'left the proprietors often in worse case than the tenants'.[101] Indebtedness worsened after 1901, and the transfer of property to moneylenders continued relentlessly, preventing any improvement in cultivation by 1920.[102]

A major factor in the stagnation was the permanent decline of wheat cultivation. Between 1891-1901 cultivation fell heavily in all districts and, though it recovered somewhat before 1920, the crop never again regained its earlier production level in the region and province.[103] This weakened the northern economy and threatened provincial finances, as wheat had contributed greatly to revenues since the first settlement.

The shift to other crops, which had begun before 1891, could not compensate the region or province for the loss of revenue and trade that accompanied the decline of wheat. In place of wheat, farmers switched to other rabi and kharif crops. As for rabi crops, it first seemed likely that linseed might fill the place of wheat, but by 1894 its cultivation was on the wane.[104] That year bad weather, fungoid diseases and caterpillars ruined the crop, and exports collapsed. Linseed contracted further during the dry years, for it required not only fertile soil but rain in September-October to maintain moisture during the winter. The crop did not make a comeback until 1909.

In its place *til*, either in the rabi or kharif, advanced after 1895. *Til* tolerated poor weather and inferior soils more readily than linseed; its yield per acre was generally higher, and it usually fetched higher prices in the market. Some districts exported *til* to Europe during the decade, and cultivation increased, especially in the more difficult years. But after 1901 the cultivation of *til* was unstable. Officials regarded its out-turn as uncertain, and disparaged it as a 'poor man's crop grown on poor soil for rent purposes'.

Generally, however, kharif crops gained from the decline of wheat, representing a setback to the region's economy.[105] Such crops usually gained lower prices than rabi crops and were on the whole less marketable. In Sagar, Damoh and Jabalpur rabi lands increasingly grew crops in the kharif. Where this shift occurred in Mandla, tribal cultivators usually grew *kodon* and *kutki* as a subsistence grain. Kharif cropping replaced rabi as the dominant form of cultivation in Seoni. The shift from wheat and rabi to the kharif was even more dramatic in the Narmada valley, which for decades had enjoyed a reputation of prosperity based on the cultivation of wheat.

Kharif crops had several advantages over rabi crops which explained their growing popularity. They grew during the monsoon and thus did not rely on the more unreliable winter rains. Crops such as *jowar* were cheap to sow, and frequently returned a good profit. *Jowar* also required less seed per acre than wheat, and was generally successful where wheat failed. *Kodon* and *kutki* were millets characteristic of poorer soils in the

Satpuras. In fact, all these crops grew on more inferior soils than wheat; they were cheaper to grow, and on the whole were less marketable, raising, where sold, lower prices in the market.

District reports demonstrated the advance of kharif crops.[106] In Sagar and Damoh agriculturists sowed increasing acreages to *jowar*, the trend continuing to 1920. In Mandla many peasants grew *kodon* in place of wheat; whereas in Seoni rice and *jowar* expanded, *jowar* outstripping the area where formerly wheat was sown. The poor seasons gave an 'immense impetus' to *jowar* in the Narmada valley up to 1920. In Hoshangabad gram and *jowar* increased in inverse proportion to wheat, and in some parts inferior crops replaced the mixture of wheat-gram then becoming popular. Cultivators in Betul switched to *jowar* on black soil in the *rabi* season as they found it difficult to procure wheat seed.

The increased cultivation of mixtures also indicated a decline in the quality of agriculture and so contributed to stagnation.[107] Farmers in the north mixed wheat and gram to reduce the soil exhaustion resulting from wheat monoculture and cut their losses if one crop failed. In Sagar farmers added linseed to the wheat-gram mixture. Observers also reported mixtures of wheat and gram in the Narmada valley. Another combination occurred in Hoshangabad, where farmers in all tahsils except Harda substituted mixtures of *jowar*, *tur*, *moong* and *urad* for the old crops and, as offcials noted disapprovingly, sowed the mixtures 'broadcast in imperfectly prepared land'. Farmers in Betul planted a fourth type of mixed crop, sowing jowar in black soil under wheat and other rabi crops.

The retreat of wheat and rabi cropping was seen in the cultivation of kharif and other crops in the second class soils once sown to wheat.[108] Some commentators suggest that wheat monoculture with improper fallowing had depleted the soils, leading to the sowing of less demanding crops, but this is difficult to substantiate. What is certain is that areas from which wheat receded were generally the inferior soils to which it expanded under pressure from British policies after 1861. The slide from such soils long predated 1891, but the process accelerated in the famine decade. Officials confirmed that poorer soils in Jabalpur division were susceptible to the effect of poor seasons. Mandla's fertile tracts were small, making agriculture there prone to deterioration from the outset. Further west in Narsimhapur:

> Large areas of inferior land were abandoned, not necessarily as a result of Mr. de Brett's assessments, but because they were only capable of producing a remunerative crop during wet years, and were

therefore bound to be abandoned as soon as a cycle of bad years came round.[109]

This experience led officials to abandon earlier cliches about the 'rich, black soils of the Narbada valley', and to see that soils varied more than they had supposed. As in Mandla, much of Betul's soil was infertile to begin with.

Another element in the stagnation of the northern economy was the continuing shortage of plough cattle. This trend was evident before 1891, but bad seasons, shortage of food and water, and disease further depleted numbers. This made cultivation impossible for many, unless they could raise credit. Though the administration opened forests for grazing, this had little effect. Cattle that did not die but were useless for work were slaughtered, while farmers who had no pasture sold off their stock. In all, officials estimated that plough cattle in Madhya Pradesh declined by 650,000 between 1891-1901.[110] Cattle numbers continued to decline after 1901 due to the growing shortage of grazing facilities, disease, and years of seasonal failure. Cattle breeding made little impact on numbers, and by 1909 the number of cattle in the Narmada valley was less than before 1891. This critical condition continued at least until 1920.[111]

Famine permanently ruined the place of crafts in the rural economy, contributing to economic stagnation.[112] During the famine decade the administration continued to allow the unrestricted entry of foreign pig iron, metal vessels, cheap European china and textiles, and some Indian manufactures as well, further destroying regional crafts. In Sagar the blanket industry declined. Foreign imports 'wholly crushed or reduced to a moribund condition' indigenous industries in Jabalpur, iron smelting, especially, suffering 'much loss'. In Seoni English piece goods displaced local fabrics, weavers wove little silk, artisans fell on 'evil times', and village industries in general declined. By 1901 foreign pig iron was on the way to ousting local iron in Narsimhapur. For Madhya Pradesh as a whole, the 1901 census reported that village industries had contracted since 1891, and that various categories of craftsmen had declined in numbers during the decade. These trends persisted up to 1920.

Industrial development in the region between 1891-1920 did little to restore the shattered economy. In 1892 Burn and Company opened a pottery in Jabalpur making tiles, pipes and earthenware; a brewery began production in the town in 1897. Enterpreneurs also developed a complex of paint and pottery factories, a distillery and some flour mills in Katni. In 1898 a Marwari seth, Radha Krishan, opened a cotton spinning factory in Hoshangabad, while other ginning and pressing factories began operating in the following year. But however noteworthy, these developments hardly compensated for the decline of the traditional economy. Some districts had no modern industries at all. After 1900 the Marwari firm of Raja Gokul Das and government agencies built additional factories in Jabalpur, and facilities for processing cotton extended in the towns of the Narmada valley. The mining of coal, manganese and limestone also expanded. But these developments could not lift the region out of stagnation, as the industrial commission underlined in 1918:

> The industrial life of the province is synonymous with its agricultural life. There has been marked activity in recent years in mining enterprise, and such excellent factories as...the Pottery Works of Burn and Co. of Jubbulpore, and the Cement Works of Katni denote a high order of industrial achievement. Yet the vast resources of the province remain untouched, and it stands today as it was, pre-eminently agricultural....Manufacturing industry, rather than agricultural, must raise the fabric of economic advancement. A new force of industrial activity must arise before any real progress can be made.[113]

Economic failure between 1891-1901 intensified the social disintegration that accompanied stagnation.[114] We have already noticed the declining number of craftsmen by 1901. On the land, moneylending *malguzars* who were absentee landlords took no interest in their tenants; and among smaller *malguzars* and tenants few had any reserves of capital at the end of the decade. The famine ruined many *malguzars*, thrusting them down to tenancy. At the same time many tenants lost their land or became ordinary tenants without security, and were thus compelled to work for others. Regular farm servants sank to the position of day labourers. During famine these sections of society were the first to be distressed. Famine also hit those in rural employment whose wages fell as prices rose. Tribal *malguzars*, peasants and labourers, concentrated as they were in the poorest areas, were especially hit during the famines.

The position had barely improved by 1920.[115] Officials, anxious to create a viable revenue base, could restore neither the society nor the economy. Many *malguzars* and peasants remained unable to meet their revenues and rents, and where indebted transferred large acreages to moneylenders. Wheat did not recover its place as the region's main export, and farmers turned permanently to less remunerative crops, particularly in the *kharif*. Poor seasons with-crop failure enhanced the difficulties of agriculturists, while famine with attendant malnutrition and disease led to recurrent high mortality. As a result the population of the region was lower in 1920 than in 1911 and, in some districts, than in 1891. Agricultural deterioration as represented in the statistics of land use persisted after the famines, and industrial growth made little headway. Between 1918-20 stagnation climaxed in a further economic crisis as more than a century of British rule in the region drew to a close. Local landowners and others chose this moment to launch a movement of non-co-operation against the administration.

The failure of the northern districts by 1920 had serious implications for Madhya Pradesh. The collapse of the economy and revenues led the Government of India to divert the revenues of Berar from the State of Hyderabad to the province from 1903. The administration employed these monies to embellish Nagpur, construct public works, and upgrade the political status of Madhya Pradesh. At the same time rising prices for cotton increased its cultivation in the southern districts of Nagpur and Berar. This led government and private agencies to develop these districts and to lose interest in districts to the north. As a result cotton and the revenues of Berar put money into the south, while the wheat districts 'had to bear the brunt of....financial stringency'[116] The gamble with wheat had failed, though it remained to be seen whether cotton alone could save Madhya Pradesh.

This article, compiled largely from official reports together with some statistical material, substantiates the claim of R.C. Dutt and twentieth-century economists and historians that British revenue assessments helped create famine. Related policies draining capital from the countryside and making farmers vulnerable to famine included the administration's coercion of revenues for 40 years up to 1901; its refusal to suspend or remit revenue until 1894, and to recognize scarcity or famine in Madhya Pradesh till 1896-97. Inefficiency in handling the situation severely aggravated the famine of 1896-97, and probably that of 1899-1900 as well. This paper also points out that if the administration created famine, so did its moneylending supporters, who exploited the need for capital over four decades and realized their debts by seizing land, leaving agriculturists without resources at times when they most needed them.

NOTES

1. This article is taken from the author's forthcoming book *Colonialism in an Indian Hinterland: the Central Provinces 1818-1920*, to be published by OUP, (India).
2. McAlpin, *Subject to Famine: Food Crises and Economic Change in Western India, 1860-1920* (Princeton, 1983).
3. The author wishes to acknowledge the help of Dr. Dharma Kumar of the Delhi School of Economics in writing this paper.
4. *Resolution in the Land Revenue Administration Department, 1896-97*, p. 7 (*LRA Resn*).
5. By 1901 Madhya Pradesh had run up an uncollected land revenue balance of Rs. 1,49,64,000, of which the administration remitted Rs. 1,16,93,000 as unpayable. Of the remaining 32.71 lakhs, it suspended Rs. 24.5 lakhs and proposed to remit further amounts. In the region by 1901, uncollected balances totalled Rs. 13.98 lakhs in Sagar, Rs. 17.86 lakhs in Damoh, Rs. 21.21 lakhs in Jabalpur, Rs. 1.85 lakhs in Mandla, Rs. 3.05 lakhs in Seoni, Rs. 11.05 lakhs in Narsimhapur, Rs. 15.28 lakhs in Hoshangabad, and Rs. 4.72 lakhs in Betul, amounting to nearly Rs. 89 lakhs.
6. *CP Administration Report, 1891-92*, p. iii (*Admin Report*). The population of Madhya Pradesh was 92,17,312 in 1901; in 1891 it was 101,51,354.
7. District census figures are taken from *Central Provinces District Gazetteers* (*CPDG*) for the districts concerned; and from the *Census of 1921*, vol. XI, *CP and Berar*, part II, *Tables*, pp. 6-7.
8. Unless otherwise indicated the footnote at the beginning of each paragraph comprises the sources of the entire paragraph. *Sanitary Commissioner's Report, 1892*, p. 1 (*SCR*); *LRA Resn, 1894-95*, p. 9; *Report of the Land Revenue Settlement, Seoni, 1894-98*, p. 24 (*RLRS*); *Census of 1901*, vol. XIII, *CP*, part I, *Report*, pp. 130-31.
9. Accounts of disease may be found in *CPDG*, and annual issues of *SCR*, *LRA Resn*, and *Admin Report*.
10. *SCR, 1896*, Resn, CC, 27 Nov 1897, p. 3.
11. *Admin Report, 1900-01*, p. 61.
12. *See SCR, LRA Resn, CPDG*; also *Admin Report, 1891-92*, p. 105; *Report of the Indian Famine Commission*, 1898, pp. 158, 172; (*FC*, 1898); P.F. McEldowmey, 'Colonial administration and social development in Middle India, the Central Provinces, 1861-1921', PhD thesis, University of Virginia, 1980, p. 229.
13. *Sanitary Report*, 1896, Resn, CC in General Department, 27 Nov 1897.
14. *CPDG*, Mandla, p. 45.
15. For details of crime see annual issues of *Police Report*, *Jail Report*, *Criminal Judicial Report*
16. *Criminal Judicial Report, 1891*, p. 2; *Jail Report, 1894*, p. 2; *Jail Report, 1895*, H. Hughes Hallett to Chief Sec (CS) to CC, 20 Mar 1896, p. 2; *Police*

Report, 1895, Resn, CC in General Dept, 20 July 1896, pp. 1, 13; *Criminal Judicial Report, 1895*, Extract Proceedings CC General Dept, 20 July 1896.

17. *Jail Report, 1896*, Extract Procs CC, General Dept, 16 July 1897, p. 1; *Criminal Judicial Report, 1896*, Extract Procs CC General Dept, 18 Nov 1892, p. 2; *Police Report, 1896*, pp. 28-29; *Police Report, 1897*, pp. 6-7; *CPDG*, Betul, p. 219.
18. Revenue and Agriculture (R+A), Famine (Fam) A, July 1898, 7, CC to Sec R+A, GOI, 10 June 1898.
19. *Police Report, 1895*, pp. 13,33; *Police Report*, 1896, p. 29; *CPDG*, Betul, p. 219.
20. I*ndian Famine Commission* (*IFC*), 1881, Appx, vol. III, p. 167; J.B. Fuller, *A Review of the Progress of the CP during the past thirty years, and of the Present and Past Condition of the People*, Nagpur, 1892, pp. 32,50 (*PPCP*); *CPDG*, Seoni, pp. 61-62; P. Harnetty, 'A Curious exercise in political economy; some implications of British land-revenue policy in the Central Provinces of India, 1861-c. 1900,' *South Asia*, 6, 1976, p. 32 (Curious exercise); W.H. Wake, 'The relations between transportation improvements and agricultural changes in Madhya Pradesh, India, 1854-1954', PhD. thesis, UCLA, 1961, p. 153.
21. *RLRS Damoh, 1866*, p. 48; *RLRS Saugor, 1887-97*, p. 39.
22. *RLRS Jubbulpore, 1886-94*, pp. 3, 21-23; *RLRS Seoni, 1894-98*, p. 28; *RLRS Mandla, 1904-10*, p. 3; *CPDG* Mandla, p. 70.
23. *RLRS Hoshangabad*, 1891-98, p. 40.
24. *RLRS Betul, 1894-99*, p. 40.
25. See *CPDG*, Mandla, p. 233; McEldowney , pp. 465-66.
26. Ibid., pp. 467-68.
27. *CPDG*, Mandla, p. 233; McEldowney, pp. 466-71.
28. *RLRS Jubbulpore, 1886-94*, p. 3; *RLRS Mandla, 1888-90*, J.B. Fuller to Sec CC, 8 Feb 1893; *RLRS Hoshangabad*, 1891-98, pp. 35-36, 40; *CPDG*, Damoh, p. 55; *CPDG*, Narsinghpur, p. 84; R.V. Russell and Hira Lal, *The Tribes and Castes of the Central Provinces of India* (London, 1916), vol. III, p. 139; Wake, p. 153.
29. *RLRS Hoshangabad, 1891-98*, p. 40.
30. Ibid., pp. 36-40; *Admin Report, 1901-02*, p. 58; *RLRS Betul, 1916-21* p. 7; CPDG, Damoh, p. 55; *CPDG*, Seoni, p. 52; *CPDG*, Narsinghpur, p. 67; *CPDG*, Hoshangabad, p. 158; *CPDG*, Betul, p. 72; P. Harnetty, 'Changes in the agrarian structure of the Central Provinces of India, 1861-1920', *Proceedings of the Seventh International Association of Historians of Asia* (Bangkok, 1979), vol. 1, pp. 450-52 (Agrarian changes); Fuller, *PPCP*, p. 29; J. Forsyth, *The Highlands of Central India: Notes on their Forests and Wild Tribes, Natural History and Sports* (London, 1871), p. 154.
31. F.G. Sly, *Memorandum on the Condition of the People of the CP during the Decennial Period, 1892-1902* (Nagpur, 1902), p. 11 (Sly, *Memo*).
32. *RLRS Betul, 1994-99*, p. 75.

33. R+A, Fam A, Mar 1897, 29, H. Priest to Sec R+A GOI, 12 Feb 1897.
34. F.H.S. Merewether, *A Tour through the Famine Districts of India* (London 1898), p. 158-59.
35. *CPDG*, Betul, 189-90.
36. *FC*, 1898, p. 290.
37. *CPDG*, Mandla, p. 185.
38. M. Sykes, *Quakers in India: A Forgotten Century* (London, 1980), p. 71.
39. D.S. Nag, *Tribal Economy; An Economic Study of the Baiga* (Delhi, 1958), p. 78.
40. *CPDG*, Mandla, p. 185-86.
41. *FC*, 1898, p. 288.
42. *Census of 1911*, vol. x, *CP and Berar*, part I, *Report*, pp. 28-29.
43. Home Establishments, Sept 1898, A.H.L. Fraser, note, 12 Sept 1898.
44. *RLRS Jubbulpore*, 1886-94, p. 30.
45. *CPDG*, Hoshangabad, p. 259.
46. R+A, Fam A, July 1898, 7, CC to Sec R/A GOI, 10 June 1898.
47. R+A, LRA, June 1899, 2, A.L. Saunders to Sec R/A GOI, 11 April 1899.
48. R+A, LRA, May 1901, 22, R.H. Craddock to Sec R/A GOI, 2 April 1901; *RLRS Jubbulpore*, 1886-94 , p. 12; *RLRS Saugor, 1887-97*, pp. 30, 63; *RLRS Mandla, 1888-90*, J.B.Fuller to Sec CC,8 Feb 1893; *RLRS Hoshangabad, 1913-18*, p. 4; *RLRS Narsinghpur, 1923-26*, pp. 25-26; Harnetty, Curious Exercise, p. 21.
49. For coercive process see annual issues of *LRA Resn, Resolution on Revenue and Agriculture in the CP* (*RACP Resn*).
50. *RACP Resn, 1900-01*, Annexure B, Narbada Division, p. 5.
51. McEldowney, p. 232.
52. R/A, Fam A, Feb 1895, 1, H.A. Crump to Sec R/A GOI, 6 Feb 1895; FC, 1898, p. 160.
53. Ibid., p. 161.
54. Ibid., pp. 161, 165.
55. *FC*, 1901, vol. III, p. 154; McEldowney, pp. 232-33.
56. *FC*, 1898, pp. 69, 163-64.
57. R+A, Fam B, March 1897, KW, F 77, Orders issued by CC CP regarding organization of famine relief, File note, T.W. Holderness, 12 Feb 1897; *FC*, 1898, pp. 72, 166.
58. Ibid., pp. 70, 72, 166.
59. R+A, Fam A, July 1898, 7, CC to Sec R/A GOI, 10 June 1897; *FC*, 1898, 1898, pp. 70, 167-68, *CPDG*, Damoh, p. 139; Merewether, p. 165.
60. R+A, Fam A, Oct 1899, 4, M.W. Fox Strangways to Sec R&A GOI, 28 July 1899; *FC* 1898, pp. 70-71, 170.
61. Ibid., pp. 71, 164, 168-70.
62. Ibid., pp. 71, 122, 169-70.
63. Ibid., p. 164; Merewether, p. 149.
64. Ibid.

65. R+A, Fam A, Oct 1899, 18, M.W. Fox Strangways to Sec R–A GOI, 7 Oct 1899; *Imperial Gazetteer*, vol. x, p. 42 (*IG*); *CPDG*, Betul, p. 191-95; D.P. Mishra et al (eds.), *The History of Freedom Movement in Madhya Pradesh* (Nagpur, 1956), p. 197 (*MPFM*); V. Nash, *The Great Famine and Causes* (np, nd), pp. 149-50; J.N. Sil, *History of the CP and Berar* (Calcutta, 1917), pp. 147-48.
66. For sections of society see *FC*, 1901, vol. III, pp. 133, 135, 141, 150, 157; *CPDG*, Narsinghpur, p. 169; *CPDG*, Betul, pp. 191 193-94. And for numbers, R+A, Fam A, CP, A, 1900 File, quoted in *Times of India*, 19 July 1900; IG, vol. XIII, p. 188; *Speeches by the Hon Sir Benjamin Robertson, CC, 1912-1920* (Nagpur, 1920), p. 169; *MPFM*, p. 197.
67. B.M. Bhatia, *Famine in India: A Study in some Aspects of the Economic History of India, 1860-1945* (Bombay, 1963), p. 253
68. R&A, Fam A, Mar 1897, 29, H. Priest to Sec R&A GOI, 12 Feb 1897.
69. FC, 1898, p. 362.
70. R&A, Fam A, Oct 1899, Memo on the several points taken by C.J. Lyall in his note of 24 Aug 1899, Note by T.W. Holderness, 24 Aug 1899.
71. R&A, Fam A, Oct 1899, 5, Lyall's Famine Administration, GOI to L.G. Hamilton, SOS, 28 Sept 1899.
72. LRA Resn, 1894-95, pp. 8,23; B.K. Bose, 'The CP Land Revenue System', in *Land Problems in India* (Madras, 1902) p. 173; *Land Revenue Administration in the CP of India*, Tenants and Landlords Association of Jabalpur (Bombay 1905), pp. 49, 51 80 (TLAJ, 1905).
73. References in this paragraph are drawn from Bose and TLAJ, 1905.
74. *RLRS Narsinghpur, 1885-94*, H.A. Crump to Sec R/A GOI, 23 Nov 1901, p. 1; *RLRS Narsinghpur*, 1923-26, p. 55.
75. R+A, LR A, May 1901, 22, R.H. Craddock to Sec R/A GOI, 2 April 1901, p. 18.
76. R+A, LR A, June 1899, 4, C.W.C. Montgomerie to Sec R/A GOI, 6 May 1899; R+A, LR A, May 1901, 22, R.H. Craddock to Sec R+A GOI, 2 April 1901; Sly, *Memo*, p. 12; *Madhya Pradesh District Gazetteers*, Jabalpur, p. 285 (*MPDG*); TLAJ, 1905, p. 50; Bose, p. 173.
77. R+A, Fam A, 1894, 2, H. Priest to Sec R+A *GOI*, 2 July 1894; *FC*, 1898, pp. 361-62; *FC*, 1901, vol. III, p. 326; *RLRS Hoshangabad*, 1891-98, pp. 35-37; *RLRS Seoni, 1894-98*, pp. 28-29; *CPDG*, Saugor, p. 123; *CPDG*, Betul, p. 145; *MPDG*, Damoh, p. 151.
78. For evidence of tenant debt see *RLRS* for the revision settlements, and *CPDG* and *MPDG* for the respective districts.
79. R+A, Survey and Settlement, CP, A, April 1901, C.E. Low, Report on proposed abatements in Hoshangabad.
80. See *RLRS Betul, 1894-97*, p. 63; *CPDG*, Saugor, p. 124; *CPDG*, Jubbulpore, p. 190; *CPDG*, Seoni, p. 102; *CPDG*, Narsinghpur, p. 121; *CPDG*, Hoshangabad, p. 160; C. Bates, 'Anthropologists, administrators and the irrationality of tribal society in the former CP of India', unpub.

seminar paper, Cambridge, 1980.

81. *RLRS Saugor, 1887-97*, pp. 33, 42; *RLRS Seoni, 1894-98*, p. 29; *CPDG*, Narsinghpur, p. 121; *CPDG*, Betul, 142; Harnetty, Agrarian changes, p. 451; Harnetty, Curious exercise, pp. 22-24.
82. *RLRS Hoshangabad*, 1891-98, p. 37.
83. *RLRS Seoni*, *1887-97*, p. 29; *RLRS Jubbulpore*, 1907-12, p. 26; *RLRS Saugor, 1911-16*, p. 40; *CPDG*, Damoh, p. 108; *CPDG*, Hoshangabad, p. 162.
84. *RLRS Saugor, 1887-97*, p. 40; *RLRS Jubbulpore, 1907-12*, p. 36; see Harnetty, Agrarian charges, Table 4.1.
85. Ibid., pp. 449, 463.
86. *RLRS Saugor, 1887-97*, pp. 43-44; *RLRS Mandla, 1888-90*, J.B. Fuller to Sec CC, 8 Feb 1893; *RLRS Seoni, 1894-98*, p. 26, R/A, LR A, Feb 1899, 24, H.A. Crump to Sec R+A GOI, 18 Jan 1899; Harnetty, Agrarian changes, pp. 459-53; Harnetty, Curious exercise, p. 22.
87. Harnetty, Agrarian changes, pp. 452-53.
88. Nash, pp. 225-26.
89. R+A Case Files, A, Sept 1892, L.S. Carey to Sec R/A GOI, 30 Sep 1892, forwarding memo by J.B. Fuller; *RACP Resn, 1896-97*, Ann. B, Report on Operations of Dept of Land Records, p. 15; *Selection from Papers on Indebtedness and Land Transfer, 1895*, GOI, 1895, p. 107.
90. Harnetty, Curious exercise, p. 24.
91. W.V. Grigson, *The Aboriginal Problem in CP and Berar* (Nagpur, 1944), p. 63.
92. Nash, pp. 196-97.
93. *IG*, vol. X, pp. 33-34.
94. Wake, p. 117.
95. See *RACP Resn*, *LRA Resn* for the decade; *CPDG*; *RLRS Seoni, 1894-98*, p. 2; *RLRS Betul, 1894-99*, p. 2; *RLRS Mandla, 1904-10*, p. 35; *RLRS Narsinghpur*, *1923-26*, p. 29; *Notes on Tour by the Vice Chairman of the Central Executive Committee,* Indian Famine, Charitable Relief Fund, April 1897, Calcutta, 1897, pp. 18-20 (*IFCRF*); Bhatia, p. 181.
96. *RLRS Seoni, 1888-97*, p. 10; *RLRS Betul, 1894-99*, p. 16; R+A, LR A, Sept 1895, 25, M.W. Fox Strangways to Sec R/A GOI, 10 Aug 1898; R+A, Fam B, Sept 1899, C.W.E. Montgomerie to Sec R/A GOI, 8 Aug 1899; R+A, LR A, May, 1901, 22, R.H. Craddock to Sec R/A GOI, 2 April 1901; *CPDG*, Saugor, p. 100; TLAJ, 1905, pp. 50, 70, 72.
97. In 1895-96 the Government of India gave the chief commissioner a free hand in suspending revenue. By the official close of the famine on 1 October 1900, of Rs. 76 lakhs of arrears in Madhya Pradesh, the administration had remitted over Rs. 40 lakhs.
98. R/A, Survey and Settlement, CP, 1900, C.R. Cleveland, Note on resettlement and debt conciliation schemes in Khurai tahsil, 11 June 1900; *RLRS Saugor, 1911-16*, p. 31.

99. R/A, LR A, July 1899, 41, C.W.E. Montgomerie to Sec R/A GOI, 7 July 1899.
100. *RLRS Jubbulpore, 1886-94*, p. 3; R/A, LR A, Mar 1899, 7, H.A. Crump to Commr, 23 Feb 1899; p. 4; R/A, Survey and Settlement, CP, A, Nov 1900, 4, R.H. Craddock to Commr Settlements and Agriculture, 22 Nov 1900; *RLRS Damoh, 1909-13*, pp. 1,3,27; *RLRS Hoshangabad, 1913-18*, p.4; *CPDG*, Damoh, p. 166; *CPDG*, Jubbulpore, pp. 300-02, *CPDG*, Narsinghpur, p. 187; *CPDG*, Hoshangabad, p. 260.
101. R/A, LR B, Mar 1902, 9, A.H.L. Fraser to Lord Curzon, 27 Jan 1902.
102. See the author's forthcoming *Colonialism in an Indian Hinterland: the Central Provinces, 1818-1920*, ch. V for evidence of this.
103. Between 1891-1901 wheat cultivation in Saugor fell from 59% to 22.9% of the cropped acreage; in Damoh from 42.5% to 25.9%; Jabalpur from 39.4% to 27.3%; Narsimhapur from 38.4% to 22.7%, Hoshangabad from 57.2% to 36.1%, and Betul from 24.6% to 16%. P. Harnetty, 'Crop trends in the CP of India, 1861-1921', in *Modern Asian Studies*, vol. II, no. 3, p. 9.
104. Ibid., pp. 16-18. For *til* see, pp. 18-19.
105. For Jabalpur division, *RLRS Seoni, 1894-98*, pp. 2,17; *FC*, 1898, p. 156; *RACP Resn, 1898-99*, p. 3; *CPDG*, Damoh, p. 87; *CPDG*, Mandla, p. 166; and for Narmada division, R/A, LR A, June 1899, 2, A.L. Saunders to Sec R/A GOI, 11 April 1899; R/A, Fam B, Oct 1901, 8, F.C. Sly, Note on agricultural statistics for 1900-01, 20 Aug 1901.
106. *RLRS Hoshangabad, 1891-98*, p. 15; *RLRS Seoni, 1894-98*, p. 2, 17; *RLRS Betul, 1898-99*, pp. 25, 29; FC, 1898, p. 156; *Report on Rail-Borne Trade, 1898-99*, p. 15 (*RBT*); *CPDG*, Damoh, pp. 87, 95; *CPDG*, Hoshangabad, pp. 118-19; *MPDG*, Sagar, p. 141.
107. *RLRS Hoshangabad, 1891-98*, p. 5; *RLRS Betul, 1894-99*, p. 25; *MPDG*, Sagar, p. 140.
108. *RLRS Saugor, 1867*, p. 30; *RLRS Mandla, 1888-90*, J.B. Fuller to Sec CC, 8 Feb 1893; *RLRS Betul, 1894-99*, p. 12; *LRA Report, 1895-96*, p. 1; *CPDG*, Jubbulpore, p. 266; 182; RLRS Narsinghpur, 1923-26, pp. 1,7; *MPDG*, Sagar, p. 182.
109. *RLRS, Narsinghpur, 1923-26*. p. 29.
110. *Admin Report, 1901-02*, p. ix.
111. *Memorandum on Rural Conditions and Agricultural Development in the CP and Berar*, Nagpur, 1926, pp. 24-25; *Report on Revenue and Agriculture in CP*, LRA report on Nerbudda Divn, 1908-09, Annexure B, p.3.
112. *RLRS Jubbulpore, 1886-94*, p. 17; *Census of 1901*, vol. XIII, *CP*, part I, *Report*, pp. 211, 224-25, 231; TLAJ, 1905, p. 95; *CPDG*, Seoni, p. 114; *RLRS Narsinghpur*, 1923-26, p. 33.
113. *Indian Industrial Commission, Minutes of Evidence, 1916-17, Bengal and CP* (Calcutta, 1918), R. Mitra, p. 631.

114. *RLRS Saugor, 1887-97*, p. 39; *LRA Resn, 1894-95*, pp. 10-11; R/A, CP, A, June 1895, F.G. Sly, Report on the condition of agriculture in Hoshangabad, 1891; Fuller, *PPCP*, p. 50; Sly, *Memo*, 1902, p. 14. R+A, Fam A, Dec 1907, 50, F.S.A. Slocock to Sec R+A GOI, 25 Oct 1907; Merewether, p. 154; Wake, p. 155.
115. For a fuller treatment of this theme see the author's forthcoming work, *Colonialism in an Indian Hinterland: the Central Provinces, 1818-1920*, ch. V.
116. *Central Provinces Legislative Council Proceedings*, vol. 1, no. 1, 4 Mar 1926, p. 5.

Gardens and Paddy Fields: Historical Implications of Agricultural Production Regimes in Colonial Malabar

RAVINDRAN GOPINATH

Variations in agricultural cultivation regimes appear to have played a significant role in shaping the history of southern India. This has been recognized in the recent historical writings on the Tamil-speaking areas of the Indian peninsula by Burton Stein, Christopher Baker and David Ludden.[1]

In this paper the attempt is to try and establish a tentative congruency between specific agricultural production regimes and the concomitant social and political relations in the context of colonial Malabar. This will enable one to relate regional and sub-regional variations in economic, social and political development to the production base.

The data base for this study is limited by marked inaccuracies in the acreage statistics of certain crops, the absence of annual acreage data at the taluka level and by the lack of annual price data on certain garden products. Further, the acreage statistics in the pre 1900-4 period are highly suspect because no systematic survey of the district had been carried out till then.

This paper deals with the two specific cultivation regimes of paddy and of garden crops. The first section introduces the district and then disaggregates it in terms of its dominant cultivation regimes. The second discusses the cost of cultivation and the intensity and seasonality of labour inputs in garden and paddy production. Section III describes the north-south differences in tenurial and land relations, the caste hierarchies and relations and, finally, the antecedent political histories of the garden cropped northern talukas and of the paddy-growing south. Section IV attempts to connect the intra-district tenurial and social variations to the dominant cultivation regimes of the sub-regions. Finally, we try to see how the garden dominated north and the paddy dominated south responded to the marked price increase and the subsequent depression in the first half of the twentieth-century.

I

For the historian, Malabar has the advantage of forming a compact geopolitical unit, with its geographical, climatic and administrative boundaries virtually overlapping one another. It may be considered a 'region' not merely in the geographers' sense of the term where the emphasis is on landscape similarities, but in socio-cultural terms as well.

The British district of Malabar was geographically separated from the rest of the Madras Presidency by the high Western Ghats in its east; it was bounded by Canara in the north and the princely state of Cochin in the south. The narrow coastal belt which forms most of the district has a maximum breadth of seventy miles in Palghat, and a minimum of five miles in the southernmost part of the Ponnani taluka.

The Western Ghats run parallel to the coast maintaining a mean elevation of 5,000 feet, forming a barrier in the path of the southwest monsoon. Being on the windward side of the Ghats, the district received an annual average rainfall of 114.5 inches, with the rainfall gradient increasing from south to north. It also received some rains in the winter months from the retreating northeast monsoons. The regularity and abundance of monsoon rains demarcated Malabar from the drier Tamil country and also saved it from famines induced by pluviometric shortfalls.

A number of passes in the Western Ghats connected Malabar with the rest of the Presidency. Commercially the most significant of these was the 25 miles long Palghat gap which permitted road and later rail communication with the eastern districts.

Malabar's separation from the country to its east was not merely in terms of climate and physical geography but also in terms of socio-political topography and history. The caste configuration of Malabar was quite different from the rest of the Presidency. In Malabar, the methods of maintaining caste ranks were much more rigid and systematized even if compared with the highly strict caste codes of the Tamil area.

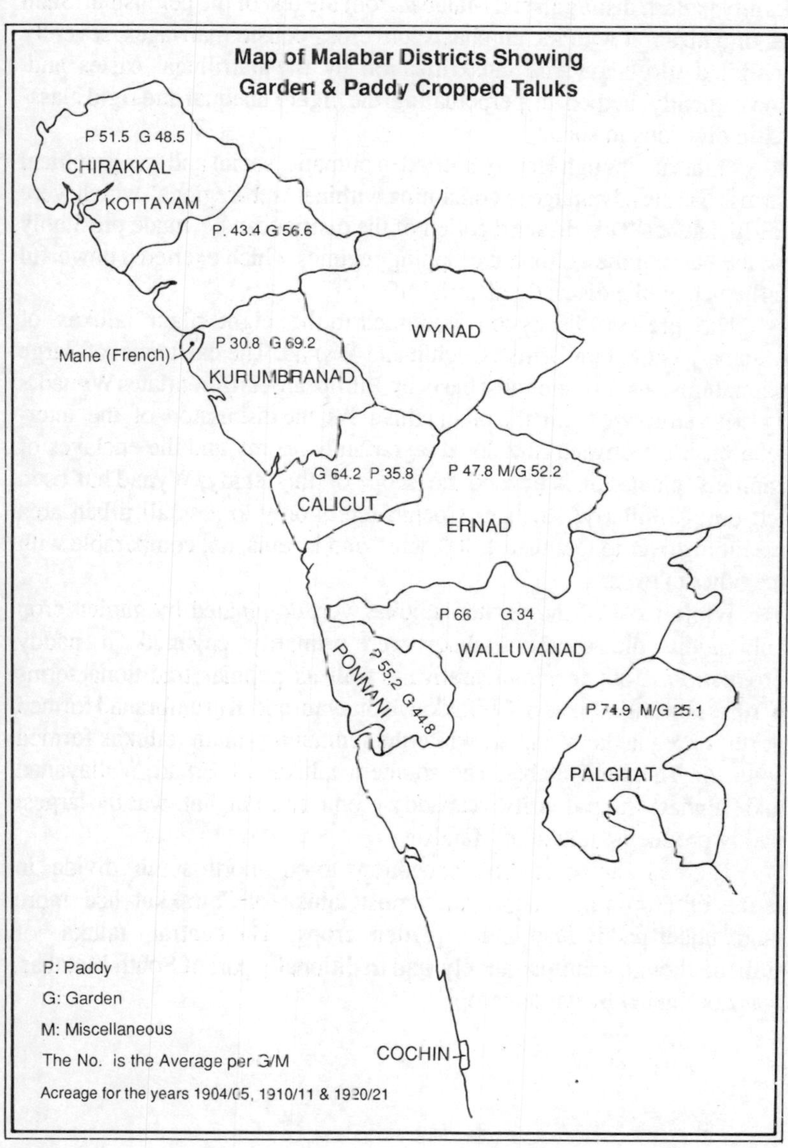

Map of Malabar Districts Showing
Garden & Paddy Cropped Taluks
P 51.5 G 48.5
CHIRAKKAL
KOTTAYAM
P. 43.4 G 56.6
WYNAD
P 30.8 G 69.2
Mahe (French)
KURUMBRANAD
G 64.2 P 35.8
P 47.8 M/G 52.2
CALICUT
ERNAD
P 66 G 34
WALLUVANAD
PONNANI
P 55.2 G 44.8
P 74.9 M/G 25.1
PALGHAT
COCHIN
P: Paddy
G: Garden
M: Miscellaneous
The No. is the Average per G/M
Acreage for the years 1904/05, 1910/11 & 1920/21

The dispersed settlement pattern in the district differentiated it from the other talukas of the Presidency. The matrilineal and avuncu-local family pattern distinguished Malabar from the rest of the peninsula. Such an organization with its emphasis on cross-cousin marriages severely inhibited efforts towards Sanskritization by the matrilineal castes and, consequently, helped in perpetuating the highly unequal and rigid class-caste divisions in society.

Malabar, though largely unified in climatic, social and geographical terms, has the advantage of containing within it 'sub-regions' which were fairly distinct. This disaggregation of the district can be made profitably on the basis of the dominant cropping regimes which exerted a powerful influence on the district's material life.

The present discussion is limited to the eight plain talukas of Malabar, excluding British Cochin and Wynad. The existence of large plantations, run on a capitalist basis by Europeans, differentiates Wynad's agrarian structure from the plain taluka. As the discussion of the inter-relationship between the local agrarian economy and the enclaves of capitalist plantation is beyond the scope of this study, Wynad has been left out. Similarly, British Cochin refers only to a small urban area extending over to less than 1,300 acres and is, thus, not comparable with the other talukas.

While most of the northern talukas were dominated by garden crop cultivation, the southern talukas were primarily engaged in paddy production. Both in administrative as well as popular traditional terms of reference the talukas of Chirakkal, Kottayam and Kurumbranad formed north or Vadakke Malabar, while the remaining plain talukas formed south or Thekke Malabar. The southern talukas of Ernad, Wallavanad and Palghat were primarily wet paddy producers. Palghat, was the largest paddy producing taluka of Malabar.

There are however some exceptions to our north-south divide in terms of crop-mix. The northernmost taluka of Chirakkal had more lands under paddy than under garden crops. The central taluka of Calicut, though administratively and traditionally part of South Malabar, was dominated by garden crops.

Table 1
Paddy and Garden Crops as percentage of GCA (Gross Cropped Area)

Taluka	Paddy as % of GCA			Garden Crops Miscellaneous as % of GCA		
	1904-05	1910-11	1920-21	1904-05	1910-11	1920-21
Chirakkal	53.29	50.71	50.38	28.96	45.84	47.97
Kottayam	54.16	42.45	33.60	37.75	56.34	66.00
Kurumbranad	30.79	30.68	35.93	65.45	67.48	62.97
Calicut	36.91	34.90	35.54	54.76	56.97	57.78
Ernad	44.86	46.04	52.46	41.49	44.61	44.28
Walavanad	75.27	60.89	61.74	11.74	29.51	31.33
Palghat	78.94	72.59	73.29	17.09	22.19	22.00
Pannani	62.78	49.37	53.59	32.01	47.22	42.54
District Total (Including Wynad and Cochin)	57.73	51.34	52.91	32.22	43.01	43.09

Source: Computed from *S.A. M.P.* for relevant years

This demarcation on the basis of crop-mix largely corresponds to the traditional Malayali division of the area north of the Korapuzha or the Kora river (which flows 12 kilometers north of present day Calicut) as *Vadakke* Malabar and that to the south as *Thekke* Malabar. As late as the early twentieth-century orthodoxy forbade a Nair woman of north Malabar from marrying into the region south of Korapuzha. If she did settle down south of the river she found herself in a region which was, in a number of ways, very different from her home.

II

The chief garden products of north Malabar were coconut, betelnut, pepper, areca, jack and other fruit trees. The following is an early nineteenth-century account of the process of cultivation in a garden:

> A strong fence is built around the area to be planted in order to keep grazing cattle off, intruding cattle being capable of destroying years

> of labour and money within a night or so. Usually an earthern dyke about six to eight feet is built if a fence is not put up. The dyke or fence has to be repaired every year after the monsoons for five or six years, which is the time the young trees take to grow out of the reach of cattle. After the land is cleared of jungle and undergrowth, an operation entailing considerable labour, the shoots are planted. The cultivator has to continuously labour and invest money for a period ranging from six to ten years before he can get any returns on them. Even after such a period the profit comes only in degrees, and it is generally allowed that an average twelve years are required to bring them to full produce.[2]

The per acre cost of cultivation is very difficult to calculate on the basis of available data. Most of the available estimates on the cost of garden production pertains to coconut cultivation usually at a point of time when the trees are in fullbearing. This sort of a cultivation budget does not take into account the expenses incurred on the trees during their long gestation period: 'On an average the coconut comes into full bearing in about its tenth year, bears vigorously for the next forty years and less and less in the last thirty years of its life'.[3] Apart from this problem, a plot of garden land usually has more than one crop. The available cultivation budgets do not give information on these other crops. According to a survey carried out in 1801, 'During the period of rearing the trees, and afterwards the charges of cultivation of the soil (for gardens) are more than the same extent of seed land.'[4] Strachey and Brown, in order to emphasize the greater care needed for garden cultivation *vis-a-vis* paddy wrote: ...'property of this description devoting to minors, women or indigent persons frequently goes to decay.'[5] They also compared these lands in order to highlight the relative contributions of the agencies of the cultivator and the environment,

> ....in the opinion of the natives founded of course on experience, the agency of man requisite for tree produce, compared to that required for grain is at least 4 to 1 as 8/10, and that of the soil only 2/10. But admitting it to be 6/10 what remains after reimbursing this agency can only be with wisdom of justice, be looked on as a fund for revenue.[6]

However, according to contemporary cultivators, the labour required for and expenditure incurred on garden cultivation is much less than on wet paddy cultivation. This seems to have also been true of the colonial period in spite of the contrary picture given by the official British sources. If garden cultivation needed such close attention and intensive labour then the district-wide shift from grain to garden cultivation cannot be easily explained. For the early colonial rulers the garden produce of Malabar was economically much more important than the rice production of the district. In such a situation it appears quite likely that the British administrators exaggerated the role of human agency in garden cultivation *vis-a-vis* paddy production. Further, the ever-changing nature of the gardens made it difficult to generalize the revenue- yielding capacity of garden lands. The imposition of a high revenue burden on these lands ran the risk of making it economically infeasible and thus destroying it.

These reservations notwithstanding, the long gestation periods (around 10 years for coconut palms, 8 years for jackfruit, 3-4 years for the pepper vine and 6-10 for pepper), and the heavy initial costs and the violent price fluctuations dictated by the vagaries of the market,[7] contributed to making the returns from garden cultivation less stable than from paddy.

Paddy was the most important crop cultivated in the southern Malabar and in Chirakkal. In spite of being the largest paddy growing district in the Presidency after Tanjore, Malabar has been a net importer of paddy from around the 18th century. Wet paddy cultivation was economically more important and widespread compared to dry paddy which was carried out on inferior lands chiefly for family consumption.

Wet paddy lands were divided into *orupuggil*, *rundupuggil* and *muppugil*, depending on whether they raised one, two or three crops in a year respectively. While two crop lands were common, three crop lands were rare as these needed irrigation in the summer months.

The Kanni crop, which is harvested between September and October, was grown in most of the *taluks* except Kurumbranad and Kottayam. The Kanni crop generally yielded more than the Magaram crop harvested from January to March. The second crop of paddy was not very important in the Chirakkal, Kottayam, Wynad and Calicut talukas.

In north Malabar, farmers who had both garden and paddy lands devote greater attention to garden. 'Paddy is cultivated more for the straw for the cattle for garden cultivation.'[8]

Throughout British rule in Malabar, officials repeatedly calculated and revised the cultivation costs incurred in paddy production. Warden's Proclamation of 1805 used the traditional customary rate, i.e., calculating the cost of cultivation at twice the quantity of seed required on any given piece of land as the cost of cultivating a paddy crop on it.[9]

In the 1880s, William Logan estimated the cost of cultivation at roughly 3.5 times the seed required. An acre of first crop paddy required 50 *edangalis* of seed and an equivalent of 178 *edangalis* were required for other expenditure. For the second crop, the seed required was 60 *edangalis* and other expenditure came to 158 *edangalis*.[10]

Moberly, Settlement Officer of the first Malabar Survey and Settlement at the beginning of this century, estimated the cost of cultivation of the best class of land at Rs. 12-8-0. Of this 55.6 per cent or Rs. 6-15-3 represented cash expenditure. The rest was incurred in kind (203 *edangalis*). The aggregate cultivation cost amounted to 7 to 8 times the quantity of seed required.[11] The Raghavayya Committee estimated the cost of cultivation at 2.5 times the seed required.[12] Finally, the Special Officer for investigating land tenures, in May 1947 recommended 20 Palghat *paras* as the cost for cultivating one acre of paddy.[13]

The Malayali festivals of Vishu and Onam mark the beginning and the end of each agricultural year. In spite of intra-district variations the agricultural cycle was more or less uniform for the whole district.[14] Given the marked differences in the cropping patterns of the north and the south one may expect the agricultural cycles in these regions to be different. However, both paddy and garden crops appear to have followed a similar cycle. This has an important bearing on the present study as it determines the seasonality of labour demand. Though our data allows for a rough estimation of the monthly and operation-wise distribution of labour inputs for paddy, similar figures cannot be calculated for garden cultivation due to lack of sources. The only garden products for which there are comparable estimates are coconut and ginger. The estimation problem in the case of gardens is complicated by the fact that the gardens grew more than these two crops planted at different times, with varying gestation periods and labour inputs. In the absence of these estimates, monthly average cultivated area in representative talukas have been used as a surrogate index for estimating the seasonality of labour inputs and the agricultural cycle (Table 3). The main problem with the use of such a surrogate is that there need not always be a correlation between acreage under cultivation and the labour demand. Our figures exhibit greater monthly variations in labour demand and area under cultivation in the garden dominated areas compared to the paddy growing southern talukas.

Table 2
Cost of Cultivating and Harvesting a Crop of Paddy in Talukas other than Wynad

Farm	Wet Lands Cost per acre		
	Rs.	As.	p.
1	12	8	0
2	12	0	0
3	11	0	0
4	10	0	0
5	8	8	0
6	7	0	0
7	5	8	0
8	4	0	0

Cost of planting, protecting and maintaining a coconut tree, an arecanut tree, a jack tree and a pepper vine until the tree or vine is in bearing

Name of tree plant	Area		Cost		
Coconut	The whole district except Wynad		2	12	0
Arecanut	"	irrigated. tree	0	12	0
		unirrigated. tree	0	2	6
Jack tree	"		2	2	0
Peppervine	- Chirakkal, Kottayam & Wynad talukas		0	6	0
	- other talukas		0	3	6

Cost of protecting maintaing a coconut tree, an areca tree, jack tree and pepper vine for one year when in bearing

Coconut	Whole district		0	2	0
Arecanut	"	irrigated.tree	0	1	3
		unirrigated tree	0	0	2
Jack tree	"	unirrigated tree	0	2	0
Pepper vine -	Chirakkal, Kottayam & Wynad talukas		0	1	6
	Other talukas		0	0	6

Source: Fort St. George Gazette, 1 March 1910, pp. 270-72.

Table 3
Average Monthly Cultivation as Percentage of Annual Total in Representative Taluka for 1930

Month	Kottayam	Kurumbranad	Calicut	Wallavanad	Palghat	Chirakkal
April	3.11	4.54	3.79	0.80	0.67	5.59
May	4.02	6.51	13.84	5.60	16.04	20.98
June	7.49	5.50	7.41	14.14	14.91	13.57
July	66.76	70.13	51.59	50.02	31.72	40.95
Aug.	2.92	3.28	4.67	4.62	4.07	5.72
Sep.	2.47	5.40	9.52	4.45	11.40	2.45
Oct.	3.65	3.08	7.50	12.01	14.74	3.02
Nov.	2.47	1.31	1.50	8.09	5.05	5.65
Dec.	0.55	0.25	0.18	0.86	1.05	1.57
Jan.	0.00	0.00	0.00	0.12	0.35	0.50
Feb.	0.00	0.00	0.00	0.00	0.00	0.00
March	0.00	0.00	0.00	0.00	0.00	0.00
Total	100.00	100.00	100.00	100.00	100.00	100.00
C.V.(%)	17.902	18.773	13.723	13.391	9.325	11.480

Source: Based on figures in SAMP 1936, p. 907 C.V= (coefficient of variation = On/x)

III

Tenurial Arrangements and Land Relations

Under British rule, the *Janmi,* the *Kanamdar* and the *Verumpattamdar* roughly approximated to the landlord, the tenant and the cultivating tenant at will, respectively, Tenurial arrangements, are only partial juridical expressions of the actual relations of agricultural production. In order to highlight this possible hiatus between juridical categories and analytical economic taxonomies a distinction between 'tenurial' arrangements and 'land relations' is maintained in the sub-title of this section. Although this broad hierarchy of land right holders prevailed throughout the Malabar district, the nature of relations in the north and the south was not the same. In the garden-producing north, the relationship between the *janmi* and the *kanamdar* approximated to that between a mortgager and a mortgagee, with the *kanam* being a proper mortgage. At the beginning of the nineteenth-century the *Janmi* , who was hard-pressed for cash, customarily borrowed from the *kanamdars*. In proportion to the principal borrowed, the *kanamdar* deducted from the *pattan* collected by him for the *janmi*, a part of the produce which was equivalent to the interest on the sum lent. The interest was calculated at certain fixed customary rates.

In cases where the interest on the principal borrowed was equal to or greater than the *janmi*'s share, the *kanamdar*'s interest in the land was called *otti*. In addition, there were other kinds of mortgages specifying the level of indebtedness of the *janmi* and the *kanumdar*'s *janmi's* right and obligations in each of these arrangements. According to Logan, the *janmi* mortgaged his right in the share of the produce. In cases where this was inadequate to meet the interest payment, he also mortgaged the rights which his status invested in him.[15]

The next broad category of land interests was the *verumpattam*. The *verumpattamdar* held land either under a *janmi* or a *kanamdar* and did not have the cultivated waste land. The customary sharing of produce of newly reclaimed land took place in gardens at the end of 12 years from the time such land was taken up. The *janmi* , when he wanted to take his customary share of the produce, had to buy it from the cultivator at customarily fixed rates.

Soon after conquering Malabar, the British recognized the *janmis* as landlords. The *kanamdars* were given the legal status of tenants. Till the 1830s this juridical revision of rights did not have any impact on agrarian relations. With the rise in agricultural product prices in Malabar in the 1830s the *janmis* started exercising their new-found legal status to the detriment of the other right holders.The earlier system based on custom was soon eclipsed by the uniform contractual relations codified by the British law courts. The traditionally lower land revenue demand on the West Coast (Malabar and South Canara)[16] increased the scope of sub-renting land. In Malabar was a maze of intermediary tenures as the following diagram suggests.

i. Zamorin demises:[17]

to	to
ii. Verumpattamdar tenant who sublets to	ii. Kanam tenant who demises to
iii. Verumpattomdar sub-tenant who cultivates through	iii. sub-kanam tenant who lets to
iv. agricultural labourers (*cherumas*, etc.)	iv. Verumpattom tenant who cultivates through
	v. agricultural labourers (*cherumas*, etc.)

Source: Malabar Tenancy Committee Report 1927-28, Madras.

The tenurial arrangement in north Malabar differed in two major respects—first, the *kanam* amount in south Malabar is invariably nominal. The *kanam* is in the nature of a lease unlike north Malabar where *kanam* amounts are quite large, mostly mortgages for securing amounts advanced as loans. Consequently, they are essentially mortgages with possession.[16] This points to the lower economic strength of the *janmis* in the north. North Malabar, unlike the south, had a much larger number of self-cultivating farmers. Further, the *kuzhikanam* tenure which guaranteed the cultivator some fixity of tenure and lower rent obligations was absent in the paddy growing south. The lower obligations on *kuzhikanam* lands were meant as an incentive for peasants to reclaim uncultivated lands. The lower rent burden and some fixity of tenure were designed to compensate for his heavy capital and labour inputs.

These features of the tenurial arrangements in north and south Malabar suggest greater concentration of land in the latter region. This is borne out by an analysis of the rent rolls and the inequality indices worked out on its basis (Table 4).

Table 4
Gini Coefficients number of pattas and revenues paid

Dominant Crop	Taluka	1910-11	11920-21	1929-30
Garden crops:	Kottayam	0.611	0.588	0.557
	Kurumbranad	0.699	0.716	0.672
	Calicut	0.686	0.627	0.655
Net Paddy:	Chirakkal	0.706	0.673	0.699
	Ernad	0.775	0.776	0.779
	Wallavńad	0.780	0.771	0.806
	Palghat	0.877	0.880	0.864
	Ponnani	0.757	0.743	0.718

Source: SAMP of the relevant years

where X_i = cumulative percentage of pattas in each revenue class
Y_i = cumulative percentage of the amount of revenue paid

The report submitted by William Logan in his capacity as Special Commissioner provides us with valuable data on the taluka-wise and crop-wise social distribution of land.[17] (see Table 5 and 6).

The data collected by Logan clearly suggests that the southern talukas had a greater number of intermediaries between the *janmi* and the actual cultivators and, subsequently, the direct leasing by the *janmis* to actual cultivators was also lower in the south *vis-a-vis* the north. Further, the *janmis* in the north retained less land under direct control than their counterparts in the south (Table 5).

Table 5
Tenurial Distribution in North and South Malabar

	North Malabar	South Malabar
No. of intermediaries per *janmi*	16.7	53.7
Lands leased to intermediaries as percentage of total land owned by *janmis*	11.8	36.6
Lands leased to actual cultivators as percentage of total lands owned by *janmis*	85.9	58.7
Percentage of lands retained by *janmis* as percentages of total lands owned by them	2.3	4.8

Source: Based on *Report of the Special Commissioner*, vol. 2, App.IV, Government of Madras, 1882.

The length of possession of lands by actual cultivators was longer in the garden lands as compared to grain lands (Table 6).

Table 6
Length of Possession of Holdings of Actual Cultivators

Length of Possession	Wet/Dry land	Garden Land
Immemorial	3.6	3.9
Above 30 years but not immemorial	34.3	43.1
12 to 30 years	18.7	22.3
Less than 12 years	43.4	30.7
Total	100.00	100.0

Source: Based on *Report of Special Commissioner*, vol. 2, App. IV, Government of Madras, 1882.

Thus, in talukas where garden cropping was more widespread and important than paddy cultivation the social distribution of land was more equitable. Consequently the economic power of the *janmis* was lesser than in the wet paddy areas. Greater fixity of tenure and lower number of intermediary tenure holders between the *janmi* and the actual cultivator also characterized the tenurial relations in these lands. The revenue burden on garden lands was also lower than on paddy lands in most of the *talukas* (Table 7)

Table 7
Average Revenue per Acre in each of the Plain Talukas, 1904.

Taluka	Wet	Garden
	Rs. As. Ps.	Rs. As. Ps.
Chirakkal	3-3-10	2-14-4
Kottayam	2-14-2	2-15-6
Kurumbranad	2-15-8	2-15-10
Calicut	3-0-6	2-8-11
Ernad	3-7-4	2-8-2
Wallavanad	4-6-6	1-15-2
Palghat	3-14-10	2-3-0
Ponnani	3-1-9	3-14-10
District Average	3-8-11	2-15-3

Source: Innes, Malabar, Vol. 1 (reprinted Madras, 1951), p. 347

Social Relations and Hierarchies

Differences in the levels of inequality in the social distribution of property resulted in the greater rigidity of caste hierarchy in the north. Eric J Miller's hypothesis on the caste system in Malabar may be extended (in a rather instrumentalist fashion) and seen as a system which effectively perpetuated the existing relations of production in the countryside. According to Miller:

> a necessary correlate of a rigid caste system of territorial segmentation which has two functions: it promotes localized interdependent relations between castes, especially at the village level, by limiting the spatial range of intercaste relations for all castes,

> by permitting greater mobility and greater spatial range of intercaste relations for those at the top than for those at the bottom. The larger and more inclusive the territorial unit in which members of a caste can move, the higher the rank of the caste.[18]

While the Nambudiris shared customs throughout Kerala, the Nayars had regional differences. The differences became progressively more pronounced as one went down the social scale The lower castes differed from chiefdom to chiefdom, while among the depressed castes from whom came the 'tied' agricultural worker, there were variations from one village to another. Thus, 'structural distance was expressed in terms of spatial segregation'.[19]

At the lower rungs of the caste hierarchy came the 'depressed' polluting castes, most of whom conveyed 'distance pollution': agricultural labourers belonged to this category. It was only in north Malabar that these castes followed the *marumakkatayam* while in the rest of the district they were patrilineal and often practised fraternal polyandry.

The most important and numerically largest of the polluting castes were the Tiyas and the Izhavas. In the north the Tiyas claimed non-polluting status because they occupied an economically and ritually higher position than the Izhavas. While the northern Tiyas followed the *Marumakkatayam* system, the Izhavas of the south practised *Makkathayam*. The northern and southern members of the caste did not inter-marry, possibly due to social differences amongst them.

As already mentioned the Kora river formed the traditional boundary between north and south Malabar. This division of the district closely approximated to our division of Malabar on the basis of dominant crop production regimes. Marriage restrictions are an important indicator of the role of the Kora river as a social frontier between the north and the south.[20]

Apart from differences in individual caste practices, status and inter-caste relations amongst the Hindus, the Mapillas of the north and the south also followed different inheritance rules. While those from the north were matrilineal like the dominant Hindu castes of the area, in south Malabar the Mapillas were patrilineal.

Another marked social difference in the two areas was the much higher concentration of Brahmins and untouchable castes in the south.[21] The population of landless agricultural labourers was also much higher in the south as compared with the 'garden producing', taluka. The greater ritual distance between the cultivators and land controlling groups in the south is accompanied by lower agricultural wages in this part of the district *vis-a-vis* the garden cropped northern talukas.[22]

The political and social history of pre-colonial Malabar appears to have been greatly conditioned by the geography and ecology of the region. Its geographic isolation seems to have minimized the impact of political developments in other parts of the peninsula. While the Western Ghats impeded overland contact with Malabar, the sea opened Malabar to influences from the Middle East and encouraged brisk commercial relations first with the Mediterranean region and then with the Arabian littoral.

Very little is known about Malabar's pre- and proto-historic past. The early Cera period does not exhibit any traces of the existence of typical Malayali social phenomenon, such as a small powerful Brahminical group, the matrilineal system and a separate Malayalam language.

It is from the later Cera period (i.e., after the eleventh-century AD or the beginning of the twelfth-century AD) that one finds the beginning of small principalities in Kerala. Even a cursory reading of the history of Kerala or of Malabar brings into relief the insignificance of powerful centralized imperial structures.

The relative lack of importance of water management and physical geographic barriers along the north-south axis also hindered centralized rule and encouraged the growth of autonomous chieftainships, especially in the north. This greater political decentralization in the North characterized the region's history right up to Malabar's annexation by the British.

IV

The differences between the garden-dominated north Malabar and the paddy growing south were not random but part of an ordered variance. This variation can be largely explained in terms of the dominant agricultural production regimes of the north and the south.

To begin with, the north-south variations in the cropping pattern seem to have been greatly dictated by the geography of Malabar. Garden crops were grown in areas with sandy and lateritic soils, whereas paddy cultivation was carried out in the alluvial river valleys. Wet paddy production, the most important mode of rice cultivation in Malabar, was extremely labour intensive compared to garden crop production. Apart from the large absolute input of labour required, the labour demand in wet paddy cultivation was highly skewed and with marked seasonal variations (Table 7). The high level of labour inputs and the distinctly seasonal nature of the demand for it explains many of the features which distinguished the paddy growing regions from garden cropped areas.

The high level of labour inputs into the wet paddy cultivation, practised in most of South Malabar and the Chirakkal talukas in the north, may be correlated with the larger proportion of agricultural labourers in these talukas in contrast to the garden cropped taluks. Francis Buchanan, at the beginning of the nineteenth-century, observed that there was a greater use of slaves in the south than in the north. This region continued to have a much larger number of agricultural labourers in the late nineteenth and in the twentieth-centuries. Buchanan also observed that the larger farmers in the northern talukas were less affluent than their counterparts in the south.

Increased ritual distance, manifested in terms of dissimilar caste practices and the low status accorded to the cultivating castes in southern Malabar, appears to have been both a product as well as a necessary condition of the accentuated social differentiation in the paddy growing areas.

Wet paddy cultivation, which needed a large servile labour force apart from an economically exploitative system of control, required an ideological system for preserving the highly unequal social relations between the surplus appropriating groups and the actual producers. The strict traditional ritual codes of purity and pollutions emphasized as well as justified the prevailing material and social inequality. The north-south difference in the degree of socio-economic inequality was also manifested in the tenurial and agrarian relations of the respective zones.

Virtually all the colonial investigations into landlord-tenant relations in Malabar refer to wet paddy lands being rack-rented while tenants on garden lands were relatively better off.[23] Garden cultivation needed a heavy initial investment with a long gestation period for the planted area to yield returns. This heavy initial outlay of capital being made by the cultivators probably checked the *janmi* from overexploiting them. Tenants on garden lands generally cultivated their plots for longer periods of time compared to tenant cultivators on wet paddy lands.

The prolonged legislative battle between the *janmis* and the *kanamdars* for gaining concessions and for reducing the rights of their adversaries finally resulted in the Malabar Compensation for Tenants Improvement Act of 1900. Under its provisions, the landlord had to pay the tenant the full market value of the improvements made by the latter. In 1911 the Government instituted an enquiry into the working of this Act and found the Act working effectively in north Malabar but not in the south. This was again largely because it was physically not possible to make any tangible substantial improvement in wet lands while they could be easily made on garden lands. While landlords all over Malabar were recognized as *janmis* by the British, the *janmi* in the north was essentially a mortgagee. Not so in south Malabar. Further the smaller economic and ritual distance between the upper caste land controllers and the cultivating communities in the north may have acted as another limiting influence on excessive exploitation.

The constantly changing physical character of the garden *vis-a-vis* the unchanging paddy flats made the latter easier to assess for revenue fixation. In addition to this, the returns from garden lands varied greatly from year to year. The fear of permanently damaging the production of the commercially valuable garden crops, along with the difficulty in estimating the returns from garden lands, possibly contributed to these lands being less heavily taxed. With the close integration of India with the world market by the second half of the nineteenth-century, the returns from garden production became closely related to the price movements in the international market, which were given to sharp fluctuations.[24]

With its abundant and regular rainfall, the availability of a large servile work force and favourable soil conditions, the returns from paddy cultivation were regular and dependable in Malabar. The higher rent and revenue charged on wet paddy lands *vis-a-vis* gardens strengthens the point that the extractables were higher in the former. This also permitted the growth of relatively larger state formations in south Malabar. Centralized imperial structures were unknown in north Malabar. Even the early Cera empire controlled only parts of south Malabar.[25] In fact, at the time of Haider Ali's invasion of Malabar in 1760, north Malabar had no strong ruling group to exercise any significant hold over its feudatories. The Kolattiri kingdom had shrunk to cover only the modern taluka of Chirakkal. And even within Chirakkal, Cannanore was held by the Ali Rajas. The south, on the other hand, was relatively much less politically fragmented with power being distributed among Zamorin and the Raja of Palghat and Cochin.

The varying nature of the dominant crop production regimes thus appears to have powerfully influenced the history and the social and political hierarchies and organization in north and south Malabar.

V

This final section examines how the regionally-differentiated Malabar agrarian economy responded to the market price from the First World War to the onset of the Depression. Since the 1830s agricultural product prices in Malabar exhibited an increasing trend, accentuated in the years between 1918 and 1925 when the agrarian economy of the district was closely integrated to the world market (Table 8).

Table 8
Prices in Malabar, Burma and Batavia

Year	Rice price in Malabar	Rangoon price of 100 baskets of 75 lbs. each	Av. Pepper price in Malabar per c	Batavia Av. price of 100 kg. (Guilders)
1920			31.9	110
1921			26.5	75
1922	7.04	448.44	25. 8	61
1923	6.83	453.69	30.9	60
1924	7.79	472.50	30.3	65
1925	7.42	480.25	46.1	78
1926	7.53	464.25	68.5	120
1927	7.40	421.50	80.3	206
1928	7.00	403.63	103.2	255
1929	6.41	392.69	88.9	230
1930	5.04	246.50	59.5	110
1931	4.18	227.63	34.2	40
1932	3.68	182.81	36.5	35
1933	3.15	150.94	26.2	35
1934	3.61	203.25	31.6	95
1935	3.81	218.63	26.5	25
1936	3.64	222.19	20.5	30
1937	3.73	224.31	21.1	25

Source: Pepper prices: Thomas and Sastry, op.cit., p. 46. Rice price: Rangoon—ThomasandSastri, op.cit., Rice price Malabar—SAMP, 1940-41.

Till 1924-25 prices of foodgrains as represented by rice and that of non-food crops showed a marked increase, with the rise being greater in the case of the latter. Malabar, as mentioned earlier was a net importer of rice. Here rice prices closely followed the Madras and Rangoon prices. Between 1910-11 and 1919-20 the price of rice increased greatly; from 1919-20 to 1925-26 the price registered a fluctuating downward trend. The continued fall began in 1926-27, reaching its lowest in 1933-34. Lowered transportation costs since the 1850s and the lower cost of rice cultivation in Burma were chiefly responsible for making Burmese rise cheaper than the Madras produce. This enabled Burma to swamp the Indian rice market. The revenue demand on rice cultivation in Burma was lower than in Madras, which partly explains the lower cost of production in Burma.

> It was estimated in 1934 that an acre under rice cost Rs. 24 in Tanjore and Rs. 17 in Burma. The cost of sea-transport between Burma and India is also lower than the rail transport between different stations in Madras. Therefore Burma rice has been able not only to beat out Madras rice from Ceylon but to sell its rice in Madras itself. [26]

Coconut and pepper prices were closely related to the level of demand in the foreign market and on international competition. The fall in the post-War price of coconut was largely the result of dumping by Ceylon, along with a lowering of demand for it due to the substitution of coconut oil by cheaper oils for manufacturing margarine[27] Pepper was in great demand in Europe as it was used as a preservative. With the increased use of fodder crops and the invention of the cold storage, its demand fell considerably. The expansion of pepper plantations in the Dutch East Indies struck a further blow to Malabar pepper. In spite of the drastic price slump, pepper production in the West Coast continued in the inter-War period; with most of it being now marketed with India. Increasing pepper prices until about 1927-28 led to an expansion of acreage under pepper. However, by the time this freshly planted land began to yield, the depression had set in and the newly augmented output further pushed down prices.

Comparing pepper and rice prices reveals that fluctuations are much more in the former. The coefficient of variation in paddy prices was 31.15 per cent during the period 1922-23 to 1924-25— it was 57.67 per cent for pepper between 1920 and 1938.

Graph I suggests that since the turn of the century paddy was losing out to non-food crops. This gap further widened during the Depression. Between 1920 and 1929 rice and pepper prices exhibit a sympathetic movement, with greater fluctuations in pepper prices. Further, at the peak of the post-war inflation, pepper prices increased much faster and to a higher level than rice prices. However, correlation of paddy acreage and

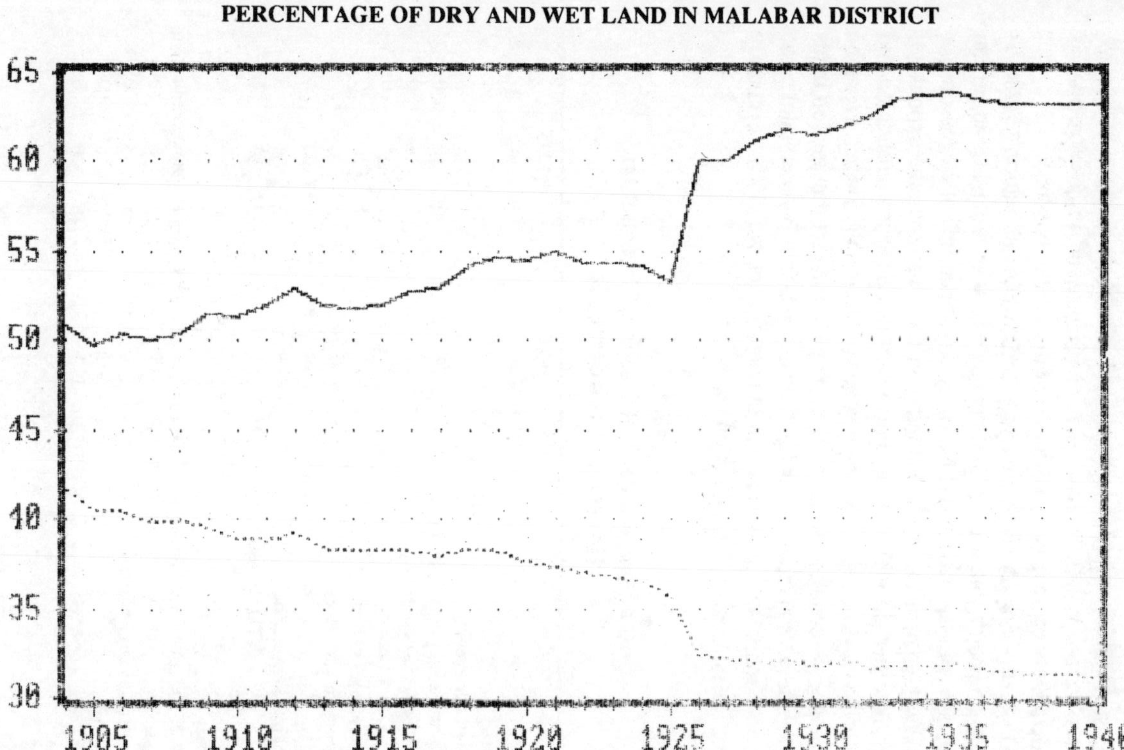
PERCENTAGE OF DRY AND WET LAND IN MALABAR DISTRICT
65
60
55
50
45
40
35
30
1905
1910
1915
1920
1925
1930
1935
1940

acreage 'under spices and condiments' yielded no statistically significant coefficient. There was also no statistical association between changes in relative prices (pepper and rice) and changes in relative acreage.[28] One possible reason may be because the price of pepper is not adequately representative of price of the garden produce.

On comparing returns from paddy and garden cultivation (Table 9) in 1925, the percentage of decline in net income was much less in garden cultivation compared to paddy. This may have been one of the reasons for a continued expansion of garden and non-food crops at the expense of paddy. Another possible factor which stimulated garden cultivation and discouraged paddy was the lower revenue burden on the former. From the late nineteenth century there are references to the fact that garden lands were less severely taxed than paddy fields. In 1935, in Ponnani taluka, the revenue demand as a percentage of the net income was 17.32 on paddy cultivation and only 8.29 on garden crops.

Table 9
Cost of Proceeds of Cultivation of Coconut on One Acre of Garden Land

	1925			1935		
	Rs	as	ps	Rs	as	ps
Expenses						
Enclosures & Fencing						
Boundaries - repairs 2 coolies	0	14	0	0	10	0
Fencing: Cost of bamboos	1	14	0	1	4	0
Coolies	1	12	0	1	4	0
Spade digging 2 colies	0	14	0	1	10	0
Ploughing: 4 times a year	3	0	0	2	0	0
Manuring	7	8	0	5	0	0
Cost of plucking coconuts	7	14	0	5	4	0
Total Costs	**23**	**12**	**0**	**17**	**0**	**0**
Proceeds						
By sale of 3500 nuts (on an average of 70 trees per acre, 10 pluckings per annum, 5 nuts from each tree)	183	15	6	112	0	0
Leaves: 560 leaves per annum	8	1	0	5	8	0
	192	0	6	117	8	0
Deduct costs	23	12	0	16	0	0
158 4	6	10	8	0		
Kist 9	6	0	9	6	0	
Net Proceeds	148 (-Rs. 56-12-6 or -38 percent on 1925 income)	14	6	92	2	0

+ Wages decreased by 50 per cent between 1925 and 1935
++ Costs assumed to have decreased by 50 per cent as average rice prices decreased by 48.96 per cent between 1925 and 1935
+++ Price of coconuts in 1925 - Rs. 52.14-5 per 1000
1935 - Rs. 32-0-0- per 1000

(Owner Cultivated)

		1925			1935		
		Rs	as	ps	Rs	as	ps
A	First Crop						
1	Repair of bunds, etc.	0	13	0	0	9	0
2	Ploughing and levelling						
3	ploughings by 5 ploughs	3	12	0	2	8	0
3	Cost of seeds - 10 paras	7	10	6	4	6	0
4	Spade cultivation after sowing	1	4	0	0	14	0
5	Manuring (mixture of cattle dung and ash) : 5 paras + transport	3	2	0	2	4	0
6	Manuring: 2nd dose (as in 5)	3	2	0	2	4	0
7	Weeding 20 women	2	8	0	1	14	0
8	Reaping and threshing (11.5 paras)	8	1	3	4	5	0
9	Watching	1	1	6	0	9	0
	Total expenses	**31**	**6**	**3**	**19**	**9**	**0**
B	Second Crop						
1	Cost of seeds (7.5 paras)	5	11	9	3	12	0
2	Cost of spade digging (1.5 man days)	0	9	0	0	6	0
3	Ploughing (6 rows, 12 ploughs)	9	0	0	6	0	0
4	Raising bunds (4 men)	1	10	0	1	2	0
5	Transplantation	2	13	0	2	9	0
6	Manuring - 10 paras	6	4	0	4	0	0
7	Weeding (less work than in 1st crop)	1	12	0	1	4	0
8	Reaping and threshing	8	1	3	4	5	0
9	Watching	1	1	0	0	9	0
10	Rent for raised plot for 1.5 months	0	6	0	0	6	0
		37	4	6	24	5	0
	Cost of cultivation of crops A & B	68	10	9	43	14	0
	Proceeds from sale of 160 paras of paddy and 20 loads of straw	117	8	0	66	4	0
	Less kist of Rs 3 14 0	113	10	0	62	6	0
	Net returns	44	45	3	18	8	0

Percentage decrease in net returns between 1925 and 1935 is 58.8 per cent
+ Wages decreased by 50 per cent between 1925 and 1935
++Cost of seed: 1925 0 12 3 para 1935 0 7 0 para
+++ paddy: 0 11 3 0 6 0

Table 10
Percentage Changes in the Extent of Land Cultivated by different Tenurial Classes in Representative Talukas 1917 to 1926

Taluka		Percentage change in the extent of land cultivated by		
	Dominant crop	Janmis	Kanamdars	Kuzhikanamdars
Kottayam		+6.02	+11.21	+13.96
Kurumbranad	Garden Crops	+1.61	+5.25	+5.26
Palghat		+14.21	-2.41	—
Wallavanad	Paddy	+11.88	+8.55	—
Chirakkal		+17.08	+3.75	-7.56

Source: Computed from figures given in the *Report of the Malabar Tenancy Committee*, vol .I, 1927-28, p. 150.

Between 1917-26 when prices increased the returns from agriculture rose. This would have resulted in an attempt by all agricultural interests to bring as much cultivable land as possible under their control.

Table 10 indicates that in the rice dominated talukas the extent of land cultivated by the *janmis* increased at a much faster rate than that cultivated by the *kanamdars* (including sub-*kanamdars*). In Palghat, which was characterized by the maximum level of inequality in the social distribution of land, *kanamdar* cultivated lands actually registered a decrease, while that of the *janmis* increased greatly.

The extent of benefit derived from the hike in agricultural product prices by different agrarian classes appears to have been determined by the pre-existing structure. It must, however, be noted that the *janmi*, *kanamdar* and *kuzhikanamdar* are essentially juridical categories. In terms of economic strength they (especially the first two) were highly differentiated internally. In spite of internal differentiation it would not be incorrect to say that the *janmis* with their superior ritual position and greater economic resources (especially in south Malabar) were able to take advantage of the price hike to the detriment of the *kanamdars*. The *janmis* after being given the juridical status of landlords by the British had the power to evict the *kanamadars* on the expiry of the lease period which they used vigorously during this period. In areas with a less inequitable social distribution of land the *janmis* appear to have lost out to the *kanamdars*, whereas in the more unequal talukas the reverse seems to have happened.

During the entire inter-War period the Net Cropped Area (NCA) as well as the Gross Cropped Area (GCA) increased in Malabar in contrast to the Tamil districts where it declined. This is explained by the fact that during the Depression period the cultivator would still continue to expand cultivation in order to maximize the absolute returns in the face of declining prices.

In conclusion, it may be said that the changes occurring under the impact of the price increase in the post-War years were mediated by the pre-existing regional differences in the Malabar agrarian economy. The antecedent configuration of power of the rural landed groups appears to have determined the extent of benefit these groups could make from the increase in agricultural product prices. The Malayali cultivators, operating in the context of a highly monetized commercial economy, appear to have responded to long run relative price trends in deciding their crop-mix over the years. Finally, the years of inflation were also years of intense struggle between the *janmis* and the *kanamdars*; with the former trying to defend their rights from encroachments and the latter attempting to displace the *janmis*. Neither was concerned about the miserable state of the small cultivator.

NOTES

1. Burton Stein, *Peasant State and Society in Medieval South* (Delhi, 1980), C.J. Baker *An Indian Rural Economy 1880-1950*, (Delhi, 1985), David Ludden, *Peasant History in South India* (Princeton, 1985).
2. Spencer, Smee and Walker, 'Revenue Survey of Rendaterran' in J. Strachey, *A Report on the Northern Division of Malabar*, 7 March 1801, Enclosure C-2.
3. Innes, *Gazetteer of Malabar and Anjengo*, p. 220.
4. Spencer, et.al. *op.cit*.
5. Ibid.
6. Ibid.
7. The coefficients of variation in the prices of rice, coconuts and pepper between 1922 and 1938 were 31.15, 31.85 per cent 57.67 per cent respectively.
8. B.O. R. No. 80 (Press), 17-10-1930.
9. Report of the Special Officer for the Investigation of Land Tenures of Malabar, May 1947.
10. Ibid.
11. Ibid.
12. Ibid.
13. Ibid.
14. See Table 10.
15. See Logan, *Malabar*, vol. 1, pp. 604-6, for a detailed discussion of *Janmi-Kanamdar-Verumpattamdar* relations.
16. Malabar Tenancy Committee Report, 1931, vol. II. p. 241.
17. For limitations of rent roll data, see Dharma Kumar, 'Land Ownership and Inequality in Madras'. *The Indian Economic and Social History Review,* vol XII, No. 3, July-Sept. 1975.
    A further problem in the Malabar rent rolls was that during the first survey and settlement operations around 1904, the cultivators were made to pay revenue directly and not through the *janmis* thereby increasing the number of *pattas*.
18. See Eric J. Miller, 'Caste and Territory in Malabar', *American Anthropologist*, vol. 56, 1954., p. 23.
19. Ibid., p. 413.
20. *Report of the Malabar Marriage Commission* (Madras, 1891).
21. Taluka-wise distribution of Nambudiris.

Chirakkal	79
Kottayam	30
Kurumbranad	70
Wynad	—
Calicut	152
Ernad	120
Walluvanad	277
Palghat	—
Ponnani	289
Cochin	—

Source: Logan, *op.cit*., pp. 119-20. Palghat draws a blank because in this taluka the Brahmins consisted of *pattars* rather than Nambudiris.

22. This is borne out by some of the wage enumerations which give taluka-wise break up wage rates, e.g., see the following table for 1897.

Taluka	Wage for a cooly for transportation per mile.		
	Rs	As	Ps
Chirakkal	0	0	6
Kottayam	0	1	0
Kurumbranad	0	1	9
Calicut	0	0	9
Ernad	0	0	9
Palghat	0	0	6

The major component of cultivation expenses was constituted by labour costs. The higher cost of cultivation for the same crop in the garden cropped talukas as opposed to paddy growing areas suggests higher wages in the former. See Fort St. George Gazettee, 1-3-1910, pp. 270-72.

Source: Proceedings of the Collector of Malabar, Bundle No. 12, Sr. No. 10219 dt. 27-1898, R-DIS.

23. See Innes, *op.cit*., Chapter XI.
24. See Table 8.
25. M.G.S. Narayanan, 'The Ancient and Medieval History of Kerala—Recent Developments and the Rationale for Inter-Disciplinary Approach', *Journal of Kerala Studies*, vol. 13, Parts III & IV, 1976.
26. Thomas and Sastry, *Commodity Prices in South India 1918-38* (Madras, 1940), p.5.
27. G.O.No. 163 (MIS), Revenue, 19-1-1937
28. Correlation Results (First Differences)

1920/21—1933/34 Pa.Ppr (unlagged) R^2 0.0759

1920/20—1933/34 Pa.Ppr (1 year lag) R^2 0.104

pa = paddy acreage Ppv = retail price of paddy.

IV

The Imprint of Ambiguity: Britain and India in the early 1930s

D. A. LOW

On 8 November 1927 Lord Birkenhead, Britain's Secretary of State for India, announced the appointment of a Statutory Commission under the chairmanship of the Liberal politician, Sir John Simon, to review the Indian constitution. No Indian was appointed to it. The Indian nationalist elite of all colours was outraged, and over the next two years there built up in India the potential for a major countrywide agitation. In October 1929, in an attempt to preempt this the viceroy, Lord Irwin, formally declared that in the British view 'the natural issue of India's constitutional progress . . . is the attainment of Dominion Status', and announced the calling of a Round Table Conference in London on constitutional reform. This, however, served to assuage very few, and in March 1930 Gandhi launched the Indian National Congress upon a major Civil Disobedience campaign. That was vigorously repressed, and twelve months later following an agreement between Gandhi and Irwin it was formally called off. But early in 1932 Civil Disobedience was renewed. This time it was even more resolutely repressed; and as a consequence Congress gradually moved towards participating once again in the constitutional politics on which the British set great store. To its delight Congress then won substantial electoral victories, first at the elections for the central legislature in 1934, and then more particularly in the provincial elections in 1937. Following upon these latter, despite some initial hesitation, Congress came eventually to form fully 'responsible' governments, in accord with the provisions of the new Government of India Act of 1935, in seven of the eleven provinces of India. But two years later in protest against the determination of the British to deny Indian political leaders anything but a merely advisory role in the mobilizing of

Indian support for the British war effort, these Congress ministries resigned, and over the ensuring year a further nationalist agitation began to mount. In August 1940 Gandhi declared that this should take the form of a succession of individual acts of civil disobedience rather than a mass movement since eight years before the British had shown how quickly they could defeat that. Sixteen months later this campaign was overtaken by very much larger events when late in 1941 the Japanese launched their assault upon the western empires in South and Southeast Asia. At this critical juncture the British Government sent Sir Stafford Cripps to Delhi to try to effect a settlement with the Congress leaders. But since the Cripps' offer fell short of their immediate demands it was summarily rejected. As it happened the Japanese were then checked at the gates of India. But not before the Congress had launched its great 'Quit India' movement of August 1942, the largest uprising the British had ever had to face in India since 1857. Whilst this was repressed, sometimes brutally, the tide had now turned, for by the terms of the Cripps' offer, the British had promised that once the Second World War was over they would grant India the independence it had sought for so long, and in 1947 proceeded to do so.

That is the conventional story of India's political history from the late 1920s to the mid-1940s, as endlessly repeated in all the standard accounts. In recent years the story has come to be filled out in four rather different directions. A great deal more is now understood about the British side. The Irwin viceroyalty, the Round Table Conferences, Willingdon's viceroyalty and that of his successor, Lord Linlithgow (not least their dealings with the Indian Princes), have all been extensively recounted. A particularly valuable addition has come from studies of the economic side of Britain's involvement in India. Upon the central political issues it is now well understood that alongside Winston Churchill's robust opposition to Indian constitutional reform, his opponents, Baldwin, Irwin, and Hoare, proceeded on the principle that if constitutional reform could be carried through skilfully it could actually strengthen British control at the centre both constitutionally (by entrenching reserved powers, particularly over financial and military matters) and politically (by calling in aid the Princes and the Muslims) even whilst relinquishing control over India's provincial governments to popularly elected ministries.

We now know much more of the Congress side as well - the quarters from which it secured support, and the processes by which this was generated. The role of 'the western educated' has been well understood for a long while now. Lately there have been several accounts of the part played by India's embryonic capitalists. More work still needs to be done on the even larger contribution of India's widespread merchant communities much more generally. But in the meanwhile the major clarification has come from tracing the long succession of adherences to the Congress of the more well-to-do peasant communities from around the end of the First World War in Bihar, Gujarat, West Bengal, and parts of the United Provinces; then quite dramatically at the end of the 1920s from the Frontier Province; and thereafter, from Madras and Maharashtra in the early 1930s, and the Princely States by the 1940s.

Simultaneously a great deal of important detail has been unearthed on the extent to which Indian involvement in the new institutions the British fashioned was characterized by self-seeking, factionalism, *et hoc genus omne*. The 'Cambridge School' has roused much ire in India; ideology and the commitment which satyagraha entailed did tend to be brushed aside. Yet it would be foolish to suggest that the political infighting with which India has been plagued since independence sprang hydra-headed only as the British departed.

More recently modern Indian historiography has been particularly enlivened by the so-called 'Subaltern' school that takes its name from Gramsci's confusing term for the non-elite. Under Ranajit Guha's energetic direction this has not only underlined the key importance of the structural contradictions which imperial rule necessarily involved, but the subordinate role imposed on very many disadvantaged communities within Indian society itself. In a succession of volumes it has produced abundant evidence of the extent to which the often different concerns of subordinate communities were both exploited and repressed by the more elitist activists in the Congress, both in the urban and more particularly in many of the rural areas of India.

In a quartet of ways the study of the Indo-British encounter in the first half of the twentieth-century has thus been greatly invigorated. Yet there have lately been two disconcerting tendencies. Principally perhaps because in 1985 the Indian National Congress celebrated the centenary of its founding - but also because the part played by ideology has not only been rather downplayed, but (as we have seen) from one quarter actively disdained - there have been disturbing signs of a reversion to uncritical paeans, even on occasion to outmoded hagiography. But perhaps the more worrying development has come from the British side. For as the British documents have become increasingly available, so the unwary have allowed themselves to be trapped into supposing that the processes of decolonization turned principally upon imperialists' decisions. That was often the surface appearance; there need be no doubt that decisions by an imperial power were of major importance. Frequently, moreover, they had a sequence to them that warrants illuminating. But it is an egregious error to suggest that this somehow unfolded within some imperialist vacuum; worse, that imperial rulers were always the olympian masters of their empire's fate.

It is not, however, too difficult to correct these two tendencies by calling in aid a perspective which the overlong tale of multiple decolonizations across the world suggests is near the mark. This suggests, for a start, that the growth and development of nationalism was ordinarily quite essential to the onset of decolonization. That was as true for Egypt and the Congo, as it was for India and Zimbabwe. Where nationalism developed relatively slowly - as in the Princely States in India, or in Malaya as compared with Indonesia, or in tropical Africa as compared with monsoon Asia - decolonization took very much longer to eventuate. Yet too myopic a concentration upon its occurrence in any one place can have the effect of seriously detracting from understanding its character there. And it is precisely at this point that it is vital to allow a major place for the distinctive attitudes taken by the corresponding imperial power. For whilst the generation of nationalist impulses was all but essential to any movement towards independence, the character of the encounter which then ensued seems to have been principally determined by the nature of the particular imperial reaction which applied there. In these terms it was far from surprising, for example, that whilst the process of decolonization in both the French and British West Africa territories was generally peaceful, that in Britain's East and Central African colonies was marked by violent revolt and major disturbances, whilst that in Algeria, Rhodesia and the Portuguese colonies was scarred by guerilla war. For these differences primarily mirrored respectively: the readiness of the British and then of the French to grant independence to all-black West African governments; the opposition of the British to proceeding similarly where there were settler minorities; and the absolute determination of the French in Algeria, the whites in Rhodesia, and the Portuguese to maintain their hold whatever the cost.

It is now time for these more general consideration to be applied to the Indian story. For despite the many new elucidations which have been brought to bear upon it in recent years one fundamental consideration has been almost neglected. It is remarkable how in all the writing on the Indian nationalist story, the sequence which events took is taken for granted; the encounter is treated as its own paradigm; there is next to no awareness of its singular characteristics; certainly far too little recognition of the contingent variables upon which these turned. The fact that it was quite distinctive, singular, even in comparative terms peculiar, struggle has somehow been seriously neglected. And the consequence is that a good many of its major themes and nuances have been very seriously underplayed.

Now it happens that the issue here can be opened up very quickly. For one of the commonest weaknesses of one-country historiographies is that they rarely take a look at what was happening close by. That seems to be quintessentially the case in the study of Indian nationalism in the inter-war period. For as soon as one does look around contemporaneously at the rest of Asia in that period a whole new, and highly illuminating, perspective promptly opens up. For running parallel to the Indian struggle there were three other, major, nationalist-imperialist encounters in other parts of Asia at this time, and they variously displayed some very different characteristics.

The essential contrasts can be put very briefly. Between the two world wars, beside the encounter between Indian nationalists and the British, there ran on the one side the engagement between Filipino nationalists and the Americans, and on the other the conflicts between Indonesian nationalists and the Dutch, and Vietnamese nationalists and the French. So far as the first of these was concerned the Americans during the 1930s not only acceded in principle to the Filipino demand for independence, but in many respects they actively sought to bring this about. In sharp contrast, close by in the Netherlands East Indies, the Dutch simultaneously decided not only to put the principal nationalist parties there out of existence, but to banish their various leaders for life. The French were even more draconian. It was not untypical of them that in Vietnam during the early 1930s they should have executed upwards of 600 of their nationalist and communist opponents.

Within this context it becomes possible to see very quickly that the Indo-British encounter took a quite different course from both the Philippines engagement on the one hand and the Indonesian and Vietnamese conflicts on the other. The starting point here is that during the inter-war period the British never considered an early move towards independence. They never, that is, emulated the Americans. But they did not rule out the prospect of independence altogether; they indeed promised that India could sometime have Dominion Status; and whilst they were perfectly prepared to suppress major agitations against them, they never thought of banishing their principal opponents for life, let alone putting them to death. They did not behave, therefore, like the Dutch or the French either.

It is necessary to be cautious about too rigid a classification of these varying imperialist positions in the inter-war period. During the 1920s, for example, the Republican regime in the United States was a good deal less sympathetic towards Filipino aspirations for independence than the Roosevelt administration which succeeded it. During the late 1920s and into the early 1930s there was a somewhat more liberal Governor-General in the Netherlands East Indies than thereafter. Following the advent of the Popular Front government in France in 1936, there was even momentarily some let-up in French repression in Vietnam. Had the great debate, moreover, in the British Conservative Party during the 1930s been won by the 'diehards' under Churchill and Lloyd, as more than once seemed on the cards, British policy in India could well have been aligned with that of the Dutch, even perhaps of the French.

But there is a good deal to be said about the fundamentals of the differing imperial positions which were supreme in the 1930s. Empire, for example, was far from being central to the self-image of the Americans, or important to their economy. The Dutch, on the other hand, believed their colonial possessions were crucial to the economic well-being of their homeland; whilst to the French such empires as they had, or so it would seem (once they had both India and Canada, and then gained West Africa and Indo-China) not only gave the opportunity for spreading the blessings of French culture to others, but seemed to them to be vital to sustaining France's standing in the world. So while the Americans could afford to go, the Dutch and the French were determined to stay.

For the British things were never quite so straightforward. Empire remained vital both to their self-image, and to their strategic position in the world. But such notions cut across their like commitments to doctrines of political liberties and their expression in parliamentary government. Moreover, they had learnt from bitter experience, first in America and more lately in Ireland, of the long term consequences of prefering the first to the second, and from their recent experience of the white Dominions, and above all, in the persons of Botha and Smuts, of South Africa, of the great advantages of prefering the second to the first.

The predominant attitudes of each of the various western imperial powers in Asia were therefore fairly firmly rooted through the 1930s, and they can thus be briefly characterized. When the later Supreme Court Judge, Frank Murphy, was appointed by President Roosevelt as Governor-General of the Philippine Islands in 1932 he roundly declared that his primary task was 'to set these people free'. By contrast, the French Foreign Legion operating in Vietnam had lately been ordered to kill nine out of ten of the prisoners taken in armed encounters with the Vietnamese communists; whilst shortly afterwards Governor-General de Jonge in the Netherlands East Indies bluntly declared that 'we have ruled here for 300 years with whip and club and we shall still be doing it in another 300 years'. Characteristically the British position lay between these polar opposites, and was invariably janus-faced. Whilst on behalf of the British Government Lord Irwin the Viceroy, for example, loudly promised Dominion Status for India in 1929, in the very same breath he also declared that this could only be 'the natural issue of India's constitutional development', which by clear implication meant that it was not to be entertained for a long while yet. He once put the British position more pithily in private when he remarked that 'it is not impossible...[to] make the shop window look respectable from an Indian point of view...while keeping your hands pretty firmly on the things that matter'.

It is then of major importance to notice just how close a conjunction there proved to be between these differing imperialist attitudes and the anti-colonial strategies adopted by the principal nationalist opposition that in each case was mounted against them. As was noted earlier for Africa, distinctive imperial stances in every case seem to have determined the corresponding primary nationalist responses. Certainly in the Philippines the nationalist elite never mounted any major popular agitation there against their American overlords; sustained lobbying in Washington sufficed to secure their ends. Since for Indonesia's nationalists there was no prospect at all of any such approach becoming possible, some of them concluded that only massive multi-class pressure could move the Dutch, whilst others reckoned that it could only be done by mobilizing a firmly cadre-led class party. Neither the nationalists nor the communists in Vietnam had any confidence that even the latter would move the French. In the early 1930s both the secular nationalists and the communists in Vietnam thus resorted to armed violence, on a scale that was paralleled nowhere else at this time.

Yet even in their differing ways these were relatively straightforward cases. It was in India that a more complex situation arose precisely because the British were so disconcertingly double-faced. Here was potentially a great risk of much disagreement. Particularly in Bengal, there were those who believed that Britain's determination to hold on to their empire meant that only a terrorist campaign against them would move them. But there were others who believed no less firmly that because of British adherence to the principles of democratic self-government, skilful negotiation with them could provide important opportunities for an advance. There were large elements of wishful thinking in both of these approaches, and it was a major part of Gandhi's genius that the approach he propounded was so quintessentially functional to Britain's inherent ambivalence. For whilst firmly eschewing violence he was in no doubt that only major self-sacrificing confrontations would make them proffer any worthwhile concessions in accordance with their liberal values. It was, indeed, Gandhi's masterly grasp of the requirements of the Indian national movement in its conflict with its profoundly ambiguous imperial masters that won him the towering position he came to hold in its ranks, rather than just his usually emphasized personal qualities. For without the former the latter would have given him as little influence as, in very different circumstances, they gave his closest disciple, Vinoba Bhave, after independence.

It was in this way that the double-think at the heart of Britain's imperial posture towards India during the inter-war years conditioned the most substantial nationalist response against it, and in consequence moulded the main forms of the inter-war Indo-British conflict which, in nature, differed so substantially from those in the rest of western dominated Asia. All that in turn had, moreover, a far more profound influence on a whole range of aspects of India's political culture after independence than has hitherto been understood.

Those are bold statements. So the rest of this chapter will be devoted to outlining three very different sequences almost at random from the years 1929 to 1933 so as to suggest their validity.

When in 1927 Birkenhead appointed the all-white Simon Commission to determine India's future over India's head, such was the anger in most Indian political circles that not only did the Indian National Congress start to limber up for another major countrywide agitation, but many of those who had broken with it to form the Indian Liberal Party started to cooperate with it once again. In an effort to head off this combination, Irwin as Viceroy issued his Dominion Status declaration on 31 October 1929, and forecast an invitation to 'representatives of different parties and interests' in India to attend a Round Table Conference in London in a year's time.

A remarkable series of events then ensued. At an early meeting in Delhi of a number of Congress and other Indian political leaders immediately after the Irwin declaration, a 'Delhi Manifesto' was issued, which despite some important qualifications, pointed in the direction of the invitation to London being accepted. Amongst the signatories was Gandhi, the more prominent Liberals, and both Motilal and Jawaharlal Nehru. Shortly afterwards, however, to Gandhi's growing alarm (let alone that of the Liberals) Jawaharlal Nehru made it plain that he could not stand by his Delhi signature. Brisk correspondence and several urgent private meetings then followed that climaxed in a Congress Working Committee meeting at Allahabad on 16-18 November. At this Gandhi seemed to hold the line agreed to in Delhi. But in the course of a subsequent meeting which some Liberals arranged with the Viceroy on 23 December, Gandhi, to their fury, finally came down upon Jawaharlal's side. Thereafter at its annual conference in Lahore at the end of the month, the Indian National Congress not only rejected any idea of Congress representation at the London conference, but firmly rejected Dominion Status as its objective, and committed itself to securing Purna Swaraj, complete independence. For good measure it then authorized Gandhi to launch forthwith a mass Civil Disobedience movement against British rule in India.

That finally broke the ranks of the Delhi signatories. But before some of the Liberals left for London later in 1930 two of them secured permission to negotiate with the Congress leaders - who had by then been put in jail - in an effort to persuade them to hold negotiations with the British after all. Whilst these negotiations failed, the fact that they were held at all indicates that some Congress leaders could not quite put the idea from their minds. When, moreover, in January 1931 the Liberals returned from the first Round Table Conference in London, negotiations were resumed, and this time eventuated in theGandhi-Irwin Pact of March 1931, one consequence of which was that Gandhi agreed to join them at the second Round Table Conference in London later that year.

Now much of this has long been well known. What has not yet been recognized is just how singular these events were. For here was a protracted debate about just how India's nationalists should respond to an ostensible accommodating British offer which - quite typically of the British - nonetheless contained no commitment to any early grant of Dominion Status (let alone complete independence). The initial response looked remarkably favourable. But the Congress leaders then became locked in an anguished debate over how precisely they should proceed, and to begin with not only came down firmly against any negotiation on British terms, but in favour of launching a full-scale Civil Disobedience movement instead. Yet six months later, despite all of that, some of the Congress leaders, Jawaharlal Nehru's influential father Motilal not least amongst them, were ready to contemplate a change of course; and when the third time around the Liberals used their good offices to bring Gandhi and Irwin together again they finally succeeded in persuading the Mahatma to go to London after all.

A glance at the parallel stories immediately reveals just how peculiar this debate was to the Indo-British encounter. In the Philippines there was no such debate over whether its nationalist emissaries should take the opportunity to negotiate in Washington; and for good reason too. During these same years when the Indian Round Table Conferences were taking place in London in the early 1930s, several Filipino delegations were involved in negotiations in Washington. But the purport of the two sets of discussions could not have been more different. In the London talks some concessions to Indian aspirations were open to discussion, but anything that smacked of independence, even of early Dominion Status, was ruled out. In Washington by contrast, Philippines' independence was the principle item on the agenda. Yet the British were showing themselves prepared to hold discussions with India's nationalist leaders. No such opportunity came to Vietnam's or Indonesia's nationalists, let alone an invitation to hold discussions in Paris or The Hague. The three sets of circumstances differed fundamentally. The Philippines, Indonesian, and Vietnamese situations mirrored quite precisely the clear positions of their particular imperial masters; and the Indian occurrences reflected no less certainly the ambiguity of the British.

That, however, is not all. For one can trace the sequels to this idiosyncracy in the years that followed. For whilst the British did eventually take India down the road which the white Dominions had trod before them, in view of the climax to the first round of the Congress debate in 1929, there was never any chance that the Congress leaders, Nehru in particular, would forego their commitment to purna swaraj, or complete independence. Recognizing this, Attlee in 1947 artfully arranged that India and Pakistan should gain their initial independence as Dominions, not by means of an Indian Dominions Act (as Churchill would have wished), but by the India Independence Act. Then to many people's astonishment India decided to remain in the Commonwealth. The rules of the association had, however, to be crucially altered so as to encompass India's determination not to remain a Dominion for any longer than was necessary. It was in these ways that the ambiguity in the British position left its mark not merely upon the high politics of India in the year 1929 to 1931 but across one principle strand in independent

India's foreign policy, and indeed thereafter upon the very character of the later Commonwealth itself.

It has always been clear that the conflict between Indian nationalism and British imperialism was not undertaken by war, nor confined to hard negotiation. The characteristic modus operandi was non-violent confrontation. Curiously there have been few historian's accounts of these in any detail, though that proves to be well worth venturing.

Following upon the Congress decision at Lahore in December 1929 to launch a mass Civil Disobedience movement, Gandhi in March 1930 embarked upon his Salt Satyagraha, in which he called upon India's nationalists to breach the oppressive British monopoly on salt manufacture and thereby display their defiance of British authority. There followed a mounting series of clashes right across the country. We have close details of one of the hundreds of these in the city of Lucknow on 25 May 1930.

Now Lucknow had been the scene of one of the two great armed clashes during the Great Rebellion of 1857. After its suppression, the British pulled down parts of the old city around the once beleaguered Residency, and drove two broad roadways—inevitably called Victoria and (after the Viceroy) Canning Street—through the remainder, so as to ensure that, should there be another revolt, they could quickly move to command its core. To the south and east of the old city they then built a large new military cantonment, and adjacent to that, abutting on Hazratganj, 'His Highness' market'—which became the principal shopping and business centre of the city (largely as it happened dwelt in by Indians)—they built for themselves a new Civil Lines; and then close by brought in the railway so as to provide an easy escape route for their wives and children should another emergency occur. Lucknow was deliberately reconstructed, that is, so as to spike another violent mass uprising from the outset.

The Congress, however, eschewed violence, and had no plans to start a mass uprising. They were concerned rather to create non-violent confrontations against the British so as to put them to shame, and place them on the defensive. In Lucknow, as it happened, the illegal making of salt could only be a farce. Following, however, upon some earlier events at the time of the Simon Commission's visit to the city in 1928, it had transpired that the city's reconstruction after 1857 had presented the local Congress with a quite perfect opportunity for demonstrating the iniquities of imperialism in a way that could not have been more dramatic locally. For in defence of their right to go about their business undisturbed in

Hazratganj—the principal business and shopping centre — the British had consistently laid it down that no political processions could be taken through its main streets. Congress now seized on the fact that it could lambast this as pure racialism, and in 1930 they very soon made their determination to break this prohibition the main focus of their civil disobedience in the city.

Over several days in mid-May 1932 the Lucknow Congress organization and the British Deputy Commissioner in charge of the city fenced upon this issue. At one stage the DC allowed a Congress procession to pass through Hazratganj so as to establish that the Congress would in fact defy his orders; but the day after he arrested a dozen of its leaders so as to demonstrate that this could not be done with impunity. At the eleventh hour he even offered to allow further processions through Hazratganj so long as his permission for these had been sought. Congress, of course, was in no mind to fall into that trap.

So on Sunday 25 May 1930 the Lucknow Congress finally laid out its trained non-violent supporters, accompanied by a large crowd of city onlookers, to march past the Lucknow Council Chamber and then up The Mall, the via sacra of Hazratganj, in deliberate defiance of the British Deputy Commissioner's prohibition. This time the DC was ready for them, a few yards before the Council Chamber. After prohibitions and warnings had been issued, and the women at the head of the procession had been carried away by the police, 200 police with their metal tipped staves were set loose on the men processionists so soon as they resisted arrest, and twenty minutes of brutal flaying followed during which considerable numbers in the attending crowd were belaboured too. Miraculously there were no deaths, but 54 people were admitted to hospital, and a large number of others were treated by their local doctors. There were no police injuries; Congress and the crowd had meticulously followed Gandhi's calls for non-violence and soon dispersed.

However, as a consequence there was deep anger in the city, not only amongst the city's crowd but amongst many members of its professional elite who had played no part in the affair. (The purpose of the Congress in defying the British had, it is clear, been amply served). The next day the British were fearful enough to post a company of British infantry and a squadron of British cavalry in the middle of the city outside the Congress' city headquarters. But as the day passed peacefully, and as night fell they were sent back to their cantonments.

Within half an hour, however, the city crowd attacked a heavily manned police station in the labyrinths of the Indian city. Bricks were thrown, a fire was lit, and 34 policemen received significant injuries. In self-defence the police under the orders of an Indian officer fired over 50 rounds of buckshot. Four people were killed, and many more were wounded. The troops were brought back to the city within the hour, and an effective embargo upon public gatherings was immediately imposed. A few weeks later Congress adopted the new expedient of despatching half a dozen volunteers daily to defy this prohibition, and, as they hoped, these were promptly arrested. So whilst following the May clashes they modified their tactics, they nevertheless maintained their non-violent defiance.

Such proceedings were the stock in trade of the Indian National Congress in its conflict with the British. There can be no doubt that an astonishing commitment to Gandhi's non-violent doctrines was displayed. But it is short-sighted to take such encounters—as most historians of modern India are prone to do—for granted. Nothing like them occurred in the Philippines—where against the Americans nothing like them was necessary—nor in Vietnam or Indonesia either—where much harsher retribution would have followed very swiftly if they had.

We can, however see from this instance just how functional satyagraha confrontations of the kind the Indian Congress employed were to its encounter with the British. Ultimately British officials would, of course, enforce their own orders, not least in defence of a racist privilege; they were clear that their prestige and their imperial primacy rested upon their readiness to do this. Nevertheless they were extremely careful by this time to control their actions carefully. They saw to it that it was Congress that escalated the encounter. When this occurred they carefully removed women processionists first, and then only used their police—brutal though these could be—even when there was a large military cantonment just a mile away. When they did send in troops it was, moreover, only a minimal number, which they quickly withdrew as soon as it seemed safe to do so. Whilst they grossly miscalculated in believing that their real enemies were only enrolled Congressmen; whilst their beleaguered police did not long hesitate to open fire when the city crowd attacked them, and whilst troops were quickly returned to the city, no punitive shootings followed, nor even any punitive arrests either.

The Congress case was much advanced by such episodes. The Lucknow Congress quite properly insisted that it had not itself prompted the attack upon the police station, and thereafter gave the city crowd no encouragement to resort to violence. When, moreover, Congress resumed its own defiance it cut this down to a symbolic minimum. All that was quite marvellously well-judged. Upon the British side these events clearly indicated that the post-1857 restructuring of the city had in one sense paid off superbly; a populist revolt had been suppressed within an hour. That confirmed for the Indian side that mass uprisings were not the best way to proceed. But since at the same time the restructuring of the city had, with delectable irony, presented the Congress with a quite perfect issue upon which to offer its own more sophisticated satyagraha, in picking on the British refusal to allow ordinary citizens to take peaceful demonstrations through Hazratganj, the Lucknow Congress was able to exemplify in wondrously penetrating way the inherent iniquities of imperialist domination in India. As angry letters that elite Lucknawis wrote to the Viceroy about the events of 25 May emphasized; as in different ways both the 'Lucknow' days which were held elsewhere in India in protest, and the Government's decision to institute a protracted public enquiry into what, after all, was a very local affair in the midst of a vast countrywide conflict, cogently demonstrated, the Lucknow Congress had evidently done its nationalist duty marvellously well in at first finding and then in piercing an imperialist Achilles heal. It had been done, moreover, without deliberately precipitating violence—and had plainly made its mark for everyone to see.

Such a mutually controlled encounter was, we may insist, both characteristic and highly revealing of the quite peculiar nature of the Indo-British conflict, and reflected with remarkable precision its quite unusual features. The Congress in Lucknow had become so well-versed in the use of satyagraha, that it persisted in using this as a principal means of bringing pressure to bear upon governments in the post-independence era. So routine, indeed, was its performance in Lucknow that for several decades after independence political processions there still used the routes followed in 1930, and mounted their demonstrations outside the Council Chamber.

A third set of occurrences to illustrate the theme advanced here spread over the latter part of 1932 and through much of 1933. The Gandhi-Irwin Pact of March 1931 had been hailed in nationalist circles as a Congress triumph. Great enthusiasm was generated, moreover, by the ensuing mass release of Civil Disobedience prisoners, and in the following months the British administration became exceedingly perturbed at the numerous indications that Congress was now preparing for an even larger assault against British rule in India. By the time of Gandhi's return from the Second Round Table Conference in London in December 1931, Civil Disobedience was indeed erupting once again in two or three provinces, and since he would not call this off Gandhi's request to discuss the situation with Willingdon, the new Viceroy, was brusquely rejected. Thereafter in January 1932 the Government of India finally took to itself emergency powers, arrested the Congress leaders and upwards of 60,000 others, and set about suppressing the movement a great deal more vigorously than ever before. There were, we may note, no summary executions (such as were concurrently occuring in Vietnam); few Congressmen were put on trial; most were simply imprisoned for indefinite periods.

In the aftermath the Government of India was absolutely determined to maintain the supremacy which it had now reasserted. They were particularly adamant that there should be no Gandhi-Willingdon Pact in repetition of the Gandhi-Irwin Pact, nor another general jail delivery either. They were especially concerned to ensure that their officials and supporters should not draw the conclusion that the end of British rule in India was at hand. In all this they clearly displayed one side of the British imperial mind at this time. Yet there was always the other side too; and as the months passed the Government of India not only became increasingly embarrassed at holding so many prisoners in jail without trial, but, as the process of constitutional reform for India proceeded in London, it began to give its mind to how it might start elbowing Congress back onto more constitutionalist paths once again.

From behind his prison walls, Gandhi was soon having to think anew about his position. Not only had Civil Disobedience been firmly repressed, Congressmen were now gravely disconcerted. Gandhi, however, was not a man to capitulate, and when he found himself in situations like this his invariable reaction was to reach for the moral high ground so as to confound his opponents from there. As a result of a decision at the Second Round Table Conference the previous year the British gave him his opportunity in September 1932 when they published their so-called 'Communal Award', which was designed to settle the plethora of disputes about the communal distribution of seats in India's future legislatures. Gandhi immediately denounced the provision in this for 'separate electorates' for India's untouchables as a device that would divide Hindu from Hindu, and forthwith embarked on a fast unto death in protest. A number of influential Indians then hurriedly worked out the so-called Poona Pact in order to adjust the Award in a way that allowed him to abandon his fast. That episode greatly enhanced his personal prestige, and won him the moral high ground which he now needed. Since, however, the British had been canny enough to allow for changes in the Award so long as there was some general Indian agreement for this, their political supremacy in India remained unaffected.

There then ensured a quite extraordinary duel between Gandhi and the Government of India which in the absence of any other major occurrences dominated the high politics of India the following year. In this Gandhi's chief concern was to maintain the moral standing he had secured, and through it the cause that he served, whilst the central concern of the Government of India was to prevent themselves from being politically worsted in the propaganda battle which Gandhi now unleashed against them. Since from behind his prison walls Gandhi was in no position to pursue his Civil Disobedience campaign directly, he committed himself instead to a major campaign on behalf of India's untouchables, Harijans, Children of God, as he called them.

To this end he immediately demanded of the Government of India that in order to pursue his Harijan campaign he should be granted on a continuing basis the freedom which he had enjoyed whilst the Poona Pact was under negotiation, and be allowed to receive all the visitors he wanted, and communicate with the press as well. Not surprisingly these demands were immediately refused. But the Government of India then relented, both because they did not want to be branded as being in opposition to Harijan interests, and because they secured from Gandhi a clear undertaking that he would not use the privileges he sought as a means of forwarding his Civil Disobedience campaign. The first round was thus a draw. By mounting his Harijans campaign Gandhi had maintained his moral ascendancy, but the British had retained their political primacy.

Over the turn of the year Gandhi tried more than once to wrong foot them in some other way. He threatened, for example, to fast on behalf of one of his high caste fellow prisoners who had been denied the right to do Harijan work. Incredibly both the British Secretary of State for India in London and the Government of India in Delhi thereupon had solemnly to consider whether or not one of their Indian prisoners should be allowed to clean out his own prison latrines or not. If this were to be conceded Gandhi would have put one over them. But to refuse would be to face the probability of a Gandhian fast on an issue on which they would clearly have been placed in the wrong. Following upon several weeks of cogitation they eventually announced that the decisions in such matters would be left to their local jail superintendents, and thereby managed to extricate themselves from a awkward corner.

It was then Gandhi's turn to feel himself boxed in. He learnt from this and similar episodes that the Government of India was not to be easily caught out; and in the meanwhile his Harijans campaign had been encountering increasing orthodox opposition. By April 1933 it was becoming very plain indeed that he was near to his wits and on both of these scores. He therefore announced that he would now embark upon a fast for three weeks, not in defiance of the British nor in opposition to the orthodox, but in response to a divine call for self-purification in the Harijan cause. In a doubly unpromising position he was clearly trying, somewhat desperately, to maintain his moral ascendency.

In response, the Government of India now set out to use all their guile against him. Since the Civil Disobedience movement had by now virtually petered out, they were increasingly anxious to release their political prisoners, Gandhi amongst them, yet without giving any suggestion that 'peace talks' could ensue. So on the day Gandhi started his fast they simply announced that since he had decided to fast upon a purely humanitarian matter they were releasing him unconditionally so that he could do so as a free man. Gandhi immediately realized they had put one over him, and within a couple of hours of his release issued a statement saying that — since he was now free to do so — he had not in any way abandoned his commitment to his Civil Disobedience campaign; that whilst his fast lasted Civil Disobedience should perhaps be suspended; and that the opportunity should be taken to effect a settlement with the Government. Since his decision to fast in the Harijan cause had now brought him to a peak of adulation, the Government of India believed this last proposal to be so threatening that they quickly issued a further statement in which they not only denounced him for using his newly granted freedom on a humanitarian matter to make a political pronouncement, but forcefully declared that there was no question of any talks being held with the Congress until Civil Disobedience had been completely abandoned. It was a very close shave for both of them.

Once the fast was over and Gandhi had somewhat recovered, it was nevertheless widely expected that Gandhi for his part would finally abandon his Civil Disobedience campaign, and that before very long the Government of India would after all negotiate with him. Neither occurred. Gandhi was never one to capitulate, while subsequent to their earlier experiences after the Gandhi-Irwin Pact the Government was utterly determined never to embark upon the formal settlement with him again. So the two titans remained locked in battle.

When the conflict then resumed in July and August 1932, the Government finally got the better of him, and this time the Mahatma was disastrously worsted. It was, however, one measure of his greatness that in defeat he was invariably able to find a way to retain and uphold his personal integrity.

The problem for him at this late stage in the Civil Disobedience campaign was to come up with some new political tactic with which to confront the Government, since the Government was now well prepared to withstand all of his old ones. From mid-July to early August 1933, tired and at the end of his tether, he simply ran the gamut of all his previous proceedings, and was more seriously routed than on any other occasion either before or after. Twice in July he asked for negotiations with the Viceroy. Both times he was sharply rebuffed. Then on 1 August, in replication of his Salt March to Dandi in 1930, he set out on a new march from Ahmedabad to Ras. But he was immediately arrested; ordered to confine himself to Poona; and upon refusing to do so sentenced to a carefully crafted 12 months imprisonment. When he then proceeded to demand the privileges he had hitherto enjoyed in prison to conduct his Harijan campaign, these were only partially granted to him. So he began a fast in protest against this. So soon as this appeared to be threatening his life, the Government of India in a brutally disdainful move released him once again unconditionally. This 'cat and mouse game' humiliated him profoundly. Politically the Government had defeated him hands down. And yet, only a month or so later, he brilliantly reasserted his moral position by declaring that although he was once again free to do so, he would refrain from taking any part in nationalist activities for the remaining term of his 12 months' sentence. That, however, was the end of his Civil Disobedience movement, and within a year Congressmen were back in the constitutional arena, once again standing in legislative elections.

By any standards this intensely personal duel was a remarkable affair. Throughout the Government of India characteristically played it quite ambidexterously. They were adamant against any challenge to their political supremacy in India, but at the same time they were exceedingly circumspect in their handling of Gandhi, and very careful too not to put themselves palpably in the wrong. With extraordinary deftness Gandhi on his side maximized the opportunities available to him within the severely limited circumstances in which he found himself; he never proferred his surrender (as we now know Sukarno did at precisely this time in Indonesia); and he succeeded in defeat in maintaining his public standing, and, by extension, that of his movement with him. Because the Government of India was never minded to crush him completely—and would have been confronted by damaging criticism both in India and Britain had it attempted to do so—the Congress he led remained intact as well, despite the growing reservations of some of its members over his leadership.

Nothing like this occurred in the Philippines; there was never any occasion for any such encounter there. Nor was there anything like it in Vietnam or Indonesia. At this stage political activists in both those countries were treated far more harshly. Whilst the Indian encounter reflected, of course, Gandhi's particular orientations, no such joust with the imperial authorities could possibly have taken place but for the ambiguity in the British position. The very possibility of any such set of occurrences turned in the first place upon that. The persistent two-sidedness of the British endlessly determined the quite peculiar form that so much of the Indian nationalist struggle took.

The further argument is apposite here as well. For the salience given by these quite particular occurrences to fasting as a political weapon helped to entrench this as a legitimate weapon in modern India's political culture after independence. It was frequently employed, for example, by Sikh leaders in Punjab, and more especially there and elsewhere during the long campaign for linguistic states. Moreover, whilst Gandhi (with others) had long been concerned with Harijan 'uplift', the primacy he gave to this as a means of securing his moral position during his period in jail in 1932-33, gave it a place within Congress' ideology that, despite continuing orthodox opposition, ensured that it became entrenched in India's constitution after independence, and periodically figured quite largely in India's future politics too. Modern India's political history bears the imprint of Britain's ambiguity in the inter-war years in many more ways than is ordinarily noticed.

BIBLIOGRAPHICAL NOTE

Since this is principally a 'work-in-progress' chapter, extensive references are not being provided. Sumit Sarkar, *Modern India 1885-1947* (Delhi, 1983) gives an up-to-date account of the Indian nationalist story. The 'Indian' literature referred to includes R.J. Moore, *The Crisis Of Indian Unity 1917-1940* (Oxford, 1974); Carl Bridge, *Holding India To The Empire* (Delhi, 1986); G. Rizvi, *Linlithgow And India* (London, 1978); S.R. Ashton, *British Policy Towards The Indian States (1905-1939)*; B.R. Tomlinson, *The Political Economy Of The Raj 1914-1947* (London, 1979), C.Markovits, *Indian Business And Nationalist Politics 1931-39* (Cambridge, 1985); D.A. Low, (ed.), *Congress And the Raj* (London, 1977); J. Gallagher, G. Johnson & A. Seal (ed.), *Locality, Province And Nation* (Cambridge, 1973); R. Guha, *Subaltern Studies I-IV* (Delhi, 1982-85); and *The Centenary History of The Indian National Congress* (Delhi, 1985). On the Philippines see T. Friend, *Between Two Empires* (New Haven, 1965); S. Fine, *Frank Murphy: The New Deal Years* (Chicago, 1979); and B.R. Churchill, *The Philippine Independence Missions To The United States 1919-1934* (Manila, 1983); on Indonesia, J. Ingleson, *Road To Exile* (Singapore, 1979); J.D. Legge, *Sukarno* (London, 1972), and S.Abeyasekere, 'Relations Between The Indonesian Cooperating Nationalists And The Dutch 1935-1942' (Monash University Ph.D. 1972); on Vietnam, J. Buttinger, *Vietnam: A Dragon Embattled*, Vol. 1 (London, 1957); A.B. Woodside, *Community And Revolution In Modern Vietnam* (Boston, 1976); and M. Osborne, 'Continuity and Motivation in the Vietnamese Revolution: New light from the 1930s', *Pacific Affairs*, Spring 1974. On the three case studies see respectively D.A. Low, 'The Purna Swaraj Decision 1929' in Wang Gungwu (ed.), *Self And Biography* (Sydney, 1975); V.T. Oldenburg, *The Making of Colonial Lucknow 1856-1877* (Princeton, 1984); and National Archives of India, Home Political 249/30; and *The Collected Works of Mahatma Gandhi*, vols. LI-LVI (Delhi, 1972-3), together with the references to the relevant National Archives files in J.M. Brown, *Gandhi And Civil Disobedience* (Cambridge, 1977).